REGIMENTAL RECORDS
OF THE
ROYAL WELCH FUSILIERS

REGIMENTAL RECORDS

OF THE

ROYAL WELCH FUSILIERS

(LATE THE 23RD FOOT)

COMPILED BY

MAJOR C. H. DUDLEY WARD, D.S.O., M.C.

(LATE WELSH GUARDS)

VOL. IV

1915—1918

TURKEY–BULGARIA–AUSTRIA

The Naval & Military Press Ltd

Reproduced by kind permission of the Regimental Trustees

Published by

The Naval & Military Press Ltd

Unit 10, Ridgewood Industrial Park,

Uckfield, East Sussex,

TN22 5QE England

Tel: +44 (0) 1825 749494

Fax: +44 (0) 1825 765701

www.naval-military-press.com

© The Naval & Military Press Ltd 2005

PRESENTATION OF COLOURS TO SERVICE BATTALIONS.

Frontispiece]

CONTENTS

PART I

THE WAR WITH TURKEY

CONTENTS

PART II
THE WAR WITH BULGARIA

CONTENTS

PART III
THE WAR WITH AUSTRIA

THE ARMISTICE AND DEMOBILISATION

APPENDICES

LIST OF ILLUSTRATIONS

LIST OF MAPS

DIVISIONAL SIGNS USED ON MAPS

7th DIVN

13th DIVN

22nd DIVN

Black braid worn on
shoulder straps.

53rd DIVN

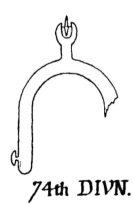

74th DIVN.

NOTE BY THE REGIMENTAL HISTORY COMMITTEE

WITH the publication of the present volume the work of enlarging and bringing up to date *Regimental Records of the Royal Welch Fusiliers* is completed.

The Committee avail themselves of this opportunity of tendering their sincere thanks to all those who, by various means and in different ways, have assisted in the compilation of the work. In particular they wish to place on record their high appreciation of the fine example of *esprit de corps* shown by Mr. Clancy (Bandmaster), the non-commissioned officers, and men of the Band of the 2nd Battalion, who, when stationed at home in 1923, gave their services free, during a tour through the Regimental District. The Committee feel sure that this spontaneous action on the part of the Band will be fully appreciated by all " Royal Welchmen." They further wish to convey their thanks to Lieutenant-Colonel C. C. Norman, C.M.G., D.S.O. (then commanding the 2nd Battalion), Lieutenant-Colonel J. R. Minshull-Ford, D.S.O., M.C. (Band President), and the officers at the various centres in North Wales where concerts were given, for their work in organising and arranging the entertainments, etc., which resulted in the tour proving so great a financial success.

CHARLES DOBELL, *Lieutenant-General, President.*
G. F. BARTTELOT, *Major, Hon. Treasurer.*

AGENDA TO VOL. II

CAPTAIN ROBERT BARCLAY

THE details of one of Captain Barclay's extraordinary walking records were published in the *Daily Telegraph* of 6th April 1929.

"The Captain rose at five one morning in 1808 and walked thirty miles grouse-shooting. He dined at five p.m., and walked sixty miles to his house at Ury in eleven hours. Then, after attending to business, he walked sixteen miles to a dance, returned home by seven a.m., and passed the day partridge-shooting. After dinner he confessed to some slight fatigue, and went to bed, having walked 130 miles, without sleep, in two nights and three days. Even Squire Osbaldeston admitted that Barclay was a 'stunner.' His example set scores of sportsmen of all ranks of society walking for wagers, and almost always on the hard high-roads." (See Vol. II, p. 385.)

"BILLY" DUFF AND "THE RAG"

IT is of interest to note in connection with Captain "Billy" Duff of the regiment that he was the originator of the nickname of the Army and Navy Club, viz. "the Rag."

The Club, of which he was a member, was opened early in 1838, and "Billy" was at this time both the terror and the amusement of London. His museum contained a very heterogeneous collection of articles curiously and sportively acquired, from the shirt-pins of his personal friends to the door-knockers and area bells of the London householder.

It may well be supposed that there were few night haunts in London which were unknown to him. In *The Autobiography of Baron Nicholson*, the presiding genius of the "Cole Hole," the "Cider Cellar," and in later days of "Judge and Jury" in Leicester Square, "Billy" Duff is mentioned more than once. In the same volume it is recorded how a certain well-known gambler, who had lost his all at Crockford's and other gambling resorts, had disappeared from the scenes, but had since been found playing coppers "at a place not inappropriately designed the 'Rag and Famish' in a turning out of Cranbourn Alley, Leicester Square."

We may be sure that "Billy" knew of this place and its character. Now, it happened that "Billy" entered the Army and Navy Club late one evening, and called for supper. The bill of fare proved to be so meagre that he angrily declared that "it was a rag and famish affair": doubtless comparing the resources of the Army and Navy Club with those of the least reputable establishment within the bounds of his experience. An admiring following considered the comparison highly humorous, and "Billy" was credited with a *bon mot*.

The title was facetiously adopted as a nickname, the sobriquet caught on, and both inside and outside the Club has been known ever since by the title of " the Rag."

Captain Duff himself was so pleased with the success attending his comment that he proceeded to design the Club button.   An original specimen of the button is preserved on the mantelpiece of the smoking-room.   The button was at one time worn by many members of the Club on evening dress.

JOHN O'HARA

JOHN O'HARA joined the 95th Foot on the 21st September 1872, and transferred to the regiment in January 1874 in the hope of getting out to Ashanti.   But he was sent to the depot and joined the 2nd Battalion at Gibraltar at the end of the year.

In June 1876, because of permanent financial stress, he threw up his commission in the regiment and became a matador in the Spanish bull-ring.

His first appearance took place at Algeciras, and was largely advertised all over the country by posters reading : " Appearance of an English officer of enormous wealth Juan O'Hara," etc.

He followed his new profession for some time, but the flamboyant character of the advertisements and posters that always heralded his appearance eventually excited the jealousy of his Spanish confrères, with the result that one day they failed to play the game and back him up—he was injured and gave up the bull-ring.

Returning to England, he enlisted in the Cavalry, and eventually became Sergeant Instructor of Gymnasia—he was always a fine gymnast.

Subsequently he went to the Cape, and joined the Cape Mounted Rifles.   Finally, he was killed while skylarking on a train between Dover and London.   While the train was in motion, he climbed on to the roof of the carriage and came in contact with a bridge under which the train was passing.

ERRATA
VOL. III

page xi: Lance-Corporal H. Weale, *not Weald*.

page 31, line 8: and Welsh Horse, *not (Welsh Horse)*.

page 59, line 38: Wynne Edwards, *not Wynne Williams*.

page 60, line 18: Clegg-Hill, *not Glegg*.

page 61, line 11: Wynne Edwards, *not Wynne Williams*.

page 62, line 5: 2nd Battalion, *not 11th*.

page 97, line 34: W. B. Garnett, *not W. G.*

page 114, footnote 2, and page 129, line 1: Major A. K. Richardson, *not Lieutenant A. K. Richardson*.

page 135, line 11: Picantin, *not Picartin*.

page 160, line 38: The Queen's Own (Royal West Kent Regiment), *not Queen's West Kents*.

page 161, line 3: Bourdois, *not Boordois*.

page 162, line 9, and page 163, lines 7 and 34: Dolling, *not Dollings*.

page 163, line 35: delete Hopkin.

page 164, line 28: right, *not left*.

page 175, line 31: Hollingbery, *not Hollingberg*.

page 175, line 37: Dolling, *not Dollings*.

page 213, line 12: Fouquereuil, *not Fouguereuil*.

page 233, line 22: Dolling, *not Dollings*.

page 246, line 29: 800, *not 300*.

page 250, line 19: N. H. Radford, *not W. H.*

page 251, line 36, and page 252, line 2: Dealing, *not Deeling*.

page 280, line 24: Kirkby, *not Kirkley*.

page 281, footnote, last line: untended, *not intended*.

page 289, lines 1 and 14: Gittens, *not Gitters*.

page 304, line 8: 22nd Brigade, *not 19th*.

page 337, line 26: Coudikerke, *not Condikerke*.

page 345, line 36: Siddall, *not Liddall*.

page 361, line 30: Longuenesse, *not Lonhuesse*.

page 384, line 14: Erie, *not Eric*.

page 389, line 27: ground, *not mist*.

page 441, line 13: N. H. Radford, *not M. Radford*.

page 466, line 30: Ainge, *not Ainger*.

page 467, footnote, line 4: E. A. Christofferson, U.S. Army, *not Christopherson*.

INDEX

Insert: Greaves, E. J., Capt., 191; wounded, 219; 464.

Delete above pages from Greaves, R.

Insert: Morgan, G. P., death, 218.

Delete: death, 218, under Morgan, C. D.

Corpl. J. L. Davies, pp. 329–330 omitted.

Delete *M. Radford*, insert N. H. Radford.

Delete *W.* from W. H. Radford, insert N.

PART I

THE WAR WITH TURKEY

THE WAR WITH TURKEY

THERE was a sharp division of opinion amongst military and civil leaders as to the value of what were called " side-shows." The argument on the one side was that the enemy's main armies could only be found and defeated on the Western Front (France and Flanders) ; on the other side it was contended that as the static war on the Western Front robbed commanders of all power of manœuvre, a flank must be found and turned elsewhere. Those who favoured " side-shows " would have received greater support had it not been for the disastrous expedition to Gallipoli : the reaction was very strong.

Three of the " side-shows " in which the regiment was concerned come under the heading of " War with Turkey." The moment Turkey entered the War, the weakness of the Allied Powers—our own great sprawling commonwealth of nations—became apparent. Sea-power alone, absolute to the extermination of all enemy craft, still left portions of the British Commonwealth vulnerable, and the initiative of extending the battle-line lay with the Central Powers : the " side-show " was inevitable.

In theory Egypt was a province of the Turkish Empire ! And Mesopotamia marched on a storm-centre which successive Indian Governments had watched with anxiety for many years. Also millions of British Mohammedans looked on the Sultan of Turkey as their religious head. Egypt leapt at once into the position of a danger-spot. The danger in Mesopotamia was not so immediate, and was more in the nature of intrigue and propaganda ; but difficult though it was, military adventure was possible, and in course of time probable.

We were committed, without alternative, to a war with Turkey, and the operations against the Ottoman Empire constitute the important ' side-shows."

Although the Balkan War of 1912–13 had led to defeat, the Turkish Army was considerable. For years German advisers had been employed in Turkey ; von der Goltz, who died in Baghdad during the Mesopotamian campaign, had been in Turkish service for over twenty years. In 1913 new blood, in the form of a Military Mission, headed by Liman von Sanders, sought to reorganise and train the Turkish Army. The guiding principle ruling the activities of the mission " was one of moderate military assistance to Turkey. During peace it comprised the reorganisation of the Army. During war it led to a limited augmentation of the German officers and to the assignment of several German formations for the Sinai front, and of some batteries, flying detachments, and auto-trucks to other fronts, and to assistance with money and war material " (Liman von Sanders). As the War progressed, this principle was lost sight of.

At the outbreak of war the Turkish standing army was between 150,000 and 200,000 strong (the Turkish Staff is uncertain), and during the War the Army attained the high figure of 2,850,000.

A total of 36 infantry divisions was increased to 70, but that figure only refers to numbering, as they never had a simultaneous existence.

The distribution before the War was in four army areas :

(1) Constantinople, Thrace, Western Asia Minor, and Anatolia : I, II, III, IV, and V Army Corps.
(2) Kurdistan : IX, X, XI Army Corps.
   (Each of the above Corps consisted of a cavalry brigade and three infantry divisions.)
(3) Syria and Cilicia : VI and VIII Army Corps.
(4) Mesopotamia : XII and XIII Army Corps.
   (The above had only two infantry divisions, and the XIII Corps only one cavalry regiment.)
Also :
   Yemen : VII Army Corps (two divisions),
   Asir : 21st Division,
   Hejaz : 22nd Division.

Each infantry division should have had one field-gun regiment of two or three battalions, each of three four-gun batteries, and one howitzer battalion of three six-gun batteries of field and heavy howitzers ; but the Turks had lost most of their artillery in the Balkan War and had not made up the deficiency in full.

War dispositions placed the First Army in Constantinople, Thrace, Dardanelles, and Panderma—five Corps at first and then the VI Corps was gradually moved from Aleppo to San Stefano—and gave command to Liman von Sanders. The Second Army was placed on the Asiatic side of the Straits, consisted of two corps, and command was given to Djemal. The Third Army was concentrated about Erzerum.

Liman von Sanders points out that during the war Turkey " nominally organised nine armies, which was contrary to good sense," as some of them consisted of complete Staffs and practically no troops.

The regiment was represented, in the war with Turkey, on each of the widely separated fronts attacked by the British Empire. The conditions under which these campaigns were fought differ widely from those on the Western Front. Occasionally similar trench warfare prevailed, but even so there was generally an open flank : the more usual condition when armies faced each other was that of defended localities and a wide neutral zone, or " No Man's Land," which favoured the small enterprise. The other outstanding features are that the artillery battle never reached the intensity of that on the Western Front, and that climatic conditions caused heavy casualties through disease, and on account of excessive heat called for a greater physical effort from our troops.

Battle casualties show that the 74th Division (our 24th and 25th Battalions) had more casualties in one battle on the Western Front than during their entire Palestine service, which included the third Battle of Gaza, the capture and the defence of Jerusalem, and the action of Tell Asur, all hardly fought engagements.

A comparison of casualties in all theatres of war that concern the regiment shows :

France	.	.	55·99 per cent., or	5 to every	9	sent out	
Dardanelles	.	22·83	,,	2	,,	9	,,
Mesopotamia	.	15·79	,,	2	,,	12½	,,
Salonika	.	.	8·60	,,	1	,,	12	,,
Egypt	.	.	6·53	,,	1	,,	15	,,
Italy	.	.	4·76	,,	1	,,	21	,,

The greater casualties on the Western Front caused those who served there to look on the task of soldiers on other fronts as easy. It was not. On the other hand, the failure of the Gallipoli venture has vested that campaign with superlative battle horrors. Artillery fire at Gallipoli never approached that on the Western Front—the enemy had not the guns or the ammunition—but troops were never out of artillery range. The truth is that the horror was psychical rather than physical—an enervating climate and a sense of failure undermined *moral* by debility ; but a state of mind and soul does not make the horror less or the soldiers' task easier.

Climatic and physical conditions must be included in the picture of every action and in every phase of the soldier's life. Dysentery was an enemy in Gallipoli, Mesopotamia, and Palestine ; jaundice and influenza, malarial fever, and the lesser but painful evil of septic sores were everywhere ; and there were extremes of heat and cold, of drought and flood.

The Turk himself has always been recognised as a stout-hearted soldier, and under German direction he accomplished some notable feats of arms. Fortunately for us, his fighting qualities were dissipated by undecided and swiftly changing ideas of war direction, more astonishing than our own changes of policy. Enver Pasha was a restless-minded leader with mercurial enthusiasm which led him into sacrificing the Third Turkish Army in operations against the Russians in the frozen and snow-covered Caucasus during the first winter of the War. Von Sanders quotes Turkish figures stating that of 90,000 men who started on this mid-winter enterprise, only 12,000 returned ; " the others were killed, captured, died of hunger, or froze to death while camping in the snow without tents." The remnant was further decimated by spotted fever.

Russia, heavily engaged on her German and Austrian frontiers, was frequently hard-pressed by the Turks ; but until her collapse in 1917 she held to our advantage a great number of Turks in the Caucasus.

We were slow in moving against the Turk—unable to do so at first—but Turks and Germans were eager for a swift descent on Egypt, and simultaneous preparations for that important operation and the Caucasian adventure were hurried forward. A holy war was declared in the hope of undermining the loyalty of British Mohammedans ; and German " military special missions " were dispatched to Afghanistan, to Persia, and to Mesopotamia.

The Turkish advance across the Sinai Desert was a well-planned and splendidly executed raid—no more. " Egypt cannot be taken by 16,000 Turkish troops," is the dry comment of von Sanders.

And then, before the Turks were prepared for further offensive action, we attacked them !

We engaged a great number of Turks on the Gallipoli Peninsula. The Fifth Turkish Army lost in this campaign no less than 218,000 men, of whom only 42,000 returned to duty. Although we failed in our local intention, in our war against Turkey the greatest blow we dealt her was on the Gallipoli Peninsula. The regiment was represented here by four battalions.

After the evacuation of Gallipoli we found ourselves arrayed against the Turk at two of the most distant points of the Ottoman Empire, and we were forced to undertake constructive work on a vast scale before an advance could be made. The regiment had five battalions in the advance into Palestine and one in Mesopotamia. The great distance which lay, in each case, between the fighting line and the heart of the Ottoman Empire seemed to give those who disapproved of " side-shows " the impression that it was useless to expect any action on either front to have a decisive effect on the War. In both cases commanders were frequently reminded by the Imperial General Staff that their primary object was to protect our interests and remain on the defensive, and, indeed, if our

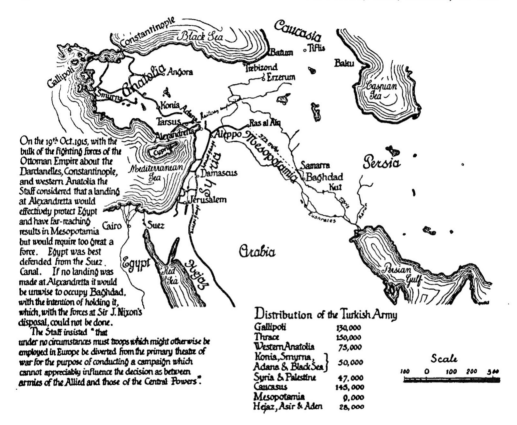

On the 19th Oct. 1915, with the bulk of the fighting forces of the Ottoman Empire about the Dardanelles, Constantinople, and western Anatolia the Staff considered that a landing at Alexandretta would effectively protect Egypt and have far-reaching results in Mesopotamia but would require too great a force. Egypt was best defended from the Suez Canal. If no landing was made at Alexandretta it would be unwise to occupy Baghdad, with the intention of holding it, which, with the forces at Sir J. Nixon's disposal, could not be done.

The Staff insisted "that under no circumstances must troops which might otherwise be employed in Europe be diverted from the primary theatre of war for the purpose of conducting a campaign which cannot appreciably influence the decision as between armies of the Allied and those of the Central Powers".

Distribution of the Turkish Army

Gallipoli	130,000
Thrace	150,000
Western Anatolia	75,000
Konia, Smyrna, Adana & Black Sea	50,000
Syria & Palestine	47,000
Caucasus	145,000
Mesopotamia	9,000
Hejaz, Asir & Aden	28,000

Scale

primary object had been to strike a vital blow at the Turk, we could not have selected worse places from which to deliver it. Of several alternative proposals that cropped up, a landing at Alexandretta was most discussed. But the procrastination of the Turk, who did not finish the Taurus Tunnel until the end of the War, left him, although unmolested, in continual difficulties at this junction of his lines of communication, which seemed such a tempting point to attack.

In spite of all our difficulties, the simultaneous advance in Palestine and Mesopotamia finally commenced to scratch at Turkish vitals. They were shaken by the loss of Baghdad, which to them was a far more serious blow than the loss of Jerusalem. They determined to retake it ; but when their Yilderim Army project reached a practical point, the immediate and dangerous threat was clearly seen by their German advisers to be in Palestine. By this time the war with Turkey was to all intents a British affair.

The German contention that her armies were never beaten in the Western Field is merely academic : Lord Allenby's final battle, in which Turkish armies were captured, came as Bulgaria sued for an armistice and Austria was at the last gasp. Apart from internal troubles the German armies might have stood on the Rhine, but in the World War their flank had crumbled and an encircling movement was in progress. In effect the Allied Powers were advancing through Turkey, Bulgaria, and Austria ; it was a complete and simultaneous collapse on all fronts save the Western Front, which, even so, was moving in the swift retreat of German armies.

At that time the regiment had, outside France and Flanders, three battalions fighting the Turks, one the Bulgars, and one the Austrians.

The regiment first entered the war against Turkey on the Gallipoli Peninsula.

GALLIPOLI

At the commencement of the Great War the whole nation " took up " the study of Military Strategy and Tactics, just as, in times of peace, they were persuaded to take a technical interest in the cultivation of sweet peas or the nutritive qualities of bread. Military problems were placed before an eager public by enterprising publishers rather in the form of " A Child's Guide to Knowledge." Mr. Hilaire Belloc, a polished writer and keen student, with considerable knowledge of military history, explained the deadlock into which the Military Commands had fallen at the end of 1914, by reducing the battlefield to the width of a street : if, he said, a trench required ten men to hold it, so long as ten men were available it could not be forced ; the breaking-point would arrive when only nine men could be produced.

Sir John French, and later on Sir Douglas Haig, and Sir William Robertson were convinced that the only way to come to a decision and end the War in our favour was " to kill Germans "—the catch-phrase was frequently used in Operation Orders—until the situation indicated by Mr. Belloc, of nine men in a ten-men trench, was secured ; and, indeed, so long as the War was viewed as a struggle in France and Flanders, there was no alternative.

But the situation at the end of 1914 was truly terrifying, and one sweeps aside the petty illustration of ten men in a trench with impatience. The Turkish Government had shown early in the War that its interests were with the Germanic Powers, but it was not until the 29th October that Turkey commenced open hostilities against Russia ; the next day the Allied Governments presented an ultimatum, and on the 5th November Great Britain and France declared war on Turkey.

Montenegro had followed Serbia into war. The complicated and mysterious policy of the Balkan States opened the door to further war combinations. Bulgaria, Rumania, Greece, were all probable combatants —potential enemies—possible allies ! In France and Flanders all movement and manœuvre were at an end, and a quick decision was out of the question—a state of interminable siege had arisen. France and Russia were tied down to their own frontiers, but the frontier of Great Britain was still the limits of the sea ! Out of such considerations the idea of an expedition to Gallipoli was born.

The sharp reaction after failure brings a flood of ill-judged criticism, enflamed accusations, and bitter condemnation. The immediate objective of this enterprise—a free passage to the Black Sea—was definite, and if successful would present opportunities as great, for example, as the capture of Douai, the occupation of Bullecourt or Passchendaele, or an advance on the Somme Front to Cambrai. But the evacuation of Gallipoli would seem to be more humiliating than getting stuck in the mud in front of Le Transloy.

Unfortunately, the Gallipoli Campaign is open to severe criticism in its execution. Its commander, Sir Ian Hamilton, had a difficult problem to solve, and his subordinates a difficult task to perform. To be an amphibious combatant is all very well, but one must be practised in changing from one element to the other, and this manœuvre was absent from our annual training programme. It is true that something of the sort was attempted a few years before the War, but the scheme was set to study defence, and was of an extremely limited nature, so that any knowledge possessed by either staff or regimental officers was of a strictly academic kind. Consequently at Gallipoli a state of bewilderment paralysed all concerned, when action, one might say movement, in any direction but one would have secured important results. As a contrast there were examples of high heroism.

But whatever the excuse offered on behalf of the Army, whatever the abuse hurled at the heads of the Government may be, a study of this campaign fails to reveal any adequate argument against the decision taken to attack the Dardanelles. We have the admission of the enemy that we were within an ace of success. Many battles have been lost on a small margin—and won !

Lord Kitchener stated bluntly that he could give no troops. The possibility of the Navy forcing the Dardanelles was not considered fantastic, and a fleet was assembled, consisting for the greater part of ships which would soon be withdrawn as obsolete. On the 16th February Lord Kitchener decided that the 29th Division could be spared, also that troops could be sent from Egypt if required (a Turkish attack on the Suez Canal had been repulsed on the 3rd and 4th February). A fleet of transports was then held at Alexandria.

The naval attack on the Dardanelles commenced on the 19th February under promising arrangements, but these were suddenly destroyed by Lord Kitchener on the 20th : pressure from the French theatre of war had, seemingly, been brought to bear, and he declared that the 29th Division could not be spared. The transports at Alexandria were then scattered.

On the 10th March Lord Kitchener again stated that the 29th Division could be spared. There were also two Australian divisions in Egypt, and a Royal Naval division under orders for Lemnos. On the 12th March General Sir Ian Hamilton was appointed Commander-in-Chief of the Mediterranean Expeditionary Force.

This able commander has given a graphic description of the problem presented to him in his first despatch. He left forthwith for the scene of operations, and witnessed the repulse of the naval attack on the 18th, " and thereupon cabled your Lordship my reluctant deduction that the co-operation of the whole of the force under my command would be required to enable the Fleet effectively to force the Dardanelles.

" . . . The northern coast of the northern half of the promontory slopes downwards steeply to the Gulf of Xeros in a chain of hills as far as Cape Suvla. The precipitous fall of these hills precludes landing, except at a few narrow gullies, far too restricted for any serious military movements. The southern half of the peninsula is shaped like a badly worn boot. The ankle lies between Gaba Tepe and Kalkmaz Dagh ; beneath the heel lie the cluster of forts at Kilid Bahr, whilst the toe is that promontory, five miles in width, stretching from Tekke Burnu to Sedd el Bahr.

" The three dominating features in this southern section seemed to me to be :

" (1) Sari Bair Mountain, running up in a succession of almost perpendicular escarpments to 970 feet. The whole mountain seemed to be a network of ravines and covered with thick jungle.

" (2) Kilid Bahr Plateau, which rises, a natural fortification artificially fortified, to a height of 700 feet to cover the forts of the Narrows from an attack from the Ægean.

" (3) Achi Baba, a hill 600 feet in height, dominating at long fieldgun range what I have described as being the toe of the peninsula.

" . . . Generally speaking, the coast is precipitous, and good landing-places are few."

The General then gives the nature and position of the various possible landing-places—W, X, Y2, Y, and V, etc. " In most of these landing-places the trenches and lines of wire entanglements were plainly visible from on board ship. What seemed to be gun emplacements and infantry redoubts could also be made out through a telescope, but of the full extent of these defences and of the forces available to man them there was no possibility of judging except by practical test."

After this reconnaissance there was no unnecessary delay. The date of the final decision to send troops, after the scattering of transports, created a fresh situation, with no happy chance of transport being available and fitted for troops ; and on the 23rd April the 29th Division sailed from Mudros Harbour to effect a landing on five selected beaches—S, V, W, X and Y. " Of these, V, W, and X were to be main landings, the landings at S and Y being made mainly to protect the flanks, to disseminate the forces of the enemy, and to interrupt the arrival of his reinforcements."

THE LANDING AT HELLES.

The landing took place early in the morning of the 25th. Four battle-ships and four cruisers, with some smaller craft, conveyed the covering parties to a point off the coast. " The morning was absolutely still ; there was no sign of life on the shore ; a thin veil of mist hung motionless over the promontory ; the surface of the sea was as smooth as glass."

The troops were transferred to small boats, and as it was light enough to see, the squadron opened a violent bombardment of the shore. To this shattering noise the Turks did not reply, beyond firing a few shells from the Asiatic side of the Straits. There was no movement, no sign of life.

The landing at S Beach was successful. The party on Y Beach, after suffering severe casualties, were re-embarked on the 26th. The landings at W and X Beaches were maintained.

Sir Ian Hamilton draws a vivid picture of V Beach :

" V Beach is situated immediately to the west of Sedd el Bahr. Between the bluff on which stands Sedd el Bahr village and that which is crowned by No. 1 Fort the ground forms a very regular amphitheatre of three or four hundred yards' radius. The slopes down to the beach are slightly concave, so that the whole area, contained within the limits of this natural amphitheatre, whose grassy terraces rise gently to a height of a hundred feet above the shore, can be swept by the fire of a defender. The beach itself is a sandy strip some 10 yards wide and 350 yards long, backed along almost the whole of its length by a low sandy escarpment about 4 feet high, where the ground falls nearly sheer down to the beach. The slight shelter afforded by this escarpment played no small part in the operations of the succeeding thirty-two hours.

" At the south-eastern extremity of the beach, between the shore and the village, stands the old fort of Sedd el Bahr, a battered ruin with wide breaches in its walls and mounds of fallen masonry within and around it. On the ridge to the north, overlooking the amphitheatre, stands a ruined

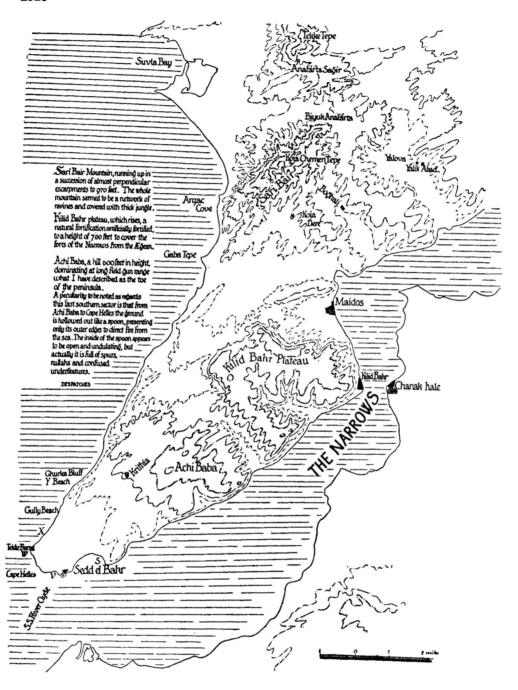

Sari Bair Mountain, running up in
a succession of almost perpendicular
escarpments to 970 feet. The whole
mountain seemed to be a network of
ravines and covered with thick jungle.

Kilid Bahr plateau, which rises, a
natural fortification artificially fortified,
to a height of 700 feet to cover the
forts of the Narrows from the Ægean.

Achi Baba, a hill 600 feet in height,
dominating at long field gun range
what I have described as the toe
of the peninsula.
A peculiarity to be noted as regards
this last southern sector is that from
Achi Baba to Cape Helles the ground
is hollowed out like a spoon, presenting
only its outer edges to direct fire from
the sea. The inside of the spoon appears
to be open and undulating, but
actually it is full of spurs,
nullahs and confused
underfeatures.

DESPATCHES

Suvla Bay

Tekke Tepe

Anafarta Sagir

Biyuk Anafarta

Koja Chemen Tepe

Yalova

Yilik Abad

Sari Bair

Boghali

Koja Dere

Anzac Cove

Gaba Tepe

Maidos

Kilid Bahr Plateau

Kilid Bahr

Chanak hale

THE NARROWS

Krithia

Achi Baba

Ghurka Bluff
Y Beach

Gully Beach

X

Tekke Burnu
W

Cape Helles
V

S
Sedd el Bahr

S.S. River Clyde

0   1   2 miles

barrack. Both of these buildings, as well as No. 1 Fort, had long been bombarded by the Fleet, and the guns of the fort had been put out of action ; but their crumbling walls and the ruined outskirts of the village afforded cover for riflemen, while from the terraced slopes already described the defenders were able to command the open breach, as a stage is overlooked from the balconies of a theatre. On the very margin of the beach a strong barbed-wire entanglement, made of heavier metal and longer barbs than I have ever seen elsewhere, ran right across from the old fort of Sedd el Bahr to the foot of the north-western headland. Two-thirds of the way up the ridge a second and even stronger entanglement crossed the amphitheatre, passing in front of the old barrack and ending in the outskirts of the village. A third transverse entanglement, joining these two, ran up the hill near the eastern end of the beach, and almost at right angles to it. Above the upper entanglement the ground was scored with the enemy's trenches, in one of which four pom-poms were emplaced ; in others were dummy pom-poms to draw fire, while the debris of the shattered buildings on either flank afforded cover and concealment for a number of machine guns, which brought a cross-fire to bear on the ground already swept by rifle fire from the ridge."

A landing on this coast was attempted, and eventually accomplished, by grounding the collier *River Clyde*. The Turks lay in wait, and though a few men succeeded in reaching the shore that day, no serious landing took place until night fell. It was a dreadful business. " Twenty-four hours after the disembarkation began there were ashore on V Beach the survivors of the Dublin and Munster Fusiliers and of two companies of the Hampshire Regiment."

At dawn on the 26th the position was, therefore, desperate. The landing had taken place, but the casualties from fire and drowning had been heavy, and the scattered remnants of units crouched on the beach itself, sheltered behind the four-foot bank that had been hollowed out by the sea. " With them," says Sir Ian Hamilton, " were two officers of my General Staff—Lieutenant-Colonel Doughty-Wylie and Lieutenant-Colonel Williams. These two officers, who had landed from the *River Clyde*, had been striving, with conspicuous contempt for danger, to keep all their comrades in good heart during this day and night of ceaseless imminent peril."

Lieutenant-Colonel Doughty-Wylie, Royal Welch Fusiliers, and Lieutenant Hayland had been detailed in the allotment of General Headquarters for the operations, for intelligence duties. At dawn on the 26th no senior regimental officers remained to lead the shaken troops. The following is an account of what happened, written by Captain Guy Nightingale, 1st Munster Fusiliers, from Gallipoli :

" The first time I saw Colonel Doughty-Wylie was on the morning of the 26th April. Senior officers were urgently required at the time, as nobody quite knew what was happening or what they were expected to do. I had come ashore myself on the previous morning, and had spent the night along the edge of the cliff immediately below the old Castle, and we were still there when two staff officers were seen coming from the *River Clyde* along the gangway to the shore.

" They were Colonel Doughty-Wylie and Captain Walford. The Colonel took charge of the situation at once, and after collecting together the whole force, which consisted of the survivors of the Munster Fusiliers, the Dublin Fusiliers, and two companies of the Hampshire Regiment under Major Beckwith, he ordered us to charge in one mass into the Castle and occupy it. He led the charge himself with the other officers, whom he ordered to form up in line in front of their respective regiments.

" The Castle was occupied finally, and the Turkish snipers found in it all bayoneted, with very small loss to us. The only way into Sedd el Bahr village lay through the Castle, which had two main entrances for this purpose. Each was a stone archway about 15 feet in breadth, but covered by a deadly fire from machine guns and marksmen hidden in the ruins of the village beyond. Anyone attempting to go through, or even walk past the gate, was killed instantly, and invariably shot through the head.

" It was here that Captain Walford, when gallantly leading a party of men later in the day, was killed, and his grave is now a few yards from the spot where he fell.

" Early in the day Colonel Doughty-Wylie had a very narrow escape here also. He was passing some distance in rear of the gateway when a bullet knocked the staff cap off his head. I happened to be quite close at the moment, and remember being struck by the calm way in which he treated the incident. He was carrying no weapon of any description at the time, only a small cane.

" When we rushed the Castle for the first time, I saw him pick up a rifle with a bayonet fixed, but he threw it away immediately after the Castle was in our possession. That was the only occasion during the whole day on which I saw him armed in any way.

" From 8 a.m. till noon we were gradually forcing our way from house to house up the village, until finally we held a line at the far end, forming up under some garden walls and in a small orchard, waiting for the order to assault Hill 141, known now as ' Doughty-Wylie ' Hill.

" At that time there were countless small incidents happening all over the village which called for fearless leadership. These occurred whenever a house containing snipers had to be rushed, or a street corner, covered by a machine gun, passed. It was greatly owing to Colonel Doughty-Wylie's example in taking the leadership whenever a party of men was held back or hesitated that the village was secured sufficiently early in the day to allow of a bombardment, and the capture of Hill 141 in the afternoon.

" I saw him on several occasions that morning walk into houses which might or might not contain a Turk ready to fire on the first person who came in as unconcernedly as if he were walking into a shop. Naturally this confidence of manner had a great effect on the men. While he was setting this splendid example, he had by no means lost touch with the battleships covering us, and the moment we had reached a point as far up the village as was possible, he went away and arranged for a bombardment, by the covering ships, of Hill 141 preparatory to an assault.

" While this was in progress Colonel Doughty-Wylie took me up one of the corner turrets of the old Castle, and pointed out to me the way he intended to carry out the assault. There was a strong redoubt on the top, but he decided that the remnants of the three battalions should assault simultaneously immediately after the bombardment. He was extraordinarily confident that everything would go well, and the hill be won by sunset, and I think it was due much to his spirit of confidence that he had been able to overcome the enormous difficulties with only such exhausted and disorganised troops as he had to deal with.

" His sole idea and determination was that the hill should be taken that day at all costs ; for he realised that it was impossible for us to hold any position between the high ground and the edge of the cliff where we had spent the previous night.

" As the time was getting near for the bombardment to cease, the Colonel gave his final orders to the few remaining officers before the assault. Major Grimshaw was to lead the Dublins. Simultaneously the Hampshires were to assault from the far end of the village and come up on the far shoulder of the hill, while the Munster Fusiliers were to advance on the left of the Dublins, and at the same time.

" When the order came to fix bayonets, however, the men scarcely waited for any orders, but all joined up together in one mass, and swept cheering up through an orchard and over a cemetery, Hampshires, Munsters, and Dublins, to the first line of wire entanglement, through which was a way out leading past the deserted Turkish trenches to the summit of the

LIEUTENANT-COLONEL C. H. M. DOUGHTY-WYLIE, V.C., C.B., C.M.G.

hill. On the top was a flat space surrounded by a moat 20 feet deep with only one entrance leading up over it, through which the assaulting troops were led by Colonel Doughty-Wylie and Major Grimshaw.

" The men lined round the top edge of the moat firing down on the retreating Turks, who were retiring down their communication trenches in the direction of Achi Baba.

" It was at this moment that Colonel Doughty-Wylie, who had led his men to the last moment, was killed by a shot in the head, dying almost immediately on the summit of the hill he had so ably captured.

" Major Grimshaw was killed shortly afterwards under similar circumstances. Colonel Doughty-Wylie was buried that evening by the men of my company, and the Burial Service was read over the grave the following morning by our Regimental Chaplain, Father Hawker, whom I had informed of the whereabouts of the grave.

" We left the hill that evening and advanced a little, and I was not able to get an opportunity of revisiting the scene for some six weeks. Later I found the grave in exactly the same place where I had seen him fall that day, and to which he had led his men from the moment he stepped off the *River Clyde* some eight hours before.

" When he took command of them, they were exhausted with the strain of the landing and depressed with what they had already experienced ; but the last he saw of them was at the moment when these same men realised the day was won, and rest close at hand, both of which they knew they owed to his gallant leadership."

Concurrently with this desperate fighting on the toe of the peninsula the Australian and New Zealand Army Corps effected a landing north of Kaba, or Gaba, Tepe, after a no less arduous and costly battle. The description given by Sir Ian Hamilton in his despatch cannot be improved —the country rises before one :

" The beach on which the landing was actually effected is a very narrow strip of sand, about 1,000 yards in length, bounded on the north and the south by two small promontories. At its southern extremity a deep ravine, with exceedingly steep scrub-clad sides, runs inland in a north-easterly direction. Near the northern end of the beach a small but steep gully runs up into the hills at right angles to the shore. Between the ravine and the gully the whole of the beach is backed by the seaward face of the spur which forms the north-western side of the ravine. From the top of the spur the ground falls almost sheer, except near the southern limit of the beach, where gentler slopes give access to the mouth of the ravine behind. *Farther inland lie in a tangled knot the underfeatures of*

IV—2

Sari Bair, separated by deep ravines, which take a most confused diversity of direction. Sharp spurs, covered with dense scrub, and falling away in many places in precipitous sandy cliffs, radiate from the principal mass of the mountain, from which they run north-west, west, south-west, and south to the coast."

A most difficult bit of country.

.   .   .   .

A diversion on the Asiatic shore was made by the French, who landed a regiment at Kum Kale, took 500 prisoners, and re-embarked on the 26th.

On the evening of the 26th the French Corps commenced to land on V Beach.

.   .   .   .

The April landing had given Sir Ian Hamilton about 5,000 yards of depth, which he tried to improve by five days of heavy fighting, commencing on the 6th May. The result, a gain of a few hundred yards, was disappointing. Thenceforth the situation changed. The moment lent itself to reflection, says Sir Ian, and it was clear that siege warfare had been imposed on him by the Turks. Still, another general attack was made on the 4th June.

There had been, then, three main battles : the landing on the 25th April, with the subsequent struggle for a foothold ; the three days' battle starting on the 6th May ; and the big effort of the 4th June—all on the toe of the peninsula and pressing in the direction of Krithia. While, north of this main field, isolated on the west coast at Anzac Cove, the Australian and New Zealand Army Corps held a small semicircle, no more than a thousand yards across, an open door " leading to the vitals of the Turkish position," playing a second part to Cape Helles by holding as large a body as possible of the enemy in front of them.

A second change in the situation is marked.

Sir Ian Hamilton's summary of his position is clear. On the 10th May, in view of the spectre of trench warfare, he cabled for two fresh divisions, and on the 17th he again cabled " that if we were going to be left to face Turkey on our own resources, we should require two army corps additional to my existing forces. . . . The 52nd Lowland Division had been sent me, but between their dates of dispatch and arrival Russia had given up the idea of co-operating from the coast of the Black Sea. Thereby several Turkish divisions were set free for the Dardanelles. . . . During the month of June I was promised three regular divisions plus the infantry of two Territorial divisions. The advance guard of these troops was due to reach Mudros on the 10th July ; by the 10th August their concentration was to be complete."

The regiment is concerned in two of these divisions, the 13th and 53rd.

. . . .

The 8th Battalion was, as its number implies, the first " Service " battalion to be raised, and it was posted to the 40th Brigade, 13th Division.

It has been noted (Vol. III) that as the war-years passed there was a steady depreciation in the quality of men drawn from the training battalions in England. But the first volunteers of the War were the cream of the nation, and of such was the 8th Battalion composed. The physique of the men was good, they were willing and keen, and it is not too much to say that the type of man was of a higher standard than that of the Regular Army.

A certain number of officers were from the Regular list : Major A. Hay (in command), Captains M. D. Gambier-Parry (Adjutant), G. H. Gwyther, M. L. Lloyd-Mostyn, M. I. H. Anwyl ; but the Reserve of Officers and the Oxford and the Cambridge Officers' Training Corps supplied the bulk : Major R. C. B. Throckmorton ; Captains G. W. D. B. Lloyd, R. B. Johnson, Walter Lloyd, F. C. T. Hadley ; Lieutenants Scott, S. Powell, T. D. Daly, A. D. M. Farrar, A. E. Allies, A. P. C. Rees, P. M. Dunn, E. K. Jones, H. G. Carter. Other officers were : D. MacBean, D. Roberts, R. N. Wilks, J. R. W. Jenkins, D. Gibby. And there were a number of Regular non-commissioned officers.

The enthusiastic volunteers were plunged at once into a life of discomfort, crowded twenty-three into a bell-tent, many of them with nothing but the clothes they stood in when enlisted ; uniforms, and even the small necessities a soldier carries, were impossible to get for many weeks. A great number of them could only speak a little English. The training hours were long, but there was a general feeling that they would be required in January, and discipline was excellent. Only some of the old non-commissioned officers gave trouble—the old soldiers' trouble, drink.

The system followed in this forced training was for the Regular officers to concentrate on the non-Regular officers. Those from the Officers' Training Corps were soon capable of training recruits, but others, with no military knowledge at all, were compelled by the exigencies of the situation to teach squad drill and elementary musketry after one week of instruction themselves. A dull and depressing experience for the men.

Under these conditions it was not surprising to find that the battalion was stale by June 1915. The orders to move brought relief.

" The battalion's strongest points were : marching, digging, boxing, football ; tactical training and musketry very fair ; discipline excellent, and physique magnificent ! " (T. D. Daly.)

Under the command of Lieutenant-Colonel A. Hay, the battalion, 1,200 strong, had moved since formation from Wrexham to Parkhouse Camp, Tidworth, thence to Draycott Camp near Swindon, and at the end of February 1915 to Blackdown, in the Aldershot Command, the whole division being there for training.

In the 53rd Division our four Territorial battalions had, at first, composed the North Wales Infantry Brigade. Their first war training was centred at Northampton. When the 4th Battalion was sent to France, the brigade was made up by the 1st Battalion Herefordshire Regiment (T.F.), and was numbered 158th Brigade.

The 13th Division was the first to receive orders to prepare for foreign service, and our 8th Battalion marched, on the 28th June 1915, to Brookwood Station, entrained for Avonmouth, and embarked (less 1 officer and 80 men, who sailed with the transport and animals on the s.s. *Eloby*) on the s.s. *Megantic*.

Captain Powell's diary contains an account of the voyage, which was, in the main, uneventful.

" A good ship and comfortable cabins. Am with the adjutant in a cabin with bathroom attached. Everyone seems rather nervous about submarines, as one was seen by this ship as she entered the harbour yesterday.

" The men sleep four in a cabin. . . . The South Wales Borderers are on board with us. E. K. Jones posted his machine guns with a view to repelling hostile attacks in the future. . . . I had a wonderful day at bridge, winning nineteen points in the train and twenty-eight after dinner.

" All port-holes are shrouded after dark so as to avoid showing lights.

" We did not move out till 8 o'clock (29th June), and then were helped out by six tugs. The captain of the ship has not been told our destination, but is merely making for Gibraltar. Had boat and alarm parade this morning with lifebelts on. . . . The men are busy singing hymns and Welsh national songs.

" Two destroyers convoyed us till 1 o'clock (30th) p.m., and then turned off home, much to our disgust."

The ship steered a zigzag course, while the officers passed the days in playing deck football and quoits, and pulled a tug-of-war. Gibraltar was passed on the morning of the 3rd July, and on the 5th Malta was sighted. A sirocco was blowing when the ship put in to the harbour early in the morning. " It is an odd, bleak-looking rock with an excellent harbour. We stayed there till 11 o'clock, and the usual swarm of pedlars collected round, and little boys dived for pennies. There was the P. & O. *Morea* lying just opposite us. She had several ladies on board, whom we inspected critically through our field-glasses. We distinctly approved of one whom we dubbed ' Ginger,' because of her red hair. There were one or two French battleships about, and their launches and boats buzzed about busily. We were not allowed to go ashore, which was a great disappointment and rather unnecessary. . . . We steamed out about 11 o'clock (a.m.) amidst great waving of handkerchiefs, and we were soon out of sight of Malta. In the evening we had a very dull boxing competition amongst the men."

On the 8th the ship touched at Alexandria, " just in time to see the *Ivernia*, with the Brigadier, Cheshires, and South Lancashires on board, preparing to go off to Lemnos, where apparently we follow them without much delay. Their boat is not nearly so comfortable as ours. Stretch, who left England a week before us in charge of the horses, and arrived here on Saturday, came on board and told us his news. He has sent on the company commanders' horses and twenty mules, and only three wagons, and has to stay here indefinitely with the rest. He is encamped twelve miles off, in the desert ; twenty men were told off to stay with him. Our base kit is going to be left here, and I had a great job packing and deciding what to leave and what to take, as there appears to be no likelihood of our being able to take on more than 35 lb."

Some of the officers managed to get a walk on shore. The voyage was resumed on the 10th.

" Have been passing the Grecian Islands all day (11th). They are barren-looking things for the most part, but we are now getting to more signs of civilisation. . . . We are at Lemnos (12th), where we arrived about 4 a.m. It is a wonderful harbour, the bay being very large. They call it Mudros Bay. The *Aquitania* is lying peacefully quite close to land, so it must be pretty deep. . . . In the afternoon some of the officers got a boat and had a bathing party, which was amusing to watch. Edmundson and Rees swam over to the *Minnewaska*, about 500 yards off, on which were Australian troops. Edmundson swam back in 14½ minutes against the tide, which was a good performance. The 38th and 39th Brigades are already in the fire trenches, so we shall probably be there in a day or two.

" 13*th July*.—Orders are out and maps issued. We may be off to the Peninsula at any hour. Wilks and 150 men are going to be left here.

Each officer is to take a bundle to carry himself, containing waterproof sheet, blanket, and toilet things. He may also take his valise, with 35 lb. in it, but he will probably not see it again. Letters are going to be very severely censored."

Everyone remained on the ship until the 15th, when : " A really most damnable day ! We started disembarking at 8, so I got up at 6 and breakfasted at 7. Finally got off at about 9. The heat was intense, and much the hottest we have had. We had a very dusty 1½-mile walk uphill to a bivouac, where we sat until 3, with not a scrap of shade. The water in our bottles was hot.

" At 12 we suddenly heard we were to go to Gallipoli to-day. Everything had been arranged for a stay of some three days, and it was just like the Staff to upset us. We left our bivouacs at 3, and went to the quay, where we waited in the stifling heat for over three hours while everything was put on board. To add insult to injury, only 500 were provided accommodation, and we were 770, so they got an extra boat, H.M.S. *Partridge*, to take the odd 270, and luckily I was with these. We had no squash on board, and they did us simply splendidly—gave us drinks, and at 9 a cold supper with the best cocoa I have ever tasted. . . . The *Partridge* was a converted liner, and had two guns forward. We got a sleep on deck for an hour or two."

Suvla Bay.

The 53rd Division received the order to proceed abroad on the 3rd July, and embarkation was completed at Devonport by the 19th. Our Territorial battalions did not arrive on the scene until the 8th August.

Meanwhile Sir Ian Hamilton was deciding how he should employ his reinforcements. He held the toe of the peninsula and the Anzac Beach, neither of which gave much hope in itself of expansion. The possible schemes were narrowed down to four.

He could throw every man on the Cape Helles shore and attempt to capture Krithia and Achi Baba. But a new system of earthworks had been constructed on the slopes of Achi Baba, so that even though he captured Krithia, the mountain would form part of the Kilid Bahr defences to the Narrows, his ultimate goal. Also the beach was restricted, and limited the number of troops that could be landed and deployed. No fresh landing-place due west of Kilid Bahr offered a fair chance of success.

The Asiatic shore ? He admits the idea was attractive, but to be successful he would have to deliver a determined attack on the peninsula as well, and his reinforcements were not sufficient for a double operation of the sort.

Bulair ? The capture of Bulair, at the neck of the isthmus, would cut the land communications of the Turkish Army, and was a better plan on paper than " on the spot." Admiral de Robeck was dead against it, as it placed the Navy in a dangerous position, open to submarine attack. The possible landing-places were not good, and so situated that the enemy would have time to organise strong opposition from Thrace. Finally, Sir Ian Hamilton was not convinced that the cutting of this neck would isolate the Turkish Army, which would still be able to draw supplies and reinforcements across the Straits.

The fourth plan, and the one he favoured, was to attack from Anzac in combination with a landing at Suvla Bay, storm " that dominating height Hill 305," and capture Maidos and Gaba Tepe. The landing conditions satisfied the Navy. The country was intricate, scarred and seared by deep ravines, the hills not high but in places precipitous and covered by thick scrub, and water was scarce. But " of these it can only be said that a bad country is better than an entrenched country, and that supply and water problems can be countered by careful preparation."

As for the date of this attack, if " large numbers of troops were to be smuggled into Anzac and another large force was to land by surprise at Suvla, it was essential to eliminate the moon. Unless the plunge could be taken by the second week in August, the whole venture must be postponed for a month."

Meanwhile the Turks were kept busy with minor operations on the toe of the peninsula.

An action had just been fought (12th and 13th July) at Helles, when the 13th Division landed and relieved the 29th Division. Our 8th Battalion arrived on the 16th, and were held in Gully Trench as Divisional Reserve. On the 17th they took over the front line from the South Lancashire Regiment.

Though rumour of attack was busy, the front remained quiet. As Sir Ian Hamilton remarks in his despatch, " The experience here gained in looking after themselves, in forgetting the thousand and one details of peace soldiering, and in grasping the two or three elementary rules of conduct in war soldiering, were, it turned out, to be of priceless advantage to the 13th Division throughout the heavy fighting of the following month."

Powell writes : " We got the first sight of the Turkish searchlight about 1, also the flash and boom of an occasional gun. Then we heard what sounded like rifle fire, but it turned out to be a park of small ammunition which had been set on fire by a shell. . . . We finally landed about 4, and the sight of the peninsula in the half-light was very strange, all sand and stones. Luckily we were not shelled as we landed. We had a very tiring three-mile walk to Gully Beach, where we are now, right on the sea-shore, which is to be our headquarters while we are on the Peninsula. They can't shell us here, which is a comfort. . . .

" Got to the trenches about 5 yesterday afternoon after a very trying, dusty march up. We settled down fairly comfortably. Food and water are rather scarce, especially the latter, and I am beginning to realise what real thirst is when you can't quench it, or have only one water-bottle to last the day."

The flies in the trenches were dreadful ; and there were unpleasant sights to greet the new-comers, such as a limb sticking out of a trench, to which was added the stench of the rotting dead. A wash was rare, and then in dirty water, but in reserve bathing in the sea was a delight. " We had a bathe, the Colonel, Parry, Allies, and myself, and it was perfect. The sea was very rough, and we stood up and let the waves break over us. No ships could get in, and all were waiting outside."

The wind was unpleasant, as it blew sand about, which entered the eyes, and food when eating. Food, too, was short—there were days when no bread was issued. And then we learn from Captain Powell what was really the most trying experience in the Gallipoli campaign :

" I am suffering very badly from the trench diarrhœa. My stomach revolts against the food provided. . . . Felt limp all day. The doctor gave me a dose about 10 o'clock and told me to starve all day and drink cold tea instead of water. . . . I have had my hair clipped short, as it is impossible to keep one's head clean owing to the sand unless you clip the hair. It looks odd, but it is rather comfortable. . . . Still feeling rather seedy and feeding on such slops as I can get. I got a bottle of French vin ordinaire for dinner, which was quite comforting. . . . Better on the whole, and at dinner-time I made my first square meal for three days—fresh meat and bottled peas. Anwyl has got some eggs from the canteen—I wonder what they will be like. My bed at night seems harder and harder, so I wake up very sore."

But on July 30th : " We were finally relieved in the Esky Lines by the Royal Scots . . . and started an awful march to V Beach, the *Clyde*, which we reached about 9. The men were travelling very heavy and were exhausted and gave a lot of trouble. I had the devil of a time whipping them in at the tail of the company. Well, we got on board the destroyer *Beagle*, parched with thirst, and they received us with every kind of drink and real ham sandwiches. It was heaven! We got to Lemnos about 2, and immediately disembarked and staggered up here, about a mile from the sea. Anwyl is feeling very ill, and so is Allies. It looks as though I may be left in charge of the company with about one other officer before casualties start. I felt better all day, and during the day ate four indifferent eggs which tasted delicious."

The date of the " great venture " had been fixed. The last reinforcements, the 53rd and 54th Divisions, were on the high seas, and due to arrive in a day or two; the moon would rise about 2 a.m. on the 7th; the first day of the attack was fixed for the 6th August.

For the purpose of " hoodwinking the Turks " Sir Ian Hamilton had arranged for a surprise landing of 300 men on the northern shore of the Gulf of Xeros; for a demonstration of French ships at Mitylene; for an attack by the Australian and New Zealand Corps on Lone Pine Trenches, which were situated on their extreme right; and a big containing attack at Helles.

The main attack on the Sari Bair Ridge was to take place at night, and was a complicated movement. The crest of the ridge runs parallel to the sea. A series of spurs run down to the shore, separated from one another by wild, scrub-covered gullies; two of these gullies lead up to Chunuk Bair, and are called Chailak Dere and Sazli Beit Dere, and another deep ravine, the Aghyl Dere, runs up to the highest peak of all, Koja Chemen Tepe (Hill 305).

Two columns of troops were to be employed to secure the crest of the ridge, each column having a covering force to whom first objectives had been given.

The right covering force was to take Table Top and clear the enemy from positions commanding the foothills between Chailak Dere and Sazli Beit Dere. This movement would not only open the way for the right assaulting column, but would also protect the flank of the left covering force. The main objective of the right assaulting column was Chunuk Bair.

The left covering force, moving north along the beach, was to seize Damakjelik Bair and gain touch with the IX Corps when it landed south of Nibrunesi Point, while the assaulting column, passing to the right of the covering force, stormed the important Koja Chemen Tepe (Hill 305).

Our 8th Battalion was to be attached to the left covering force with the primary duty of holding the line, but was split, two companies going to hold, with the 1st Australian Light Horse Brigade (under Chauvel), No. 3 Section of Defence, and, if all went well, to co-operate in the consolidation of the line Quin's Post–Scrubby Knoll, while Battalion Head-quarters, with the other two companies, the 3rd Australian Light Horse Brigade, and the 8th Cheshire Regiment, were to occupy No. 4 Section, the line Russell's Top–Walker's Ridge to the sea.

We know now that General Liman von Sanders, commanding the Turkish Fifth Army, which defended the Peninsula, received reports on the 16th July that between 50,000 and 60,000 men were being concentrated on the Island of Lemnos. Other reports gave greater numbers. He was certain that an attack was pending, but there was no indication of its direction. To the south, the British front might be reinforced but could not be extended, as both flanks rested on the sea. Of Anzac he says : " The British southern wing had made several attempts to gain ground. The only result was that the Turkish left was slightly bent back. On the British north flank a detachment, little more than a battalion, had been detached from the flank and pushed some distance to the north. It appeared to me of some significance, but Essad Pasha did not see any danger in it. Several attempts to drive the detachment back—adding even the Headquarters Guards to the attack—met with strong resistance and failed. These were the only indications which pointed to an intention to extend the front in that quarter. The indications were rather insignifi-cant." There was, too, the possibility, ever present in his mind, and always provided for, of a landing to attack Bulair and cut the narrow neck of the isthmus. To guard against this last possibility he had placed two divisions, the 7th and 12th.

He was also watching the coast between Helles and Anzac, and placed there the 9th Division under Colonel Kannengiesser.

North of Essad Pasha's troops, that is to say, between the north flank of the Anzac position and those two Turkish divisions about Bulair, the coast was guarded by two battalions of Gendarmerie (the Brussa and the Gallipoli Battalions) and a battalion of the 33rd Turkish Infantry Regiment, with one squadron of cavalry and four batteries of artillery, under Major Willmer, a gallant and capable Bavarian officer, who appeared again, in Palestine, to command a division on a stricken field.

Who will say that Sir Ian Hamilton's plan was a bad one ? It is true that the Turks had Colonel Kannengiesser's division for immediate reinforce-ment against the main attack from Anzac, but our IX Corps, landing at Suvla, had only three battalions and four batteries against them, for the two divisions on the upper Xeros Gulf were not immediately available.

Our Intelligence was not at fault—the Turks were given a margin. IX Corps Orders give three battalions " located in or about the Anafarta villages, also one battalion at Ismail Oglu Tepe, and another at Yilghin Burnu, with outposts at Lala Baba and Ghazi Baba. A few mounted troops and gendarmerie were also reported in the country north of Anzac, and it was considered possible that the hills due east of Suvla Bay were held by a party of gendarmerie."

The first troops detailed to land at Suvla were the 11th Division, two Highland Mountain Batteries, and six machine guns from the Royal Naval Air Service, the force under the command of Major-General F. Hammersley. A brigade of Field Artillery and the 10th Heavy Battery were to be landed beforehand at Anzac, and as the action moved forward were to join the 11th Division by way of the beach. The disembarkation of the 11th Division was to be closely followed by the 10th Division, less one brigade, the 29th.

The Corps Orders are clear. The 11th Division, after securing certain landing-places, had the following tasks : (a) Secure the enemy posts at Lala Baba and Ghazi Baba, and establish a footing on the ridge running north-eastward along the coast through Karakol Dagh and Kiretch Tepe Sirt, thence as far as possible, as Point 156. (b) Occupy the positions Yilghin Burnu–Ismail Oglu Tepe. (c) Seize the road junction at Baka Baba, and establish connection northwards between this point and such troops as have been detailed under (a) to advance on Point 156.

It was pointed out that the security of Suvla Bay would not be assured until the heights between Anafarta Sagir and Ejelmer Bay were denied to the enemy. When this was accomplished, " the G.O.C. IX Corps will endeavour to give direct assistance to the G.O.C. Australian and New Zealand Corps in his attack on Hill 305, by an advance on Biyuk Anafarta, with the object of moving up the eastern spur of that hill."

. . . .

Our 8th Battalion remained on the Island of Lemnos until the 4th August, when they sailed for Anzac. No kits, coats, or blankets were taken. They arrived at 9 p.m. The landing took place without a hitch, although shells were falling in the Cove and a continuous rattle of musketry seemed quite close. Nerves were taut before the knowledge of their purpose and the mystery of an unknown country. The battalion bivouacked in the shelter of White Gully.

The 40th Brigade, with which we are immediately concerned, operated entirely on the left of the Anzac attack. Theirs was no easy task in an unknown country, for they had been detailed as the left covering force. Two battalions, ours and the 8th Cheshire, were to hold the existing line in conjunction with Australian troops, while Brigade Headquarters, the

4th South Wales Borderers, and the 5th Wiltshire seized and held Damak-jelik Bair.

On the 5th August C and D Companies, under Daly and Anwyl, were sent to No. 3 Section, while Headquarters and A and B, under Graham and Walter Lloyd, went to No. 4 Section.

Daly was sent with his company to Quin's and Courtney's Posts, and received an enthusiastic welcome from the Australians. The trenches were from 5 to 10 yards apart, and " there was no chance," says Daly, " of using artillery against the Turkish trenches " (a condition imposed on the Turks by General Liman von Sanders : " A distance of a few paces between the hostile lines would inhibit the fire from the ships, which would now equally endanger the troops of both sides." This was explained to the leaders and to their troops.)

The awful stench of dead bodies in the narrow strip of No Man's Land permeated the air. The Australians claimed that their snipers had the upper hand, but, says Daly, " the Turks were very active " and all movement behind the front line was fatal. The front line was, apparently, the " safest place," as the Australian officer who took Daly round the line refused to use a periscope and pointed out landmarks over the parapet. There was a shortage of bombs, in spite of which two were always thrown to the enemy's one (which suggests that the supply was not inadequate, although the trench reserve may have been small). The Turks were very alert, and it was their habit to fire " mad minutes" at regular intervals.

Other points noted by the new-comer were the shortage of water, which was limited to half a gallon per man per day ; the melted state of bully beef ; the swarms of flies that covered everything ; the sides of the trenches, which were revetted with tins, and, of course, the intense heat. The Australians and New Zealanders worked in shorts, often without a shirt, and were burned dark brown : the New Zealanders were a remarkably fine set of men.

The preliminary attack, " to bamboozle the Turk," commenced on the right of our Anzac line at 4.30 p.m. At Helles it had opened at 9.30 a.m. and was in full swing. We need not follow its course, but it is important to glance at the account furnished by General Liman von Sanders :

" Essad Pasha at first believed that the decisive attack was directed against his left wing [*the right of our Anzac line*]. But on the evening of the 6th it was discovered that from the beach at Ari Burnu [*Anzac*] the enemy was moving northward along the coast, and that still farther north strong forces were being disembarked at various points . . . [*this must refer to*

Anzac, not Suvla]. Immediately upon receipt of the foregoing report I telephoned to the 7th and 12th Divisions on the Upper Xeros Gulf, ordering that they be alarmed and made ready to march at once. About an hour later orders were sent to start both divisions at once in the general direction of Usun-Hisirli, east of Anafarta Sagir. Essad Pasha that evening alarmed the 9th Division and ordered it to march northward."

The attacking columns were advancing up the slopes of Sari Bair. The left covering force, the 40th Brigade, under Brigadier-General Travers, reached No. 3 Post about 9.25 p.m. and advanced in lines of companies moving to a flank in fours, with an advance guard. They passed Bauchop's Hill and Walden Point, still held by the enemy, and encountered the enemy in a trench across the Aghyl Dere. The enemy fled before the determined advance—other trenches on the slopes of Damakjelik Bair were rushed—the hill was captured.

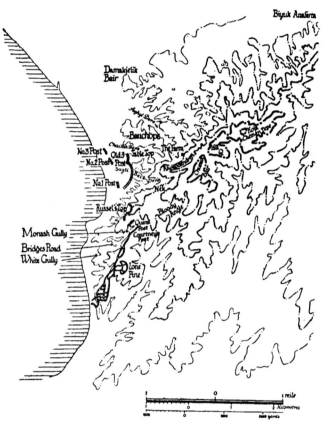

Success attended the efforts of the right covering force, and all seemed going well. At 3.30 a.m., under orders for attack, our 8th Battalion (A and B Companies) marched from Russell's Top to Monash Gully. The 3rd Australian Light Horse were to rush a place called The Nek at 4.30 a.m., and if successful our battalion was to attack other lines of enemy trenches.

Soon after 5 a.m. a message reached the Commanding Officer of success. A and B Companies were already moving up the gully, following a track. A wire entanglement was found, which the Royal Engineers demolished;

the track then split, and A Company was ordered to go right, which would lead them to about the centre of the Turkish line, while B Company went left, to the top of the gully : they were to work inwards when they reached the Turkish position.

The gully itself was covered with thick scrub, and the sides at the head of it were extremely steep with a lot of loose earth at the top offering a precarious foothold. A Company were topping the ridge when they were attacked with bombs and a machine gun from a trench on the very crest. Casualties occurred at once, and the leading men, falling back, knocked over those in rear who were struggling up the loose-sided slope.

An examination of the position forced a decision to withdraw : the loose earth, the steepness of the gully bank, and the restricted front, confined by thick scrub, afforded no chance to rush the Turkish trench, and the company was ordered to turn and follow in rear of B Company.

But B Company had already reached the top of the ridge on their side, and had been checked by the fire of machine guns, which had wiped out the leading platoon.

At this point a staff officer arrived to say that the Australians had failed to take the Nek, and no further advance was to be made by the battalion. The two companies therefore remained under cover in the gully until the evening, when they returned to Russell's Top. Here they remained until the 9th, when they moved back to Bridges Road in Army Corps Reserve.

Our 8th Battalion did not move again until the 15th, but we must follow the general action at Anzac with the landing at Suvla in order to get the Territorial battalions of the regiment properly placed in the picture.

The 40th Brigade, as covering party on the left, had captured Damakjelik Bair, and the left assaulting column had entered the Aghyl Dere. This deep gully splits into a northern and a southern arm ; the 4th Australian Brigade took the northern, to make for Koja Chemen Tepe, while the 29th Indian Infantry Brigade took the southern fork to Hill Q.

Nothing could be more graphic than Sir Ian Hamilton's despatch. " . . . The country gave new sensations in cliff climbing even to officers and men who had graduated over the goat-tracks of Anzac. The darkness of the night, the density of the scrub, hands-and-knees progress up the spurs, sheer physical fatigue, exhaustion of the spirit caused by repeated hairbreadth escapes from the hail of random bullets—all these combined to take the edge off the energies of our troops."

An admirable country for defence, and the advance everywhere was slow. At daybreak the 4th Australian Brigade was on the line of the

Asma Dere,[1] and the 29th Indian Brigade on the ridge west of the Farm. A little later they were in touch with the right assaulting column on the top of Rhododendron Spur, " a quarter of a mile short of Chunuk Bair—i.e. of victory."

At the end of the day Sir Ian Hamilton writes : " Our aims had not been fully attained, and the help we had hoped for from Suvla had not been forthcoming." He is unable in his despatch to conceal his anger and bitter disappointment, for the troops of the 11th Division, leaving Lemnos after dark, were successfully landed, but had achieved nothing. The original plan had been to land at two points south of Nibrunesi, but at the request of General Stopford a third landing was agreed to in Suvla Bay : it was here that confusion started. Some of the lighters grounded in the shallow water, and fire was opened by enemy pickets at Lala Baba and Ghazi Baba. Still, the 34th Brigade was landed : south of Nibrunesi the 32nd and 33rd Brigades were unopposed.

Every allowance must be made for the 11th Division during the night 6th/7th August. The country was unknown, and out of the inky darkness came fire from an enemy whose strength could not be appreciated. There was some control, for news of the difficulties of the 34th Brigade caused the 32nd Brigade to be moved to their support, but there is little doubt that our troops fired on each other. One unit, however, the 11th Battalion Manchester Regiment, seems to have been kept well in hand, and advanced resolutely in the night to Karakol Dagh. At daybreak the Turks commenced for the first time to shell, and set fire to the scrub about Hill 10, where the 34th and 32nd Brigades were assembled.

Dawn also brought the 10th Division into the Bay. The position assigned to this division was on the left, but the first six battalions were landed on the right and had to march by Lala Baba and Hill 10 under a flanking fire from Major Willmer's Turks. How many Turks were on the spot we do not know, but his total strength in infantry was little over 2,000. The remaining battalions of the 10th Division were landed at Ghazi Baba. At the same time the two Highland Mountain Batteries and one battery 59th Brigade Field Artillery were landed south of Nibrunesi.

The situation, when it was light enough to see, was that the infantry of a whole division was ashore, with three batteries, and a stream of battalions of a second division were landing behind them. " I have failed in my endeavours to get some live human detail about the fighting which followed," says Sir Ian Hamilton. The operations of the 11th Division are difficult to follow : the 10th Division, saved from the confusion of a

---

[1] The next ravine north of Aghyl Dere.

night landing, but split by the accident of their landing, made an advance with the 31st Brigade to Yilghin Burnu (Chocolate Hill) on the right, and along the Kiretch Tepe Sirt on the left. And that was all that happened on the 7th August.

On the 8th, at Anzac, the battle was resumed early in the morning. On the right, New Zealand troops reached the crest of Chunuk Bair and held on with the 7th Gloucestershire in a most heroic and determined manner. In the centre, about the Farm, enemy opposition was strong and defeated all attempts to advance, and on the left the Turks repulsed the Australian attack on Koja Chemen Tepe. " So matters stood at noon. . . . The expected support from Suvla hung fire, but the capture of Chunuk Bair was a presage of victory. . . . "

Taking everything into account, heat, thirst, fatigue, green troops, and making every allowance for the confusion caused by the first clumsy movements in a difficult country, there remains a complete lack of effort at Suvla Bay. There were, at General Stopford's disposal, five brigades of infantry and three batteries on shore, while at sea the warships were ready to give fire support. And the Turks were inactive. Except for a little artillery fire in the early morning, the enemy guns were silent throughout the day, and rifle and machine-gun fire was negligible.

General Liman von Sanders is most interesting. His account is given in the general manner of an Army Commander—there are no details, for instance, of Major Willmer's manœuvres—and he tells us that during the afternoon of the 7th August the Commander of the XVI Turkish Corps, consisting of the 7th and 12th Divisions, reported the arrival of his Corps from the neighbourhood of Bulair. Troops, he said, no doubt with pride, had made a double march that day. The Corps Commander was ordered to attack the British troops landed on the Anafarta Plain.

But on the morning of the 8th August von Sanders rode to the ground on which the XVI Corps was to form up for attack and found no one. Finally, he discovered a staff officer of the 7th Turkish Division, who said he was selecting an outpost position, and that troops were far in rear. The General gave orders for the attack to commence at sunset.

Major Willmer reported that evening that no troops had arrived. The Corps Commander stated that the fatigued state of his troops precluded any attempt to attack. He was promptly relieved of his command.

An odd situation. Nothing to choose between Turks and British.

Sir Ian Hamilton, with victory within his grasp, with the gallant New Zealanders on Chunuk Bair, wanting but a slight effort to fix his grip firmly on the high ground which would give him command of the plain

A FRINGE OF BEACH PROTECTED FROM SHELL-FIRE.   *[Crown Copyright.*

GABA TEPE.   *Crown Copyright.*

behind Helles and bring him within measurable distance of the Narrows, felt that something was wrong at Suvla, and went there.

He found Corps Headquarters on the *Jonquil* talking with confidence of an attack in the morning. "But when I urged that even now, at the eleventh hour, the 11th Division should make a concerted attack upon the hills, I was met by a *non possumus*. The objections of the morning were no longer valid; the men were now well rested, watered, and fed." And so they were. And on the 8th two British officers and a corporal reconnoitred Tekke Tepe to the summit and found it empty, except for two small patrols who fled: there were no enemy troops to resist an advance to the fatal heights.[1]

The Commander-in-Chief then landed on the beach and found all quiet. He spoke to General Hammersley commanding the 11th Division, who declared it was a physical impossibility to get out orders for a night attack, the time being 6 p.m. Troops were scattered; orders were out for an attack in the morning; nothing could be done. In fact the situation at 6 p.m. did not seem to justify the confident anticipation at Divisional and Corps Headquarters of the attack in the morning. One brigade only, the 32nd, was considered capable of movement, and the Commander-in-Chief directed that this brigade should anticipate the morning attack by occupying the heights that night. The orders reached the 32nd Brigade Headquarters at 7.30 p.m. at Hill 10.

The 32nd Brigade Staff was, however, as much out of touch with its battalions as the other Brigade Staffs. The attack did not commence until 4 a.m. on the 9th, and was made by the 6th East Yorkshire, a Pioneer battalion, supported by the 8th West Riding Regiment.

On the Turkish side command had been given to an energetic officer, Mustapha Kemal, who had whipped up the laggard Turkish divisions to attack before dawn on the 9th. They met the 6th East Yorkshire on the top of Tekke Tepe and drove them down again—an entire company was captured together with Colonel Moore, who had led them, and who was murdered by the Turks.

While this was going on, all through the night of the 8th/9th August, still another division was being disembarked on the beach. Headquarters of the 53rd Division was dumped on the beach at 7 p.m. on the 8th, and was met by orders to send two brigades to the 11th Division. Only one battalion had landed, so the order could not be complied with. From early morning, however, battalions were being sent singly to the front line.

---

[1] James T. Underhill, of Vancouver, was one of the officers of the 6th East Yorkshire who reconnoitred the hill. See *The Times*, 14th February 1925.

At 5 a.m. the 33rd Brigade made the attack which had been planned the previous day, in the direction of Ismail Oglu Tepe, and met the considerable fire of troops from the 16th Turkish Corps already in position. The attack failed.   No less than seven battalions of the 53rd Division were sent piecemeal into the fight, so that when night fell this new division was as scattered and out of control as the 11th had been.   Nevertheless, the Corps Commander decided to make another attempt on the Anafarta Ridge the next morning with the 53rd Division.

But on the 10th the result of the Suvla Bay inertia on the 8th became apparent.   Mustapha Kemal, of whom General Liman von Sanders held a high opinion, had received further reinforcements from the southern group, and launched an attack on Chunuk Bair, Hill Q, and the Farm.   The New Zealanders had been relieved by two battalions of the 13th Division ; these were overwhelmed under the weight of the Turkish attack and Chunuk Bair was lost.

The attack of the 53rd Division at Suvla, launched under the most unfavourable circumstances, did nothing to influence events on the important heights of Sari Bair.   The commander of the 160th Brigade sat on the beach with no troops, his battalions having been scattered in all directions, so that General Lindley had only two brigades at his disposal.   The 159th Brigade had also been sent up to the fighting line by battalions, but as all of them were in the neighbourhood of Sulajik it appeared possible for this brigade to organise a short preliminary advance to the foot of the ridge.   The 158th Brigade, to which our three Territorial battalions belonged, had lost the Herefordshire, but had the 2/10th Middlesex attached : the brigade was to pass through the 159th and carry out the main attack.

THE 5TH, 6TH, AND 7TH BATTALIONS.

Our three Territorial battalions had disembarked on C Beach early in the morning of the 9th, and remained there throughout the day (Lala Baba).   Orders for attack were issued that evening.   The 159th Brigade would commence the advance at 6 a.m.

From the beach on which our battalions were bivouacked there was very little movement, and no opportunity of seeing the country in front. One company of the 5th Battalion carried spades to the front line, but that was at dusk, and little was seen.

Verbal orders seem to have been given by the Brigadier-General, and so we find a contradiction in the order of battle.   The 5th Battalion believed that they were to be in the centre with the 7th on their right and the 6th on their left ; the 7th Battalion believed they were centre, with the 5th on their right.   At all events, the 5th led in the approach march.

Apparently a warning order only was issued on the night of the 9th. Réveillé was at 3.30 a.m., when the men had hot tea.   At 4 a.m. details of the attack were learned.

At 6 a.m. the 159th Brigade commenced to advance.   It is impossible to give positions with any degree of accuracy ; reports are vague and confused.   The line of advance was over a flat country covered with scrub, stunted trees, and hedges, and officers were unable to locate themselves (or the enemy) on the maps supplied.   To add to these difficulties, the 159th Brigade Staff spent the night trying to find the brigade units.   " The most that could be done was to give orders to commanding officers of three battalions, who, however, were not in a position to say where their battalions were, except the 4th Welch " (Brigade Diary).   Also the Staff was not in communication with the 158th Brigade Staff, whose whereabouts were unknown.

A line did advance at 6 a.m., 1½ companies of the 7th Cheshire and slightly stronger elements of the 4th Cheshire and 5th Welch.   It was a feeble affair, and after groping about for a while in a spiritless manner, troops stood still.

The 158th Brigade had left the beach about a quarter to five, our 5th Battalion leading.   They headed across the bed of the dried Salt Lake, and soon found themselves in sticky mud, in some places six inches deep. Half-way across the Lake the battalion opened out into artillery formation under shrapnel fire, which caused a few casualties.   Some 200 yards beyond the Salt Lake unaimed rifle fire was encountered, and the battalion deployed.

Kenneth Taylor, of the 5th Battalion, says : " The hill, or rather ridge, in front of us had a gradual rise at first, which was covered with trees, hedges, bushes, and oak scrub about waist-high.   It was practically impossible to keep any sort of formation or keep touch, and we were soon split up and rather disorganised."   All battalions met with the same experience, and their accounts of the action suffer accordingly in accuracy ; they gave what they believed to be true, and what seemed to them to be happening during their advance over an unknown country.

Lieutenant-Colonel Jelf Reveley, commanding the 7th Battalion, says : " It was apparently not known that the 159th Brigade had had to retire on the right, so that we were surprised at coming under rifle fire directly we reached the east side of Salt Lake, which we crossed under shrapnel fire from the hills in front.   Under the shrapnel fire the battalion was opened out into artillery formation, remained very steady, and suffered few casualties, the shrapnel appearing to burst too high up. The heavy rifle fire from the direction of Hill 50 drew our line, which was now extended in that direction, resulting in the swing to the right taking place too soon, so that our whole line was too much to the right—the 6th Royal Welch Fusiliers, who should have been on my left, being on my right. Messages were sent to the various companies of my battalion to work across more to the left, and by the early afternoon they were facing south-east on a line running north-east from Sulajik."

The 5th Battalion state that they passed through troops of the 159th Brigade, who were mostly entrenched behind hedges, and that at about 11.30 a.m. " fire was opened " ; they were then some 200 yards from the position held by the enemy. The leading line was reinforced by successive lines, and by a company of the 6th Battalion. Lieutenant-Colonel B. E. Philips (5th) was joined by Lieutenant-Colonel T. W. Jones (6th), and an assault was ordered.

The best account comes from Kenneth Taylor. After passing over troops of the 159th Brigade : " The situation became a little less obscure, as we could now see the ridge in front of us, and knew where the fire was coming from. The ridge must have been 150 to 200 yards away from us. About 50 yards away was a bank, and after that was all oak scrub.

" We started off again in waves with big intervals, and the first 50 yards was a hell-for-leather race, no cover and every chance of striking eternity. That 50 yards accounted for a good many, and my only recollection of it is the splendid way the men behaved. We arrived at the bank and had another breather. . . .

" I was out of touch now with anyone on my left, although I tried hard to find them. Shortly the order came down to fix bayonets and get ready to charge. I believe our own Colonel and Colonel Jones, of the 6th Battalion, were together at this time, about 100 yards on my right, and soon the order came to charge. The density of the oak scrub absolutely ruined all chance of a decent charge, as we had to follow goat-tracks and water-courses in single file to get through. Either the Turk could not see us or he was preparing to retire, as few bullets came over, and we had little difficulty in getting to the top, and to my immediate front everything was quiet. But being split up into small parties by the scrub caused more confusion, because so many parts of the line were out of touch, and it became impossible to tell how things were going on in other spots.

" After a while, I have no idea how long, everything seemed quiet, except on the right. Soon we saw a retirement taking place on the right, and it gradually crept closer to where we were."

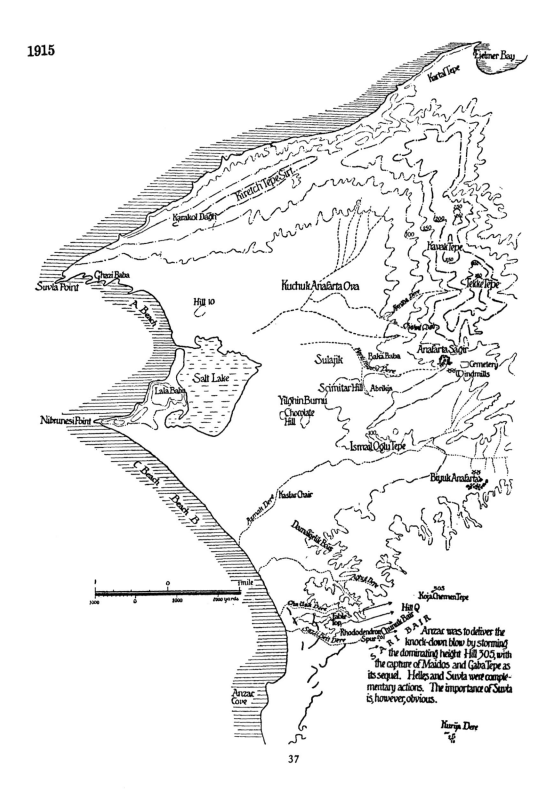

Lietner Bay

Kartal Tepe

Kireich Tepe Siri

Karakol Dagh

1200
750
600
850
Kavak Tepe
850

Ghazi Baba

Suvla Point

Hill 10

A Beach

Kuchuk Anafarta Ova

Tekke Tepe

Anafarta Sagir

Baka Baba

Cemetery

Salt Lake

Windmills

Sulajik

Lala Baba

Scimitar Hill   Abrikja

Nibrunesi Point

Yilghin Burnu
Chocolate
Hill

100

Ismail Oglu Tepe

C Beach

Biyuk Anafarta

Beach B

Kastar Chair

Aerioli Dere

Damakjelik Bair

305
Koja Chemen Tepe

1 mile

1000   0   1000   1000 yards

Table
Top

Hill Q

Rhododendron
Spur

S A R I   B A I R

Anzac was to deliver the
knock-down blow by storming
the dominating height Hill 305, with
the capture of Maidos and Gaba Tepe as
its sequel. Helles and Suvla were comple-
mentary actions. The importance of Suvla
is, however, obvious.

Anzac
Cove

Kurija Dere

37

We must now turn to Lieutenant-Colonel Reveley's account of what seemed to him to be happening on the right. " In the early afternoon heavy casualties were experienced when my men were just coming up to the leading (?) trenches owing to the retirement from them *of troops of another brigade*, who carried my men with them for a short distance. The retirement was checked and the advance was resumed."

An officer sent by Taylor to find out what was happening returned with the information that a retirement had been ordered. It is more probable that the 7th Battalion drew the whole line back with them. Lieutenant-Colonel Philips, leading his battalion, had been killed on the top of the ridge, and the same confusion existed there as on the immediate front of Kenneth Taylor.

The times mentioned by officers are vague ; no doubt minutes seemed hours. All this must have taken place before midday. At 1 p.m. the Corps Commander ordered a second attack to take place at 5 p.m.

" At 5 p.m. the leading line was still about 400 yards short of the ground on which we were to relieve the 159th Brigade, so a general advance was ordered at that hour. This was carried a short distance, but failed to get through to the required ground, casualties again being very heavy " (Reveley).

Kenneth Taylor, who dropped back with his company to the entrenched troops he had passed over, writes of them as the 160th Brigade, and never mentions the 159th Brigade. " I remember the kindness of a Queen's officer giving us a drink "—and this confirms Lieutenant-Colonel Reveley's statement that the whole of the 158th Brigade swung too much to the right. But all are agreed that the ridge assaulted was the first objective allotted to the 159th Brigade. By 5 p.m. the Turks were firmly established and the British advance had failed.

The situation is well described by Taylor : " We could locate very few of our own men, as everybody was so mixed up—battalions, brigades, and divisions all jumbled up together—so we decided to move to a big tree about 100 yards to the left and have a look round.

" We decided that we must find Major Head, who was now in command of the battalion, and get some orders and information if possible. Borthwick [Adjutant] went off in search of Head, Tom [Parry] in search of a hospital, and I in search of the remainder of our scattered battalion. I found a few men and collected them behind a bank and hedge just in rear of our tree, a place Borthwick had decided on as our rendezvous. Borthwick returned later with a few more men and the news that we were to collect all the men we could possibly find, and remain where we were in support,

LIEUTENANT-COLONEL B. E. PHILIPS.

in case of necessity.   Head, I think, knew less of the situation than we did, and was beating up stragglers in the rear.   Later on we found Colonel Jones.   Captain Porter had a few men of the 6th Battalion on our right, in the same boat as ourselves, and looking very miserable."

Sir Ian Hamilton had watched the battle, and in the evening ordered the Corps to entrench on the positions held.   The 11th Division was given the right, the 53rd Division the centre (from Sulajik to the foot of the slope rising to Kiretch Tepe Sirt), the 10th Division the left.   Our battalions were on the right of the divisional front, and did not participate in the attack of the 54th Division on the 12th August, launched with the object of clearing the wooded plain of Anafarta Ova, or that on the 15th August when the 10th Division, supported by the 54th, sought to clear the ridge Kiretch Tepe Sirt.   This attack was considered by General Liman von Sanders as being the third crisis in the Suvla Bay landing.   But again, under the able leadership of Major Willmer, whose Gendarmerie had been reinforced by all available troops, including battalions from the Asiatic shore, a timely counter-attack drove our leading troops from the ridge they had won, the reinforcements that had been promised them not arriving in time.   Once more it seems to have been a matter of a few minutes only.   Liman von Sanders attached the greatest importance to this ridge, and saw himself in grave peril if it was lost.   He thinks that we could and should have occupied the Kiretch Tepe Sirt on our first landing.   He sees us squatting on the beach and cannot understand why we don't advance at all costs.   " The opponent, of course, does not know the reasons of the enemy.   Since the weakness of the Turks in the Anafarta section was known, the British leaders may not have thought that reinforcements could be brought up so quickly, the more as large forces were tied to the two battle-fronts by heavy attacks simultaneously made on them.   Perhaps they had difficulty getting their young troops quickly forward over the cut-up and rocky terrain where there was hardly a road."   But to parry the blow he had to denude the Xeros Gulf of troops, " and on the whole Asiatic coast there were but three battalions and a few batteries left as coast-guards."

But the lesson of Suvla will not be learned by putting the responsibility of failure on the battalions of young soldiers—battalions of the same quality and under similar conditions fought gloriously at Anzac, holding on to positions to which they had been led when all officers were down.

On the evening of the 15th August General Stopford handed over the command of the IX Corps.

The high ground of Sari Bair remained in the hands of the Turks, and the net result of our operations was to extend our left flank from Anzac Cove.

Of the first week after the failure at Suvla, Lieutenant-Colonel F. Mills, then a Company Commander but later commanding the 6th Battalion, says : " We then had a terrible week, occupying a shallow Turkish trench, very little water, few rations, cold at night, and a blazing sun during the day. The smell was indescribable, dead and wounded everywhere, and no means of burying the dead. After sweating in the sun all day, the dust caked on everyone's face, and for want of water everyone's lips were black with caked blood ; the blood cracked if one opened one's mouth, and it streamed down one's chin."

At Anzac our 8th Battalion left Army Corps Reserve on the 15th and took over the front line at the apex. Promptly they attempted a small enterprise. The Turks had erected three loopholes in a trench on a small knoll about 30 yards from the crest line. Lieutenant Allies took out a small party to destroy the post—a foolhardy exploit in broad daylight which might from its recklessness have succeeded—and he was seen to enter the trench. But the Turks saw the raid coming at the last moment : the party was scattered, and Lieutenant Allies and 5 men were reported missing.

The attempt was repeated twice the next day by Lieutenant McC. Jones with a bombing party, who each time reached the trench but was bombed out again by the garrison. This post was finally captured by an organised brigade attack !

The climate was beginning to undermine the health of troops. The sick casualties were high ; boils of a painful description were common.

Captain Powell, of the 8th Battalion, says :

" *9th August.*—Left about 12 and joined the rest of the battalion and moved off to Johnson's Gully to support the Connaught Rangers, who were supposed to be exhausted. It was nice seeing all the others again, and we had a good night.

" *10th.*—Made an early start about 6.40, before we could get any water or have breakfast, and moved for about two hours right up to the left of our position. We passed streams of wounded walking, and saw a few on stretchers until we got to the clearing-station, where we rested an hour, and I was able to fill my water-bottle. The wounded were lying about in thousands, and sometimes the moaning was very trying. Then we pushed on up the gully and passed more wounded and several dead bodies. We got to our rest-place about 1 and stayed until 7.30. Then we moved up to the top of this very steep gully. D Company had to form a covering party while the rest of the battalion dug all night. It was a jumpy job, as we had to lie down in front of the trench all night. We lost 16 men—3 killed and 13 wounded.

" 11th.—I have a nasty boil on my neck that has been troubling me. The doctor says it is a carbuncle, and to-day opened it in a most unpleasant manner. We rested all day, and then moved up the gulley and dug a trench all night. No sleep is beginning to tell, and there is no water to be had. You must drink the little you get, so washing is impossible. The supply of food is limited to bully beef and biscuits. In fact things could scarcely be more miserable.

" 12th.—We were badly shelled this morning and our cook had his head blown off. Also we had got some water for the men, and they were all collected round it when a shell came and killed and wounded about six and knocked all the water-cans to bits, and there is no more to be had. . . . About 7 we heard we were not to dig that night.

" 14th.—Unless we can get some vegetables to eat we shall have trouble, as the men are breaking out in sores. The issue of lime-juice is ludicrous—yesterday we had 7 pints to the battalion !

" 17th.—A very tiresome day, as we had to move our bivouac three times, owing to two battalions of the Canterbury New Zealanders coming up to take on the fire-trenches with us in reserve. The authorities look upon the taking of this advanced Turkish trench as a matter of great importance, and it was arranged that the N.Z.s should have a go at them last night. At 7 o'clock we were told that we should have to lie up all night in support of them, and we moved off at 9 and tried to take up a position in the open brushwood, but the country was so awful and the bush so thick that we were withdrawn on to the track, and we stayed there all night with fixed bayonets, standing to arms at 12.30 and 4. The N.Z.s attacked, but the Turks had a listening-post out ready for them, and these dashed back, and the Turks immediately reinforced heavily and drove the small attacking party off.

" 19th.—We had a few drops of rain this morning—the first we have had since leaving England. It is getting cold at night and I wish I had a blanket.

" 20th.—Nothing much happened all day, except the eternal finding of fatigues. If the men don't get a rest they will collapse. . . . I am getting weak again with diarrhœa.

" 21st.—About 3 o'clock they started to attack on the left : the 9th Army Corps, consisting of the 10th and 11th Divisions and a Territorial division in which our 5th and 6th Battalions are.[1] It was a wonderful sight

---

[1] Our Territorial battalions were not concerned in this attack.

watching the bombardment and then the advance through glasses. We looked to be having a lot of casualties, but we certainly took three lines of trenches, if not more.

" *22nd.*—We hear they did a very good advance on the left yesterday, and as it is only about two miles across (!) there, they may get to the sea any day, which would put the end in sight. Pray God they do ! " (Powell.)

Until the 4th September the 8th Battalion took regular duty on Cheshire Ridge. The front was very quiet and, except for sickness that frayed tempers, there was little to grumble at. The battalion then left, and marched to Lala Baba.

" We suddenly heard, early in the morning, that we were going to move at 8 to-night, so we had a great hustle all day getting ready. As usual, in moving we had a terrible time. The Newfoundlanders who relieved us were late, and we did not leave till 11 p.m. Then the guide, who was a perfect fool, lost his way, and B and A Companies, owing to a mix-up in orders, failed to meet us at the expected place. After two hours they were found by the Sergeant-Major, and then the tail of the column managed to lose touch with the others and again lost themselves. Meanwhile, T. M. [Throckmorton] was livid with rage most of the time, and finally we struck a trench occupied by the Gloucesters, who put us on our track."

Meanwhile, with the 53rd and 54th Divisions holding the line from Sulajik to Kiretch Tepe Sirt, the 29th and 11th Divisions had once more attacked Ismail Oglu Tepe, on the 21st August. The Turks were by that time well entrenched, and after suffering heavy losses the two attacking divisions failed to make any appreciable advance. Except for the disturbance caused by this attack, all was quiet on the 53rd Division front. Casualties from shell or rifle fire were small—from sickness they became heavy. A dreadful wastage set in.

Our 7th Battalion had been sent on the 14th August to Mudros, where they were engaged in guarding Turkish prisoners, making roads, loading and unloading stores and ammunition. They did not return to Suvla until the 14th October, when their strength was 20 officers and 496 other ranks. By this time the strength of the 5th and 6th Battalions was so reduced that they were amalgamated on the 9th under Lieutenant-Colonel C. S. Rome.

EVACUATION.

Sir Ian Hamilton was recalled on the 17th October, and General Sir C. Monro was sent out to report (*a*) on the military situation on the Gallipoli

Peninsula ; (b) to express an opinion whether on purely military grounds the Peninsula should be evacuated, or another attempt made to carry it ; (c) the number of troops that would be required (1) to carry the Peninsula, (2) to keep the Straits open, and (3) to take Constantinople.

Fresh on the scene, Sir C. Monro viewed the position that had been secured on the fringe of the coast-line with amazement. None of the principles of any textbook was possible—the Turks had observation, depth, every conceivable advantage, and, no doubt, according to textbooks, should have swept us off the Peninsula with ease. It was all too true— the golden opportunity had passed. Evacuation was decided upon.

The 10th Division was the first to move, in October, to Salonika, where they joined two French divisions. But the order to evacuate was not given until the 8th December.

As the weather cooled, the wastage through sickness decreased, but our battalions, always within range of the Turkish artillery, whether in or out of the line, resting, or on fatigue, were not only weak in numbers but in a state of physical debility. On the 26th November torrential rain heralded a blizzard and severe frost. The dry watercourses at Suvla became swift-flowing rivers ; trenches were filled, and had to be abandoned ; and then frost and snow ! At Anzac and Helles the damage was not extensive, owing to the protection of the surrounding hills, but at Suvla there was no such protection : over 200 deaths occurred from exposure, and some 10,000 sick were evacuated during the first few days of December. Our four battalions were caught in this and suffered severely. It was a most unusual time of year for a storm of such violence, but it was a warning against undue delay.

"... Our flimsy piers, breakwaters, and light shipping became damaged by the storm to a degree which might have involved most serious consequences, and was a very potent indication of the dangers attached to the maintenance and supply of an army operating on a coast-line with no harbour and devoid of all the accessories such as wharves, piers, cranes, and derricks for the discharge and distribution of stores, etc." (Despatch.)

" 25th November.—Nothing very much happened during the day. Went round the trenches again with the C.O. Suddenly, late at night, an enormous fatigue was commanded. We found 450 men, which meant cooks, officers' servants, ourselves, etc., all had to turn out, and sick men did guard. It was on from 1.15 and we did not get back till 5.30. We dug two pentagonal trenches with a place for five machine guns and linked it up with the firing line and towards the beach. It was frightfully cold, but the Engineers gave me a topping cup of coffee.

" 26th.—We heard that we were not going to the fire-trenches for three or four days, probably owing to the giant fatigue. About 5.30 a dreadful thunderstorm burst over us, and it seemed as though all the furies of hell had broken loose. All our dugouts were washed out and the stream was two feet deep in the trenches. It continued till 10 p.m. and then cleared a bit, and I turned up my breeches, took off my socks, and waded round the company to see how they were, and I was delighted to find them in fair spirits. I have never known such a storm in any part of the world, and the force of the wind was appalling. Well, I hope the authorities realise their responsibility in not having fixed us up with head covering, and things like gum-boots.

" 28th.—The day did not clear and the night set in to rain and snow. We did our best to dig away the mud, but as fast as we did so the snow and rain filled it up again. Indeed, it was quite impossible to cope with the situation. They are evacuating all the sick they can. . . . Of course all blankets and bedding are soaking. Food has, of course, been mere bully and biscuits, with an occasional bit of horrid bacon. I simply can't swallow the stuff. However, it was a wonderful bit of work getting rations up at all.

" 29th.—Were told that some of us had to go up and relieve those in the firing-line, and accordingly I and my 3 officers and 100 men dragged up there about 2 in the rain and through the mud knee-deep. On the way we met numerous cases of men desperately ill, staggering down, and one or two had gone mad from exposure. Two fellows had got hold of a bottle of rum each and were dead drunk. . . . To add to our troubles it has started to freeze hard and nobody can feel their feet at all. The whole business is rank bad luck. We ought to have been off the Peninsula by now. The night watches were perishing.

" 30th.—The men are in a very bad state and I have had to send any amount down with bad feet and rheumatism. One's clothes, already soaking, freeze on one, and the only thing to do is to keep on the move the whole time. We have got a certain amount of braziers going in the trenches, but it is very hard getting the men any tea or hot food, indeed, almost impossible. The nights cannot be described. To add to my troubles I have got bad diarrhœa. I hear the Turks are in an awful bad condition, and we can see them running about in the open trying to keep warm. However, we shoot as many as possible, but some of the rifles are in such a condition they won't go off. My feet are agony to walk on. . . ." (Powell.)

Plans were maturing. Orders for the withdrawal of certain guns were issued on the 27th November, and a more detailed scheme was issued on the 29th. The evacuation was to be carried out in three stages : (*a*) the preliminary, (*b*) the intermediate, (*c*) the final stage. The preliminary consisted of the evacuation of stores and a certain proportion of troops.

There was a rumour that the 53rd Division would be the last to go, but troops were so weak that it was decided to send them first. The whole division, 217 officers and 4,522 other ranks, embarked on the night of the 11th December, and sailed for Alexandria.

The next day orders were issued to push forward the intermediate stage, which included the withdrawal of men and guns not actually required for the final defence.

The last stage was carried out during the night 18th/19th December. The battalions holding the line were 6th Loyal North Lancashire, South Lancashire (38th Brigade), Warwickshire, Worcestershire, Staffordshire (39th Brigade), Cheshire, South Wales Borderers, Royal Welch Fusiliers (40th Brigade).

" *17th December*.—My watch was from 4 to 6, and as soon as it started rain fell heavily for a couple of hours and made the trenches slippery, muddy, and beastly. After that the wind changed round and the rest of the day has been lovely and warm. Received our final orders for evacuation. The bulk of the battalion go to-morrow, 88 men of C Company, myself, and Lopp being left behind with the Cheshires to hold the line for another twenty-four hours. . . .

" *18th*.—The plans are all altered, and it was decided that I should not stay but go down with the rest of the battalion, the line being held by the Cheshires and S.W.B.s. We were relieved by the latter at 2, and having buried or destroyed everything of value, we left the dear old trenches at 5.30 in absolute silence. I had carefully inspected the company twice to see that they had nothing on them that could rattle, and their mess-tins were tied up in their waterproof sheets. . . . We crept off at intervals of about 50 yards between companies, and got down to the beach about 7.30 without a casualty. Not a single shell was fired and very few stray bullets came across. The beach presented an extraordinary deserted appearance. We had to spread over an area of about 400 yards and light fires to keep up appearances. There were plenty of spare rations lying about, and I collared cases of tinned milk and butter for the company.

" *19th*.—I can't describe the relief of having got my company down so far without a casualty. They are still shelling the beach, but there is fair cover. The men, who are in extraordinarily bad condition, not having marched for months, were very tired last night. Taylor and 42 men embarked last night as an advance party. I was told off for a fatigue at

6 o'clock to load 750 boxes of ammunition and embark with it. I got on board the *Snowbell* transport by 8.30, having loaded the ammunition in the record time of sixty-five minutes. To our amazement we were told that we were bound for Imbros ! " (Powell.)

To prevent any suspicion arising in the mind of the enemy all hospital tents were left standing, and parties were detailed to set fire to the depot stores after the last body of troops had embarked.

The embarkation was carried out without incident in bright moonlight. The sea was smooth, no one hurried, it might have been a peace-time parade.

The enemy were heard sniping away at the sandbagged trenches in entire ignorance that they no longer contained defenders. At 3.50 a.m. the last few men were boarding the lighter, and shortly after 4 a.m. the weird glare from the burning depot lit up the sky.

" *20th December.*—Got to Imbros about 2, and got up to the camp, two miles off, at 3.30, where we discovered a hot meal waiting for us. The men were in a bad state of exhaustion, and they don't seem to have any reserve power at all. The Gurkhas marched right past us, carrying enormous packs, and it made me feel quite ashamed at the state of my men."

Powell and his men sailed for Mudros on the 23rd and " When we got on shore we discovered there was a three-mile march to the camp, and as it was raining pretty heavily this did not cheer us up. We finally fetched up in camp rather bedraggled about 10, and found Glazebrook [1] had prepared an excellent breakfast for the officers and men. The camp is a neatly-set-out one, surrounded by hills which look wonderfully picturesque at dusk and early morning. I share a tent with Stretch and the Adjutant. In the afternoon I went to Porticudos, a village about 1½ miles off, and purchased oranges for the company for to-morrow, and tried to buy various other things, but the Greeks are such frightful robbers. A large mail came in, but there is a great deal more still to come.

" *25th, Christmas Day.*—A lovely day and, appropriately enough, quite a large mail of letters and parcels turned up. It was delightful getting these after so many weeks with no news. Church parade at 10.30. The men had plum pudding, and also a free issue of a pint of beer per man. There was only enough beer for two companies, so mine got it, as I was senior company commander. The only gift I could procure for the men was an orange per man. In the evening we had quite a good dinner, finishing up with nuts, figs, and oranges. The mincing machine has arrived, so that now the meat is eatable.

[1] Quartermaster.

" 26th.—. . . Started off early for Thermos to get a bath in the hot springs there before the rush came. It is a jolly walk about four miles along the valley. There were crowds of ambulance Tommies already there, and one or two whole battalions, but I managed to get a bath after waiting half an hour, and it was delicious—just the right heat. But best of all, afterwards we had two omelettes apiece, honey and biscuits, and really good tea, and then a leisurely walk back. I enjoyed the whole thing, although I feel I have no energy, and don't want to read or write or walk or work ! However, I am very fit and better for the change of food." (Powell.)

The evacuation of Suvla Bay being complete, the next problem was to get the troops away from Cape Helles. It was known that the Division was under orders to take over a sector of the line at Helles, and on the 30th our 8th Battalion sailed in the *Redbreast*. " Disembarked about 10, and after a weary march with our heavy packs got to our bivouacs at Gully Beach about 1 a.m., hungry and exhausted." (Powell.)

In the line they found that nothing had been done " since last July by way of improvement, and no attempt has been made to improve the road, which is a foot deep in mud. The firing-line is most bewildering, but very interesting ; in some places about 15 yards from the Turks and nowhere more than 100 feet. The Turkish artillery was active.

Liman von Sanders tells us that the long-coveted German artillery ammunition reached him in November. At the same time an Austrian 24-cm. mortar battery arrived, and was followed in December by a 15-cm. howitzer battery, also manned by Austrians. At the end of November he was at work on a plan for an attack on the junction of our Anzac and Suvla Bay forces, with the hope of far-reaching results. Fresh troops were promised by Turkish Headquarters, and technical troops were to come from Germany. Divisions were taken out of the line and practised the attack. And then, suddenly, Anzac and Suvla Bay were found to be deserted !

He turned his attention to Helles, or, as he calls it, Sedd el Bahr. A plan of attack was prepared, again on the assumption that technical troops would be sent from Germany, and that eight Turkish divisions would be given him, besides the four already in place.

Monro's despatch mentions the German ammunition and the extra artillery released by our evacuation of Anzac and Suvla, also daring and frequent patrolling of our trenches by the enemy, and extra aerial activity. The preparations for final evacuation went on.

On the 7th January General Liman von Sanders ordered the 12th

Turkish Division to carry out the attack planned on the left of our line at Helles. It almost coincided with the evacuation. Our 8th Battalion was " packing up."

" Had a good sleep until ' stand to ' at 6, and felt all the better for it. Hickman was sent up at 10 a.m. to command A Company, and so I returned to my own company in support about 11. We then got the order to send away all packs, blankets, and water-proof sheets, and I sent my valise, stuffed full with some of Home's things, and some of those belonging to Rigby, a nice little fellow of the Wilts who had been attached to me. From 11.30 to 1 they shelled us heavily with big H.E. shells, and we stood to arms, as we realised that an attack was pending. Mercifully most of my men were away on fatigue, carrying packs down to the beach, and the trenches were fairly empty. On the other hand, this made me very anxious, as I only had about ten men with me with which to reinforce if called upon. Headquarters cooks, orderlies, officers' servants, were sent up to reinforce us, and presently also my fatigue men returned in driblets, and we cheered them as they arrived. Then the shrapnel started at the rate of about four shells a second, and rapid fire started from the firing-line, and I got a message from the Worcesters that the attack had started. . . . It turned out later that the only place where they came out of their trenches was opposite the North Staffs, on our left, and not one of them got back to their trenches. About 5 everything was quiet, and we were able to think of a little food." (Powell.)

So far as our battalion was concerned, the length of line they held was heavily bombarded from midday until 4.30 p.m. Then the rifle fire broke out and bayonets could be seen over the Turkish trenches, while Turkish officers moved rapidly along the line apparently urging the men to advance. On the left of our battalion, on the 39th Brigade front, the Turks did leave their trenches, but were easily repulsed. At Fusilier Bluff two mines were fired by the Turks, but their efforts were half-hearted and they gained nothing.

Our battalion had about 30 casualties, and the parapets and communication trenches were considerably knocked about.

In the evening the first troops to be evacuated embarked after dark.

The next night Captain A. P. C. Rees, with a rearguard of 120 N.C.O.s and men, held the line until 11.45 p.m., the battalion having left the line at 8 p.m. Embarkation was carried out from W Beach. The weather was not kind : a stiff breeze got up, and the last few lighter-loads were in difficulties for a while. Battalion Headquarters and 300 men were taken off in a destroyer which ran for Lemnos, but owing to the sea they sought

SUVLA BAY.

OCEAN BEACH, NORTH OF ANZAC COVE.

shelter at Imbros, where they were transhipped to a paddle steamer which took them safely to Lemnos. The whole battalion was collected there by noon on the 10th—strength slightly over 400.

There does not seem to have been any of the sanguinary encounters reported to General Liman von Sanders ; in spite of the rising sea we were away before the Turks knew we were moving. Of course great quantities of stores were left, and a few guns, which Sir C. Monro describes as worn out, but which were no doubt used by the enemy.

On the 26th January the 8th Battalion sailed on the s.s. *Grampian* and landed at Port Said on the 30th.

Perhaps the best comment on the whole business is to quote Liman von Sanders :

" The tribute of tenacious and steadfast prowess cannot be withheld from the Turkish troops, of whom at the height of the fighting twenty-two divisions stood in the primary and secondary fronts or as reserves under the command of the Fifth Army. They had held their ground in unnumbered conflicts with a brave enemy who ever renewed his attacks and was supported by the fire of his fleet.

" The total loss of the Fifth Army in the Dardanelles campaign is very high, and corresponds to the duration and severity of the fighting. It amounted to about 218,000 men, of whom 66,000 were killed ; and of the wounded, 42,000 were returned to duty."

Our casualties, including the Navy, and deaths from disease, were 119,696, of whom 34,072 died.

IV—4

MESOPOTAMIA

THE little expedition known as Force D, which was composed of the 16th Infantry Brigade, 22nd Company Sappers and Miners, and 1st Indian Mountain Artillery Brigade, was sent by the Indian Government to the head of the Persian Gulf before any declaration of war against Turkey, ostensibly to protect our oil interests in Persia, " but in reality to notify to the Turks that we meant business and to the Arabs that we were ready to support them. . . . With the Arabs on our side a jahad is impossible, and our Indian frontier is safe from attack." Troops did not, however, land or commit any act of violence until the 6th November 1914.

The remainder of the 6th Indian Division (Poona) arrived on the 13th.

Under cover of naval guns, Fao was occupied on the 6th November. Our landing was feebly opposed ; according to a Turkish writer, 110 rifles and 4 guns resisted the British, although some 5,000 men were available. Within a few days Basra was occupied and an advanced post was established at Qurna, the junction of the Tigris and the Euphrates.

About the time that Sir Ian Hamilton was landing at Gallipoli, Sir John Nixon arrived at Basra (9th April) to take command of a force that had swelled to two infantry divisions and one cavalry brigade. By the end of May it had moved forward to Amara on the Tigris, and later to Nasiriya on the Euphrates. Inevitably the question of an advance on Kut was discussed.

Always caution was recommended. Tireless efforts were being made to conciliate Arab tribes, to enlist them on our side—and always a situation developed that demanded action.

From the commencement there seemed to be a lack of firmness in our dealings with Turkey, which were complicated by the delicacy of the Persian and Indian Frontier situations.

Also, as an additional confusion to clear vision, our operations against Turkey, in this field, were conducted by two Governments linked in the person of the Secretary of State for India. Each Government seemed to have its hands full, the Home Government with the war in France and Flanders, the Indian Government with the North-west Frontier and the provision of troops for France. Turkey embarrassed both of them, but something had to be done.

The landing at Suvla Bay coincided with a discussion of Baghdad as an objective in Mesopotamia ; and the high hopes of defeating the Turks at Gallipoli had already been shattered when the battle of Kut was fought (28th September 1915). Being then fifty miles from Baghdad, and with an estimated force of between eight and nine thousand Turks with some thirty guns to oppose us, the Government sanctioned an advance on the city. Two Indian divisions were promised from France.

It was a worried Government that came to this decision. The evacuation of Gallipoli was already under discussion, with a situation which set two hundred thousand Turks free to operate elsewhere. Lord Kitchener feared a general rising of Arabs in Egypt combined with a Turkish advance ; and the tribes of the North-west Frontier of India were still on the warpath.

On the 22nd/23rd November the Battle of Ctesiphon was fought, revealing the Turks in unexpected strength, and leading to the retirement of General Townsend's force on Kut (2nd December) and its investment by the Turks.

General Nixon handed over his command to General Lake on the 19th January. We had failed in a first attempt to relieve the forces in Kut, and were opposed by well-entrenched Turkish troops. One word describes the conditions under which the struggle was being carried on—mud !

A second attempt at relief was made on the 8th March, and two more on the 5th and 22nd April.

But by this time the Regiment was concerned.

. . . .

Our 8th Battalion embarked on the s.s. *Grampian*, and sailing from Lemnos on the 28th January, arrived two days later at Port Said. The 13th Division took over those defences of the Suez Canal which lay next the sea, and training commenced. A bombing school was opened ; this primitive weapon was considered important. Within ten days the division was under orders for Mesopotamia.

The work of re-equipping the infantry and artillery brigades was put in hand immediately, and in rotation. The division commenced to move from Port Said for embarkation at Suez on the 12th February : our battalion sailed on the s.s. *Briton* on the 14th. The voyage was uneventful.

Arriving at Kuwatt Bay on the 24th February the Battalion was transhipped to the s.s. *Thongwa* on the 26th, and proceeded up the Shatt el Arab to Basra, where they disembarked at Margill Wharf and encamped three and a half miles up the river—this on the 28th. It was the season of flood, and the state of the ground was dreadful. All along the Tigris British troops were employed strengthening the banks in a vain endeavour to control the swollen river. The mud in the flat country in which they were about to operate was as bad as anywhere in France.

Notes were issued by the Divisional Staff which covered " the offensive spirit," " security," " discipline," " march discipline," " fire discipline," " inspections," " intelligence," " punctuality," " reconnaissance," " signalling," " sanitation," etc., on the lines of the training manuals. They dwelt on a condition which prevailed in all theatres of war—the waste of equipment. " The indiscriminate waste and loss of articles of clothing, equipment, stores, etc., which has prevailed throughout the War are necessarily having an adverse effect upon its duration, quite apart from the diminution of efficiency in the unit resulting from the deficiency in these articles, and it is the duty of subordinate commanders to take steps to ensure that such irregularities shall cease. Under certain circumstances losses are unavoidable on active service, but the wilful waste of articles ranging from supplies, clothing, and equipment down to items such as field-glasses, wire cutters, iron rations, or even razors, which are constantly carried on the person of the soldier, is inexcusable."

On the 8th March the battalion started on a voyage up-river in a steamer towing two lighters. This was a dreary, tiresome journey, relieved by the one exciting adventure of a man falling overboard : he was rescued by Private Tellery, a difficult and hazardous adventure in that swift-running stream.

Arriving at Sheikh Saad on the 15th March, the Battalion went into camp to wait for the remainder of the division. Here the order was to practise bombing, and the instructions followed the official formation recommended at that time in France, from which, as a matter of interest, the following extracts are taken :

" The efficient use of grenades as a factor in modern warfare is of such immense importance that subordinate commanders are once more reminded that it is imperative that grenadiers should not only be most carefully selected as regards character, courage, determination, and skill, so that it should be the aim and object of every good soldier to become a grenadier, but that the numbers should be constantly maintained at a minimum of 2 officers and 64 other ranks in reserve to replace casualties. Special concessions as regards fatigues and other duties should be granted to battalion grenadiers at the discretion of the Infantry Brigade Commander."

The formation recommended was :

2 bayonet men, to prevent the throwers from being rushed ;

2 throwers, each thrower to carry 12 grenades ;

2 carriers to supply the throwers, each to carry a bucket (if available) full of grenades, or as many as could be conveniently carried ;

1 observer, generally a N.C.O., to observe and direct the thrower ;

1 damper, to deal with hostile grenades ;

4 spare men.

(*Note.*—All above to be interchangeable in their duties.)

If rifle grenades were available, 2 to 4 men firing from the hip were to accompany this party.

Then came :

Blockers (for advance trench), 10 or 12 ;

Blockers (for side trench), 2 bayonet men, 2 throwers, followed by 10 or 12 men, the odd numbers of which carried 12 grenades, and the even numbers shovels. As many blocking parties as there were side trenches were to be detailed.

Then came :

Clearers, 4, each to carry 12 grenades to clear dugouts ; a main body, from 50 to 200, to garrison and consolidate all ground gained, odd numbers carrying 12 grenades, even numbers a shovel ; a rear party of 4 to 6 grenadiers, each with 12 grenades, to prevent the party being cut off by the enemy working behind.

All men, excepting grenade throwers, were to carry 10 empty sandbags tucked into the belt.

The whole of this period is covered by Captain Powell's interesting diary, including the journey up the Tigris, but not in the same ship as the battalion. He was on leave at Cairo, and sailed from Suez on the 26th February. The ship reached the mouth of the Tigris on the 10th March.

" We started up the river about midday, being kept owing to the tide. Two hospital ships passed us to-day. The river is about ½ mile wide here, the banks being very green with cactus plants and palms. The country is very flat. We passed a large town with an unpronounceable name, but important owing to the oil works there, and anchored in midstream about six.

" 11*th March*.—Left in the afternoon about two and got to our final anchorage about seven in the evening and stayed on board all night.

" 12*th*.—We were on board all day, but the Military Landing Officer came on board and told us we should not disembark until to-morrow morning. From this officer we got some very interesting news. There has been an action during the last few days in which we lost 2,000 casualties but apparently gained our object, a force under Gorringe crossing the river to the left and marching to a spot only 6 miles from Kut, where Townsend is bottled up. [*This refers to General Kemball's attack on the Dujaila Redoubt on the 8th March.*] They are in communication with him, and are able to drop mule-meat and money to him from aeroplanes. The Arab menace is apparently serious, and there is a large horde within striking distance of Basra, but they are kept in check by a bribe of a lakh of rupees a month. On the other hand, the Arabs on the right (Persia) side of the river are friendly.

" 13*th.*—Landed about midday and were able to make several useful purchases at the Ordnance. We learnt through the telephone that the battalion have gone on, but that there are still a few of the 40th Brigade at Maheena Camp, about two miles north of the town. After a little shopping in the quaint town called Asher, we went by bellum (a cross between a punt and a canoe) to Maheena, and were then directed to Margill Camp, where we discovered about 100 of the Wilts and a few officers who were very good to us. The Colonel and I and Brown slept in a large tent, and I was very glad to get to bed, as I had a splitting livery headache, owing to my first day in a sun-helmet. We were not able to get a meal all day, but fed on buns and chocolate purchased in Asher. I wish I had my revolver, as it is not safe to wander about without one, and there have been several cases of murder and mutilation by the Arabs. We go up the river to-morrow.

" 14*th.*—Felt much better for my night's rest, but the ground felt hard after sleeping on soft beds. Went into Asher again by bellum with the Colonel and purchased some food to help down the rations and enough to last us till we catch up the battalion, which ought to be in five days' time. We bought tinned milk, butter, fruit, mugs, plates, biscuits, etc. We came aboard the river paddle-boat about 3. There is barely room to turn round. The officers are in the fore part of the deck, about 30 feet square, and the 400 men occupy the rest. There are lighters attached to each side of the boat containing horses, mules, etc., and the whole cavalcade looks weird. There is a good awning over the ship, and I have my deck-chair. We did not get off till about 7 o'clock, and then, after a scratch meal, settled down for the night, each having enough room to lie down and no more.

" 15*th.*—Woke about 7, and washing was rather a farce. There is one bathroom, but as thirty clamour for it at the same time it is hardly worth trying for. It was dull all day, and there is no room to move about. I had two quite good games of bridge. About 5 o'clock we passed the tomb of the Prophet Ezra. It had a wonderful dome of turquoise-blue tiles. The colour is wonderful, and I believe they are unable to produce work like it nowadays, as the secret is lost. The tomb must be very old. The country is very bare and marshy, and we frequently stick on the mud.

"16th.—Had a very unpleasant night. It rained hard and everything got soaked. The mosquitoes are beginning to appear. I spent most of the day on the awning with Murphy, the Wilts Adjutant, with whom I have many friends in common. We bought eggs from the Arabs in the morning at prices ranging from 9 to 16 a rupee. The Arab children are most amusing, running about stark naked. It is great fun to watch them scramble for pennies. We made poor progress to-day owing to the river winding in and out, and we stuck in the mud every half-hour. We tied up about 6.30, as last night, and put out a small outpost to guard against thieving Arabs. I stretched my legs on shore for half an hour after supper.

"17th.—Reached Amara, our immediate base, about 2.30, and tied up there for the night. The bazaar was most picturesque and amusing. They have a large pontoon bridge across the river there, which swings open when anything wants to pass. The Arabs seem very friendly, but they are treacherous brutes.

"18th.—Left Amara this morning with a heavy gale against us, and it was cold and unpleasant, and we made bad time.

"19th.—Better weather during the day, but there was a fierce thunderstorm in the night.

"20th.—Arrived at our destination about midday, and found the division encamped at a place called Sheikh Saad. At night we have outposts in trenches all round the camp, which is about seven miles from the firing-line, and native cavalry patrol the district during the day. About 6 yesterday a large Arab patrol chased one of our Indian patrols, who were trying to draw them into our outposts, but they merely exchanged a few shots and disappeared.

"21st.—For some reason I slept rottenly. Jackals howled round the camp all night, and you could hear the faint booming of the guns now and then. About midnight I heard a certain amount of machine-gun fire, but I don't know what caused it ; probably one of our outposts on the other side of the river firing at an Arab patrol.

"22nd.—Had a brigade route-march and practice attack. One of our flank guards got into touch with a Turkish patrol, but no damage was done, although several shots were exchanged."

It was a strange situation which awaited the arrival of the 13th Division. After their Gallipoli experience the officers and men might well have considered that Mesopotamia presented at least plenty of elbow-room. The known situation they had left on the peninsula, with its deep nullahs and rugged escarpments, and the limited plain encircled by hills, explained the trench fighting, the bombing, the hand-to-hand fighting ; but looking at the map of Mesopotamia, there was excuse for supposing they might find ample room for manœuvre. It was not so. The country was flat ; the season of the year was the time of flood, when the Tigris overflowed its banks and vast areas became swamps, and the lack of sufficient transport pinned the British forces down to the course of the river. These two conditions combined to create a situation quite similar to that in France, where the sea and the Swiss frontier enclosed a definite defensive line : the Turks, astride the Tigris, had their flanks secured on swamps and marshes ; there was by no means unlimited elbow-room, and trench warfare, sapping, and bombing must be a prelude to advance.

The 13th Division arrived at a critical moment. On the 10th March the Turkish Commander, Halil Pasha, wrote to General Townsend, pointing out the futile efforts that had been made to relieve him, and suggested surrender. General Townsend had to face the exhaustion of his food-supplies about the middle or end of April. Time was, therefore, short.

A vain hope, constantly recurring in the early days of the War, especially on the Western Front, that the Russians, who in this distant country had troops in the neighbourhood of Erzerum and at Karind, in Western Persia, might do the job for us, was fluttering through the conferences between India, London, and Expeditionary Force D. But this unavoidable side-show was becoming an operation of importance, insisting on recognition, with disconcerting demands for the diversion of troops and supplies from the main theatre of war where the final decision, it was thought, would be won. Action was imperative.

General Gorringe, in command of the operations for the relief of Kut, planned to take Hannah, on the left bank of the Tigris, with the 13th Division supported by the 7th. He would then take Abu Rumman, on the right bank, with the 3rd Division, which movement would be followed by the capture of Sannaiyat on the left bank. This preliminary operation should be concluded by the 8th April : the next step would be the actual relief of Kut. Meanwhile, the water-level of the river rose and fell, at times in an unexpected manner.

On the night 31st March/1st April the 13th Division was ordered forward to take over trenches held by the 7th Division in front of Hannah.

.   .   .   .

RELIEF OF KUT : THIRD ATTEMPT.

ACTION OF FALLAHIYA, 5TH APRIL, 1916.

" *25th March.*—Have got the news that in the very near future we are to make a frontal attack upon the enemy's position on the right bank of the river. We are to be in the front line and to start the assault without a preliminary bombardment, so as to create a surprise. From information received we appear to have three times as many guns as the enemy [1]— 140 to 40. In addition, batteries of machine guns will cover our advance on each flank. On paper everything reads perfectly, and everyone hopes that this time we shall succeed in getting them on the run. Everything is to be kept secret as long as possible. We have never before been over the parapet and attacked trenches, so there is a lot of practice. I hope to goodness their barbed wire is not strong. The artillery will try to smash this up on previous nights. Well, we have got the real thing at last, and pray heaven we succeed and behave ourselves creditably.

" Went out on night operations, and on our return about 11 o'clock heard that we have to go up to the trenches to-morrow with the C.O. in a monitor which leaves Sheikh Saad village at 8.15. I had meant to lie long and have a late breakfast. Such is life !

" *26th.*—A very tiring day. The monitor was a very small one and got us up to Hannah about 10.30. Then we had a three-mile walk up to the trenches, very hot work. The trenches are good ones, but dug in a great hurry, and so are not very elaborate and comfortable. The 7th Division (Indian) are sapping forward and getting our front line as near the enemy as possible. They hope to get within 100 yards. Having examined the trenches, we ate our frugal meal about 2.30 and walked back, reaching the monitor well tired out.

" *27th.*—No further details. Practised bayonet charges all day ! The men still seem feeble and weak and slow on their pins, but I hope they will come up to the scratch all right when the day comes.

" *28th.*—The C.O. on parade this morning informed the battalion as a whole what was in front of them. Apparently we are to creep out of the trenches before dawn and attack at the first streak. Everything depends on the surprise being effected. We practised getting out of trenches with fixed bayonets to-night, and everything went off quite well. Our main objective seems to be to take two lines of enemy trenches, and, if we can do

---

[1] A fairly accurate estimate. General Gorringe had an effective strength of just over 30,000 rifles and 127 guns. The Turkish strength, from their own and German accounts, both vague, was 18,000 rifles and from 80 to 90 guns.

this with comparatively little loss, to push straight on to relieve General Townsend at Kut, 20 miles farther on.

" 29th.—Had a great practice attack on a facsimile of the enemy trenches procured by means of a photo from an aeroplane. Plans have been slightly changed, and the Wilts are to take the first trench and the R.W.F. the second—a far more difficult and dangerous job.

" 30th.—All operations are put off twenty-four hours.

" 31st.—Packed everything up during the day. My company was doing advance guard, and were to have started at 7.15, but a thunderstorm came on, and we did not move until 9. It was still raining hard and the ground was in a horrible state, and it was 11 o'clock before the long column, with guns and transport, finally got on the move.

" 1st April.—It was 5.30 before the brigade struggled into Orah Camp in an exhausted condition. It was a pitch-dark night, and rendered worse by blinding lightning, so that one's eyes could not get used to the darkness properly. We stuck to the telephone poles all the way, and the ground was in a ghastly state of slippery mud. Got no sleep all day, and it rained so hard that we could not get up to the trenches as was intended.

" 2nd.—Had a real good sleep, and mercifully by the morning the rain had stopped. I went down to the river to superintend the landing of luggage from lighters. This took all morning. We finally paraded at 6.30 and moved to the trenches at 7. The assault has again had to be put off twenty-four hours owing to the state of the ground. We got up to the trenches at 11, and a tiresome journey it was.

" 3rd.—Got very little sleep, as it was so cold and my blanket did not arrive. The trenches are frightfully uncomfortable, with no room to do anything, and not enough water to wash. In fact, we are in the midst of the old discomforts again, and they are at their worst. We had to move off to the left in the evening to give the 39th Brigade room. It rained about 5, and a thunderstorm got up about 10 and spoilt all our night for us."

. . . .

The country through which our battalion was about to advance was the old Babylonian Plain, which lies below the high-water level of the Tigris and Euphrates. At that time of year, that is between March and May, the temperature is moderate and the rainfall slight ; the floods are caused by the melting of the snow in the Caucasus and the hills of Asia Minor.

The first stage of the march, undertaken at night, was to Orah, and just after our battalion started a heavy thunderstorm burst which made the sandy soil slippery and greasy, added to which many water-cuts had to be crossed, with consequent delays to the transport : the march was, therefore, slow and wearisome. The battalion bivouacked in the early hours of the morning.

The next day they crossed over the Tigris by a bridge of boats, and took over a section of the trenches. Here they remained until the night of the 4th April, when they took up their battle position.

The division was extended with the 38th Brigade on the right, 39th centre, 40th on the left. Each brigade attacked with one battalion; in the 40th Brigade the Wiltshire were in the first line and our battalion in immediate support. The orders were to occupy a position at Fallahiya, with advanced troops as far forward as possible with a view to attacking the Sannaiyat line.

The advance commenced at 4.55 a.m. on the 5th April in absolute silence and without artillery preparation. But three minutes later the artillery opened on the enemy's third line of trenches.

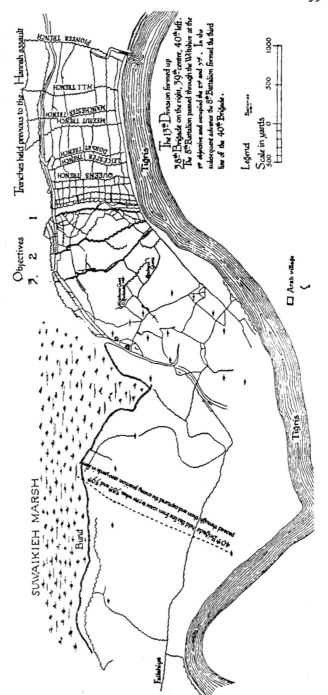

The Wiltshire found the first line of trenches unoccupied. Our battalion in rear then passed through the Wiltshire and advanced on the second line : this also was found unoccupied. But here, according to orders, there should have been a pause while the artillery bombarded the third line. The absence of opposition, however, seems to have caused confusion and doubt ; a mixed body of men of various regiments pressed on and ran into the fire of our own guns.

Where officers could retain control, men remained in the second line. But Captain Powell, seeing the disaster in front of him, left the shelter of the trench and, running forward, attempted to turn the men back. He reached the third line, which was by that time full of men, and, sitting on the parapet, tried to signal to the artillery observers with a bit of rag on a stick. He was struck down by one of our own shrapnel bullets. Many of the men succeeded in getting back to the second line ; some remained unscathed through our bombardment. At 5.35 a.m. the artillery lifted and the third line was finally occupied.

This unfortunate accident left our battalion much scattered and disorganised. Indefatigable Colonel Hay gathered the bulk of his men together again.

After a pause of a couple of hours, the 40th Brigade was ordered to advance while the other two brigades re-formed. Our battalion then fell back to the third line in the advance. The leading troops came under rifle fire and machine-gun fire, but secured the position ordered—in fact, they were about 700 yards beyond it.

It appeared from statements made by the few prisoners captured that the Turks had evacuated their lines because of the floods, but they were in full force in front of the 40th Brigade, so much so that when General Maude ordered the 38th and 39th Brigades to move up on the right and left of the 40th Brigade, they were pinned to the ground several hundred yards in rear by the volume of Turkish fire.

Nothing more could be done that day. Squeezed in between river and marsh, there was no alternative to a frontal attack over ground devoid of cover. Also it was an exceedingly hot day and the distorting mirage was strong. The total advance that had been made was about six miles. The transport had accompanied the brigade, but machine guns, ammunition, tools, grenades, sandbags, artillery screens, and red marking-flags were all carried forward by hand. Each man had carried 220 rounds of ammunition, 2 Mills grenades, 3 sandbags, a pick or shovel, and 2 days' rations.

At dusk, about 7.30 p.m., the 38th and 39th Brigades were able **to** move, and passing over the 40th rushed and secured the Fallahiya position. Our battalion then bivouacked on the river-bank.

First Attack on Sannaiyat, 6th April.

The captured position was taken over that night by the 21st Brigade of the 7th (Indian) Division, relief not being completed until after midnight. A lot of movement was taking place during the night. The 7th Division had been ordered to assault, at 4.55 a.m. on the 6th, the left of the Turkish position, which they were to turn. The rapid rising and falling of flood water had created what appeared to be a favourable situation—the water from the Suwaikieh Marsh had receded, and the brigades of the 7th Division were to slip in between the marsh and the Turkish trenches. The whole of the 7th Division was therefore on the move, the 21st Brigade to relieve the 13th Division, and the 19th and 28th Brigades to gain a position from which to assault before dawn. To guide them in their night march, the two latter brigades were to keep their left on a communication trench and a flood bank.

Briefly, the movement was unhappy from the start. Delay was caused by meeting the units of the 13th Division coming out of the line, and also the wounded (the casualties had been 1,868 in the 13th Division). There **were**, too, a number of ditches across the line of advance, and several times brigades lost themselves, in spite of the guiding bank. At dawn the attacking brigades were uncertain of their position, but they advanced " into the blue," were badly cut up by rifle and machine-gun fire, and were held about 400 yards from the Turkish trenches.

General Gorringe, in command of the relieving force (with General Townsend's time-limit in his mind), ordered the attack to be renewed during the night of the 6th/7th, the 7th Division to be reinforced by the 40th Brigade. The 40th Brigade, therefore, moved forward to the Fallahiya position, our battalion occupying some of the old Turkish trenches. Before the troops had got into position, however, the trenches occupied by the 7th Division were inundated by the rapidly rising Tigris, aided by a north-west wind, and had to be evacuated. The attack was cancelled.

Second Attack on Sannaiyat, 9th April.

After a good deal of conferring and some reconnoitring—which opened the possibility of crossing the marsh—General Gorringe decided to attack on the 9th with the 13th and 7th Divisions. Our battalion received the orders at 3 p.m. on the 8th, and that evening, about 8.30, marched out of camp and took up a position already marked out some 800 yards from the enemy lines.

The formation for the attack, ordered by the 13th Division, after consultation with the three Brigadiers, was battalions in mass, but with platoons in single rank—the men would be shoulder to shoulder, with 50 yards between lines. Each man would carry 200 rounds of ammunition ; magazines would be charged, but rifles were not to be loaded.

The night was very still, not a shot being fired ; but it was excessively cold, and by dawn the men were thoroughly chilled.

At 4.20 a.m. on the 9th the whole division commenced to move forward in quick time, with orders to break into a double when within charging distance of the Turkish trench. The line of battle for the 40th Brigade was 8th Cheshire, 8th Royal Welch Fusiliers, 4th South Wales Borderers, and 5th Wiltshire ; on their right was the 38th Brigade, and the 39th (with only three battalions) was in reserve. The orders were to go through to the third line of Turkish trenches.

The attack failed miserably. Flares from the enemy lines revealed this mass of men advancing, and immediately fire was opened on them. The assaulting troops wavered, lost direction, and eventually broke—a few got into the Turkish line, but were bombed out after a short stay. The rapidly growing light of day revealed a situation of the utmost confusion. The mass of infantry in lines had been stirred until not only battalions but brigades were inextricably mixed. In our battalion no attempt could be made to reorganise until dusk. At 7.30 a.m. Lieutenant-Colonel Hay went to the 40th Brigade Headquarters and announced that the attack had failed. The wildest rumours had been circulated, even that the attack had been successful, which had caused General Gorringe to order the 7th Division to move forward in pursuit !

The whole plan was based on the assumption that it was possible to assault the enemy line by surprise. There was no preliminary artillery fire, but the artillery behind the division were to be ready to fire on the flanks of the objective, and the artillery on the right bank on the rear lines of the Turkish trench system ; the machine guns of the 3rd Division, on the other side of the river, were to fire on certain portions of the objective, and those of the 7th Division were only to fire on the Turkish left if the enemy opened fire.

All day long the Turks kept up a continuous sniping fire, directed against any movement—including stretcher-bearers, who were gathering in the wounded. At dusk efforts were made to reorganise. By midnight rather less than half of the 40th Brigade had been found. The 38th and 39th

Brigades were withdrawn, leaving the 40th to hold the line with their left on the river.

The next day (10th) there was a severe hailstorm, accompanied by a strong wind. The bund broke in places, and water from the Suwaikieh Lake flooded some of the front trenches held by our battalion.

On the 11th the 40th Brigade was relieved, and our battalion went into bivouac near Fallahiya.

General Gorringe then decided to transfer his efforts to the right bank of the Tigris. Once more the forces of Nature intervened on the side of the Turks—fresh snow was seen on the Persian hills, and the shifting waters, from marsh and river, moved across the front of the 3rd Division. Still, a little progress was made, and Bait Isa was occupied.

ACTION OF BAIT ISA (AISSA), 17TH/18TH APRIL.

The garrison in Kut had reached the last stages of resistance ; General Townsend had cut their rations to the lowest possible amount, but even so supplies could only last a few days. Preparations were made for a final effort by the relieving force. The attack was to be renewed by the 3rd Division, supported by the 13th, which was moved on the 16th to the right bank of the Tigris. Actually the 40th Brigade moved at 4 a.m. on the 17th and took up a position near Abu Rumman Mount, in reserve.

The first phase of the attack was successful. The 3rd Division, advancing under a protective bombardment, jumped into the Turkish trenches, captured some 180 prisoners and 8 machine guns. The 7th, 8th, and 9th Brigades consolidated the line, and the 13th Division was ordered to relieve them at dusk, when they would concentrate for a further advance.

Under the expectation of early relief some of the units of the 3rd Indian Division allowed their reserve of small-arm ammunition to remain low—owing to the flooded state of the country transport was difficult to arrange, but, on the other hand, the 3rd Division had a different mark of ammunition, and could not use any that the relieving units might bring into the line—and when, about 6.30 p.m., the advanced troops discovered that the Turks were concentrating for an attack, it was too late to make up deficiencies.

The Turkish artillery opened on the British lines, and at 7 o'clock the Turkish infantry assaulted.

Some parts of our line gave way under the weight of this attack, which was repeated and continued through the night. Our battalion was not involved. The 38th and 39th Brigades moved forward in close support, the 40th moved from Abu Rumman towards the Narrows. It was an anxious night of much confusion.

By 6 a.m. on the 18th all was once more quiet. The Turks had gained some trenches ; masses of their dead cumbered the ground ; insignificant as was their gain of terrain, they had succeeded in postponing any further British advance.

During the day the 13th Division relieved the 3rd Indian Division, the 39th Brigade relieved the troops north of Twin Pimples, and the 40th took over a thousand yards of line south of that place, our battalion being on the left of the brigade, and there they remained for the rest of the month while attempts were made to eject the enemy from various positions on the right and left banks of the river (a third attack was delivered against Sannaiyat on the 22nd April). Kut was surrendered on the 29th.

Our battalion was now weak. The casualty return for the month of April gives 4 officers killed (including Captain S. Powell, G. L. Sinnett-Jones, and 2nd Lieutenant A. Birch), 2 died of wounds, 16 wounded, and 3 missing ; and of other ranks 27 killed, 4 died of wounds, 241 wounded, and 32 missing.

During the first days of May—the 3rd and 4th on our battalion front—Turkish parties, under a flag of truce, were allowed to bury their dead. A general feeling of depression descended on the troops, at what seemed to them with the fall of Kut the end of their efforts. The Turks evacuated their front-line system, and on the 19th May two battalions of the 40th Brigade went forward and occupied the Chahela line. On the 20th our battalion was relieved by the 8th Gurkhas of the 20th Brigade and went into rest-camp at Mason's Mounds.

For several days the temperature was 108 degrees in the shade. The approach of summer put an end to active operations, and on the 28th our battalion marched to Orah, thence on the 29th to Sheikh Saad, where they encamped on practically the same ground as in March.

And here they remained through the months of June, July, and August. " Constant fatigue parties were called for almost daily to unload stores from steamers and lighters ; in addition, the guard duties were extremely heavy. . . . Nothing occurred to call for special mention. In their turn the battalion furnished escorts for supply columns to Sodom, and also garrisons for outlying blockhouses. With a view to Sheikh Saad being ultimately held by only two battalions, a line of blockhouses connected with barbed wire was commenced. On 25th August orders to move to Amara—transport animals and horses belonging to the battalion left with the remainder of mounted troops. . . . Moved camp to the river bank on 7th [September]. A steamer came alongside on the 12th. On 13th embarked, and battalion left at 5.45 a.m. The river was very low in places, and there were numerous sandbanks. The steamer got stuck a few miles below Sheikh Saad for over seven hours. Tied up for the night. Arrived at Amara at 7.30 p.m. on 14th. Camp pitched 15th. A great reduction of temperature was noticeable from the middle of the month." (Battalion Diary.)

The strength of the battalion at the end of October was 20 officers and 685 other ranks.

.   .   .   .

During these months of inaction through the hottest part of the year, when the temperature was 120 degrees in the shade, many and far-reaching changes were made. The conditions under which D Force was fighting—especially questions of supply and medical organisation—were the subject of an inquiry by the Home Government. It revealed an unsatisfactory state of affairs. The decision arrived at earlier in the year that the War Office would take over control of the operations in Mesopotamia had been misunderstood at least by Mr. Austen Chamberlain (Secretary of State), either through inadequate discussion or a badly worded order ; at all events, divided responsibility still existed, the direction of the operations being with the War Office in London and the administration of the Force being with India. In future the Commander-in-Chief in India was to be responsible to the Army Council in London for the administration of the Force, and was to be assisted by officers appointed by the Army Council.

A general shifting of command took place. General Gorringe, commanding the Tigris Corps, was succeeded by General Maude, whose command of the 13th Division was taken over by General W. de S. Cayley on the 11th July. In August General Maude succeeded General Lake as Chief in Command of D Force.

These were matters easily decided ; more difficult was the policy to be followed. The costly, straightforward, battering-ram effort of the Somme was in progress in France. The Chief of the Imperial General Staff (Sir William Robertson) stated bluntly that no additional units could be sent to Mesopotamia. No help could be expected from Russia, for the weak force under General Baratoff, in the neighbourhood of Kermanshah, had retired at the end of June before a superior force of Turks and continued to do so through the next months. The Chief of the Imperial General Staff was clearly out of sympathy with the whole enterprise. He asked

IV—5

what D Force was doing there, and that he himself should clearly understand what the policy of His Majesty's Government was.

Sir William Robertson wired to General Maude his opinion that " We must concentrate all possible strength in main theatres. No appreciable effect on the War would be produced even if we could later occupy Baghdad, and before attempting to go there we must be strong enough to defeat without doubt all enemy concentrations feasible. We cannot hope to do this." He wished to withdraw the line to Amara. " Anything is better than continuing the present difficult, costly, and objectiveless plan."

Oil ! Was that the only object ? An army of a hundred thousand men wasting with fever to protect the oil-fields !

I Corps (Lieut-General A.S.Cobbe)
3rd Divn (Maj-Gen H d'U Keary)
7th Divn (Maj-Gen V.B.Fane)
astride the Tigris, in front of
Sannaiyat on the left bank to the
Dujaila Redoubt on the right bank.

III Corps (Maj-General W.R.Marshall)
13th Divn (Maj-Gen W de S Cayley)
14th Divn (Maj-Gen R.E.Egerton)
carried the line along the Dujaila
depression

15th Divn. Group Headquarters
(Maj-Gen. H T.Brooking)

Detachment (Colonel L.N.Yonghusband)

19th November 1916

General Maude and Sir Beauchamp Duff pointed out that D Force was on the flank of a possible road to India, via Persia. And Sir William Robertson replied, " Although it is realised the Force is indirectly doing more to secure Persia than merely holding up some 20,000 Turks in the vicinity of Kut, we ought to derive greater value than we have hitherto from the large force employed." He proceeded to lay down the mission of D Force as decided by the Government on the 28th September.

The Mesopotamian Expeditionary Force was to protect the oil-fields and pipe lines in the vicinity of the Karun River ; maintain our occupation and control of the Basra *vilayet* ; deny the enemy access to the Persian Gulf and Southern Persia. The question of an advance on Baghdad was still left undecided, but when possible British influence was to be extended over the Baghdad *vilayet*.

General Monro was sent to report on the situation, and upheld the local view. General Maude was given a certain range of freedom. A concentration of the Army for further active operations was completed on the Tigris on the 11th December.

THE MARCH TO THE HAI.

Our battalion remained at Abu Shitaib Camp, Amara, until the 28th November. During this time there was a marked decrease in the sick-rate, which was attributed to the fall in temperature, better rations, and fewer guard duties and fatigues. But the battalion was not idle—training was carried out regularly ; there was a rifle range and a grenade range available on certain days of the week, and field work was also carried out. They were carefully nursed by Lieutenant-Colonel Hay, a feeling of confidence was established—the men felt fit.

On the 28th the battalion marched out of camp and took the road for Twin Canals, arriving at Sheikh Saad on the 6th December and Twin Canals on the 7th.

The I Corps had the 7th Indian Division on the left bank of the Tigris, and the 3rd Indian Division on the right bank from opposite Sannaiyat to the Nasifiya canal. The III Corps carried on the line on the right bank to the vicinity of Atab with the 14th Indian Division in the line and the 13th Division concentrated at Imam al Mansur. Our battalion marched to this last place on the 13th December.

In order to deceive the enemy, all tents were left standing during the concentration. And on the 14th the I Corps, on the left bank, were to bombard the Sannaiyat positions and do all that was possible to make the Turks believe an assault was about to be launched on their first system of trenches. The duty of the III Corps was to occupy a line from the Calf's Head to the Hai, and thence to a point north-west of Basrugiya.

At 3 a.m. on the 14th the 13th Division commenced the advance.[1] Our battalion, after moving to the point of deployment with the 40th Brigade, proceeded independently to seize a small redoubt north-west of Atab, on the Hai, and cover the crossing of the 5th Wiltshire lower down the river.

Excitement was tense. Bayonets were fixed, and the orders were to charge into the fort and take the garrison by surprise. But a reconnoitring patrol soon reported that the fort had been abandoned by the enemy. Not a Turk was seen. Dawn broke and revealed the River Hai with a trickle of water in it. A bridge was thrown over below Atab. For the rest of the day the battalion was strung out about 2,000 yards north of Atab, in front of the 38th Brigade, and when night fell was withdrawn into reserve.

[1] The Divisional Artillery engaged were the 55th R.F.A. Brigade (12 guns), 66th R.F.A. Brigade (16 guns), A/69th Howitzer Battery (4 howitzers), 72nd Battery R.G.A. (4 howitzers).

The next day our battalion remained in line while the cavalry probed the country ahead. But on the 16th the whole of the III Corps crossed the Hai, our battalion taking over a line about Besouia and digging trenches through the night. Everything was quiet. C Company occupied a small hill in advance of the line on the 17th, and after nightfall the battalion was withdrawn to Umm as Saad as divisional reserve.

THE ATTEMPT TO CROSS THE TIGRIS ABOVE KUT.

During the next two days a slight redistribution was effected in the III Corps. The 13th Division was astride the Hai with the 38th Brigade on

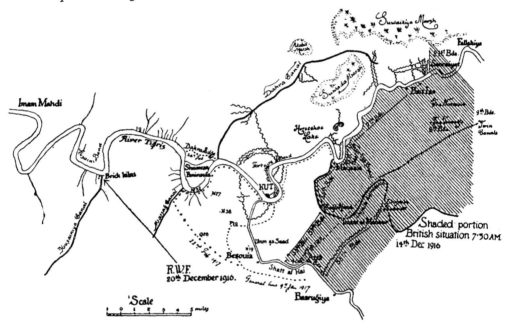

the east bank and the 39th on the west; the 36th Brigade (14th Indian Division) was on the left of the 39th. A column was assembled, consisting of the 7th Cavalry Brigade, the 40th Infantry Brigade, B/55th Field Battery, a section of the 88th Field Company, and the Bridging Train. This column was given as an objective the Brick-kilns on the Husaini Bend, and their orders were to secure a crossing and throw a bridge across the Tigris.

Marching first in a south-westerly direction, to escape shell fire, twelve miles were covered before the column reached the objective. The cavalry found the Turks on the alert, but the infantry dropped into the dry bed of the canal and approached the bank of the Tigris under ideal cover.

At 11.30 a.m. the Cheshire Regiment was ordered to the east of the canal, while our battalion lined the bank of the Tigris, with A, B, and C Companies from the Brick-kilns to the canal.

Supported by the fire of the two battalions, the Bridging Train attempted to launch a pontoon.   The fire from the Turks was too severe—in a moment, out of the 29 men employed, 10 were hit (Captain Piers Mostyn was badly wounded in our battalion)—and it was decided to attempt a crossing higher up.   Before this could be proceeded with, however, a telegram from General Maude ordered General Crocker to withdraw his column unless a crossing had been effected before receipt of the message.

Shortly after 2 p.m. General Crocker withdrew his troops, but the movement required care, and the concentration was not complete until 5 p.m. The column then marched about six miles and bivouacked in the desert.

Considering the nature of the operation—and the strength of the enemy, which was estimated at 350—the casualties were small : 54 for the column. Our battalion had Captains Mostyn and Gibby and Lieutenant Owen wounded, 2 other ranks killed, and 9 wounded.

The next day the battalion took over a bit of line from the 7th Gloucestershire, which they occupied until the 29th.   It was peaceful.   Patrols went out every night, but found no sign of the enemy within a mile and a half of the line.

The wet weather had set in, and the line to the west of the Hai was shortened.   The 40th Brigade was withdrawn on the 30th.

As an indication of the conditions of this campaign, the casualty return for the month gives 3 officers wounded, 2 men killed and 7 wounded, 3 men died of wounds, 1 man missing, and 102 men sick.

·   ·   ·   ·   ·   ·   ·

THE BATTLE OF KUT, 1917.

9TH JANUARY–24TH FEBRUARY.

The rainy season now set in.   Lieutenant-Colonel Hay notes on the 6th December the " first rain, except slight shower on 5th November, since April.   Gentle rain the whole day, making ground very difficult for wheeled traffic."   It rained for days on end, with an occasional break of a day or two.   The mud was appalling.

Although no major movement could be undertaken, by the end of December the infantry were established on the bank of the Tigris opposite Kut, with the Turks entrenched in the bend of the Hai where it runs into the Tigris.   The Hai had become a river of considerable depth, and several bridges across it had become impassable.

General Maude planned to clear the right bank of the Tigris, and to commence his operations by seizing the position known as the Khudhaira Bend. The attack was ordered on the 9th January, and was to be undertaken by the 8th and 9th Brigades, 3rd Indian Division.

From the 1st to the 8th January our battalion remained in camp, in reserve, providing large fatigue parties to cut brushwood for the making of a road to Imam ; it was, however, a relief to have a fixed camp after the continual moving throughout December.

CAPTURE OF THE KHUDHAIRA BEND, 9TH–19TH JANUARY.

On the 9th the battalion moved at 4.30 a.m. into reserve to the 3rd Indian Division. The attack that day was only partially successful, the Turks counter-attacking strongly, and the battalion was held at the Pentagon, and remained there until the 11th, when it returned to Besouia. The clearing of the Khudhaira Bend had not proved an easy task, and the last Turk was not across the river before the night 18th/19th.

CAPTURE OF THE HAI SALIENT, 25TH JANUARY–5TH FEBRUARY.

The next step was the Hai Salient, and General Maude considered that the lessons of the Khudhaira Bend pointed to an advance by means of the limited objective (the system employed in France). A paper from I Corps, issued at this date, is most interesting.

" 1. The recent fighting has again emphasised the necessity for methodical progress in the attack on a trench system.

" 2. It has been found that with sufficient preliminary bombardment and an efficient artillery barrage (within 40 or 50 yards of which our troops are able to advance), we can successfully assault and capture the enemy's first line or system, killing or capturing the garrison.

" 3. Shortly after this, the time varying according to circumstances, the enemy launches a counter-attack mainly on the unprotected flanks, and this is the vital time which decides whether we retain or lose our success.

" 4. The time in which this counter-attack is delivered varies according to the actual frontage of our assault, compared to the whole front on which we might assault, and which the enemy has consequently to make provision for.

" 5. In the Khudhaira Bend the enemy's front line was some 2,600 yards ; we assaulted on 600 yards front, leaving some 1,800 yards of hostile position on our right flank, whilst the left flank attained the river-bank and was protected. In this case the enemy's counter-attack was delivered against our right flank about an hour after our assault.

" In the Hai Bridgehead system the probable hostile front on which we might have attacked was some 4,000 yards. We attacked on about 1,330 yards, and it was about two hours before the enemy's counter-attack was launched.

" On our front at Sannaiyat, where the enemy might assume that our assault would be launched from our left on 800 or 900 yards front, counter-attacks might be expected much earlier, if we attacked on this front.

" 6. It has again been emphasised that the most dangerous part of this counter-attack to deal with is the portion which comes bombing down the trenches. The portions coming over the open are met by the artillery and, if the trench gained has been prepared rapidly to fire over the parados, by infantry and machine- and Lewis-gun fire. Under these circumstances they can be dealt with successfully and with heavy loss to the enemy.

" 7. The bombing attack down the trenches leading into the captured portion meets our bombers progressing up these and possibly at some distance from the captured position, owing to rapid progress at first. These parties are apt to be cut off or overwhelmed, with the result that the hostile bombers are able to close on the men consolidating the main position, deprived of their protective bombers, and the whole position is in danger of being rolled up.

" 8. This danger is greatly increased if the initial orders giving the first objective include orders to extend the flanks by bombing immediately the first objective has been gained. This extension of the flanks immediately following a successful assault can frequently be rapidly carried out, but it tends to send the bombers and their supports into the air, and in any case leaves them to meet a hostile counter-attack whilst somewhat disorganised owing to rapid advance and without protective blocks.

" 9. The orders for the attack must therefore lay down the first objective to be gained in detail, and stringent orders must be given that no advance is to be made beyond this, however tempting to the victorious infantry, until the position has been thoroughly consolidated. If then the enemy, as hitherto, counter-attacks, he does so against a position more or less consolidated according to detailed plans which have been thought out and practised beforehand, and his counter-attack should be repulsed with very heavy losses, after which he retires to his next position, and our preparations to deal with this are not much disturbed.

" 10. *The important points to consider in consolidating a position won are :*

" (i) The conversion of the trench to fire over the parados ; this latter is frequently high, and unless a fire-step is rapidly made or the parados cut down, it prevents our men and Lewis guns firing over it, and also prevents them observing the approach of the enemy over the open.

" (ii) The rapid double blocking of every trench leading from the captured objective to the enemy. The ones on the flank are particularly important. This blocking must be done rapidly, under cover of bombing parties in advance of it and Lewis guns in rear of it.

" (iii) *Artillery Barrage during Consolidation.*—It is impossible to provide sufficient ammunition to keep up a continuous barrage during the process of consolidation ; much of such fire goes merely on to open ground, effecting no useful purpose. A short time after the successful delivery of the assault, the rate of artillery fire has to be decreased and then stopped, the artillery coming under the F.C.O.s, who watch for any enemy issuing into the open to counter-attack. This is quite effective to meet a counter-attack over the open, but hostile movement down trenches is not so easily seen nor so easily stopped by artillery fire. It is essential, therefore, that one or two guns, firing in enfilade where possible, should be accurately registered on to every trench which has to be blocked ; these guns can barrage these trenches in front of the blocking parties with comparatively little expenditure of ammunition. They should not be switched on to other objectives, but should be told off specially for the purpose.

" 11. Bombing parties with their supports must be supported by other bombing parties. Infantry following up a small bombing party which happens to be overwhelmed by hostile bombers becomes helpless in a trench, and if they get out of the trench they are shot down.

" (Signed) H. P. BROWNE, *Brigadier-General,*
General Staff, I Corps."

Preparations for the next move were made at once. The 40th Brigade took over the line opposite the apex of the Hai Salient on the 12th January, and found that it consisted of a series of lunettes, connected by a narrow communication trench, and having a few strong-points in rear. But " No Man's Land " was a considerable width, and it was proposed to reduce it by night digging. The work was hampered at first by rain, but the 14th was a bright, fine day, and much progress was made that night.

The first date selected for the attack was the 20th. At a conference held on the 15th, however, the Brigadier pointed out that the early date did not allow time to dig the necessary lines, which should be continuous and about 200 yards from the enemy. The weather was the main difficulty.

The attack was therefore postponed to the 25th.

Meanwhile digging proceeded every night. The ground between the opposing lines was perfectly flat, with practically no cover, and the enemy was well aware of what was going on ; the work was carried out under continuous sniping fire.   But persistence triumphed, and two continuous lines were dug, with eight communication trenches, and, on the 40th Brigade front, within 350 yards of the Turkish front line.   It represented a

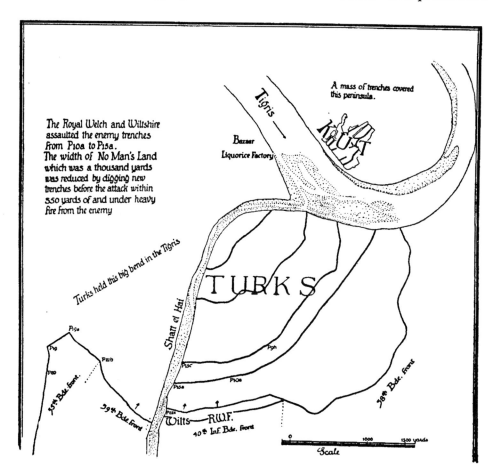

forward move of some 650 yards on a 1,200-yards front, and the digging of over five miles of trenches.

Everything was ready on the 24th, and on the morning of the 25th the attack commenced.

Success depended on the ability of the artillery to keep the enemy at the bottom of his trenches until the moment of the infantry advance. Artillery fire was directed for the first five minutes on the second line, and then from 9.35 a.m. to 9.46 a.m. on the front line. When the guns lifted, the assaulting troops were 50 yards from the Turkish trench.

Our battalion was on the right of the 40th Brigade front, attacking with the Wiltshire. A, C, and D Companies made the advance in four waves, on a frontage of 500 yards. The first wave was led by Daly, Trench, Hubbard, and Dyke, all dressed in the service dress of private soldiers so as not to attract the attention of snipers, and all except Daly smoking long cigars. All except Daly were hit ! In spite of the artillery, the enemy was able to inflict a number of casualties as our troops crossed " No Man's Land."

The front line was entered and bombing parties moved out from flanks and down communication trenches, while the captured trench was consolidated under Captain A. D. M. Farrar.

The Turks launched counter-attacks by bombers, but they were easily beaten off with severe loss, a party under Captain Carter defeating a particularly heavy attack. By dusk the battalion had reached the enemy's second line, and had secured a frontage of 1,200 yards.

The casualties in the brigade amounted to 14 officers and 282 other ranks ; as against this the brigade had captured 107 prisoners and buried over 400 Turks ; in material, beyond a large number of rifles, only one Austrian machine gun and three trench mortars were taken.

The 39th Brigade on the west bank of the Hai had not met with equal success. Having gained their objective, they were driven out by counter-attacks, and by 4 p.m. were back in their original line. Attacks next day, however, gained ground, and continued, the 40th Brigade again taking part in a general advance on the 1st February, when the Cheshire assaulted the third enemy line successfully. On the 2nd February the 40th Brigade was relieved by the 8th Brigade, and marched to Besouia.

The relief was only an affair of a few hours. The brigade was ordered to cross the Hai, and left camp at 9.30 p.m., marching to the line M32—Q28. The operation ordered was to run a line of pickets across the big bend in the Tigris from Kut to the Shumran Peninsula. The whole of the 13th Division was taking part in this effort to enclose the Turks, but the two other brigades were closer in, connecting the Hai and Tigris. The 14th Division was to carry on the attack along the west of the Hai.

Our battalion arrived at Q28 at 1 a.m. From this point they moved forward on a bearing of 360 and commenced digging a line of picket posts 350 yards apart. Each post was designed to hold 50 men. (See sketch, page 68.)

The ground was very hard, and digging progressed very slowly. Six posts were commenced, but all attempts to prolong the line met with resistance from the enemy, and at dawn the sixth post was found to be about 100 yards from a trench and dry water-course held by the Turks. There were the ruins of three houses there, too, which afforded excellent cover for snipers.

Captain Daly, who was in command of A Company, gives an account of the operation :

" The battalion was tired after the strenuous fighting, and needed a day or two's rest. However, after the Brigade Commander had pointed out the state of the brigade to higher authority, it was decided to proceed with the operation.

" The brigade filed out, the South Wales Borderers leading, followed by the Royal Welch Fusiliers.

" A long march with frequent halts. Edmund Candler,[1] riding a small pony and dressed in an odd kit, accompanying the column, was arrested by a zealous officer as a spy, but was soon released.

" About 2 a.m. we had arrived at what was believed to be the objective.

" Corps reconnaissance the previous day [2] had indicated that the Turks were not in position. However, a few shots rang out, and the Brigade Commander determined to go more warily. The plan was to dig four company lunettes and be below ground before dawn broke.

" The Royal Welch Fusiliers, at Colonel Hay's wish, took over the task, the rest of the Brigade taking cover in a nullah. It was pitch-dark, and this led to delay in the issue of tools.

" About an hour before dawn the battalion commenced to site its position and dig. The men were tired out and the soil more difficult to dig than ordinarily. When dawn broke, it was discovered that the Turks were holding a position immediately in front of the battalion.

" The writer was at the time in command of A Company, and can only state that at dawn the men had got down some 2 feet and every movement drew fire. There was nothing to be done except dig in a lying position and site Lewis guns to meet any attack. During the whole day it was impossible to gain touch with the rest of the battalion. Orderlies were killed directly they left the trenches to take messages. It was a remarkably uncomfortable day, especially owing to the uncertainty of the situation.

" Towards dusk the Adjutant, Captain Graham, reached A Company

---

[1] " Eye-witness," the author of *The Long Road to Baghdad*.

[2] The Cavalry Division had operated in the direction of Shumran the previous day and had captured a few prisoners.

and told us that the Colonel and Captain Dunn amongst others had been killed, that Major Farrar in attempting to come up and take over command had been seriously wounded, and that orders had been received from Brigade that we were to withdraw under cover of darkness."

Lieutenant-Colonel Hay had gone forward to see for himself what the situation was, and was crawling along the shallow trench. Rather than allow a private soldier to expose himself unnecessarily, he got up to jump over him, and was shot dead. Captain P. M. Dunn was killed while telephoning the news to Headquarters. Major Farrar, who was at No. 4 picket, about 1,000 yards to the south, seeing that the forward and vital post was without an officer, went forward to take command, and had to run the gauntlet over the open country, which was under rifle and machine-gun fire. He was slightly wounded, but reached the forward post. Later in the afternoon he was seriously wounded.

Captain Graham went up to the advanced post after dusk, taking stretcher-bearers with him. He brought away with him five bodies and three stretcher cases ; also all stores, ammunition, and grenades. The garrison withdrew without loss.

The other posts were then withdrawn, and on the 5th the battalion marched back to R19, where the brigade was in Divisional Reserve.

Captain Daly says : " It was remarkable that the Turks made no attempt to assault the battalion in its exposed position. The nullah was on slightly higher ground, and every movement could be seen by them. It is probable that they were weak numerically, but strongly posted and with machine guns. Any attempt by us to rush them would have been stopped at once. We had no artillery support and no machine guns up."

Captain M. D. Gambier-Parry, the D.A.Q.M.G. 13th Division, took over command, with Captain Graham as second-in-command, and Captain Daly as Adjutant. The Company Commanders were then : " A," Carter ; " B," Gibby ; " C," Wancke ; " D," Davies.

.   .   .   .

A Special Order, issued by Brigadier-General A. C. Lewin, pays a remarkable tribute to Lieutenant-Colonel Hay.

" The Brigadier-General Commanding desires to express his deep sorrow, which he knows is shared by every officer, N.C.O., and man of the brigade, on the death of the late Lieutenant-Colonel Hay, commanding the Royal Welch Fusiliers, who has fallen at the head of the battalion, which he raised at the outbreak of hostilities, trained, and subsequently so ably commanded during two years of active service, first in the Dardanelles, and later in Mesopotamia.

LIEUTENANT-COLONEL A. HAY.

" The success of the recent operations, during which the brigade drove the enemy from the east bank of the Hai, was in no small measure due to the untiring energy, coolness, and forethought displayed by him.

" The intimate knowledge of the exact situation which he possessed at all times was only gained by complete disregard of all personal danger, and was of the utmost value, materially affecting the issue. Had he lived Lieutenant-Colonel Hay would no doubt have reaped the reward of all his labours, but it was not to be, and he has died as he would have wished to, in the forefront of the battle, at the head of the gallant regiment of which he was so proud, and by whom he will always be remembered with pride.

" The Brigadier-General knows he is but voicing the wishes of all ranks in tendering their deep sympathy to the relatives of the late Lieutenant-Colonel Hay, and in thus placing on record the high regard in which he was held by all who knew him, both as a tried soldier and a brave comrade."

. . . .

Capture of the Dahra Bend, 9th–16th February.

From the 5th to the 9th February the battalion remained in camp, reorganising, checking equipment, and refitting ; specialists were also exercised. They then moved forward to some rear trenches, and on the 12th to a nullah on the east bank of the Hai.

The line had altered considerably while the battalion was in reserve. Pressure was never relaxed—there was, occasionally, a lull in the fighting, as when a storm on the 11th February raised such dust that the artillery could not fire—and the Turks were slowly squeezed into the Dahra Bend, and were now well in the bight of it.

General Maude, methodical and secretive, decided it was time to drive the enemy out of the Bend, and after discussion with Generals Marshall and Egerton the first plan for attacking the Turkish right was discarded, and his centre was given as the main objective.

The assault was to be made by the 40th Brigade with one battalion of the 38th Brigade. The 14th Division on the right and the 39th Brigade on the left were to give support with rifle and machine-gun fire directed mainly against the left bank of the Tigris, from which the Turks could enfilade any advance.

The orders were received by our battalion on the 13th to attack on the 14th, but on arriving at the assembly trenches a new front trench was found to be only partially dug and very unfavourable as a starting-point. The attack was therefore postponed until next day, while other battalions completed the work, our people returning to a trench in rear.

At 4 a.m. the battalion moved into position. Three companies were disposed in four waves on the right of the brigade front. The South Wales Borderers, in the same formation, were in the centre, and the 6th Loyal North Lancashire on the left.

The attack went like clockwork. The bombardment started at 8.30 a.m. and lifted at 8.45. The leading wave advanced steadily, followed by the 2nd, 3rd, and 4th at intervals of 50 yards. The rifle and machine-gun fire from the Turks was not intense, but our machine guns, massed on either flank, rattled out a stream of bullets.

There was little resistance, and an hour after the assault had commenced the whole position was in our hands, our battalion alone taking some 300 prisoners.

The wedge driven by the 40th Brigade into the enemy position created a favourable opportunity for troops on the flanks, and by the morning of the 16th, in spite of heavy rain which commenced to fall during the night, the 35th Brigade had completely cleared the Dahra Bend.

This put an end to two months of continuous fighting to batter a way through twelve miles of country heavily entrenched.

Details of the fight are not abundant. Captain Daly, who was then Adjutant, states that : " After about an hour the situation from Battalion Headquarters seemed uncertain, and the Adjutant was instructed to find out the situation. The Turkish position was about 600 yards away, and ' No Man's Land ' was quite flat. He started the 600 yards' sprint with Edmund Candler and an orderly. The orderly was hit at once, and the two lone figures soon discovered they were under direct fire of a machine gun. Edmund Candler, the wiser man, decided to proceed by strategy ; the Adjutant, thoroughly frightened, decided to make a dash for it, and arrived exhausted but happy. About ¼ an hour later Edmund Candler rejoined him quite calm and unruffled.

" The situation was odd. The Turks appeared to be holding a series of Soviets. The Brigade Orders were to hold the ground occupied, and a subsequent advance was to be carried out on the right. About 3 p.m., after a preliminary bombardment, our troops could be seen advancing steadily under a barrage. Almost immediately vast masses of Turks, like a football crowd, swarmed over the top towards us, all waving white handkerchiefs—where they got them from is curious. This was our first visible sign of the breakdown of Turkish *moral.*"

CAPTURE OF SANNAIYAT, 17TH–24TH FEBRUARY, AND THE PASSAGE OF THE
SHUMRAN BEND, 23RD–24TH FEBRUARY.

Kut itself was a place of little importance ; but the favourable situation
created by the Army pointed to a general advance on both banks of the river.

Troops of the I Corps were still in front of the Sannaiyat trenches,
and the successful operations on the right bank of the Tigris had forced
Halil to extend his forces over a wide front.   General Maude decided to
attack both enemy flanks simultaneously—that is, Sannaiyat and the
Shumran Peninsula.

Preparations were put in hand to force a crossing at the Shumran Bend,
but the weather interfered, and heavy rain, with floods, caused a postponement.   Still, following the principle that the enemy must not be allowed to
recover his *moral*, the 7th Indian Division delivered an attack against
Sannaiyat on the 17th February.   The Turks were found as strong as ever
in defence, and the attack, through the mud, failed.

The weather, however, improved, and the big operation was fixed for
the 22nd February.   The I Corps was to attack the Sannaiyat lines with the
7th Division and two battalions of the 3rd Division, and, on the opposite
bank, was to show " general activity " up to the Hai.   The I Corps had
also to carry out a raid during the night 22nd/23rd across the Tigris at
Maqasis.   The III Corps was to commence the crossing of the river at
Shumran on the 23rd.   The 14th Division was to carry out this difficult
operation, while the 13th Division held the line from the Hai westwards.
The 40th Brigade held the river-bank from the Hai to M32.   (See sketch,
page 68.)

The Sannaiyat position was by this time recognised as a strong one,
and the attack was limited to two lines of trenches.   It was successful,
although our casualties were fairly heavy.   The crossing at Shumran was
fixed for the first streak of daylight on the 23rd.

Our battalion played a very small part in this affair.   Captain Daly
says : " The 14th Division was selected for the actual crossing, much to
our discontent, as we wanted to be in at the kill at Kut.   At that time no
one breathed of Baghdad ! "   But the battalion sent 50 volunteers for the
hazardous business of ferrying troops across the river at Shumran, and
during the night 22nd/23rd the battalion was engaged in moving about and
making noises as though preparations were being made to cross the river
by the Liquorice Factory.   They moved heavy planks about, carts were
driven creaking along the river-bank, men were sent to splash in the river,
a few lights were occasionally shown.

The desired effect was produced. The enemy was taken by surprise, and the 14th Division accomplished the crossing ; it was a hard task, and most gallantly done. The artillery at the end of the day was reduced to the ammunition in their limbers.

The Turks had concentrated at Sannaiyat, where the 7th Division was waiting to continue their attack on the 23rd. Our troops were confronted by a maze of trenches, across a perfectly flat and featureless country, and although the Turks were preparing for immediate retirement, the evening of the 23rd saw the 7th Division no farther than the fourth line of the enemy defences.

But the Engineers had now constructed a bridge at Shumran, and on the 24th a general advance by the 14th Division and the 7th Indian Division resulted in a rapid retreat by the Turks, and Kut was found deserted on the morning of the 25th.

A general pursuit was ordered, and on the morning of the 25th our battalion crossed the bridge to the left bank of the Tigris.

" At dawn a wonderful sight met our eyes. The Tigris was alive with monitors. The fleet—the Tigris flotilla—was going upstream full steam ahead. We cheered them lustily.

" We saw many signs of the Turkish hurried departure—dumps of ammunition—but few prisoners. We saw our first German prisoners, doubtless machine gunners who had stayed longer than the others." (Daly.)

The Pursuit to Baghdad, 25th February–10th March.

The crossing of the Tigris marks the commencement of a long march after the retreating Turks.

" We were not to wait long before coming into action again. The Turkish rearguard was fighting well, being prodigal of their artillery ammunition. Towards dusk we were ordered to go up and relieve the leading brigade. [*The advance guard was held up, and the 40th Brigade was ordered to turn the enemy flank.*] We advanced in artillery formation, and 5·9's crumped all round us. It seemed impossible that we should come through unscathed—but we did. The Turkish fire was in the nature of a *feu de joie*. The Turks bolted at dusk, and we were marched back to our lines, tired and sleepless, to a wonderful meal that our Quartermaster, Glazebrook, had prepared for us.

" The next days were march—march—march. Rations down— administration could not keep up." (Daly.)

The problem of supply was causing grave concern : it meant a change in future from rail to river, and the Tigris was in flood, so that, although river-craft were plentiful, their progress up the river was extremely slow.

Telegrams were passing rapidly between General Maude, Sir William Robertson, and General Monro, the Commander-in-Chief in India. The situation was interesting. Our flotilla had caught an orderly Turkish retreat, and by pressing boldly on had converted it into a rout. The moment was propitious for a close pursuit, but the question of supply arose.

Sir William Robertson was not enamoured of the idea of occupying

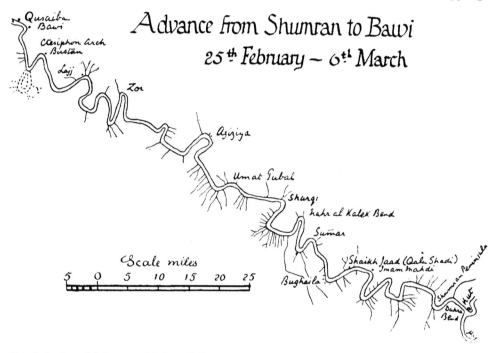

Baghdad, which would be difficult to hold if attacked in force ; General Monro was in favour of getting there as quickly as possible, and so was General Maude. The Inspector-General of Communications, General MacMunn, only asked, however, for a few days' delay—the 5th March—when he could guarantee constant supply.

One of the most encouraging decisions made at this time was that the 13th Division, which had been earmarked for withdrawal, was to remain in Mesopotamia. Thirteen fresh Indian battalions were also on their way from India.

The pursuit was not therefore forced, and the marches of our battalion took them to Um at Tubal on the 1st March ; Aziziya on the 2nd ; Bustan, a mile south of the ruins at Ctesiphon, on the 3rd ; and the neighbourhood of Diyala on the 7th.

The advance guards had scrappy encounters with the enemy. " Turkish rearguards fought and stopped us, and went at dusk.

" In addition to marching, outpost duties were onerous. Maps were bad, and our air force had no supremacy. [*They were successful in bombing the retreating Turks.*]

" At one of the halts the officers, armed with ship's cutlasses, went after pig. We rounded up one beauty—250 lb. He made for the Tigris, followed by our officers on weary chargers, charged a bell-tent, and died, ingloriously dispatched by the axe of the battalion cook.

" The Navy were our friends. They organised pig-hunts—men as beaters, officers with service rifles.

" After scrappy fighting we reached the Diyala, where the Turks had taken up a strong position. Baghdad was on everyone's lips—would the Turk defend it ?—burn it down ?—what ?

" Many attempts were made to cross the Diyala—costly ones. The Wiltshire eventually forced a surprise crossing." (Daly.)

The first intimation that something more than scrappy fighting might take place was found by the cavalry at Lajj on the 5th March. The wind had increased to a storm, and the swirling sand covered the flat plain with clouds of dust. Unable to see farther than a few score of yards, the 13th Hussars charged some straggling infantry, only to ride against an entrenched position beyond. They extricated themselves with credit, though their losses were heavy.

The advance guard to the III Corps, composed of the Corps Cavalry, a field artillery brigade, and the 38th Infantry Brigade, came within four miles of Diyala village early in the morning of the 7th. Reconnaissance revealed that the bridges, at Diyala village and the artillery bridge higher up the river, had been removed.

The first attempt to cross was made that night by the 6th King's Own, but the pontoons, with their passengers, were quickly riddled with bullets and the attempt was abandoned. The same day the 35th Brigade crossed from the left to the right bank of the Tigris at Bawi.

Meanwhile the greatest indecision had been shown by the Turks. They had turned on crossing the Diyala, but had taken no steps to avail themselves of the possibility of flooding the low-lying country to the south of the river and round the city of Baghdad. (As it was, water-cuts, canals, and marshes hampered our movements.)

PASSAGE OF THE DIYALA, 7TH–10TH MARCH.

General Maude, however, did not delay his preparations for overcoming the obstacles which lay between him and the enemy.   The Engineers bridged the Tigris at Bawi, and the Cavalry Division crossed to the right bank, followed by the leading brigade of the 7th Indian Division before dark.   And that night (7th/8th) the 38th Brigade made a second attempt to cross the Diyala, a gallant and costly attempt, which left about 100 of the 6th Loyal North Lancashire on the right bank to maintain themselves until the morning of the 10th.

Towards the evening of the 9th the Turkish dispositions had been so

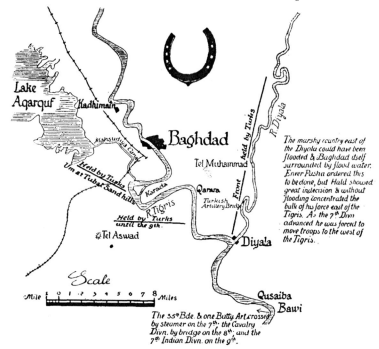

The marshy country east of the Diyala could have been flooded & Baghdad itself surrounded by flood water. Enver Pasha ordered this to be done, but Halil showed great indecision & without flooding concentrated the bulk of his force east of the Tigris. As the 7th Divn advanced he was forced to move troops to the west of the Tigris.

The 35th Bde. & one Batty. Art. crossed by steamer on the 7th; the Cavalry Divn. by bridge on the 8th; and the 7th Indian Divn. on the 9th.

altered that the bulk of their forces were opposing General Fane's Cavalry Division and the 7th Indian Division on the right bank of the Tigris.

Efforts to cross the Diyala were renewed, first by the 8th Cheshire, who tried to slip up the Tigris in motor-lighters and land above the Diyala, and then by the 5th Wiltshire, who finally succeeded in the early morning of the 10th in joining the small party of Loyal North Lancashire.

The 39th Brigade, as advance guard, then crossed the river, followed by the 40th Brigade.   Our battalion crossed at 8.30 a.m.   The Turks had, by this time, disappeared, and were not found for some hours.

On the right bank of the Tigris, fighting of a difficult nature took place. The sand-storm was so bad that vision was restricted to about 150 yards, consequently progress was very slow.   Nearer the rivers, where there was less dust, conditions were not so bad.

Advancing from the Diyala the 39th Brigade found the enemy on a line through Tel Muhammad, and at 5 p.m. the 40th Brigade, with the III Corps Cavalry and the 66th Field Artillery Brigade, moved to encircle the enemy's left flank.   Our battalion bivouacked on the river-bank that night after a trying and dusty march.

Although movements were slow, they were too fast for the Turks—Halil gave the order for retreat at 10 p.m.

Our patrols discovered the enemy gone in the early morning of the 11th, and a general advance commenced on Baghdad.   The 35th Brigade, on the right bank of the Tigris, led by the 5th Buffs, entered that part of the city before 9 a.m.   On the left bank the 40th Brigade, led by our battalion and two squadrons of cavalry, marching through Tel Muhammad, passed by the east wall of the city, and so to the north, where they occupied the cavalry barracks.   Officers and men were forbidden to enter Baghdad. Later in the day the 13th Division concentrated at Es Salekh.

" Reaction set in after the first rejoicings.   We felt we had attained our object—Baghdad was ours !

" These feelings were soon dispelled.   Our tactical situation was not good—there was much more to be done.   The 13th Division, and especially the 40th Brigade, were from now on continuously on the move.

" A noteworthy feature of these days was the friendliness of the inhabitants.   For the first time we came into friendly contact with the Arabs.   Our rations became more varied, and we had melons, limes, lemons, cucumbers, etc., not to speak of sandgrouse and partridges, with an occasional goose, duck, or pig.   Fish were bombed." (Daly.)

.   .   .   .   .   .

A good many of the Royal Welch never saw more than the distant view of Baghdad, and were able to preserve their illusions—beautiful from a distance, the city was indescribably filthy.   A few troops were sent in to preserve order.   Our battalion with the 40th Brigade moved slowly up the left bank of the Tigris, while the 7th Division and attached troops engaged the enemy on the right bank and drove him farther north.

On the 24th March the 40th Brigade moved forward to the edge of the most northerly belt of Palm Groves, and occupied Diltawa and Sindiya, our battalion collecting in the latter village a quantity of light-railway material.

A defensive line, some 3,000 yards in length, was prepared from the river.   In the distance small bodies of Turks could be seen, and the battalion was occasionally shelled.   By the 27th the Turks, who appeared to have increased in numbers, were seen to be digging.

The defence of Baghdad was no easy matter.   Although the Turkish XVIII Corps had lost heavily, the remnants of it, estimated at about 5,000 rifles, were still in being with Army Headquarters at Samarra.   A small force was also approaching from the west of Baghdad, and across the hills to the east was the Turkish XIII Corps, ordered by Enver Pasha to effect a junction with the XVIII Corps.

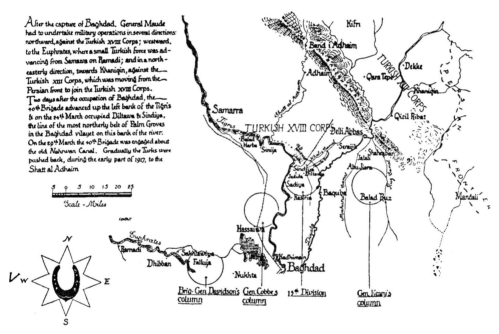

After the capture of Baghdad, General Maude had to undertake military operations in several directions: northward, against the Turkish XVIII Corps; westward, to the Euphrates, where a small Turkish force was advancing from Samawa on Ramadi; and in a north-easterly direction, towards Khaniqin, against the Turkish XIII Corps, which was moving from the Persian front to join the Turkish XVIII Corps. Two days after the occupation of Baghdad, the 40th Brigade advanced up the left bank of the Tigris & on the 24th March occupied Diltawa & Sindiya, the line of the most northerly belt of Palm Groves in the Baghdad vilayet on this bank of the river. On the 29th March the 40th Brigade was engaged about the old Nahrwan Canal. Gradually the Turks were pushed back, during the early part of 1917, to the Shatt al Adhaim

Scale - Miles

A column under General Keary was operating to the east of Baghdad, and was already in touch with the enemy.   The danger lay in this direction.

On the 27th General Maude informed his commanders that the Turkish 2nd and 6th Divisions beyond the hills and advancing on the left bank of the Diyala were estimated to be 6,000 rifles and 26 guns ; that the Turkish 14th Division, estimated at 2,400 rifles and 10 guns, were on the right bank of the Diyala about Delli Abbas ; and that the 51st and 52nd Divisions, estimated at 4,500 rifles and 24 guns, were advancing from the Adhaim. The threat from Shatt al Adhaim and Delli Abbas—a concentration with the object of helping the XIII Corps beyond the hills—was to be met by striking first at the Shatt al Adhaim force, and then passing on to the Delli Abbas force. The III Corps telegraphed the 13th Division to attack the enemy vigorously.

AFFAIR OF DELLI ABBAS, 27TH-28TH MARCH.

During the evening of the 28th the 38th Brigade took over the line, and the 40th concentrated on the Nahrwan Canal.

The 40th Brigade, advancing along the line of the Canal, was to make a holding attack, to be pushed home if circumstances were favourable, while the 39th Brigade made an enveloping movement of about 10 miles round the Turkish left flank. The Wiltshire and South Wales Borderers led the 40th Brigade ; our battalion was held in reserve all day. The 39th Brigade were most hotly engaged, and succeeded in their task, the whole Turkish force retiring. But the battle took place on the Marl Plain, over a surface which " was as smooth as a liquid which has congealed on a still night ; there were stretches where you could not find an inequality that would give bias to a marble," and the men suffered accordingly. The mirage during the day was extremely bad, distorting all objects. Some 180 Turks were captured, and they left about 200 dead on the ground. Our battalion went up during the following night to assist in consolidating the captured position.

On the 30th the battalion was back in the old bivouacs near Deltana Wood.

Our battalion casualties for the month were 2 men wounded, 117 sick.

Away on the right, General Keary's column had also been engaged, and had occupied the Jabal Hamrin, while the advanced troops of General Baratoff's force had arrived near Qasr Shirin, a few miles from Khaniqin. The Turkish XIII Corps, however, had extricated itself from a dangerous position, and was moving in the direction of Kifri.

AFFAIR ON THE NAHR KHALIS CANAL, 9TH-15TH APRIL.

The junction of the British and Russian forces seemed on paper to promise far-reaching results, but the revolution was now in full blast. Baratoff's force was very weak, and the Russians were in any case determined not to make any serious effort. But the junction led General Maude to re-dispose his troops. General Keary, who had the greater part of the 3rd Division under his command, withdrew his column to the I Corps area, on the right bank of the Tigris.

Preparation was then commenced to advance on Samarra, which, owing to the necessity of using the Tigris as the line of supply, would have to be carried out on both banks of the river. The left-bank force, in which was the 13th Division, was commanded by General Marshall ; the right-bank force by General Fane.[1]

The general advance commenced. The 13th Division moved on the 6th to the north end of Kuwan Reach, where the 40th Brigade were given a bad camping area, in a barley-field which was filled with grasshoppers. The cavalry were in touch with the enemy, and having driven some Turkish troops across the Adhaim, they were relieved on the 7th by the 40th Brigade along the line of the river.

The next day (8th) General Marshall was ordered to stand fast, as the Turkish XIII Corps was found to be advancing from Delli Abbas, on the north, or right, bank of the Khalis Canal, across the bare and waterless plain. The Turks, however, took their time, and it seemed at one moment that they did not intend to advance, so that the first plan, which was to wait for them, had to be changed on the 11th to an order to advance.

During the night 10th/11th our battalion had marched along the railway line to a point about five miles west of Chaliya, and at 5.30 a.m. had halted for breakfast. At this moment no news of any enemy movement had been received, and General Marshall's orders were to push forward against the enemy between Delli Abbas and Diltawa. But by 8 a.m. the cavalry reported that the Turks were advancing in force.

The situation was that the cavalry was retiring before rapidly advancing Turks : swift decision and alteration of plans were necessary. The cavalry was ordered to hold a line of mounds in the middle of the plain until the 40th Brigade came up to relieve them. The mounds were some two miles from the spot where the 40th Brigade was halted, and our battalion with the 8th Cheshire on their right set out to take up the position.

Ordered to move at 8.30 a.m., the two advancing battalions were approaching the mounds when the cavalry gave ground. Then commenced a race for the mounds. About 9.30 the leading lines of infantry reached the top of the mounds ; the Turks were caught and, completely taken by surprise, lost heavily, 94 dead being counted on our battalion front alone.

It was the right flank of the Turkish force that was at first stopped and then driven back by the fire from our battalion and the Cheshire. Echeloned on the left of our battalion was the 39th Brigade, and wide to the left of them a cavalry brigade. A turning movement had been ordered and was commenced. But on the right there was a wide gap between the 40th

---

[1] Left-bank column : a mounted force consisting of two squadrons 32nd Lancers, 21st Cavalry, and one section each from S Battery, R.H.A., and D/66th Battery R.F.A. ; 13th Division ; 134th Howitzer Brigade, R.F.A., 2/104th Battery (60 pounders), and No. 80 Anti-aircraft Section ; a bridging train ; and C Flight, 30th Squadron, R.F.C.

Brigade and the 2nd Gurkhas (attached), who were on the bank of the Khalis Canal ; on the far side of the canal was the Cavalry Division.

The Turks, with their right driven back by the 40th Brigade, halted their left about Shaikh Muhammad Ibn Ali.

The situation which had developed after the occupation of the mounds was interesting and seemed to promise great results.   The 39th Brigade, with a brigade of cavalry on their left, were moving forward, driving the enemy in

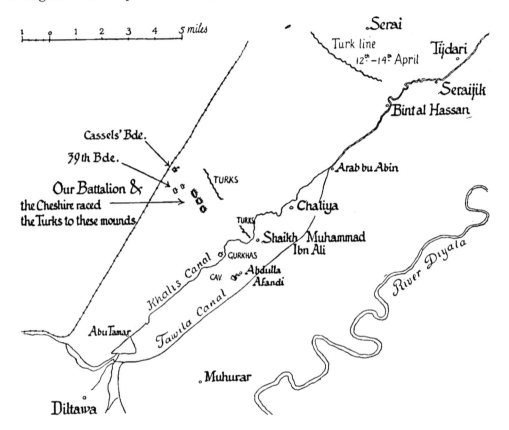

front of them as they executed their encircling manœuvre, when General Cayley became apprehensive of his right flank, and ordered the 39th Brigade to withdraw.   This was done, with some loss, and the Worcestershire were sent to prolong the line of the 40th Brigade and fill the gap between them and the Gurkhas.   The remainder of the 39th Brigade were held in reserve.

The mirage now became very bad and the heat was intense.   Troops in contact remained on their ground, the Turks attempting to dig in.   But throughout the day a concentration of troops drawn from the Diyala—

Sindiya defence line was carried out on our right flank, preparatory to a turning movement on the south, or left, bank of the Khalis Canal—most difficult country, much cut up by water-cuts and old canals. A small advance was made late in the day, the Turks offering little resistance.

The next morning the enemy was found to have retired. His exact position could not be ascertained, and it was not until 1.30 p.m. that the 40th Brigade received orders to continue the advance, with the 35th Brigade on their right. The time given to move was 3 p.m., but the brigade was holding over four miles of front, and the concentration was not complete until some time later, about 5 p.m. The head of the brigade came under shell fire, and the line halted about 1½ miles short of Bint al Hassan. During the night the Wiltshire and South Wales Borderers, who had led the advance, pushed their line forward some 1,000 yards.

On the 13th April the advance was continued, commencing at 5.30 a.m. on the right, where the 35th Brigade experienced some difficulty in the cut-up country. The 40th Brigade did not move until the afternoon.

The heat in the morning had been dreadful. At 1 p.m. our battalion received orders to attack. They were then in reserve, some two miles in rear of the front line, and the advance did not commence until 3.30 p.m. On a one-company frontage of between 400 and 500 yards they won about a mile. They were then under fairly heavy fire, especially from three machine guns on their right flank, and with no one on either side of them. At nightfall the line was dug in, and the 40th Brigade was relieved by the 39th, our battalion marching back to bivouac some three miles in rear. The whole of the day's operation had been over flat, open country, and the men suffered greatly from the heat—there were many cases of heat-stroke—and lack of water.

The heat was so great on the 14th that no further advance was attempted. In the evening, however, our battalion, with the 40th Brigade, marched in a north-westerly direction for a couple of miles, accompanied by 100 transport carts, to give the enemy an impression of movement in that direction. They returned after dark.

The next day the enemy was found entrenching on the foothills, and as General Maude did not wish to become involved in the hills, the attack was broken off.

Our battalion remained at Bint al Hassan until the 22nd, when they marched and took over portions of the Tawila Canal-Abu Tamar-Sindiya line.

Other movements were taking place. On the 18th April the 38th Brigade had crossed the Adhaim near its mouth, and on the right bank of the Tigris an action was commenced which ended in the occupation of Samarra on the 24th April.

AFFAIR ON THE SHATT AL ADHAIM, 30TH APRIL.

Believing that the Turkish XIII Corps would again attempt a junction with the XVIII Corps, General Maude determined to attack and defeat them about Band i Adhaim before their concentration was completed. Our battalion commenced to move, to Dahuba on the 26th, to Tulul en Nar on the 27th, and to a point in the bed of the Adhaim, about four miles from the Turks, on the 28th.

The Turks were holding a position astride the river, and about six miles south of Band i Adhaim, their advanced troops having been driven in on the 24th April as the result of a successful engagement in which the 38th Brigade took part.

On the 29th the 40th Brigade took over the front line on the left bank ; behind them was the 38th Brigade ; and across the river was the 35th Brigade.

The ground was the usual flat, hard plain, with a few mounds dotted about, and a few dry water-courses. But the river flowed in a deep depression from 1,000 to 3,000 yards wide with cliff-like sides, which opened suddenly in the flat plain.

The Turks were disposed with their 14th Division on the left bank and their 2nd Division on the right. General Marshall determined to concentrate against the 14th Division, and then deal with the 2nd.

The 38th and 40th Infantry Brigades attacked in line, while the 7th Cavalry Brigade (less two regiments) moved round the right flank to cut off the enemy's retreat.

Under cover of an artillery bombardment the advance commenced at 5 a.m. on the 30th April. The 38th Brigade captured the Mound, but came under heavy fire from the north and remained there. The 40th Brigade attacked with the 4th South Wales Borderers and 8th Cheshire. Under an artillery barrage, and the dust it raised in front of them, they advanced easily and carried the first and second lines of Turkish trenches. Their orders were to stop at the second line, but the majority of troops, not realising that they had taken the second line, carried on to what was the third line. The Cheshire, in hot pursuit of the enemy, took the village of Adhaim, and went beyond.

The line they were on was behind a position known as the Boot, on the right bank of the river, from which the Turks now poured a galling

TYPICAL BATTLEFIELD.   [*Crown Copyright.*
The tremendous heat and the mirage complicated active manœuvre in this desolate country.

ARTILLERY OBSERVATION POST.

fire. Our attacking troops were, however, much scattered in the broken ground in and about the depression down which the river ran.

The situation at that moment was by no means unfavourable, as the Turkish 14th Division were reported by the 35th Brigade to be in full retreat. But communication with Brigade Headquarters had not been established, and all observation was suddenly blotted out by a dust-storm.

The artillery had ceased fire when a report of the situation reached Brigadier-General Lewin about 7 a.m. He immediately ordered our battalion and the 5th Wiltshire to go up in support.

Attacks by the 35th Brigade on the right bank had failed to dislodge the Turks from the Boot, from which machine-gun fire was causing a lot of trouble amongst the scattered parties of South Wales Borderers and Cheshire. On the left bank the Turks, recovering from their first panic, organised and launched a strong counter-attack. At first they came on slowly, but our men were short of ammunition, and at 7.30 a.m. the enemy was seen advancing in a solid body.

The South Wales Borderers and Cheshire were driven back out of the village, but by this time the Royal Welch and Wiltshire had reached the second line of Turkish trenches, and here the enemy was repulsed.

This part of the fighting was entirely an infantry affair, as the artillery could give no support owing to the dust-storm. Even the 38th Brigade, on the Mound, knew nothing of the Turkish counter-attack. Later in the day, however, the storm subsided, and the artillery fired on the village with good results ; but they could not drive the Turks from the Boot on the far side of the river. So all remained stationary, except the Turks, who, under cover of heavy gun fire, commenced to retire into the hills. The next morning they had disappeared.

The heat during those last three weeks of April had been above the average, rising to 110 degrees in the shade. It was time to break off active operations. The column commenced to disperse to summer quarters.

Our battalion remained clearing the battlefield until the 5th May, when they marched to Tulul en Nar, to Dahuba, and on the 7th to Barura. And then on the 11th, as a demonstration while the Russians made a move in the direction of Kifri, they marched back again through Dahuba to Tulul en Nar. On the 17th they returned to hold the line at Sindiya, and for training in summer camp at Sadiya.

.   .   .   .

Situation, Summer 1917.

Training was carried out vigorously early in the morning while our battalion was in summer camp. A draft joined in May, consisting of men who had never fired a musketry course, and they were instructed on a 30-yard and on a 400-yard range. Besides physical training, squad drill, arms drill, etc., classes were formed for signalling, Lewis gun, bombing, and machine gun. Field work for battalions and for the brigade was also carried out.

There were ominous signs that the future might contain difficult moments for the Mesopotamian Army. The Russians, who had a considerable force on the Persian frontier, 22,000 sabres, 31,000 rifles, and 102 guns, were summed up by the British liaison officer with the Caucasian force : *British gold may keep the Russians in Persia, but it will not make them fight. The old Russian Army is dead, quite dead. Our efforts, therefore, to resuscitate it stand useless.* General Maude was driven to the conclusion that he must not count on any concerted action with the Russians. General Baratoff's force had retired from Khaniqin and the banks of the Diyala, and the Turks were along the line Kifri–Qara Tepe–Qizil Ribat– Mandali. Reoccupation by the Russians of the Diyala line was considered out of the question. (See sketch, page 85.)

But although we had cause for anxiety, the situation the so-called side-shows had created was of the greatest value. General Maude's success and the capture of Baghdad had a great moral effect. Enver

Pasha had sworn to retake Baghdad, but Russian pressure had, up to the summer of 1917, prevented any important reinforcements being sent to the Turkish Sixth Army. Now that the Russians were crushed by revolution, Enver could give his attention to that important battle-centre.

Whether he foresaw the defeat of Germany at that date one cannot say, but in spite of the Turkish successes at Gallipoli the War had entered the Ottoman Empire. Sir Archibald Murray had crossed the Sinai Desert and had a considerable force over the borders of Palestine. True, the first battle of Gaza had been inconclusive, and lucky for the Turks, and the second had been for them a victory; but the threat was still there. And in Mesopotamia there had been a considerable gain by the British: obviously they must be driven into the sea!

The desire of Enver Pasha to recapture Baghdad, which became with him an obsession and blinded him to what was going on in other parts of the Ottoman Empire, gave birth to the celebrated Yilderim Army. The Army Group was to be composed of Turkish Armies to which the German Asiatic Corps was to be attached, and the whole was to be under the command of a German General, with a staff of German officers.

The German Asiatic Corps was not a very imposing force on paper. Its backbone was three infantry battalions, Nos. 701, 702, and 703, and three machine-gun companies of six guns each. There was a complement of trench-mortars, artillery, and cavalry, and we are told that they were picked men.

Although Ludendorff says that German G.H.Q. agreed to Enver's plans with little enthusiasm, General Falkenhayn was given command of the Yilderim Army Group, and, what is perhaps more significant, a sum of £5,000,000 in gold was set aside to help this enterprise. From June onwards divisions commenced to assemble at Aleppo, with the idea of marching down the Euphrates, and offering a direct threat to the rear of the British Forces at Baghdad.

Although the Yilderim Group never operated in Mesopotamia, the change of Turkish plans demonstrates the progress of our operations against Turkey, which must be considered as a whole, with the reactions consequent to the fighting in which our 8th Battalion was concerned in Mesopotamia, and the fighting in Palestine in which our 5th, 6th, 7th, 24th, and 25th Battalions were involved. In Mesopotamia the summer months passed under the menace of the Yilderim Group.

During the period two new divisions appear in General Maude's Army. He had completed, by adding to a number of units already in Mesopotamia, the 15th Division, and had been sent the 17th Indian Division. A few units of the 18th Division had also arrived, but it was far from complete in November.

Second Action of Jabal Hamrin, 18th–20th October 1917.

Our battalion remained at Sadiya through the months of June, July, and part of August. On the 14th/15th August they moved to Imam abu Khamed. In the month of September they had to provide strong fatigue parties for digging in the defensive line, and training had to be abandoned. The battalion marched to the village of Qubba during the month to enable the Provost-Marshal to arrest some members of a hostile Arab tribe ; otherwise the month was one of work with the spade.

But the Army commenced to operate. After an abortive attempt in the heat of the summer to capture Ramadi, a further action was fought between the 27th and 29th September which gave us possession of that place. At the same time (24th) General Maude occupied Mandali on his right flank, the Turkish garrison taking to flight.

This preliminary move caused the enemy great inconvenience : the loss of Ramadi was looked upon as a disaster which had opened the Euphrates to the British, while the loss of Mandali seriously affected the supply of the XIII Corps.

The next move, made during the month of October, was to occupy the Jabal Hamrin on the left bank of the Diyala, with the object of controlling the mouths of the various canals leading down-stream.

A forward concentration commenced on the 13th October. The 40th Brigade concentrated at Abu Saida and the group moved on the 15th to Bint al Hassan.

In this move to the hills General Marshall, commanding the III Corps, divided his force into three groups, the infantry and cavalry of the right group being the 36th and 37th Infantry Brigades and the 7th Cavalry Brigade ; the centre group the 35th Infantry Brigade ; and the left group the 38th and 40th Infantry Brigades and the 12th Cavalry Regiment (less two squadrons). The operation was quite successful, and entailed only 37 casualties. Our battalion was not involved in any skirmish, but moved to a position astride the Khalis Canal on the 16th, to the Marfooha Canal on the 17th. On the 18th they returned to Tijdari and the line of the Asaighi, which consisted of lunettes 800 yards apart.

The month of November was spent in work on the Asaighi Canal, which was dry, and was deepened for lateral communication and made capable of defence by the construction of a fire-step. Also a great deal of wiring was done.   At the end of the month the battalion received its full complement of 16 Lewis guns.

One must note at this time that the men suffered considerably from septic sores.

The month, however, was a tragic one, for on the 17th the Army Commander, quartered at Baghdad, was attacked by cholera, and on the 18th Sir Stanley Maude died.

THE EFFECT OF SIR E. ALLENBY'S OPERATIONS.

But before this catastrophe occurred, the situation had altered. General von Falkenhayn had arranged that the Seventh Turkish Army, of the Yilderim Group, should concentrate at Aleppo and, marching down the Euphrates, where it would be joined by the German Asiatic Corps, commence an offensive against the British left early in December.

At the end of October and commencement of November Sir E. Allenby had attacked the Turks on the Beersheba–Gaza line and driven them in full flight into the hills round Jerusalem.

The preparations for this battle had caused General von Falkenhayn to alter his plans.   By the end of August he was arguing with Enver Pasha (who was all for recovering Baghdad) in favour of shifting the famous Yilderim Army to Palestine.

The situation we had produced can be gathered from a document sent to Enver Pasha by Mustapha Kemal.   After summarising the position :

" In the west we are not in contact with the enemy. . . . In the Caucasus the situation is one of stalemate, and it is impossible for us to make headway. . . . In Iraq the British have gained their objectives. . . . Thus the exigencies of the military situation require us . . . to forestall the enemy's advance which he is preparing on the borders of Syria.   In the present state of affairs it is useless to think of the recapture of Baghdad with our last reserves.   The nearest enemy, the most powerful and most prepared, is in Sinai.   He cannot'be ignored. . . .

" Though it is necessary to escape from the predicament in which we find ourselves in company with Germany, I am opposed to their policy of taking advantage of our misfortunes and the prolongation of the War to turn us into a German colony and exploit all our resources. . . .   To continually keep oneself in the background will not inspire respect or justice in any ally, especially the Germans.   The more we give the more they will grasp.   Falkenhayn, even now, is bold enough to say that he is a German before everything and that German interests come first.   In Aleppo, and Syria, and on the Euphrates, it is impossible to be blind to what German

policy and German interests mean.   If a German commander is in a
position to order Turks to die in thousands, it is obvious that the interests
of the State are not being watched.   From the day on which Falkenhayn
arrived, he sent German lieutenants to the chiefs of the tribes to establish
direct relations.   ' The Arabs are enemies of the Turks.   We can gain
their friendship, as we are neutral,' said Falkenhayn to me, an Army Commander.   He understood from the first that the Iraq project was hopeless,
so he adopted the exploitation of the country as his aim.   In truth he has
taken all Arabia under his protection, and has now begun the second phase
of his plan.   Abandoning his Iraq objective, he now discusses the chance of
an offensive in Sinai.   What will it be in two months, attack or defence ?
The talk of an offensive is only an alluring pretext by which the Germans
hope to seize Syria and Arabia.   If in two months the offensive is unfavourable and the defence of Palestine with all the troops proves feasible, there
is no doubt we shall be very indebted to Falkenhayn if he gains a great
success.   But in that case the Government and country will pass from our
hands and we shall become a German colony.   To this end Falkenhayn
is wasting the gold in our treasury and shedding the blood of the last Turks
whom Anatolia can produce."   (Official History.)

An intelligent appreciation.

The effect of all this is seen in a telegram sent by Sir William Robertson,
Chief of the Imperial General Staff, to General Marshall, who was appointed
to the command in succession to Sir Stanley Maude.

" On your assumption of the command in Mesopotamia I think it
advisable to recapitulate the instructions issued to your predecessor.

" 1. The prime mission of your force is the establishment and maintenance of British influence in the Baghdad *vilayet*.   Your mission is,
therefore, primarily defensive, but while making every possible preparation
to meet attack, you should take advantage of your central position and of
the superiority of your communications over those of the enemy to make
your defence as active as possible, and to strike at the enemy whenever he
gives you an opportunity of doing so with success.

" 2. You are further charged with the protection of the pipe lines and
oil-fields in the vicinity of the Karun River, and with denying hostile access
to the Persian Gulf. . . .

" 3. . . . You should endeavour to enlist the co-operation of the
Russians in blocking the Persian frontier, and are authorised to supply
such portion of General Baratoff's force as may come forward to the Persian
frontier, if you can do so without detriment to the maintenance of your
own force.

" 4. It is important to enlist the co-operation of·the Arab tribes. . . .

" 5. As far as it is possible to judge the situation here, the destruction of the enemy's advanced bases at Ramadi and Tikrit, together with the successes gained in Palestine and the consequent diversion of the enemy's reserves to that theatre, make it impossible for the enemy to bring against you this year a force sufficient to threaten you seriously, and make it doubtful whether he can do so before the hot weather of 1918. Much depends on the extension of the enemy's railway to Mosul, and it is important to obtain all possible information as to this, as well as to get timely notice of the enemy's concentration either on the Euphrates or on the Tigris.

" 6. The general situation makes it important that no more troops than are absolutely necessary for the carrying out of your mission, as defined in paragraphs 1 and 2, are locked up in Mesopotamia during the hot weather in 1918, and I therefore wish you to keep in view the possibility of reducing your forces before then, and to make all possible preparation to economise force to the fullest extent by strengthening your defences and improving your communications." [1]

THIRD ACTION OF THE JABAL HAMRIN, 3RD–6TH DECEMBER 1917.

General Maude had commenced a move towards the hills, and soon after taking over command General Marshall decided to attack the Turks in the Jabal Hamrin and along the right bank of the Diyala. The British III Corps faced them on the line from the main crossing over the Kurdarra River, north of Mansuriya, to the Khalis Canal : the 14th Division was on the left bank, and the 13th Division on the right of the Diyala ; there was also a Russian detachment under Bicharakoff at Chahriz.

The Cavalry Division attempted to find a passage through the hills on the 2nd December, but discovered that the hills were strongly held by the enemy. While this was going on, the 37th Brigade Group concentrated at Kurdarra crossing ; the 35th Brigade Group at a spot seven miles north-east of Shahraban ; the 38th Brigade Group north of Mansuriya ; and the 40th Brigade Group about four miles west of Delli Abbas ; but our battalion had not yet joined them.

The forward movements of the various groups commenced after dark on the 2nd December. In the 40th Brigade the South Wales Borderers and the Cheshire had been selected for the assault, and they found the enemy trenches on the plain at the base of the foothills unoccupied. By dawn they were established in the hills.

Our battalion (and the Wiltshire) in Tijdari boarded 200 Ford vans

---

[1] *Mesopotamian Campaign.*

IV—7

and 39 lorries, and moved off at 2.30 a.m. The experiment of motor transport was a complete success : there were four men, exclusive of the driver, in each Ford, and the cars were drawn up on markers for each company.

At 7 a.m. on the 3rd December our battalion formed up on the left of the Cheshire, and a general advance of the brigade commenced in the direction of Sakaltutan Pass, over very intricate and difficult country. The artillery soon found themselves in trouble. They came across deep, soft, impassable sand, and had to make a wide detour which left the infantry unsupported during this phase of the operation.

On the right the South Wales Borderers found the enemy, and while the greater part of the battalion was held up, a patrol managed to get through and capture some Turks and guns. But the situation was vague, and about 11.30 a.m. our battalion was halted and ordered to move in to their right, as touch had been lost with the Cheshire. Up to this time no opposition had been encountered, but our men had suffered considerably from a good deal of counter-marching over very stony country.

At 3 p.m. our battalion was ordered to capture the Sakaltutan Pass with the support of the 26th Mountain Battery, which had managed to follow. Just before the advance commenced a body of Turks, with some mountain guns, was noticed moving along the main ridge of the Jabal Hamrin towards the Pass, and when our battalion came within 1,500 yards of the Pass these enemy troops were seen manning the defences, and soon a hot machine-gun fire was being directed against our leading men.

The country consisted of a series of broken hills and ridges, gradually increasing in height towards the Pass—very difficult to negotiate. But strong patrols, covered by the fire of massed Lewis guns and a section of machine guns, won ground, and by nightfall our leading troops were about 800 yards from the Pass.

Various attempts by patrols to make progress after dark met with no success until soon after 11 p.m., when an officers' patrol went out and found the Pass open. Three hours later it was secured by two companies.

Two squadrons of the 12th Cavalry then went through the Pass and joined some of the Cossacks advancing from Kishuk ; they were engaged all day with the enemy in the vicinity of Qara Tepe. But the 40th Brigade went on, our battalion being in reserve, and finding no opposition secured the bridge at Narin Kopri by 9 a.m. Here they remained for the rest of the day. Horses were watered for the first time in 36 hours. That night our battalion occupied an outpost line on the left bank of the Narin River.

On the 5th December the enemy on Qara Tepe was attacked by the

40th Brigade, supported this time by the Field Artillery, with success, and our battalion moved up from reserve and occupied the position.

This concluded the operation. Our battalion returned to Narin Kopri on the 6th, to Suhaniya on the 7th—this was an unpleasant march in a high wind and much dust, with the transport in difficulties over the Pass —and to Tijdari on the 8th.

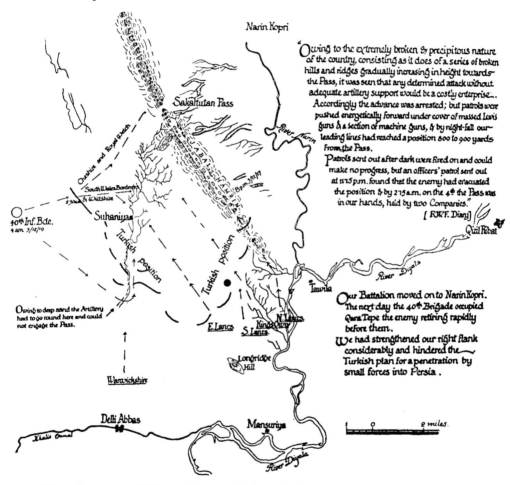

Narin Kopri

"Owing to the extremely broken & precipitous nature of the country, consisting as it does of a series of broken hills and ridges gradually increasing in height towards the Pass, it was seen that any determined attack without adequate artillery support would be a costly enterprise... Accordingly the advance was arrested; but patrols were pushed energetically forward under cover of massed Lewis guns & a section of machine guns, & by night-fall our leading lines had reached a position 800 to 900 yards from the Pass.

Patrols sent out after dark were fired on and could make no progress, but an officers' patrol sent out at 11.15 p.m. found that the enemy had evacuated the position & by 2.15 a.m. on the 4th the Pass was in our hands, held by two Companies."

[R.W.F. Diary]

Sakaltutan Pass

40th Inf. Bde. 4 a.m. 3/12/19

Suhaniya

South Wales Borderers

Owing to deep sand the Artillery had to go round here and could not engage the Pass.

Warwickshire

Delli Abbas

Khalis Canal

Mansuriya

River Diyala

E. Lancs   S. Lancs   N. Lancs

Kingston

Longridge Hill

Tawila

Qizil Ribat

Our Battalion moved on to Narin Kopri. The next day the 40th Brigade occupied Qara Tepe the enemy retiring rapidly before them.

We had strengthened our right flank considerably and hindered the Turkish plan for a penetration by small forces into Persia.

8 miles

For the rest of December and the whole of January, February, and March training was carried out when possible. There was a week of intense cold in December, and during the other months periods of heavy rain, but on the whole the health of the troops was good. The effective strength of the battalion at the end of February was 26 officers and 836 other ranks.

The Effect of Operations in Other Theatres of War.

Since October 1917 operations directly affecting Mesopotamia had been carried out by Sir E. Allenby in Palestine. After following the Turks into the Judean Hills, he captured Jerusalem on the 9th December. As affecting the war against Turkey, events in France were exerting a powerful influence. Indeed, in making a general survey of the War one has to skip about the map in a bewildering fashion. Russia was breaking away from war altogether, and making peace with Germany and Turkey ; Italy had suffered some severe defeats, and was seeking the help of France and Britain ; France was breaking up divisions ; we were 100,000 men below establishment, and commenced reducing our brigades from four to three battalions. But Germany, thanks to the defection of Russia, could bring against the Allies on the Western Front something between thirty and forty divisions from her Eastern Front.

It was the panic period for the Allies on the Western Front. Exhausted by the Third Battle of Ypres, Haig and Robertson were scraping men from anywhere. British battalions were to be replaced where possible by Indian. In pursuance of this policy the 7th Indian Division was taken from the Mesopotamia Force to go to Palestine (December), and was soon followed by the 3rd Indian Division (March). War, on a serious scale, practically ceased in Mesopotamia, and the diplomat and secret agent became active. General Dunsterville was sent cruising about south of the Caucasus and in Persia. It was hoped that a certain number of Russians under General Bicharakoff would remain on the Persian Front. Armenians, Georgians, and Tartars were uncertain elements in Transcaucasia. Kifri was a centre for German and Turkish intrigues.

Military operations were not entirely abandoned, however, and throughout March 1918 a force under General Brooking, manœuvring in the direction, and beyond Hit, after some sharp engagements broke up the 50th Turkish Division, capturing 5,254 prisoners, 12 guns, 47 machine guns, and quantities of small arms and ammunition.

News of the German successes in France now began to have an effect on Persia, and General Marshall decided that it would be well to drive the Turks from the Tuz Khurmatli–Kifri–Qara Tepe area. Plans were discussed with General Egerton, commanding the III Corps.

Action of Tuz Khurmatli, 29th April 1918.

As a result of this decision we find our battalion moving to a brigade concentration area on the 24th April, marching through the Abu Hajar

Pass on the 25th, to Narin Kopri Bridge on the 26th, to Lesser Naft River on the 27th, and, in two stages, to Kulawand on the 29th.

The Turkish XIII Corps, which was widely scattered, had Headquarters at Kirkuk. In the area which General Marshall was about to deal with was the Turkish 2nd Division—estimated strength 100 sabres, 2,900 rifles, and 23 guns.

Against this enemy force four columns were organised : A Column—a cavalry column with field artillery and attached units, which included an infantry Lewis-gun detachment in 50 Ford vans ; B Column—which was subdivided into B1, a column of all arms containing the 38th Infantry Brigade, less the 6th South Lancashire, but with the 9th Royal Warwickshire attached, and B2, a column of all arms containing the 40th Infantry Brigade and the 7th Gloucestershire ; C Column—a column of all arms containing two battalions of the 37th Infantry Brigade ; D Column—a cavalry column (14th Lancers), with a Royal Horse Artillery battery and a section of a Light Armoured Motor Battery.

On the 27th April A Column took Kulawand. The next day Kifri was occupied by C Column. On the evening of the 28th April General Cayley, commanding B Column, issued the order for the 40th Brigade (B2) to be at a point two miles north of Kulawand by 5 a.m. and attack northwards, by which time B1 Column was to be across the Aq Su, north of Khasradala, and would attack Yanija and Tuz. It was understood that A Column would get astride the Tuz–Tauq road by 5 a.m., and the intention was that the 40th Brigade should seize the northern heights of Naft Dagh before dawn, and then push across the Aq Su and cut off the enemy line of retreat along the road shown as running across the hills northeast of Tuz.

Our battalion moved at 1.30 a.m., in advance of the main body, with instructions to reconnoitre the enemy positions astride the Tuz–Kifri road, and if they were found to be held to occupy the high ridge to the east, turn the enemy position, and eventually cross the Aq Su. In this they would be supported by the main body, which marched at 3 a.m. Colonel Gambier-Parry had with him the 26th Mountain Battery (less two sections) and one section of the 40th Machine-gun Company.

D Company, under Captain H. A. Davies, was detailed as the advance guard to the march forward. Proceeding along the line of the road a few shots were fired at 3.20 a.m. A Company, under Captain Bowen-Jones, was sent forward to support Captain Davies, while patrols ascertained the strength of the enemy. The battalion halted on the road.

It was soon discovered that the advance guard was in touch with the trenches across the road, and that the enemy held them in strength, so Captain Bowen-Jones was ordered to move on to the high ground on the right, but to keep well south of the trenches reported by aeroplane, and shown on the map as running parallel to the road.

Captain Davies was ordered to rejoin the main body of the battalion.

Captain Bowen-Jones, however, although he made a wide detour, did not get round the trench, which was afterwards discovered to extend a mile farther along the hills than shown on the Intelligence map. A Company was within 600 yards of the foothills when they were seen and fired on by the enemy. The Turks seemed to be in some strength, and disclosed at least four machine guns. The battalion, still somewhat scattered on the road, in the formation of the original advance, was revealed in the swift-breaking dawn, and casualties commenced to mount up. It was impossible, in the exposed position in which they found themselves, to form up for an attack, and companies were withdrawn to a nullah running parallel to the road and on the western side of it.

In the shelter of the nullah the battalion was reorganised, but had been seen, and it was now daylight. To the machine-gun fire the Turks added artillery fire, which was very accurate and fairly heavy.

On an early report of the situation Brigadier-General Lewin ordered the Wiltshire to move up into the hills, sweep along the crest of the ridge, and relieve any pressure on the Royal Welch. The movement was clearly seen by the Royal Welch, who gave covering fire from their nullah. The crest was gained by 5 a.m., but the Wiltshire were immediately held up by a strong point commanding the length of the ridge.

There was a pause in the advance while arrangements were made for artillery support, and under cover of a bombardment from the howitzers the Wiltshire then carried the strong-point.

About 9.30 a.m. it was noticed from the Royal Welch position that the enemy was preparing to withdraw. By 10 a.m. he was in full retreat, with our battalion moving in pursuit. The 40th Brigade bivouacked on the left bank of the Aq Su for the remainder of the day.

The battalion casualties in this engagement, which was sharp and strenuous, were 3 officers wounded (Captains C. P. Martin and H. W. Cothay, and 2nd Lieutenant Fryer), 3 men killed, 5 died of wounds, and 52 wounded.

Over 200 dead Turks were buried, 1,000 prisoners were taken with 12 guns, 20 machine guns, and much ammunition. Our total casualties were 194.

Our battalion was employed for the next few days in clearing the battlefield and repairing roads.

It had become obvious that although the Turks would never stand against a mounted attack, a close pursuit of them would lead us into great

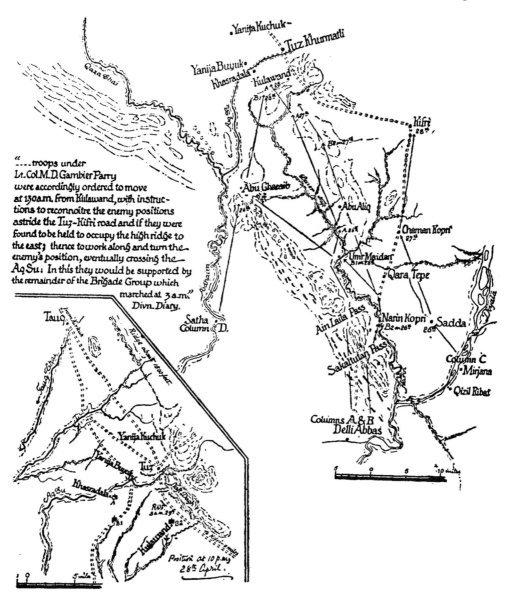

difficulty in maintenance. On the other hand, German agents in Persia, and the influence of the German successes in France and Flanders, were making great headway in that country. And it seemed that the kaleidoscopic events in Transcaucasia would shortly crystallise into Turkish domination. The War Office, therefore, telegraphed to General Marshall recommending him to strike hard in the direction of Kirkuk–Sulaimaniya in order to divert troops which the Turks intended to send to Persia to support a general rising of the Persians.

General Marshall gave orders immediately for the capture of Kirkuk, but informed the War Office of the difficulties which confronted him beyond that point. To capture Kirkuk meant that the whole of the III Corps would have to be on reduced rations while operations lasted. Summer was approaching, and to hold long lines of communications by isolated posts in a country lacking shelter and water would be disastrous to the health of his troops. A long discussion went on by telegraph.

For the capture of Kirkuk the columns were reorganised. A Column, consisting of one field battery, two light armoured motor batteries, two cavalry regiments, and the Lewis gun detachment in Ford cars, and B Column, consisting of one squadron of cavalry, eighteen guns, and the 38th Infantry Brigade, were to be the striking force, while the line of communication was to be held by Brigadier-General Lewin with two squadrons of the 22nd Cavalry, two batteries of the 55th Brigade R.F.A., the 40th Infantry Brigade, and No. 237 Machine-gun Company.

The expedition was entirely successful, the Turks retreating from Kirkuk ; but it could not be held, and before the end of May all troops were back again on the line of Tuz Khurmatli and Kifri. Our battalion did not have a very enviable time on this adventure. Lieutenant-Colonel Gambier-Parry had, attached to his battalion, one squadron of cavalry, the 273rd Machine-gun Company less one section, one section from B Battery 55th Brigade R.F.A., and two sections of the 39th Brigade R.F.A. This little force concentrated on the right bank of the Aq Su during the evening of the 3rd May. The next day they marched nine miles in heavy rain, and on the 5th reached Tauq.

On the 6th Parry's force was ordered to attack and capture the Turkish position at Taza, and to occupy the Qaza Ali Dagh and Chardagly Dagh by nightfall. The Turks were found to have evacuated these positions.

On the 7th rain fell heavily. The roads were converted into rivers and the bivouac camp was flooded out, the water being in some places a foot deep. The drenched soldiers had to perch themselves on some small mounds.

The next day the force found itself completely isolated. The telegraph wires were all broken, and all attempts to get into communication with division and brigade failed. The question of food became serious. The cavalry were sent out to forage, and returned with some sheep and goats. Fortunately, the river fell a little, and the ford at Taza, which had been impassable, could be used. Late in the evening Ford vans arrived with rations.

The battalion remained at Taza, repairing roads, until the 14th, when their work was finished and they returned to Tauq ; an eight-mile march on the 15th ; to Tuz (where their camping area was infested with flies) on the 16th ; a fifteen-mile march on the 17th ; to Kifri on the 18th ; to Sallahiya on the 19th ; to Qara Tepe on the 20th, and there selected a site for their summer camp.

THE ADVANCE ON MOSUL, 23RD OCTOBER–5TH NOVEMBER 1918.

It had been agreed with the War Office that General Marshall should not undertake any active operations during the hot weather. His army was widely distributed : on the right from Kazvin to Kifri and Tuz Khurmatli ; in the centre the I Corps was about Samarra ; and on the left the 15th Division at Ramadi had detachments at Hit and Sahiliya. Our battalion spent the summer in improving their camp, in constructing and maintaining a swimming-pool, and in growing crops, which they harvested.

The interest of the Higher Command centres during this period in the doings of General Dunsterville in Persia and at Baku. Bicharakoff, the Commander of the Russian force that had been co-operating with us in Mesopotamia, had gone to Baku, where the Menshevik party was attempting to stem the Bolshevik tide, and both parties were being menaced by the Turks. The 39th Infantry Brigade and part of Dunsterville's force were sent to try to save the town, but eventually it fell to the Turks, our troops being evacuated in time.

The general war situation was so dreadfully complicated at this period that it was easy to make a false war-policy move. The spectacular successes of the Germans in France and Flanders not only swayed the Persians to their side, but convinced Enver Pasha that the British could not attack in Palestine : he turned his attention once more to the retaking of Baghdad, and operations in the direction of Persia and the Caucasus. Although it was obvious that exhaustion had already fallen on the Ottoman Empire, influence over the Caucasus and Persia was a political lifebuoy. Similar considerations were exercising German minds, but their interests were not in sympathy with those of Turkey.

Dawn, on the 18th July, gave birth to a new situation in France, and the great Allied advance which drove the Germans back to the borders of their frontier commenced. On the 19th September General Allenby struck in Palestine, and a few days after the fall of Baku the following summary was issued by the British Government for the guidance of the British Minister in Tehran :

" The complete destruction of the whole Turkish Army in Palestine leaves Syria open to invasion. Every anti-Turkish element in the country will support the advancing British. The communications of the Turkish force in Mesopotamia are thus seriously threatened, and in all probability it will be forced to abandon Mesopotamia altogether. Arabia is completely lost to them and the fall of Medina is now imminent. Turkey, in addition to being faced with the loss of three-quarters of her Asiatic territory, is gravely threatened in Europe by the Allied advance in the Balkans, which since the 15th September has continued uninterruptedly. The Bulgarian Army is in a critical situation and a slight further advance by the Allies will sever it in two. To meet all these dangers on so many fronts the Turks have only one army left, which is now in the Caucasus and Persia. General Allenby's victory has already compelled them to transfer to Constantinople a division which was destined for Tabriz ; and the situation in the Balkans and Palestine will completely paralyse Turkish operations in the Middle East, and in all probability will lead very soon to the evacuation of Persia. Thus the whole situation has been transformed in the last few days, and the Turks must now think only of protecting their own territory and not of further aggression."

General Marshall, ordered to take advantage of this situation, felt himself hampered by lack of transport. Doubts were soon dispelled by the retirement of the Turks from Persia, and a forward movement by the I Corps, with a small column under Brigadier-General Lewin on the right flank, up the Tigris, with Mosul as their ultimate objective. Between the 18th and 30th October this force, under General Cobbe, captured 11,322 prisoners, 51 guns, and 130 machine guns, the total British casualties being 1,886. On the 1st November advanced British troops twelve miles south of Mosul were met by a flag of truce ; the armistice with Turkey had come into force on the 31st October.

In this last advance our battalion played but a small part. Their agricultural and other pursuits continued at Qara Tepe until the 8th October, when A Company was sent to Kifri. And on the 16th C and D Companies were ordered to Tuz to join Lewin's column ; half of C Company was left at Tuz, and the remainder proceeded with the column to Kirkuk, arriving on the 26th.

At the end of October our battalion was distributed as follows :

Abu Hajar .	Two platoons B Company, with twelve sabres, 12th Cavalry, under Captain Carter.
Narin Kopri.	One platoon B Company, under Lieutenant A. E. Birch.
Qara Tepe .	One platoon B Company and twelve sabres, under 2nd Lieutenant A. H. Philp.
Kingerba .	One platoon A Company and twelve sabres, under Lieutenant A. Bouchier.
Kifri . .	A Company, less one platoon, and twelve sabres, under Captain Bowen-Jones.
Tuz . .	Half C Company and twelve sabres, under Lieutenant C. E. L. Locke.
Tauq . .	One platoon C Company and twelve sabres, under Lieutenant C. A. Lawrenson.
Taza . .	One platoon C Company and twelve sabres, under 2nd Lieutenant J. Quigley.
Kirkuk .	D Company, under Captains H. A. Davies and A. T. Robinson.

Towards the end of November the echelons commenced moving back, and our battalion, less B Company, joined C Echelon at Abu Hajar, near which place they went into camp.

On the 1st December 2 officers and 117 other ranks left for the base *en route* for Salonika. The battalion was lectured on the subject of demobilisation, but continued training ; they entertained the Corps Commander by a practice attack on Longridge Hill.

At the beginning of January preparations were made to move down the Tigris, and on the 11th a string of 173 Army Transport carts arrived to take the battalion baggage to the station at Table Mount. Heavy rain fell as our battalion left camp on the 12th ; they left in two trains, with some details of the North Staffordshire, on the 13th, arriving at Kut at 2 p.m. on the 14th. Special provision had been made for feeding the troops before embarkation ; there were ample stew, tea, and cakes. Thence by boat to Amara, arriving at dawn on the 15th. The camp was at Tabar, seven miles below Amara.

The battalion had practically ceased to exist ; most of the men had been sent home, miners going first ; but the cadre remained through the summer, arriving eventually at Wrexham on the 16th August, and was finally disbanded on the 21st August 1919.

PALESTINE

IN August 1914 the British troops in Egypt were the 2nd Devonshire, 1st Worcestershire, 2nd Northamptonshire, 2nd Gordon Highlanders, the 3rd Dragoon Guards, a battery of Royal Horse Artillery, a Mountain Battery, and a Field Company of Royal Engineers. The situation in France and Flanders required the instant recall of this handful of troops, and they were relieved on the 27th September by the East Lancashire Division, Territorial Force, sailing on the 30th. In October, Indian troops began to arrive.

Egypt, after years of British administration, was still nominally a province of the Ottoman Empire. The Khedive was actively pro-Turk, and when war was declared on Germany he went to Constantinople. Officially war was not declared on Turkey until the 5th November, but the situation in Egypt was impossible from the commencement of the great struggle. Technically Germans could roam about Egypt at will, German ships could use the harbours! The 5th November put an end to a stupid condition of affairs.

The sole anxiety of the Home Government was to suppress any rising that might break out and defend the country from invasion; the Suez Canal must be kept open. Egypt as a base for operations against the Turks was the last thing they contemplated.

Egypt was declared a protectorate on the 18th December, the reigning Khedive, Abbas Hilmi, was deposed, and his uncle, Prince Hussein Kamel Pasha, was raised to the throne with the title of Sultan.

German and Turkish hopes of a formidable rising against the British were soon killed. There was some trouble with the Sultan of Darfur, and with the Grand Senussi, but in each case it was of little importance. The first serious enemy attempt was in January 1915, when the Turks tried to cross the Suez Canal; from that date to July 1916, when they again crossed the Sinai Desert, all military operations consisted of the pursuit of a few tribesmen. The end of 1916 saw, however, the commencement of the offensive-defence of Sir Archibald Murray. We were then across the Sinai Desert.

THE SITUATION.

Egypt, then, became a British Protectorate in 1914. The Turkish frontier ran from Rafah to the Gulf of Aqaba, but no attempt was made by us to guard this frontier, as between it and the Suez Canal lay the Sinai Desert. The desert is a serious though not an insuperable obstacle. In the *Guerre d'Orient : Campagnes d'Egypte et de Syrie*, published by General Bertrand, we are told how Napoleon tackled the business.

" The desert which separates Syria from Egypt extends from Gaza to Salhiya ; it is seventy leagues [a French league is 4,850 yards]. Caravans march eighty hours to cross it. Gaza is one hundred leagues from Cairo. The desert is divided into three parts. First from Salhiya to Qatiya there are sixteen leagues of arid sand ; one finds no shade, no water, and not a vestige of vegetation ; the caravans march for twenty hours. The French troops covered the distance in two days, but three are necessary for the camels, wheeled vehicles, and artillery. Near Qatiya are moving sands, very tiring for transport. Qatiya is an oasis ; there were two wells, rather bitter but nevertheless drinkable ; there were about a thousand palm trees which could provide shade for four or five thousand men. . . .

" The second part extends from the oasis of Qatiya to that of El Arish, a matter of twenty-five leagues. Caravans are thirty-two hours on the march ; the French Army took three and a half days for the journey. One passed on this road three wells which marked the stations, but these wells only contained supplies for one or two battalions. . . .

" El Arish is an oasis much more extended and much more productive than that of Qatiya. There are six wells that can provide for the needs of an army of from fifteen to twenty thousand men, and several thousand palm trees that can give it shade. There was a large stone village, containing five or six hundred inhabitants, and a stone fort. . . .

" The third part of this desert extends from El Arish to Gaza, a matter of twenty-nine leagues. Caravans are twenty-three to twenty-four hours on the road. French troops took three days to cross it. Four leagues from El Arish one finds El Kharruha ; four leagues farther the wells of Zowaiid ; four leagues from Zowaiid the wells of Rafah ; two leagues farther the castle of Khan Yunis ; Syria commences here. From Khan Yunis to Gaza there are seven leagues ; it is no longer the desert ; it is an intermediary state, between desert and cultivated country. All along the road one follows the coast at a distance of a league or half a league. . . .

" A big army requires then twelve days to cross the great desert and the isthmus of Suez, counting one day spent at Qatiya and one at El Arish. . . .

" It is a very exhausting and delicate operation to cross the desert in summer. First, the heat of the sand ; second, the lack of water ; third, the lack of shade, are all capable of perishing an army, or of weakening it, or of discouraging it more than can be imagined.

" Of all the obstacles that can cover the frontiers of empires a desert, similar to this, is incontestably the greatest."

The conditions had not changed, but the Suez Canal had been dug with a fresh-water canal on the Egyptian side of it, so that the advantages of holding the Canal line rather than the frontier are obvious.

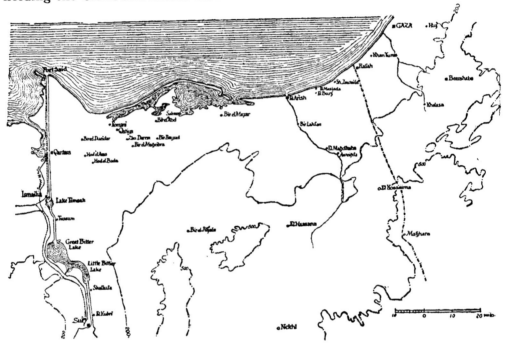

Before the end of the year the number of Indian battalions sent to Egypt, and retained for the defence of the country, was sufficient to form the 10th and 11th Indian Divisions. In addition, Australia and New Zealand sent their first contingents to train in Egypt : Australia, one light horse brigade, and one infantry division complete with artillery ; New Zealand, 2,500 mounted troops, 5,000 infantry, and one field artillery brigade.

The Canal defences, divided into three sectors, were held by the two Indian divisions and by five British and three French ships. General Maxwell, who had relieved General Byng in command of the Force in Egypt, was well aware that some enterprise was in preparation by the Turks.

It was thought by the War Office that the largest number of Turkish troops that could venture a raid across the desert was 5,000, but early in January 1915, French airmen reported that a large force of three divisions was assembled on the frontier near Beersheba. The Turkish advance commenced.

The raid was repulsed, but it gives us an insight into the character of the commander we had to meet in subsequent actions.

Djemal Pasha had been appointed Commander-in-Chief in Syria and Palestine, and his plan was to invade and conquer Egypt. The operation was placed in the hands of Colonel Djemal Bey, who had the able General Kress von Kressenstein as his Chief of Staff.

There were three roads across the desert, marked by a succession of wells. The old caravan road, and the best, was along the coast, but it was within range of warships ; the second best, through Nekhl to Suez, was also commanded by warships in the Gulf of Aqaba. The third, through Jifjafa to Ismailia, could not, because of the size and number of its wells, carry many troops. All our calculations had been based on these three roads.

The great desert which covers the Sinai Peninsula varies in quality. The southern half is mountainous, and is fringed by sand-dunes which are impassable for large bodies of troops. The northern half is, in the main, hard, although it contains drifts, sometimes several miles wide, of soft sand. Kress struck a course for himself over this hard desert, and he moved between 20,000 and 25,000 troops to the banks of the Canal without losing a man or beast.

Naturally enough, although the attack on the 3rd February was repulsed, this demonstration of what could be accomplished was disturbing to those responsible for holding the Canal. But it did not, at that time, suggest the possibility of attacking Turkey from Egypt. Attack was contemplated, but Alexandretta, Gallipoli, and Salonika were the spots under consideration. Gallipoli was finally selected, and caused a diversion which, while it lasted, freed Egypt from serious attack.

The Gallipoli adventure came to an end, but before its close Bulgaria had decided to attack Serbia, and the Allies were committed to support the Serbians by throwing a force into Salonika. This decision came as an aggravation to the Turkish problem. For a moment it had seemed that General Townsend's advance towards Baghdad offered opportunities for an effective supporting blow, and Alexandretta once more came under discussion.

The breathing-space afforded Egypt by the Gallipoli campaign had been used by the Turks to push their narrow-gauge railway down to Beersheba ; the gaps in the railway line above Alexandretta had not been completed, but work was going on apace, and the road had been remade ; at all events, the work done had greatly improved their facilities for attacking Egypt, and Djemal was determined to continue the narrow-gauge railway across the desert. If we could cut the Turkish communications at Alexandretta, it would affect their position in Mesopotamia, and protect Egypt from serious invasion.

The Alexandretta scheme was eventually squashed by the French, who would have none of it, so that when the evacuation of Gallipoli, then under discussion, was finally agreed upon, Egypt was faced with the prospect of speedy invasion. The local opinion was that the Turks would bring 250,000 men to cross the desert ; the Imperial Staff thought half that number.

To meet this menace a great deal of work had been done before the evacuation of Gallipoli commenced. A defensive line, 11,000 yards to the east of the Canal, had been sited and was under construction, with second and third lines behind it.

The expedition to Salonika, the evacuation of Gallipoli to its main base, Egypt, the defence of Egypt itself, created a situation in the Mediterranean which called for reorganisation. Sir William Robertson had just succeeded Sir Archibald Murray as Chief of the Imperial General Staff. Sir Archibald was sent to Egypt in supreme command of the whole Mediterranean Force, including Salonika : his command was afterwards modified. But when he arrived on the 9th January 1916, work on the Canal was in full swing, and a pipe-line was being laid to take fresh water into the desert.

At that time there was a very large force in Egypt, and the policy of the Imperial General Staff was indicated by Sir William Robertson :

" You will realise that the force under your command in Egypt is of the nature of a general strategical reserve for the Empire.

" It is at present quite uncertain what the future action of the enemy in the East and Near East may be. The Turks may elect to make their main effort in Mesopotamia, while demonstrating against Egypt, or they may make their main effort against the latter country. Again, they may decide to employ their forces in Europe, set free by the evacuation of Gallipoli, to assist the Central Powers and Bulgaria in operations in the Balkans or against Rumania.

" The War Committee has decided that for us France is the main theatre of war. It is therefore important that as soon as the situation in the East is clearer, no more troops shall be maintained there than are absolutely necessary, but circumstances may make it necessary to reinforce our troops either in Mesopotamia or in India or in both. You should, therefore, be prepared to detach troops from Egypt when and if the situation makes this advisable.

" Both for the defence of Egypt and the creation of an effective strategical reserve, the first requirement is to reorganise the troops in Egypt, and to get the depleted and tired divisions from Gallipoli in a condition to take the field."

REORGANISATION IN EGYPT.

The great exodus from Gallipoli was in progress. The 53rd Division, with our three Territorial battalions, the 5th, 6th, and 7th Royal Welch, arrived at Alexandria on the 19th December 1915, and moved into camp near a little village called Wardan, on the banks of the Nile.

The strength of battalions in the division was such that the 5th and 6th Royal Welch had, as we know, been amalgamated. Their strength, as given at the end of the month of December, was : 5th Royal Welch, 2 officers, 176 other ranks ; 6th Royal Welch, 14 officers, 184 other ranks. The 7th Royal Welch, which had retained its identity, from a strength return on the 12th December, consisted of 16 officers and 205 other ranks. After landing in Egypt Lieutenant-Colonel F. H. Borthwick took command of the 5th Battalion and Lieutenant-Colonel C. S. Rome retained the 6th Battalion.

For the first four months of 1916 the 53rd Division was much scattered, units being required to hold posts and protect various works widely apart. In the middle of February the 158th Brigade, with our three battalions, was sent to relieve the 159th at Wadi Natrun, a small village with a salt and soda factory near a chain of salt-water lakes. This post included the protection of the Khatatba Canal, which supplied Alexandria with drinking water.

Major-General A. G. Dallas had assumed command of the division on the 11th January. On the 1st April he was appointed to command what was known as the North-western Force. The disposition of troops in this command covered Alamiein, Moghara, Abbassia, Wadi Natrun, Beni Salama, Faiyum, Minia, Sohag, and Suez. The 158th Brigade were still at Wadi Natrun ; at Beni Salama we find the 1st Montgomeryshire Yeomanry ; at Minia the 4th Dismounted Brigade. Troops at Faiyum and Wadi Natrun were watching the west, where the Grand Senussi and his tribesmen were giving trouble. The 159th Brigade was sent on the 1st May to Sollum, which was in the thick of the Senussi rising.

IV—8

Two Yeomanry units, the South-eastern and the Eastern Mounted Brigades, had been in Gallipoli from the 7th October to the 31st December, and had then arrived at Sidi Bishr ; with them was the Welsh Horse. The two brigades were amalgamated and renamed the 3rd Dismounted Brigade, and in February were sent to Kubri, north of Suez.

The 4th Dismounted Brigade was composed of the South Wales and the Welsh Border Yeomanry Brigades, and had sailed from Devonport on the 5th March 1916. Amongst the units of this dismounted brigade were the Denbighshire and the Montgomeryshire Yeomanry Regiments.

These three Yeomanry regiments (Welsh Horse, Denbighshire and Montgomeryshire) were later to form the 24th and 25th Battalions, Royal Welch Fusiliers.

Our three battalions in the 158th Brigade led a heated existence at Wadi Natrun, which was below the level of the sea. In May they moved to Zeitoun, near Cairo, and on the 21st June to No. 2 Section, Canal Defences, where the 53rd Division was taking over from the 2nd Anzac Division.

The Canal Defences, running from Suez to Port Said, were divided into three sectors, or sections. No. 2 Section ran from Kabrit to Ferdan, with Headquarters at Ismailia.

When Sir Archibald Murray was Chief of the Imperial General Staff he had examined the question of defence, and had come to the conclusion that the better-watered district round Qatiya should be denied to the enemy. He now contemplated going much farther, to El Arish, which would give him control of all the water along the old caravan route. Sir William Robertson, however, did not view an advance to El Arish with favour ; he agreed to the occupation of the Qatiya area, and work on the railway and pipe line was pushed ahead in that direction. Troops holding the Canal line worked on completing and perfecting the trenches.

The danger of invasion, which was real, although not to the extent feared by Sir Archibald Murray, was reduced during the early months of 1916 by the victories won by the Grand Duke Nicholas at Erzerum and Trebizond. The condition of affairs in Mesopotamia was not too good, as we know.

As the railway was pushed out into the desert, so mounted troops patrolled wider circles and stood farther out in the desert. Occasionally shots were exchanged with small enemy parties ; occasionally our mounted troops raided camps and wells, destroying both : the Turks made a successful raid against Qatiya, and cut up the Yeomanry, who put up a gallant fight. But one can say that the enemy remained quiet until the end of July.

This dull and uneventful period was, however, of the greatest importance to our three Territorial battalions. Their Gallipoli experience had been shattering ; it had left them not only weak in numbers but in health. Sickness meant slackness, which had to be cured ; drafts of recruits had to be absorbed ; and each battalion had to undergo a process of rebuilding. Every battalion in the division was in like case.

No better commander for the job could have been found than General Dallas. He was ably supported by Lieutenant-Colonels F. H. Borthwick, C. S. Rome, and T. H. Harker, and although some of the younger officers thought they were being unnecessarily worried, there is no doubt that the depressed battalions which arrived from Gallipoli became, during this year spent on the edge of the sandy desert, well-trained, fighting troops.

The 158th Brigade, with our three battalions, was in camp in the neighbourhood of Moascar. Tents were plentiful, as " it was part of the higher policy to induce enemy aeroplanes to believe that there was a large force at Ismailia, and to this end a large number of tents were pitched," but troops experienced tremendous heat. " We began serious training in the digging of soft sand trenches, and found what immense labour was involved in throwing out enough sand to get any sort of depth. A trench had to be eighteen feet wide to get down five feet. When the required depth had been reached, the walls of the trench, whether of hurdles or sandbags, were built, and then the sand was all shovelled back against them. The pressure of the sand would then frequently crush the whole thing inwards, and it had to be done afresh, supplemented with heavy cross-pieces at the top and bottom." [1]

THE BATTLE OF ROMANI, 4TH–5TH AUGUST 1916. AREA EAST OF THE CANAL AND NORTH OF ISMAILIA.

Nothing occurred to upset the even passing of uneventful days until the 17th July, when enemy aircraft suddenly became active. On the 19th July our own aircraft discovered a concentration of Turks at two hitherto deserted oases. It was soon apparent that the enemy was preparing the long-expected advance. The 158th Brigade was ordered to Romani.

Romani lies between Qatiya and the coast, but, in relation to the front, behind Qatiya, and it marked rail-head. It was in No. 3 Section, and was held by the 52nd (Lowland) Division, occupying a line that rested on the sea, running like a fish-hook round Romani Station, and sited on a line of sandhills. From many points the palm groves of Qatiya Oasis could be seen across the wide intervening stretch of bare, rolling desert. The 158th Brigade arrived at Romani on the 21st July.

[1] Captain Ashton, Brigade Major : *History of the 53rd (Welsh) Division.*

Sir Archibald Murray was quite prepared for the Turkish attack, and had rightly anticipated that it would be launched against the right of our Romani position. He had, echeloned to his right rear, the New Zealand Mounted Rifle Brigade at Dueidar and Hill 70, and at Hill 40 the 1st Dismounted Yeomanry Brigade.

At Romani the line ran : 155th Brigade, 158th Brigade (less our 5th Battalion), and the 157th Brigade ; our 5th Battalion and the 156th Brigade were held in reserve at Romani Station.

The Turks, under Kress, came on slowly, preparing, as they advanced, successive lines of defence. Australian Mounted troops kept in touch with them. Sir Archibald Murray's plan was to make as stout a resistance as possible about a mound called Katib Gannit, and to this end two brigades, the 1st and 2nd Light Horse Brigades, under General Chauvel, had reconnoitred a position between Katib Gannit and Hod el Enna, on the edge of a tumbled area of sand-dunes that cropped up suddenly across the flat desert. When the enemy was committed against this position, he was to be attacked in flank from Dueidar and the Canal Defences, while a mobile column swung wide round his flank to take him in rear.

The Katib Gannit position was not entrenched ; the main position, held by the 52nd Division, was a series of redoubts. Off the coast, about Mahamdiya, British monitors were able before the end of the month to shell the advanced Turkish troops. The 42nd Division had been moved from Qantara, along the railway, at Gilban Station, Hill 70, and Hill 40.

The honours of the battle of Romani lie with the mounted troops. The Turks advanced against our right flank during the night, 3rd/4th August, and found the gullies leading to the sand-dune area held. The battle commenced about 2 a.m., but no sound reached our battalions until about 3.30 a.m., when rifle fire was heard from the south-east, and a report circulated that the mounted troops were being pressed back.

Soon after 5 a.m. the battle was brought to Romani Camp by four enemy aeroplanes, which flew round for about an hour and dropped some thirty bombs without inflicting much damage.

No sooner had the aeroplanes departed than the Turkish artillery commenced to shell the oasis. But up to 7 a.m. no sign of enemy movement had been observed on the 158th Brigade front ; a few troops were then seen in the far distance.

Our counter-movement against the enemy's left flank did not commence until 5.35 a.m., and by that time the mounted troops opposing the Turks had been slowly forced back almost to Pelusium Station. The Turks also launched an attack against the bend in the hook of the main line, but it was never pushed home, and our 6th and 7th Battalions had only a fleeting glimpse of the enemy.

At Romani the 156th Brigade, with our 5th Battalion attached, waited. The heat of the day and the strong fight put up by the mounted troops began to tell on the enemy ; towards evening New Zealanders and Yeomanry drove the Turks from Mount Royston, and at 5 p.m. the 156th Brigade was ordered to attack Wellington Ridge.

Brigadier-General Girdwood launched the 7th and 8th Cameronians just before it was dark, and the 8th Cameronians, with D Company of our 5th Battalion in support, were held up by rifle fire within a hundred yards of the crest of the ridge. Here they remained through the night.

When the advance was resumed at daybreak, the Turks were exhausted. White flags and a forest of arms went up : 1,500 prisoners were taken about Wellington Ridge.

It was thought that the enemy was demoralised, but General Kress was an able soldier and, falling back on the successive lines he had prepared, he escaped in good order. Altogether we captured about 4,000 Turks.

The casualties of our 5th Battalion are returned as 11 ; no return was made for either of the other two.

On the 14th August the 158th Brigade went back to El Ferdan, where they remained for the next three months training, cooling themselves by bathing in the Canal, and seeking such amusement as occasional journeys to Port Said provided.

Yeomanry Dismounted. The 24th and 25th Battalions.

The diary of events which led the British Army across the Sinai Desert is given in *Military Operations : Egypt and Palestine* as commencing with the occupation of the Qatiya basin in April ; Turkish surprise attack on the mounted troops, 23rd April ; occupation of the Romani Oasis—railway and wire road laid to Romani (23 miles) through April and August ; railhead 8 miles east of Salmana (54 miles)—pipehead Romani (23 miles), 17th November ; railhead east of Mazar (64 miles), 1st December ; occupation of El Arish (90 miles), 21st December ; pursuit of Turks and destruction of rear-guard at Magdhaba, 23rd December ; capture of Turkish force at Rafah, on the Palestine frontier (117 miles), 9th January 1917.

The last six months of 1916 were devoted to the Battle of the Somme in France, the battering-ram policy. In Mesopotamia General Maude commenced to move in December 1916, but the battle that swept the Turks from Kut only started on the 9th January 1917. The Government and the Imperial General Staff, looking at the War as a whole, found no outstanding success which could be exploited ; their policy with regard to Egypt and the war with Turkey generally was indefinite.   Before the Battle of Romani Sir Archibald Murray's suggestion to occupy El Arish was approved with something like enthusiasm—at that moment the Arab revolt in the Hejaz had just broken out, and the Somme offensive had not begun—but after Romani Sir Archibald's force was reduced by five dismounted Yeomanry regiments, his divisions were below strength, and any spark of enthusiasm for war in Palestine died.

Sir Archibald wanted five divisions—he had four.   After occupying El Arish he wished to pursue an offensive defence and hold enemy troops which might otherwise be engaged against the Sherif of Hejaz, the Russians, or in Mesopotamia.   " The Egyptian Field Force must always be necessary, and to reduce it below a certain figure, which I consider has now been reached, relegates it to a purely defensive rôle which might lead to its being ignored ; whilst if we keep it to its present strength, the offensive action it is capable of must draw the enemy forces against it. . . ."

Then, in December, Sir William Robertson was approached by the new Prime Minister, Mr. Lloyd George, who thought that the capture of Jerusalem would have a wide moral effect, and seemed for a moment to favour more active operations against Palestine.   He wired : " A success is badly needed, and your operations promise well."   But this was quickly followed by a more cautious telegram : " In order that any possibility of misunderstanding may be removed, I wish to make it clear that, notwithstanding the instructions recently sent to you to the effect that you should make your maximum effort during the winter, your primary mission remains unchanged, that is to say, it is the defence of Egypt.   You will be informed if and when the War Cabinet changes this policy."

Other telegrams of a like nature were sent, and on the 17th January the War Office ordered Sir Archibald to send one of his divisions to France— the 42nd was chosen.   This entailed a rearrangement of his force.

General Headquarters were in Cairo, a distant centre made necessary by the peculiar political situation of Egypt ; and in October Sir Charles Dobell, who, after his successful operations against the Germans in the Cameroons, had commanded the Western Frontier Force of Egypt, was given command of the force on the Canal and in Sinai ; he was given the title of G.O.C. Eastern Frontier Force.   He had under his command the Imperial Mounted Division, Anzac Mounted Division, Camel Brigade, the 52nd, 53rd, and 54th Infantry Divisions, to which was added a new division.

Sir Archibald had the 2nd Dismounted Brigade, which was made up of the Highland Mounted Brigade and the South-western Mounted Brigade ; the 3rd Dismounted Brigade, made up of the South-eastern and Eastern Mounted Brigades ; and the 4th Dismounted Brigade, made up of the South Wales and the Welsh Border Mounted Brigades. These units now became definitely infantry units for the period of the war, and were posted to the new 74th Division.

The Welsh Horse had originally been in the Eastern Mounted Brigade ; the Denbighshire Yeomanry in the South Wales Mounted Brigade ; the Montgomeryshire Yeomanry in the Welsh Border Mounted Brigade. The Denbighshire Yeomanry, commanded by Lieutenant-Colonel Clegg, then became the 24th Battalion Royal Welch Fusiliers—they had been moved from the Western Frontier zone to Sherika—and on the 2nd February 1917 were inspected by the Commander-in-Chief in their new rôle as infantry. The Montgomeryshire and the Welsh Horse Yeomanry Regiments were fused into the 25th Royal Welch Fusiliers on the 4th March at a place called Helmia.

The reorganisation of his mounted troops gave Sir Archibald Murray the Australian and New Zealand Mounted Division and the Imperial Mounted Division, each of four brigades.

The reorganisation meant the transfer of many units from garrison duties in Egypt to Sir Charles Dobell's Eastern Frontier Force. The War Office had, however, been forming and sending abroad battalions of old soldiers, and men suffering from some disability which prevented more active employment, for garrison duty. Amongst those sent to Egypt were the 2nd (Garrison) and 6th (Garrison) Battalions Royal Welch Fusiliers.

We have to deal now with the 5th, 6th, 7th, 24th, and 25th Battalions with the Eastern Frontier Force, and the 2nd and 6th (Garrison) Battalions in Egypt.

THE 2ND (GARRISON) BATTALION.

The 2nd (Garrison) Battalion was formed on the 21st October 1915, out of drafts from the 3rd Royal Welch Fusiliers, 3rd South Wales Borderers, 3rd Cheshire, and 3rd South Lancashire (Prince of Wales' Volunteers). The new battalion was stationed at Garswood Park, near Wigan, and was commanded by Lieutenant-Colonel W. Hussey Walsh.

This battalion sailed from Devonport on the 6th March, and arrived at Alexandria on the 15th March 1916. The battalion went to Zagazig, and sent A Company to Tel el Kebir and D Company to Belbeis. On the 21st April the battalion was sent to Cairo.

At the memorial service for Lord Kitchener, held on the 13th June (which was attended by the 5th, 6th, and 7th Battalions), the buglers of the 2nd (Garrison) Battalion sounded the " Last Post."

They left Cairo on the 27th February 1917, for Alexandria, *en route* to Sollum Bay, which had been the centre of the Senussi trouble. Here they remained.

THE 6TH (GARRISON) BATTALION.

The 6th (Garrison) Battalion was formed at Aintree, Liverpool, on the 18th September 1916. It is somewhat remarkable to find that included in its ranks were 350 men who had already seen active service. With such a backing the battalion was soon ready for service, and sailed on the s.s. *Tofua* on the 23rd January, under the command of Lieutenant-Colonel Lushington. On arrival in Egypt the battalion was stationed at the Citadel, Cairo.

ACROSS THE DESERT.

By the 31st December 1916 the Egyptian Province of Sinai was free from the enemy invasion. Our three Territorial battalions were still employed on the Canal defences (eating a frugal Christmas dinner at Romani), but on the 18th January the 53rd Division, with Headquarters at Mahamdiya, were ordered to concentrate at Mazar by the 31st of the month. The 160th Brigade had already moved forward to Bir el Abd, and the division, in two columns, followed them on the 20th, arriving at El Abd on the 27th. Their destination was then changed to El Arish, where they were ordered to relieve the 42nd Division.

Our men had become accustomed to a landscape of sand, and the march across the desert was monotonous, but to some it contained a mysterious charm, especially at dawn and in the evening. Before the sun is high the mounds and ridges cast shadows over the still wilderness of sand ; the changing light is fascinating. And there was mystery, too, in the sudden discovery of oases—they were usually close below a ridge of sand, completely hidden, little patches of shading palm trees. And then came the magical change on crossing the Wadi el Arish—from waste to growth, from sand to green grass.

Looking from the desert there lies before you a country of rolling downs. On the hillside there are patches of barley, and in the spring all is covered with the brilliant colour of red and yellow poppies, pink dianthus, white and pink convolvulus. Towards the sea a long valley divides the downland from a coastal fringe of high, soft, sandhills, and along the valley runs the old caravan road to Gaza.

It is a dry and treeless land, but where there is water fig-trees and olives flourish.   The town of Khan Yunis is surrounded by gardens, edged with enormous cactus hedges ; and there were small villages, little hamlets.

From inland heights the great Wadi Ghazze runs across this front, a wide cleft in the soft soil, cut by the flood of winter rain ; and into it, from the downland, there runs a countless number of tributary wadis, deep, angry-looking scars in the hillside.   On the left bank of the Wadi Ghazze there are a few landmarks such as Tel el Jemmi, Tel el Fara, In Seirat, and Raspberry Hill, but on the right bank there is a definite ridge culminating at Sheikh Abbas in a curious sort of cliff.

From Sheikh Abbas, across an open plain, the hill Ali Muntar, surmounted by a mosque, marks the outskirts of Gaza, hidden in a forest of olive trees.   Across the plain runs the road to Beersheba.

The pipe-line reached El Arish on the 15th February 1917.   Khan Yunis was occupied by the Desert Column on the 28th February.   The Turks held a strong position at Shellal.

What was known as the Desert Column consisted of the Australian and New Zealand Mounted Division (less the 1st Light Horse Brigade), the Imperial Mounted Division (less the 4th Light Horse Brigade), and the 53rd Division, under the command of General Chetwode.   General Dobell held under his own hand the 52nd and 54th Divisions, the 229th Brigade from the 74th Division now forming, and the Imperial Camel Brigade.

The 53rd Division had concentrated at Sheikh Zowaiid on the 22nd February.   Sir Archibald Murray's intention was to attack the Turkish position at Shellal when, on the 5th March, the Turks suddenly withdrew to Gaza and Tell esh Sheria.   His instructions from the Imperial Staff remained the same—that no advance was to be made into Palestine until the autumn ; but at the beginning of March they were modified to include " pressure on all fronts."   His contemplated attack on Gaza fell in, therefore, with the policy of the War Cabinet.

THE FIRST OFFENSIVE.

FIRST BATTLE OF GAZA, 26TH–27TH MARCH.   AREA NORTH OF THE LINE
BEERSHEBA–BELAH.

Owing to water and transport difficulties, Sir Archibald limited his plan to a cutting-out expedition, for which the disposition of the Turkish forces was favourable : with a strength of 16,000 rifles in the line, the Turks had their main forces between Abu Hureira and Beersheba, and a detachment at Gaza.

Sir Archibald Murray was able to maintain the whole of the Eastern Force at Rafah, but was not in a position to employ more in this operation than the portion of it known as the Desert Column—two mounted divisions and the 53rd Infantry Division—commanded by General Chetwode. But the 54th Division was to move forward and protect the right flank of the Desert Column against any enterprise from the Abu Hureira–Beersheba line, and the 52nd Division, denuded of all but the 1st line Transport, was in reserve east of Kahn Yunis.

The high ground which encircles the west and southern sides of the plain east of Gaza runs down to the Wadi Ghazze in three ridges. Then comes the old caravan road from the desert to Gaza, then the sand-dunes. The Turks did not hold the line of the Wadi Ghazze, and allowed the lower slopes of the ridges on its right bank to be reconnoitred. " They were rather jolly outings," says Captain Ashton, Brigade Major of the 158th Brigade. " One would make one's way slowly and steadily out all morning, till one reached the desired spot, when one would have a real good look with glasses and a map. A picnic lunch followed, an hour's easy, and one would start off home again, and everything was so green and fresh with the ground fairly covered with little scarlet tulips." [1]

The Turkish defences encircled the town, lying on the edge of the groves and gardens, and including the hills to the south and east, the most important of which were Green Hill, Ali Muntar, and Clay Hill.

Sir Charles Dobell's plan was a bold one. On the morning of the 26th March the two mounted divisions were to cross the Wadi Ghazze south of El Breij and, riding in a wide circle, throw a strong protecting screen round Gaza : the Australian and New Zealand Mounted Division from the sea near Wadi Hesi, north of Gaza, through Deir Sneid to Nejile and Huj ; the Imperial Mounted Division to continue the line from Huj through Khirbet el Resum to the Gaza–Beersheba road. The 54th Division was to follow the cavalry and occupy Sheikh Abbas. The Imperial Camel Corps were to clear the right bank of the 54th Division. With the arena held by these troops, the 53rd Division was to attack the town.

Of the 53rd Division, one battalion of the 160th Brigade, with a cavalry regiment and a section of artillery, were to demonstrate on the sand-dunes with the object of holding the enemy in his works south-west of Gaza.

The bulk of the Division would cross the Wadi Ghazze between El Sire and El Breij, and occupy the line El Sheluf–Kh. Mansura–Tell el Ahmar. A " visual reconnaissance will then be made of the enemy's

---

[1] *History of the 53rd Division.*

position about Ali Muntar, and arrangements made for the attack of that position."

In preparation for the attack the 53rd Division moved to Rafah on the 21st March, and on the 24th to Khan Yunis, a squalid little town out of which the tower of an old Crusader's fort thrusts itself ; but it is surrounded by a wide fringe of gardens and fruit groves which afforded good cover from the air.

The next day the division moved to Deir el Bulah, another wooded area. The officers reconnoitred the ground for the approach to battle on the 26th. They sat on the forward slopes of In Seirat, which gave them a good view across the Wadi Ghazze, while General Dallas pointed out the lines of advance of the three brigades. The officers then went down to the wadi to the crossings allotted to their units, and, in the case of the 158th Brigade, surveyed the route back to the starting-point of the brigade, behind Druid's Hill, north of Deir el Bulah. "It was an infernally difficult route, as various small wadis had to be crossed, but we got it pretty clear, with plenty of notes and compass bearings." The reconnoitring party returned to Druid's Hill as the brigade was marching in, about 6 p.m.

The latter part of the day's work was, however, wasted, as an order was issued at 9 p.m. that the brigade would proceed by a taped route and that a guide would be provided.

The starting-hour was 1 a.m., and the head of the column, our 5th Battalion, appeared punctually—and waited. The guide was lost ! Officers were sent out to search for him ; he was found about 1.30 a.m.

It was a clear, starlit night with no moon. The long column started out, marching through nearly full-grown barley and green crops ; there was a heavy dew, and all ranks were soaked to the waist. Soon it was found that the guide had not the vaguest notion where he was ; his strips of canvas had been removed by some irresponsible person, and he had not reconnoitred the route. Brigadier-General Mott, who had an excellent eye for country, led the column himself on a rough compass bearing, and found the El Breij hut, about half a mile from the Wadi Ghazze. A crossing was discovered—not the right one—and the brigade finally stood on the right bank at 4.35 a.m., nearly an hour late, and dawn breaking !

The brigade was scarcely across the wadi when a thick sea-fog rolled inland, blotted out the dawn, and reduced visibility to about 50 yards. Already an hour late, and conscious of the importance of time, the Brigadier led his brigade—"the most amazing fine leading : dashing off on a horse, and aided by a natural sense of country "—and at 8.30 a.m. the whole column was snugly tucked away in a covered position near Mansura.

The fog had by this time dispersed on the high ground, and the 158th Brigade got into touch with the 160th at El Sheluf, on the ridge on the left. The 159th Brigade had crossed the Wadi Ghazze after the 158th, but had remained, according to orders, on the right bank. A message requesting orders sent about this time received the reply that the brigade was to stay where it was.

A sea-fog is by no means an uncommon occurrence—it had been experienced by our battalions during the latter stages of their march across the desert—but it was unusual at that time of year. The time-table provided no margin, and the Higher Command was greatly exercised in mind when the fog descended. Nothing could, however, be done, as the whole of the Desert Column was already on the move : the leading brigade of the Australian and New Zealand Mounted Division crossed the wadi when the fog was at its thickest, and at 9 a.m. the 2nd Light Horse had reached Beit Durdis. By 11 a.m. the 7th Australian Light Horse had reached the sea, north of Gaza.

By 10.30 a.m. the masking of Gaza was completed : the 54th Division was on the Sheikh Abbas position, digging a line of trenches facing east ; the camel brigade was away on their right flank, and the two mounted divisions were just completing the circle to the sea. And before that hour the attacking units were in position : the 158th Brigade at Mansura ; the 160th at El Sheluf ; the 159th (ordered to move from the right bank of the wadi at 9.30 a.m.) was marching towards Mansura ; the two artillery brigades, 265th and 266th, were ready to fire (the 266th had actually fired at Ali Muntar at 10.10 a.m.).

It was said that the sea-fog snatched complete success from the Desert Column by depriving them of so many hours of daylight, but as a study of events will show, there were contributory causes far more serious than the fog.

The 158th Brigade were at the curious cliff-edge of Mansura at 9 a.m., and officers were looking over the side at the great plain between them and Gaza.

The 159th Brigade had asked repeatedly for orders, but were held on the bank of the Wadi Ghazze until 9.30 a.m., when the Brigadier was also ordered to attend a conference at Mansura : all officers called were present at 10.15.

General Dallas allotted objectives to brigades, the 158th Brigade's task being to attack Ali Muntar from the east with the 159th Brigade on their right ; but Brigadier-General Travers stated that the 159th Brigade, only having received orders to move at 9.30, had not really got on the move until 10 a.m. and would require at least 1½ hours to cross the three miles of rough country to Mansura. Also Brigadier-General Le Mottee made the curious statement that his artillery would not be in position for two hours, which suggested the probable hour of advance would be 12.30 p.m.

At the termination of the conference Commanding Officers were informed of the plan of attack, and viewed the position, after which everyone rested. (" I had a desperate job to keep awake."—Ashton.)

General Chetwode had hoped that the attack would be launched at 10 a.m., and at 10.15 wired to General Dallas impressing on him the need for speedy action. General Dallas replied at 10.50 that there had been difficulty in bringing up the artillery, but he hoped to attack at noon. At 11.30 General Chetwode wired again ordering General Dallas to start his attack forthwith.

The 158th Brigade was suddenly ordered to advance.

Our three battalions were ordered to attack in line ; the Herefordshire were held in Brigade reserve. The actual times recorded in battalion and brigade diaries do not always agree, but the sequence of events is easy to follow.

Brigade and Divisional Headquarters were in close touch, both being at Mansura. General Dallas himself showed the Desert Column messages to Brigadier-General Mott, and when he ordered the advance to commence, before the 159th Brigade had arrived, is stated to have said that he thought Ali Muntar was unoccupied, as our cavalry had been seen to the north of Gaza. General Dallas also said that the artillery would be under Divisional control.

Orders for the attack had been given verbally, and were embodied in a short written order which was delivered later :

" The Division will attack the Ali Muntar position as follows :

" 160th Brigade along the main ridge from the south-west on Ali Muntar ;

" 158th Brigade from the east, also on Ali Muntar ;

" 159th Brigade, less one battalion, on the hill north-east of Ali Muntar, indicated to G.O.C. 159th Brigade, at the same time covering the right flank of the 158th Brigade ;

" The artillery of the division will support the attack under order of the C.R.A. ;

" The G.O.C. 159th Brigade will detail one battalion in divisional reserve at Mansura."

Lieutenant-Colonel Borthwick, commanding our 5th Battalion, was ordered to move from the protecting rim at Mansura in an easterly direction for about a thousand yards, and then to wheel on Ali Muntar on a two-company front. The 6th (Lieutenant-Colonel Rome) and 7th (Lieutenant-Colonel Harker) Battalions were to follow, each wheeling left 500 yards beyond the point of deployment of the last.

Soon after noon our 5th Battalion had deployed on ground that fell gently towards the steeper slopes of Ali Muntar. They were in full view of the enemy, but not a shot was fired until they commenced to advance down the slope, when the Turks opened artillery fire. The shrapnel, however, burst high.

The battalion moved rapidly towards the Cactus Gardens, about 800 yards from Ali Muntar ; as they neared the Garden heavy machine-gun and rifle fire was opened on them by the Turks. The battalion lay down and waited for the rest of the brigade to come up.

Now the 6th Battalion came into line, followed by the 7th. The story is graphically told in the 7th Battalion Diary :

" During the advance the enemy's artillery opened a pretty hot shrapnel and high-explosive fire on the brigade ; fortunately few casualties occurred during that period. This advance was carried out perfectly by the troops, and also the wheel facing north. Each battalion as it completed its wheel went quickly forward towards its objective till the firing-line was held up by heavy rifle and machine-gun fire about 500 yards from the enemy position. I must point out that the last 1,500 yards of our advance was in full view of the enemy and an absolutely open glacis ; the battalion nevertheless worked a magnificent advance in splendid order, showing the greatest bravery and determination." (Harker.)

Our 5th Battalion remained for an hour under heavy fire from Green Hill and Ali Muntar before the wheel was completed. The Brigadier was in communication with Lieutenant-Colonel Borthwick, and learned that Green Hill, on the left of the 5th Battalion, was strongly held. The 159th Brigade had arrived at Mansura about noon, and was immediately ordered by General Dallas to prolong the right of the Royal Welch line ; battalions were streaming out across the rear of the firing-line, so eager that long stretches were covered at the double. But it was obvious to Brigadier-General Mott that his brigade had struck in rather too far north, and that his left was his weak spot. He therefore decided to put in his reserve battalion, the Herefordshire, to advance on Green Hill.

The Herefordshire moved out about 1.45 p.m. ; the 159th Brigade were level with the Royal Welch soon after 2 p.m. The whole line remained stationary until 3.50 p.m.

At this time the advance of the 160th Brigade, which would have materially assisted the Royal Welch, was held. They had captured the Labyrinth, a maze of trenches and cactus hedges, south of Gaza, but their losses had been severe, troops were much shaken, and further advance was out of the question—indeed, stragglers began to trickle back through the batteries of the 265th Field Brigade.

The whole of the 53rd Division was committed, excepting the 7th Cheshire held in divisional reserve.

General Dobell had informed General Dallas that he could have the 161st Infantry Brigade and the 271st Field Artillery Brigade if he required them, and early in the morning (10 o'clock) General Dallas had telegraphed to Desert Column to be informed of the position of the 161st Brigade. Desert Column replied that the brigade was at Sheikh Nebhan ; but the brigade had been ordered by Eastern Force to move from Sheikh Nebhan to El Burjabye, a position from which it could support either the 53rd or 54th Divisions, and, having reached that position, the Brigade Commander, thinking it too exposed, moved into the valley between Burjabye and Es Sire Ridges. Consequently, when General Dallas opened his attack and wired an order to the 161st Brigade to move up to Mansura, that order never reached the brigade. At 1.10 p.m. a separate order from Eastern Force moved the brigade to Mansura, and it arrived there about 3.30 p.m.

The moment the 161st Brigade arrived, General Dallas sent his Cheshire Battalion to join the 159th Brigade, and ordered the 161st, less one battalion, to capture Green Hill and fill the gap between the 158th and 160th Brigades. The brigade commenced to advance at 4 p.m.

Our three battalions had remained motionless until 3.50 p.m. Captain E. W. Walker, of our 7th Battalion, on the extreme right of the 158th Brigade line, had managed, with 2nd Lieutenants Latham, Thomas, and Westcombe, to get within 200 yards of the enemy position. " I now sent back a written message to my Commanding Officer, stating that with the help of supports I was in a position to assault, and asking that bombardment be lifted. I afterwards learned that this message did not reach him. This was about 14.30 hours, and I waited in the hope of support for about an hour. This delay caused me many casualties, but we were not under machine-gun fire. Mr. Westcombe was hit during this time, after excellent work. I was greatly helped by overhead machine-gun fire from the ridge behind me, and by the Lewis gun with me brought up by the 5th Welch Regiment. Mr. Roberts from D Company here came over to me, and I found that he was suffering more heavily than I was, and could obtain no support. All the supports of his own brigade behind him had come up. Apart from a machine gun in a gully, which I could plainly see firing to my left, there was extraordinary little fire on our position. Just after this there was a direct hit on the machine gun in the gully, and the artillery bombardment seemed mostly on foreside of the position. I saw Mr. Roberts, Mr. Lastin, and an officer of the 5th Welch Regiment, and we assaulted. I was here separated from Mr. Latham, who assaulted through the prickly-pear hedge, while I went up the gully to machine gun, which, however, offered no resistance.

" I then sent parties round the trenches, and turned out and collected about 20 Austrian and German prisoners, some of whom were officers, and about 12 Turks. Unfortunately a second machine gun managed to get away into the trenches farther to the left, from where it caused us several casualties. I reported capture of hill, machine gun, and prisoners to my Commanding Officer in duplicate, but I learned that neither message reached him.

" The time was, as far as I can remember, 15.50, but I subsequently lost my notebook. At this time, about five minutes after the capture of the hill, I was reinforced by a strong party of the 7th Cheshire, under Colonel Lawrence, who then took command and consolidated the position." (E. W. Walker.)

Second Lieutenant C. Latham, after charging through the cactus, " continued clearing cactus gardens, and rounding up all prisoners under a heavy sniping fire. I then met a major of the Cheshire Regiment, who asked me to organise all men I could get hold of, and build up a line of defence along the prickly pears running north-east, and commanding a good view of Gaza town, which was a splendid position for a counter-attack. This position was held at night by several units, men reporting from all quarters of the fighting area, and were all put on duty to strengthen the defence, and reorganise into their own units, which chiefly consisted of the 7th Royal Welch Fusiliers, 5th Welch Regiment, and 7th Cheshire Regiment." (C. Latham.)

This effort of our 7th Battalion started a general advance along the whole line. The 159th Brigade stormed Clay Hill, a nasty hummuck with a lot of cactus hedges, at 4.45 p.m. At 5.30 p.m. the 161st Brigade had driven the Turks from Green Hill. All the high ground overlooking Gaza was in our hands, for the 160th Brigade still held the Labyrinth, and mounted troops were pressing down on the town from the north.

The situation on Ali Muntar Hill is described by the Brigade Major of the 158th Brigade, who rode over as soon as it was captured. " We found a strange scene of turmoil, masses of dead and wounded of both sides, a lot more people nearly frantic with thirst and excitement, and a great mixing of units. . . .

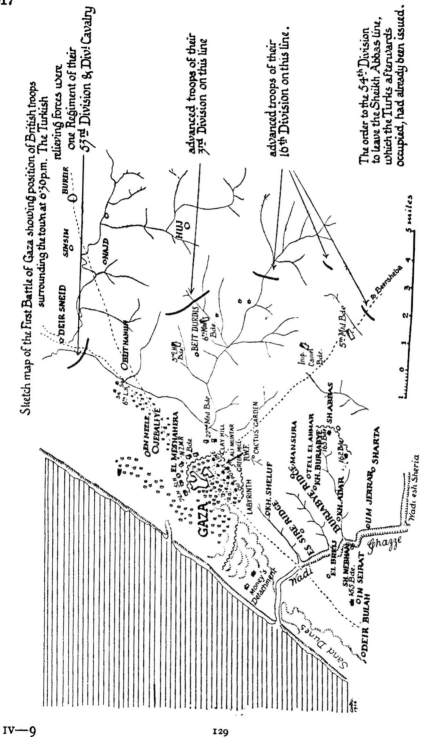

Sketch map of the First Battle of Gaza showing position of British troops surrounding the town at 6·30 p.m. The Turkish relieving forces were one Regiment of their 53rd Division & Divl Cavalry

advanced troops of their 3rd Division on this line

advanced troops of their 16th Division on this line.

The order to the 54th Division to leave the Shaikh Abbas line, which the Turks afterwards occupied, had already been issued.

" Desultory firing was going on on the far side—though it was now quite dark—where a certain amount of the enemy were still sticking in the gardens and cactus hedges which cover that side [*opposite the 160th Brigade*]."

This was between 5 and 6 o'clock. The Brigadier had intended to ride over to Ali Muntar with his Brigade Major, but as he was mounting he was called to the telephone, and was instructed by General Dallas to remain where he was for the present, as General Dallas was about to speak to Eastern Force. " He mentioned the possibility of retirement, at which the Brigadier protested, as the contingency appeared to the Brigadier as out of the question."

The above entry in the Brigade Diary refers to a conversation with General Chetwode, not General Dobell. General Chetwode had been nervous all day—first the fog, and then the delay in launching the infantry attack, had increased his anxiety. Soon after the infantry had started their advance he had ordered the mounted troops to attack from the north, and had chafed under the unavoidable delay, necessitated by reorganisation, in carrying out his orders until 4 p.m. There was, however, no news of any Turkish advance to relieve the Gaza garrison until after 4 p.m., and then only news of small detachments. It seems as though he had made up his mind that he must withdraw his mounted troops to water their horses by 6 p.m.

The first news of any considerable number of advancing Turks came from the Imperial Mounted Division in a message timed 4.50 p.m. : " 3,000 Infantry, 2 squadrons cavalry, advancing from Huj in south-westerly direction." That an advance would be made by the main Turkish force had, of course, always been obvious, and the lack of news had been puzzling. The 54th Division had had a warning order to be prepared to move to their left closer in to the 53rd Division, so that they could give more adequate protection, and at 5.30 p.m. General Dobell ordered them to move to the Burjabye Ridge, with their left a mile north of Mansura. This order was communicated to Desert Column, but not to the 53rd Division.

So we have, about 6 p.m., a direct chain of communication between Brigadier-General Mott, who was in the act of getting on his horse to ride up to Ali Muntar, and General Dallas, who was telling him to stay where he was while he, General Dallas, talked to General Chetwode.

Military Operations state that the order to the mounted troops to retire was issued at 6.10 p.m., and that as the order " was being dispatched, a report came in from General Dallas that a redoubt north-east of Ali Muntar had been captured, and that the enemy was retiring stubbornly. This information did not seem to General Chetwode to warrant any change in his orders," and adds that " it was not until some time later that he heard of the retreat of the enemy from the whole ridge." The hour given for General Chetwode's conversation with General Dallas is " shortly before 7 p.m."

General Dallas was then informed by General Chetwode that the mounted troops were being withdrawn, and was ordered to " make touch with the 54th Division." General Dallas objected forcibly, only to receive in the end a peremptory order to draw back the right of the 53rd Division to the left of the 54th.

During this conversation and argument, two points were ignored by both Generals—the extent of the 53rd success and the position of the 54th.

One can sympathise with General Dallas when he wrote in his report : " At 1 o'clock in the morning I learned from my own staff that troops of the 54th Division had appeared in the open plain north of Mansura, having apparently closed in on my right for some two miles. . . . Further, at daylight I learned, for the first time, that the 54th Division, less the detachment that had been placed at my disposal, had been withdrawn during the night from Sheikh Abbas to the line Mansura–Tell el Ahmar– El Burjabye–El Adar. Had I known that the 54th Division was moving to close in on my right, I should have held on to the positions gained, possibly with the exception of the hill north-east of the Mosque Hill [*Clay Hill*], and have consolidated the ground gained. I would also have followed my intention of pressing down into the gardens and town, and so of widening and strengthening the position."

The feelings of the 158th Brigade may be imagined when this order for withdrawal was communicated to them. But, as the Brigade Major wrote in his diary, " orders were orders, and the necessary instructions were sent out to units, and at midnight the withdrawal was begun. As a matter of fact, small parties of heroes had pushed down the slope into Gaza, notably one under Walker and George Latham of the 7th (R.W.F.), and never got the order, only coming away at dawn, when they found that there was no one else about. One such party met some Anzac Cavalry who had come right through the town from north to south. It showed to what a pitch the Turks had sunk. The whole remnant of the garrison, and Gaza itself, was like a large plum, and no one to pluck it. . . . We got back behind our cliff-edge at Mansura somewhere about 2 a.m., and literally fell asleep in a heap across each other." [1]

General Dobell did not learn the true situation until 11 p.m., and by

---

[1] *History of the 53rd Division.*

that time he had additional information, which had been unaccountably delayed for several hours, in the form of intercepted wireless messages between Major Tiller, the German in command at Gaza, and General Kress, at Tell esh Sheria. They were of a despairing nature. The British were in the town—the Turks would not fight any more—papers were burned—the wireless was blown up !

On receipt of the first of these messages General Dobell promptly instructed Desert Column that General Dallas " *should dig in on his present line, throwing back his left flank and connecting his right with the 54th Division.*" This order was not transmitted to the 53rd Division, as it was considered to be a confirmation of the previous order given verbally by General Chetwode to General Dallas.

The tragedy of this business was completed when at 10.30 p.m. General Dallas issued his order for the 53rd Division to retire, and telegraphed to Desert Column the line he was going to take up—Tell el Ujul (a point one mile north of Esh Sheluf)–Mansura–Sheikh Abbas—and that he would join up with the 54th Division " on the western slopes of Sheikh Abbas." The information conveyed nothing to Desert Column.

The 26th March had been a fairly cool day, but one must consider what our three battalions had done. Starting at dusk on the 25th, they had marched seven miles to Deir el Bulah ; after a halt of about three to four hours they had started on the trying march to Mansura—seven miles by daylight, but in the fog and with their bewildered guide considerably more ; they had then fought throughout the day and had finally marched back to Mansura, arriving at 2 a.m. on the 27th.

At 5 a.m. on the 27th General Chetwode understood what had happened, and orders were then issued to send out patrols, and support them if Ali Muntar was found unoccupied by the enemy. The 160th and 161st Brigades pushed forward and found that Green Hill and Ali Muntar were indeed unoccupied. From the 158th Brigade the Herefordshire were sent to Ali Muntar.

The Turks were, however, getting active. Our three battalions were ordered to prolong the line across the plain from Ali Muntar, and moved from their " bivouac "—where they had fallen in a heap to sleep—at 8 a.m. under enemy shell fire from Sheikh Abbas, which, since its evacuation by the 54th Division, had been occupied by the relieving Turkish Forces. Before they got well into position, Turkish attacks were developing against Ali Muntar.

While our battalions were moving out, an interesting wire, explaining the early-morning situation, was sent by General Dallas to Desert Column :

" The enemy has appeared on Sheikh Abbas, and he is shelling my reserves and back while I am holding and fighting on the line Ali Muntar–Sheluf. The 54th Division is facing Sheikh Abbas on line north-east of Mansura and along the line Tell el Ahmar–Burjabye–El Adar. We are in a bottle-neck, but can hold our position provided Ali Muntar can be retaken by fresh troops. Enemy has only recently appeared on Sheikh Abbas, and cannot have yet deeply entrenched."

The Turkish attack along the high ground on the left had swept our troops from Ali Muntar and Green Hill—the 158th Machine-gun Company abandoned 7 guns—and the position of our 5th and 7th Battalions, out on the plain, was precarious. They had to conform and fall back.

About 11.30 a.m. our 5th Battalion reported large numbers of the enemy concentrated in cactus gardens to their front, but they did not fire, as they had left a number of their wounded there. The Turks did not advance.

The heat was now tremendous, as the khamsin had been blowing all the morning. The weary men lay and watched. At 4.30 p.m. our 5th Battalion again reported a large body of Turks approaching Gaza.

Brigadier-General Mott telephoned to Divisional Headquarters asking that camels might be sent up with food and water for the men. He pointed out that he had no reserves, and wished to get his battalions back in rotation to rest and feed. General Dallas replied that an event of great importance would happen at 9 p.m., and that no camels could be sent up before then, and asked if the brigade could wait until that time. The Brigadier thought the General referred to reinforcements, and so informed Commanding Officers by telephone. Actually a general retirement was in contemplation. The situation was, as General Dallas said, a bottle-neck—the artillery of the 53rd Division was in fact back to back with that of the 54th on Mansura Ridge, and in the valley, between Burjabye and Es Sire Ridges, a congested mass of camels which had been brought forward during the night was trying to get back.

Soon after 4.30 p.m. the verbal order came from General Dallas for a general withdrawal behind the Wadi Ghazze, but no information was given as to the route to be taken, nor was the 158th Brigade told to cover the retirement, consequently precious time was wasted and officers were unnecessarily fatigued by being sent to reconnoitre one route which, on receipt of written orders from the division, was found not to be the one selected by them.

Battalions commenced to arrive at the assembly point at 10 p.m. The officer sent from the 436th Welsh Field Company as guide was, fortun-ately, very certain of the route, and led the brigade over difficult country, much cut up by wadis, to the banks of the Wadi Ghazze. After filling water-bottles and resting for about an hour, the brigade marched to bivouac 1½ miles to the north of Deir el Bulah.

Casualties had been heavy, especially amongst officers. The 5th Battalion returned 4 officers killed—Lieutenants T. Bate, W. G. Griffiths, E. Ll. Thomas, and 2nd Lieutenant E. L. H. Jones ; 33 other ranks killed ; 8 officers wounded—Captains W. E. Trickett, T. H. Parry, A. Kingsbury, T. H. Armstrong, 2nd Lieutenants W. B. H. Ladd, W. P. Dodd, W. Brandreth, H. S. Shaw ; 186 other ranks wounded ; 9 other ranks missing.

The 6th Battalion returned 3 officers killed—2nd Lieutenants A. L. Williams, W. E. Ireland, A. Rogers—and 10 other ranks ; 11 officers wounded—Captains T. M. Whittaker, D. F. J. Morgan, E. H. Evans, 2nd Lieutenants J. H. Jenkins, A. E. E. B. Williams, J. Arnell, J. Baird, E. Close, G. R. Sparrow, W. Harris, G. C. Davies—and 138 other ranks ; 3 other ranks missing.

The 7th Battalion returned 9 officers killed—Captain Iros T. Lloyd-Jones, Lieutenant V. Gwynne James, 2nd Lieutenants H. W. Fletcher, S. Garvin, O. G. Jones, R. Parry (other names not given)—and 36 other ranks ; 7 officers wounded, and 220 other ranks ; 15 other ranks missing.

The result of this battle was precisely nil ! But to Sir Archibald Murray, who had moved his Headquarters to El Arish during the fight, it seemed hopeful. He wired to the Chief of the Imperial General Staff : " We have advanced our troops a distance of 15 miles from Rafah to Wadi Ghazze to cover construction of railway. On the 26th and 27th we were heavily engaged east of the Ghazze with a force of about 20,000 of the enemy. We inflicted very heavy losses on him : I estimate his casualties at between 6,000 and 7,000 men, and we have in addition taken 900 prisoners, including General Commanding and whole Divisional Staff of the 53rd Turkish Division. This figure includes 4 Austrian officers and 5 German other ranks. We captured two Austrian 4·2-inch howitzers. All troops behaved splendidly, especially the Welsh, Kent, Sussex, Hereford, Middlesex, and Surrey Territorials and the Anzac and Yeomanry mounted troops."

In a slightly more detailed account telegraphed on the 1st April he said : " The operation was most successful, and owing to the fog and waterless nature of the country round Gaza just fell short of a complete disaster to the enemy. . . . None of our troops were at any time harassed or hard pressed. It is proved conclusively that in the open the enemy have no chance of success against our troops, but they are very tenacious in prepared positions. In the open our mounted troops simply do what they like with them."

In spite of the hopeless muddle which terminated the operation, there was only one misleading statement in these accounts—that the attack had been made on 20,000 Turks.

General Liman von Sanders gives a few details : " At 10 a.m. Gaza was surrounded. In the city were the 125th and 79th Infantry Regiments and the 2nd Battalion of the 81st Infantry, with machine guns and artillery. After noon they could be communicated with by wireless only. Height 83 in front of the city was the focus of the action. The British succeeded in taking it in spite of an obstinate defence, and in entering the batteries in rear. . . . The groups at Dschemame (Jemmami) and Tell Scheria had been alarmed at once. . . . Their action did not become effective on the 26th, as both columns were several times checked during the march, and it was 9 a.m. on the 27th March before they were near enough to Gaza for the relief to become sensible."

In the telegrams that passed between Sir Archibald Murray and Sir William Robertson a change is seen in the War Cabinet's policy. The news from Mesopotamia was good ; the Turks were anxious about the situation on the Tigris, and were diverting reinforcements to that front. " In these circumstances, and as you are assured of reinforcements during the summer, your immediate objective should be the defeat of the Turkish forces south of Jerusalem and the occupation of that town. . . . Your subsequent operations after you reach Jerusalem must depend largely on what the Russian Caucasus Army is able to achieve." Sir William Robertson also pointed out the state of affairs in England after the battles of the Somme. " Everyone is now feeling the strain of war, and this strain will certainly increase ; therefore the moral effect of success is of great importance, both in strengthening the hands of the Government and in making the public more ready to bear their burdens. . . . War Cabinet are anxious therefore that your operations should be pushed with all energy."

SECOND BATTLE OF GAZA, 17TH–19TH APRIL. AREA NORTH OF THE LINE
BEERSHEBA–BELAH.

The German commander, Kress, was not disposed to risk defeat a second time. By the middle of April he had at Gaza the Turkish 3rd Infantry Division ; between Gaza and Tell esh Sheria the reinforced 53rd Division ; at Jemmame the Turkish 3rd Cavalry Division ; at Tell esh Sheria the 16th Infantry Division ; and the 54th Turkish Division assembling at Beersheba, with the 7th Division *en route*. The opportunity which had been afforded Sir Archibald Murray was not to be repeated.

The attack was, however, to be repeated, but the Commander-in-Chief and Sir Charles Dobell were well aware that it must be a bigger affair. Aeroplanes reported Turkish activity ; the centre of their defensive system shifted from Beersheba to Gaza.

Railhead was brought up to Deir el Bulah, and water was stored in the Wadi Ghazze. The third artillery brigades of the 53rd and 54th Divisions were brought up from the Canal defences, also twelve 60-pdrs., and a siege battery of two 8-inch and two 6-inch howitzers. The 52nd, 53rd, and 54th Divisions held the line of the Wadi Ghazze until the beginning of April, when the 74th Division appeared.

The movement of the three dismounted brigades from the Western Front (Egypt) to form the 74th Division commenced with the New Year. The 2nd Dismounted Brigade were at Moascar on the 5th January, El Ferdan on the 15th, Qantara on the 5th March, and El Arish on the 6th : this Brigade was numbered the 229th Brigade. The 3rd Dismounted Brigade went to Sidi Bishr on the 2nd April, and to Deir Belah on the 9th : it was numbered the 230th Brigade. The 4th Dismounted Brigade went to Assiut on the 1st January, Zeitoun on the 1st March, Helmia on the 1st April, and Khan Yunis on the 6th : it was numbered the 231st Brigade.

General Girdwood, commanding the new division, arrived at El Arish on the 4th March.

The interval for preparation between the end of March and the 17th April permitted the German General, Kress, to present a problem of some difficulty to Sir Charles Dobell. It is summarised in Sir Archibald Murray's despatch :

" It became clear that five divisions and a cavalry division had now appeared on our front with an increase of heavy artillery. Not only were the Gaza defences being daily strengthened and wired, but a system of enemy trenches and works were being constructed south-east of Gaza to the Atawine Ridge, some 12,000 yards distant from the town. This put any encircling movement by our cavalry out of the question, unless the enemy's line in front of us could be pierced."

And before Gaza, " strong defences known as the Warren, the Labyrinth, Green Hill, Middlesex Hill, Outpost Hill, and Lees Hill running southwards along the ridge from Ali Muntar. This position, which commands all approaches to the town from the south-west, south, and south-east, has been very strongly fortified and well wired, in addition to the natural obstacles formed by thick cactus hedges, and had been made into a nest of machine guns largely manned by Germans. The right of the line, between Gaza and the sea, ran in the arc of a circle west and south-west of the town. This section consisted of a double line of trenches and redoubts, strongly held by infantry and machine guns, well placed and concealed in impenetrable cactus hedges built on high mud-banks, enclosing orchards and gardens on the outskirts of the town."

Now that the Turks had shifted their forces nearer the sea and left the Beersheba flank weak, the possibility of attacking this flank was considered, but quickly rejected on account of water difficulties. An attack in depth along the shore was also considered, but also rejected, as it did not allow General Dobell to use his mounted troops. The plan finally agreed upon was a repetition, with certain modifications, of the first Battle of Gaza.

It was, of course, no longer possible to mask the town with the mounted troops, but the attack was to be made by two divisions from Mansura and Sheikh Abbas ; and on the sand-dunes, instead of a detachment, a division would advance on the seaward side of the town.

The main effort, from Mansura and Sheikh Abbas, was to envelop the ridges covering the town from the east, while the mounted divisions and the camel brigade were to protect the right of the infantry by an attack on the Atawine and Hureira trenches, and be prepared to go through the gap which would be created either to pursue or to complete the envelopment of the town from the north.

The first phase of this operation was carried out on the 17th April, when the 52nd and 54th Divisions occupied the Sheikh Abbas–Mansura line with practically no opposition. The 53rd Division was on the left holding the line of the Wadi Ghazze, and on the 17th completed a new line running from Kurd Hill to Cliff Fort. Our three battalions had done a lot of digging in the sand prior to this date, at night, to the unearthly tune of howling jackals.

General Dallas had resigned his command, and Brigadier-General Mott succeeded him on the 10th April. Brigadier-General C. S. Rome took over the 158th Brigade, and Lieutenant-Colonel F. Mills assumed command of our 6th Battalion.

Brigade Headquarters were in a delightful spot known as St. James's Park, a grove of pomegranates, citrons, and large eucalyptus trees. The Turks, well aware that an attack was pending, had commenced to shell heavily at intervals on the 14th April. On the 15th Brigadier-General Rome held a conference at his Headquarters, under the shade of the trees, when the enemy artillery commenced to bombard the grove. There was a hasty exit to the hot but comparatively safe sand-dunes. Lieutenant-Colonels Borthwick, Mills, and Harker learned, however, that theirs would be a minor rôle when the battle opened, as the 159th and 160th Brigades were to attack. They were not concerned in the first phase, on the 17th.

The Brigade Headquarters moved up to Tell en Nujeid on the 18th, and our 5th Battalion held the new line that had been constructed.

On the 19th the big attack commenced. The 160th Brigade on the right and the 159th on the left formed up in rear of the new line, between Money Hill and Cliff Fort, and advanced through our 5th Battalion at 7.15 a.m. It was a dreadful-looking bit of country to move over. The so-called ridges were just drifts of sand, the rest flat with a few miserable stunted, thin bushes scattered widely apart. The advancing troops were in full view of the gardens on the high ground near Gaza, and long-range machine-gun fire was troublesome. The advance was slow.

The big battle was fought by the 52nd and 54th Divisions, with the 74th Division in reserve. Our 24th and 25th Battalions, held on the right bank of the Wadi Ghazze since the 17th, crossed to a position between Tell el Ahmar and the Wadi Nukhabir soon after midnight, and had great difficulty in getting there in the darkness, " the difficulty being added to by troops of the 52nd Division being already bivouacked in the same area. These moved off about 4.15 a.m., and the units of the brigade had all gone to ground in the deep wadis by 5 a.m." (Lord Kensington, commanding 25th Royal Welch.) There they remained throughout the day.

Briefly, the battle was a costly failure. General Liman von Sanders puts the case in a nutshell. " In one attack against the left wing of the 53rd Division (Turkish) the British came under the flanking fire from the 16th Division, and in an attack on the right of the 53rd Division under the flanking fire from the 3rd Division." To complete the unhappy tale, our own official history says : " This was a dogged advance against imperfectly located entrenchments, and in the face of fire from hidden artillery, without adequate support from that arm on the side of the attackers."

The attack of the British 53rd Division was rather a fumbling business, and ended with the capture of Samson Ridge. The 158th Brigade, less the 6th Royal Welch (under 259th Brigade), were ordered to relieve the 160th Brigade on Samson Ridge that night. The Herefordshire were already in the line, and when our 5th and 7th Battalions arrived there was much confusion. " The night was very dark and the sniping considerable, but the main difficulty lay in the way the trenches were held. The 160th Brigade manned the line from the left—Kents, Middlesex, half Herefords, Sussex, half Herefords, Queen's " (Brigade Diary). Our two battalions had to relieve the West Kent, Middlesex, and Sussex.

The 52nd Division had made a gallant effort, but the defences round Middlesex Hill and the broken ground to the west of it proved too strong. When darkness fell, the order was that the battle would continue in the morn-

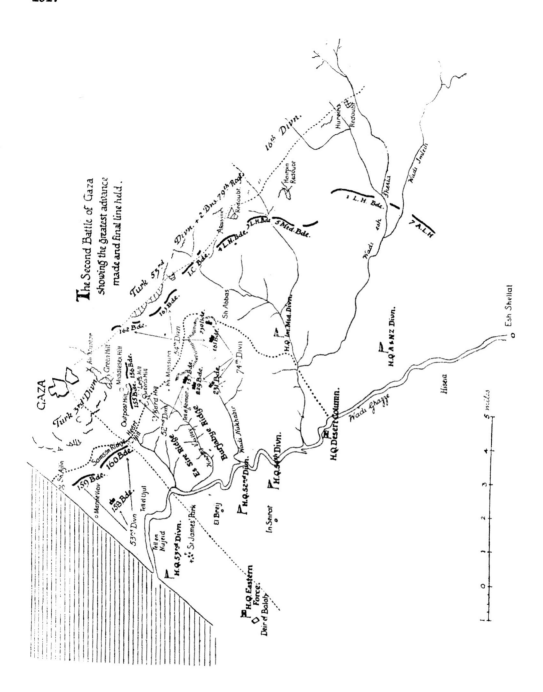

The Second Battle of Gaza showing the greatest advance made and final line held.

ing, but after consulting with his subordinate commanders, General Dobell offered his opinion that the prospects of success were not sufficient to justify the heavy casualties which would undoubtedly be incurred : he suggested the consolidation of the position on which his troops stood. Sir Archibald Murray agreed.

A matter of minor interest in the second Battle of Gaza was the employment of tanks (eight), which, however, did not prove successful either in the broken hilly country or on the sand-dunes, although one did good work at El Arish Redoubt, beyond Samson Ridge ; also the use of gas shells, which had little apparent effect, but, according to subsequent information from the Turks, did damage.

The line as finally settled ran from Sheikh Abbas along the edge of the plateau through Mansura to Lee's Hill—all this part was widely separated from the Turkish line—thence to Heart Hill, across Samson Ridge to Sheikh Ajlin on the shore : this last part was in close touch with the enemy. At Sheikh Abbas the British line returned to the Wadi Ghazze, and the Turkish line swung back to Beersheba, so that a great open plain, many miles in width, lay between the combatants.

The left of the Samson Ridge sector, held by our 5th Battalion, and which had been dug in the dark, was found to be under a sand-ridge with no field of fire at all ; this had to be rectified and the whole position well wired. On the 23rd the 6th Royal Welch relieved the Queen's, and our three battalions were then in line. The work of consolidation was hindered by excessive heat ; the khamsin commenced to blow, and continued for several days.

This khamsin, or sirocco, is a wind that blows from the sun-scorched deserts of the interior. The temperature may be low when it starts, but as the wind increases the thermometer rises, a fine mist of sand obscures the sun ; men become prostrate with thirst and fever ; vegetation shrivels ; sometimes the sand on the wind is so thick one cannot see at all. A diary of the 74th Division, covering the 19th and 20th, tells us : " Woke to find the khamsin upon us. Not much wind yet, but getting thick and very hot. . . . Wind got cooler, but more of it towards evening, and we had an awful night—mess-tents blown down, most people's bivvies, too. . . . Woke at intervals during this terrible night and found myself covered in inches of sand, but no use moving, so stuck it till dawn, when it got better." The motor-ambulances at Deir el Bulah were going about in the daytime with headlights.

The khamsin blows chiefly in the spring, otherwise a time of year when the climate of Palestine is most delightful. The rainy season—and the ruling climatic condition is the positive division of the year into dry and rainy seasons—begins to tail off in March. From May to October one rarely sees a cloud pass over the deep blue sky, although morning mists, and thick ones, are not uncommon. Sometimes the nights are chilly. But the point is the yearly drought from May to October, when the land dries up and all vegetation is scorched and dies.

The great heat engendered by these unbroken months of blazing days of sunshine is usually mitigated by a cool wind from the north-west, which rises between 10 a.m. and midday and continues until sunset. The khamsin winds, from the east, south-east, and south, are fortunately infrequent and irregular.

At the end of October summer ceases and heavy rains commence to fall ; this is the time of tillage in the cultivated areas. December, January, and February are the months of the full rainy season, with hail and sometimes snow.

The difference in temperature between winter and summer is very great, sufficient to influence military operations. In Palestine, as in Mesopotamia, no major operation was undertaken in the full heat of summer. But the difference in altitudes and the broken nature of the country modified conditions in particular spots. Thus in the lower ground about the Wadi Ghazze the hottest period of the day was between noon and 5 p.m.— " during those hours one lay in the sweltering bivouac shelter, tormented by flies and heat." The same observer [1] writes of El Shauth that it was " a series of pleasant little gardens, full of almond and apricot trees, surrounded by cactus hedges," and that as it stood on high ground it was much cooler than " down near the Wadi Ghazze. The afternoon breezes, although they blew the dust about, were moderately cool, and the flies were not nearly so bad." El Israain was similarly a popular place.

The heat of the summer put an end to further operations. During the quiet months that followed the second effort on Gaza the 53rd and 74th Divisions moved in the ordinary course of relief to various sectors of the line. Our 24th and 25th Battalions were at first in reserve near Tell el Jemmi ; the Brigade was then attached to the 54th Division in the Sheikh Abbas sector, and later moved to Lee's Hill. At night patrols went out as far as the Cactus Garden ; in daytime a lot of traffic could be seen in the distance, out of range. On one occasion our 25th Battalion caught about 80 Turks in the Cactus Garden while on patrol, and attacked them with the bayonet—they killed 8, captured 2, and put the rest to flight. They also discovered that the Turks were using a large number of dogs as " sentries " and to carry messages.

[1] Captain John More (6th R.W.F.), *With Allenby's Crusaders.*

Our 5th, 6th, and 7th Battalions moved from the sand-dunes into reserve, in the neighbourhood of Sheikh Nebhan. The health of the troops was good, but septic sores were prevalent. On the 19th May our 5th and 7th Battalions relieved the Imperial Camel Brigade on the line of the Wadi Ghazze ; on the 26th they moved to relieve the 230th Brigade, 74th Division, at Gamli : the whole Brigade assembled here. On the 19th June they moved to El Shauth area, and trained.

The right sector of the line, along the right bank of the Wadi Ghazze, consisted of a series of redoubts, covering the water and crossings at Gamli, El Fara, El Shellal, and Hiseia. At night mounted troops had standing patrols out in front of the infantry, by day they made wide sweeps across the plain towards the Turkish lines, and sometimes got in touch with the enemy, but the infantry was seldom worried. Battalion Headquarters and reserve companies were back in the crevices and crannies of the wadi itself, quite snug. The sector was seven miles from end to end, and brigadiers went round in Ford cars, which ground through the thick dust at a speed of about four miles an hour, with clouds of steam issuing from the radiators.

The Wadi Ghazze itself became the main thoroughfare, with railways, pipe-lines, and pumping centres as the Royal Engineers developed local water-supplies. The pipe-line from the Suez Canal was the basis of the water-supply, but wells were sunk in the bed of the Wadi—the 74th Division sank one which yielded 1,600 gallons per hour ; there were also a large number of pools in the Ghazze, but the water was mostly foul and difficult to control. Old wells were found to be infested with leeches, and were cleaned out ; they were reinforced with canvas tanks. All local sources were developed, and the best wells fitted with oil-engine pumps.

Summer pests made their appearance. Flies were dealt with by means of crude oil and sacking ; incinerators were kept going ; definite eating-places were established, so that scraps of food could be dealt with.

Lice were prevalent, and fleas. Septic sores were very bad. Diphtheria and scarlet fever were present. Scorpions and spiders of many colours and sizes were unpleasant companions.

On the other hand, every effort was made for the entertainment and recreation of the vast camp and bivouac town which had arisen along the banks of the Wadi Ghazze. Sports, horse shows, with competitions of all kinds, were organised ; bands and concert parties were formed by all divisions ; the canteen service was immensely improved ; and leave to Cairo was frequent : the result was a regular social life. Before the next battle seven infantry divisions, three mounted divisions, and a host of army troops were assembled.

The 74th Division left the line and went into reserve at Dorset House, by the Wadi Nukhabir, on the 9th/10th July ; they then moved to a camp in the sand-dunes west of Wadi Ghazze, and a period of intensive training took place. Battalions were reorganised into sections of Lewis gunners, riflemen, snipers, and bombers, and the men went through courses of instruction and training in these weapons. There followed outpost schemes, night marching, night attacks, and field-firing : there was plenty of room for the latter over the desert.

The 53rd Division remained on the right of the line, the brigade in reserve carrying out field training, and on the 1st August was relieved by the 60th Division, which had arrived from Salonika on the 1st June, and took over from the 54th Division on the sand-dunes.

Trench warfare was active in this sector. Patrolling was energetic, and our 5th and 6th Battalions secured several prisoners in " No Man's Land." The 53rd Division was relieved on the 24th/25th August, and went to the Southern Reserve Area, beyond the Wadi Selka, behind Deir el Belah, where training for open warfare commenced.

THE SECOND OFFENSIVE.

THIRD BATTLE OF GAZA, 27TH OCTOBER–7TH NOVEMBER 1917. AREA NORTH OF THE WADI GHAZZE.

Since the second Battle of Gaza many changes had taken place. Sir Archibald Murray relinquished his command in June ; Sir Philip Chetwode had succeeded Sir Charles Dobell. The summer had put an end to active operations in Mesopotamia and Palestine, but the war in Europe had been pursued with vigour. The Battle of Arras on the British front in April, followed by Nivelle's abortive and costly experiment, dragged on until one might well have imagined that the final decision would be reached over the ruins of Bullecourt. In June the successful Battle of Messines took place, and then July saw the commencement of that fearful holocaust, the third Battle of Ypres. To add to the uncertainty of the Allied cause, Russia had definitely collapsed.

On the other hand, America had entered the War in April.

Sir E. Allenby succeeded Sir Archibald Murray, and, reinforced, commenced to reorganise his Army. Within a few weeks he telegraphed his plan to the War Cabinet.

The full length of Syria between the Arabian Desert and the sea lay in front of him.   From the Lebanons, in the north, the Jordan flows for 160 miles down a depression which, starting at sea-level, drops at the Dead Sea to 1,292 feet below sea-level.   To the east of this great rent in the earth lies a range of hills rising to 2,000 feet (mean height) above sea-level ; on the west of the Jordan, from the Lebanons to the south of the Sinai Peninsula, runs a great ridge of limestone broken by the Plain of Esdraelon.

South of the plain, through Samaria, the ridge crops up in groups of hills, but they form the one great mass known as Mount Ephraim, then solidify again into the Tableland of Judea, and so, south of Hebron, slide down to the desert.

The descent from the ridge to the Jordan is precipitous, but on the Mediterranean side a second range of hills, of a different formation, lies up against the Judean hills ; this range is called the Shephalah.

All these great features run through the length of Syria, and seen in section from the British position, there was on the left the Maritime Plain " of gentle contours, and with a strip of sand along the coast—the soil of the plain is brown, broken by gullies containing a greyish shingle, puddles of water, and reeds ; then the Shephalah, a country of short, steep hills, a lot of brushwood and oak scrub, scrags of limestone, and rough torrent-beds ; then the Plateau of Judea, a stony moorland, with no water, no streams, some rough scrub, and a few dwarf trees—stones, boulders, rocks, and glaring sun ; and then comes desolation, hills like gigantic dustheaps, twisted, contorted, with an outcrop of jagged rock, and falling in broken chaos to the Dead Sea, the awful, enervating, fantastic ditch." [1]

The configuration of the country has always led invaders of Judea up the Maritime Plain.   The first pass on the way north is the Wadi el Alfranj to Beit Jibrin, where several Roman roads converge from the hills of Judea ; the second, at Tell el Sufi, the Blanchgarde of the Crusaders, is marked by the Wadi el Sunt and leads to Bethlehem ; the third is Wadi el Surar, used by the railway to Jerusalem ; the fourth is the Valley of Ajalon, a broad, fertile plain headed by three gorges which run up to the two Beth-horons and so to Jerusalem.

Covering Syria, the Turkish Army extended over a front of, roughly, 30 miles from the sea.   Gaza was now a fortress ; the remainder of the line was held by strong-works at Sihan, Atawine, Baha, Abu Hureira, and Beersheba.   General Allenby decided to attack the Turkish left.

His force had been augmented.   Besides the 60th Division he had the 10th and 75th.   Eastern Force and the Desert Column disappeared, and

---

[1] *The 74th Division in Syria and France.*

the Army was organised in two Corps, the XX, commanded by General Chetwode and composed of the 10th, 53rd, 60th, and 74th Divisions ; the XXI, commanded by General Bulfin, and composed of the 52nd, 54th, and 75th Divisions ; and the Desert Mounted Corps, commanded by General Chauvel, and composed of the Yeomanry Mounted Division, the Australian Mounted Division (late Imperial), and the Australian and New Zealand Mounted Division (Anzac). The Imperial Camel Corps remained a separate unit, in Corps Reserve.

Opposing General Allenby the Turkish order of battle, as given by Liman von Sanders, was 7th, 53rd, 54th, 16th, 27th Infantry Divisions and the 3rd Cavalry Division in line, the 3rd Infantry Division was in reserve at Huj ; the 26th Division, from Rumania, was assembling at Ramleh with the 24th, and the 19th Division was to follow there ; the 59th, less artillery, was at Aleppo ; the departure of the 20th from Haidar Pasha commenced on the 12th September. The movement of other divisions was also contemplated.

There had been during August a complete change in the Turkish plans. The Yilderim Army, as we know, was being assembled to drive the British from Baghdad. The plan arranged was that the Seventh Turkish Army would assemble at Aleppo, and that in October the Turkish portion of it would proceed to Hit and join the German Asiatic Corps. But during August General von Falkenhayn developed grave fears for the Palestine front, and after a good deal of argument upset Enver Pasha's pet scheme to recapture Baghdad. Liman von Sanders gives the order wrung from Enver : " the Seventh Army pertaining to Yilderim will be transported to the Sinai front. The troops now on the Sinai front will be under the Army Group Yilderim as long as the Seventh Army remains on the Sinai front. The Army Group Yilderim will conduct its operations independently on the Sinai front and in the separate Sanjak of Jerusalem, but Yilderim will keep the Commander-in-Chief in Syria and West Arabia informed."

The Turkish troops under General Kress now became the Eighth Army, under the orders of Yilderim, or Falkenhayn. The friction that existed between German and Turk caused Mustapha Pasha to resign command of the Seventh Army early in October.

At the date of General Allenby's attack Falkenhayn was on his way to Jerusalem ; Kress, commanding the Eighth Army, was at Huleikat ; and Fevzi Pasha, commanding the Seventh Army, was preparing to take over command of the left of the line.

.   .   .   .

In order that officers might become acquainted with that wide expanse

IV—10

of country that lay between the British right and the Turkish left, and also to accustom the Turks to the presence of cavalry on the plain, a number of reconnaissances in force were organised. The cavalry would ride out at night and occupy a line of outposts by dawn next morning. " Behind this line of protecting posts, the infantry corps and divisional commanders, and innumerable lesser fry, disported themselves in motor-cars and on horse-back. The senior corps commander and his staff used to be irreverently referred to as ' the Royal Party.' " [1]

The first move out into this " No Man's Land " by the 158th Brigade was made on the 19th July, when our 5th and 6th Battalions sent each two companies forward in position to support mounted troops, but it was more for the purpose of watching reported movement of the enemy than for reconnoitring ground.

On the 4th August Brigadier-General Rome, who was a cavalryman, was on the point of handing over command to Brigadier-General Vernon, having been given command of a mounted brigade, and the two Brigadiers and staff, with the Commanding Officer and one other from each battalion, and the machine-gun officer, reconnoitred as far as the Fara–Beersheba road. The ground was difficult and time was limited. " Officers concerned got a rough idea of their areas, but a further reconnaissance was necessary " (Brigade Diary). On the 28th September officers from our 5th and 6th Battalions examined the line from Beersheba road to the Wadi Saba, and were freely fired on by snipers. Several other reconnaissances took place. " We would start from Bulah in Ford cars about 10 a.m., and driving via Shellal (about 25 miles), arrive at El Buggar, our usual rendezvous, about 1 p.m. Here we would take to horses, which had been sent over to Shellal the day before and out to El Buggar during the morning, and reconnoitre various parts of the allotted line behind the cavalry screen from Tuweil el Khebari down to Wadi Saba one way, and through Pt. 820 to Pt. 810, and forward nearly as far as Pt. 790 in the other. We would potter about, dodging a few shells generally, then back to El Buggar and the homely Fords, and finally home to dinner about 8 p.m."

From the high ground accessible to these reconnoitring parties the Beersheba defences were plainly visible, the position of the town itself being indicated by the minaret of the Great Mosque. From his trenches the Turk had good observation over the intervening wide, rolling plain.

Officers from our 24th and 25th Battalions carried out the same programme.

The mounted troops found these " outings " somewhat trying : they

1 R. M. P. Preston, *The Desert Mounted Corps.*

lasted for thirty-six hours across a country that was like a stony desert, with no protection from the sun and the thermometer frequently up to 110 degrees in the shade, with innumerable flies, no water for the horses, and only the full water-bottle carried for the man. The Turks brought out light field guns and lay in wait to fire on troops crossing wadis. Colonel Preston says : " It was with a sigh of relief that the troops saw the last of the motor-cars of the Royal Party disappear in a cloud of dust."

The instructions issued were covered by Force Orders, dated 22nd October, which contain the following :

" It is the intention of the Commander-in-Chief to take the offensive against the enemy at Gaza and at Beersheba, and, when Beersheba is in our hands, to make an enveloping attack on the enemy's left flank in the direction of Sheria and Hureira.

" On Z day the XX Corps (with the 10th Division and the Imperial Camel Brigade attached) and the Desert Mounted Corps (less one mounted division and the Imperial Camel Brigade) will attack the enemy at Beersheba with the object of gaining possession of that place by nightfall.

" As soon as Beersheba is in our hands and the necessary arrangements have been made for the restoration of the Beersheba water-supply, the XX Corps and the Desert Mounted Corps complete will move rapidly forward to attack the left of the enemy's main position, with the object of driving him out of Sheria and Hureira, and enveloping the left of his army. The XX Corps will move against the enemy's defences south of Sheria, first of all against the Kauwukah [Qawuqa] line and then against the Sheria and Hureira defences. The Desert Mounted Corps, calling up the division left in general reserve during the Beersheba operations, will move north of the XX Corps, and will be prepared to operate vigorously against and round the enemy's left flank if he should throw it back to oppose the advance of the XX Corps.

" On a date to be subsequently determined, and which will be probably after the occupation of Beersheba, and twenty-four to forty-eight hours before the attack of the XX Corps on the Kauwukah [Qawuqa] line, the XXI Corps will attack the south-western defences of Gaza with the object of capturing the enemy's front-line system from Umbrella Hill to Sheikh Hasan, both inclusive.

" The Royal Navy will co-operate with the XXI Corps in the attack on Gaza and in the subsequent operations which may be undertaken by the XXI Corps.

" On Z –4 day the G.O.C. XXI Corps will open a systematic bombardment of the Gaza defences, increasing in volume from $Z-1$ to $Z-2$ day and will be continued until $Z-4$ day at the least.

" The Royal Navy will co-operate. . . .

" The XX Corps will move into position during the night $Z-1$/Zero, so as to attack the enemy at Beersheba on Zero Day south of the Wadi Saba with two divisions, while covering his flank and the construction of the railway east of Shellal with one division on the high ground overlooking the Wadis Sufi and Hanafish.

" The objective of the XX Corps will be the enemy's works west and south-west of Beersheba as far as the Khalassa–Beersheba road, inclusive.

" The Desert Mounted Corps will move on the night $Z-1$/Zero from the area of concentration about Khalassa and Asluj, so as to co-operate with the XX Corps by attacking Beersheba with two divisions and one mounted brigade.

" The objective of the Desert Mounted Corps will be the enemy's defences from the south-east to the north-east of Beersheba, and the town of Beersheba itself.

" The G.O.C. Desert Mounted Corps will endeavour to turn the enemy's left flank with a view to breaking down his resistance at Beersheba as quickly as possible.   With this in view the main weight of his force will be directed against Beersheba from the east and north-east.   As soon as the enemy's resistance shows signs of weakening, the G.O.C. Mounted Troops will be prepared to act with the utmost vigour against his retreating troops, so as to prevent their escape, or at least drive them well beyond the high ground immediately overlooking the town from the north.   He will also be prepared to push troops rapidly into Beersheba in order to protect from damage any wells and plant connected with the water-supply not damaged by the enemy before Beersheba is entered.

" Special instructions will be issued to G.O.C. Mounted Corps. . . .

" The Yeomanry Mounted Division will pass from the command of G.O.C. XX Corps at 05.00 on Zero day, and will come directly under Headquarters as part of the general reserve. . . .

" When the situation as regards the water at Beersheba has become clear, so that the movements of the XX Corps and the Desert Mounted Corps against the left flank of the enemy's main position can be arranged, G.O.C. XXI Corps will be ordered to attack the enemy's defences south-west of Gaza in time for this operation to be carried out prior to the attack of the XX Corps on the Kauwukah [Qawuqa] line of works."

All instructions for the operation were most jealously guarded. General Chetwode had to write on the 30th September " that one division has issued preliminary operation orders, containing the most secret and confidential matters. . . . I consider that this is most unnecessary and, indeed, most dangerous, and I direct that all copies, except those issued to Infantry Brigade Commanders and ' Q ' of Divisions, be at once withdrawn. . . . Nothing in type or writing should be outside Divisional Headquarters (G.S. or Q offices), or at most Infantry Brigade Headquarters, and no departmental officer should have anything written in his possession until the last possible moment."

With a great army such as Sir E. Allenby had assembled on the banks of the Wadi Ghazze such secrecy was essential : natives from the villages and living out on their farms were in touch with the troops, and it was not difficult for the Turks to slip agents into the very midst of the Army.

It was, of course, impossible to conceal the movements of so big a force, but General Chetwode wrote privately to each of his Divisional Commanders asking them to employ " every device by which enemy airmen may be deceived, such as leaving your present bivouac areas looking as much occupied as possible by leaving tents standing and digging holes wherever you have blanket shelters, not pitching brigade field ambulances or showing their flags, and allowing no new ground to be used whatever." Strict air discipline was enforced, and no motor lights were shown east of the Wadi Ghazze until after Zero day.

In spite of all precautions, the Turks knew an attack was imminent, but fortunately imagined that it was to be once more against Gaza.

The Capture of Beersheba.

All our battalions were to attack the Beersheba flank. The first unit to move towards the concentration area was the 158th Brigade from the vicinity of Bulah on the 20th October, at the close of a beautiful autumn day ; they marched 15 miles to the Shellal defences and took over the Kent Fort from the 161st Brigade, 60th Division. On the 24th they were relieved by the 159th Brigade and moved into the bed of the wadi, " a grisly squash, hot and dusty, and entirely airless."

The 74th Division was round Nakhrur and did not move until the night of the 25th October, when they went to Abu Sitta, thence to Gamli.

On that same day, the 25th, the 158th Brigade marched out from the wadi at 5.30 p.m. to take up the Imara outpost line, our 6th Battalion being on the right, with the 5th Battalion in support, and our 7th Battalion on the left with the Herefordshire in support. Beyond this outpost line there was, by day, a mounted brigade occupying the line El Buggar, Points 720, 630, and 550 ; at night the mounted troops withdrew, leaving standing patrols at Khasif, Pt. 510, and Dammath.

On the 27th the 53rd Division were ordered to occupy the line held by the mounted brigade (the 8th, under Brigadier-General Rome) and moved forward covered by the 5th Royal Welch and Herefordshire. While the division was on the move, the Turks suddenly attacked the mounted troops.

This reconnaissance in strength, in which the Turks employed some 3,000 men of all arms and succeeded in wiping out one or two mounted posts (although our 5th Battalion, followed by the rest of the 158th Brigade, hurried forward, the distance was too great, and they could not help), was a curious affair. It commenced at dawn and continued well into the afternoon. The Turks occupied the high ground and had a view of the whole plain, which, an observer says, was " crammed full of troops . . . there were batteries, camel convoys, ambulances," the whole of a great movement plainly visible, and yet the advance on Beersheba came as a surprise to the Turks.

An attack was finally organised and launched at 4 p.m., but the Turks did not wait for it, and the 53rd Division occupied the outpost line without opposition. Railway construction was then hurried on to Karm.

The time-table of work in preparation for the battle covered fifteen days before Zero day. The systematic bombardment of Gaza was to commence at Z–6 day ; the railway was to reach Karm on Z–3 day, and the station was to be completed on Z–1 day. At the time of this brush with the enemy Gaza was, therefore, being bombarded, and the Royal Engineers had three clear days to finish the railway.

Except for the 229th Brigade, which was attached to the 53rd Division, the 74th Division remained at Gamli until the 29th, when they moved to covered positions at Khasif, and were rejoined by the 229th Brigade on the 30th. The attacking divisions then moved into their battle positions.

The XX Corps orders provided that while the Desert Mounted Corps attacked the enemy's defences from the south-east and north-east of Beersheba and the town itself, " the 60th Division will attack the Beersheba works on the right of the 74th Division, as far as the Khalasa–Beersheba road, while the 53rd Division, with attached troops, will cover the left flank of the corps from a position on the general line between Kh. el Sufi and El Girheir. The 74th Division and attached troops will attack, capture, and consolidate the enemy main line between H29 (work Z8) and the Wadi Saba. . . . The following troops attached to the 74th Division will be known as ' Smith's Group,' under the command of Brigadier-General C. L. Smith, V.C.—the Imperial Camel Brigade, less two companies, two battalions of the 158th Infantry Brigade. The rôle of these troops is to hold the ground from the Wadi Saba . . . to the right of the 53rd Division, to deal with any counter-stroke against the left of the 74th Division, to prevent the transfer of troops to reinforce the enemy on the front of the 60th and 74th Divisions by holding the enemy to his trenches north of the Wadi Saba."

.   .   .   .

The 53rd Division was holding the line of outposts on the high ground. At dusk on the 30th October the left of the 53rd Division (our 5th and 6th Battalions) was taken over by the 30th Infantry Brigade of the 10th Division, and the 74th and 60th Divisions, moving up in rear, commenced to deploy on the right of the outpost line. While brigades marched up to their positions the horizon flickered with the distant bombardment of Gaza. The 229th Brigade, which had been attached to the 53rd Division, returned to the 74th and provided the advance guard ; they were followed by our 5th and 6th Battalions, who were part of Smith's Group. Positions had to be found in absolute silence, but " We in Smith's Force, i.e. the brigade less two battalions, marched at 5.30 p.m. to our old haunt, El Buggar, and then east along the Beersheba-Fara track in rear of the 229th Brigade, until we got to Tuweil Khebari, which is at the top of the slope whence the ground runs down gently to Beersheba. The 5th and 6th Royal Welch Fusiliers then turned right-handed and marched down to their allotted positions. There was some shelling away out on the right and occasional rifle fire, but otherwise all was silent in front of us—but not so behind us ! The noise of tractors bringing up guns was overpowering, as if the whole British Army was on the move, and sounded like the roar of London traffic from a little way off. The whole plain behind us hummed with mechanical noises, and I marvelled that the enemy in their trenches could not hear it. They afterwards told us they were taken by surprise, but it is indeed hard to believe." [1]

The attack was carried out in two phases, the first being an assault on some advanced works, called 1070, by the 181st Brigade, 60th Division. " During this period the 231st and 230th Brigades will co-operate as follows : A screen of infantry accompanied by machine guns will be pushed forward and will perform a double rôle—(a) assist in the advance of the 60th Division on the 1070 works ; (b) cover the deployment in depth of the remainder of each brigade.

" The 231st will conform to the advance of the 181st Brigade, and will endeavour to occupy the tributary wadis of the Whale Wadi, and will engage by fire the enemy trenches Z16, Z15, and Z7."

[1] Captain Ashton in *The History of the 53rd Division.*

When the 1070 works had been captured, the field artillery would advance to wire-cutting distance, and while this operation was in progress the assaulting infantry would take every opportunity of creeping forward. The time for assault would be decided by the G.O.C. 60th Division, and the 231st Brigade would again conform to the advance of the 181st Brigade on its right.

While this preliminary bombardment was in progress, the Desert Mounted Corps was riding hard round the flank of the unsuspecting Turk.

At 5.55 a.m. the artillery opened. At 7 a.m. the dust caused by the bombardment was so intense that the artillery had to cease fire so that observing officers might see the targets. The bombardment was then resumed and the 181st Brigade advanced and captured the works with little trouble. Our 24th and 25th Battalions conformed, followed by the 230th Brigade with the Buffs and Norfolk to the front. They encountered heavy and accurate shrapnel fire, but fortunately the country was crossed by numerous small wadis which afforded some protection. But the crossing of wadis made it difficult to keep direction and our two battalions edged too much to the right, so that the support companies of the Buffs had to fill a gap.

The advance was over a rolling plain, and as the line of advancing troops topped each swell in the ground they were met by a hail of low-flying bullets ; the advance slowed down as successive sky-lines became more fatal. By 10.40 a.m. our two battalions were within 600 yards of the Turkish lines.

The Turkish trenches on the far side of a deep depression were cut in white limestone rock with a strong belt of wire from 70 to 100 yards in front of them. There was a pause in the advance while the artillery cut the wire and bombarded the trenches.

The heat was tremendous as the men lay waiting on the stony ground. There was no cover and casualties mounted up. It was during this wait that Corporal Collins, of our 25th Battalion, repeatedly carried wounded men back to what little cover was to be found.

At 12.30 p.m. the artillery delivered a final burst of rapid fire, before lifting, and the machine gunners swept the enemy line with a hail of bullets. The whole attacking line rose and advanced across the depression. The wire in front of our two battalions was found to be little damaged, and had to be cut by the men. Again Corporal Collins " was conspicuous in rallying and leading his command. He led the final assault with the utmost skill, in spite of heavy fire at close range and uncut wire. He bayoneted fifteen of the enemy, and with a Lewis-gun section pressed on beyond the objective and covered the reorganisation and consolidation most effectively, although isolated and under fire from snipers and guns. He showed throughout a magnificent example of initiative and fearlessness." (Gazette.) For these various acts he was awarded the Victoria Cross.

From a distance the final assault could not be seen for the dust raised by the artillery bombardment. The support battalions followed on and carried the advance some 2,000 yards beyond the captured trenches, but the Desert Mounted Corps were having some trouble on the far side of Beersheba, and opposition was by no means overcome.

Our 5th and 6th Battalions, with Smith's Group, had advanced in touch with the 229th Brigade, and had done what they could with long-range machine- and Lewis-gun fire, but " we were not really in the picture. As the attack was designed only against the defences south of the Wadi Saba, the enemy in front of us, in trenches across the road, where there was a particularly nasty-looking, heavily-wired place called the Barricade, was not being disturbed." General Girdwood was, however, anxious about this place, especially as Smith's Group reported it held, and he obtained permission to attack (provision had been made for this in his orders). The 230th Brigade cleared the works, which were found to be lightly held, and our 5th and 6th Battalions moved up to a position along the Beersheba-Fara road, across the Barricade, and in touch with the 230th Brigade. The Australian Light Horse were already in the town (6 p.m.).

. . . .

During the night the 53rd Division was ordered to relieve the cavalry pickets north of the town, and occupy the line Towal abu Jerwal-Muweileh, with the Imperial Camel Brigade operating on the right.

At dawn (1st November) the 158th Brigade, less our 7th Battalion and the Herefordshire, with a battery from the 266th Field Artillery Brigade, a R.E. Section, and an ambulance detachment, moved as advance guard to the division. Our two battalions, the 5th and 6th, marched on parallel lines, the 5th going through Beersheba, which was found to be a small and fairly modern town, " with Abraham's Wells still functioning," but in Captain More's eyes it was " a filthy hole " with the roofs and doors stripped off most of the houses. " We were now in the country which had been fouled by the Turks, consequently the flies were appalling and our sanitary authorities had their hands full." The 6th Battalion, skirting the town, proceeded about a mile to the west of it. They marched by compass-bearing on Jerwal, which they reached about 7 p.m., the last five miles being over a mountainous, trackless, and stony country which was punishing to the men, accustomed for so long to sand ; and in places the passage of limbers was difficult, as the country was a network of deep fissures. Drage's Column, marching straight across country from a position a good deal north of the Beersheba–Fara road, joined the Brigade during the afternoon. The outpost position taken up was beyond the Lekiyeh Caves, with the Camel Brigade on the right and the 159th Brigade in rear to the left. Away in the distance Beersheba was seen to be enveloped in a solid cloud of dust, stirred up by the movement of the XX Corps.

It was a depressing finish to a trying march, as the ration convoy lost its way and the men had neither food nor water.

The khamsin commenced to blow up on the 2nd November. A certain amount of water reached the troops, but the shortage was serious and caused much suffering. There was no move forward that day. In the distance large bodies of Turks could be seen passing from the plain into the hills in front of the division. The 229th Brigade, 74th Division, was marched up to take over the left of the 53rd Division line. On the coast the XXI Corps attacked against Gaza.

On the 3rd November the 53rd Division was ordered to advance and gain touch with the mounted troops operating in the direction of Khuweilfeh, and the 74th to move up to a position of assembly on the left flank of the 53rd.

The 158th Brigade passed into Divisional Reserve, but our 5th Battalion was sent as escort to some of the artillery, which, owing to the dreadful nature of the country, had to make a wide detour to the east in search of a road.

The fighting that day was terrible owing to the heat of the khamsin and the grim nature of the hills. Our 5th Battalion, sweeping round on the right, gained touch with the mounted troops a little after midday and were soon engaged with the enemy on the lower slopes of Khuweilfeh. The remainder of the division fought their way up and were level by the end of the day.

An abortive attempt was made to capture Khuweilfeh on the 4th, doomed to failure by the khamsin and the absence of water for the troops— the ration convoy had again lost its way. At nightfall the XX Corps issued orders that the 53rd Division would not attack Khuweilfeh without direct sanction from the Corps. The 74th Division went up into the line on that day, and orders were issued for an attack on Sheria.

.   .   .   .

The forecast of the battle was not quite in accordance with the situation. At the end of the first movement, the capture of Beersheba, the 60th Division should have been in the town, the 74th between the Beersheba–

CORPORAL J. COLLINS, V.C.

Fara road and Kh. el Sufi, and the 53rd covering the left of the 74th on the line Kh. el Sufi–Bir Imleih–El Girheir.   The 10th Division was seen at Shellal.

The attack on the left of the British line, towards Gaza, along the sand-dunes, was to follow immediately, and that had been done (the XXI Corps had secured Sheikh Hasan).

The next move in the plan had been that the 53rd should make a frontal attack on the Qawuqa System, while the 74th and 60th took the whole of the fortified area in flank and reverse.

But the mounted troops had made no impression on the Turkish forces north of Beersheba and the 53rd Division had been diverted into the Judean Hills ; the 74th had moved up on their left ; the line was then carried on by the 60th and 10th Divisions to Abu Irgeig.   The 53rd had continually edged to the right, and some of the ground first occupied by them had been taken over by the 74th Division.

The modification of the original plan to meet the situation directed the 60th Division on the Qawuqa System, and gave to the 74th the enveloping movement.

The 53rd Division was now placed under the orders of the Desert Corps and, for the attack, was directed to take up the line Khuweilfeh–Rujm edh Dhib.   Their special task was to protect the right of the XX Corps and by taking advantage of any retirement of the enemy to press forward and seize the Nejile and Jemmame water-supplies.

The line of the 74th Division attack was a divergent one, and behind the junction of the 53rd and 74th Divisions was the Yeomanry Mounted Division ready to close the gap as it occurred.

The interest in this plan of operation lies in the situation facing the 53rd Division.   General Mott had two of his brigades facing north and in close contact with the enemy on Khuweilfeh, and was convinced that there were strong forces assembled about that dominating height.   As a matter of fact his appreciation of the situation was correct, as General Kress had moved his general reserve into the hills at Khuweilfeh to strike at the outer flank of the turning movement and get outside it.   General Chetwode's order meant that the 53rd Division would have to side-slip to the left, to the lower slopes of the hills, and leave Khuweilfeh to be dealt with by mounted troops.

General Mott did not think that mounted troops could take Khuweilfeh, and so long as it remained in Turkish hands the threat of a counter-stroke was present and an easy road of retreat for them was provided over Hebron.

General Mott's views do not seem to have made any impression on General Chetwode, whose order held good until the Commander-in-Chief visited the 53rd Division Headquarters on the 5th November and consented to the Divisional Commander's proposal to attack Khuweilfeh simultaneously with the advance of the XX Corps.

Plans for the attack had already been prepared. It was entrusted to the 158th Brigade, with the Herefordshire on the right, the 6th Royal Welch in the centre, the 7th Royal Welch on the left, and the Sussex protecting their left flank ; the 5th Royal Welch were in reserve.

The great difficulty the 53rd Division had was in moving guns in that rocky and precipitous country.

The plan of the 74th Division included the building up of a flank on their right. The objective of the division was the railway line between Qawuqa and Sheria. The 229th Brigade on the left would direct, the 230th and 231st advancing successively echeloned to the right. The 231st Brigade, however, was to keep in touch with the Yeomanry, and after making good the high ground to the north be prepared to resist any counter-attack against the flank of the division. The line of the enemy's entrenched position ran diagonally across the line of advance of the 74th Division, so that while the 230th and 231st Brigades would be engaged at once, the 229th, starting before them, had 4,000 yards to go to the nearest group of works on their front.

The country in front of the 74th Division was of a gently undulating character, very open, and with a stony surface. There was no cover of any sort.

The battle opened at 5 a.m. on the 6th November. The remarkable point of the 74th Division achievement was the speed of their advance over an open country, with very little artillery support in the earlier and difficult stages. The 231st Brigade found some unmarked and unsuspected works on the right flank which were captured after some stiff fighting. At 3.15 p.m. the final assault was delivered on the railway, the 231st Brigade forming a flank facing north. Sheria was entered in the early morning of the 7th.

The fight of the 53rd Division was, however, of paramount importance and interest. The line in front of the Khuweilfeh position was held that night, 5th/6th, by our 5th Battalion and the 2/10th Middlesex.

The position to be attacked was clearly marked. Although the country was broken with steep minor hills and precipitous-sided ravines which were most confusing, there were two conspicuous features in the Turkish position —on our right, in front of the Herefordshire, a flat-topped hill, and on the left, in front of the 7th Royal Welch, the commanding Khuweilfeh Hill. The flat-topped hill was at the head of a long, wide valley, on the opposite side of which was Ras el Nagb : it marked the junction of two ranges of hills.

The artillery barrage opened at 4 a.m., and with it sixteen guns of the 158th Machine Gun Company. At 4.20 a.m. the barrage started to lift 100 yards at a time, and the advance commenced.

Our 7th Battalion gives a good account of the arrangements : " The battalion formed up in column of route. Lewis-gun ammunition was man-handled, the Lewis-gun mules being used to carry spare ammunition and bombs. Arriving at the line of deployment, the battalion formed up on a four-platoon front in five lines at twenty-five yards' distance, the fifth line being formed by Lewis gunners withdrawn from their platoons. The whole frontage of the battalion was 500 yards. Two water-bottles were carried and 170 rounds of ammunition, also the unconsumed portion of the day's ration, one extra day's ration, and the iron ration. All ranks were clearly made to understand that on no account, without an order from the C.O., was any ammunition to be fired, and all work was to be done with the bayonet. At 4.23 a.m., three minutes behind scheduled time, the battalion moved off to attack Khuweilfeh Hill under cover of the barrage, and gained its objective at 5.3 with apparently few casualties."

Brigadier-General Vernon states that the whole attack went like clockwork ; the barrage was so good that the objective was reached just as dawn was breaking with practically no casualties. The Turks were cowed by the creeping barrage, and were bayoneted in large numbers.

The Turkish front line had gone, and the leading waves of Herefordshire and 6th Royal Welch had reached gun positions to the north of the flat-topped hill—a company of the Herefordshire had charged and put to flight or bayoneted the personnel of nine field guns, in the act of limbering up—when a thick mist swept down, enveloping the hills.

On the left the 7th Royal Welch had cleared the enemy from the top of Khuweilfeh Hill, and through the waves of mist saw below them, on their right, a mass of troops which they took to be Turks. They called for artillery fire—it was a mistake easily made in the confusion of the moment—and the advance elements of our 6th Battalion and the Herefordshire were driven back by our own artillery ; the guns and the flat-topped hill had to be abandoned.

This unhappy accident, and the fact that the mist prevented troops supporting each other, gave the Turks an opportunity of rallying ; their machine gunners knew the ground and where they should fire through the mist, and the Turkish line, which had been on the point of dissolving, stiffened.

The situation was exceedingly puzzling for the Brigadier who was conducting the attack. After a while he ordered the artillery to cease fire and all troops to remain where they were until the fog lifted.

" At 0700, being rather nervous about my right flank, where numerous counter-attacks were reported, I ordered one company of my reserve battalion, the 5th Royal Welch Fusiliers, under Captain Wigan, in support. Owing to the fog it was extremely difficult to clear up the situation exactly, so I ordered all artillery to cease firing, and troops to remain where they were until the fog lifted. When it was possible to see, the line was found to be as follows : On the left the R. Sussex Regiment holding their objective ; the 7th R.W.F. holding the Tell, their objective ; the 6th R.W.F. and Herefordshire holding the spur (*which shot out from the Khuweilfeh Hill*) with the 3rd Imperial Camel Corps prolonging and slightly in advance of their line. This line was practically my objective." (Brigadier-General Vernon.)

But with the light the front of the 6th Royal Welch and Herefordshire was so swept by machine-gun fire that they were pinned to the ground. The artillery, however, prevented the enemy from reoccupying the flat-topped hill, although they made several attempts to do so.

On the left the Turks launched a strong counter-attack against our 7th Battalion, and by sheer weight of numbers succeeded in pushing them off the crest—but only for a moment. After a short artillery bombardment the position was retaken at the point of the bayonet.

Nothing more could be done. The fog had robbed the 158th Brigade of the full fruits of their gallant attack which would have meant the capture of large numbers of Turks, and possibly have closed to them the one exit to Jerusalem over the Judean Hills. But their achievement enabled the attack across the plain bordering the foothills to be driven home without molestation. At 11.30 a.m. the Commander-in-Chief telegraphed to General Mott : " I congratulate you and your troops on admirable success of your efforts, and troops' gallant conduct. You have drawn enemy into very position required to facilitate success of main operations of XX Corps. Your operations have given us most favourable prospects of success, which now depends on valour of 53rd Division."

The heat of the day now fell across the battlefield. The khamsin commenced to blow, and the men, whole and wounded, suffered agonies of thirst. The air was thick with clouds of flies !

Throughout the day the Turks kept massing behind the flat-topped hill, but prompt artillery action dispersed them. At 3.30 p.m. they resolved to recapture Khuweilfeh Hill and made two determined attacks,

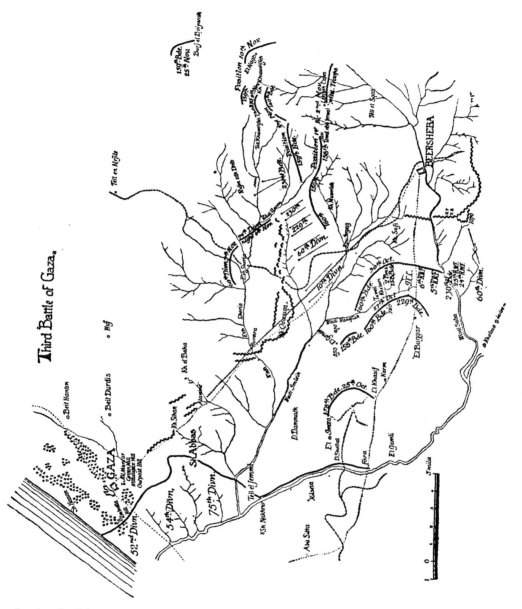

both of which were broken up by the combined fire of the artillery and 7th Royal Welch.

At dusk the 2/10th Middlesex relieved the 7th Royal Welch, and the 5th Royal Welch took over the rest of the line.

Fighting had been practically continuous. From the moment the Turks recovered from the first blow they did their utmost to restore the situation. The line held by our 6th Battalion was a sketchy one, enfiladed in many places, below commanding underfeatures in others, so that the battalion was under a continual strain all day. Captain Fox Russell, the Medical Officer attached to the battalion, showed the greatest gallantry in rescuing and attending the wounded in the exposed and precarious position until he was killed. He was awarded a posthumous Victoria Cross.

.   .   .   .

The 74th Division (231st and 230th Brigades) held a line astride the Wadi Esh Sheria, facing north-east, when the 60th Division entered Sheria at dawn on the 7th November. About the same time the 10th Division captured the Hureira Redoubt. A gap—the word which always raised a smile in France—had now been made for the mounted troops, who were soon streaming through, harrying the Turks until dark. On the extreme left the XXI Corps found Gaza evacuated. But the Turks still faced the 53rd Division on the right.

The 53rd Division was placed under the orders of General Barrow, as part of a force known as Barrowsdett, and was ordered to stand fast. Early in the morning reports were sent bank by front-line troops that the enemy was retiring ; several large bodies were caught by our artillery fire.

Only one platoon of our 5th Battalion carried out a small enterprise under cover of a rifle-grenade bombardment which gave them a commanding ridge. On the 8th, patrols found the enemy had gone.

The 158th Brigade was moved to el Sqati to ease the supply difficulty.

The 74th Division cleared up the battlefield and marched to Irgeig on the 9th, Karm on the 10th—the khamsin blowing strongly—Shellal on the 17th, and Deir el Belah on the 18th.

Pursuit of the Turks.

The 158th Brigade remained at el Sqati, a dreary bit of country, infested with flies which were greatly encouraged by numbers of dead horses and camels. All available transport was required for the pursuit ; water and supplies generally were short ; septic sores broke out ; but the discomforts were cheerfully borne, as victory was in the air, and each evening it was possible to mark on the maps a further advance towards Jerusalem.

The pursuit of the retreating Turks by the Desert Corps was relentless, but the water question was serious and the Turks marched well, destroying

THE BROKEN COUNTRY SOUTH-EAST OF GAZA.   [*Crown Copyright.*

[*Crown Copyright.*

AIN SINAI ON THE LEFT AND YEBRUD ON THE RIGHT. TAKEN FROM THE JERUSALEM
—NABLUS ROAD.

what they could as they went. At one time portions of the Australian Mounted Division advanced three days and four nights without watering their horses. On the 10th November the Desert Corps was 35 miles from railhead. It was for these reasons that the XX Corps was left out of the pursuit and as much transport as possible was switched over to supplying the XXI Corps.

The Turks made a stand on the 13th between El Kubeibeh and Beit Jibrin. The battlefield was the open Maritime Plain, dotted with villages surrounded by mud walls, with plantations of trees outside the walls. Attacked by the Desert Corps and 52nd Division, the Turkish Army split, the one part going north, the other east on Jerusalem. The Anzac Division chased the right wing of the Turkish Army across the River Auja, and the Yeomanry Division pursued the left wing through the Vale of Ajalon into the Judean Hills.

Once in the hills, however, in spite of the gallantry of the Yeomanry, who penetrated at one time as far as Beitania, the Turks stiffened, and it became clear that Jerusalem must be captured by more deliberate methods. Work was commenced at once on the roads.

The two principal defiles into the hills follow up the course of the Wadis Ali and es Surar ; the high-road to Jerusalem goes through the one and the railway through the other. All the defiles are difficult roads to travel, leading frequently to the loose shingle beds of mountain torrents. In the summer the sun beats down on the limestone, and the heat rises in suffocating waves from the ground ; with winter and the rainy season approaching black mud lay in the valleys, or a torrent rushed down.

The 74th Division started to march north on the 23rd November, when battalions bivouacked east of Gaza, and troops were able to visit Ali Muntar, to find that our bombardment had done no great damage to the Turkish trenches.

On the 25th the division was at Majdal ; on the 26th at Nahr Suqreir ; 27th at Junction Station ; 28th Latron. The 60th Division were already there ; the 10th followed ; the 53rd remained about Khuweilfeh, divorced for the moment from the XX Corps and attached to G.H.Q. as " Mott's Force."

Just before our 24th and 25th Battalions marched into the Judean Hills, the Yeomanry Division had been heavily attacked and had been forced to give ground.

The march from Junction Station to Latron is only seven miles, but the climb and the nature of the road may be gauged from the fact that the 231st Brigade took four and a half hours to cover the distance. They

IV—11

arrived at 12.30 p.m. and were off again at 7 p.m. under orders for Beit Anan via Enab. It was found impossible to take the transport beyond Enab ; the Brigade arrived at Anan at 4.30 a.m. on the 29th. By that time the men were thoroughly exhausted, having marched 26 miles since the morning of the 25th.

THE AFFAIR AT BEIT UR ET FOQA.

At 7 p.m. Lord Kensington, commanding our 25th Battalion, received a telephone message from Brigade warning him to be prepared to move at once and take up a line Hill 1750–Beit Ur et Foqa ; or failing to occupy the village the left of the battalion should rest on the Wadi Zait.

Shortly afterwards written orders from Brigade arrived to relieve the 8th Mounted Brigade and placing the 24th Royal Welch on the right between the 181st Brigade and Beit Dukka, the 10th Shropshire to Hill 1750, and the 25th Royal Welch to the Wadi Zait. This was followed by a second illuminating telephone message from the Brigade that there was no one to relieve !

The 10th Shropshire had moved earlier in the day to the line Dukka— Kh. Jufna, so that the new order meant they must swing their left forward through the village of Et Tireh to get in touch with Hill 1750. From the Shropshire Lord Kensington learned that the village of Et Tireh was in enemy hands, but that two companies would advance on the village at 9 p.m.

Lord Kensington had a difficult task before him. It was a brilliant moonlit night, but there were no roads through this jumble of hills and precipitous-sided wadis, only native tracks ; and he was in the hands of two natives guides, who knew but one track to his position leading through Beit Dukka and Et Tireh. Knowing that the Shropshire were going to clear the village of Et Tireh, he decided to place himself at the mercy of his guides.

The road was so bad that although the battalion left Beit Anan at 11.15 p.m., they did not reach Dukka until 1 a.m. Here the heavily laden men rested while an effort was made to find an easier way ; none was found, and the march to Et Tireh was resumed.

The Shropshire had discovered the enemy in possession of Et Tireh and had turned him out about 10.15 p.m. A further advance was opposed by fire from Hill 1750, but a position was taken up north of Et Tireh.

When Lord Kensington arrived he sent one company forward to capture Hill 1750, supported by the fire of the Shropshire and two Royal Welch platoons, with a machine gun on a knoll to the left. The hill was captured, 10 Turks being killed and two prisoners and two machine guns captured.

Major Rees was then ordered to push forward to Beit Ur et Foqa with five platoons and a machine gun.

Major Rees, with his little force of eighty rifles, scrambled along rough tracks, and up and down the sides of wadis until, just as dawn was breaking, he found himself behind the village, east of it. He also saw a large body of Turks parading on the western side of the village, while to the south of it, on a ridge which lay between him and the British lines, several small posts were revealed by the light of fires they had kindled ; they were evidently preparing a morning meal under shelter of the ridge.

Quick action was imperative ; in a few minutes it would be daylight. He decided to attack, and extended his force—three platoons, under Lieutenant Neale on the left, and he himself with the remaining two to the right. The whole then advanced on the village from the east.

As they were closing on the place a Turkish officer, mounted on a grey pony, rode up. He was seized, made to dismount, and put in the ranks of the leading platoon, his pony being led.

The party reached the walls of the village and through the guide called on the garrison to surrender.

The bewildered Turks seemed at first as though they were about to do so, and then to consider a charge with the bayonet. Finally, they made a pretence of surrender and suddenly opened fire with six machine guns. Happily the garden walls and cactus hedges protected Major Rees's command, and well-directed rapid fire spread terror in the Turkish ranks ; they promptly threw up their hands. In a few minutes the whole garrison had surrendered.

About 450 prisoners were collected and sent back to the British lines under a small escort, Major Rees remaining at Beit Ur et Foqa. As the prisoners stumbled along to the west, the escort hoping to find our lines, they were fired on by the enemy, and also by our own troops, and in the confusion a good many escaped ; but the escort managed to reach the Wadi Selman with 308 Turks.

Major Rees then tried to get in touch with the British line by flag, and sent runners to find Battalion Headquarters. In neither case was he successful. After the capture of Hill 1750 Lord Kensington had followed a track to the Wadi Shebab, but had run into the enemy lines, had been caught by machine-gun fire, and had been forced to retire. He had found an Australian picket at the junction of the Wadis Shebab and Selman ; but this was some distance in rear of where he was expected to be.

At Beit Ur et Foqa the Turks soon realised that it was held by a small force and commenced to close on the village from all directions. At 8 a.m. Major Rees was practically surrounded, under fire from all sides, and reduced to thirty rifles and four officers. Isolated as he was, he decided to fight his way south and try to join up with the British line.

His retirement was admirably carried out, and he reached Et Tireh at 9.45 a.m.

The original capture of Beit Ur et Foqa was not known at Divisional Headquarters until 10 a.m., and the loss of it until 5 p.m. There were many observers, including General Girdwood, who could see the line from Beit Anan, but no one could make out what was happening at Et Foqa. The whole field of battle was frightfully confusing, our own troops and Turks appearing in the most unexpected places.

After Major Rees had retired, the Turks soon made Hill 1750 untenable, and then Et Tireh, so that the Shropshire had to fall back behind the Wadi Selman. By that time the situation was more or less understood at Divisional Headquarters, and the 229th Brigade was sent up to restore the line and recapture Et Tireh, Hill 1750, and Beit Ur et Foqa. Fierce fighting went on until the 3rd December, and by that time the fact that Et Foqa was commanded from the Zeitun Ridge, Kh. Kereina, and an unnamed hill, separated from the village by a deep ravine and only 500 yards distant, was clearly appreciated.

CAPTURE OF JERUSALEM.

Area: North and East of the Line Hebron–Junction Station.

The XX Corps took over the line from the XXI Corps, the relief being complete on the 2nd December. Our line of battle then ran 60th, 74th, 10th Divisions, in touch with the Australian Mounted Division on the left.

A conference was held at Enab on the 3rd December to discuss the capture of Jerusalem. General Mott, commanding 53rd Division, attended ; he had already had some correspondence on the subject.

The new proposal was to attack with the 60th and 74th Divisions in an easterly direction, from Ain Karim–Beit Surik, and throw the two divisions astride the Jerusalem–Nablus road ; Mott's Force would advance from Hebron, protect the right flank of the attack, and threaten the city from the south. The notes of the conference give the whole situation.

" The enemy are holding a line covering the Hebron–Jerusalem road, with works in the neighbourhood of Ras Esh Sherifeh, behind which are trenches near El Khudr, and round Bethlehem from about Kh. esh Shughrah, on the south-east, across the road to Kh. Kebah, and thence northward. . . .

" North of the railway the enemy have a series of trenches and redoubts from just west of Malhah to Nabi Samwil.

" Facing the XX Corps are believed to be anything from 500 to a maximum of 1,200 on the Hebron road, and a maximum of 15,000 from the right of the 60th Division to the left of the 10th Division at Suffa, including the reserves.

" The enemy defences are not deep, and once through them the troops have only difficulties of terrain to contend with. . . . [The rearrangement of the front] will give to the attack two complete brigades of the 53rd, the whole of the 60th, and it is hoped two brigades of the 74th Division.

" It is obvious that the form the attack will take will depend a good deal on the action of the enemy on the advance of the 53rd Division towards Jerusalem. The two brigades of this division reach a point to-night from which they are two ten-mile marches from the position north of Bethlehem, which they will have to reach to co-operate with the remainder of the corps.

" Should the enemy decide to strengthen his defences in front of the 53rd Division by pushing troops south of Jerusalem, the attack will take the form of the 60th and 74th Divisions driving straight on to the Jerusalem –Nablus road, the 60th Division throwing out a flank to the south-east, the object of the move being the prevention of the escape of the enemy opposing the 53rd Division, either by the Nablus or the Jericho road.

" Should, however (as is more probable), the enemy recognise the danger of such a movement, and withdraw from the front of the 53rd Division, the attack will take the form of a direct advance on the part of the 53rd Division on Jerusalem, and a wheel by the 60th and 74th Divisions, pivoting on the Beit Izza and Nabi Samwil defences, designed to drive the enemy northwards, and with the following objectives : (a) a position covering the Jericho road to be occupied by a portion of the 53rd Division, (b) the 60th and 74th Divisions to seize the general line Shafat–Nabi Samwil, or, if possible, the point 2670–Kh. Ras et Tawil–Nabi Samwil.

" In order to inflict a severe blow on the enemy before he has time to arrange to meet the attack, it seems obvious that the advance of the 53rd Division must be as rapid as possible once it moves from its present position, and the G.O.C. 53rd Division must endeavour to ensure, by careful reconnaissance of routes, that his brigades are on the general line Sur Bahir–Sherafat by the early morning of Zero-day.

" Should the enemy retire from before the 53rd Division, or only oppose that division lightly, the general attack will take, roughly, the following form :

" 1st Phase.—The capture as soon as possible after dawn by the 60th Division of the enemy works from the railroad to the main Enab road, and by the 74th Division of the works covering Beit Iksa, as far north as the Wadi el Abbeideh. After this advance it will be necessary to advance more guns of the 60th Division.

" 2nd Phase.—The advance of the 53rd and 60th Divisions to the general line Jerusalem–Lifta. It is recognised that difficulties of terrain may prevent the 53rd Division from advancing from Sherafat northwards, and that they may have to work up the main road nearer to Jerusalem before they can gain close touch with the 60th Division.

" 3rd Phase.—The advance of the 60th and 74th Divisions to the general line of the track running out of the main road one mile north of Jerusalem. . . . During this phase the left brigade of the 53rd Division, if there is any room, will assist the right of the 60th Division. Otherwise the brigade will drop into reserve. . . . The right brigade of the 53rd Division will endeavour to place itself in a position covering the Jericho road, and the east and north-east of Jerusalem.

" 4th Phase.—The further advance of the 60th Division to a line astride the Jerusalem–Nablus road about Shafat, and, if possible, to Pt. 2670, Ras et Tawil. During this phase the 74th Division will improve its position by throwing its right into Beit Hannina."

.   .   .   .   .   .

The preliminary moves to get into position for the attack on Jerusalem were made between the 4th and 7th December. The 10th Division, having relieved the 74th on the night 4th/5th, extended its line to cover Beit Dukka.

On the 5th/6th the 231st Brigade relieved the 60th Division on the Beit Izza–Nabi Samwil line. The line here was a salient, and the pivoting point on which the attack might turn (and did). The point of the salient was a commanding hill, on which was a mosque, held by us, but the enemy were from 15 to 20 yards away from it. Our 24th Battalion was posted here, but, owing to the nature of the ground they were holding and the nearness of the enemy, could give little help to the advance of the 230th Brigade when the attack commenced on the 8th December. The 230th Brigade suffered from enfilade fire from Nabi Samwil, probably from caves or trenches below our troops. Our 25th Battalion was on the north-eastern face of the salient.

The attack of the 6oth and 74th Divisions went forward well, but the difficulty that day was the advance of the 53rd Division.

General Mott's orders were : " The 53rd Division, less one brigade group, with the Corps Cavalry Regiment attached, will advance on 6th December from the Dilbeh area to the Bethlehem–Beit Jala area, which must be reached on the 7th December." The corps do not seem to have appreciated the difficult country in front of Mott's Force. General Mott had wired after the conference at Enab : " We shall be doing well if we make the vicinity of Bethlehem in two days from here, on the assumption that we are unopposed. Though the road is good, the gradients are punishing to gun teams and transport animals." And he repeated the opinion on the 4th : " Very pretty country, but map distances give no idea of the distances men have to march—sometimes two hairpin corners to get down a hill, and long ones at that."

The 53rd Division was late—unavoidably so. Extracts from General Mott's report give the situation accurately : " We had pushed along the main road until the enemy held up our advance on the road with artillery and rifle fire. The hills in which we were advancing were enveloped in clouds, and the rain was torrential at intervals. . . . From the reports of previous air reconnaissance it was certain our advance troops must be quite close up to the system of Bethlehem defences, but the weather had denied us any glimpse of the terrain, or the position of the enemy trenches on which to base a plan of attack next morning. All we did know was that the terrain on either side of the road was very steep and rocky. It was clearly impossible to make any further advance until dawn." Those who took part in the march remember it as a sort of nightmare of rain, mist, and cold.

Our battalions, however, did not take part in the advance on Jerusalem. The 158th Brigade was left at Beersheba, repairing roads and keeping the line of communication across the hills.

Dawn on the 9th heralded a fine day. The 53rd Division had advanced to the outskirts of Bethlehem, and patrols reported to the 74th Division units that the enemy had retired. At 8.30 a.m. the Mayor and Chief of Police approached the lines of the 60th Division and surrendered the city. The 74th Division advanced and occupied the line Tell el Fal–Beit Hannina –Nabi Samwil, and during the day the left of the line was extended to include the front held by the 10th Division—a fearful move over inundated country through which the camels and mules could not move. The 231st Brigade remained in the line with their left on Beit Ur et Tahta for several weeks. A frost followed the rain—conditions were hard.

The 158th Brigade was left by itself in the neighbourhood of Beersheba. On the 6th December the 5th Royal Welch were moved to a little spring called Ain el Unkur, the 6th Battalion to near Dhariye, and the 7th Battalion to Sqati. Their principal job was the repairing of roads.

On the 7th, leaving one company at the spring, the 5th Battalion moved into Hebron. The road to Hebron was seen to be " a most magnificently engineered road, all hairpin bends and corkscrew curves, through most wild and picturesque country. Hebron proved to be most beautiful, a city of gardens, with the square tomb of Abraham in the middle." The town lies in a broad valley, the surrounding hills being terraced with vineyards.

A curious story, unusual but not unique, is told of Hebron : that one of the men was accosted by a native in Welsh, and recognised a brother who had disappeared some years before the War and was presumed to be dead. The Welshman had married a native woman and was settled in the town.

On the 14th Brigade Headquarters moved to Hebron, and Brigadier-General Vernon with the Military Governor, Sir F. Curtis, paid ceremonial visits to the officers of the new Civil Government.

The attitude of the inhabitants was described as unsettled, not to say unfriendly. They had pro-Turk leanings on religious grounds, but they were also frightened, as the Turks had expressed the intention of returning at an early date. For moral effect an armed force, in which our 5th Battalion and a company from our 6th Battalion were included, marched through the town headed by the Military Governor. " When the brigade left the town, owing to the benefits of settled government, the good behaviour of the troops and the moral effect of this armed display, the attitude of the people had changed, with very few exceptions, to one of complete friendliness."

The Jews of Hebron, who were described as a repulsive-looking lot, with long oily ringlets down their necks, professed to be pleased to see the British, but the pleasure was more noticeable in their women-folk, who were generally good to look upon, with fine complexions and magnificent black eyes ; they were also, in appearance, much cleaner than their men-folk !

On the 16th December the brigade was ordered to concentrate at Wadi el Arab by the 19th. Unfortunately the weather broke and there was continual rain until the 21st ; the march was one of great discomfort and fatigue.

The brigade moved from the Wadi el Arab to Burak, and on the 21st to the outskirts of Jerusalem. On the 22nd our 5th Battalion was ordered to relieve the whole of the 159th Brigade in the line.

The 159th and 160th Brigades were found to be holding an outpost line to the east and north-east of the city. The Valley of Jehoshaphat runs across the northern side and the eastern side of the city, and then turns to the east. Shallow to the north, the valley is marked by the ridge on the far side of it, about 1½ miles out, running east, then turning south, the bend in the ridge being the Mount of Olives. This ridge formed the line of defence held by us, with our outpost line well down the forward slope, which was steep and rocky. Brigade Headquarters were in the Kaiserin Augusta Viktoria Hospice, on the Mount of Olives, a magnificent building, luxuriously furnished, ornamented with statues and frescoes (some of the Kaiser), and containing a staff of servants which included a German housekeeper and cooks. Wonderful views were obtained from the tower.

Christmas Day dawned " in the usual torrents of rain," and the Valley of Jehoshaphat, in which the 158th Brigade was bivouacked, became a rushing torrent. By nightfall the whole brigade, less our 5th Battalion, was under cover in some of the large monasteries. The next day the 6th Royal Welch and Herefordshire took over the line ; the 5th Royal Welch went into reserve at the Russian Hospice, south of the German Hospice ; the 7th Royal Welch in reserve at Sir John Grey Hill's house, north of the German Hospice.

Brigade Headquarters, watching the rain as they sat in the tower of the German Hospice, knew that when it ceased they would get the order for a general advance, and that perhaps their next Headquarters would not be so comfortable.

DEFENCE OF JERUSALEM, 26TH–30TH DECEMBER. AREA : NORTH AND EAST OF THE LINE HEBRON–JUNCTION STATION.

The contemplated attack of the XX Corps was designed to pinch off the salient made by the Turkish line toward Jerusalem. Not a salient as understood in France, for it had but one side ; nevertheless it was a salient, as the eastern side of it was the God-forsaken, tumbled, and broken country that fell into the valley of the Jordan. The 53rd and 60th Divisions were given objectives north of Bireh and Ram Allah—the direction of the Right Attack would, therefore, be north. The centre of the XX Corps front was lightly held by the 231st Brigade, from Beit Izza to Et Tireh. The Left Attack was to be carried out in its initial stages by the 229th Brigade (74th Division) and the 31st, 29th, and 30th (10th Division) in an easterly direction.

All was settled. The rain ceased during the night 26th/27th December, and a small preliminary affair was undertaken on the 231st Brigade (74th

Division) front by the 24th Welch Regiment, which was not brought to a successful conclusion until the morning. Everyone was ready for the general " push " on the left of the corps front.

But on the right an interesting situation had arisen. During the advance from Beersheba a lucky capture had been the Turkish wireless code, which put General Allenby in immediate possession of any plans transmitted by wireless. He had known for some days that the Turks were preparing an attack to recapture Jerusalem, and learned, at the last moment, that it was to take place during the night 26th/27th. He decided that it would take place, and orders for the XX Corps Right Attack to proceed were not issued ; but when the Turks were well committed against the 53rd and 60th Divisions, the Left Attack of the XX Corps was to take place as arranged.

While the Welch Regiment was busy capturing Hill 1910, in preparation for the general advance on the left, the right of the corps was violently attacked by the Turks.

The 60th Division took the first blow, and when dawn broke, on a fine but misty day, the attack spread to the 53rd Division front. But not against the 158th Brigade ; the 60th Division, on their left, were driven from some of their advanced posts, and the 160th Brigade on their right had a tough fight, during which the Queen's had to abandon White Hill, an important position commanding the Jericho Road, but succeeded in preventing the Turks from occupying it. A very feeble effort was at one time made against our 6th Battalion, but it was easily dispersed. Towards evening the 158th Brigade was ordered to take over all that part of the 160th Brigade line north of the Jericho Road ; this meant the recapture or reoccupation of White Hill, which was carried out behind a barrage by our 7th Battalion at 1 a.m. By that time there was no opposition.

The Left Attack was entirely successful. The 229th Brigade and the 10th Division captured their first objective, Sheikh Abu ez Zeitun–Kh. er Ras by 9.20 a.m. The line was now in a sharp salient, and at 10.15 a.m. our 24th Battalion, who had concentrated during the night in the Wadi Selman, in front of Beit Dukka, attacked Kh. Dreihemeh and Hill 2450. In each case the crest of the hill was reached, but the companies were faced with one of those difficult situations which abounded in that country of sharply rising hills : each crest could be swept by machine guns placed on the forward slope of the other while the Turkish gunners remained safe in dead ground. The two companies on Hill 2450 were counter-attacked again and again and were finally forced down the reverse slope. An artillery bombardment was organised and a second assault delivered, but the Turkish machine gunners, cleverly concealed on the neighbouring hill Kh. Dreihemeh, held the crest clear by their fire, and the attempt failed.

The line remained in a sharp salient that night.

The next morning the Turks had retired from the 231st Brigade front,

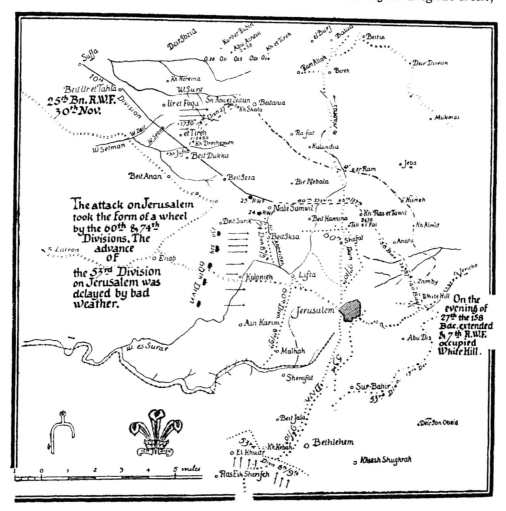

and in the advance the brigade was squeezed out by the 230th, and withdrawn into reserve south of Beitania.

The Right Attack was continued on the 28th December by the 60th Division advancing north. The 53rd Division was given the task of protecting the right flank of the 60th. This operation entailed the capture of three separate hills by the Herefordshire and our 6th and 7th Battalions.

The advance commenced at 3.45 p.m. The first hill, Anata, was quickly taken by the Herefordshire ; on the right Grey Hill was as swiftly taken by Captain Emrys Evans, of our 6th Battalion ; but the third hill was a harder job.

White Hill was occupied by our 7th Battalion and was connected with Suffa, the objective, by a saddle, about a mile long. Colonel Harker directed his attack (1½ companies) along the length of the saddle ; but the hills on the flank were held by the enemy, who were able to keep the whole line of advance under machine-gun fire. The advance commenced with a dash, but soon slowed down and at 4.30 p.m. ceased. The 7th Royal Welch were responsible for Zamby, White Hill, and the Jericho road, and more troops could not be spared to give fresh impetus to the attack ; but in the evening the 5th Royal Welch took over the line, and the 7th, as a battalion, assaulted and occupied the hill at midnight.

After the capture of Suffa all was quiet. Our 7th Battalion again took over White Hill and Zamby in addition to the position won ; our 5th Battalion concentrated at Anata ; our 6th Battalion held the line from Wadi Ruabeh to Kh. Almit ; the Herefordshire carried it on to about Hismeh, where they joined with the 159th Brigade.

On the rest of the corps front the 60th Division units had to fight in one or two places, but the general advance on the 29th was not otherwise opposed. The final line occupied by the XX Corps was Deir Ibn Obeid–Hismeh–Jeba–Beitin–El Burj–Ras Kerker–Deir el Kuddis.

.   .   .   .

All through these winter months of rain and cold our battalions with the 158th and 231st Brigades when not in the line were mostly engaged on road making and repair, in common with others. The grind of heavy lorries made the work of repair incessant. The native population was drawn upon, and men, women, and children were employed carrying stones from the hillsides.

Rest out of the line was hard work. The mud was dreadful ; the cold was piercing. The men adapted themselves to the hard conditions, and some of them became exceedingly clever in the construction of stone shelters in their bivouac camps.

With the rain there was a certain amount of snow, and frost was frequent, with the result that frost-bitten feet afflicted a number of men. The Higher Command issued violent threats, and the Quartermasters tins of whale oil as a palliative.

In the villages drying-rooms of a primitive nature were constructed by blocking up windows of empty houses and lighting innumerable wood fires in the rooms ; socks were the articles of clothing that required the greatest attention.

But the hardships suffered by the men were not greater than those suffered by the animals, especially the camels. These poor brutes, with their great padded feet, could not get a hold on the muddy roads, and were constantly falling ; they died in hundreds from the cold and wet. Donkeys suffered almost as much.

There was a heavy fall of snow just after the 53rd Division took over the Burj–Beitin line on the 4th January, our battalions being on the right.

In rear of the right of the line was a deep wadi through which our battalions made roads during their periods of " rest."

The British line across Palestine was thrown back on the right, where troops looked down from the heights into the wonderful sunken Valley of the Jordan. In the right sector held by the 53rd a fine view was obtained from Kh. Nisieh across a few wooded valleys to the mass of tumbled, bare desert hills, a ghastly sort of wilderness which fell abruptly into the valley. Beyond the Valley of the Jordan the hills of Moab could be seen. General Allenby decided that he must move down into the valley.

The task was given to the 60th Infantry Division and the Anzac Mounted Division. The 53rd Division drove the Turkish garrison from the village of Rummon, but our battalions had little to do beyond patrolling and watching the road across their front and protecting the flank of the whole operation. This was one of the occasions when all our battalions may be said to have met. The 231st Brigade was lent to the 60th Division and our 25th Battalion was in close support to the line which eventually held the escarpment on the edge of the Valley of the Jordan on the 20th February : they were withdrawn after the capture of Jericho to Ras et Tawil, and relieved the 158th Brigade on the 26th and 27th. The 158th Brigade had then been in the line for 33 days, 16 of which had been wet.

.   .   .   .

At this time another change took place in the Turkish command. Our old redoubtable opponent Liman von Sanders was asked by Enver Pasha to take command of the Turkish Armies in Palestine. He took with him a number of his Turkish staff who had worked under him since 1914. His account of the journey is amusing. He left Constantinople on the 24th February and found that someone had hitched " the Headquarters squadron of Turkish Headquarters " bound for Aleppo on to his train. The overloading caused the train to be late, " so at the station of Ekischehir I simply ordered the uncoupling of the cars of the squadron. Neither it nor Headquarters ever went to Aleppo. The squadron was peacefully taken back to Constantinople." But " after numerous changes of trains caused by the incomplete state of the Taurus tunnel and by the differences of gauge south of the Taurus, I reached Samach on Lake Tiberias at noon on 1st March."

He says that after Jericho " had been given up," the XX Turkish Corps had crossed to the east bank of the Jordan. West of the Jordan the line was held by the III Turkish Corps. " The left flank of the corps was in the air, the interval of twenty kilometres between the main position and the Jordan being guarded only by a few small detachments." Von Sanders therefore ordered the XX Corps to recross the Jordan and take post between the III Corps and the Jordan.

After a tour of inspection he returned to the III Corps front on the 8th March and found that the last units of the Turkish XX Corps had just arrived.

ACTIONS OF TELL ASUR, 8TH–12TH MARCH.   AREA : WEST OF THE JORDAN, AND NORTH OF THE LINE JERICHO–RAM ALLAH–JAFFA.

The arrival of Liman von Sanders coincided with orders to our own XX Corps for a further advance. General Allenby was thinking of operations on the east of the Jordan and wished to deprive the enemy of the use of the few roads leading to the lower Jordan Valley, and force him, if he wished to transfer troops, to make a wide detour to the north. His orders to the XX Corps were to secure Kh. el Beiyudat and Abu Tellul, in the Jordan Valley north of the Wadi Auja. The chaotic mass of arid hills falling from the highlands into the valley were left out—no troops could manoeuvre there—but on either side of the Jerusalem-Nablus Road the advance was to be to the line Kefr Malik–Kh. abu Felah—high ground south of Sinjil— ridge north of the Wadi el Jib, running through Kh. Aliuta–Jiljiliya– Abwein–Arura, thence to Deir es Sudan–Neby Saleh.

The 60th Division was down in the Jordan Valley. Above the great rent was the 53rd Division ; then the 74th ; then the 10th. The country on the line of advance was wild and picturesque ; it was sparsely dotted with ruins and villages, with fig and olive groves, and vineyards painting the hillsides with varying shades of green, but apart from these cultivated pockets it was a succession of scarred hills, separated by deep and sometimes precipitous valleys. To cover what appeared a short distance on the map required a great physical effort.

The 53rd Division would have to build up a flank as they advanced in touch with the 74th. General Mott gave the main attack to the 158th Brigade, and to the 159th Brigade the task of building up a flank ; the

10th Middlesex were to see to the gap which would occur between the left of the 158th Brigade and the right of the 74th Division.

The 74th Division had the 231st Brigade on the right, and the 230th on the left, in touch with the 10th Division.

The shifting and indefinite position of the Turkish line frequently gave a considerable width to " No Man's Land." [1] On the night 6th/7th March the 159th Brigade advanced several thousand yards to get in touch with the enemy. On the 74th Division front two such advances were made by our 24th Battalion.

All was ready on the 8th March, the day the XX Turkish Corps came into line.

. . . .

A panoramic view of the line of advance shows a mass of hills—no ridges, no definite line. When our 5th, 6th, and 7th Battalions started out at 2 a.m. on the 9th March, they had given them as objectives various hills, and these hills, not easily located, had small features, bumps, false crests, and so on, which are not shown on maps but which were tactical features of vast importance in the struggle to capture the objectives.

A preliminary advance on the night 6th/7th had placed the 158th Brigade line west of Taiyibeh, where the Herefordshire formed up on the right and our 5th Battalion on the left. Advancing on a two-battalion front, the Herefordshire were given Drage Hill and then Chipp Hill ; our 5th Battalion had Cairn Hill. When these points were taken Tell Asur was to be attacked from the east.

We are told that Chipp Hill was a hill " in succession to Drage Hill," and that Cairn Hill was " a kind of hump between Drage Hill and Tell Asur." Tell Asur with its slopes covered with vines and fig trees was a high, steep hill rising straight out of the valley which separated it from Cairn Hill, and " we somehow assumed that the country would fall on the other side in the same way ; most hills do. Actually Tell Asur was the edge of a high plateau." Tell Asur was, in fact, the highest point of all, and north-west of it, on the forward slope of a hill, was Selwad, the first objective of the 231st Brigade, to be taken by the Shropshire Light Infantry with our 25th Battalion in support. The directions of attack seem strange.

The 158th Brigade advanced from the position west of Taiyibeh at 2 a.m., our 7th and 6th Battalions being in support. A long march lay before them over a rough country, but free of enemy posts. As dawn approached, a thick fog enveloped the hills : the fog interfered greatly with communication, but does not seem to have been so thick in the valleys.

---

[1] Officers of the 7th Field Survey Company, R.E., worked frequently far beyond the front line.

About 6 a.m. the 5th Royal Welch approached Cairn Hill, and were fired upon by the enemy on their immediate front and also from Tell Asur. Lieutenant-Colonel Borthwick had kept his battalion in close formation up to the last moment, but he was now forced to deploy. Companies then advanced up the hill into the thicker fog, the enemy retiring before them. The hill was occupied, but much time was spent in reorganising and regaining control of men who had wandered in all directions in the fog. Meanwhile, the Herefordshire had advanced up Drage Hill, which they found was already partly in the hands of the 4th Welch Regiment, from the 159th Brigade on the right.

Back at Brigade Headquarters no one could see or obtain direct information of what was happening. Our 5th Battalion was completely hidden, but unauthorised reports came to the brigade. One, repeated several times, was that Tell Asur had been captured, and Brigadier-General Vernon moved the 6th and 7th Battalions up in close support in some dead ground, the 7th behind Drage Hill, the 6th behind Cairn Hill.

The Herefordshire then became involved in severe fighting in which they won and lost Chipp Hill, and while this was going on the Brigadier heard that Tell Asur had not been captured. Lieutenant-Colonel Borthwick had, however, reorganised his battalion, and under artillery support assaulted and captured Tell Asur without much difficulty.

Our 7th Battalion was then ordered to relieve the Herefordshire companies on Drage Hill, and our 6th to relieve the 5th on Tell Asur. The relief was not complete until 11.30 a.m., the fog having by that time dispersed.

The Herefordshire, freed from the responsibility of Drage Hill, continued to attack Chipp Hill without success until about 6.30 p.m., when they secured a position on the crest and were then relieved by our 7th Battalion. The relief was not complete until 10 p.m.

On Tell Asur our 6th Battalion had no sooner got into position at midday than they were counter-attacked in force, and a regular " dog fight " took place in which our battalion was at one time pushed off the top of the hill, but regained it by a counter-charge. The position they held was the highest point, but what they describe as the " plateau " fell in a very slight gradient before them and was covered with great boulders. The Turks were on the plateau, finding splendid cover behind the boulders, so that the capture of Tell Asur was only partial.

The difficulties on this front reacted on the 231st Brigade, actually attacking on the left, but at some distance.

The Shropshire Light Infantry had captured Selwad after a company of our 25th Battalion had dislodged some machine guns on the right, and when the village was secured the 25th Battalion deployed on the right of the Shropshire. In front of them lay the Wadi Nimr, below a steep escarpment. Further advance was a hard problem. Only two paths could be discovered leading down to the rock-strewn bed of the wadi, and both were under machine-gun fire from Lisaneh and Sheikh Saleh. Tell Asur to their right rear was still in the hands of the Turks, against whom sections of the 210th Machine-gun Company were in action. On the left the 230th Brigade had not yet taken Burj Bardawil, and the 231st Brigade stood with both flanks in the air. Burj Bardawil was eventually captured at 10.30 a.m., but the 230th Brigade was not ready to move forward until 2.30 p.m. They then moved on to the escarpment overlooking the Wadi el Jib, into which the Wadi Nimr runs, in line with the 231st Brigade.

With his two attacking brigades in this position, General Girdwood postponed any further advance in daylight, and telegraphed to General Mott to this effect. The time was 5 p.m.

Night brought no rest to our three battalions on Chipp Hill and Tell Asur. The 7th Royal Welch were attacked twenty minutes after taking over from the Herefordshire, and after severe and close fighting repulsed the enemy, but gave a little ground themselves.

At 3 a.m. on the 10th March our 7th Battalion was ordered to advance north. The Herefordshire came up again and took over the line ; our battalion commenced to advance at 4 a.m. They had not gone far, however, when they bumped into a large body of Turks also advancing. The Turks spread out and opened fire at once, but our 7th Battalion stood their ground. There they remained in close touch with the enemy.

On Tell Asur our 6th Battalion had repulsed five separate attacks since taking over the position. They were ordered to advance at 6.30 p.m. on the 9th, and their line was taken over by our 5th Battalion. The 6th Battalion had one company holding Cairn Hill, and three companies only commenced to advance along the boulder-strewn plateau. They were not in sufficient strength, and the Turks were well placed amongst the boulders. No advance was made.

It was a trying and nervous night for all Commanding Officers. Orders were issued from Brigade which did not reach their destination for some hours, and it was impossible to co-ordinate the advance of widely separated battalions. The attempt of our 6th Battalion to go forward on Tell Asur was supposed to be part of a general advance ordered when Chipp Hill had been taken by the Herefordshire. Chipp Hill was only partly taken. Our 7th Battalion, as stated above, did not commence the forward move until the early hours of the morning, while the 6th Battalion started at 6.30 p.m., which was about the time the Herefordshire got a footing on Chipp Hill. Between these two hours of assault Brigadier-General Vernon decided that he was stuck on both flanks and that his best course was " to push one battalion as a wedge through the centre " and get behind the Turks on the forward slopes of Tell Asur. The Brigadier expected this movement to be carried out before midnight, but the order did not reach Lieutenant-Colonel Mills until 10 p.m., and then directed that one company should be left on Cairn Hill, to which the whole battalion had been withdrawn. A second order followed that the last duty should be undertaken by our 5th Battalion, and this was not carried out until 4 a.m.

The 6th Battalion commenced to advance at 4.5 a.m., which was the hour when our 7th Battalion commenced to move forward on Chipp Hill, only to meet with an unexpected advance by the Turks. The check on Chipp Hill was believed by Lieutenant-Colonel Mills to be a retirement, and he therefore halted his battalion and waited for fresh orders.

When orders arrived, Lieutenant-Colonel Mills advanced and found that the enemy had retired. This was after daylight.

Similarly, on the 74th Division front darkness on the 9th March meant renewed activity. The paths found by our 25th Battalion leading down the escarpment could be negotiated in single file after dark, and by 8.30 p.m. our battalion was deployed in the bed of the Wadi Nimr, with the Shropshire on their left. The descent had not been too bad, except for gradients, as the enemy was then sweeping the hillside at random. Having got down in the valley, they had now the job of climbing out the other side, up the precipitous Lisaneh Ridge. Expressed in time, the arduous nature of this climb in the dark is 6½ hours—terraces, impassable except in one or two spots, which had to be found, obstacles which men had to overcome by mounting on each other's shoulders—and the enemy's position was only reached at 3 a.m., but carried after a sharp hand-to-hand fight.

The enemy was not content, however, and launched three counter-attacks before dawn—all strong bombing attacks—which were repulsed.

On the left the 230th Brigade had some hard fighting, which continued all through the day. In the afternoon our 25th Battalion was twice counter-attacked, but succeeded each time in stopping the storming troops. In the evening the 230th Brigade was well forward, and the 231st Brigade advanced on Sheikh Selim, without opposition, but over steep rough country and in pouring rain, and brought the line level, with their left on the high ground near El Tell.

On the 53rd Division front our 5th Battalion relieved the right of the

6th and carried on to near Kh. Abu Felah. Kh. Abu Felah was occupied next day by the 159th Brigade.

It had been a difficult advance, entailing great physical effort and much severe fighting. The final line occupied by the corps was Kefr Malik-ridge overlooking Wadi el Kola–Burj el Lisaneh–Kh. el Sahlat–Kh. Aliuta–Jiljiliya–Abwein–Arura–Deir es Sudan. Summing up the operations, General Allenby's dispatch states : " The descent of the slopes

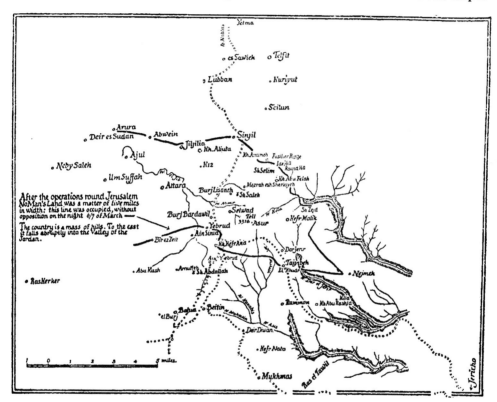

leading down to the Wadis en Nimr and el Jib and the ascent on the far side presented great difficulties. The downward slopes were exceptionally steep, almost precipitous in places. It was impossible for companies and platoons to move on a wide front. The slopes were swept by machine-gun and rifle fire and the bottom of the wadis by enfilade fire. The ascent on the far side was steeply terraced. Men had alternatively to hoist and pull each other up under fire, and finally to expel the enemy from the summits in hand-to-hand fighting. . . . The result of this operation was the capture of a line with great natural facilities for defence, and of eleven officers,

160 other ranks, eleven machine guns, and considerable amounts of ammunition and other booty."

Liman von Sanders remarks with pride that the British effort to take Nablus did not succeed until six and a half months later, and that the spirit of the Turkish troops after the three-day battle was full of confidence. He was rightly pleased with his decision to redistribute his troops.

. . . .

On the 13th March the 53rd Division was relieved by the 74th. On the 3rd April the 74th Division was informed of the War Office decision to replace British by Indian troops as far as possible, and that they would proceed to France. The great German offensive commenced on the 21st March, and Haig's " back to the wall " order was issued before the division left Palestine.

The division concentrated at Ludd on the 14th April, with Divisional Headquarters at Qantara, to be followed during the next two days by the three infantry brigades. By the 3rd May embarkation at Alexandria was complete.

. . . .

The 158th Brigade Group was in the neighbourhood of Jerusalem, and on the 23rd March our 6th and 7th Battalions were ordered to march to Talaat ed Dumm, on the road to Jericho.

General Allenby had turned his attention once more to the east of the Jordan, and the 60th Division and Australian Mounted Division were advancing on Amman.

On the 29th our 7th Battalion was moved to a position beyond the Ghoraniyeh Bridge on the Jordan, and the rest of the brigade commenced to march to Talaat ed Dumm from Jerusalem.

This is the shortest road from Jerusalem to Jericho. There are no passes from the depths of the Jordan Valley to Judea—although there are many gorges, they are too narrow and crooked to carry roads—and the roads follow the ridges rather than the valleys. The first consideration in either ascent or descent is the oasis, and most roads follow the line of oases through this grim and barren wilderness of hills ; but there is no water-point on the road followed by our battalions across the blistering limestone rocks and over bare hills without shadow or verdure. Red streaks in the stone give the name to Red Khan, the Chastel Rouge of the Crusaders, and to Talaat ed Dumm, or " the ascent of blood ! "

Beyond the heat in the valley, which was intense, there is nothing to record. Visitors to Jericho found it disappointing. Talaat itself still preserved the ruins of a Crusader castle, and there were monasteries, particularly the one on the Mount of Temptation (Kuruntul), which attracted attention.

On the 1st April the order came to return to Ram Allah. The brigade marched to Jerusalem on the 4th, Ram Allah on the 5th, and relieved the 230th Brigade on the 74th Division front (left subsector) on the 7th.

This sector was astride the Jerusalem–Nablus road, with excellent observation over the Turkish positions from Beachy Head—which stuck out like a cape into the wide green valley to the north—and the Sinjil Ridge. The main road runs between Beachy Head and Sinjil Ridge, across the valley and so into the hills beyond. On Sinjil Ridge the 158th Brigade joined hands with the 10th Division.

" No Man's Land " was wide. The front line was held at night only, and consisted of a series of sangars and breastworks protected by barbed wire ; in daytime troops retired behind Beachy Head or the crest of the Sinjil Ridge.

Behind the front-line system the serried ranks of hills were divided into defended localities ; some of them, such as Burj el Lisaneh and Burj Bardawil, were easily recognised by the ruins of ancient castles on their summits.

The right subsector, into which the brigade moved in due course, ran along the edge of a high escarpment, at the bottom of which was the Wadi Samieh—it was a tremendous ravine. On the right was Nejmeh, a detached locality from which troops could look down a drop of some 4,000 feet into the Jordan Valley. The view from the detached post was weird and magnificent. The Dead Sea, half hidden in haze, lay still and mysterious to the south, reflecting in its near surface the mountains of Moab, on the far side of the Valley. A snake-like white road ran from the hills to the green patch of Jericho, and beyond, running the length of the wide valley, were the green banks of the Jordan ; and then on the far edge of the valley the hills of Moab, with a range of colour that beggars description ; " added to a family of browns, chocolates, and yellows, always present, there are other families of purples, mauves, and violets, and of all imaginable shades of grey, salmon, pink, and blue ! "

In the early part of the year the ground in the valleys was carpeted with a blaze of small flowers, a certain amount of grass grew on the hillside, the young vine leaves were a beautiful shade of light green contrasting with the dark green olive trees which were most plentiful. Later in the year only the olives and vines remained—the rest was burned a drab dust-colour.

Indian battalions began to arrive. The composition of the division began to change, and did not settle down until the 1st August, when our 5th and 6th Battalions were amalgamated and known as the 5th/6th Battalion. The new battalion remained in the 158th Brigade, which was now composed of the 4/11th Gurkha Rifles, 3/153rd Indian Infantry, 3/154th Indian Infantry.

Our 7th Battalion was moved to the 160th Brigade, with the 21st Punjabis, 17th Indian Infantry, and the 1/1st Battalion Cape Corps.

The heat of the summer put an end to all major operations. Our battalions settled down to a regular routine, and life was not so difficult. Also news of a change of fortune in France began to trickle through, although it meant very little to the men in Palestine.

Reorganisation went on all through the summer and was completed in August.

Opposite us General Liman von Sanders was having a lot of trouble. He declares that he was well aware, from the moment of taking over command of the Yilderim Group, that the British could break through his line at any point they chose. He supplies himself an excellent reason for the state of affairs, and from the British point of view a justification of their efforts against the Turks—the aggressive efforts, for it was we who attacked. In a letter to Count Bernstorff, Ambassador at Constantinople, complaining of the action of Turkish Headquarters in giving orders for the withdrawal of all German troops in Palestine, he says : " Through the advance into Persia, against which I urgently warned, the Turks have lost Baghdad ; through the initiation of the Yilderim enterprise planned against Baghdad the Turks have lost Jerusalem ; and now through the bottomless advance into Transcaucasia they are going to lose all of Arabia, Palestine, and Syria." The letter is dated the 21st June.[1] The " side-shows " had their value.

THE BATTLE OF NABLUS, 19TH–25TH SEPTEMBER 1918.

AREA : BETWEEN THE HEJAZ RAILWAY AND THE SEA, NORTH OF THE LINE DHABU STATION–MOUTH OF JORDAN–ASSUF.

The Turkish Seventh and Eighth Armies, opposing us on the west of the Jordan, stood within a rectangle 45 miles wide and 12 miles deep.

" The northern edge of this rectangle was a line from Jisr ed Damieh on the Jordan, through Nablus and Tul Keram to the sea. All the enemy's communications to Damascus ran northwards from the eastern half of this line, converging on El Afule and Beisan some 25 miles to the north. Thence,

---

[1] Liman von Sanders, *Five Years in Turkey.*

with the exception of the roads leading from El Afule along the western shore of the Sea of Galilee, his communications ran eastwards up the Valley of the Yarmuk to Deraa, the junction of the Palestine and Hedjaz railways. Thus El Afule, Beisan, and Deraa were the vital points on his communications. If they could be seized, the enemy's retreat would be cut off. Deraa was beyond my reach, but not beyond that of mobile detachments of the Arab Army. It was not to be expected that these detachments could hold the railway junction, but it was within their power to dislocate all traffic.

" El Afule in the Plain of Esdraelon, and Beisan in the Valley of Jezreel, were within reach of my cavalry, provided the infantry could break through the enemy's defensive systems and create a gap for the cavalry to pass through. It was essential that this gap should be made at the commencement of the operations, so that the cavalry might reach their destinations 45 and 60 miles distant before the enemy could make his escape."

The above was General Allenby's plan epitomised in his despatch. The break-through was entrusted to the XXI Corps, on the Maritime Plain, who had in front of them the hills of Samaria, which are not a series of piled-up ranges like the Judean hills, but run to a point. The Desert Mounted Corps, less the Australian and New Zealand Mounted Division, was assembled behind the XXI Corps to ride through the gap when made. The XX Corps were to advance on the evening of the day on which the coastal attack took place, " or later, as circumstances demanded." But on the night previous to the attack the 53rd Division were to cross the Samieh basin and place themselves in a better position to block the exits from the hills into the lower Valley of the Jordan when the general advance was ordered.

Zero day for the big attack was the 19th September. General Mott's plan for the preliminary move of the 53rd Division was to attack with the 160th and 159th Brigades. The 160th was to cross the great basin of the Samieh and sweep round the far rim of it, while the 159th, carrying out a series of frontal attacks, would meet them on the northern side of the basin. As the 160th Brigade crossed the basin, their left was to be covered by two companies of the 5th/6th Royal Welch.

The long, peaceful summer was at an end ; the old camps, where guard-mounting had become a smart and impressive parade, were to be left standing, so that no change could be noted from the air, and battalions were to move forward into olive groves, of which there were quite a number.

The secret regrouping of the Army was a great achievement. The moving of guns and the shifting of a mass of cavalry from one flank to the other were moves that required the most careful timing and thought, but they were done without exciting any suspicion.   Liman von Sanders claims that he knew the attack would be on the coast, and the Turkish Intelligence Service issued a warning that an attack must be expected on the 18th, but they also issued a map which showed all mounted troops, except the 5th Cavalry Division, on the British right.

At 4.30 p.m. on the 18th the 160th Brigade, protected in the air by two fighting aeroplanes, assembled in rear of a hill between El Munatir and Rock Park.   The setting of the sun did not bring darkness, but a soft light, a dimming of visibility in which troops could still distinguish the Mountains of Moab, 40 miles away, and every feature of the opposite side of the basin.

At 7.15 p.m. a slow rate of artillery fire was opened on Keen's Knoll to drown the noise the leading battalion might make scrambling down the precipitous side of the basin.   The 17th Indian Infantry advanced, a long column, more or less in fours, showing clearly against the yellow escarpment, and reached a wide ledge, three-quarters of the way down, before they were observed by enemy posts beyond the wadi.   The Turks sent up signal lights and started wild rifle shooting.   For some time there was no artillery response to their signals, and when it came it was scattered and did little harm.   The 17th quickened their pace and were soon in a position to assault the Wye Hill defences.

A slight pause, waiting for Zero hour, which was in this case a direct order from Brigadier-General Pearson.   And then with a crash a twenty-minute bombardment started.

The assault followed and was entirely successful, the 17th establishing themselves on the opposite rim of the basin.

The attack was of the " leap-frog " kind.   The Cape Corps took up the running, guided by smoke shells fired at intervals by the artillery. They passed behind the Valley View positions, posting pickets overlooking the Valley of the Jordan as they went, and finally took up a position near Square Hill and Kh. Jibeit.   Our 7th Battalion had then to carry on the advance.

As the Cape Corps turned away from the basin at End Hill, the 7th Royal Welch passed inside them, but also behind the Valley View position, which was attacked by the Punjabis, who had turned left, inside the Royal Welch.   The bewildered Turks fled before the Indian battalion, but broke back only to fall into the hands of our battalion.

They pushed on.   The track they were following, marked on the map and seen from the air, was through thick scrub and consequently easy to miss ; the battalion had strayed to the north, moving in two columns, when

Lieutenant-Colonel Harker discovered that he was on the slopes of Square Hill on the right of his objectives, Boulder's Boil and Hill 2362. However, the position was clear, and he ordered the leading company of his left column to take Sheikh Azeir and the support company to push straight on and take Hill 2362. He directed the companies of his right column on El Mugheir and Boulder's Boil.

The Turks were taken by surprise. Each objective was rushed as fast as the men could go, and only three shots were fired by the Turks. At Boulder's Boil there was a standing bivouac camp ; at El Mugheir a Battalion Headquarters, including the commanding officer, was captured. Altogether 20 officers, 192 other ranks, two 4·2-inch howitzers, and 15 machine guns were captured. In the whole advance our battalion had only two men wounded.

At dawn on the 19th September all objectives on the northern side of the basin had been taken excepting Malul, on the left. In the centre the 4th/5th Welch Regiment had advanced rapidly and had captured a key position, a hill called Hindhead, and our 5th/6th Battalion was ordered to relieve the Welch Regiment before or after dark and continue the advance to the line Kulason–Plateau. Two companies had been in the neighbourhood of Keen's Knoll, and the remainder of the battalion attached to the 159th Brigade who had fought their way along the western rim of the basin.

The 53rd Division stood fast on the 19th and did not expect to resume the advance until forty-eight hours after the commencement of the main attack by the XXI Corps. That attack was launched early in the morning of the 19th and was entirely successful; by 7.30 a.m. the 5th Cavalry Division was riding through the gap followed by the whole of the Desert Mounted Corps, and by midday were behind the Turkish Army.

The success was so rapid that soon after midday General Allenby ordered the XX Corps to advance during the night 19th/20th. The trouble with the 53rd Division was that they were in the worst bit of country for the movement of artillery, the artillery was already firing at the limit of range, and Malul had not yet been taken. General Chetwode left General Mott to decide whether he would advance that night or the next morning : he decided to attack at dawn.

On the evening of the 19th Malul was captured by the 4th/5th Welch Regiment and the 2/153rd Indian Infantry.

Our 5th/6th Battalion had assembled at 1 a.m. on the 20th and occupied a position on the edge of the Plateau. All infantry not employed in the line were working on a road along the Wadi Forth, and as soon as that was completed the 158th Brigade were to advance on the line Pt. 2006–Kh. Bkt. el Kusr, the 159th Brigade, echeloned on the left, to Ras el Tawil, and the 160th Brigade would picket the right flank until troops in the Jordan Valley relieved them of that duty.

Early in the morning of the 20th, however, the Turks counter-attacked the Cape Corps Battalion on the right, and severe fighting continued until the early afternoon. While this was going on the advance of the 158th Brigade in the centre hung fire.

The 158th Brigade had been much scattered, units being attached to other brigades and working on roads, etc. Our 5th/6th Battalion was in position on time, but when Brigadier-General Vernon arrived to take command of his brigade, ours was the only battalion present. " My orders," he says, " were to attack at dawn, but I was unable to comply as I had no troops to do it with."

The Gurkhas and the 3/153rd Indian Regiment arrived at 8.30 a.m., and the Gurkhas marched through the Royal Welch as advance guard directed on Pt. 2006–Kh. Bkt. el Kusr, a line of hills across the main plateau. But the Turkish rearguard was well supplied with machine guns and the brigade was held (see map, page 288). No artillery support was available, as all guns which might have helped the 158th Brigade had been turned on to the 160th Brigade front, where the Turkish counter-attack was in progress. Further advance was, therefore, postponed until after dark.

In the evening General Mott had news that the cavalry had occupied Beisan, 25 miles to the north. There was now some danger that a large portion of the Turkish Army might escape into the Valley of the Jordan. The nearest road they could use ran from Nablus through Mejdel Beni Fadl to the Damieh Bridge over the Jordan, and was only 4 miles away. Ten miles away were two other roads, one through Beit Furik, the other through Beit Dejan, which joined below the desolate Ghor country. If the 53rd Division was to carry out its task, the road to the Damieh Bridge must be cut. The Corps order was to advance " absolutely regardless of fatigue of men or animals."

The 158th Brigade was ordered to be on the Damieh Bridge road at Kh. el Nejmeh by dawn on the 21st ; thence their advance would be on Akrabeh. The 159th Brigade would be on their left, the 160th on their right watching the Jordan Valley.

Our 5th/6th Battalion, as advance guard to the brigade, moved forward at 11 p.m. on the 20th and found that the Turks had retired. The objective on the Damieh Bridge road was occupied at 5 a.m., when the whole brigade halted for breakfast.

Visibility was good. Before them was an open country affording distant views. Captain John More, of our 6th Battalion, who was then Brigade Major to the 158th Brigade, describes this country from the top of El Nejmeh hill as a fan-shaped plain with rounded hills on the east and west sides, and on the north of it a steep range of hills " at the foot of which nestled Akrabeh and Yanun." The country they had passed through was singularly bare, but in front of them was a " more fertile and green country."

The Turkish rearguard had been located on a low ridge about 2½ miles away ; 9 miles away was the tall hill of El Tuwanik, and on the left of it the Damieh Bridge road emerged from a gorge. Suddenly a large body of the enemy was seen marching out of the gorge, but instead of following the road to the Damieh Bridge, and incidentally to the waiting 158th Brigade,

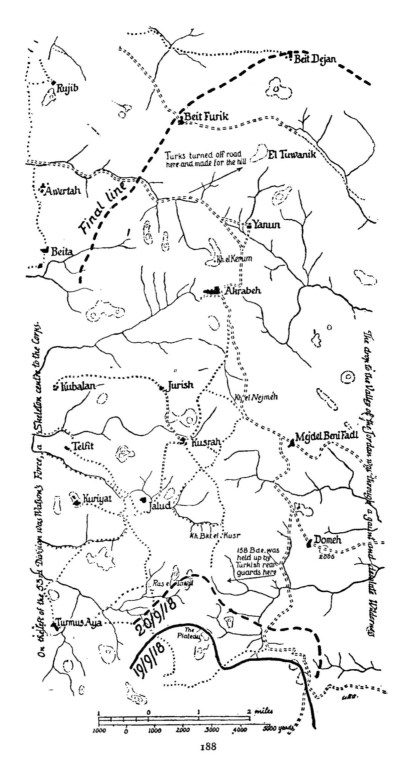

Rujib

Beit Dejan

Beit Furik

Turks turned off road here and made for the hill

El Tuwanik

Awertah

Final line

Yanun

Beita

Kh. el Kenum

Akrabeh

The drop to the valley of the Jordan was through a grim and desolate wilderness

Kubalan

Jurish

Kh. el Nejmeh

Telfit

Kusrah

Mjdel Beni Fadl

On the left of the 53rd Division was Watson's Force, a Skeleton centre to the Corps.

Kuriyat

Jalud

Domeh
2886

Kh. Bkt. el Kusr

158 Bde. was held up by Turkish rear guards here

Ras el Tawil

20/9/18

Turmus Aya

The Plateau

19/9/18

1   0   1   2 miles

1000   0   1000   2000   3000   4000   5000 yards

they turned off, climbed the Tuwanik Ridge and escaped down the precipitous and desolate hills into the Jordan Valley.

The brigade was ordered forward at once, and our 5th/6th Battalion advanced over the plain in artillery formation. " It was a fine sight to see the orderly little groups of men in single file, moving off in perfect formation across the open ground, never deviating to the right or the left as the shells began to fall." (More.)

As our battalion advanced they were ordered to picket the hills on the right, and during this operation one Lewis-gun team surprised and captured 12 officers, 143 other ranks, and 5 machine guns.

The 3/154th Indian Infantry then secured Kh. el Kerum, driving the enemy before them, and at 3 p.m. the 3/153rd Indian Infantry, assuming the lead, passed over El Tuwanik to Beit Dejan. The roads were all finally blocked.

That night the 5th/6th Battalion moved to El Tuwanik, arriving about 10 o'clock, and at 6.30 a.m. on the 22nd the division received the news that the Turkish Army west of the Jordan had ceased to exist.

In the graphic words of Colonel Garcia, G.S.O.1 of the Division, " from the depths of war we passed in the twinkling of an eye into the depths of peace." The exhausting strain of the last few days ceased so completely that even the protection of an outpost line was ignored.

The 158th Brigade concentrated at Jurish and moved to Akrabeh during the afternoon.

Our 7th Battalion, with the 160th Brigade, had remained on the right flank watching the Jordan Valley. All brigades were ordered to work on the Nablus road, and on the 26th the whole division moved back to the Tell Asur area.

On the 8th October the division moved to the Latron–Ludd area, and on the 26th to Sidi Bishr.

The armistice with Turkey did not come into force until the 31st October.

.   .   .   .

The 2nd Garrison Battalion, at Jollum, sent A Company to Alexandria to relieve the 6th Garrison Battalion, who were sailing for Salonika. On the 7th November Lieutenant-Colonel W. Hussey-Walsh was appointed Commandant at Beirut, and was succeeded by Major W. R. Howell. Gradually the companies were sent to Alexandria : C Company on the 10th November ; B Company on the 24th ; D Company on the 10th December.

The 6th Garrison Battalion had also been ordered from Cairo to Jollum on the 7th May 1918, but on arrival found a counter-order to return to Alexandria. Here they remained until October, when they were ordered to Salonika.

PART II

THE WAR WITH BULGARIA

SALONIKA

To the British people generally Balkan politics seem a tangle of incomprehensible intrigues, but Bulgarian hopes and desires at the beginning of the Great War are not difficult to follow. The Bulgars had enforced an old claim to Macedonia—based on nationality—by an appeal to arms against Turkey, in which they allied themselves with the Serbs and Greeks. They defeated Turkey, but over-reached themselves in their demands, fell to quarrelling and finally to war with their late allies, and lost the greater part of Macedonia.

Wars with erstwhile allies naturally lead to great bitterness, and the outbreak of the Great War, centred on Serbia, opened, to the Bulgarian view, possibilities of recovery. The Bulgars had a single aim, but prejudice existed, and although a series of victories for the Allied Powers would, no doubt, have stayed Bulgarian intervention, their armed support on the side of Serbia was improbable.

On the declaration of war, Austria had launched her armies against Serbia and had suffered several severe defeats. But it was obvious from the commencement that lack of supplies would more than counterbalance the gallantry of Serbian troops : the country was completely cut off from communication with the Allied Powers, except through neutral States whose intentions were dubious. Also there were no striking victories which might have affected this neutrality and relieved the pressure on Serbia. Even the decision of Italy, who declared war on Austria on the 23rd May 1915, was of no assistance to the Serbs, who by that time were quiescent.

King Ferdinand and his Bulgar advisers waited, but they were convinced that the Central Powers had established their supremacy and the die was cast. A general mobilisation was ordered on the 10th September, and Serbia was attacked on the 29th.

The development of this situation was not sudden, but when it became a *fait accompli* it exposed not only Serbia but our Gallipoli Army to immediate danger. A fresh invasion of Serbia was imminent, and the supplying of Turkey, particularly with heavy artillery, was now simplified—and, as we know, our position in Gallipoli was not good !

The Allied Powers then made a decision which, if not aggressive, was

IV—13   193

a very high-handed action and morally indefensible, although justified by military and political expediency. M. Venizelos, the President of the Government, was in sympathy with the Allied Powers, but the King and the majority of the Greek nation were not. The Allies wrung from Athens an unwilling consent to a landing, and our presence at Salonika must be considered as due to *force majeure*.

With this decision came another which determined the evacuation of Gallipoli, and one might look upon the landing at Salonika as an attempt to close up the Allied forces in face of a fresh development. The two forces, one in Gallipoli, one in Serbia, had been separated by neutral States, one of which had now declared against us : our command of the sea made that element as much a defended line as any on land ; so the withdrawal of a force at Gallipoli and the introduction of one at Salonika to gain touch with the Serbs made the operation a rectification of the battle-line.

The 10th Division left Gallipoli and, with the French 156th Division, commenced to land at Salonika. Naturally enough, great excitement prevailed in Greece.

The 11th Battalion.

Our 11th Battalion had done little more than pass through France. They had joined the 22nd Division in the autumn of 1914 when it was formed under Major-General R. B. Montgomery at Seaford, and the whole division had moved to the Wellington and Stanhope lines and Rushmore and Tweseldown Camps at the beginning of June 1915. Within a few days of its arrival at Aldershot, Major-General the Hon. F. Gordon, C.B., D.S.O. (from the 19th Infantry Brigade), assumed command.

The division commenced to leave Aldershot on the 3rd September, and by the 6th the crossing to France, via Folkestone and Boulogne, was completed. They were posted to the XII Corps, then forming, with Headquarters at Doullens, but were attached to the X Corps for training. They detrained at Amiens and Longueau. Our battalion went to Vignacourt, and on the 9th to Rainneville.

" At present it is understood that we shall take our place in the line on the left of the X Corps." On the 11th our battalion moved to the Bois des Tailles, where they came under the 14th Brigade, 5th Division, for instruction. The next move was to be south of the Somme, where British troops were taking over from the French.

In due course the 22nd Division took over the southern sector, and the 27th Division the northern sector of the French 154th Division front. Our battalion was at Fontaine les Gappy on the 19th and at Proquart on the 20th. On the 25th they relieved the 9th Border Regiment at Framerville.

On the 20th October news came of a move to an unknown destination, and the next day our battalion went to Domart. By the 23rd the whole division had been relieved by the 6th French Division and were at Villers Bretonneux.

They entrained on the 25th for Marseilles, and on the 30th embarked on the good ship *Huntsend*, with the Major-General and his Staff, the 8th South Wales Borderers, and a portion of the Shropshire Light Infantry, and sailed at 4.30 p.m.

The ship made a good passage with no submarine scares, and anchored in Salonika harbour about noon on the 5th November. The division was ordered to concentrate in a camp on the right bank of the Galiko River, north of the Salonika–Uskub Railway.

The situation was not good. The French had wandered out into a corner of Serbia, just over the Greek frontier about Lake Doiran, and were extended on a line to Krivolak. We had one brigade on their right, otherwise the British Force was round Salonika. The Serbs were being hard-pressed by a horde of Germans and Austrians descending from the north, and from the east by Bulgaria. Their Army Headquarters were at Kruse-vatz, and their Government was established at Kralyevo, in the northern half of the kingdom. South of these places the Bulgars had driven in as far as Uskub. South-east of Uskub there was a small force of Serbs near Veles, but retiring to the south on Prilep. The left of the French was some twenty miles south-east of Veles, and they were not in practical touch with the Serbs.

On the 2nd November a report of a heavy attack on the Serbian Army on the right bank of the Morava came through Montenegro to Scutari, by wireless to Rome, and so back to Salonika : such indirect communication, either through Rome or Brindisi, was the only possible one with the main Serbian Army. Later news stated that the Serbs had been driven from Kraguyevatz, but had blown up the arsenal there. By the 30th November Serbian Headquarters were at Scutari, and their Army, reduced from 400,000 to a half-starved 150,000 men, was retiring on the Albanian coast, for the time being out of the War.

All through this tragic period the unfortunate Serbs made continual appeals for help, but owing to our lack of transport we could do nothing from Salonika—just as well, perhaps, for we, too, might have ended in Albania. The Allies simply held the small semicircle of Serbia from Lake Doiran to Prilep.

When our battalion arrived at Salonika, the French Army, under General Sarrail, consisted of the 156th, 57th, and 122nd Divisions. The 156th Division was advancing slowly against the Bulgars north of Lake Doiran, on a line that ran Calkali–Kajali–Hill 350, thence along the left bank of the River Vardar to about Vojsan. The 57th Division carried on along the left bank of the Vardar to Krivolak and Gradsko, where the line turned west towards the Baborna Pass, which was then still held by two Serbian Regiments.

Galiko Camp, where the 22nd Division was concentrating, was 8 miles from the quay at Salonika. The road was congested, being used by all the transport of the French and also the Greeks, who were concentrating their III, IV, and V Corps round Salonika. There were no traffic regulations or attempts at control.

General Sarrail, with his troops beyond the Greek frontier, was feeling uncomfortable and asked that our 10th Division might be sent up on his right. Doiran village at that time was still inhabited, and a certain amount of food could be bought there. The road from Doiran to Radrovo ran in a long valley with steep hills on the north side of it and was cut by the river Bojomia, which could not be crossed by lorries. From Radrovo to Strumitza the road ran under very rocky and mountainous country ; the width of the valley, from 2 to 4 miles, lay to the south of it, and then another great mass of mountains. In this country limbered wagons could move in the valleys, but for an advance into the hills pack transport was absolutely essential.

Generally speaking, the country was deserted and supplies non-existent. There was little cultivation beyond mulberry trees, but water was plentiful and good.

General Monro's[1] despatch states that " the task of moving troops into Serbia and maintaining them there presented many difficulties. No road exists from Salonika to Doiran, a few miles of road then obtains, which is followed within a few miles by a track only suitable for pack transport. Sir B. Mahon had therefore to readjust his transport to pack scale, and was dependent on a railway of uncertain carrying power to convey back his guns and all wheeled transport in case of a withdrawal, and to supply his troops while in Serbia."

On the 20th November the 10th Division took over the Kosturino–Ormanli–Prstan position from the French. On the same day our 11th Battalion moved with the 22nd Division to a new camping ground on the Salonika–Monastir road, about 6 miles from Salonika. The political

---

[1] In command of the Mediterranean Force, with Headquarters in Cairo.

situation with Greece was then so acute that troops were practically confined to camp ; but they carried out brigade exercises and general training until the next move, which commenced on the 12th December.

The Serbs were now out of the fight, and it became obvious that the Allies were in a precarious position. There was a big German-Bulgar concentration in the Strumitza Valley, and General Sarrail decided to withdraw from Serbia, pivoting on the British 10th Division.

Before the withdrawal was completed, the 10th Division was heavily attacked on the 6th, 7th, and 8th December. The men were suffering terribly from the cold. They had been through a blizzard and were only clad in khaki drill. But they " extricated themselves from a difficult position with no great loss."

The weather was very trying. Lieutenant-Colonel Lloyd, commanding our battalion, was ill and went to hospital, and the battalion marched north on the 12th under the orders of Major Yatman.

The whole of the 67th Brigade, in a thick fog, struck across country for the Seres road ; but what with the fog and the heavy state of the ground, progress was exceedingly slow : at 5 p.m. the brigade halted for the night at Ayvatli. Beyond Ayvatli motor transport was impossible, the track was in such a condition that double teams would be required for the limbered wagons ; vehicles sank up to the axles in the mud and the track was frequently intersected by deep nullahs. It was decided that only two battalions, the 11th Royal Welch and the 7th South Wales Borderers, should go forward.

The start the next morning was much delayed by the Greek Army, which had commenced to move south along the Seres road ; but when our battalion left the road conditions were worse than ever : the transport was divided into four sections, and each section was escorted by a company to pull it through difficult places. Only 4 miles were covered on the 13th before the men and animals became exhausted. The battalions halted at Baldza.

The next day (14th) they marched through the Baldza Ravine and heavy clay, over the hills above, and so to the banks of the Pirnak, south of Daudli, which they reached at 2.30 p.m. in heavy rain. From this spot they commenced to construct a great system of defences protecting Salonika. They worked north of a hill called Matterhorn, making use, when suitably sited, of old Greek trenches. Occasionally parties were sent road making, but the main work was trenches, and during the remaining weeks of December the assembled 67th Brigade completed 4,000 yards of trench, which, in view of the fact that parts of the line had to be hewn out of the solid rock, was good work.

They worked on trenches and what were called " devilish devices " all through the winter and into the spring. Brook Camp was their home until the 17th April, when the brigade moved to the Plough Sector, and continued digging. The weather, on the whole, was good, with occasional falls of snow and one blizzard in January. Our men, not having been in Gallipoli, did not arrive in khaki drill.

Training, with a few field days, broke the monotony of digging, and retained the smartness of the battalion. As an exercise the brigade sometimes attacked the trenches they had been digging. An amusing test was made one evening in February, when twenty-five of our men, in skeleton marching order and with fixed bayonets, were pursued from the front line to the support line by other twenty-five of our men in greatcoats : the object of this strange competition was to test the efficacy of searchlights ! That same day, the 8th February, is also noted as the commencement of the regular occupation of the front line they had been constructing by three platoons, acting as an inlying picket.

All this work, carried on through the winter, was consequent to an order to transform Salonika into an entrenched camp. The line Topshin–Dogandzi–Daudli was entrusted to the French ; Daudli–Lakes of Langaza and Bezik–Rendina Gorge to the sea was given to the British. All the advanced positions held by British and French troops were now in Greek territory, as the whole of Serbia, including Monastir, was in the hands of the enemy.

The general situation was fantastic. Lord Kitchener visited this front in December 1915, and wished to evacuate the whole place, where so many troops were being held to no purpose. Salonika itself was a hot-bed of intrigue and espionage, with enemy consuls, very properly, working for their own countries, and being helped in every way by the Greeks. The consuls were all arrested and the Salonika area was declared a war-zone. Diplomacy, in which General Sarrail was necessarily involved, became very active ; the General was nominally in supreme command of the Allied Force. The Greek Army, mobilised ostensibly to guard the frontier against German and Bulgarian aggression, was looked upon with mistrust and suspicion by the Allies, who sought to persuade the Greek Government to disband it. The suspicion was well founded, for when the Bulgars advanced into Greek territory during May 1916, the IV Greek Army Corps surrendered without a blow (with the exception of 2,000 men) and were marched off in friendly captivity.

About this time, the 9th May, Lieutenant-General G. H. Milne took over command of the British Salonika Army.

Our battalion moved from the Plough Sector on the 22nd May, halted for the night at Ambarkoj, just south of Kukus, on the 23rd, and so to Janes, where they commenced to work on the roads.

They moved again on the 8th June to Vaisili, sending three platoons of C Company and two of D Company to take over from the 260th French Regiment on some heights east of Deresfelo. They were off again on the 20th to Seremento, thence to Galiko Rest Camp, to Salamili Rest Camp, to a camp west of Akbunas on the 23rd.

From the 10th to the 27th July they took over the duties of the battalion at Army Headquarters (Kalamaria). It was now the full heat of summer, and all duties mounted without jackets or puttees, while packs were taken in limbers to the various guards. And then, having handed over to the 2nd Royal Irish Fusiliers, our battalion, in shorts and slouch hats, commenced to trek again—30th July, north of Table Hill; 31st, Galiko River (return of strength shows 29 officers, 754 other ranks); 1st August, two miles north of Sarigol; 3rd, to Jenikoj (joined rest of brigade). Steel helmets were issued on the 7th, and on the 10th the battalion worked on trenches at Pivoines; they rejoined the brigade on the 27th and marched to Orco Vica.

On the 7th September they relieved the 7th South Wales Borderers in the line in Sector 4.

Doiran Operations, 1916.

The supreme command wielded by General Sarrail was not of a united force : we are told that he never exercised that absolute authority which is an indispensable condition of success ; he was said to have a taste for petty political intrigue. In August 1916 he commanded, besides the French and British contingents, a resurrected Serbian Army of 120,000 ; some 10,000 Russians, who had arrived in July ; and an Italian division which had just landed (30,000). It was a considerable force, and as Rumania had now decided to throw in her lot with the Allies, an offensive was in preparation.

The movements of the British Army from the time of his assumption of command are detailed in General Milne's despatch : " . . . I entered into an agreement with General Sarrail by which the British Force should become responsible for that portion of the Allied Front which covered Salonika from the east and north-east. . . . On the 8th June troops commenced to occupy advanced positions along the right bank of the River Struma and its tributary the River Butkova, from Lake Tahinos to Lozista village. By the end of July, on the demobilisation of the Greek Army, this occupation had extended to the sea at Cajagzi. . . . On the 20th July I began to take over the line south and west of Lake Doiran and commenced preparations for a joint offensive on this front. . . . On the 10th of that month [August] an offensive was commenced against the Bulgarian defences south of the line Doiran–Hill 535. The French captured Hills 227 and La Tortue, while the British occupied in succession those features of the main 535 Ridge now known as Kidney Hill and Horseshoe Hill and, pushing forward, established a series of advanced posts in the line Doldzeli–Reselli. . . .[1]

" As a result of these operations it became possible to shorten considerably the Allied line between Doiran Lake and the River Vardar, and on the 29th August . . . I extended my front as far as the left bank of the river, . . . the position then held extending from Hill 420 to the Vardar River just north of Smol. . . .

" On the 17th August the Bulgarians, who at the end of May had entered Greek territory by the Struma Valley and moved down as far as Demirhisar, continued their advance into Greek Macedonia, . . . unopposed by the Greek garrison, and it was estimated by the end of August the enemy's forces, extending from Demirhisar southwards in the Seres sector of the Struma front, comprised the complete 7th Bulgarian Division with two or three regiments of the 11th Macedonian Division. . . . Opposite the Lower Struma was a brigade of the 2nd Division, with a brigade of the 10th Division in occupation of the coast and the zone of country between Orfano and the Drama–Kavala road. . . . As a result of this advance and of a similar move in the west, General Sarrail decided to entrust to the British Army the task of maintaining the greater portion of the right and centre of the Allied line.

" On the 10th September detachments crossed the river above Lake Tahinos at five places between Bajraktar Mah and Drajos, while a sixth detachment crossed lower down at Neohori. The villages of Oraoman and Kato Gudeli were occupied, and the Northumberland Fusiliers captured Nevoljan. . . .

" On the 15th similar operations were undertaken, six small columns crossing the river between Lake Tahinos and Orljak Bridge . . . villages . . . were burned. On the 23rd a similar scheme was put into action."

Our battalion went into the front line just before these raids on the

---

[1] On the 31st July the dispositions of the British Army were as follows : 80th Brigade, mouth of the Struma and Neohori ; 27th Divisional Cavalry, Krusoves ; 7th Mounted Brigade, from the sea to the area of Orljak ; 28th Division, Orljak to Lozista ; one battalion of 85th Brigade, Petkovo ; 28th Division Cavalry, guarding Lozista Radile, point of junction with the French 57th Division ; 22nd Division, Hirsova area ; 26th Division, Vergetor area ; 27th Division, less one brigade, Hortiach ; 10th Division, less one brigade, Dremiglava ; one brigade 10th Division, on the Salonika–Seres road (kilos 22–36) ; Headquarters, XII Corps, Kirec.

Struma front started—on the 7th. They were on the Doiran-River Vardar front. Here " there remained, as before, the whole of the Bulgarian 9th Division, less one regiment, a brigade of the 2nd Division, and at least two-thirds of the German 101st Division, which had entrenched the salient north of Macukovo on the usual German system. . . . I ordered the salient to be attacked at the same time as the Allied operations in the Forina area commenced." (General Milne.)

ACTION OF MACUKOVO, 13TH–14TH SEPTEMBER.

AREA : BETWEEN THE SELIMLI DERE AND RIVER VARDAR.

Macukovo was opposite our battalion ; " No Man's Land " was an extensive tract ; the salient, entrenched in the German fashion, lay some way beyond Macukovo ; knowledge of the ground was essential. Immediately on taking over, a patrol from our battalion was sent out, but returned without meeting any of the enemy.

In the morning it was seen that the enemy's position gave them observation over all our advanced works, but good scouts, working in pairs, could pass to the north of our line by day. The enemy works to be attacked were on a narrow, steep-sided spur, the southern slopes being intersected by ravines running into Macukovo village—the Y Ravine and Macukovo Ravine were found to be choked with brambles. The point of the enemy salient, Piton des Mitrailleuses, was on an outcrop of rock separated from the Dorsal by a slight dip ; the whole work, in which there were many dugouts cut into the solid rock, was protected by two belts of wire from 10 to 20 feet in width. In itself it was a strong position, and, as was afterwards made clear to everybody, was supported by the works called the Dome, Petit Clou, and Jumeau, from which enfilade fire could be brought to bear.

On the 9th, Lieutenant W. S. B. Walker and 2nd Lieutenant Lewis of the South Wales Borderers, with 12 of our men, went out at night to the west of Macukovo, but could not get to the village owing to the presence of enemy patrols. They managed, however, to reconnoitre the Piton de l'Eglise thoroughly. East of the village Lieutenant John penetrated into Y Ravine.

The next night Captain Spooner, Lieutenant Farrant, and 25 men again went to the outskirts of the village without seeing any sign of the enemy. On the 12th Major Bruce took a patrol right through the village.

These patrols gained some knowledge of the ground at least half-way to the point of attack. The orders were to attack the Dorsal from the south-east and, if the wire was cut, to advance on the Piton des Mitrailleuses from the south ; but if the wire was not cut, only the Dorsal was to be assaulted and bombers would work down into the Mitrailleuses. The intention was to hold the position and link it up with our main line of defence.

Two Groups, A, consisting of the 14th King's Liverpool Regiment, half-section of the 65th Machine-gun Company, and 1 section of the 99th Field Company, and B, consisting of the 12th Lancashire Fusiliers and similar attachments, were to carry out the assault. Two flank guards were detailed, on the right the 9th East Lancashire Regiment, on the left the Royal Welch, each with a half-section of machine guns and a section of the 127th Field Company.

On the night of the 12th/13th our battalion moved into what was known as the Ravin des Cuisiniers.

There was no surprise about this operation. The wire-cutting batteries commenced to fire at 7 a.m. and continued until 5 p.m. It was then seen that the steep slope of the Mitrailleuses had had some effect on the fire and the wire was not cut, but that a good wide gap had been cut on the south-east face of the Dorsal.

Our battalion had now taken over the works A 11 to A 14, and the two assaulting groups had gone into the Ravin des Cuisiniers.

It was a notable occasion : the first attack in which our battalion took part—the first attack of the 22nd Division ! Major-General Gordon spoke to the assaulting groups, and addressed to the Royal Welch the following letter :

" Royal Welch Fusiliers !

" You will be called upon to perform a most important operation to-morrow evening. You will be sure to meet the enemy (there are Germans opposed to us). I trust that you will show that you can deal with Germans in the same effective manner as Welshmen have been doing in France ever since August 1914.

" You must keep your presence of mind when the fight is warm. Do not fire wildly—aim low and fire slow.

" It rejoices the enemy to hear rifle ammunition being blazed off into the darkness high above his head. Look out for the enemy's counter-attacks—they will certainly be delivered against your battalion. You are properly placed to repel them. Watch your flanks—keep constant touch. If rifle fire and bombing do not stop the enemy, a bayonet charge will certainly do so. Our enemy has courage of a brutal sort, but experience proves that they shrink from facing a British soldier who is prepared to use his bayonet with effect. From my heart I wish the Royal Welch

Fusiliers Godspeed in their important work, upon the success of which much depends.

" Finally, as a commander and a friend of all ranks, I urge upon each and all the pressing necessity to bear in mind the stern nature of the duty you are about to undertake.

" I am well aware that among my battalions there are men of various Churches and forms of religious beliefs, but two years of unceasing war have to a great extent blotted out points where men differ as to religion, and the vital points common to all religions stand out as alone of eternal importance : the existence of God who loves all men ; His Son and Saviour who died for us.

" Let us all pray that our sins may be forgiven and commit our cause into God's hands.   Then we may safely go to battle hopeful of victory.

" God bless you all.

" From your General and comrade,

" FREDERICK GORDON."

At 7.30 p.m. on the 13th Brigadier-General Herbert, who was in command of the operation, gave the order to advance, and the assaulting groups began to move forward through gaps in our wire which had been opened after dark.   On the left flank Captain Spooner led our scouts forward, and behind them came a screen of infantry.   All men were in " skeleton " marching order, with rolled capes ; excepting the scouts, they each carried two extra bandoliers, two bombs, six sandbags, and either pick, shovel, or wire.

The scouts reported Macukovo and Piton des 4 Arbres clear of the enemy.   B Company took up a position in Bangor Ravine and Macukovo Ravine ; D Company in the north-west of the village about Piton de l'Eglise ; A Company continued the flank-line to the River Vardar ; C Company and Battalion Headquarters were in a ravine some 400 yards south-west of Piton de l'Eglise.   All companies were in position by 9.30 p.m., and D and A commenced to entrench and wire while C carried up material for them.

The assaulting groups reached the position of assembly to the east of the village at 10 p.m., and sent patrols to examine the enemy's wire.   On the right the 9th East Lancashire came in contact with a strong enemy patrol, which they dispersed by fire.

Everyone then waited in the darkness, which was suddenly cut by a searchlight in the German lines sending its beam across 4 Arbres to the river.

When the patrols returned, they reported gaps to a satisfactory extent except on the south face of the Mitrailleuses, where the wire was not sufficiently cut to warrant an attack at that point. But they also reported that the enemy appeared to have manned his trenches in some strength.

All information was passed back to Divisional Headquarters, and General Gordon approved the order to attack. The assaulting groups then moved forward to positions of deployment, and at 1.55 a.m. were a hundred yards from the German wire.

The artillery (two 18-pdr. batteries) were still firing on the enemy trenches, and the arrangement was that they should lift clear of the Dorsal and Mitrailleuses on the word either by telephone and at the same time a series of dashes from several signal lamps, or as an alternative, the firing of red Verey lights. The first signal was only received by one battery, and there was an unpleasant delay until Verey lights were fired: all fire then ceased.

The assault was delivered at 2.10 a.m. and the Dorsal was taken by the 14th King's Liverpool Regiment with little opposition. The Mitrailleuses gave more trouble to the 12th Lancashire Fusiliers, but Brigadier-General Herbert was able to report the whole of the position captured at 2.40 a.m.

As the assault was delivered the whole of B Company of our battalion moved into Cardiff Ravine.

Everything, so far, was quite successful. Most of the German troops holding the work retired into the deep dugouts on the northern slopes of the spur and were either captured or bombed; a few escaped over the hill.

The consolidation of the captured position then proceeded without interruption from the enemy, whose protecting barrage fell across the north-east of Macukovo, through l'Eglise to the river, and our troops were able to walk freely across the crest of the spur.

About 8 a.m., however, the enemy turned his artillery on the whole of the Dorsal-Mitrailleuses system. The shelling continued all day. Our B Company remained in Cardiff Ravine, but A and D Companies, leaving a few posts in the trenches they had dug, withdrew behind l'Eglise and into the Headquarters Ravine.

The situation commenced to alter. The enemy's batteries raked the Dorsal position and increasing casualties caused the Right Group to dribble back over the crest of the spur. Seeing this, the German bombers advanced from the Dome and the Ravin des Muriers, and a bombing fight continued for some hours. Communication by telephone was continually cut, and the enemy infantry pressed with increasing persistence.

At 2 p.m. a counter-attack in strength launched from the Dome and Petit Clou drove the King's Liverpool down the southern slopes of the spur.

This enemy success on the right opened the way to an attack on the Lancashire Fusiliers, and at 3 p.m. our B Company reported that the enemy had gained a footing in the Mitrailleuses.

Major Dumbell had promptly ordered Lieutenant John with a platoon

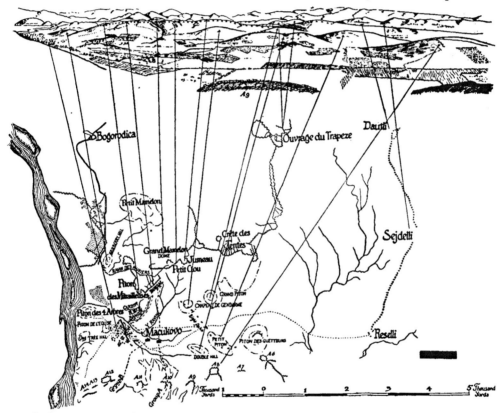

and the company bombers to support the Lancashire Fusiliers, and under the impetus given by this party the enemy was driven out of the Mitrailleuses; but it was only a temporary success.

Bulgarian infantry was now reinforcing the Germans; the enemy were making a desperate effort to regain the lost salient, and fresh troops were seen advancing towards Mulberry Hill. A lot of confused fighting followed, during which one of our men with a broken leg was cut off by a party of German bombers, but was rescued by Private Roberts, who had to carry him over a rocky spur under the excited fire of the enemy : it was a miraculous rescue.

The end was, however, approaching. At 4.30 p.m. Brigadier-General Herbert informed General Gordon that the whole spur was enfiladed from the Dome and Petit Clou, and " was the target for the concentrated fire of the enemy's artillery," and that " the British and French counter-batteries had been unable to cause any appreciable diminution in its volume." He said that his two battalions holding the south side of the crest were in a precarious position, had suffered many casualties, and were worn out with continuous close fighting. He proposed to withdraw at dusk, and General Gordon agreed.

All the wounded, together with the German prisoners, were sent back. At 6 p.m. Lieutenant John returned to B Company and reported that the Lancashire Fusiliers had withdrawn. Our Battalion (B, D, C, and A Companies) followed, and by 10 o'clock all were behind our own wire.

In view of the intention to hold the captured line and include it in our own system, the operation was not a success.   Like so many of these minor operations, it showed that we could capture a position, but that the attacking troops would be blown out of it by concentrated artillery fire.

The captured Germans, 71 in number, were of the 59th Regiment, and a few of the machine gunners were of the 230th Regiment.

Our battalion casualties were : 1 other rank killed ; Captain Spooner and 3 other ranks died of wounds ; Lieutenant W. S. B. Walker and 20 other ranks wounded.

.   .   .   .

In the intervals of holding the line our battalion worked on improving and erecting wire entanglements, and on preparing winter quarters at Glen Smol Camp. While in the line, patrolling was carried out regularly with few incidents.   One fighting patrol of 6 officers and 120 men, under Captain H. R. Curtis, was sent on the 4th November with the deliberate purpose of attacking advanced enemy posts in the Cardiff Ravine and Piton des 4 Arbres, and " inflicting loss." No surprise was effected, and they found the enemy waiting for them behind a bank. Captain Curtis extricated his command from the nasty position with the loss of only 6 men.

Winter was approaching.

SITUATION, AUTUMN 1916.

The fighting during the autumn fell mostly on the Serbs. The First Serbian Army was holding the line between Majadag and Kupa with the Moravian Division and with the Vardar Division in reserve at Topshin ;

the Second Army was holding from the river side Dere–Kovil–Pozar–Rodivo with the Shumadiya Division, and the Timok Division was in the Sendil–Necekli area ; the Third Army had the Danube Division in the line from Gornicevo–Banica–Leskovec with detached elements westwards, one battalion at Florina, two battalions operating in the area between north-west of Florina and Prespa Lake, and volunteer battalions were still farther westwards near Goritza, and two brigades at Vlodova ; the Cavalry Division, about 3,000 strong, was being converted into infantry and was in the Seres area, east of Salonika.

On the 18th August the Bulgars attacked the left flank of the Allies in considerable force. The Serbs met the attack and were driven back, the Bulgars occupying Florina, and the Serbs retiring to a line between Petersko and Ostrovo Lakes.

On the 21st the Serbian left flank was seriously threatened and they shortened their line, with their left flank resting on the west edge of Ostrovo Lake. After that the Serbs held.

On the 29th August Rumania declared war on Austria. On the 30th some of the Greek Army and Gendarmerie joined the Allies.

Rumania was very soon in trouble, and an Allied offensive was commenced on the 12th September along the whole front covered by the First and Third Serb Armies, French and Russian troops taking part in it. Progress was made, but the fighting was heavy.

On the 9th October Turkish troops were reported opposite the mouth of the Struma.

The 12th, 13th, and 14th November were days of severe fighting for the Serbs. Monastir was recaptured on the 19th.

On the 29th November the 35th Italian Division was relieved by the 83rd Brigade (28th Division) and the 68th Brigade (22nd Division). The British then held a continuous line from the River Vardar to the sea.

Still, the fighting on the Serbian Army front continued well into December, but with little more result. Incidentally there was a good deal of inter-Allied squabbling during, and as a result of, this offensive.

About the middle of December the British 60th Division arrived at Salonika.

·   ·   ·   ·   ·   ·   ·

The winter passed. There was a good deal of snow, occasionally blizzards. Our battalion remained in the line with periodic rests at Glen Smol. In January the strength of the battalion was 35 officers and 974 other ranks.

RAID ON THE MITRAILLEUSES.

Towards the end of January it was suspected that the German 59th Regiment had been relieved by Bulgars, and the Commander-in-Chief ordered the 67th Brigade to secure prisoners and confirm the report.

The task was given to our battalion.

Patrolling by the enemy had always been active, although he afforded no opportunities for the taking of prisoners, and the order to our patrols to close with the enemy whenever met gave no result. A sharp interchange of rifle fire occurred on the night 2nd/3rd February, but our patrol was too weak and was compelled to retire. Subsequently patrols were strengthened, but the enemy was aware of his peril and twice drew our pursuing troops into a barrage which inflicted loss and enabled him to escape.

It was decided to raid. A scheme for a surprise raid, without artillery support, was discussed, but an examination of the enemy's wire showed that it was not possible. The decision was therefore made to bombard the Mitrailleuses, Dorsal, and the Nose for three days, to cut the wire on the third day in front of all three places, and after feint attacks on the Dorsal and the Nose to enter the Mitrailleuses.

The heavy rain and severe frosts had cut up the roads, and large fatigue parties were required to repair them for the regrouping of artillery. All guns were in the required positions by the 17th February, when the bombardment opened.

The 18-pdr. wire-cutting batteries commenced their task on the 19th. The light was poor, and, in spite of good shooting and the expenditure of much ammunition, the wire proved obstinate. At 3 p.m. there was no gap at any point, and the Brigadier asked for the raid to be postponed. But that night a further bombardment—during which patrols went up to the wire and fired Verey lights and the artillery " lifted "—drew heavy artillery barrage fire from the enemy.

On the 20th the wire cutting by 18-pdrs. and 4·5 howitzers continued. The belt was smashed and rolled into heaps so successfully that at 3 p.m. the gaps were found to be sufficient for the raid.

At 7.45 p.m. the feint raids, with bombardment and " lift " signals, were repeated, but drew nothing from the enemy beyond beams from his searchlights. Our artillery, however, continued to fire short bursts on the three gaps until 10 p.m.

Some 200 men took part in the raid, which was under the command of Captain J. W. McKill. These were divided into two search parties, under

Captain D. S. Gibbon and Lieutenant J. L. W. Craig, four " blocking " parties, and a left flank guard. The 8th South Wales Borderers provided a right flank guard and a demonstration party.

Our left flank guard of 75 men, under Lieutenant T. E. Evans, started from our lines at 8.30 p.m. and were in position by 10 o'clock. The raiding party started at 9 p.m. The enemy were apparently nervous—they sent up Verey lights and their searchlights played over " No Man's Land." The party reached Bangor Ravine.

Captain McKill says : " The searchlights and Verey lights were very troublesome. Having reached the point where Bangor Ravine bends round to the east, we crossed over the open to the eastern branch of Cardiff Ravine. There were people talking in a listening-post outside the wire. We endeavoured to get the people in the listening-post, but failed to do so. I have no doubt about this post being occupied, as I heard them talking ; presumably they went back to their own trenches when they heard us. We again advanced until we got out of the ravine, and then halted.

" I sent up one man to find the wire, and on his return sent up four to examine it. We found that we were about 100 yards south of the wire. This would be about 0030 or 0040 hrs. I at once began to get the lamp signal going. One lamp threw a very faint light, the other was all right, but to get the bearing of M 4 was very difficult ; both Lieutenant Goulder, R.F.A., and myself worked at it. After trying the lamp for ten or fifteen minutes I got a green Verey light from Lieutenant Goulder, and we fired off the arranged signal together. [*This was the emergency signal.*]

" The artillery reply to our signal was very smart, the first shells being over before the Verey light went out. Under the artillery fire we crawled up to the wire and got through the opening of both belts of wire ; the gap appeared to be about 10 or 12 yards wide. On our right was a huge mass of tangled wire 10 to 12 feet high. We lay down in this opening until our guns lifted off the front-line trench, when we immediately rushed into the trench ; it was at once seen to be well filled with men, in fact to contain a strong garrison. Our men were at hand-grips with them at once ; some, refusing to surrender, were bayoneted, others were seized and hauled out by the raiding parties. As soon as the prisoners were well clear of the wire I blew the signal to retire. The prisoners were secured under five minutes.

" The ground we were on was like a ploughed field ; I cannot speak as to the state of the trench. There was no firing on our part and no bombs were thrown, as far as I could observe from my position.

" The ' retire ' being repeated, all the raiding and blocking parties

IV—14

rushed out of the trench, making for the eastern branch of Cardiff Ravine, except Sergeant Hedley, who was in charge of our right local protection. When he had been recalled, we all rushed for Bangor Ravine, which we struck about 150 yards up from the road.

" When we were north of Macukovo, near the two cottages behind the yellow house, Lieutenant Goulder and myself put up two white Verey lights towards the enemy lines as the signal for the flankers to withdraw. All the way through Macukovo we had a lot of rifle fire on us and could see shells falling to the Y Ravine end of the village. Shells fell about the yellow house and to the west after we had passed. We were all right from the white house.

" From my observation of the party with me I remarked specially Captain D. S. Gibbon, Lieutenant Farrant, and also Lieutenant Goulder, R.F.A.

" The last I saw of Lieutenant Craig was when I was getting Sergeant Hedley recalled. He was bounding down towards Cardiff Ravine and did not appear to be wounded. He called out to me as he was passing, ' Hello, Mac ! '—he had passed me before I retired."

When the party returned, it was found that two officers—Lieutenants Chassereau and Craig—were missing. Lieutenant Chassereau was a Sapper who had done excellent work widening the gap in the wire by means of Bangalore torpedoes. 2nd Lieutenant S. L. L. Brunicardi and 32 other ranks went out to find them. They discovered Lieutenant Chassereau wounded in Macukovo, but they could not find Lieutenant Craig, who was afterwards reported wounded and a prisoner.

Our total casualties were 3 officers and 16 other ranks wounded.

Other officers who took part in this raid and did well, where all did well, were Lieutenants G. Y. S. Farrant, 2nd Lieutenants D. J. Meecham, J. H. Gannon, W. A. Pickard, E. S. Brown.

The prisoners were all of the 59th German Regiment.

.   .   .   .

The weather began to improve and the Higher Command thought of offensives. A plan was put in preparation for an attack by the XII Corps west of Lake Doiran with the Doiran–Krastali road as first objective. The 60th Division was to take over from the 22nd Division, and the 22nd and 26th Divisions were to carry out the attack from Doiran to Hill 380. The Corps artillery was made up to nine 60-pdr., four 6-inch guns, and seven 6-inch howitzer batteries for this offensive.

The enemy also commenced to move. From the 18th to the 20th March the XII Corps front was subjected to a heavy bombardment with gas shells, phosgene, and lachrymatory. Our battalion came under this unpleasant bombardment on the 19th, and lost 4 men killed, 3 wounded, and 18 slightly gassed.

Another meeting with the enemy took place in " No Man's Land " on the 27th March. It had been a fine day, but as night fell it began to rain and the night was very dark. The usual patrol, with Lieutenants T. E. Evans and S. S. Jones Savin and 2nd Lieutenant T. Rowlands, went out to reconnoitre and occupy the Piton de l'Eglise. They had reached One Tree Hill Ravine when they were joined by a patrol of the 2/19th London Regiment (60th Division), who, under two guides from our battalion, were making for 4 Arbres.

The London Regiment patrol was put on its way, and Lieutenant Evans led his patrol towards the Piton de l'Eglise. Advancing by bounds, he detailed Lieutenant Jones Savin and 7 men to make good the cottages on the south-west corner of Macukovo village. But before Jones Savin had gone far, a noise of many men moving was heard ; suddenly the enemy was revealed to front, right, and left—a strong patrol was advancing in horseshoe formation and the whole of our patrol was inside its horns.

A burst of rifle fire and machine-gun fire from the cottages discovered to Jones Savin the peril he was in ; he tried to rejoin the main patrol, but was instantly killed and most of his men were wounded.

Lieutenant Evans and his party retired hastily, but halted some 70 to 100 yards away to wait for wounded.

The heavy firing brought the London Regiment patrol back, and their appearance caused some of the enemy to move, as about 20 were seen scampering away in the darkness.

Casualties were then found to be 2 officers and 2 men missing and 10 men wounded.

The firing died down, and a relief patrol under 2nd Lieutenants W. A. Pickard, H. A. Allison, and D. J. Meecham arrived to take over. The evacuation of the wounded and the recharging of Lewis-gun magazines took some time in the dark, but all this was eventually done and the first patrol withdrew.

Meecham then went forward with a small party and soon reported finding five enemy dead. Pickard told him to continue his search and bring in all papers found on the bodies.

Pickard then left Allison in charge of the main body of the patrol, and with 12 men proceeded to complete the reconnaissance of the Piton de l'Eglise. He soon came across the body of Jones Savin, and at the same time the enemy appeared. He opened fire, upon which Allison brought up the main body of the patrol, and the enemy vanished.

Unfortunately Meecham, on the outburst of firing, had also attempted to join Pickard, and was killed while crossing the sunken road.

Dawn was now breaking, and Pickard, taking with him the body of Jones Savin, withdrew his patrol.

Meecham, Rowlands, and one man were missing, so Lieutenant J. O. Williams and a party of scouts went out to search for them. They recovered Meecham's body, and found traces on the ground that led them to believe that Rowlands had been hit and made prisoner. The enemy had evidently searched the ground thoroughly before our scouts arrived, and had removed their dead and wounded, but the ground was littered with German bombs, and the scouts also found heaps of them dumped for use.

The result of the encounter was distressing : 2 officers killed, 1 missing and prisoner of war, 1 other rank missing, and 13 wounded.

Lieutenant-Colonel Yatman rejoined the battalion from leave on the 30th March, and relieved Major G. W. G. Lindesay, who had been in command since the 24th February. On the 2nd April the 181st Brigade (60th Division) took over from the 67th Brigade, who in turn relieved the 77th Brigade in Corps Reserve at Galavanci.

BATTLE OF DOIRAN

24TH–25TH APRIL AND 8TH–9TH MAY 1917. AREA : BETWEEN DOIRAN–KARASULI RAILWAY AND THE RIVER VARDAR.

The 60th Division had now been introduced on the left of the Corps front, between the 22nd Division and the River Vardar. On the 21st April the bombardment for the planned attack, together with a general Allied offensive, commenced, and the infantry assaulted on the 24th. The enemy's trenches were entered along the whole XII Corps line, but the 26th Division was eventually forced back to its original line ; the 22nd Division retained the positions won.

On the Salonika front there had been no movement at all since the capture of Monastir, and the enemy was well dug in. On the British front to the east of Lake Doiran, or what was called the Struma front, the opposing lines were widely separated ; west of Lake Doiran, on the XII Corps front, they were in places quite close together. As so frequently happened, the positions we occupied were overlooked by the enemy, who held great blocks of hills like the Grande and Petite Couronnes, and west of them what were known as the P Ridges. On these superior heights dugouts had been bored out of the solid rock, and everywhere the enemy had excellent cover.

The most commanding position we held had the descriptive name of

La Tortue, which was separated from the Petite Couronne by the Ravin des Jumeaux, but it was dominated by the Grande Couronne on the right (near Lake Doiran) and the P Ridges on the left.

In the April attack the positions on the Grande and Petite Couronnes proved too strong for us. Our losses were heavy.

But on the left an advance had been made and retained. Our battalion returned from Corps Reserve as the last enemy counter-attack was repulsed on the 29th April and bivouacked in Shelter Ravine ; the next day they took over Kidney Hill (A, C, and D) and Clichy Ravine (B).

On the night 8th/9th May, at 9.50 p.m., the XII Corps attacked selected portions of the front : the attack of the 22nd and 60th Divisions was successful to a depth of some 500 yards, but again the 26th Division on the right, after entering the enemy trenches, were withdrawn, after suffering heavy casualties.

On the whole General Sarrail's offensive of the spring in 1917 was not a success, and it was followed by a long period empty of action.

On account of ill-health General Gordon was compelled to hand over his command at this time (7th May) to Brigadier-General J. Duncan. And in June the Corps lost the 60th Division, and soon after the 10th, both going to Egypt.

The 22nd Division then held from Lake Doiran to Mamelon Vert (exclusive).

·   ·   ·   ·   ·   ·   ·

In a political sense the Salonika expedition was extremely active from June 1916 to June 1917.

On the 21st June 1916 the Allied Governments sent a note to Greece demanding the demobilisation of her Armies and a change of Government. King Constantine agreed, but did not carry out the demand in spirit or letter.

If Rumanian intervention in the War had any effect on Greece, it soon evaporated ; active Rumanian support of the Allies was crushed, and within a year nothing at all was left.

In September 1916 M. Venizelos formed a Provisional Government in Crete, which was to act in opposition to the Government in Athens, and on the 23rd October this Provisional Government, having moved to Salonika, declared war on Germany and Bulgaria. It was war without any troops ; but although the Greek nation, as a whole, did not wish to fight, Venizelos had strong support in the country. He set to work to raise an army.

By the middle of November the first Greek Regiment was in the field. By way of encouragement to M. Venizelos, the Allied Governments then demanded of the Athens Government that the Ministers of the Central Powers be removed from Greek territory, also the surrender of war material.

Naturally enough the situation was a difficult one for the Allied Powers, and naturally enough the Greeks resented their action. The Allies made a demonstration of force at Athens and some 200 French soldiers were ambushed and killed. This tragedy made the situation still more difficult ; there was nothing for it but another ultimatum demanding the withdrawal of all Greek troops from Thessaly—which the Athens Government accepted.

The Athens Government then issued a warrant for the arrest of M. Venizelos on a charge of high treason, and we countered by recognising the Venizelos Government. But no definite steps were taken to put an end to the impossible position until the 28th May 1917, when an Anglo-French Conference in London came to a decision to depose King Constantine. A demand for the abdication of the King was presented to the Athens Government on the 11th June ; and M. Jonnart, a former Governor-General of Algeria, was given the powers of High Commissioner for the Allies.

M. Jonnart acted swiftly. Troops and ships commenced to move, and under the threat of naval guns and the landing of French and Russian troops (British troops were already at Corinth) the King abdicated the throne in favour of his second son, Prince Alexander.

M. Venizelos assumed power at Athens on the 27th June, and the declaration of war made by the Provisional Government became effective for the whole of Greece. By this time the Provisional Government had managed to put three divisions, known as the National Defence Army Corps, into the field. The Provisional Government was at an end.

The task of reorganising the Greek Army and hunting out the supporters of the pro-German ex-King was now undertaken by the French—a work of some magnitude. A Greek Army that served a useful purpose gradually came into being.

But a further complication in the turmoil of the War had already arisen with the Russian Revolution, which commenced on the 12th March : the Tsar abdicated on the 15th.

.   .   .   .

All through the heat of the summer our battalion took its turn in the front line, and worked on the defences and roads. On the 16th August they went back into Corps Reserve at Chaîne Tehomis. The strength of the battalion was then 15 officers and 704 other ranks.

They relieved the 9th King's Own Regiment in the left subsector on the 3rd September ; 7th October saw them once more in Corps Reserve at

Cuguinci; on the 9th November they relieved the 7th South Wales Borderers in the right sector.

On the 21st December General Guillaumat took over command of the Allied Forces from General Sarrail.

All action was at a standstill during the bitter winter months. Patrols went out in the snow in white overalls, but there was no clash with the enemy until the month of May.

RAID ON O 2, 6TH MAY 1918.

Enemy artillery commenced to be active in May. A raid on his front line—a portion known as O 2—was already in preparation. The idea was that the defensive belts of wire should be cut by the artillery on the 6th May, and the trenches and dugouts subjected to a bombardment. At dusk, harassing fire by the artillery, trench mortars, and machine guns was to be directed at intervals on the gaps that had been cut.

At 9.50 p.m. a bombardment of the enemy's front line would commence and lift after ten minutes, when Lieutenant Pickard and a party of 12 other ranks would " demonstrate " to make the enemy man his trenches. He was given five minutes to do this, and then every gun and trench mortar was to open on the front-line trench.

Normal harassing fire was then to continue until 11.15 p.m., when D Company, under Captain W. E. Whall (4 officers and 119 other ranks), would rush through the gaps in the wire, the artillery putting a " box barrage " round the position.

After a lapse of fifteen minutes a bugle call would be the signal to retire.

In the phraseology of the War, " all went according to plan." The raiding party formed up in front of Wylye Sap in columns of platoons in file, at about 30 yards' interval and 50 yards' distance, with three platoons in the front line and one in support.

Captain G. Y. S. Farrant commanded the left platoon and had as his objective a large dugout, which he hoped to destroy ; the centre platoon was under 2nd Lieutenant L. Davies ; the right platoon was under Lieutenant J. Bould, with a pill-box[1] as objective. The supporting platoon was under Captain Whall.

Two sappers were detailed to each of the flank platoons, and in addition seven men were allotted to the right platoon, each carrying a specially prepared box containing 15 lb. of guncotton, and four men to the left

---

[1] The name given to the concrete shelters which were, as a rule, machine-gun emplacements.

platoon carrying two Bangalore torpedoes, each charged with 121 lb. of ammonal.

A party of bombers was told off for the protection of the " demolition " parties.

The wire-cutting artillery had done their work well—the wire was found to be no obstacle—and the raiders advanced rapidly on their objectives. But they were at once seen by the enemy, who put down a barrage from batteries on the Piton Chauve and the lake side ; this was thickened by a heavy trench-mortar barrage. All this protective artillery fire was directed on the enemy's own trenches, and it continued throughout the operation.

The scene, viewed from a short distance, was weird. The enemy was sending up hundreds of Verey lights, and the beams from searchlights on the Piton Chauve hit the scene of the raid, making a great patch of light in the darkness which only revealed a whirling cloud of dust and smoke !

Captain Farrant, on the left, met with some opposition from a party of about fifteen Bulgars posted near the dugout ; five of these were bayoneted, and the remainder plunged down into the dugout, only to be followed by bombs. But the sappers with the Bangalore torpedoes, which were to be used for demolition, could not be found, although they were with Captain Farrant's platoon when they passed through the broken belt of wire. They had become casualties.

Captain Farrant looked at his watch and found that it was a minute past the time for withdrawal. Realising that something had occurred to prevent the bugle sounding the " retire," he passed the word for his platoon to withdraw.

The centre platoon, under 2nd Lieutenant Davies, met with no opposition. They took up a covering position and withdrew when ordered.

The right platoon, under Lieutenant Bould, surrounded the pill-box. Two Bulgars came out and one attempted to light a flare ; both were killed. Whether the pill-box was seriously damaged or not is, in the words of a subsequent report, " not clear, each survivor having a different account ; but it is certain that five out of the seven boxes of guncotton were stacked and exploded against the northern face of the structure. Captain Whall was present for a short time, and Private Evans, one of the carrying party, states that it was he who eventually gave instructions as to where to place the charge. A statement by Corporal Patterson, R.E., that they were interfered with by a party of Bulgars was not borne out by Private Evans, nor can it be reconciled with the general situation, for, besides Captain Whall, Lieutenant Bould and Sergeant Davidson are reported to have approached the pill-box at different times during the fifteen minutes that the party was at work, and neither saw nor heard any enemy. A trench-mortar shell bursting close to the pill-box just as the carrying party arrived, wounded five out of the 7 carriers."

Captain Whall unfortunately disappeared, and was reported wounded and missing. He was last seen going from the pill-box to the dugout, but he never arrived there. As he and his orderly were the only two persons carrying bugles, no signal of withdrawal was made.

On the return of the raiding party, their casualties were found to be : 1 officer missing, 3 officers wounded ; 9 other ranks missing and 60 wounded.

On the 11th May both sides mounted a sort of Chinese attack. At about 8.15 p.m. some shouting and the explosion of bombs were heard in the Bulgar lines, and a red light was fired which produced a heavy bombardment of our trenches. At midnight our battalion sent out three patrols to shout and fire rifle grenades. Immediately red lights were fired all along the enemy front and a heavy barrage was put down. The searchlights were active from Piton Chauve and Kohinoor.

The battalion then continued the even tenor of trench warfare through June and July, the only incident being that a post in Snake Ravine was bombed out of its position by a Bulgar patrol on the 2nd July. The enemy did not hold the post, which was reoccupied.

But the Salonika situation changed during these months. The great losses in France, caused by the German spring offensive, resulted in a general combing out of battalions from all fronts. Eight battalions were taken from the XII Corps, brigades were reduced to three battalions.

BATTLE OF DOIRAN

18TH–19TH SEPTEMBER 1918. AREA : DORA TEPE–DOIRAN–KARASULI
RAILWAY AND THE RIVER VARDAR.

On the other hand, French operations on the left of the front were successful during the month of June, and on the whole front desertions from the enemy commenced to grow in number. On the British front, in the Struma Valley, they were more numerous than elsewhere. All the deserters stated that the enemy intended to launch an attack on the 15th June, but that the Bulgar troops were in a state of mutiny and were reluctant to attack. These enemy schemes never came to anything.

On the 17th June General Franchet d'Esperey took command of the Allied Armies, replacing General Guillaumat.

On the left, French and Italians made important gains in July, and towards the end of July General d'Esperey issued instructions for the preparation of a general offensive to take place during the first fortnight in September. A general staff conference took place on the 12th August at British General Headquarters, and the plan, which was that the Serbs and French were to break through in the centre, was discussed. The rôle assigned to the British was to attack the formidable heights on the Doiran sector, with a view to holding the Bulgars there. The main attack on the British front was against the P Ridges and the neighbouring high ground, which included the Kohinoor and Grande Couronne. On the right the Cretan Division and the Seres Division of the Greek National Defence Corps were to carry out a holding attack.

The left, or chief British attack, was to be made by the 22nd Division, the 77th Brigade, and one regiment of the Seres Division ; the right attack was to be carried out by the Seres Division less one regiment, supported by the 83rd British Brigade less two battalions, and was to be launched against Doiran Hill, Teton Hill, and the Petite Couronne.

Training for the offensive was commenced. On the 18th August our battalion was in a new camp at Fly Nek, and did not return to the line until just before the attack.

It has been pointed out that the enemy positions were of exceptional strength ; they were tactically good, and after two and a half years the trenches and dugouts were perfect, and the thickness of wire entanglements exceptional. Added to the natural superiority and domination of the enemy lines, the country itself was difficult to cross, being much cut up with deep water-courses which had steep, rocky sides overgrown with bushes. The soil is sandy, and gets very dry in summer, with the result that a bombardment raised thick clouds of dust through which it was impossible to see.

The task before our battalion was no easy one.

As a further handicap to successful issue, the whole corps was visited by an epidemic of influenza ; and the exceptional heat of the summer (average shade temperature over 100 degrees) brought on malaria[1] and dysentery. The strength of battalions dwindled. Indeed, all conditions conspired to produce a gloomy view. It was quite clear that no reinforcements would be sent by British or French or Italians, for the Government opinion of each country was that nothing could be gained in Salonika. But as preparations were pushed forward the situation in the main Western Theatre, which had been

---

[1] Malaria was the great trouble throughout the campaign. As protection against mosquitoes sentries wore veils over face and hands, and moreover were smeared with an evil-smelling concoction which announced their presence long before they could be seen on an ordinary night. Malaria casualties put whole battalions out of action until the decision to abandon low ground during the summer was arrived at.

so depressing in the spring, improved ; the brilliant French counter-attack on the 18th July was followed by sweeping Allied victories in August ; and yet, even with such hopeful prospects of ultimate victory, the soldier in Macedonia might be forgiven for looking gloomily at the Couronne and P Ridges.

The Allied Forces now consisted of 8 French Divisions, with 2 cavalry regiments, and some odd unattached battalions ; one strong Italian division ; 6 Serbian divisions, and one cavalry division ; 10 Greek divisions ; and finally 4 British divisions. These units, however, were of different values, as we were already reduced to 9 battalions per division, as were the Serbians, Greeks, and all but 3 French divisions. The approximate strength in rifles was :

French	45,000
Greeks	40,000
British	32,000
Serbs	30,000
Italians	10,000

The total artillery was about 1,600 guns.

In his despatch General Milne writes that " it was now clear that the enemy suspected an impending attack, but did not know where the blow was to fall. His reserves were reported to be in the Vardar Valley. To prevent their withdrawal, and to deceive him as to the sector chosen for the main Allied attack, operations were begun on the afternoon of the 1st September, after heavy artillery preparation, against the rocky and strongly fortified salient north of Alcak Mahale, on the right bank of the Vardar. The troops engaged were the 2nd Battalion Gloucestershire Regiment, and the 10th Battalion Hampshire Regiment of the 27th Division. The undertaking proved an entire success. Not only were determined counter-attacks launched fruitlessly against our new trenches, but on the right the division was able to occupy the enemy's outpost line, thus gaining suitable positions for a further advance. With this operation and with the unhindered advance of the posts of the 1st Hellenic Corps in the Struma Valley about a week later, the preliminaries on the right section of the general offensive were completed.

" On the morning of the 14th September the general attack began. All along the 80-mile front from Lake Doiran to Monastir the artillery bombardment of the hostile positions became intense. Twenty-four hours later the Franco-Serbian troops, under the command of Voivode Mischitch, stormed the Bulgar trenches on the mountain heights from Sokol to Vetrenik. Before noon the enemy's first and second lines were in the possession of Allied troops. This initial victory forced a withdrawal on the flanks. The gap of 12 kilometres was enlarged to one of 25 kilometres. The way was open for an advance to the heights of Kozak.

" The success on which an assault on the Doiran sector was conditional had been attained. Early on the 15th September I received orders from General Franchet d'Esperey that the troops under my command were to attack on the morning of the 18th."

Meanwhile the enemy's positions from Doiran Lake to P Ridge were being heavily shelled, and his wire cut.

In his description of the position, General Milne says : " To an observer from the centre of the line from which the Allied attack was to take place, the medley of broken hills forming his position [Bulgar] baffles detailed description except at great length. There are steep hillsides and rounded hills. There is little soil. The hard rocky ground makes consolidation of a newly won position difficult, and gives overwhelming advantage to the defender, well dug into trenches that have been the careful work of three years. Deep-cut ravines divert progress and afford unlimited opportunity for enfilade fire. But in all the complexity of natural features the P Ridge and Grande Couronne stand out in conspicuous domination. The former, from a height of over 2,000 feet, slopes southward towards our lines, overlooking our trenches and the whole country south to Salonika. To its right the country dips and rises to a less sharp but no less intricate maze of hills, that mount, tier upon tier, from Petite Couronne with its steep and rugged sides, above Doiran Lake to Grande Couronne, itself little lower than the summit of P Ridge. The enemy had taken full advantage of his ground. He was strongly entrenched in three lines, with communicating trenches deeply cut into the rock, and roomy, well-timbered dugouts, with concrete machine-gun emplacements, and on the crest between P Ridge and Grande Couronne with concrete gun-pits. It was the key position of the Vardar–Doiran defences, and he held it with his best troops."

The Bulgar troops on the Doiran front were the 17th, 33rd, 34th, and 58th Regiments.

Operations were commenced on the morning of the 18th September. They were divided into a Right and Left Attack.

The Right Attack by the Seres Division (less the 3rd Infantry Regiment), supported by the British 83rd Infantry Brigade, and with the 2ème bis Régiment de Zouaves and 12th Corps Cavalry Regiment in reserve, was to advance over the Petite Couronne to the line Doiran Hill–Teton Hill and Hill 346, and to operate against the Orb, and finally seize the Grande Couronne in conjunction with the Left Attack.

The Left Attack, under the command of Major-General Duncan, was made by the 22nd Division (less the 65th Brigade in Army Reserve), the 77th Infantry Brigade, the 3rd Greek Regiment of the Seres Division, and the 65th and 67th Machine-gun Companies. The final objective was the line Grande Couronne–Kohinoor–P 2–Dolina.

These positions were protected by three lines of trenches known as the X, W, and T lines and, on the crest of the ridge west of Grande Couronne, a fourth line known as the Grand Shoulder–Kohinoor–P 2 line. The W and T lines were strongly entrenched, provided with bomb-proof shelters, and protected generally by three belts of wire : the lines were situated in terraces, one above the other.

What was called the P Ridge, on the left of our attack, was defended by strong works labelled P 4½, P 4, P 3, Dolina, and P 2.

The wire was cut on the 16th and 17th by howitzers assisted by 2-inch and 6-inch trench mortars, and, we are told, " was generally well cut and the attack was never held up by wire, but, owing to the fact that only two gaps could be cut on the front of each battalion, the wire added greatly to the difficulty of the infantry, which had to advance over a narrow front."

During the night 17th/18th harassing fire by 18-pdrs. and machine guns was kept up all night. From six and a half hours before the time of the assault the enemy's camps in the trench system and his battery positions were subjected to a gas bombardment. It must be noted that gas was used for the first time on the Macedonian front, but " its effect on both the enemy's infantry and artillery was far less than had been anticipated."

For two hours before the assault smoke shells and harassing fire were directed on the enemy's front system to hide the troops assembling, and to drown the noise of their movement ; but the night was fine, flooded with a full moon, and it was impossible to conceal the assembly.

The assaulting troops assembled in Shropshire and Jackson Ravines, about 450 yards from the enemy first line. The barrage was timed to start at 5.8 a.m. and the assault of the first line at 5.11 a.m.

Following the attack from the right, the Greek Seres Division captured Doiran Hill and Teton Hill at 6.10 a.m., and an hour and a half later were on Hill 340.

The 67th Brigade attacked with the three battalions in line—11th Royal Welch Fusiliers, 11th Welch Regiment, and 7th South Wales Borderers—with the O 6 work and trenches on the east slopes of Sugar Loaf as a first objective ; the Hilt, Knot, and Tassel as a second ; the Rockies and the west face of the Grande Couronne as the third.

B Company, commanded by Captain Stockdale, and D Company, commanded by Captain Bone, advanced against O 6, B advancing by Claw Ravine, and D by Snake Ravine.

B Company entered the trenches with little opposition at 5.18 a.m., but as they advanced against Dagger Ravine they were met by a strong counter-attack. Sharp and costly fighting followed, in which all the company officers became casualties ; but the company held and the enemy were driven back, about 30 prisoners and a trench mortar remaining in the company's hands. About 6.45 a.m. touch was obtained with Greek troops from the direction of Petite Couronne.

D Company had moved on the work up a more precipitous slope and met with considerable opposition which caused many casualties. All officers became casualties, but Private D. Roberts rallied the men and led them on towards the Hilt, which was being attacked by the remainder of the battalion.

A Company, under Captain Curtis and C Company, under Captain Jones, attacked the trench to the east of Sugar Loaf, and during their first advance came under heavy machine-gun fire from the Knot. The trench was rushed and the garrison destroyed. The two companies then swung right-handed across the Jumeaux, over the lower slopes of the Blade, and up to the wire protecting the Hilt ; here there was a pause to allow the barrage to lift, and also to reorganise, for the companies had run into our own gas and had been obliged to put on their masks.

At about 5.38 a.m. the advance was continued through the gap in the wire, but now the companies were being swept by machine-gun and trench-mortar fire from the upper Hilt, and suffered many casualties. The trenches were strongly held, and when all opposition was overcome, after heavy fighting, companies were reduced to half. All officers and all but two non-commissioned officers had become casualties, and the survivors were greatly exhausted through having to wear gas-masks. Counter-attacks came from the Knot Ravine, and finally the men gave way and fell back on the Doiran–Krastali road.

Back at Battalion Headquarters, Lieutenant-Colonel Yatman heard nothing definite. The first wounded men, returning from B Company about 6.30 a.m., had stated that the line had been occupied with little opposition, but that strong counter-attacks had started soon afterwards. No information of any kind was received on the situation at the Hilt, and the dust and smoke from trench-mortar and artillery fire were so thick nothing could be seen. The Commanding Officer decided to advance his Headquarters to the Doiran–Krastali track, only to meet, on arrival, a counter-attack delivered from the direction of O 6. The remnant of B Company, under Sergeant O. Roberts, was mixed up in this fight, and the enemy was finally beaten off.

Lieutenant-Colonel Yatman soon realised the extent of his casualties, and that he had an insufficient number of unwounded men to continue the advance, so he decided to hold the line from O 6 to the Doiran–Krastali

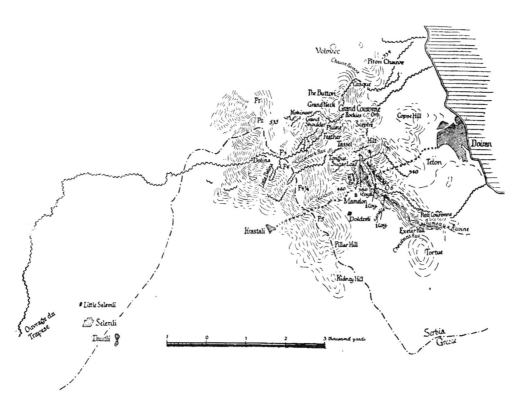

road, keeping in touch with the Greeks at Sabre Trench, and with the 11th Welch Regiment at Fang.

The 11th Welch Regiment had also been obliged to resort to gas-masks on account of our gas, and suffered some casualties in their advance to the east of Sugar Loaf, but they reached the Knot and Tassel, and a party got in touch with our battalion on the Hilt. At about 7.30 a.m. the Bulgars counter-attacked, and the Commanding Officer of the Welch, seeing that the Greeks were falling back, ordered a retirement to Shropshire Ravine, whence they had started. Later the Welch tried to reoccupy the Sugar Loaf, but were driven off by fire.

The 7th South Wales Borderers passed over the Sugar Loaf and Tongue trenches on to the lower slopes of the Feather, where they were joined by a considerable number of Greek troops, and continued their advance to the Rockies. But in the approach up the Feather machine-gun fire was opened on them from both flanks, and although a few reached the Rockies, casualties were too heavy for the men and the battalion fell back on the Tongue. Later they went back to the top of Shropshire Ravine.

The 3rd Greek Regiment reached the Warren, but machine-gun fire from the Grande Couronne and P Ridge caused heavy casualties, and a counter-attack from the Grand Ravine drove them out of the Bulgar main line. They gradually fell back to their position of assembly.

On P Ridge the 66th Brigade lost 65 per cent. of their strength. After gallant attempts against the fearful P defences, they fell back on their original position.

" At about 9 a.m.," says General Duncan, " I came to the conclusion that the attack had failed, and I informed the Corps Commander that I considered it would be useless waste of life to try to press the attack further."

But the Corps Commander ordered the attack to be resumed the next day, released the 65th Brigade from Reserve, and placed it with the 2ème bis Zouaves at the disposal of General Duncan.

The plan was for the 77th Brigade to attack the Grande Couronne and Plume works via the Knot–Tassel–Tongue works, keeping the Vladaja Ravine on their left ; the 2ème bis Zouaves were to capture the Corne and Warren, with the Vladaja Ravine on their right ; the 65th Brigade were to assault P 4¼ and P 4.

It was a disastrous day. The Zouaves, on their way to their position of assembly, came under light harassing fire along the road they were using ; this stopped them, and they never resumed their advance.

" As soon as I heard that there was some doubt whether the 2ème bis Zouaves had advanced, I telephoned to G.O.C. 77th Infantry Brigade that unless the French came up on their left they were not to advance beyond the line Knot–Tassel–Hilt, and informed Corps and Seres Division of my order.

" I also sent a message at 0500 hours from P 5 to the O.C. King's Own Royal Lancashire Regiment, who was 500 yards away and who was going to attack P 4¼ and P 4, that in consequence of the delay of the French the assault on P 4¼ was not to take place at 0535 hours as originally arranged, but

TYPICAL COUNTRY ON THE BALKAN FRONT. [*Crown Copyright.*

Roads were few and extremely bad. The difficulties in moving a great army over these hills will be appreciated.

[*Crown Copyright.*

DOIRAN. THE 22ND DIVISION ATTACKED OVER THESE HILLS.

at 0555 hours, and that the barrage would remain on until that hour, and that if by that time he found that the French were not advancing, he was not to attack P 4¼ at all.   Unfortunately this message did not reach the 9th King's Own until about 0600 hours.   The battalion, after waiting some minutes, advanced into our 18-pdr. barrage and had some casualties." (General Duncan.)

The attack again failed.   The total casualties in these operations were given as 155 officers and 3,710 other ranks in the British 22nd Division, including the 77th Brigade, and about 1,350 in the Greek Regiment.

Late in the night of the 19th September our battalion was relieved by a company of the Border Regiment and went back to Exeter Ravine.

The Pursuit to the Strumitza Valley, 22nd–30th September.

The British Army claimed that the two days' fighting had "administered a severe blow to the enemy on the most vital and best defended part of his front," and not only pinned down his reserves at a most critical period for him, but actually induced him on the second day to increase his strength on this front.   In spite of the heavy British and Greek losses, a greater number, it was estimated, had been suffered by the Bulgars—1,200 prisoners had been taken.   At all events, the Franco-Serb forces were advancing rapidly on the left.

On the 20th and 21st no infantry action took place on the Anglo-Greek front, but the air reports stated that there was great activity behind his front lines, and that dumps at Hudova station, Lestova, Furka, and Tatali were in flames !   The Kosturino–Strumitza road was densely packed with troops and transport, and was bombed and fired on by low-flying British aeroplanes all day on the 21st.

On the 22nd Division front patrols found the enemy gone, and his main line was in our possession without opposition on the morning of the 22nd.   The pursuit of the enemy was commenced, and by 1 p.m. British and Greek forces had reached the line Kara Oglular–Harzali–Paljorca to one mile south of Bogdanci.   Over 4,000 prisoners had been captured, and the retreating enemy, who were packed on the roads, were still being bombed and fired on by the Royal Air Force.

Our battalion had moved on the 21st from Exeter Camp to Tortoise Camp, and on the 23rd marched over the Grande Couronne to Volovec, thence to Kara Oglular, where they were in support to an attack by the 83rd Brigade.

At this point in the general advance the British Forces were reorganised. The XVI Corps Headquarters was moved from the right to the left of the British Army.   The XII Corps, now on the right, consisted of the 22nd and

IV—15

28th Divisions, the 228th Brigade (Garrison Battalions), the Surrey Yeomanry, the Cretan Division, and the 2ème bis Régiment de Zouaves. The XVI Corps was composed of the 26th and 27th Divisions, the Lothian and Border Horse, the Derbyshire Yeomanry, and the 14th Greek Division.

Early in the morning of the 25th September the Derbyshire Yeomanry entered Bulgaria—the first of the Allied troops—and the 22nd Division commenced to clamber up the Belasica Range. Our battalion moved to Zeus Junction, in support of the 65th Brigade, who were attacking Visoka Cuka.

Bulgarian parlementaires approached the British lines and were passed through to the Allied Commander-in-Chief.

The 22nd Division, in numbers no more than three battalions, was ordered on the 27th to assemble in the vicinity of Kara Oglular–Volovec, leaving the Cretan Division in the front line.

On the 30th September an armistice was signed, and hostilities ceased at midday.

On the 5th October the 22nd Division marched back to Grande Couronne, and thence, in a thunderstorm, to Pillar Hill. The Bulgars had been ordered to return to Bulgaria by the shortest route, and arrangements were in hand for the delivery of all war material to the Allies. And then a change took place in the general plan of operations.

General Milne was directed to collect a force consisting of the 22nd, 26th, and 28th British Divisions and the 122nd French Division and to move them to the Turkish frontier. He was to seize the bridge over the Maritsa, occupy Adrianople, and advance on Constantinople.

The railway between Doiran and Seres had been totally destroyed, and there were practically no roads in Eastern Macedonia ; the change of plans, therefore, meant a rapid march of some 250 miles for the British Army.

Our battalion halts were on the 11th the old transport lines at La Marraine ; 14th, to Janes ; 15th, to Sarigol Station ; 16th, to camp north of Dremiglava ; 17th, to Tumba, west of Beshik Lake. And then it was decided that the 22nd Division, which was ordered to concentrate in the Guvesne area by the 23rd, should be transported by sea to Dede-Agach.

To Stronlongoo station on the 19th ; to Stavros on the 20th ; on the 25th embarked on H.M.S. *Alarm.* The division was being carried by seventeen destroyers, and the landing was to be covered by monitors. But, having put to sea, the weather made it impossible to land and they returned to Stavros.

On the 27th the battalion embarked again, and the whole division was successfully landed at Dede-Agach on the 28th, and commenced to move to the Maritsa River with the object of seizing the bridgehead at Ipsala. The strength of our battalion was then 10 officers and 359 other ranks.

Again there was a redistribution of troops. The Turkish peace delegates arrived at Mudros on the 27th, and a wire on the 30th announced that an armistice had been signed and hostilities with Turkey would cease at midday on the 31st. The 22nd Division was ordered back to the base area, and entrained for Drama on the 12th November ; proceeded by motor to Kinella on the 13th ; marched to Mustenja on the 19th ; to Orfano on the 20th ; to Tash on the 21st ; and on the 22nd to Stavros.

By the end of the month the British Forces were disposed with the 28th Division Headquarters at Chanak ; the 82nd Brigade in the Asiatic forts guarding the Dardanelles ; the 84th Brigade in reserve in Gallipoli ; the 85th Brigade with its Headquarters at Biyuk Dere, one battalion in the European forts of the Bosphorus, one battalion at Pera, and one north of Constantinople ; the 27th Division was in the Janes–Sarigol area ; the 26th Division at Rustchuk ; and the 22nd at Stavros.

General Milne arrived in Constantinople on the 18th December. General Wilson had arrived there on the 12th November to stay in the same hotel as General Liman von Sanders : at that time there were many German troops in Constantinople.

Our battalion moved on the 12th January to Gueunei (Flynek Camp). And then, on the 27th February, commenced to move to Constantinople. Lieutenant-Colonel Yatman took over the stores and equipment of the 2nd East Surrey Regiment at the Tash Kishla Barracks, and absorbed the personnel of the regiment with the exception of a cadre on the 26th March. The strength of the battalion was then 14 officers and 317 other ranks.

The 6th Garrison Battalion arrived at Salonika on the 1st November to perform useful guard duties. Lieutenant-Colonel Lushington was taken ill on board ship and admitted to hospital on landing. Command was taken over by Major Charles de Robeck.

After a brief stay at Salonika the battalion embarked for Bulgaria and landed at Dede-Agach on the 10th November 1918, and was employed immediately in guarding the Salonika–Constantinople railway.

During the winter Major de Robeck was invalided home, and command passed to Major E. Greenfield. No incident worthy of note occurred. All duties which affected the Bulgar population were carried out with extreme tact by officers and men, so that the battalion earned not only commendation from higher Authority but the gratitude and respect of the Bulgars themselves.

PART III

THE WAR WITH AUSTRIA

ITALY

In *The Seventh Division*, G. T. Atkinson remarks that " it was strange that a division with the Seventh's record should have been stranded in a backwater in the great crisis of the War." The fire-eating regimental officer, yearning to be where the fight was hottest, would agree with him ; but the regiment, with its twenty-one fighting battalions scattered over the battle front on three Continents, has reason to ask that the remark should not be taken as meaning that any effort of any one of the battalions was useless.

It was on the 23rd May 1915, during the Battle of Festubert, that Italy declared war on Austria and fighting commenced on the Italian frontier. The first Battle of the Isonzo was fought from the 29th June to the 7th July, and during the next two years the battles on the Isonzo mount up to eleven, while the Austrians made one offensive in the Trentino during May 1916.

The Italian frontier from Lake Garda to the Adriatic ran in a rough semicircle with Venice as the centre. The Italians, with their minds on Trieste, had been banging away on the Isonzo, and the Austrian offensive in 1916 had been delivered on the left of the semicircle, about Asiago, which offered great possibilities. In Ludendorff's opinion—and he is at one with Falkenhayn, who was then in command—the attack had been undertaken with too few troops, and should have been supported by an offensive on the Isonzo : the result was that after a preliminary success the Italians were able to transfer troops from the east to the west of their line and hold the Austrians. He tells us, too, that he was tempted to repeat the operation in 1917 ; but although the Austrian Army was to be stiffened with some nine German divisions, it was now in an exhausted state and not fit to break through from the Tyrol. He therefore chose the region of Caporetto.

The attack was launched on the 24th October and the Italian line was pierced. In a few days the whole of the Isonzo line was crumbling, and the northern sweep of the semicircle as well. The enemy attacked in the Tyrol, but the Italians held them there fairly well.

The German success was, however, great and the plight of the Italians desperate—they simply scrambled across river after river, and finally stood on the Piave.

French and British divisions were sent to help the Italians. The British 23rd, 41st, and 48th Divisions had already moved when the 7th was ordered to Italy. General Plumer, from playing a minor rôle on his own front at Ypres, was sent to command.

The journey was uneventful, but rather long. The division commenced to entrain on the 17th November, and the first train arrived at Legnago on the 22nd. Our 1st battalion was divided in half (see page 361, Vol. III), but the two sections joined up at Sossana on the 26th. Reporting on the situation, General Plumer said : " The situation was certainly disquieting.

THE ITALIAN FRONTIER

The Italian retreat had been arrested on the River Piave....... The general impression conveyed....was that the Austrians were being encouraged to persevere with their attacks in the hope of getting down into the plains for the winter. [Plumer Despatch]

The Italian Army had just received a severe blow, from which it was bound to require time to recover and reorganise, and although every effort was being made to dispatch the French and British forces to the theatre of operations, it was obvious, owing to the limited railway facilities, that some time must elapse before these forces could be regarded as a material factor." The 7th Division Order No. 1, issued on the 25th November, opens with the information that " the situation on the Piave River remains unchanged. The 23rd and 24th Divisions are moving forward to the line of the River Brenta."

There followed days of marching for our battalion : on the 27th to

Mossano ; 28th to Villafranca ; 30th to Rustega ; 2nd December to Istrana ; 5th to Trevignano ; 10th to Riese, where the 7th Division was in reserve to the XXXI French Corps ; 11th to Loria.

Divisional Headquarters opened at Vedelago on the 10th December, and the orders were that the division would be prepared to move north, east, or west. The Italian line was now firm, but attacks were expected, and on the 13th the 22nd Brigade was warned to stand by to support the French, who had no reserve division and, with the Italians on their left, were being strongly attacked. The Austrians were, however, repulsed.

The line held by the British divisions was known as the Montello Sector. The 7th Division did not go into the front line until the 19th January 1918, when they relieved the 41st Division. Our battalion had moved into billets at Altivole on the 17th, and on the 18th relieved the 10th Royal West Kent Regiment in reserve on the extreme right of the British line with Battalion Headquarters at Bavaria. On the 26th they were relieved by the 9th Devon Regiment and marched back to Volpago.

Our battalion took over the front line on the 2nd February, relieving the 22nd Manchester Regiment. The enemy was exceedingly quiet. The River Piave, broad and swift, lay in the middle of " No Man's Land," at that time of year a most effective obstacle to patrolling. Relieved on the 10th February by the 2nd H.A.C., they did not go into that sector again.

On the 23rd February the division was ordered to entrain for France at an early date, and our battalion commenced to march back to the entraining area : on the 26th to Casa Corba ; on the 1st March to Loreggia, where the St. David's Day dinner [1] was held (42 sat down to dinner) ; on the 3rd to Villafranca ; on the 7th to Bosco di Nanto.

The order to return to France was cancelled, but repeated on several occasions before the final advance in Italy. The date of the first order

---

[1] An interesting letter was received on this occasion :

"FIRLEY HALL, YORK.

" 27th February 1918.

" DEAR COLONEL,

" I send my sincere good wishes and affectionate remembrances to all with you on the 1st March

' and St. David.'

" I have just been looking up the menu of March 1st, 1870, which was my first St. David's Day, and the 1st Battalion was quartered at Devonport. It reads strangely in these days of simple meals, which happily commenced before ever rationing came in, and I hope you will all be having a bottle of the best and are not limited to 1 lb. of meat per head per week.

" The menu of 1870 consisted of soups and fish, 6 entrées, 8 rôtis, 6 relevés, 8 entremets ! Hackett, V.C., was mess president and all the servants wore white kid gloves ! The two silver ' obelisks ' were on the table for the first time. . . .

" Yours sincerely,

" E. H. CLOUGH TAYLOR."

will be appreciated : actually the 41st Division did return to France during March.

Leaving all personnel surplus to 120 per company at Bosco di Nanto, the battalion marched to bivouacs near Rovolon on the 18th for a few days' training in mountain warfare. They practised field firing, night firing, and hill climbing. During these exercises there was a distressing bombing accident due to a moment of forgetfulness on the part of an instructor : two old and tried sergeants were killed and there were 14 casualties in all.

The Battalion returned to Bosco di Nanto on the 21st, and four days later commenced to march to Grantorto ; to Quinte on the 27th ; to Villa-verla on the 28th ; to Thiene on the 29th ; and by Fiat lorries to Capriola, in the mountain area, on the 30th. They were then in the Asiago Plateau sector, where the 7th Division was taking over from the Italians. That evening our battalion relieved the 12th Durham Light Infantry at Ghelpac.

RAIDS ON THE ASIAGO PLATEAU

The 7th Division was to stay on the plateau until August, 4,000 feet above sea-level. It was an uncomfortable bit of line, as the heavy haul from the plain deprived troops of all that was not absolutely necessary, and the altitude made it very cold ; there were plenty of trees, however, to provide them with fuel. And life in the rigorous climate was not made more bearable by the news from France.

The Ghelpac was a deep, narrow ravine and the front line was on the edge of it : the Plateau opens out into a wide saucer-like shape about 1½ miles to the east. Snow was still lying on the ground and the battalion took over alpenstocks and ice-grips !

On the 7th April our battalion led off with the first of a series of raids made by the 7th Division. Particulars are meagre. Two parties from D Company, led by Captain D. B. Anthony and 2nd Lieutenant L. C. Phillips, entered the enemy trenches near Ambrosini—a much-battered house in the Austrian lines—inflicted casualties estimated at 17 killed or wounded, and returned with one prisoner of the 17th Infantry Regiment, Kronprinz 6th Division. Captain Anthony and 2nd Lieutenant L. C. Phillips were slightly wounded, but remained at duty ; one other rank was missing, but rejoined three days later.

The next day the battalion was relieved and marched back to huts on M. Brusabo.

A similar sort of raid, but with artillery support, was made on the 3rd May by A Company. Ambrosini was again the point chosen. " No Man's Land " was fairly wide, and unfortunately, while getting to their selected jumping-off spot, the company was seen by the enemy, who opened heavy rifle and machine-gun fire. It was not yet Zero hour. The company was suffering casualties—the situation was distinctly unpleasant. One reads the cold, unadorned entry in the Brigade Diary with gratification : " As it was not yet Zero time they charged, and the enemy retired ! " The soldierly spirit and bearing of the 1st Battalion were remarkable.

The raid yielded one Austrian officer and two other ranks. Our own casualties were, in comparison, heavy : 7 killed, 1 died of wounds, 12 wounded, and 2 missing. 2nd Lieutenant C. H. Lloyd Edwards was amongst the wounded, also Lieutenant-Colonel Holmes, but he, luckily, only slightly, so that he stayed at duty.

After this affair the battalion moved on the 4th to billets at S. Dona on the plains. They were in reserve and support during the rest of the month of May ; and then the division came out of the line and our battalion went into camp at Beregana until the 11th June, when they moved to camp at Monte di Grumo. The weather was fine,[1] and it proved to be a real rest, disturbed once only, on the 15th June, when the division stood to during an attack on the 48th Division ; the 91st Brigade was hurried up on to the plateau, but the other two brigades did not move. An attack on the Val d'Assa was practised during the month.

On the 24th June our battalion relieved the 5th Gloucestershire at M. Pau, and on the 25th the 5th Warwickshire at Busibollo ; thence into the Cesuna Switch to work on dugouts and wire.

The month of July was peaceful. The moves during the first half of the month were to Magnaboschi, 4th ; Serona, 9th ; huts at Carriola, 19th ; and on the 20th into the front line to relieve the 1st Staffordshire Regiment.

A raid was discussed and prepared. Early in August prisoners stated that the enemy was withdrawing to the Val d'Assa–Camporovere line, and to test this statement raids were ordered on the British, French, and Italian fronts, starting with ten raids on the British front on the night 8th/9th August. The arrangements already made for our raid were adhered to, but slightly enlarged.

There were some interesting details in the divisional preparations made for the four raids lettered A, B, C, and D. It was decided, as there was no moon, to use searchlights, and experiments carried out on the nights of the 6th and 7th showed that if the lights were directed over the heads of the attacking troops, the downward glow would enable them to see without being seen. One light on M. Lemerle was, therefore, directed on the barracks at Interrotto, the other, from Buco di Cesuna, on Orato Spilleche ; and officers

---

[1] The troops had khaki drill and helmets issued.

were detailed to see that one or other of the lights was constantly shining. The raiding parties were to remain within the enemy lines for two hours, and the signal for withdrawal was to be a beacon fire lighted on the top of M. Lemerle ; the fire would also serve to guide the raiders on their return, and was to burn for half an hour.

The artillery was to fire on a normal plan until Zero hour, which was midnight, when a " crash " of three rounds gun-fire was to be put down on all four points to be raided.

Most of the wire had already been cut by the artillery, although a little trimming was required on A raid front, which was ours, and on C raid front.

Our area included part of Manchester Trench, the Railway Cutting, and the Quarry—a rough triangle with a depth of about 500 yards. Two companies were used, one to occupy a line north-east of the Railway Cutting, the other to mop up Manchester Trench, the Quarry, and the intervening ground.

The objective was approached by Vaister Spur, a long convex-shaped spur along which our patrols had found no difficulty in working up to the enemy's wire.   On the evening of the 8th, at dusk, a patrol of 1 N.C.O. and 16 men was sent out with instructions to patrol " No Man's Land " in front of the area to be raided, to cover the forming up of the raiding party, and to send back accurate information of the enemy's attitude.

The raiding party was formed up on Vaister Spur fifteen minutes before zero.   A few shots were heard on the left flank, but nothing developed from that direction.   At midnight the crash of artillery came down on the enemy's front line.

The reflected light from the searchlight beam was of the greatest assistance, and although the companies did not strike the gaps in the wire at once, our men were in Manchester Trench two minutes after Zero.

The enemy stood, but their fire was wild.   Everything went " according to plan " : the line north-east of the Railway Cutting was occupied, the Quarry and the intervening ground mopped up.   In the Quarry, 9 Austrians with a machine gun and a trench mortar were captured by an officer with one man ; but B Company found a communication trench from the Quarry to the front line in which were concrete dugouts containing a whole company —3 Austrian officers and 115 other ranks were quickly rounded up, 5 wounded men were picked up later.

The order was to remain in the enemy's line for two hours.   One hour and a half had passed before any counter-attack developed—it came from Little Spur and Post Spur, and was easily broken by rifle fire.

And then the beacon fire on M. Lemerle flared up and the companies withdrew, taking with them their prisoners, 3 machine guns, 3 trench mortars, 1 searchlight, and 7 mules. It was estimated that about 50 of the enemy were killed.

Our casualties were Lieutenant Kenyon and 5 other ranks wounded ; 1 other rank killed and missing.

All four raids had been successful, but the " bag " of the Royal Welch headed the list. H.R.H. the Prince of Wales called in person on Battalion Headquarters at 9 o'clock next morning to congratulate the battalion. This was the last raid on the Asiago Plateau. The division was relieved and went into G.H.Q. reserve, in the Cornedo area.

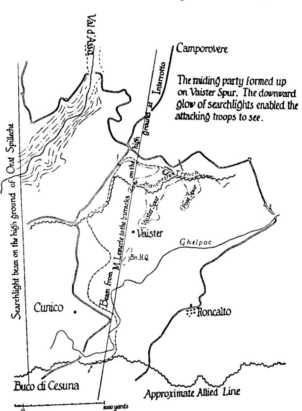

The Earl of Cavan's despatch dated the 14th September covers this period. He assumed command on the return of Sir Herbert Plumer to France on the 10th March, and he points out that the situation on that date " was very different from that which had faced Sir Herbert Plumer on his arrival in this country. Four months of rest and quiet had given ample time to re-form those Italian units which had suffered severely in the fighting of October and November 1917. . . . All ranks were looking with confidence and resolution to the campaign of 1918."

THE BATTLE OF VITTORIO VENETO, 24TH OCTOBER–4TH NOVEMBER 1918.

In his next despatch, dated 15th November, Lord Cavan refers to the improbability in September of any offensive action being undertaken in Italy in the near future, and to a consequent decision to assist France with some or all of the troops in Italy. " In accordance with this idea the 7th,

23rd, and 48th Divisions were reduced from 13 to 10 battalions, and the 9 battalions thus released were dispatched to France on the 13th and 14th September. The 7th Division was already at rest, and it was intended to dispatch this division as soon as a battle-worn division should arrive from France to replace it." The latter proposal did not, however, come to anything. The battalions that left were the 9th Devonshire and the 20th and 21st Manchester Regiments.

The whole of the month of September was spent in training at Cornedo : the billets were excellent and the surrounding country delightful. On the 5th October our battalion marched to Monteviale, where they were under orders to move at short notice.

We must turn to Major Alston's account.

" The division had been enjoying itself for a long spell in good rest-billets. Our move to France was imminent in relief of a tired division from there, and our opposite numbers had actually arrived to reconnoitre the line and billets. On this day (1st October) the return to France was cancelled.

" Even so we did not expect that we were to fight a battle in Italy. The offensive across Val d'Assa or the Asiago Plateau had been on and off so regularly during the summer, and now the season was getting late.

" However, the division was put at short notice to move in battle order, and at the same time field days were planned, the schemes for which were all exercises in moving warfare.

" On the 12th October a brigade field day was ordered. The battalion was to do advance guard, which meant a five-mile march to the starting-point. The exercise had just commenced when all troops were ordered back to billets to pack up on arrival and prepare to march at once. Detailed orders would follow.

" We reached billets at 11.30 a.m. simultaneously with the arrival of entraining orders. At 3 p.m. the battalion, who had already marched some ten miles, started on their thirteen-mile march to Villaserla. Packing up and giving everyone a meal in the meantime had been a strenuous effort.

" The entraining station, a long open siding, was reached at 6.30 p.m. A drizzling rain had been falling throughout the latter part of the march ; there were no trains waiting for us, and we had to remain on that wretched siding until 11.30 p.m., when we were able to entrain. A hard day for everyone.

" At 3 a.m. the train left. The greatest secrecy had been observed and we had no idea of our destination."

Lord Cavan himself did not go to Comando Supremo until the 6th

October, and he says that at this interview General Diaz offered him command of a mixed Italian-British Army with a view to undertaking offensive operations at an early date. Secrecy was vital, and in order to make as little change as possible General Diaz suggested that the 48th Division should remain in position on the Asiago Plateau under the temporary command of General Pennella, commanding the XII Italian Corps.

General Diaz explained his plan at a conference on the 13th. The main attack was to advance across the Piave with the Tenth, Eighth, and Twelfth Italian armies, to drive a wedge between the Fifth and Sixth Austrian Armies, forcing the Fifth Austrian Army eastwards and threatening the communications of the Sixth Austrian Army through the Valmarino Valley. At the same time the Fourth Italian Army was to take the offensive in the Grappa sector.

The task allotted to the Tenth Army was to reach the Livenza between Portobuffole and Sacile, and thus protect the flank of the Eighth and Twelfth Armies in their move northwards.

The Tenth Army was at first to consist of the XI Italian and the XIV British Corps. The XIV British Corps was to concentrate in the Treviso area on the 16th October.

The problem of crossing the Piave, which the Tenth Army had to face, was not an easy one. The river, dotted with islands, was about one and a half miles across. The current in the main channel was ten miles per hour. The enemy held the Grave di Papadopoli, the principal island, as an advanced post, and it was decided that this island must be occupied as a preliminary step to a general advance.

Our battalion detrained at Istrana at 9 a.m. on the 13th and marched to Preganziol. On the 16th they took over billets from the 8th Devonshire at S. Lazzaro.

No one had any idea of what was afoot, and all were content to assume that they were to take over a portion of the line from the Italians. But on the 17th " the battalion was marched to the River Sacile and practised embarkation in small boats, being ferried across that fast-running stream by Italian boatmen. A pointer at last !

" That evening a very sudden brigade conference of Commanding Officers was called, and the attack on the Grave di Papadopoli, an island in the Piave, was ordered and objectives roughly outlined. At this time the Brigade Commander [Steele] contemplated using the 2nd H.A.C. only."

On the 19th the battalion marched to the Catena area, and the next day took over from the 121st Regiment, 37th Italian Division, B and D Companies in the front line, A and C in support.

" The handing over had its amusing side.   The Italians held their line with their men almost shoulder to shoulder, according to our views, and with a large number of machine guns in the line.   Further, our idea of handing over the responsibility for areas to be manned, broadly speaking, as the relieving units thought best, did not come into their scheme of things. Their equivalent of our platoon commander, or machine-gun sergeant, would not consider themselves relieved except there arrived a relieving party of equal strength in men and weapons to their own.   As our numbers were considerably less than half of theirs, such a relief was manifestly impossible, and a good deal of persuasion and some stratagems were used in order to satisfy their requirements.

" There is an authenticated tale of one of the Divisional Machine-gun Battalion Officers, who started from one flank of his front with a gun and team, and moving from post to post relieved each Italian gun in turn with the same team.   Our Allies having evacuated the front line, this officer was then free to make his own dispositions.

" The Italian officers were very hospitable and friendly.   Their Regimental Commander was convinced that our attack would be successful. French, English, and schoolboy's Latin, the last written on account of the difference in pronunciation, were our means of talking to each other. The sum-total of the knowledge that both sides had of these three languages was minute, but the results were satisfactory.

" A further brigade conference had been held on this day (20th), and it was still intended that the 2nd H.A.C. should be ferried across the river for a frontal attack."

On the 21st the 11th West Yorkshire took over from C and D Companies, who moved to the right of A and B and relieved the two left companies of the 2nd Royal Warwickshire.   (Alston.)

" At 12 noon it was notified that the attack would be carried out ' at a time and place to be notified later,' and at 12.30 p.m. the Brigade Commander informed the Commanding Officer (Alston) that the 1st R.W.F. would take part in the attack also, each battalion attacking with three companies."

PASSAGE OF THE PIAVE, 23RD OCTOBER–4TH NOVEMBER.

" It would be best to explain the nature of the operation now.

" The intended battle front extended from the Asiago Plateau to the sea near Venice.   Lord Cavan had been given the command of the Tenth Army, and he was to attack across the middle Piave.   The XIV Corps, under

MONTE CAVALETTO, ASIAGO PLATEAU.

TRENCHES ON THE BANK OF THE PIAVE.

Sir Francis Babington, was to cross the river between Palazzon and Salettuol with the 7th and 23rd Divisions.

" On the 7th Division front the river was from a mile to a mile and a half broad, and in the middle was the Grave di Papadopoli, a large island held by the enemy as an outpost, separated from our shore by the main stream of the river, but from the Austrian shore by small fordable streams only.

" The river itself is peculiar compared with the rivers of northern Europe. It consists of a broad shingle bed down which many small streams wander, and also one larger stream, the main one, which will run at a faster rate through the deep channel it has cut itself. To make the system even more confused, this main stream itself will often fork, flowing as two streams for a mile or two, and then again rejoining as one. The system is liable to heavy and sudden floods, and the deep channels change their course frequently as a result of the floods.

" Though surveyed, the maps showing the river system were quite inadequate in furnishing any useful information, and this is not to be wondered at.

" The country on both banks is particularly difficult, consisting of low-lying stretches of land covered with dense scrub, and at this time of year we could find no recognisable landmarks or roads. This description applies to the island of Papadopoli also.

" The Italians had prepared their defence in three lines, the first on the water's edge, then the second line, and finally along a high bank built to contain the river when in flood—this was called the Bund.

" There was also a similar Bund on the enemy side, and it was clear that they held their front in a similar manner.

" From our side, observation on to the enemy's line was impossible, and this defect laid a difficult and anxious task on us all as we made our reconnaissances and plans for the attack.

" There were two suitable points for crossing.

" 1. One from near Salettuol across an island called Veneto, near our bank, and thence across the main stream.

" 2. Across another island on our side called Cosenza, thence across the main stream to a beach at the western end of the Papadopoli called Lido.

" At this time, although not in actual spate, the river system was filling, and the main streams were flowing at a sufficiently rapid rate to cause anxiety to the corps of Italian boatmen who were to ferry us across. They also feared that instead of the river abating, its flood conditions would become worse.

IV—16

" The island of Papadopoli itself is some three miles long, and varies in breadth from 200 yards at the north-west corner to some 2,000 yards in the centre.   The eastern half of the island had been cultivated, but the rest was a mere low-lying swamp.   In the centre of the island was a fosse varying from three to ten feet deep, and ten wide, which was afterwards a useful means of communication and came to be called the Fosse.   The whole of the island was perfectly flat and densely covered with scrub.   It appeared to be held in two main lines : the front line, well wired, was to the edge, and the support line along the centre of the island.   The stream on the northern side, besides being bridged by numerous foot-bridges, was also fordable, so that it was practically part of the mainland.[1]

" The operation was to consist of a frontal attack on a two-battalion front, the 2nd H.A.C. to be on the right.

" [On the 22nd] the Italian boatmen required a postponement of twenty-four hours to allow the river to subside.   Still maintaining the decision to hide the arrival of the British on the front [*Orders were issued that all troops visible to the enemy should wear Italian uniform, and that no British gun should fire a single shot previous to the general bombardment*], the British guns were in position and were being calibrated by a Royal Engineer survey party, but the attack was to be a surprise one and no artillery support would be given.

" The next twenty-four hours, day and night, were spent in reconnaissances, searching the island by day from every conceivable point, hoping without success to get observation on it—by night mostly in the stream itself, sounding for fords on to Veneto island.

" On this day Lieutenant-Colonel Holmes rejoined from leave, only to go into hospital with pneumonia immediately afterwards.

" There was fairly heavy gas shelling, mostly lachrymatory, on Maserada, the site of the memorial to the 7th Division, at that time a fairly congested traffic junction for wheeled transport."   (Alston.)

It was now the 23rd.   Operation Orders for the frontal attack had already been typed when Company Commanders were called to a conference. The Orders were to be modified, the direction of the attack changed.   The objective, the Grave di Papadopoli, was to be attacked from the north, that is, the Cosenza crossing was to be used instead of the Veneto, and Lido was to be the place of disembarkation.

" [Between the Lido and Cosenza] was a known shallow.   After dark Captain Odini would reconnoitre this previous to starting the ferry service.

---

[1] Until the night of the 25th/26th October, all attempts at bridging the Piave between the right bank and the Grave di Papadopoli failed, owing to the strength of the current.

He would decide either that we should jump out and drag our boats across the shoal, or to arrange a second fleet on the far side of the bank into which we should tranship.

" The boats were flat-bottomed, rowed by two Italian watermen, gondolier fashion, and carried a complete section [of men]. They were under the command of Captain Odini, always known as ' the admiral,' who, with his men, won the highest admiration from British troops.

" The new plan meant attacking the enemy's right flank, and seemed full of promise. It would now be carried out on a one-battalion frontage with the 2nd H.A.C. in the front line.

" The change of embarkation point involved heavy work on the transport and the 2nd Royal Warwickshire, who furnished all the carrying parties, as all dumps of ammunition and stores had to be moved about 1½ miles upstream ; and in addition the administrative orders, previously issued, were in course of execution. No easy task sorting out loads and transport in the dark on a congested road, and dispatching them to a fresh and unknown rendezvous.

" Company Commanders received their orders ; nothing further to do except wait for Zero hour. The 2nd H.A.C. would cross first ; then A Company, under Captain R. M. Stevens, would embark in support of the H.A.C., covering their left rear as far as the inter-battalion boundary. Headquarters would follow. Then B Company, under Captain J. M. Davies, and then D Company, under Captain D. B. Anthony. The advance from the landing beach would be resumed by B Company, followed by D.

" The boats could only ferry one company at a time. B and D would be formed up on the Lido and dispatched to their task ; reaching their boundaries, they would hold the Austrian line facing north.

" There was every chance of parts of the two regiments engaging each other in the dark ; as a precaution the R.W.F. wore deep white arm-bands, the Italian cloaks and helmets were to be discarded after dark.

" At 7 p.m. Captain Odini and an officer of the H.A.C. reconnoitred the shoal opposite the Lido ; they discovered three main streams had to be crossed, separated by two sandbanks. Both the first two were unfordable ; the last stream was fordable. Boats would be dragged across the sandbanks separating the first two streams.

" Their reconnaissance appeared to be unnoticed by the enemy.

" The battalion closed up on to the front line on the water's edge. Meanwhile the H.A.C. embarkation was about to commence.

" At 9.15 p.m. the enemy barrage crashed down on the Italian lines. It was found that Cosenza Island, although small, escaped most of the barrage, and the three companies were led on to it from the front-line trenches, which were receiving a hammering. They were disposed about the island and were practically untouched by shelling.

" A beach master from each battalion was responsible for the regulation of the embarkation of the troops into the boats as they became available, and later for sending stores across. In this capacity Captain C. T. Davies embarked the battalion. As they lay about in parties in the scrub he sent his runners to guide them to their boats on the water's edge, and so well arranged were his preparations that the embarkation passed without a hitch. Lieutenant G. Bromley crossed with the battalion to carry out similar duties on the disembarkation shore.

" The battalion embarkation began at 9.45 p.m. The foreshore and river-bed were being shelled heavily ; as heavy shells burst in the river they would lift large columns of water into the air, and in addition to splinters, stones and pebbles were thrown by the explosion. The Italian boatmen were working splendidly in two shifts, one remaining on the beach while the other made a journey. The embarkation was carried out in as quiet and orderly a manner as if on parade. The steadiness of the men was splendid, in spite of the shelling, and there was never any sign of confusion. At ten minutes past midnight the whole battalion had disembarked.

" A Company had already moved in touch with the H.A.C. Headquarters were established on the Lido beach. News was received that A Company was making progress.

" At 1.50 a company of the West Yorkshire, from the 23rd Division, disembarked ; they occupied some old trenches on the Lido, thus covering the left rear of the new position when occupied, and protecting the disembarkation beach.

" At half-past two B Company reported progress but still fighting.

" At 2.45 a.m. Battalion Headquarters moved to a forward site selected by the Scout Officer. The guides lost their way, and eventually Headquarters returned to the beach. All this time a post on B Company's front was still holding out and causing trouble. A heavy fog had risen, which made progress more difficult than ever, and for some time there was a doubt whether in attacking this post B Company was not engaging our own side : this was now cleared up.

" At 4.30 a.m. A Company had occupied their objective ; they were in touch with a company of the H.A.C., but the latter were out of touch with their Headquarters.

" At 5 a.m. one machine gun and 52 prisoners from the H.A.C. and B Company arrived.

" By 5.10 the Scout Officer, Lieutenant D. M. John, had seen the Officer Commanding the H.A.C., whose right and rear companies were all right. He had got touch with our D Company, who were in touch with the H.A.C. : they had advanced some 600 yards beyond their objective.

" At 6 a.m. B Company's situation cleared up.   They had encountered

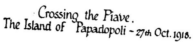

Crossing the Piave.
The Island of Papadopoli - 27th Oct. 1918.

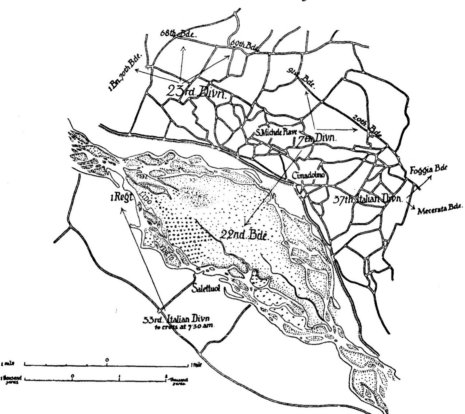

numerous strong, isolated parties, and getting touch with A they were able between them to mop these up and had also driven some into the H.A.C. and *vice versa.*

" The battalion objectives were now definitely occupied, and more had been taken.   The H.A.C. had been equally successful.

" The fog was still very thick, visual signalling with Battalion Head-quarters was impossible, and the power buzzer we had taken across could not work over the river. Previous to crossing, bearings between the objectives and Brigade Headquarters had been measured off the map, and it was hoped that we might be able to resect back. An attempt was to be made to keep signal lamps burning on which to take our bearings. The fog stopped all this, but it had the advantage of allowing the ferry service to be used in daylight, and a runner was sent back to Brigade Headquarters with the situation. Battalion Headquarters moved to B Company's Headquarters.

" The battalion was now firmly established, with D Company holding an outpost line between Papadopoli and the mainland on the Isola di Francia. The shelling throughout the day was heavy and the river rising. We now expected to get news of the crossing of the 91st and 20th Brigades.

" At 6.35 p.m. Lieutenant Abbott, Brigade Intelligence Officer, arrived with verbal orders that the 20th and 91st Brigades would cross the Piave and attack through the troops on the island, who would then follow them.

" This had been an anxious day on the island, raining most of the day. The river was rising very rapidly, and we were now faced with the possibility of having our communications become more difficult than ever. But the rain had cleared the mist away to an extent and the two battalions were able to locate their positions with accuracy. Up to now this had been a matter of guesswork.

" The enemy did not seem anxious to counter-attack, but he shelled very heavily and the Lido beach was under machine-gun fire all day."

The dividing line between the 7th Division and the XI Italian Corps cut through the Grave di Papadopoli, and on the night 24th/25th the Italians attempted to capture the south-east end of the island, but failed.

Also, owing to the downpour of rain and the rising of the river, the main attack, which had been ordered for 6.45 a.m. on the 25th, was cancelled. The river current was exceedingly swift and all attempts to build a bridge at Salettuol failed.

" Major Macfarlane and Captain A. C. Cameron, both attached to the Divisional Staff, crossed in the night (24th/25th) ; they brought back news that the attack of the other two brigades had been postponed. Lieutenant-Colonel R. N. O'Connor, commanding the H.A.C., then took command of all the troops on the island.

" At 10.45 p.m. C Company, under Lieutenant T. B. Edwards, and the remainder of Headquarters, under Regimental Sergeant-Major T. Hannon, crossed to the island. [*They were to have crossed by bridge at Salettuol, but as this was impossible, they were marched to the Lido and ferried across.*] One platoon was left in position to strengthen the defence of the Lido beach, undertaken by the West Yorkshire ; the remainder of the company came into Battalion Reserve.

" At 10.20 a.m. (25th) an Austrian plane was shot down in flames by the battalion. It fell near three Austrian posts. Captains Stevens and Anthony and Lieutenant John over-impulsively rushed out to where the plane had fallen, whereupon about 15 men ran out from the Austrian posts ; of these they captured 3 and wounded 1, the remainder running away. The airmen had been killed by the fall of their machine.

" We were told that we could call for artillery support in cases of great urgency. It is worth noting that not one round had so far been fired by our own or the Italian artillery in support of the two battalions. In point of fact this artillery support was never called for.

" At 5 p.m. Captain G. Camberledge arrived after a dangerous crossing, and there was a conference at the H.A.C. Headquarters. The remainder of the island had to be cleared that night in order to allow the 37th Italian Division to come through and form on the right of the 7th Division for the attack on the enemy's main line. The battalion should have carried out this attack, but the task of reconnaissance and re-forming could not possibly have been carried out in the short hours of daylight left, while the H.A.C., who had been on this ground for two days in touch with the enemy, would be fighting on ground fairly well known to them and, being on the spot, could start their preparations at once. A Company of the battalion were to move behind the H.A.C. covering their left rear, and dropping posts to garrison the north side of the island, and the battalion would extend their front to free the H.A.C., a matter of two kilometres.

" At 5.30 p.m. the Brigade Commander himself arrived [Steele]. He had had a most difficult crossing, had been slightly stunned by a machine-gun bullet, which had struck his helmet in front and passed out behind, and, of his two boatmen, one was wounded and the other jumped overboard. A second attempt to cross was successful. He announced that the 2nd Royal Warwickshire were crossing to relieve the battalion, freeing them to take over the H.A.C. front and hold it in strength. The battalion front after the relief was to be held with B and D Companies in the front line and C Company in reserve.

" At 9 p.m. the H.A.C. attack started. For some half-hour previous to this the Austrian shelling had recommenced as heavily as ever."

The attack was successful and resulted in the capture of some 300 prisoners.

" By 4.30 a.m. (26th) the Warwickshire were beginning to arrive. At 5.30 a.m. both battalions [H.A.C. and R.W.F.] were counter-attacked.

The relief by the Warwickshire had been completed twenty minutes earlier.

"The counter-attack was on D Company's front—very near to their junction with the posts dropped by A Company as they moved forward with the H.A.C.—and extended on to B Company's front. B and D Companies stopped the attack completely—it lasted for about forty minutes. An Austrian officer was captured in whose boot a reasonably accurate map of our position was found. The H.A.C. were equally successful in beating off the attack made on them. [*It was a very determined counter-attack, accompanied by an intense barrage on the island itself. Again some 300 prisoners were left in our hands.*]

"By daylight the H.A.C. situation was clear. The whole of the island had been captured. To sum up, the operation, consisting of two night attacks unsupported by artillery, had been successful." (Alston.)

On this three-mile front the main channel of the Piave was now behind the 7th Division and the 37th Italian Division—all was ready for the major attack. Not a single gun had fired and the artillery kept silent until 11.30 p.m. on the 26th, when the bombardment of the whole enemy front commenced.

During the day a footbridge had been completed at Salettuol, under cover of a thick mist, an attempt the previous night having failed. A second footbridge was commenced after dark at Lido and was completed by 11 p.m.

By 2 a.m. on the 27th the 20th and 91st Brigades had crossed to the island by the Salettuol bridge and were forming up to attack through the 22nd Brigade.

Zero hour was at 6.45 a.m., and the advance was met with moderate artillery fire but considerable resistance from the enemy infantry at certain spots. Although the main channel of the river was behind them, the assaulting troops still had several minor channels to wade through, with the water up to their waists and over ; and the enemy's wire had, in most places, to be cut by hand under active machine-gun fire. By nightfall the division had taken some 2,000 prisoners, a few guns, and were on the line Camminada–Tezze.

There had been some difficulty on the right, the XI Italian Corps front, and also on the left, the VIII Italian Corps front, where the whole width of the Piave lay in front of the attacking troops, and consequently the advance of the British XIV Corps was restricted ; but the Bund on the enemy's side was in our hands. On the 23rd Division front a strong counter-attack recaptured the village of Borgo Malanotte, but a second assault secured the place with the enemy garrison.

The Piave still hindered the general advance, and on the left of Lord Cavan's Army the Eighth Italian Army, although they had succeeded in landing on the opposite bank, found the current so strong that their bridging operations failed. Comando Supremo therefore allotted their XVIII Corps to Lord Cavan, so that he could pass it over the British bridges. Needless to say the British bridges were terribly congested. The conversion of the footbridge at Salettuol into a medium pontoon bridge was at first successful, but later the whole bridge broke away ; the new bridge was only open to traffic on the evening of the 28th. In spite of these difficulties, one brigade of the Italian 56th Division and one regiment of the Italian 33rd Division were passsed over to the left bank during the afternoon.

Our left flank being refused, the brigade from the 56th Italian Division commenced the advance at 9 a.m. on the 28th, while the XIV Corps, moving in conjunction with them, only commenced to advance at 12.30 p.m. There was not much opposition, and by nightfall the 7th Division were on the line Raivazzola, with patrols well in front.

On that day Major Alston, commanding our battalion, had to go to hospital, and Captain E. G. Hawes assumed command. The battalion billeted at S. Michele Piave.

The Pursuit.

From reports of the fighting it became evident that the enemy's resistance was slackening ; but it was established that he held the line of the Montecano River with strong detachments of machine guns.

Our 22nd Brigade was ordered on the 29th to march to Fontanella, but the advance of the 20th and 91st Brigades was slower than was expected, and orders were soon issued to halt at a point south of Vazzola. The Montecano line had held up the 20th Brigade, and the 91st, although they had succeeded in crossing the river, had heavy fighting in Cimetta, which changed hands several times in the course of the day. The whole corps were, however, across the river by nightfall.

The orders for the 30th were that the 22nd Brigade should pass through the 91st at 9 a.m. and attack, with the 20th Brigade in support ; the 91st were to rest and follow in reserve. The final objective for the day was given as the River Livenza. But at 7.45 a.m. the Brigadier commanding the 91st Brigade found that the enemy was retiring on his front, and he at once followed them up.

The 22nd Brigade were not far behind. With our battalion on the right and the Warwickshire on the left, the brigade pushed forward and passed through the 91st. The Corps Mounted Troops went out beyond.

" From this moment," says Lord Cavan, " the defeat became a rout." Still, a few enemy machine guns and light field guns remained on the left bank of the Livenza.

The advance up to this point had been a very exhausting affair, and, owing to the bridging difficulties, and the congestion on such bridges as the XIV Corps had constructed being occasioned by Italian infantry divisions and cavalry, our troops had been on short rations. It was a relief to find no

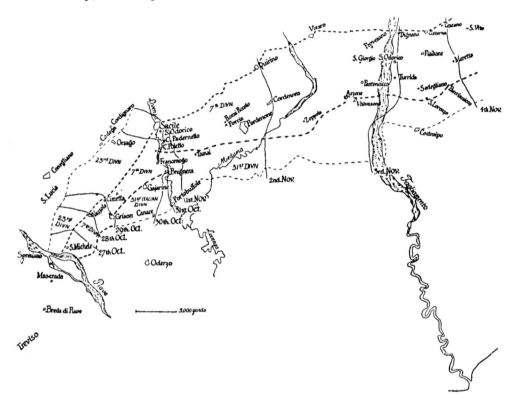

orders for the 31st October while preparations were made for bridging the Livenza River. And the orders for the 1st November were to establish bridgeheads but not to make a prolonged advance. On our battalion front patrols from C Company had crossed during the night, using the debris of the bridge at Brugnera ; they reported that the left bank was clear of the enemy. Patrols from A, B, and D Companies then crossed. The battalion held the line of the road Odorico–Tamai.

The next day the advance was continued with the 2nd Warwickshire as advance guard to the 22nd Brigade. By evening they were on the line of the Meduna River, from Pordenone to Cordenons, and in touch on each flank.

Some delay was caused in establishing bridgeheads over the Tagliamento on the 3rd. The advance had been taken up by the H.A.C. when the General Officer Commanding the 4th Italian Cavalry Division requested the 22nd Infantry Brigade to remain on the west bank of the Tagliamento, as an armistice had been declared. As a result of this, a battalion was not passed over the river until the evening, and was then withdrawn. Our battalion went into billets at Pastoncicco. At 2 a.m. on the 4th a message arrived at Brigade Headquarters to the effect that no armistice had been signed. An officer's patrol was sent across the river, and at 7.30 a.m. the battalion commenced to cross. No opposition was encountered, and by 9 a.m. they were on the line Turrida–Rivis, where they reorganised for an advance on the Pantianicco–S. Lorenzo line.

The situation was most peculiar at this time, as the Austrians were protesting that an armistice had been signed, and that they should not be called upon to surrender. Lieutenant J. C. L. Edwards entered Turrida with a patrol and found some 200 Austrians had dumped down their arms ; he took them prisoners.

At 10 a.m. the Commanding Officer was informed that an armistice had actually been signed which would come into force at 3 p.m., and that all territory occupied at that hour would be held, but no further advance would take place. All enemy troops taken before that hour would be prisoners of war ; after 3 p.m. the enemy would withdraw at least three kilometres from the line held by the battalion.

Operations ceased on the line Romano–Coseanetto.

Curiously enough, the 48th Division, which had been left on the Asiago Plateau, with the Sixth Italian Army, reached Vezzena on the 2nd November and, Lord Cavan claims, " was therefore the first British division to enter enemy territory on the Western Front."

Almost at once the 7th Division was withdrawn. On the 6th our Battalion was in billets at Provesano, where Major Alston rejoined from hospital ; on the 8th at Rorai Piccolo ; on the 9th at Orsago ; on the 10th at Vazzola ; on the 11th at Breda di Piave. The battalion was actually halted, the normal halt on the march, in the centre of the River Piave, on Palazzo Bridge, when Brigadier-General Steele informed Major Alston that Germany had accepted the terms of the armistice. On the 13th the battalion moved by train from Treviso to Montechio Maggiore.

THE ARMISTICE AND DEMOBILISATION

THE ARMISTICE AND DEMOBILISATION

No one has yet laid bare the soul of the soldier, the representative soldier who fought in the Great War. Books have been written, plays have been performed, and picture-stories have been unreeled in cinema houses, but no one has succeeded in showing the intense fortitude, the incredible courage, of those millions of civilians who became soldiers for the period of the War. Most writers seek to interest and gain the sympathy of readers and audiences with the portrayal of a coward or a nerve-racked man ; the cinema hero is merely ludicrous. The individual soldier was, maybe, a lout with no more than brute intelligence and feeling, or he might have been a sensitive lad engaged in some artistic profession to which he was drawn by an innate love of beauty—all sorts came together in a platoon, and the platoons made companies, battalions, divisions, the Army that fought. Neither nerves nor cowardice were the outstanding features of this great adventure, but the rare exceptions which are most hideous to recall. Death, mutilation, fear ? These things do not come first in war memories—but the men do ! There is something akin to a great love for the men, and it is they who spring foremost to the mind.

Those philosophical sentries who stood in the fierce heat of a semi-tropical sun or the drenching downpour of icy rain ; those calm figures sitting round a brazier, with its choking fumes, or stripped to lie naked in a patch of shade ; those cursing, sweating men, staggering under loads which they carried over incredible ways ; those gallant, stumbling, but tenacious men who advanced over the open at Zero hour ; those men who chose to sing songs at most inappropriate moments, were dumb when they might well have spoken, and chattered when they should have been silent as the grave ! When old soldiers gather together it is of them they speak, recalling their jokes, their opinions, their faults and qualities ; and they say of the War that it was a damned good time !

It is only natural that certain scenes should have impressed themselves indelibly on the mind : certain battlefields with the dead lying thick in strange attitudes, and amongst them the bodies of friends ! But to the great majority of men such sights were not horrible—only small things are horrible—they were too impressive, too big ; there was an awesome grandeur, the fate of man in the immobility of that army of fallen : it was as though the Creator's secret had been approached—something seen but not understood.

But the thought that passes in a soldier's mind gives no indication of his action, his strength, his sacrifice, and his sense of right towards a comrade, his self-control and determination ; and this applies as much to a single orderly with a message as to a company relieving another company.

A brave officer, mentioned several times for his gallantry in a regiment of men who were all gallant, takes a young friend, lately joined, for a walk after tea :

" I wanted to get him accustomed to the unpleasant sights, which seemed to upset him less than I expected. There were a lot of yesterday's dead lying in front of the trenches—to-day's attacking troops were a little way down the far slope. The dead lay there in all their equipment, most of them shot in the head. When Casson was at Winchester he did not anticipate that he would be walking about on a fine April evening among a lot of dead men. It struck me as unnatural at the moment, probably because the stretcher-bearers had been identifying the bodies and had arranged them in seemly attitudes, their heads pillowed on their haversacks.

" Young Casson was trying to behave as though it was all quite ordinary ; he was having his first look at the horrors of war. While we were on the hill there was a large explosion down by Fontaine Wood, as though a dump had been blown up. On our way home we stopped to inspect a Tank which had got stuck in the mud while crossing a wide trench. But I was thinking to myself that sensitive people like Casson ought not to be taken to battlefields. I had grown accustomed to such sights, but I was able to realise the impact they made on a fresh mind. Detached from the fighting, we had merely gone for a short walk after tea, so to speak, and I couldn't help feeling as if I had been showing Casson something obscene. Nine years afterwards the whole business has become incredible. Unfortunately young Casson is not alive to share my sense of the incredulity of that little evening walk."

Such scenes were common enough, but they did not break the millions of civilian soldiers who saw them : how much longer they would have held one cannot say—the life, in which such scenes were incidents, was to so many a " damned good time " !

The gallantry of the Army inspired admiration, and the unselfishness of the soldier commanded affection. All lived near reality, saw it, and were not afraid. The teachings of civilisation which bid the young turn from blood, although it flows through their own veins, to affect disgust at the wonderful inner machinery of the human body although their own is similar, and to fear death although they will surely meet it to-day, did not exist on the battlefield.

It may be said that death was not a horror to the soldier, but every one of them had sympathy and understanding for the maimed ; the handicap of physical disability is obvious.

" The truth is that infantry soldiering in the battle-zone was an overwhelming physical experience. Such human elements as food, warmth, and sleep were the living realities, and it may not have occurred to many a writer of military histories that the weather was a more effective general than Foch, Haig, or Ludendorff.

" A bad blister on a man's heel might be the only thing he remembered after a week of intense experience which added a battle honour to the colours of his regiment. For those whose active unit was company, platoon, or section, physical sensations predominated. Mental activity (detached from feet and belly) was strictly limited to gross physical actualities. Whatever exploits a fighting man might afterwards claim he had achieved, his achievement could usually be recorded in a few short sentences. But how lifeless, how meagre and incomplete, that epitome would seem to one who understood but had not shared the experience, unless it was interwoven with those details of discomfort, so difficult to remember, which constitute the humanity of infantry soldiering ! If I were wearing a certain pair of wire-torn puttees and scraping the caked mud off them with a rusty entrenching tool, I should be able to remember quite a lot about the War ; as it is, the War emerges from its dugout in my subconscious memory as a very blurred personal experience of a time when I expected every day to be my last—a very ordinary infantry emotion." (Sassoon.)

And yet it was perhaps the greatest surprise of the War for the civilian soldier to discover how much pain and discomfort his body could resist : the discovery gave him confidence in himself, although for the moment the discomfort claimed his whole attention and consciousness, so that he was unable to see and give even a credible story of adjacent action in battle.

Sassoon, however, was a man of exceptional sensitive character, which seems to have led him more easily to pity than to admiration (generally speaking, the popular reaction to the War has turned from brave achievement to sympathise with pitiful impotence), but his observation is keen and his accounts and descriptions particularly vivid. What he says of physical sensations is true enough, but all soldiers did not suffer from discomfort and minor ailments all the time—the note does not commence to reveal the private soldier.

IV—17

The personal experience, which is so illuminating, is not easy to get. Power of expression was not a quality possessed by officers or men—indeed, in these records the fullness of the contributions from Dunn and Sassoon, and one or two others of the same unit, is detrimental to other battalions, whose records seem meagre in detail by comparison.   Regimental records are the most fitting place for the intimate though restricted view of the battle, but to chronicle jokes whose points, if any, lie at the bottom of Palestine ravines, or stark statements such as that someone found a dozen bottles of beer, seems not worth while ; and yet these are the kind of subjects which make up the majority of letters from the front and the jottings in diaries.   In itself this absence of comment is illuminating—it was not necessarily from a desire to spare the feelings of others.   The sole record of some battalions is the cold official account of actions—an adavnce or failure to advance from one point to another.

In the wider view of regimental work it is well for young officers and soldiers to realise that war consists of success and failure, of difficulties, obstacles, disappointments in all directions, and that it is the spirit in which duties are undertaken and performed that makes for ultimate success. The regiment, swollen to 42 battalions, steered its way through four years of war.   The highly trained Regular soldiers and Reservists dwindled in numbers ; inevitably the high standard of regimental training was reduced :· it was the great difficulty that had to be met and dealt with—on one side attrition, on the other expansion.   In spite of all efforts to preserve the integrity of the two Regular battalions, the War took its toll and the exigencies of the Service had to be met.

What would have been said if in January 1914 a proposition had been made to raise the strength of the regiment to 42 battalions practically within a year ?   It would have seemed a mad project.   There would have been gloomy forecasts of complete ruin, destruction of regimental spirit, the transformation of a highly trained and disciplined regiment into a mob !

The regiment was singularly fortunate in the number and quality of Regular, Reserve, and Retired officers and non-commissioned officers who served throughout the War : so much so that an examination of the records of battalions reveals no startling errors of leadership and training to note and guard against in future.   The magnitude of the War and the conditions under which it was met might well lead one to expect a lack of quality in what were known as the Service battalions, those special battalions raised for the period of the War only.   These records show that it was not the case.

It would be idle to say that all battalions had an equally successful record, but it is not possible to compare the tasks and conditions of one battalion with those of another, so that in fact it is never a question of battalions, but of the regiment. This becomes evident from the scattering of Regular, Reserve, and Retired officers and non-commissioned officers throughout the regiment—they served in all battalions. There was grumbling—it is a well-known soldier's privilege to ease his humour in this manner—but the grumbles were invariably belied by results. The difficulties existed and the difficulties were surmounted—and that is the proud claim of the regiment.

Some of the difficulties were formidable. Our 1st Battalion emerged from the first Battles of Ypres less than 90 strong ; drafts arrived, and the battalion was built up to strength. In 1916 the same thing happened on the Somme, although drafts being immediately available it is not so apparent ; and in 1917 the battalion was again shattered. In each case the names of certain officers and non-commissioned officers had cropped up in reports of patrols and raids to establish them as known and tried leaders of men, and in each case we find them in the fatal list of casualties. Gradually there seems to be no one left of the old battalion [1] ; their places can be filled, but how can the dash and tireless energy of Stockwell's men be replaced ? Holmes's men did the same.

In 1918 the 9th Battalion is practically destroyed on each of three successive occasions that it went into the line, only to rise from the fire of each battle as tough and unbreakable as before.

The more complete records of the 2nd Battalion show the colossal strain of steady depletion triumphantly met—a grip of steel—unshakable purpose !

The records of the 10th and the 19th (Bantam) Battalions are noble epitaphs on their brief careers.

None of these battalions can be said to have been exceptionally lucky— the tasks they were called upon to perform are truly appalling ; but there is an onward sweep without check in the record of their actions. On the other hand, the five Service battalions of the 38th Division, the three Territorial battalions of the 53rd Division, and the one Service battalion of the 13th Division received staggering blows in their first engagements. They recovered. But here was another difficulty the Regiment had to meet and deal with—a psychological difficulty, a disaster as an opening experience of war.

No parallel can be drawn between Mametz Wood and the first Battles of Ypres, or between any actions in France and those on the Gallipoli

---

[1] Two officers with continuous service in the 1st Battalion were Captain E. C. Hawes as Company Commander, and Captain B. Reeves as Adjutant. They were untouched and unshaken.

Peninsula. Officers who were present at Mametz Wood, and who have contributed to these records, are all agreed that it was a bungled affair. It was not a baptism of fire, but a slaughter of inexperienced troops working under confused orders—and they lost their leaders in the holocaust. Lieutenant-Colonel R. C. Bell, of the 15th Battalion, was the only commanding officer who came through untouched.

The result of such a disastrous entry into war is frequently seen : the battalion, drawn from the same pool of men as others, remains without spirit, enterprise, or determination to do anything ; a vicious circle of depression moves from officers to men and from men to officers, and it seems beyond the power of man to arrest it : the breaking-up of the unit is the only remedy. The men are then found to be good and normal soldiers. The mystery is covered by that blessed word " psychology " !

In the case of these five battalions it is the psychology of the regiment that becomes a mystery. After a term of inaction—which in itself presents a grave danger of staleness—they swept over the Pilckem Ridge in the third Battle of Ypres, and never looked back.

Gallipoli was a very different story, but it developed in the same way. After a year in Egypt the three battalions became the heroes of the first and third Battles of Gaza. Here, as in Mesopotamia, climatic conditions were often more trying than the inclement weather in Flanders and Northern France.

Powell's diary is a most human document. By his account of his own sufferings and indomitable courage he reveals the true nature of the Mesopotamian campaign. Here we come back to the physical condition—nothing is more depressing and exhausting than diarrhœa and kindred ailments. " The men still seem feeble and weak, and slow on their pins. I hope they will come up to the scratch all right," he wrote. And the men did come up to the scratch.

There was yet another ailment that visited troops in all climates and was officially recognised—war weariness. On the top of all others this was an anxious trouble. The strain of living under fire had, no doubt, much to do with it, but perhaps the chief cause was the enforced circumstances of life, which were easy but led to a gradual loss of personal care and pride. It was a fatal lethargy of body and mind that brought about a disregard and neglect of duty that was perilous. It affected the bravest, the iron-nerved. The official cure was a few weeks' leave, perhaps to England ; but the strain of fighting it was really on the company officers.

After all, the front-line trench was a ditch, and would carry out the natural draining functions of a ditch. However well tended, it was a dirty place. The soldier lived in a ditch, and that is all to be said of it ; there are none of the amenities of home life in a ditch. Dugouts were also crude, dirty habitations.

The support line was a ditch with dugouts, or maybe shelter was obtainable in a ruin. In reserve, billets might be tolerable.

Personal baggage was, naturally, whittled down to a minimum, the most important articles of which were a bit of soap and a razor.

The soldier sat on the earth, slept on it, became well acquainted with it. For days he was forbidden even to remove his boots, so that he might be ready to rise on the instant and fight. All delicate and decent convention was abolished. Body-lice abounded. He found it impossible to keep himself clean and smart. He became accustomed and indifferent to dirt, which was on his clothes and body, in his food and drink. If left to himself, the soldier lost all self-respect rapidly.

And the same influence was at work on the company officer. A tired officer had to goad himself at times to wash and shave in a cup of water, especially after several days of wallowing in mud. It seemed so inadequate, such a vain and useless pretence !

It was an easy life, as easy as that of a tramp who sleeps under a hedge. Feeding was easy. It was somebody's duty to dump food at a certain spot, and the soldier went and fetched it. He cut the meat into small pieces, threw them in a tin with a little water, and set them over a fire to stew. His tea was made in another tin—or perhaps in the same one as the stew. The company cooks had the field equipment, but the principle of cooking was much the same, whether done in bulk or by the individual. The soldier then sat on the ground to eat his stew and drink his tea. If he had nothing else to do, he lay down and slept, like a tramp under a hedge.

The strain of keeping a battalion up to the mark in cleanliness and smartness was as great as any in the War. Circumstances were always forcing the men back into a state of dirt. When in the line the first and principal duty of a soldier was to keep his rifle clean—nothing else really mattered. If water was plentiful, he was expected to shave ; if scarce, shaving was omitted.

The moment a company left the line there was a "clean-up," a scraping of mud from uniforms and polishing of buttons—the men had only one uniform. Every effort was made to give them baths and clean underclothing (under favourable circumstances once a fortnight). A travelling oven, a " de-lousing machine," dealt with the cast-off underclothing, which was then passed to the laundry. At the beginning of the War the 1st and 2nd Battalions instituted laundries of their own, but later the laundry became a divisional organisation.   The opportunity of de-lousing the men's uniforms was so rare it can be ignored, although some battalions carried ordinary household flat-irons for that purpose.   In any case, when washed and provided with clean underclothing the man returned to a shed or room which was invariably infested with lice, and so back to the mud, dust, and stench of the ditch.

The efforts to keep billets clean were restricted to picking up bits of paper, cigarette ends, and food.   It was occasionally possible to improvise a broom, but the floors of rooms could not be scrubbed, and the majority of billets were floorless barns.   Grease and bits of food thrown on the ground were removed or covered over by means of a shovel.   All refuse collected was burned in an incinerator.

In the trench or ditch everyone floundered about in mud when it rained—there was nothing to be done ; but in dry weather the company officer kept his eyes open for bits of paper, cigarette ends, and scraps of food.   The easiest way for men to get rid of these things was to heave them over the parapet.   In France, at the beginning of the War, bully-beef tins lay thick amongst the wire entanglements ; but the evil was soon recognised, and all trench refuse had to be collected in sandbags and buried by the sanitary men, who also disposed of the contents of latrine buckets in the same way, so that in course of time the ground was infested.

It was all easy and simple, and the monotony of it produced a weariness of soul as the months and years slipped by, and the bravest commenced to " bob," as the men said.   The first signs of war-weariness occurred during the winter of 1914–15, when the practice of growing beards and allowing unpolished buttons crept through the Expeditionary Force.   It was readily excused in those uncertain days, but the Army suddenly woke up and realised where they were drifting and the evil was stopped.   From that moment ceaseless vigilance on the part of company officers and non-commissioned officers within the regiment kept the battalions at the highest possible pitch of smartness, but it was weary work.

The burden was increased at the end of the War, the conscript period, when a type of man was drafted into the Army who was not only unused to discipline but lacked also the sense of duty that had inspired the volunteer, and although he responded to orders, he was not generally inclined to move ahead of them.   In the back areas, where so many organisations for supply and administration had cropped up, and where supervision was frequently lax, men with no excuse for slovenliness seemed to take a delight in being untidy and dirty.   The men of fighting units regarded them with contempt, but it was a bad example for some of the newer drafts.   At the same time the enormous war consumption had resulted in a shortage of material, so that new uniforms were no longer issued from Ordnance as a matter of course. Old uniforms had to be returned to be patched with material of a different shade and texture and reissued to the troops. The result was not encouraging, and the tendency of all this was to undermine self-respect and discipline.

The difficulties of the British officer were equally the experience of enemy officers. The Germans, at the very commencement of the War, had talked at length of their " will to conquer." They were highly disciplined, wonderfully organised. But war weariness fell on them and their Allies, and cracks in their defence became visible.

It was the lesser degree of war weariness that brought us victory and enabled us to attack in the final advance with vigour. The spirit was alive, but when the " cease fire " order was given it was rather tired.

And the men were physically tired. The German retreat was well carried out, the demolition of railways, cross roads, and bridges was complete, and the task of pursuit was a far greater physical effort than retreat ; but they drove forward until the last moment, and then " from the depths of war we passed in the twinkling of an eye into the depths of peace " (Garcia, 53rd Division). Everywhere it was the same—the Army halted to await orders !

Nothing happened. Nothing, in the dramatic sense, could happen ! Attempts have been made by the use of dramatic words in descriptions of the last minute of war to create an atmosphere of drama which did not exist. Units on the move merely halted, and if the question, What do we do now ? was not asked, it represents the state of mind throughout the combatant troops.

In Italy the bridging difficulties in the last advance had resulted in short rations, and the men had waded through rivers and marched until their clothes and boots dried on them, so that their first thought was probably a welcome rest. They were, however, moved back immediately to the Vicenza area. There was no demonstration.

Ll. Evans, Adjutant of the 2nd Battalion, records an attempt, even as the gunners in some batteries vied with each other to fire the last gun, to create excitement and enthusiasm.

" What a glorious autumn day it was ! Dry, hazy, and with promise of sunshine—a rare, crisp, good-to-be-alive-in winter's day. There was excitement in the air, too, because rumours were rife, hopes high, and spirits never brighter since somehow we had begun to *feel* that the end was very near, and a sensation of release, which we had hardly dared express, was persistent in our hearts. . . .

" On that morning of mornings we were taking it easy, for the scattered enemy were ' out somewhere in front ' and worrying us neither with shell nor machine-gun fire, except but fitfully and from afar. Our centre, Aulnoy, was what had been a most important enemy railhead up to a few days previously, and at the station with its rows of metalled fairways was grim evidence of the effect of our night raiding bombers and long-range gun fire.

" Early on this day, however, there was calm around, but excited expectation in the breasts of all of us, since by now that premature rumour which had excited Britain from Land's End to John o' Groats—and from Penmaenmawr to Pontypridd also—had reached us out there, so that somewhere about 9 a.m., when came the official message from Brigade that ' an armistice was signed at 08·00 hours to-day—hostilities will cease therefore at 11·00 hours,' one felt a sense of anti-climax ; the long-sought-for moment so recently hoped for and a feeling of certainty seemed tame and ungraspable after all, leaving an inexplicable sensation of flatness.

" But momentary, and perhaps peculiarly personal, for some cheers were rising and the good news spread as only the best of news can.

" A, B, C, and D Companies were spread out in the village beyond, under arms or on outpost duty. I have a copy of the last message issued in the War before me as I write :

" ' To A, B, C, D Coys : H.Q. and Q.M.

" ' Official information has been received that an armistice was signed at 08·00 hrs. to-day AAA Hostilities will cease at 11·00 hrs. AAA Troops will then unfix bayonets and unload rifles at that hour and will stand by for further orders AAA.'

" The morning wore on, but still that sense of its being unbelievable also prevailed. As 11 o'clock approached, ' orders ' were evidently being obeyed with zeal, for rifles were being ' unloaded ' into the air, as also were pouches and all stray S.A.A. around.

" A band appeared from somewhere and played. I well remember it, ' Ap Shenkin,' that rousing march of the gallant 41st, and later our march, ' The Men of Harlech,' rent the air.

" There was a ' pay-day ' atmosphere, and flags and bunting appeared miraculously in almost every cottage, kept heaven only knows where throughout those long four years of occupation !

" A prisoner was brought in that afternoon. A youth, dazed and bewildered, knowing not where his comrades were, nor how to seek them. Humorously a card was placed on him, ' The very last ! ' But to the men experienced in war, the capturers of prisoners in their thousands, this field-grey youth seemed a novelty to-day, and he soon became a pet. They fed him and gave him ' fags,' turned him eastwards with his face towards the Fatherland, and sent him off with their good wishes that he should reach there safely and unharmed.

" Beyond the village there was tragedy—men killed and men wounded on the very morning of peace, on the fringe of that village of prophetic name, ' Wattinges sur Victoire ' !

" Armistice night came ; that night when London and ' home ' went mad with joy. But no outbreak of joyous madness took us up in its flight. Verey lights blazed away all round, sounds of singing came from barn and estaminet, burning dumps flared on the horizon, but that was all. It was over ! A fact too stupendous to realise, all in one day.

" There was no rumbling of distant guns ; no staccato of machine guns ; no zooming of enemy or other aircraft to wreck the uncanny stillness of that night—and, perhaps, that was why I could not sleep at all ! "

It was a tame affair—even the firing of rifles in the air was not general. In the villages the civilians made some show of Gallic delight, kissed the nearest soldiers, and from some cellars produced wine ; but the French peasant was not disposed to slake the thirst of the British Tommy, and the bottles were restricted in number. It was otherwise in England. Many accounts have been written of the extraordinary scenes in London ; Mr. Winston Churchill's is one of the best. Captain Moody, of our 2nd Battalion, after three and a half years in France, was sent home for six months' rest as an instructor at a Corps School—he writes :

" With three colleagues, officers in the Royal Scots, Argyll and Sutherland Highlanders, and Rifle Brigade, I went to see what London was doing on Armistice night. Parades had been ordered for next day, the 12th, but they were cancelled tacitly, then formally. We arrived in town early in the evening in the rain, and it continued to rain. Thinking it necessary to book a table for dinner, we made a weary round of restaurants that were full up, before coming to rest at a little place in Wardour Street, owned by a Frenchman. Very bedraggled we were, for the London populace was in a state of wild excitement, especially the feminine part, who seemed to think that anyone in uniform was fair game.

" The doors of the restaurant were closed immediately after we got in, and customers were told that Monsieur X, the proprietor, wished to make a speech. Standing on a table he spoke, partly in French, partly in broken English, with much gesticulation. He said the doors had been closed because of the crowds, and that it would be unsafe for those who had been fortunate enough to get in to leave until late at night. He had an eye to business ! Dinner was ordered, but before the fish had been eaten it was obvious that no more food would be served owing to the waiter's preoccupation with the opening of champagne bottles. Songs were started by the French community and rendered with excessive noise, fervour overcoming the singers. The Scottish officers could not stand it ; they insisted on providing real music, so every Scottish song ever written was given in turn. The popularity of the Scots overcame all thought of food. Everyone in uniform had to be the guest of civilians. All present were soon on the best of terms. The scene of amity was indescribable. We danced ; we toasted the Entente Cordiale many dozens of times ; but as time wore on, the novelty of the experience wore off, so we contrived to give our new-made friends the slip and have a look at what the rest of London was doing.

" The scenes outside were extraordinary. Coventry Street and Leicester Square were packed with people whose chief object seemed to be to shake hands with any Service man. Girls formed rings, in the centre of which was pushed and pulled any officer or man they could seize. By this means the four of us got separated for a time, but by good luck we met again in Coventry Street. The feeling of the people was really genuine, there was no disorder. Everyone was extraordinarily kind and generous ; it seemed that most of the better-class people were taking a personal interest in each soldier they met.

" About 1 a.m. on the 12th I found myself alone, having seen the going of my friends. Number One had taken strong objection to a small under-sized Jew, and expressed his intention to ask the little man ' what he had done in the Great War.' His victim, seeing that something out of the ordinary was about to happen, turned and bolted through the crowd, closely pursued by Number One.

" Number Two disappeared on the roof of a private limousine, dancing a reel.

" Number Three was left giving a good exhibition of squad drill, using a squad of policemen who had just come out on duty from Vine Street. A space had been cleared, and the police were willingly carrying out his orders, to the amusement of the crowd.

" Number Four, his hand black and swollen with much handshaking, arrived at the Piccadilly Hotel that was more than overcrowded. After a clean-up I descended to the grill-room, where most of the occupants seemed to be dancing on the tables or steeplechasing over the furniture that had been pushed against the walls. I had not been in the room a second before a party of perfect strangers insisted that I had been a friend of the family for more years than they cared to remember and compelled me to be a guest for the rest of the night. So there was I among about twenty people, being hilariously entertained. Having had nothing to eat since lunch-time, I tried to impress on my new-made friends that food was all-important. The protest was ignored, and champagne was ordered.

" A day or so later the original party of four met again and tried to reckon up the number of people who had ordered champagne on their behalf. It had been quite impossible to share in all that had been ordered —many dozens of bottles of champagne must have been wasted." The last statement is probably not correct !

The celebrations were carried on in England for a number of days. Men overstayed their leave to the United Kingdom, but there were no cases of desertion in the regiment. Gradually the jubilations died down.

Technically we were still at war—it was merely an armistice that had been signed—but actually it was peace ; no one believed for a moment that hostilities would recommence. A colossal task was over, and—a colossal task remained to be done.

In November 1918 the total number of men under arms in the British Empire was estimated at 5,389,607. Of these, British and Colonial troops numbered 4,089,226. At home, in England, there were 1,383,311 British and 220,073 Colonial troops ; abroad, in the various theatres of war, 2,075,275 British, 304,400 Colonial, and in India 93,670 British (these were chiefly Territorial and specially enlisted troops). The meanest intelligence could perceive the gigantic problem that faced the Government, but unfortunately the cheaper Press showed strong partisan and personal bias, became opportunist, and supported the worst elements in the Army, who commenced to ask when they would be sent home.

Nothing of a very serious nature occurred. In France demonstration was generally limited, where any was made, to a refusal to go on parade. In England a mob of foolish men gathered in Whitehall on several occasions, some of them having taken lorries and driven up from outlying camps. But there is no burking the fact that the powerful Press support given to the agitators created a serious and dangerous situation.

The scheme for demobilisation, in brief, was based on what were called " key industries," of which mining was one, and batches of men were withdrawn from battalions for repatriation. Incidentally the key industries had, during the War, recruited workers from other trades and occupations, who, in the main, preferred learning a new craft at home to risking their lives in support of the national family in trouble. The support these workers had given to the fighting men was, in most cases, commensurate to the wages they were able to wring from a harassed Government by strikes, and, naturally enough, the newly recruited workers joined the Trade Union of their selected industry. Consequently the demobilised soldiers found that their old jobs were not waiting for them, but that they were expected to wait until the industry absorbed them, unless the temporary workers who had taken their places went willingly back to their previous and actual trades. The majority, however, did not propose to take the latter course, and quite a number of them, mercifully gifted, had attained minor positions in the official ranks of Trade Unionism.

.   .   .   .

The 1st Battalion was billeted at Montechio Maggiore. " The Battalion dwindled away till the cadre came home. Time was spent in sports and athletics of all sorts. Education (!) was introduced into the Army : it was a new toy, and higher powers liked to see it, and disliked one if they did not see it. All sorts of vocational classes were started. The Transport Officer found his men being demobilised quicker than his animals—an animal-management class solved his difficulties. There were several race meetings. For the officers, polo, paper-chasing, a tandem, and a four-in-hand helped to fill in the time." (Alston.)

The battalion (cadre) left C. Valle on the 23rd February, 1919, and arrived at Wrexham on St. David's Day.

From the 2nd Battalion we get more details of what happened in France, and it may be assumed that they apply in essence to all the battalions.

" The battalion remained at Aulnoy until a few days after Christmas 1918. Billets were comfortable and a common regimental mess was established by Major R. A. Adamson, who had come to us some time in October, in what had been the refreshment-room of the station.

" A considerable number of officers and men joined us during these weeks, from base camps, courses, detached duties, etc. Many of the officers were fresh from England, not having reached France until after the Armistice.

" Demobilisation commenced almost immediately, the priority of various occupations directing the class of men to be released first. Miners were called for very early, and one of the first of these to seek his move back to the pit was Lance-Corporal (then Sergeant) W. Evans, the ubiquitous ' O.C. runners.' . . . The sequel justifying this recollection was in a letter from Colonel Cockburn, in about 1920, wherein he mentioned he had but recently heard from the ' plucky little bird,' writing from Constantinople, where he was then serving with the Royal Army Service Corps. Evidently the call of the mine had proved a fickle one.

" Colonel Cockburn returned to us before we left Aulnoy, remained there a short time, and returned to Oswestry to assume command of the 1st Battalion, then preparing to proceed to India.

" During December an Army Order was issued allowing Regular infantry battalions to send an escort for their colours if they wished. Colonel Norman was now acting as Brigade Commander and de Miremont was again promoted to Acting Lieutenant-Colonel in command. 2nd Lieutenants J. Roberts and Roberts-Morgan, who had transferred to us from the 13th Battalion, and three senior non-commissioned officers made the trip to Wrexham for our colours. The sentiment was, perhaps, admirable, but the worry of having so valuable a regimental possession in our keeping in such temporary quarters as we occupied hardly justified the additional pomp and circumstance thus acquired.

" Christmas Day was spent where we had seen the War end, but a few days later the unit was moved to hutments outside Blangy-Tronville, some 8 to 10 kilometres out of Amiens, just off the Albert road. A good deal had to be done to make the camp comfortable, but, in spite of cold weather, things were soon as comfortable as ingenuity could make them.

" Demobilisation continued meanwhile, reducing the companies' strength week by week. Officers also were going off as the weeks followed each other—some home, some to jobs such as the charge of various ' clearing-up ' areas, and some to the Rhine as educational officers ; and some went to Boulogne, together with men whose terms of service did not expire, with a view to further service in Egypt and the East. Whether they ever went I cannot say, for rumours were heard of much trouble and mutinous opposition to this scheme being made by some of the men assembled there for this purpose. [*Our 26th Battalion went to Egypt.*]

" Route marching, camp duties, and fatigues were the order of the day at that period, and a recreation hut and canteen was established for the men, completed with ' chip fryers '—an innovation that was very popular until the night when the fat blazed into flame and burnt the whole hut to the ground.

" Besides the colours, the regimental band and goat came out to join us while we were at Blangy. Both arrived together, the band fifty-six strong, under Bandmaster Clancy, and the goat, habitually stubborn, in charge of one of the musicians.

" The arrival of the band was much welcomed, making route marches occasions, guests' nights functions, and church parades ceremonials. It was in great demand throughout the division the whole time we were there.

" The bandboys had to attend school as well as band practice, and strict ' bounds ' were enforced on them within the camp area—only to be broken with disastrous results on one occasion, for a party of them, inspecting a German dump, set some bombs off, with the result that eight or nine were wounded, and one, Boy Williams, aged fifteen, was killed.

"Some time in the spring we were ordered to send a half-company, armed with Lewis guns, to surround an island in the Somme, somewhere near Bray, known to be the headquarters and base of a number of Australian and French deserters who were terrorising the neighbourhood. This party set out and completed their task without difficulty, for the 'enemy' were completely surprised and caught in their beds and pyjamas.

"While here the battalion received two visits from Royalty. Early in January His Majesty the King visited every division in turn, and when visiting the 38th he was accompanied by the Prince of Wales and the Duke of York. Later H.R.H. the Prince of Wales spent most of a week with the 38th, staying at Headquarters with General Cubitt. One of these days he spent with the 2nd Battalion, arriving before lunch, for which he stayed, and leaving late in the afternoon. He held an informal inspection of the men in their lines, dispensing with the enormous 'tail' which followed him, and chatting freely with our men.

"Taffy's Day, 1st March 1919, was celebrated in time-honoured fashion, General Cubitt and his Staff, as well as all Brigade Staffs, being our guests. Colonel Norman presided on that occasion. With the presence of the band, drums, and goat, the ceremony lost little of its peace-time ritual, and the leek was eaten as time-honoured custom ordained.

"Our horses were being collected for disposal at a huge horse depot at Havre, and opportunity was given to officers who wished to purchase their chargers if passed fit for export. Yates purchased Girlie.

"Yates was busy with a mystic form G1098, making up a complete equipment for a full-sized battalion, down to horse-shoes and spare pins, for conveyance home when the time came.

"Orders for proceeding to England came in May. We were now but a skeleton, a cadre battalion, except for complete transport and stores and equipment. The officers were Yates, Fox, Howells Evans, Roberts Morgan, and myself. Albutt was Regimental Sergeant-Major, and veterans like Quartermaster-Sergeant Jack Hughes, Company Sergeant-Major 'Dodger' Green, Sergeant Drummer Dyer, Childs of the Transport, the old water-cart man, whose name I forget, and sundry other well known in the battalion, were amongst those forming the cadre, together with the band and goat.

"We entrained at Longeau, outside Amiens, for Havre, where more than a week was spent in camp at Harfleur.

"We shared a boat with the 1st Wiltshire cadre and band, but before moving off the goat business began.   Weeks prior to this I had, according to orders, obtained a permit from the Board of Agriculture and Fisheries to bring over the goat, but on endeavouring to embark on our transport the skipper would not allow it to set foot on his boat, despite my authority from England—it had to be one from the port of embarkation.   I had nothing less to do than taxi from the landing-stage in search of some competent authority, meanwhile keeping the boat, all ready to sail, waiting for me.   The local Embarkation Officer was at last traced to his lair, only to be found dubious of his authority to issue a permit.   So off I went to someone higher up, and thence higher up still, regulations and orders being consulted while I held my paper tightly in my hand, as it was too laborious a process to take it out of my pocket and put it back again.

" Eventually I got back with the necessary chit, and sped with all haste to the impatient transport, to find that all was ' set ' except that our bandmaster and the Wiltshire ditto hadn't even then decided who was senior in order to conduct the massed bands as we moved from French soil.   Finally, the Wiltshire man had it, and we left the port to the strains of ' Auld lang syne,' the ' Marseillaise,' ' Men of Harlech,' and other suitable airs.

" Arriving at Southampton, we were moved to a comfortable camp on the Winchester Road, and unloading began.

" But now the goat wasn't allowed to be landed.   But somehow or other we smuggled it to the dock-side and stealthily lugged it to our camp. After the unloading, we entrained for Blackdown.   Smuggling the goat was practised as a habit, as apparently station-masters and guards equally objected to its conveyance, pleading foot-and-mouth disease, or some such impediment.

" At Blackdown we were the guests of the Loyal North Lancashire, to whom our complete mobilisation stores had now to be handed over.   While Yates was making a ritual of this transference—had every bit laid out, inspection fashion, checking off each nail and strap on his beloved G1098 in company with his opposite number—we had nothing at all to do.

" On completion of the handing over, we entrained, after a last alter-cation on the goat question, for Wrexham, arriving there on a Saturday (1st June), to be met by the band of the 1st Battalion and Colonel Cockburn, the Mayor and Corporation in their robes of office, and most of the inhabitants."

.   .   .   .

From every front drafts arrived at the demobilisation centres, and finally the cadres.   The 11th Battalion, at Constantinople, absorbed a certain number of men from the 2nd East Surrey Regiment, when that regiment was reduced to cadre strength, and were not disbanded until the 14th October 1919. The 6th Garrison Battalion had been disbanded in Salonika on the 24th June.

The final year's work of the 26th (4th Garrison) Battalion is of interest, especially in view of the agitation for immediate demobilisation. The battalion embarked at Dunkirk on the 7th May for two weeks' leave in England, returning on the 21st—strength, 30 officers and 678 other ranks. Two days later they left for Marseilles, embarked on the 28th and arrived at Alexandria on the 4th June. They proceeded to their station at Damanhur by rail on the 9th. In August they moved to Tanta.

In September 150 other ranks were drafted to the 7th Battalion (T.F.), 80 were demobilised, and the battalion (307 other ranks) sent to Sidi Bishr. The cadre did not arrive in England until the 10th January 1920, to be disbanded on the 20th.

And so the many gallant Service battalions disappeared, the Territorial battalions also (for the Force was entirely disbanded, only to be recalled a few months later as the Territorial Army), and the Garrison battalions. The regiment, reduced to two battalions, commenced the work of rebuilding.

" Read and re-read the story of your regiment if you wish to know what men can do and have done, . . . and you will have received an impulse that, in whatever walk of life you may be, will make your hearts beat high and lead you to a life worthy of those magnificent soldiers of Wales who, in peace or war, in life or death, have set us so great an example." Thus Lieutenant-General Sir Francis Lloyd, Colonel of the Regiment, in his introduction to the short History of the Regiment. It was he who unveiled the memorial at Wrexham on the 15th November 1924, that monument of stone to the immortal memory of the Royal Welch Fusiliers.

Make your hearts beat high ! Can the story fail ? In England it has been the practice of civilians to make war ; the most peaceful body of men in the land are the soldiers who fight the wars. If these records serve no other purpose than to show how men of the Royal Welch fulfilled their engagements to the King and State, your hearts must beat high—for no man can do more.

APPENDICES

LIEUTENANT-GENERAL SIR FRANCIS LLOYD, G.C.V.O., K.C.B., D.S.O.

APPENDIX I

SUCCESSION OF COLONELS OF THE ROYAL WELCH FUSILIERS

LIEUTENANT-GENERAL SIR FRANCIS LLOYD, G.C.V.O., K.C.B., D.S.O.

LIEUTENANT-GENERAL SIR FRANCIS LLOYD, G.C.V.O., K.C.B., D.S.O., of Aston Hall, Oswestry, and Rolls Park, Chigwell, was appointed Colonel of the Royal Welch Fusiliers on the 2nd February 1915, on the death of Sir Luke O'Connor, V.C., K.C.B.

Francis Lloyd was born in 1853, and was the son of an old Grenadier. He was educated at Harrow, and commenced his military career in the 33rd Foot (Duke of Wellington's Regiment) ; within a few months of joining, however, he transferred to the Grenadier Guards (18th March 1875).

In 1885 he served as signalling officer to the Guards Brigade in the Suakim Expedition, and was mentioned in despatches after the Battle of Hasheen. In 1898 he was again in Egypt as second-in-command to the 1st Battalion Grenadier Guards, and was awarded the D.S.O., being again mentioned in despatches.

During the South African War he served for two years in command of the 2nd Battalion, and was severely wounded at Biddulphsberg.

He commanded the 1st Guards Brigade at Aldershot from 1904 to 1908. Being promoted Major-General, he was given command of the Welsh Division, Territorial Force, in 1909 ; and of the London District in 1913.

During the War the London District was one of the most important commands in the British Army, and Sir Francis Lloyd held it for five years. His name was known to every British soldier. A man of remarkable character and forceful personality, he combined the firmness of a strict disciplinarian with a rare kindliness of heart, so that he was able not only to rule London with an iron hand, but to preserve the affection he had won in the old Army during the creation and existence of the new Army. It was a triumph of firmness and tact.

He retired in 1920 and became Food Commissioner for London and the Home Counties. He died on the 26th February 1926, and was buried at Oswestry. The 2nd Battalion detailed the Band and funeral party.

SIR CHARLES MACPHERSON DOBELL, K.C.B., C.M.G., D.S.O.

SECOND son of Richard Reid Dobell, of Beauvoir Manor, Quebec, Canada ; born 22nd June 1869. Received his commission as 2nd Lieutenant in the Royal Welch Fusiliers on 20th August 1890 ; became Lieutenant 13th July 1892, Captain and Brevet Major

275

8th March 1899, Major and Brevet Lieutenant-Colonel 29th September 1907, Brevet Colonel 4th November 1910, promoted out of the Regiment to rank of substantive Lieutenant-Colonel 4th May 1912. Served with the 1st Battalion in the Hazara Expedition, North-west Frontier of India, 1891, receiving medal and clasp. Was appointed Adjutant 2nd Battalion 7th November 1896, and served with that Battalion during the International Occupation of Crete from March 1897 to December 1898, for which he was mentioned in despatches and received the brevet of Major.

He took part in the South African War, first doing duty with the Royal Canadian Regiment, then as A.D.C. to the G.O.C. 2nd Cavalry Brigade, during the Relief of Kimberley and the operations which resulted in the surrender of General Cronje and his army at Paardeberg, subsequently in command of the 2nd Battalion Mounted Infantry from 24th February to 15th July 1900. For his services he was mentioned in despatches, awarded the D.S.O., and granted the Queen's Medal with clasps for Relief of Kimberley —Paardeberg—Driefontein—Johannesburg—Diamond Hill—Wittebergen.

In July 1900, trouble having broken out in China, he resumed his duties as Adjutant 2nd Battalion, arriving in Pekin in August, shortly after the relief of the Legations. He took part in subsequent minor operations and was awarded the medal. He attended the Staff College during 1903–4.

In January 1905 he went to Northern Nigeria to command the 1st Battalion Northern Nigeria Regiment, West African Frontier Force. Here he took part in expeditions first against the Munshi tribe on the Benue River and then against the King of Hadejia, who, at a critical period in the history of Nigeria, had revolted against our rule.

While still in the Munshi country he was ordered to move his column, consisting of artillery and infantry with porter transport, as quickly as possible to Zungeru, then the capital of Northern Nigeria. The journey, which lasted several days, was made by water, but it was the height of the dry season and the rivers were very low, consequently progress was slow. From a point on the Kaduna River it was possible, by marching across a large bend of the river, to save considerable time. This was done, and a distance of 87 miles was covered in 47 hours. The troops were in heavy order, carrying capes, blankets, and 100 rounds of ammunition besides arms and equipment. The carriers were all laden with 60-lb. to 65-lb. loads. Time had not admitted of previous arrangements being made for the comfort and supply of the column during this forced march ; that not a man fell out speaks volumes for the discipline and marching qualities of the Nigerian troops. Was twice mentioned in despatches, received the medal with clasp and Brevet Lieutenant-Colonel.

He was employed as a General Staff Officer at Army Headquarters in the Directorate of Military Operations at the War Office from 1907 to 1911, the section of which he was in charge dealing especially with our Dominions and Colonies. In January 1908 he was awarded the certificate on vellum of the Royal Humane Society for saving life.

On 4th November 1910 he was appointed an Aide-de-Camp to His Majesty King George V, and was granted the brevet of full Colonel. As an A.D.C. to the King he took part in the Coronation ceremonies in 1911 and received the Coronation Medal.

On 4th May 1912 he was appointed to command the 2nd Battalion Bedfordshire

Regiment, quartered in South Africa. On the 1st September 1913 he was appointed Inspector-General West African Frontier Force with the rank of Brigadier-General. During the ensuing winter he visited and inspected the troops in Nigeria, the Gold Coast Colony and Ashanti, Sierra Leone, and the Gambia.

On the outbreak of the European War in August 1914 he was appointed by the British and French Governments to command the Allied troops operating in the German colony of the Cameroons. His conduct of the ensuing operations was so successful that by March 1916 the country, which had an area of nearly one-third of a million square miles, was entirely cleared of Germans, and by the following month it was possible to withdraw all troops. He was rewarded with the C.M.G. on 1st January 1915 ; was specially promoted to Major-General for service in the field in June 1915 ; and after the conclusion of the operations was created a K.C.B. The French conferred the Legion of Honour, Croix de Commandeur, on him. On arrival in England he was summoned to Windsor, where the King conferred the K.C.B. on him.

In June 1916 he joined the Egyptian Expeditionary Force, and was appointed to command the Western Force with a front extending from Sollum on the Mediterranean to Assuan on the Middle Nile, a distance of roughly 900 miles.

In September of that year he was transferred to command the East Force, which included all troops on and east of the Suez Canal, and was appointed a temporary Lieutenant-General. Under his orders successful actions were fought at El Arish— Magdhaba and Rafah, at each of which the enemy received telling defeats and the loss of many thousand unwounded prisoners.

In March 1917 he attacked the enemy entrenched about Gaza ; in this battle he advanced his army, consisting of one Mounted Corps (2 Divisions and Camel Brigade), 52nd, 53rd, and 54th Divisions, with ancillary troops, in one jump of 15 miles across a waterless desert. He eventually was obliged to break off the engagement owing to lack of water, but remained in occupation of the Wadi Ghazzi, about 3 miles from Gaza.

In April he again attacked, but although he forced the enemy back and entrenched his force close under the defences of Gaza, he was unable to inflict the crushing defeat on the Turks he had hoped for. Very considerable reinforcements had reached the enemy in the intervening weeks, while he had only received some portions of the recently formed 74th Division.

He returned to England in May. For his services in Egypt he was twice mentioned in despatches.

In July 1917 he went to India to command a division. In connection with the internal trouble which broke out in India in the early months of 1919 he received the thanks of the Government of India.

May 1919 found him in the Khyber Pass in command of his (the 2nd) Division, taking part in the third Afghan War. For this he received a mention in despatches and medal with clasp.

In January 1920 he assumed command of the Northern Army, and in February of that year was nominated by the Commander-in-Chief in India (General Sir Charles Monro) to command on the Khyber and Kurram fronts in event of hostilities again breaking out with Afghanistan. This, at that time, looked very probable, as the Afghans had already crossed the frontier into British territory in Chitral and at Paiwar

Kotal, at the head of the Kurram Valley. As hostilities did not ensue, he came home in August of that year. He received one more mention in despatches for his services in India, and for the Great War received the 1914 Star as well as the War and Victory Medals.

He was not again employed, but was placed on the retired list in November 1923, after being three years on half-pay.

In 1926, on the death of Lieutenant-General Sir Francis Lloyd, G.C.V.O., K.C.B., D.S.O., he had the great satisfaction of being appointed Colonel the Royal Welch Fusiliers.

He is included among the twenty-two General Officers whose portraits go to make up the picture " Some General Officers of the Great War," by the late Mr. John Sargent, R.A., painted for the nation and now hanging in the National Gallery. He was educated at Charterhouse and at the Royal Military College, Kingston, Canada. He married, on 3rd March 1908, Elizabeth Annie, daughter of Major Meyrick Bankes, of Winstanley Hall, Wigan, and of Letterewe, Ross-shire, and widow of Captain F. Livington Campbell, R.N.

APPENDIX II

THE CAMPAIGN IN THE CAMEROONS

A SHORT account of the operations of the Allied expedition which conquered the German West African colony of the Cameroons will not be out of place here, since the chief command was held throughout by an ex-Royal Welchman and several other officers of the regiment took part.

Germany's African possessions consisted, in 1914, of German East Africa, German South-west Africa, the Cameroons, and Togoland. The first three comprised an area of about one-third of a million square miles each, while Togoland was considerably smaller. An expedition was sent from India to operate against German East Africa. General Botha, at the head of forces of the Union of South Africa, conquered German South-west Africa, while in Togoland and the Cameroons the French and British acted together and allied expeditions were employed.

Brigadier-General C. M. Dobell, D.S.O., A.D.C., had in 1913 been appointed Inspector-General of the West African Frontier Force, and, by common consent of both nations, he was selected for the command of the Allied forces in the Cameroons.

The troops employed, both French and British, were drawn from the native African forces recruited and trained in the West African colonies of the two nations.

The General Headquarters Staff of the expedition left England in August 1914, arriving off the coast of the Cameroons on the 23rd September. The task which had to be accomplished was not an easy one. The country, which is situated between Nigeria and French Equatorial Africa, is vast, roadless, much of it can boast of possessing the worst climate in the world, and the dense tropical forests which stretch back for a

LIEUTENANT-GENERAL SIR CHARLES DOBELL, K.C.B., C.M.G., D.S.O.

hundred miles along the whole sea-coast are all in favour of the side acting on the defensive.

The Germans were well armed, well trained, and the proportion of Europeans with their African troops was very high. In the first instance a landing had to be effected and the force established on shore. This operation was rendered peculiarly difficult owing to the dangerous bars at the mouths of the rivers and to the presence of mango swamps along the coast and on the banks of all rivers and creeks, while the Germans had obstructed the Cameroon river on which the capital, Duala, stands, by sinking eleven ocean-going steamers in the channel; this obstacle being in its turn protected by two mine-fields. In spite of this, on the 27th September, only four days after the arrival of the expedition, a threatened landing of troops to the east of Duala conducted in conjunction with a bombardment of the town by H.M.S. *Challenger* caused the German Governor to surrender the town of Duala and retire some 200 miles to the east, where he established his seat of government at Taunde.

This initial success was followed by eighteen months of hard and continuous fighting in the most trying and difficult circumstances in a country of dense forests and under almost incessant rain. On the 1st January 1916, however, General Dobell's expeditionary force, with which had been co-operating a force under Brigadier-General F. J. Cunliffe from the northern district of Nigeria, and another composed of French and Belgian troops, under General Aymerick from French Equatorial Africa, entered Taunde on the heels of the retiring Germans. The enemy was given no leisure, but was constantly harassed during his rapid flight to Spanish Muni, which had now become his goal. After eluding their pursuers, the remnants of the German forces, some 1,000 Europeans and 6,000 blacks, laid down their arms and were interned by the Spaniards.

By the middle of February 1916 no Germans remained in the Cameroons, and the conquest of the country was complete.

Among the horrors and savageries which we are accustomed, with only too much reason, to associate with our enemies on all fronts during the War, the following little incident is interesting as showing that they were not all at all times devoid of chivalry. A patrol of 1 N.C.O. and 5 men of the Gold Coast Regiment was sent out on reconnoitring duty in April 1915. This patrol never returned and no news was forthcoming about its fate. Some months later, when an advance was made, we found a mound over which the following inscription had been placed in German : " Here lie six soldiers of the Gold Coast Regiment who died for the honour of England and for the glory of their country."

The following officers of the Royal Welch Fusiliers served with General Dobell in this very successful campaign :

Major (temp. Lieutenant-Colonel) J. B. Cockburn commanded the 1st Battalion of the Nigeria Regiment and greatly distinguished himself. From first to last he was always where the fighting was most severe ; he brilliantly conducted many important and difficult operations, always with the greatest success. The end of the campaign found him in command of the British contingent of the force.

For an act of most conspicuous gallantry, in jumping overboard into the Cameroon River, which is infested with crocodiles, when in high flood, in an attempt to save a bluejacket of H.M.S. *Cumberland* who had fallen overboard, he was awarded the Silver

Medal of the Royal Humane Society. For his services throughout the campaign he received a brevet of Lieutenant-Colonel, was twice mentioned in despatches, and was decorated by the French with the Legion of Honour. In his final despatch addressed to the Secretary of State for War, Field-Marshal the Earl Kitchener, General Dobell paid him the following tribute : " Of those officers whose names I bring to your Lordship's notice for distinguished and meritorious service, I am anxious to give particular prominence to Brevet Lieutenant-Colonel J. B. Cockburn, Royal Welch Fusiliers, and Major (temp. Lieutenant-Colonel) A. H. W. Haywood, D.S.O., Royal Artillery. Both these officers, in their capacity as battalion or column commanders, have experienced the brunt of the hard fighting which has fallen to the British force. In no case has their judgment or discretion been at fault, and I am greatly indebted to both."

Captain G. E. R. De Miremont was Aide-de-Camp to General Dobell, but frequently, owing to shortage of officers, he took part, with the Sierra Leone Battalion, with which unit he had been serving before the War, in important activities. He received the honour of a mention in despatches.

Captain J. G. Bruxner-Randall served throughout with the 1st Battalion Nigeria Regiment under Colonel Cockburn.

Captain L. D'A. Fox served with the Sierra Leone Battalion.

Temp. Lieutenant R. Stirrup, 12th Service Battalion, Royal Welch Fusiliers, joined the force on the 30th June 1915, and was posted to the Gold Coast Regiment. His services earned him a mention in despatches.

Temp. Lieutenant E. L. Hills, also of the 12th Service Battalion, arrived in the Cameroons on the 15th June 1915, and was posted to the 1st Battalion, Nigeria Regiment. This gallant young officer was killed in action on the 25th November 1915.

During the campaign and at its conclusion General Dobell was the recipient of many rewards. In January 1915 he was awarded the C.M.G., while in June of that year he was specially promoted to the rank of Major-General for " distinguished service in the field." He was then, with one exception, the youngest Major-General in the Army.

In April 1916, when on his way home, a very singular compliment was paid him by the French. Monsieur Cloyel, the Governor-General of French West Africa, intercepted the steamer on which he was travelling by a wireless message inviting him to visit Dakar, the capital of French West Africa. On arrival, he was called on by the G.O.C. the troops and the A.D.C. to the Governor-General. Later he landed and drove to Government House through streets which were lined with troops in his honour. In the evening the Governor-General gave a banquet, during the course of which he conferred on him, in the name of the President of the French Republic, the honour of Commander of the Legion of Honour, decorating him with the star and collar of the Order which he himself had been wearing.

Soon after reaching England, he was summoned to Windsor Castle, where His Majesty conferred on him the honour of knighthood and invested him with the insignia of a Knight Commander of the Most Honourable Order of the Bath (Military Division).

APPENDIX III

NOTE TO THE ATTACK ON THE BEAUREVOIR LINE

PAGES 479–81, VOL. III

LIEUTENANT-COLONEL C. C. NORMAN (2nd Battalion) says :

" This line had long since been prepared for defence by the Germans. Not all the trenches had been dug, but concrete machine-gun emplacements had been built into it, deep dugouts had been prepared, and it was protected throughout its length by a thick double-barbed wire entanglement. For the most part the line ran through open country, giving a wide field of fire from the trench. An attack by daylight under these circumstances could be carried out only under a very heavy barrage and after wire cutting had been completed. A night attack was, therefore, decided on.

" The 115th Brigade were ordered to attack that portion of the line which lay in front of the village of Villers-Outreaux at 1 a.m. on 8th October. Simultaneously the 113th Brigade was to attack farther north as far as Mortho Wood. At 8 a.m., when the line should have been broken, the 114th Brigade were to pass through and continue the attack beyond.

" Preparations for that attack were necessarily hurried, and although the night was dark and very wet the leading battalions succeeded in forming up for that attack on the fronts allotted to them. The detailed plan for the 115th Brigade was as follows : The 17th Battalion Royal Welch, on the left, was to break through the line, and passing by the northern edge of Villers-Outreaux was to join hands in the open ground beyond the village with the 10th South Wales Borderers, who had been allotted a similar rôle on the south side of the village. At daybreak the 2nd Royal Welch, accompanied by three tanks, were to mop up the village itself, a task which would have been an easy one in view of the fact that the flanks and end of the village would have been cleared of the enemy.

" The attacks by the 17th Royal Welch and the 10th South Wales Borderers completely failed after most gallant attempts by both these battalions to penetrate the wire entanglements. As evidence of their determination, daylight disclosed the bodies, lying well within the entanglement, of officers and men who were killed in their efforts to cut their way through. The 113th Brigade met with hardly more success. They succeeded in getting through the line in places, but were ultimately held up by defences only a short way beyond.

" Heavy machine-gun fire was being directed by the enemy all along the front, and the task of reorganising the 17th Royal Welch and the 10th South Wales Borderers in the open country in broad daylight became an impossibility. A sunken lane, running towards some high ground to the south-west of the village, had been fixed upon for the forming up of the 2nd Battalion, preparatory to undertaking the task of mopping up. This was found, on their arrival, to be already choked with parties of 10th South Wales Borderers, machine gunners, and advanced parties of the 114th Brigade, seeking cover from a rain of machine-gun bullets which were sweeping over the top. The situation, in these circumstances, presented a far from promising outlook. It appeared to be impossible either to organise a fresh attack or to extricate battalions. A complete deadlock seemed to have been produced. Suddenly, however, while in this predicament, the three tanks, whose progress to the rendezvous had been delayed by bad going, arrived on the scene. There appeared to be some chance of relieving the situation with their aid.

" A fresh plan was hurriedly made under which two tanks, supported by B Company, were to endeavour to force their way through the defences and establish themselves on the north-west corner of the village. A and C Companies were held in readiness to exploit any success. The third tank was directed, in conjunction with C Company, to cover the right flank.

" The plan only partially succeeded, for two of the tanks were very quickly out of action. The third, however, most gallantly followed by B Company, under Captain Kirkly and Lieutenant Nickson, both of whom were wounded, successfully crossed the wire and pushed on beyond to the outskirts of the village.

" The effect was almost instantaneous. The Germans, on either flank, finding their position turned, and perhaps not realising that so small a force had penetrated their line, began gradually to withdraw. A Company, closely followed by C Company, were immediately sent through the gap, the former to secure the northern edge of the village, and C to turn right-handed and secure the southern outskirts and thus enable D Company to push on.

" The result was beyond all expectations. The whole German line now began, without hesitation, to retreat. C Company on the right had the unusual view of a disorganised crowd of German infantry streaming across the open country not 800 yards away. They opened fire, but the excitement of the moment hardly lent itself to good shooting. It was an opportunity for cavalry to complete the success, but one which could hardly have been foreseen.

" Meanwhile the 17th Battalion Royal Welch and the 10th South Wales Borderers reorganised with remarkable rapidity, and on their own initiative pushed on to their original objectives. By 11.30 a.m. the 114th Brigade, supported by the Divisional Artillery, were enabled to continue the pursuit, and by nightfall had driven the enemy back and established themselves on a line east of Malincourt, three miles beyond the Beaurevoir Line, and handed over to the 33rd Division."

APPENDIX IV

THE WELSH HORSE

1/1ST EASTERN MOUNTED BRIGADE DIARY.

THE Welsh Horse, who with the Montgomeryshire Yeomanry formed the 25th Battalion, served in Gallipoli. These extracts from the interesting Brigade and Battalion Diaries complete the record of war service for the 25th Battalion. They are exceptionally well kept diaries.

8th October 1915.—Attempted to land the brigade, less Welsh Horse, at Walker's Pier, Anzac, but as this proved impossible we put back into Imbros Harbour. One man of Field Ambulance shot dead while on board off Walker's Pier. Welsh Horse, on board H.M.T. *Partridge*, landed successfully about 20·30 hrs. at Walker's Pier in bad weather, having arrived off the land at an earlier hour.

IMBROS. *10th October.*—Weighed anchor and started for Anzac. Landed Norfolk Yeomanry, Suffolk, Ambulance.

ANZAC. *11th October.*—Joined up with Welsh Horse, who were in rest camp in Burnt Gully.

12th October.—Attached 54th Division. Welsh Horse selected for pioneer and mining work in trenches of 163rd Brigade. Deep underground trenches the speciality and line very strong for defence.

13th November.—Secretary for War visited Anzac with General Horne.

15th November.—The five mines on Hill 60, dug by Welsh Horse, were exploded at 17·00 hrs. Fifteen casualties in the division occurred from falling debris. The mine craters were not occupied and the line not advanced. The explosion caused two mounds of earth, which proved rather disadvantageous from our point of view. Result of explosion disappointing. No casualties in Welsh Horse from explosion.

20th November.—Turks blew up a mine on Hill 60, burying Lieutenant Renwick and 8 men of the Welsh Horse. Lieutenant Renwick was dug out by 20·00 hrs. and was carried to hospital. The 8 men all perished, as they could not be got out.

24th November.—Welsh Horse mainly employed on Hill 60, mining and sapping, and finding a reserve of 150 men by night.

18th December.—From midnight (17th/18th) until daylight an enormous fire on Anzac Beach, caused by the accidental ignition of a store dump—very regrettable under the circumstances. Several of our aeroplanes and one German were up during the day. After dark an aeroplane appeared low over Anzac. Reported to be German —a disturbing factor.

19th December.—At 8 a.m. Turks exploded a mine near Ivy Lane on Hill 60. Two Gurkhas killed, 5 Welsh Horse and 8 Gurkhas wounded. Turks shelled Hill 60 heavily. The bombardment was quite three times as heavy as any morning bombardment which we have experienced during our stay on the Peninsula. This bombardment, taken in conjunction with the appearance of the aeroplane over Anzac yesterday, made one think the Turks had suspicions as to our intended evacuation. We had in mind also the unfortunate conflagration on Anzac Beach.

20th December.—At 8 a.m. heard that evacuation had been completed without loss. Proceeded to Mudros.

22nd December.—Left Mudros. Sea calm. Weather fair.

25th December.—Disembarked Alexandria and marched Sidi Bishr.

(BATTALION DIARY.)

September.—Early in September the regiment received notice to hold itself in readiness.

23rd September.—To Liverpool. Embarked on *Olympic*.

1st October.—Arrived Mudros. Remained on board.

8th October.—Transhipped to *Partridge* and to Anzac Cove.

Within two days of its arrival the regiment was detailed to take over and carry out all the extensive mining and sapping on and in front of Hill 60, which had been commenced but which had been delayed owing to lack of experienced miners. The work continued under the direction of G.O.C. 54th Division some six weeks, when the 54th Division evacuated and a considerable readjustment of the line necessitated moving of the Eastern Mounted Brigade closer to the front line. The Welsh Horse still continued mining and digging new saps, and in addition were put in charge of five important bombing posts.

12th December.—Very secret information was conveyed to senior officers of the Commander-in-Chief's intention to evacuate the Peninsula.

15th December.—A strong party left.

19th—20th December.—The Welsh Horse were detailed to find the last garrison on Hill 60, consisting of 4 officers and 39 men, which formed part of the Eastern Mounted Brigade rearguard of 100 men, under the command of Lieutenant-Colonel Lord Kensington.

The rearguard was withdrawn and embarked on trawlers at 4 a.m. on the 20th and proceeded direct to Mudros, where it arrived 12 noon. The major part of the regiment, having been withdrawn earlier in the evening of the 19th, embarked elsewhere, and it was not until the 26th December that the whole was concentrated once again at Sidi Bishr Camp, Alexandria.

After concentration the next three months were spent in re-equipping, etc., after the arduous work on the Peninsula, which work was most favourably commented on by General Officers. It resulted in one of the biggest explosions of the whole operations, resulting in the total destruction of the Turkish front line for some 200 yards.

APPENDIX V

"PALS" BATTALIONS

THE 13th Battalion was a so-called Pals Battalion. The idea was to recruit gangs of friends who would serve together. On the 3rd September 1914 the new battalion sanctioned by the War Office had no regimental name—it was simply a North Wales Pals Battalion—and it did not become the 13th Royal Welch until it was posted to the 128th Brigade, 43rd Division. The brigade was renumbered 113th and the Division 38th on the 29th April 1915.

Recruiting was rapid, and in November the new battalion was so much over strength that the surplus was taken to form the 16th Battalion.

The 14th Battalion was raised on the same principle as the 13th by Lieutenant-Colonel Owen Thomas, who commanded the 128th Brigade. It was a Carnarvon and Anglesea Battalion.

The same with the 15th Battalion, but this was the 1st London Welsh, and was raised by a civilian committee of which Sir Vincent Evans was chairman. Apparently they were not very optimistic in London, as they fixed a possible strength of only 500 men, between the ages of nineteen and thirty-five.

It is interesting to note how these " raising " committees worked. They were to clothe, feed, and house the units raised, and were made responsible for finding the first training instructors. They were to select temporary officers, the final appointments to be approved by the War Office. The money for equipment was fixed at £7 5s. per man, but was not to provide a khaki uniform but " the initial clothing and personal necessaries," which took the form of a blue or grey dress of military pattern.

The Welshmen of London swarmed up to Gray's Inn, which had been given by the Benchers for a recruiting depot and headquarters, and registered their names. Anyone with the slightest knowledge of drill became an instructor—it was a strange sight to see men in every conceivable kind of civilian costume doing squad drill on any available corner of ground. A disused hotel (Inns of Court) in Holborn was lent by the owners and provided lecture-rooms, mess-rooms, etc.

Unfortunately there were some confusion and delay in attesting recruits, and many of them became impatient and joined other units. But in spite of all difficulties the 15th Battalion, 1,100 strong, left on 5th December for Llandudno, where it was posted to the 1st North Wales Brigade, or 128th Brigade, which eventually became the 113th.

Recruiting continued in Gray's Inn, and the 18th Battalion was formed as the 2nd London Welsh. They remained at Gray's Inn until the 9th June, when they moved to Bangor. This battalion was definitely detailed to supply drafts as a reserve battalion on the 7th July, and sent men to the five battalions in the 38th Division.

Another reserve battalion was formed of the 25 per cent. of strength which the battalions of the 38th Division were ordered to leave at Kinmel Park Camp when the division moved to Winchester in June 1915. This was the 20th Battalion.

There were also at Kinmel Park the 21st and 22nd Reserve Battalions.

APPENDIX VI

HIS MAJESTY KING GEORGE V

His Majesty made frequent visits to his Armies in France. His visits are not always recorded in Battalion Diaries, but special mention was made of the following occasions.

1st Battalion found a Guard of Honour on the 1st December 1914.

2nd Battalion found a Guard of Honour on the 2nd December 1914.

9th Battalion sent a party who had received awards for gallantry in the field to an inspection by the King, 14th August 1916.

4th Battalion sent a similar party to an inspection at Querrieu Château, 13th August 1918.

14th Battalion was visited by His Majesty on the 3rd December 1918.

H.R.H. THE PRINCE OF WALES

HIS ROYAL HIGHNESS was on Lord Cavan's Staff, and was up and down the Front a great deal. His visits to battalions are also not invariably recorded. He had tea with the officers of the 2nd Battalion on the 10th November 1916, and visited the battalions in the 38th Division before and after the Third Battle of Ypres, 1917. The 9th Battalion provided a Guard of Honour when he visited Bertrancourt on the 12th December 1918.

APPENDIX VII

THE ALBERT MEDAL

AN officer of the 10th Battalion, 2nd Lieutenant A. Nevitt, won this rare decoration. On the 4th September 1916 he, with another officer and two men, was in a trench giving bombing instruction when one of the bombs fell back in the trench. Nevitt groped in the mud and water for it, and was successful in finding it at the second attempt, and threw it over the parapet, where it exploded.

Again, on the 24th September, while bombing instruction was going on, another bomb fell into the trench, and the men in their confusion nearly knocked Nevitt down, but he searched for the bomb and, having found it, threw it, when it at once exploded. On both occasions his courage and presence of mind undoubtedly saved the lives of others.

APPENDIX VIII

ROYAL WELCH FUSILIERS
ROLL OF HONOUR 1914-19

EXPLANATION OF ABBREVIATIONS

b.	.. ..	born.
e.	.. ..	enlisted.
d.	.. ..	died.
d. of w.	.. ..	died of wounds.
k. in a.	.. ..	killed in action.
F.	.. ..	France & Flanders (including Italy).
M.	.. ..	Mesopotamia.

G.	.. ..	Gallipoli.
I.	.. ..	India.
E.	.. ..	Egypt.
P.	.. ..	Palestine.
S.	.. ..	Salonika.
Se.	.. ..	Serbia.
Gib.	.. ..	Gibraltar.
E.A.	.. ..	East Africa.

OFFICERS

3 ACKERLEY, Ronald Hermann, Lt., k. in a., 16/5/15 (att. 1/Bn.).

1 ACKLAND - ALLEN, Hugh Thomas, Lt., k. in a., 23/10/14.

9 ACTON, Charles Annesley, Major (Tp.), k. in a., 25/9/15.

11 ADAMS, John Bernard Pye, Lt. (Tp.), d. of w., 27/2/17 (12).

17 ALLEN, Alfred James Benedict, 2/Lt. (Tp.), k. in a., 3/3/16.

8 ALLIES, Alfric Evan, Lt., k. in a., 16/8/15.

3 ALLISON, Harry, Lt., k. in a., 27/8/18 (att. 13/Bn.).

ALLTREE, Charles Derek, Lt. (Tp.), d. of w., 27/3/18 (in German hands) (att. 9/Bn.).

19 ANDREWS, Glyndwr Levi, Capt. (Tp.), k. in a., 21/8/18 (att. 16/Bn.).

14 APSIMON, Arthur Injwerm, Lt. (Tp.), d. of w., 4/8/17.

12 AUBERTIN, William Aldworth, Major, d., 20/2/19.

13 AYER, Leonard Stuart, Capt. (Tp.), d. of w., 15/7/16.

BALL, Samuel George, 2/Lt., k. in a., 20/3/18.

12 BANCROFT, Stanley Fleming, Lt. (Tp.), k. in a., 19/8/16 (att. 10/Bn.).

2 BANKS, Arthur Chaplin, 2/Lt., k. in a., 22/6/16.

BARKER, Randle Barnett, D.S.O., Brig.-Gen. (Tp.), k. in a., 24/3/18 (Major, R. of Off.). (Staff.).

1 BARKER, Richard Vincent, Capt., k. in a., 31/10/14.

BARRETT, Adrian Hamilton Silverton, 2/Lt. (Tp.), k. in a., 10/7/16 (att. 14/Bn.).

18 BARTLE, George, 2/Lt. (Tp.), k. in a., 2/11/16 (att. 9/Bn.).

14 BARTLEY, John, M.C., 2/Lt. (Tp.), k. in a., 31/10/18.

9 BAXTER, Ian Alexander, M.C., Capt. (Tp.), k. in a., 30/5/18.

1 BAYNES, R. H. B., Lt., k. in a., 14/7/16.

16 BENNETT, Herbert, 2/Lt. (Tp.), k. in a., 22/4/18.

16 BEVERS, Isaac Gwilyn, 2/Lt. (Tp.), d. of w., 2/8/17.

10 BINNY, Steuart Scott, D.S.O., Lt.-Col. (Tp.), k. in a., 3/3/16 (R.O., 19 Hus.).

12 BIRCH, Howard, 2/Lt. (Tp.), k. in a., 9/4/16 (att. 8/Bn.).

10 BLAKE, George Penderell, Capt. (Tp.), k. in a., 20/7/16.

11 BONE, Victor Arnold, Capt. (Tp.), k. in a., 18/9/18.

3 BOTTOMLEY, Frederick, 2/Lt. (Tp.), drowned, 4/5/17.

15 BOWES, Roy, M.C., T/Lt. (A/Capt.), d. of w., 5/8/17.

3 BOWLES, Reginald Julian Albany, Lt., d. of w., 20/7/16.

3 BRENNAN, John Henry, Capt., k. in a., 19/10/14.

1 BROCKLEBANK, Ralph Royds, 2/Lt., d. of w., 16/5/17.

3 BRODIE, William Alan, 2/Lt., d. of w., 13/5/18.

3 BROWN, John, 2/Lt. (Tp.), drowned, 4/5/17 (Garr. Bn.).

10 BROXUP, John William, 2/Lt. (Tp.), d. of w., 24/4/17.

3 BRUNT, Henry John Francis, Lt., k. in a., 25/9/15 (att. 1/Bn.).

1 CADOGAN, Henry Osbert Samuel, Lt.-Col., k. in a., 30/10/14.

2 CAMIES, Ernest Arthur, 2/Lt. (Tp.), k. in a., 15/7/16.

CAMPBELL, Victor Robert Wilkie, 2/Lt. (Tp.), k. in a., 7/9/18 (3/Garr. Bn.) (att. 23 Ches. R.).

10 CAPELL, Arthur Edward, 2/L. (Tp.), k. in a., 13/11/16.

2 CASSON, Randal Alexander, 2/Lt., k. in a., 26/9/17.

8 CAWLEY, Robert, Lt. (Q.M.), d., 30/6/18.

1 CHANCE, Guy Ogden de Peyster, Lt., k. in a., 19/10/14.

CHAPMAN, Herbert, 2/Lt. (T/Lt.), d. of w., 29/5/15.

14 CHARLES, George Harold, 2/Lt., k. in a., 31/10/18.

2 CHILDE - FREEMAN, John Arthur, M.C., Capt., k. in a., 25/9/15.

COLES, Herbert Stonehouse, Capt., k. in a., 16/5/15.

3 COLQUHOUN, Ernest Forbes Campbell, 2/Lt., k. in a., 26/9/17 (att. 2/Bn.).

2 CONNING, Thomas Rothsay, M.C., Lt., k. in a., 27/5/17.

1/2 COSTER, Ernest M.C., T/2/Lt. (A/Capt.), k. in a., 26/9/17.

9 COWIE, William Anderson, M.C., Lt. (A/Capt.), k. in a., 30/5/18.

10 CREE, Adrian Victor, 2/Lt. (Tp.), k. in a., 17/2/16.

CROSLAND, John Herbert, Lt., d., 13/4/19 (att. K. Afr. Rifs.).

2 CROSLAND, Trevor Allington, 2/Lt., k. in a., 22/6/16.

10 CURRAN, Henry, 2/Lt., k. in a., 25/4/17.

11 CURTIS, Harry Reginald, Major (Tp.), k. in a., 18/9/18.

1 DADD, Edmund Halton, Capt. (Tp.), k. in a., 3/9/16.

17 DANIEL, Ralph Picton, Capt. (Tp.), k. in a., 31/7/17.

22 DANIEL, Thomas George, Lt. (Tp.), k. in a., 23/11/17 (att. 19/Bn.).

DARWELL, Thomas Walter,

2/Lt., k. in a., 18/9/18 (att. 14/Bn.).

10 DAVIES, David, 2/Lt. (Tp.), k. in a., 13/11/16.

10 DAVIES, David Ethelstone, Lt. (Tp.), k. in a., 18/6/17.

19 DAVIES, Ernest Glyn, Capt. (Tp.), k. in a., 5/7/16.

15 DAVIES, Evan, Major (Tp.), k. in a., 27/7/17.

18 DAVIES, John Charles, 2/Lt. (Tp.), d. of w., 12/4/17.

16 DAVIES, John Morris, 2/Lt. (Tp.), k. in a., 8/10/18.

16 DAVIES, John Wesley, Lt. (Tp.), k. in a., 26/3/16.

8 DAVIES, Joseph Ithel Jehu, 2/Lt. (Tp.), d. of w., 3/9/16 (att. 1/Batt.).

13 DAVIES, Robert Humphrey, 2/Lt. (Tp.), k. in a., 23/8/18.

9 DAVIES, Sydney George, 2/Lt. (Tp.), k. in a., 31/7/17.

13 DAVIES, William Lloyd, 2/Lt. (Tp.), k. in a., 31/7/17.

2 DAVIS, Thomas Edward George, 2/Lt. (Tp.), k. in a., 27/5/17.

2 DIGGLE, Joseph, 2/Lt. (Tp.), k. in a., 23/8/18.

10 DIXON, Ernest, 2/Lt., k. in a., 19/8/16.

1 DOBELL, Colin Macpherson, Lt. d. of w., 30/5/18 (att. 9/Bn.).

2 DOLLING, Caledon Robert John Radcliffe, 2/Lt. (Tp.) (A/Capt.), k. in a., 20/8/16.

1 DOONER, Alfred Edwin Claud Toke, Lt., k. in a., 30/11/14.

DOUGHTY - WYLIE, Charles Hotham Montagu, V.C., C.B., C.M.G., Lt.-Col., k. in a., 28/4/15. (Staff.)

1 DOVE, Etienne Howard, 2/Lt. (Tp.), k. in a., 30/3/17.

8 DUNN, Philip Morgan, Capt. (Tp.), k. in a., 3/2/17.

8 DYCHE, John, Lt. (Tp.), d. of w., 28/1/17.

18 EDMUNDS, Gwynne Rhys, Lt., k. in a., 20/7/16.

23 EDRIDGE-GREEN, Henry Allen, 2/Lt., d., 5/11/18 (and R.A.F.).

17 EDWARDS, Algernon Stuart, Lt. (Tp.), k. in a., 31/7/17.

3 EDWARDS, Henry Laidley Garland, Lt., d. of w., 16/5/15 (att. 1/Bn.).

3 EDWARDS, John Francis Coster, Lt. (A/Capt.), d. of w., 10/11/18 (att. 24/Batt.).

2 EDWARDS, John Ivor Jones, 2/Lt. (Tp.), k. in a., 31/10/18 (att. 24/Batt.).

13 EDWARDS, Kenneth Grenville, Lt. (Tp.), k. in a., 8/5/18.

EGERTON, Rowland Le Belward, 2/Lt., k. in a., 30/11/14.

3 ELLIOTT, George Keith, Lt., k. in a., 8/9/18 (att. 25/Bn.).

15 ELLIS, Ceredig, 2/Lt. (Tp.), d. of w., 19/7/16.

1/2 ELLIS, Hughie Lodwick Maldwyn, 2/Lt. (Tp.), d. of w., 5/5/17.

19 ELLIS, Robert Thomas Hugh, 2/Lt., k. in a., 13/10/17.

13 EVANS, Bertram Trevor, 2/Lt. (Tp.), k. in a., 22/4/18.

3 EVANS, David Edward, 2/Lt., k. in a., 26/8/18.

17 EVANS, David Owen, Lt. (Tp.), k. in a., 12/2/16.

1/2 EVANS, David William, 2/Lt. (Tp.), k. in a., 8/10/18 (att. 14/Batt.).

1 EVANS, John, 2/Lt., k. in a., 19/9/18.

17 EVANS, Norman Edward, 2/Lt. (Tp.), k. in a., 4/11/18.

8 EVANS, Oscar James, 2/Lt. (Tp.), k. in a., 5/1/16.

EVANS, Richard Parry, 2/Lt. (Tp.), k. in a., 14/5/17.

EVANS, Thomas Richard, D.S.O., T/Major (A/Lt.-Col.), k. in a., 3/10/18 (att. 1/6 N. Staff. R.).

3 EVANS, William Edwards, 2/Lt., k. in a., 1/5/17 (13) (att. 13/Bn.).

FARREN, William Ignatius George, Lt., d., 29/3/18.

3 FENN, Edward Gerald Palmer, 2/Lt. (Tp.), k. in a., 19/9/18 (Garr. Bn.) (att. 1/5 Essex R.).

15 FLEMING, Reginald Henry, 2/Lt. (Tp.), k. in a., 11/7/16.

9 FLETCHER, Horace William, 2/Lt. (T/Lt.), d. of w., 26/3/17 (att. 7/Bn.).

FLETCHER, Joseph Harold, Capt. (Tp.), k. in a., 25/11/17 (att. 19/Bn.).

FLETCHER, Walter George, 2/Lt., k. in a., 20/3/15 (att. 2/Bn.).

13 FLOWER, Oswald Swift, Lt.-Col. (Tp.), d. of w., 12/7/16.

10 FOLLIT, Charles Albert Roy, D.S.O., Capt. (Tp.), d. of w., 20/8/16.

FOXALL, Thomas William, 2/Lt. (Tp.), k. in a., 2/10/18 (3/Garr. Bn.) (att. 25/Garr. Bn. K. L'pool R.).

10 FREEMAN, Edward, Major (Tp.), k. in a., 3/3/16.

3 FRENCH, Robert Mason Jackson, Capt., d. of w., 19/2/16.

1 GABBETT, Richard Edward Phillip, Lt.-Col., k. in a., 16/5/15.

3 GANNON, John Howard, 2/Lt. (Tp.), killed, 9/10/17 (att. 11/Bn.).

9 GARVIN, Samuel, 2/Lt., k. in a., 27/3/17 (att. 1/7 Bn.).

16 GEORGE, Thomas, 2/Lt. (Tp.), k. in a., 27/8/18.

3 GLADSTONE, William Glynne Charles, Lt., k. in a., 13/4/15.

10 GODFREY, Leonard George, 2/Lt., k. in a., 20/7/16.

3 GORE, Gerard Ribton, 2/Lt., d. of w., 20/12/14 (att. 2/Bn.).

1 GREEN, George Binch, 2/Lt. (Tp.), k. in a., 11/6/18 (att. 7/Shrop. L.I.).

2 GRIFFITH, Arthur Charles Fleming, Lt., k. in a., 8/10/18 (att. 17/Bn.).

15 GRIFFITH, William Henry, M.C., 2/Lt. (Tp.), d. of w., 5/7/17.

1 GRIFFITHS, William George, 2/Lt. (Tp.), k. in a., 9/3/18 (att. 5/Bn.).

10 GRIFFITHS, William Percival, Capt. (Tp.), k. in a., 30/3/16.

3 GROSER, Arthur Hugh, 2/Lt., k. in a., 22/9/16 (att. 1/Bn.).

10 HALE, William John Douglas, Capt. (Tp.), k. in a., 28/4/17.

16 HANCOCK, Harold, Lt. (Tp.), k. in a., 19/9/18.

9 HANDLEY, Walter, 2/Lt. (Tp.), k. in a., 25/3/18.

19 HARGREAVES, Frank, Lt. (Tp.), k. in a., 12/7/16.

18 HARRIES, Howard Lock, 2/Lt. (Tp.), k. in a., 13/11/16 (att. 10/Bn.).

1 HARRIS, Arthur Harold, 2/Lt., d. of w., 4/7/18 (att. 16/Bn.).

HARRIS, Charles Henry, 2/Lt., d. of w., 19/9/18 (att. 11/Bn.).

9 HARRIS, Nathan Leonard, M.C., Capt. (Tp.), k. in a., 28/8/18.

17 HARRIS, Percy George, 2/Lt. (Tp.), k. in a., 11/8/17 (and R.F.C., 21 Sqd.).

16 HARRIS, William Handel, 2/Lt. (Tp.), k. in a., 26/8/18.

14 HARRISON, Brian, 2/Lt. (Tp.), k. in a., 10/7/16.

8 HAY, Archibald, Major, (T/Lt.-Col.), k. in a., 3/2/17.

3 HEASTEY, George Rodney, 2/Lt., k. in a., 20/7/16.

16 HEATLY, Charles Frederick, 2/Lt. (Tp.), d. of w., 17/4/18.

13 HEATON, Harold Sinclair, 2/Lt. (Tp.), k. in a., 22/4/18.

HEATON, Lionel James, 2/Lt., k. in a., 29/8/18 (att. 17/Batt.).

8 HERINGTON, Percy Godfrey, 2/Lt. (Tp.), k. in a., 15/2/17.

2 HEYCOCK, Edwin, 2/Lt. (Tp.),

BRIGADIER-GENERAL A. W. G. LOWRY-COLE, C.B., D.S.O.

Commanded the 25th Infantry Brigade of the 8th Division. His brigade played a prominent part in the Battle of Neuve Chapelle. He was killed while directing operations against the Aubers Ridge on 9th May 1915.

k. in a., 27/8/18 (att. 14/Bn.).

HILL, Hugh, M.V.O., D.S.O., Bt.-Lt.-Col., k. in a., 10/9/16. (Staff.)

8 HILL, William, Hon. Lt. & Qr.-Mr., d., 11/10/15.

12 HILLS, Ernest Leslie, Lt. (Tp.), d. of w., 26/11/15 (att. N. Nigeria R.).

15 HINDS, William Pugh, Lt. (Tp.), d. of w., 2/2/16.

15 HODKINSON, Leonard, 2/Lt. (Tp.), k. in a., 14/9/17 (and R.F.C., 53 Sqd.).

9 HOGG, Lewis Stephen, Capt. (& Adjt., Tp.), k. in a., 25/9/15.

3 HOLLINGBERY, Raymond Archibald Robert, Lt., k. in a., 6/7/16.

12 HOLME, Bertram Lester, Lt. (Tp.), d. of w., 25/4/16.

19 HOPE-EVANS, Timothy Idwal, Capt. (Tp.), k. in a., 23/11/17.

1 HOSKYNS, Edwin Cecil Leigh, Lt., k. in a., 20-21/10/14.

17 HOWELL, George Woodbourne, 2/Lt., k. in a., 22/6/18 (att. 1/2 Bn.).

9 HOYLE, Basil William Edmond, Capt. (Tp.), k. in a., 25/9/15.

8 HUBBARD, Alfred William, 2/Lt. (Tp.), k. in a., 25/1/17.

1 HUGHES, Horatio Clement, 2/Lt. (Tp.), k. in a., 18/9/18 (att. 11/Bn.).

3 HUGHES, Hugh Darrell, 2/Lt., k. in a., 14/1/17 (att. 8/Bn.).

10 HUGHES, John Edwyn, 2/Lt. (Tp.), d. of w., 19/8/16.

20 HUGHES, John Gwilym, Lt. (Tp.), killed, 3/11/16 (att. 9/Bn.).

20 HUGHES, Maurice Thomas, 2/Lt. (Tp.), k. in a., 30/5/16 (att. 13/Bn.).

10 HUGHES, Tegerin, Capt. (Tp.), d. of w., 1/4/16.

10 HUGHES, William, 2/Lt. (Tp.), k. in a., 3/3/16.

HUGHES, William Francis, M.C., M.M., 2/Lt. (Tp.), d. of w., 7/9/18.

19 HUMPHREY - JONES, Cecil, Capt. (Tp.), k. in a., 24/11/17.

14 HUNKIN, William Burrows Clement, M.C., Lt. (Tp.), k. in a., 3/11/18.

13 HUTCHINS, Frederick Charles, 2/Lt. (Tp.), k. in a., 22/4/18.

10 HUXLEY, Joseph, 2/Lt. (Tp.), k. in a., 22/4/18 (att. 14/Bn.).

1 JACKSON, Dudley William Gerald, Capt., d. of w., 13/4/16.

2 JACKSON, James Battle, 2/Lt. (Tp.), k. in a., 23/4/17.

9 JAGGER, Arthur Stannus, 2/Lt. (Tp.), d. of w., 1/10/18.

10 JAMES, Albert John Stanley, D.S.O., M.C., T/Major (A/Lt.-Col.), k. in a., 28/3/18 (att. 8/Bn., K.O.R.L.R.).

14 JAMES, Enoch Lewis, 2/Lt. (Tp.), k. in a., 18/2/17.

13 JAMES, Gwilym, 2/Lt. (Tp.), d. of w., 8/10/18.

JAMES, Vivian Gwynne, Lt., k. in a., 26/3/17 (att. 7/Bn.).

13 JAMES, William David, M.M., 2/Lt., k. in a., 8/10/18.

3 JAMES, Walter Ibbe, Lt., k. in a., 25-27/9/15.

19 JAMES, Wilfred Sydney, 2/Lt. (Tp.), k. in a., 24/11/17.

3 JENKINS, Cyril Donald Thomas, Lt., killed, 2/10/16.

3 JENKINS, Sidney Oswald, 2/Lt., k. in a., 22/8/18 (att. 10/K. Shrop. L.I.).

20 JENNINGS, Gouldbourne Hayward, 2/Lt., k. in a., 10/8/16 (att. 10/Bn.).

10 JOHNS, Bernard Digby, Capt. (Tp.), k. in a., 17/2/16.

14 JONES, Arthur Lloyd, M.C., Capt. (Tp.), d. of w., 3/9/18.

11 JONES, Cecil Hughes, Capt. (Tp.), k. in a., 18/9/18.

15 JONES, Clifford, 2/Lt. (Tp.), k. in a., 2/8/17.

3 JONES, Daniel Thomas, 2/Lt., k. in a., 4/5/17.

3 JONES, Edwin Tudor, Capt., k. in a., 3/9/16 (att. 1/Bn.).

8 JONES, Ernest Kerrison, Capt. (Tp.), k. in a., 3/7/16.

12 JONES, Evelyn Llewellyn Hustler, 2/Lt., k. in a., 26/3/17 (att. 5/Bn.).

2 JONES, Francis Leonard Clarence, M.C., M.M., 2/Lt., k. in a., 1/9/18.

17 JONES, Harold Madoc, Lt. (Tp.), k. in a., 31/7/17.

13 JONES, Harold Vivian, Lt. (Tp.), k. in a., 10/7/16.

10 JONES, Henry Myrddin, 2/Lt. (Tp.), k. in a., 13/11/16.

10 JONES, Hugh, 2/Lt. (Tp.), k. in a., 3/9/16.

1 JONES, John Harold, 2/Lt. (Tp.), k. in a., 1/10/17.

3 JONES, Leonard, 2/Lt., k. in a., 16/5/15 (att. 1/Bn.).

14 JONES, Stanley, 2/Lt. (Tp.), d. of w., 25/2/17.

JONES, Stanley, Capt., k. in a., 16/5/15.

2 JONES, Thomas Stephen, 2/Lt., k. in a., 26/9/17 (att. 10/Bn.).

13 JONES - BATEMAN, Francis, Capt., k. in a., 4/11/18.

11 JONES - SAVIN, John Savin, 2/Lt. (Tp.), k. in a., 27/3/17.

2 JONES-VAUGHAN, Evan N., Capt., k. in a., 26/10/14.

3 KEEPFER, William Robert Cyril, 2/Lt., k. in a., 4/11/16 (att. 2/Bn.).

9 KILVERT, Harry, 2/Lt. (Tp.), d. of w., 1/8/17.

15 KING, David, 2/Lt. (Tp.), k. in a., 31/7/17.

1 KINGTON, William Miles, D.S.O., Capt., k. in a., 20/10/14.

13 LACK, Reginald Walter, 2/Lt., k. in a., 29/9/16 (att. 1/Bn.).

LAW, Harry, Lt., d. of w., 7/7/15.

9 LAWES, Charles Gilbert, Lt. (Tp.), k. in a., 27/10/16.

1 LEWIS, Arthur Starkey, Lt. (Tp.), k. in a., 4/5/17 (Garr. Batt.).

16 LEWIS, David Elwyn, 2/Lt., d. of w., 18/9/18.

17 LEWIS, Joseph Henry, T/2/Lt. (A/Capt.), k. in a., 8/10/18 (att. 1/7 Ches. R.).

17 LEWIS, Llewellyn, 2/Lt. (Tp.), k. in a., 1-12/7/16.

1 LEWIS, Thomas William, 2/Lt. (Tp.), d. of w., 27/10/17.

3 LINDSLEY, George Vincent, 2/Lt., d. of w., 16/3/17 (att. 2/Bn.).

16 LINTON, Frederick Tom, 2/Lt. (Tp.), k. in a., 22/4/18.

LLEWELLYN, Edward Thomas, Lt. (Tp.), d. of w., 18/5/18 (4/Garr. Bn., att. 9/Bn.).

14 LLEWELLYN, Vivian, 2/Lt. (Tp.), k. in a., 3/11/18.

10 LLOYD, Charles Gordon, Lt., d., 9/6/15.

13 LLOYD, Frank Stuart, Major (Tp.), d. of w., 5/9/17.

1/2 LLOYD, James Percival, 2/Lt. (Tp.), k. in a., 25/7/17 (att. 16/Batt.).

1 LLOYD, M. E., Capt., k. in a., 23/10/14.

LLOYD, Robert Love, Major, d. of w., 9/12/15.

8 LLOYD, Walter, Capt., k. in a., 7/8/15.

15 LLOYD, William Robert, 2/Lt. (Tp.), k. in a., 12/7/18.

3 LORD, Arthur George, 2/Lt., k. in a., 20/7/16.

10 LORD, Charles Henry, Major (Tp.), d., 30/12/14.

LYNCH, Harold Francis, 2/Lt., k. in a., 16/5/15.

10 LYONS, William Thomas, Capt. (Tp.), k. in a., 3/3/16.

McINTOSH, Joseph Francis, Lt. (Tp.), drowned, 10/10/18 (att. 2/Bn.).

1 McKAY, Frederick, Lt., d. of w., 28/2/17.

McBEAN, Donald, Lt. (Tp.),

k. in a., 15/3/16 (att. 10/Bn.).

9 MCCAMMON, Charles Duncan, 2/Lt., k. in a., 3/7/16.

1 MADLEY, Lewis George, 2/Lt. (Tp.), k. in a., 14/5/17.

9 MADOCKS, Henry John, Lt.-Col. (Tp.), k. in a., 25/9/15.

3 MAIR, George Hay, Lt., d., 14/12/18 (att. R. Sussex R.).

9 MANDERS, S. G., Capt., d., 9/12/18 (and R.A.F.).

2 MANN, John Charles, M.C., A/Capt., k. in a., 26/9/17.

3 MANN, Robert Leonard, 2/Lt., k. in a., 9/10/14 (att. 16/Bn.).

9 MANWARING, Jack Lancaster, M.C., 2/Lt. (Tp.), d., 15/11/16.

3 MARTIN, William Howard, 2/Lt. (Tp.), k. in a., 31/7/17 (att. 2/Bn.).

11 MEECHAM, David Jeffreys, 2/Lt. (Tp.), k. in a., 27/3/17.

MILLER, Reginald de Hoche-pied Marillier, 2/Lt. (Tp.), d. of w., 27/10/18 (3 Garr. Bn.).

14 MILLS, Robert Henry, Major (Tp.), k. in a., 10/7/16.

15 MORGAN, Emlyn Thomas, Lt. (Tp.), d. of w., 7/2/16.

19 MORGAN, George Hamilton, Capt. (Tp.), k. in a., 23/11/17.

1 MORGAN, Geoffrey Penney, 2/Lt. (Tp.), k. in a., 14/7/16.

MORGAN, Guy Williams Stuart, Capt., k. in a., 25/9/15.

MORGAN, Herbert Glyn Rhys, 2/Lt. (Tp.), d. of w., 31/7/17.

1/2 MORGAN, John Towlson, Capt., k. in a., 29/10/18 (and R.A.F.).

1 MORGAN, Wilfrid, 2/Lt. (Tp.), k. in a., 18/9/18 (att. 11/Bn.).

MORRIS, Arthur Cukelyn, Lt. (Tp.), k. in a., 17/2/18 (att. R.F.C.).

MORRIS, Charles Herbert, Lt., k. in a., 13/4/17 (and R.F.C.).

MORRIS, John Torrington, 2/Lt., k. in a., 16/5/15.

9 MOSS, Enoch Frank, 2/Lt. (Tp.), d. of w., 17/9/16.

NAYLOR, Rowland Edmund, Lt., k. in a., 16/5/15.

1 NEWTON, Vivian Frederic, 2/Lt., d. of w., 15/9/16.

14 NICHOLLS - JONES, Thomas Cyril, Lt., (Tp.), k. in a., 1/8/17.

3 ORME, Edward Leslie, Lt., k. in a., 27/5/17 (att. 1/Bn.).

1 ORME, Francis Reginald, 2/Lt., k. in a., 7/11/14.

1 ORMROD, Lawrence Moreland, M.C., Capt., d., 25/8/17.

14 ORMSBY, Harold Sydney, T/Lt. (A/Capt.), d. of w., 18/2/17.

15 OSBORNE-JONES, Noel, 2/Lt., k. in a., 8/5/16.

16 OWEN, Henry James, 2/Lt. (Tp.), k. in a., 24/8/18.

2 OWEN, John Morris, T/Lt. (A/Capt.), k. in a., 23/4/17.

3 OWEN, Thomas John, 2/Lt., d. of w., 19/2/17 (att. 8/Bn.).

13 OWEN, Thomas Starr, 2/Lt. (Tp.), k. in a., 8/10/18.

9 OWEN, Vernon Elias, 2/Lt. (Tp.), d. of w., 29/11/15.

16 OWEN, William, 2/Lt., d. of w., 27/8/18.

15 OWENS, Arthur Owen, 2/Lt., k. in a., 22/4/18 (att. 16/Bn.).

10 PAGE, Henry, 2/Lt., k. in a., 20/7/16.

PALFREYMAN, A., 2/Lt., d. of w., 9/10/18 (att. 16/Bn.).

PARKER, Colin, 2/Lt., d., 25/10/18 (3/Garr. Bn., whilst P. of W. in enemy hands).

PARKES, Horace Frederick, 2/Lt., k. in a., 12/3/15.

10 PARRY, James Hywell, Lt. (Tp.), d. of w., 5/9/17.

9 PAYNE, Edward Geoffrey, Capt. (Tp.), k. in a., 25/9/15.

PENSON, Thomas Edward, 2/Lt., k. in a., 18/9/18 (att. 25/Bn.).

17 PERRETT, Fred Leonard, 2/Lt., d. of w., 1/12/18.

2 PHILLIPS, Arthur, 2/Lt., k. in a., 23/4/17.

9 PHILLIPS, James Williams, Capt. (Tp.), k. in a., 30/5/18.

2 PHILLIPS, Ralph Noel, Capt., d. of w., 27/12/14.

1/2 PICKARD, Harry Lawson, M.C., 2/Lt., k. in a., 20/10/18 (att. 9/Bn.).

3 PILLING, William, M.C., 2/Lt., d., 22/10/18 (att. 2/Bn.).

20 PORTER, Graham Hawksworth, Lt. (Tp.), k. in a., 3/10/16.

8 POWELL, Scott, Capt. (Tp.), d. of w., 4-5/4/16.

3 PRITCHARD, T. L., Capt., d. of w., 9/11/14 (att. 2/Bn.).

1 PRITCHARD, David, 2/Lt., k. in a., 19/3/16.

PRITCHARD, Henry, 2/Lt. (Tp.), k. in a., 7/4/18 (att. Hood Bn.).

13 PRITCHARD, John, 2/Lt., k. in a., 4/9/17.

1/2 RABY, William Donald, 2/Lt. (Tp.), k. in a., 8/10/18.

15 RADCLIFFE, Ernest Charles Derwentwater, 2/Lt. (Tp.), k. in a., 31/7/17.

RAMSAY, William James, Lt., k. in a., 27/3/18 (and R.F.C.).

1 REES, Albert Lloyd, Lt. (Tp.), k. in a., 6/11/17.

19 REES, Edgar George, 2/Lt., k. in a., 23/11/17.

REES, Edward Davies, 2/Lt. (Tp.), k. in a., 13/6/17 (att. 16/Bn.).

3 REES, Edris, 2/Lt., d. of w., 27/10/17 (att. 1/Bn.).

16 REES, Henry Hugh Tregarthen, 2/Lt. (Tp.), k. in a., 11/7/16.

REES, John Trevor, 2/Lt., k. in a., 22/1/15.

15 REES, Roland Gwyn, Lt. (Tp.), k. in a., 10-11/7/16.

14 REES, Tom, Lt., k. in a., 17/9/16 (and R.F.C.).

1 RICHARDES, Roderic Alexander William Pryse, 2/Lt., d. of w., 18/9/18 (whilst P. of W. in Bulgarian hands).

14 RICHARDS, Gwilym Owen, 2/Lt. (Tp.), d. of w., 23/4/18.

16 RICHARDS, John, 2/Lt. (Tp.), k. in a., 15/3/18.

17 RICHARDS, Llewelyn Thomas, 2/Lt. (Tp.), k. in a., 4/9/15.

1 RICHARDSON, Mervyn Stronge, Capt. (Tp.), d. of w., 19/3/16.

14 ROBERTS, Alan Sheriff, 2/Lt. (Tp.), k. in a., 10/7/16.

9 ROBERTS, Cadwalader Glyn, Lt. (Tp.), k. in a., 3/7/16.

1 ROBERTS, Frederick Sheriff, 2/Lt., k. in a., 28/8/18 (att. 9/Bn.).

14 ROBERTS, Howel Dilwyn, 2/Lt. (Tp.), k. in a., 31/10/15.

17 ROBERTS, Henry Sheriff, Capt., k. in a., 27/8/17.

17 ROBERTS, Idris, 2/Lt. (Tp.), d. of w., 3/9/18.

ROBERTS, Thomas Owen, 2/Lt., k. in a., 18/9/18 (att. 14/Bn.).

3 ROBERTSON, Helenus Mac-Aulay, Capt., k. in a., 26/1/16 (att. 2/Bn.).

2 ROBINSON, James Thompson, Lt. (Tp.), k. in a., 7/9/18 (att. 24/Batt.).

3 ROWLAND, Stanley Jackson, Lt., k. in a., 2/11/17 (att. 1/8 Scot. Rifs.).

ROWLAND, William Henry, 2/Lt., d., 22/2/19 (att. 26/Bn.).

10 ROWLANDS, Charles William, 2/Lt. (Tp.), k. in a., 26/9/17.

9 RUCK-KEENE, Ralph Edgar Lt. (Tp.), killed, 16/1/16.

12 RUDD, William Ferris, Capt., k. in a., 13/11/16.

2 SAMSON, Arthur Legge, M.C., Capt., k. in a., 25/9/15.

13 SAMUEL, James Frederick, 2/Lt. (Tp.), k. in a., 22/4/18.

SAUNDERS, Gwilyn Essex, 2/Lt. (Tp.), k. in a., 18/9/18 (att. 16/Bn.).

SAVAGE, John Brown, 2/Lt., d. of w., 16/5/15.

10 SCALE, George Devereux, Capt. (Tp.), k. in a., 20/7/16.

19 SHANKLAND, Llewelyn Ap Tomas, Lt. (Tp.), d. of w., 25/11/17.

20 SINGLETON, William James, Lt. (Tp.), drowned, 10/10/18 (att. 3/Bn.).

8 SINNETT-JONES, Gilbert Lloyd, Capt. (Tp.), k. in a., 4/4/16.

3 SINNETT-JONES, James Victor, 2/Lt., k. in a., 10-12/7/16 (att. 17/Bn.).

1 SNEAD-COX, Geoffrey Phillip Joseph, 2/Lt., k. in a., 20/10/14.

11 SPOONER, Ronald Alan, Capt. (Tp.), d. of w., 23/9/16.

2 STABLE, Lascombe Law, Capt., k. in a., 26/10/14.

12 STANLEY, Robert Oliver, 2/Lt., k. in a., 9/4/16.

11 STOCKDALE, Frank, Capt. (Tp.), d. of w., 19/9/18.

2 STONE, Ellis Robert Cunliffe, 2/Lt., k. in a., 26/10/14.

17 STYLES, Arthur Horatio, Lt. (Tp.), d. of w., 26/7/16.

SUTCLIFFE, Sydney, 2/Lt., k. in a., 2/10/17 (and R.F.C., 11 Sqd.).

13 SWAIN, Robert Ernest, 2/Lt. (Tp.), d. of w., 8/7/16.

3 SWEETLAND, Rupert Girard, 2/Lt., d. of w., 26/1/17.

9 SYMONS, Charles Fleming Jelinger, Lt. (Tp.), k. in a., 25/9/15.

1 SYRETT, Alfred Montague, 2/Lt. (Tp.), k. in a., 4/5/17.

11 TAGGART, Herbert, 2/Lt., k. in a., 8/5/16 (att. 15/Bn.).

16 TANNER, David Thomas, Lt. (Tp.), k. in a., 31/8/16.

1 TAYLOR, Guy Collins Vernon, Lt., k. in a., 2/10/17.

15 THOMAS, Basil Llewellyn Boyd, Lt. (Tp.), k. in a., 9/4/17 (att. 27/M.G.C.).

THOMAS, David Arthur, 2/Lt. (Tp.), k. in a., 4/5/17.

3 THOMAS, David Cuthbert, 2/Lt., d. of w., 18/3/16.

15 THOMAS, David John, 2/Lt. (Tp.), k. in a., 22/4/18 (att. 13/Bn.).

10 THOMAS, George, 2/Lt. (Tp.), k. in a., 13/11/16.

2 THOMAS, George Oliver, Capt., k. in a., 26/9/15.

3 THOMAS, Herbert Gordon, 2/Lt., k. in a., 13/11/16.

1 THOMAS, Noel Lavender, 2/Lt., k. in a., 18/9/18 (att. 11/Bn.).

THOMAS, Reginald Spenser Dudley, 2/Lt., k. in a., 18/9/18 (att. 25/Bn.).

9 THOMAS, Richard Nixon, 2/Lt. (Tp.), d. of w., 23/8/15.

16 THOMAS, Rufus William, 2/Lt. (Tp.), k. in a., 9/5/18 (att. 113 T.M.B.).

16 THOMAS, Thomas, 2/Lt. (Tp.), k. in a., 10/1/16.

17 THOMAS, Thomas Oliver, 2/Lt. (Tp.), k. in a., 10-12/7/16.

19 THOMAS, Tudor, 2/Lt. (Tp.), k. in a., 25/11/17.

14 THOMPSON, Arthur George, 2/Lt. (Tp.), k. in a., 2/6/16.

3 THOMPSON, Edward James Vibart Collingwood, 2/Lt., d. of w., 10/9/14.

3 THOMPSON, Walton Downing, Lt., d. of w., 2/9/18 (att. 1/6 H.L.I.).

TOBIAS, Leslie Mark, Capt., d., 25/2/19 (2/Garr. Bn.).

1/2 TYRRELL, Walter, 2/Lt. (Tp.), d. of w., 4/9/18 (att. 17/Batt.).

3 VAUGHAN-JONES, Edward, Lt., k. in a., 11/5/18 (att. 11/Bn.).

14 VENMORE, James Frederick, Lt. (Tp.), k. in a., 11/7/16.

10 VERNON, Leonard Patrick, M.C., Lt. (Tp.), k. in a., 18/6/17.

1 VYVYAN, William Geoffrey, Capt., d. of w., 24/10/14 (in German hands).

10 WALKER, John Arthur, Capt. (Tp.), k. in a., 19/2/16.

14 WEBB, Joseph Gilbert, M.C., Lt., d., 9/5/18.

WEBB-BOWEN, Hugh Ince, Capt., d. of w., 23/5/15. (Staff.)

13 WHITE, John Stephen Grantham, Lt. (Tp.), d. of w., 31/7/17.

3 WILDING-JONES, Hugh Wynn, Lt., d. of w., 22/9/18 (att. 11/Bn.).

13 WILLIAMS, Arthur Ivor Meakin, Capt., d. of w., 9/10/18.

10 WILLIAMS, Arthur Owen, 2/Lt. (Tp.), k. in a., 16-19/8/16.

15 WILLIAMS, Arthur Trevor, 2/Lt. (Tp.), d. of w., 4/9/17 (att. R.F.C.).

17 WILLIAMS, Bleddyn, Capt., k. in a., 22/1/16.

10 WILLIAMS, Edwin Gordon, 2/Lt., d. of w., 13/5/17.

10 WILLIAMS, Evan, 2/Lt. (Tp.), k. in a., 10/4/17.

12 WILLIAMS, Gwilym, 2/Lt. (Tp.), d. of w., 21/5/16 (att. 17/Bn.).

WILLIAMS, Howell, 2/Lt. (T/Lt.), d., 21/2/17 (att. Gold Coast R.).

14 WILLIAMS, Hugh Powell, Capt. (Tp.), k. in a. 5/6/16.

17 WILLIAMS, Hywel, Capt. (Tp.), k. in a., 10-12/7/16.

1/2 WILLIAMS, Idwal, 2/Lt., k. in a., 26/9/17.

WILLIAMS, James Griffith, Lt., k. in a., 27/8/18 (att. 17/Bn.).

19 WILLIAMS, James Morgan, 2/Lt., k. in a., 9/5/18 (att. 17/Bn.).

19 WILLIAMS, John, Capt. (Tp.), k. in a., 30/6/17.

10 WILLIAMS, Lewis, 2/Lt. (Tp.), k. in a., 18/8/16.

10 WILLIAMS, Peter, 2/Lt. (Tp.), k. in a., 13/11/16.

19 WILLIAMS, Philip Ernest, M.C., Capt. (Tp.), d. of w., 24/11/17.

9 WILLIAMS, Reginald Joseph, 2/Lt. (Tp.), k. in a., 25/9/15.

17 WILLIAMS, Richard, 2/Lt., d. of w., 2/4/18 (att. M.G.C.).

10 WILLIAMS, Richard Henry, 2/Lt. (Tp.), k. in a., 13/11/16.

17 WILLIAMS, Richard Lloyd, Capt. (Tp.), d. of w., 2/8/17.

WILLIAMS, Roderick Mathafar, Capt., k. in a., 12/8/17 (2/Garr. Bn.) (R.F.C., 32 Sqd.).

3 WILLIAMS, Thomas Benjamin, 2/Lt., k. in a., 27/5/17 (att. 2/Bn.).

15 WILLIAMS, Vivian Pedr., 2/Lt., k. in a., 22/4/18.

3 WILLIAMS, William, 2/Lt., d., 27/2/17 (att. 1/Bn.).

17 WILLIAMS, William George, Capt. (Tp.), d. of w., 29/8/17.

9 WILLIAMS, William Henry, 2/Lt. (Tp.), k. in a., 6/11/17 (att. 7/Bn.).

1 WILLIAMS, William Ifor, 2/Lt., d. of w., 18/3/18 (att. 16/Bn.).

16 WILLIAMS, William James, M.C., 2/Lt., k. in a., 19/9/17.

3 WILLIAMS, William James Minister, 2/Lt., k. in a., 7/2/16 (att. 2/Bn.).

14 WILLIAMS, William John, Lt. (Tp.), k. in a., 25/2/17.

WILLIAMS-MEYRICK, Edmund Oswald Griffith, Lt. (Tp.), d., 7/5/16 (Garr. Batt.).

3 WILSON, Neville Inchbold,

M.C., Lt., k. in a., 6/4/18 (att. 4/Bn.).

3 WILSON, Philip Stanley, 2/Lt., k. in a., 20/8/16 (att. 2/Bn.).

13 WINTER, Thomas Barron, 2/Lt., k. in a., 24/4/18.

3 WOLFF, Gustav Frederick, A/Capt., k. in a., 21/3/18 (att. M.G.C.).

WOOD, Charles Edmund, Capt., k. in a., 11/3/15.

15 WOOD, William Leslie, 2/Lt. (A/Capt.), k. in a., 7/5/17.

WOODWARD, Charles Francis, Lt., d. of w., 20/5/15.

17 WRIGHT, William Clifford, Lt. (Tp.), k. in a., 10-12/7/16.

10 WYNNE-WILLIAMS, Humphrey Evan, 2/Lt. (Tp.), k. in a., 30/3/16.

DENBIGHSHIRE YEOMANRY
24th Batt. R.W.F.

ALLISON, Robert Stafford, 2/Lt., k. in a., 16/6/17.

JAMES, Alyn Reginald, Capt., k. in a., 24/3/18 (and R.F.C.).

MILLER, John Kingsley, Lt., k. in a., 19/9/18.

ROOPER, William Victor Trevor, Capt., k. in a., 9/10/17 (and R.F.C.).

SANDBACH, Gilbert Robertson, Capt., d. of w., 3/7/17.

THOMAS, Llewellyn, 2/Lt., k. in a., 27/12/17.

MONTGOMERYSHIRE YEOMANRY
25th Batt. R.W.F.

CAPPER, Edward Walter, Lt., k. in a., 14/4/17 (and R.F.C.).

CHARLESWORTH, Frederick Raymond, Capt., d. of ., 19/9/18.

ELLIS, Rae Adam, Capt., d. of w., 22/9/18.

FITZHUGH, Godfrey, Capt., k. in a., 31/10/17.

LANGRISHE, Hercules R., Lt., killed, 16/2/17 (and R.F.C.).

NORRIS, William Eric, 2/Lt., killed, 14/1/18.

ROBERTS, Harry Cureton, Lt., k. in a., 27/12/17.

WELSH HORSE YEOMANRY

JONES, Herbert Wyman, Lt., d. of w., 24/3/18 (and M.G.C.).

ROCH, William Protheroe, Lt. (A/Capt.), k. in a., 11/3/18.

SHIRLEY, Archibald Vincent, 2/Lt., k. in a., 8/6/17 (and R.F.C.).

THOMAS, Owen, Capt., d., 21/8/17.

4th (DENBIGHSHIRE) BATTALION (TERRITORIAL)

BARTLETT, Arthur, 2/Lt., d. of w., 12/4/18 (in German hands).

BEYNON, William Charles, 2/Lt., d. of w., 3/5/17.

BLAXLEY, Stewart Lenton, 2/Lt., k. in a., 23/4/17.

BROWN, Ernest James, 2/Lt., k. in a., 31/7/17.

CROOM-JOHNSON, Brian, Lt., k. in a., 9/5/17.

DAVIES, John Howard, 2/Lt., k. in a., 4/7/17.

DAVIS, Reginald Percy, 2/Lt., d. of w., 5/10/15.

ELLIS, John William, 2/Lt., k. in a., 27/5/18.

ELLIS, William John, 2/Lt., k. in a., 23/3/18.

EVANS, Francis Graham, Lt., d., 26/9/16.

EVANS, John Arthur, 2/Lt., k. in a., 27/1/17.

EVANS, John Eric, Capt., d. of w., 9/5/15.

EVANS, Robert Cecil, Lt., k. in a., 6/4/18.

EVANS, Rhys Trevor, 2/Lt., k. in a., 1/9/17.

FRANCE - HAYHURST, Frederick Charles, Lt.-Col., k. in a., 9/5/15.

HAZELDENE, John Turner Clough, 2/Lt., killed, 9/5/15.

HOLLAND, Thomas Welsby, Lt., k. in a., 18/9/18.

HOWARD, John Brereton, Capt., d. of w., 6/4/18.

HOWE, Claude Arthur, Capt., k. in a., 20/11/17.

HUGHES, John Arthur, Lt., d. of w., 26/1/15.

JONES, Thomas Esmor, Lt., k. in a., 6/4/18.

MILLS, John Birchell, 2/Lt., d. of w., 16/4/17.

MINSHALL, Thomas Charles Wynn, Capt., d. of w., 25/3/18.

MORSE, Gerald Ernest, 2/Lt., killed, 31/10/17 (and R.F.C.).

NASH, Harold John, Lt., k. in a., 24/3/18.

PHILLIPS, David Charles, 2/Lt., k. in a., 16/8/17.

PRICHARD, John Walter, 2/Lt., k. in a., 18/9/18.

QUICKE, Henry, Lt., k. in a., 23/3/18.

SHAW, Bernard Lynton, Lt., k. in a., 23/4/17.

SHINGLER, John Stanley Marsh, M.C., Capt., d. of w., 4/9/18.

WALSHE, James, Lt., k. in a., 6/4/18.

WELSH, Alexander Torburn, 2/Lt., k. in a., 3/5/17.

5th (FLINTSHIRE) BATTALION (TERRITORIAL)

ARNOLD, Frederick Marshall, Lt., k. in a., 27/3/18.

BATE, Thomas, Lt., k. in a., 26/5/17.

BECKTON, William, Lt., killed, 23/3/18 (and R.F.C.).

BRADLEY, Horace Walter, 2/Lt., k. in a., 10/2/17.

BRASH, Edmund, 2/Lt., d. of w., 2/9/18.

EVANS, A. F., Lt., k. in a., 30-31/10/18 (and R.A.F.).

HAYES, John Henry, 2/Lt., k. in a., 31/7/17.

HEAD, Bernard, Major, k. in a., 12/8/15.

JERVIS, Percy William, 2/Lt., k. in a., 3/4/17.

JONES, John Humphrey, 2/Lt., k. in a., 8/10/18.

LELAND, John Henry Frederick, 2/Lt., k. in a., 10/8/15.

LOVELOCK, Clifford Andrew, 2/Lt., d., 20/11/18.

MOCATTA, Robert Menzies, 2/Lt., k. in a., 10/8/15.

MORRIS, Tom Bernard, Lt., d. of w., 23/7/17.

NICHOLS, Clifford, Capt., k. in a., 31/7/17 (and M.G.C.).

OVERTON, John, 2/Lt., k. in a., 22/3/18.

PHILIPS, Basil Edwin, Lt.-Col., k. in a., 10/8/15.

ROBERTS, Arthur Howell, 2/Lt., k. in a., 20/10/18.

SYNNOTT, Fitz Herbert Paget, 2/Lt., k. in a., 10/8/15.

THOMAS, Evan Llewellyn, 2/Lt., k. in a., 26/3/17.

TREGARTHEN, Ernest William, Lt., killed, 18/3/18.

TRICKETT, William Edwin, Major, d., 21/11/17.

WALTON, Robert Clare, 2/Lt., k. in a., 10/8/15.

WILLIAMS, Hugh Osborne, Lt., d. of w., 12/8/15.

WOODCOCK, Geoffrey Herbert, 2/Lt., k. in a., 6/4/18.

6th (CARNARVONSHIRE AND ANGLESEY) BATTALION (TERRITORIAL)

ANSON, Walter Frank Vernon, 2/Lt., k. in a., 8/11/17.

ANTHONY, John Richard, Capt., d. of w., 25/5/17 (and R.F.C.).

BAGNALL, Philip Walter Jowett, 2/Lt., k. in a., 10/8/15.

BEAN, Bevis Heppel, Lt., k. in a., 18/6/17 (and R.F.C.).

CRADDOCK, Percy Frederick, Capt., k. in a., 25/2/17.

DAVIES, Arthur Charles, Capt., k. in a., 10/8/15.

EDWARDS, John Henry, 2/Lt., k. in a., 21/9/18.

EVANS, Griffith William, 2/Lt., k. in a., 22/4/18 (att. R.A.F.).

FOSS, Frederick George, Lt., k. in a., 6/11/17.

GRIFFITHS, Edwin Harold, 2/Lt., d. of w., 23/10/18.

BREVET LIEUTENANT-COLONEL HUGH HILL, D.S.O., M.V.O.

Was Brigade Major to the Jullundur Brigade, Lahore Division, which arrived in France in September 1914. In May 1915 he was appointed D.A.A. and Q.M.G. ; in August A.Q.M.G. with the acting rank of Lieutenant-Colonel. In October he became G.S.O.1 to the 8th Division. After the First Battle of the Somme the division was moved to the Bethune front, and it was here that Lieutenant-Colonel Hill was killed by a sniper while inspecting the front line. He was buried at Bethune.

IRELAND, Walter Ernest, 2/Lt., k. in a., 26/3/17.

JONES, Evan, 2/Lt., k. in a., 6/11/17.

JONES, Gwilym Rhys, 2/Lt., k. in a., 10/8/15.

JONES, Owen Morris, Lt., k. in a., 31/10/18.

JONES-MANLEY, David Henry George, Capt., k. in a., 6/11/17.

MILLER, John, Capt., k. in a., 19/8/15.

PARKINSON, Thomas, 2/Lt., k. in a., 12/9/18.

PERRY, William Johnstone, 2/Lt., killed, 21/5/16.

ROGERS, Arthur, 2/Lt., k. in a., 26/3/17.

WILLIAMS, Arthur Llewellyn, 2/Lt., k. in a., 26/3/17.

WILLIAMS, George Stewart Louis Stanislaus Stevens, 2/Lt., k. in a., 8/9/18.

7th (MERIONETH AND MONTGOMERY) BATTALION (TERRITORIAL)

AXTENS, Harold Surridge, Lt., k. in a., 6/4/18.

BEADON, Basil Herbert Edwards, Capt., k. in a., 10/8/15.

BEANLAND, Joseph Wilfred, T/Capt., k. in a., 14/8/15.

BROWN, Herbert James, Lt., k. in a., 6/11/17.

BUCKLEY, Edmund Maurice, 2/Lt., d. of w., 12/8/15.

BURDETT, Thomas George Deane, M.C., Capt., k. in a., 6/11/17.

DAVIES, Albert Gordon, 2/Lt., d. of w., 1/8/17.

EVANS, Hywel Llewellyn, 2/Lt., k. in a., 26/9/17.

GOFF, William Setten, M.C., Lt., k. in a., 22/4/18.

GRANT, Albyn Evan Powell, 2/Lt., k. in a., 14/8/15.

GREGORY, Kenneth Stuart, Lt., k. in a., 10/11/17 (and M.G.C.).

HAILSTONE, George Rupert, Capt., k. in a., 6/11/17.

HARRIES, Eric Guy, Capt., d. of w., 17/8/15.

HUGHES-DAVIES, Arthur Gwynne, M.C., Lt., k. in a., 20/9/18 (and M.G.C.).

HURLBUTT, Percival, M.C., Hon. Capt., d., 8/6/18 (att. 25/Bn.).

JAMES, Ralph Lionel, 2/Lt., d., 3/8/17.

JONES, Ivor Wyn, 2/Lt., d. of w., 9/6/17.

JONES, Owen Cecil, Major, d. of w., 30/12/17.

JONES, Owen Gwilym, 2/Lt., k. in a., 26/3/17.

JONES, Russell Hafrenydd, 2/Lt., k. in a., 10/8/15.

JONES, Titho Glynne, Lt., k. in a., 20/4/17.

JONES, Vavasor, 2/Lt., k. in a., 19/5/15.

JONES, Wilfrid Griffith, Lt., k. in a., 6/4/18.

JONES, William Hugh, 2/Lt., k. in a., 21/6/17.

LLOYD-JONES, Edward Wynne, Capt., k. in a., 10/8/15.

LLOYD-JONES, Ivor Thomas, Capt., k. in a., 26/3/17.

NEWMAN, Leslie Cambridge, Lt., d. of w., 27/12/17 (in German hands).

OWEN, Humphrey Francis, Lt., k. in a., 24/3/18.

PARRY, Robert, 2/Lt., d. of w., 26/3/17.

PLOWDEN, Godfrey Bruce, Capt., d., 2/2/17.

REED, Andrew Gordon, Capt., k. in a., 10/8/15.

ROBERTS, John William, 2/Lt., d. of w., 23/3/18.

ROBERTS, William, Lt., k. in a., 27/12/17.

ROBERTS, William Lloyd, Lt., k. in a., 6/11/17.

SILCOCK, Bertram Baker, 2/Lt., k. in a., 10/8/15.

THOMAS, Edward Geoffrey, Lt., d., 10/10/18.

VALIENT, James, Lt., d. of w., 28/10/17.

WALKER, Edward William, Capt., k. in a., 6/11/17.

WATSON, George Walker, 2/Lt., killed, 29/12/16.

WHEELER, Augustus Henry, Major, k. in a., 10/8/15.

WHITTINGHAM, Lewis Stuart, 2/Lt., k. in a., 28/2/17.

WILLIAMS, Frederick, Lt., k. in a., 24/6/18 (and R.A.F.).

WILSON, John Edward Goodwin, 2/Lt., k. in a., 16/8/17.

WINDSOR, Harold George, 2/Lt., k. in a., 8/10/18.

OTHER RANKS

1st BATTALION

ABRAHAMS, J., b. Bradford, 47220, Pte., k. in a., F., 1/10/17.

ACKERLEY, J. H., b. Rossett, 18858, Pte., k. in a., F., 25/9/15.

ACTON, F., e. Liverpool, 53705, A/Cpl., k. in a., F., 14/5/17.

ADAMS, T., b. Lymn, 5105, L/Cpl., k. in a., F., 5/6/16.

AINSWORTH, H., b. Denton, 4219, Pte., k. in a., F., 15/7/16.

AIRD, W. J., b. Birmingham, 6494, Pte., k. in a., F., 4/5/17.

AMBROSE, H. G., b. Damerham, 4402, Sgt., d. of w., F., 29/11/14.

AMPHLETT, T. W., e. Wrexham, 17643, L/Cpl., k. in a., F., 25/9/15.

ANDREWS, G., b. Dowlais, 17451, Pte., k. in a., F., 18/7/15.

ANDREWS, G. A., b. Newport, 5666, L/Cpl., d. of w., F., 28/9/15.

ANDREWS, H. H., b. Bristol,

17001, L/Cpl., k. in a., F., 28/8/16.

ANKERS, S., b. Wrexham, 4893, Pte., k. in a., F., 16/5/15.

ARMSHAW, G., b. Birmingham, 9884, Pte., k. in a., F., 13/4/15.

ARMSTRONG, G., b. Liverpool, 18186, Pte., d. of w., F., 15/3/15.

ASHDOWN, E., b. Birmingham, 6849, Pte., d., F., 19/6/17.

ASHLEY, P. W., b. Runcorn, 23722, Pte., d. of w., F., 13/1/17.

ASQUITH, W., b. Liverpool, 17920, Pte., k. in a., F., 27/8/16.

ATKINS, E., b. Birmingham, 5011, Pte., k. in a., F., 16/5/16.

ATKINS, F. C., b. Birmingham, 19309, Pte., k. in a., F., 5/6/16.

ATKINS, W., b. Wolston, 9717, A/Sgt., k. in a., F., 25/9/15.

ATWELL, F. R., b. London, 9919, Pte., d. of w., F., 20/10/14.

AUSTIN, J., b. Newcastle, Staffs,

56300, Pte., k. in a., F., 30/3/17.

BACON, H. A., b. Normanton, 24809, Pte., k. in a., F., 15/5/17.

BAILEY, J. E., b. Thornton Heath, 23854, Sgt., d. of w., Home, 9/1/18.

BAILEY, W. A., b. Birmingham, 19308, Pte., k. in a., F., 15/5/17.

BAKER, W., b. London, 10337, Pte., k. in a., F., 21/10/14.

BALDWIN, E., b. Higher Walton, 4594, Pte., d. of w., F., 8/11/14.

BALL, H., e. Southport, 266873, Pte., d. of w., F., 1/10/17.

BALL, T., b. Birmingham, 11353, Pte., k. in a., F., 25/9/15.

BALNAVES, F. F., b. Birmingham, 11384, Pte., d. of w., F., 14/3/15.

BANNER, J., b. Worcester, 9930, Pte., k. in a., F., 21/10/14.

BANNING, A. H., b. Birmingham, 10421, Pte., k. in a., F., 21/10/14.

BARGUSS, G. W., b. Slough, 9824, Cpl., k. in a., F., 16/5/15.

BARKER, J., b. Birkenhead, 18193, Pte., k. in a., F., 28/8/16.

BARNES, D. A., b. London, 27536, L/Cpl., k. in a., F., 17/10/16, M.M.

BARNES, R. J., b. Millbrook, 31630, Pte., d., F., 8/7/16.

BARNES, W., b. Arnold, 19758, Pte., k. in a., F., 25/9/15.

BARNETT, H., b. St. John's Kenilworth, 9016, Pte., k. in a., F., 19/10/14.

BARNETT, P., b. Aldershot, 9018, L/Cpl., d., F., 25/2/15.

BARRATT, J., b. Wigan, 17215, Pte., d., F., 15/9/15.

BARTER, J. T., b. Cardiff, 9791, Pte., k. in a., F., 30/10/14.

BATCHELOR, R., b. Hungerford, 6225, Pte., d. of w., F., 13/10/17.

BATEMAN, T., b. Birmingham, 9661, Sgt., k. in a., F., 14/5/16.

BAYLIS, B. J., b. Barnsley, 10836, Pte., k. in a., F., 30/10/14.

BAYLIS, E. T., b. Birmingham, 9623, Pte., k. in a., F., 4/5/17.

BEALE, W. E., b. Carnarvon, 10471, L/Sgt., k. in a., F., 30/10/14.

BEARDWOOD, H. B., e. Liverpool, 53950, L/Cpl., d. of w., F., 6/5/17.

BEECH, G., b. Stockport, 11463, Pte., k. in a., F., 17/5/15.

BEEKS, J. A., b. Hereford, 10969, L/Cpl., k. in a., F., 30/10/14.

BELLIS, E. W., b. Wrexham, 5329, Pte., k. in a., F., 25/9/15.

BENCH, C., b. Leamington, 10812, Pte., k. in a., F., 21/10/14.

BENDALL, F., b. Prestwich, 28499, Pte., k. in a., F., 5/12/16.

BENNETT, I. E., b. Cinderford, 61370, Pte., d., Italy, 12/3/18.

BENNETT, S., b. Northop, 5845, Sgt., k. in a., F., 14/7/16.

BERRIDGE, A., b. London, 10291, Pte., k. in a., F., 30/10/14.

BERRY, W., b. Rhiwderin, 18100, Pte., k. in a., F., 25/9/15.

BEVAN, J., b. Wrexham, 4913, A/Cpl., k. in a., F., 9/12/16.

BENYON, R. G., b. Swansea, 19783, Pte., k. in a., F., 3/9/16.

BINGHAM, J., b. Birmingham, 10869, Pte., k. in a., F., 7/1/15.

BIRCHALL, R., b. Latham, 53771, L/Cpl., k. in a., F., 14/5/17.

BISHOP, A., b. Llangibby, 18145, L/Cpl., k. in a., F., 28/5/16.

BISHOP, T., b. Warwick, 9658, Sgt., d. of w., F., 27/10/17.

BLAKE, E., b. Horninglow, 6479, Cpl., k. in a., F., 19/10/14.

BLAKE, W. G., b. Chipping Norton, 10683, Pte., k. in a., F., 30/10/14.

BLAYLOCK, H., b. Crewe, 33214, Pte., k. in a., F., 3/9/16.

BLOOMFIELD, W., b. Stockport, 7829, Pte., k. in a., F., 30/10/14.

BLOOR, R., b. Runcorn, 17335, Pte., d. of w., Home, 7/10/15.

BOLTON, G. H., b. Harborne, 5920, Pte., k. in a., F., 21/10/14.

BOOTH, A., b. Claycross, 36590, Pte., d. of w., F., 7/7/16.

BOUGHEY, J. L., b. Fenton, 5727, Pte., k. in a., F., 16/5/15.

BOULD, G., b. Shrewsbury, 19383, Pte., k. in a., F., 3/9/16.

BOULTER, H., b. Oxford, 8636, Pte., k. in a., F., 6/3/16.

BOUNDY, C. E., b. Carnarvon, 7723, Sgt., k. in a., F., 20/10/14.

BOUNDY, F. H., b. Wrexham, 10202, Sgt., k. in a., F., 16/5/15.

BOURKE, J., b. Manchester, 55712, Pte., k. in a., F., 3/5/17.

BOWEN, W. J., b. Ferndale, 5019, Pte., k. in a., F., 13/3/15.

BOWHAY, H. H., b. London, 10800, Pte., k. in a., F., 7/11/14.

BOWKER, E. V., b. Bangor-on-Dee, 8482, Cpl., k. in a., F., 4/5/17.

BOWLER, J., b. Ashton-under-Lyne, 7649, Pte., k. in a., F., 30/10/14.

BOWLES, A., b. Oswestry, 5723, Pte., d. of w., F., 19/12/14.

BOWLES, C., b. Rogerstone, 5094, Pte., k. in a., F., 16/3/15.

BOYTON, G., b. Cheltenham, 17300, Pte., k. in a., F., 16/5/15.

BRACE, I. J., b. Aberdare, 24421, Pte., d. of w., F., 9/7/16.

BRACKLEY, T., b. Grangetown, 9939, Sgt., k. in a., F., 30/10/14.

BRADLEY, J. S., b. Liverpool, 67753, Pte., k. in a., F., 2/10/17.

BRADSHAW, F., b. Hadfield, 3820, Pte., k. in a., F., 22/11/14.

BRADSHAW, J., e. Colwyn Bay, 53677, Pte., k. in a., F., 11/1/17.

BRADSHAW, L. R., b. London, 10753, Pte., k. in a., F., 20/10/14.

BRADSHAW, W. T., b. Ardwick, 8310, Pte., k. in a., F., 5/7/16.

BRAIN., H., b. Southam, 9009, Sgt., k. in a., F., 25/9/15.

BRATHERTON, G., b. Chester, 5501, Pte., k. in a., F., 16/5/15.

BRAZENDALE, A., b. Kirkdale, 53772, Pte., k. in a., F., 4/5/17.

BRETON, J., b. Islington, 22632, Pte., d. of w., F., 13/10/17.

BRIDGMAN, W. H., b. Ashsted, 10363, Pte., k. in a., F., 16/5/15.

BRINDAL, A. S., b. Cardiff, 31942, Pte., k. in a., F., 2/10/17.

BROADHURST, E., b. Birmingham, 9790, Pte., d., F., 30/11/14.

BRODERICK, M., b. Bristol, 9171, Cpl., k. in a., F., 25/9/15.

BROOKES, W., b. Nannerch, 15855, Pte., d., Home, 29/10/18.

BROOKS, C. W., b. London, 35048, Pte., k. in a., F., 3/9/16.

BROOMHALL, R., b. Walton, 9259, L/Cpl., k. in a., F., 25/9/15.

BROTHERTON, S., b. Birmingham, 10825, Pte., d. of w., F., 10/12/14.

BROTHERWOOD, A., b. West Ham, 17446, L/Cpl., d. of w., F., 10/12/16.

BROWN, J., b. London, 8160, Pte., k. in a., F., 30/10/14.

BROWN, J., b. Chester, 33038, Pte., k. in a., F., 12/5/17.

BROWN, J., b. Hednesford, 19747, Pte., k. in a., F., 27/8/16.

BROWN, T., b. Dublin, 10004, Pte., k. in a., F., 23/8/15.

BROWN, W., b. Whitchurch, 241799, Pte., k. in a., F., 2/10/17.

BROWN, W. E. A., b. London, 27517, Pte., k. in a., F., 2/11/16, M.M.

BROWNSEY, A. H., b. Rimpton, 56608, L/Cpl., k. in a., F., 3/9/16.

BRUTON, W. A., e. Mountain Ash, Glam., 70449, Pte., k. in a., F., 26/10/17.

BUCKLEY, P., b. Aberavon, 11781, Pte., k. in a., F., 16/5/15.

BULLIVANT, G., b. Birmingham, 8480, Pte., k. in a., F., 7/11/14.

BUNCE, W., b. Saltney, 11096, Pte., k. in a., F., 30/10/14.

BUNNELL, A., b. Tarvin, 5839, L/Cpl., k. in a., F., 16/5/15.

BUNNEY, T. J., b. Penrhiwceiber, 10542, Pte., d. of w., F., 1/11/14.

BURGE, G., b. Longeaton, 16787, Pte., k. in a., F., 30/10/14.

BURTON, J., b. New Mills, 36003, A/Cpl., k. in a., F., 15/5/17, D.C.M.

BURTON, W., b. Garw Valley, 13673, Pte., k. in a., F., 5/7/16.

BUSTIN, R. J., b. Birmingham, 7985, Cpl., d. of w., F., 25/2/17.

BUTLER, J., b. Bradford, 19162, Pte., k. in a., F., 28/6/15.

BUTWELL, W. A., b. Birmingham, 8104, Pte., k. in a., F., 16/5/15.

BYRNE, G., b. Liverpool, 11098, L/Cpl., k. in a., F., 25/9/15.

CADMAN, H., b. Wolverhampton, 4424, Pte., k. in a., F., 16/5/15.

CALDWELL, G., b. Birmingham, 6809, L/Cpl., k. in a., F., 25/9/15.

CAMPBELL, J., b. St. Helen's, 45588, Pte., k. in a., F., 21/7/17.

CAMPOUSER, J., b. Swansea, 6209, L/Cpl., k. in a., F., 16/5/15.

CAPELIN, B., b. Wrexham, 53604, Pte., d. of w., F., 1/4/17.

CAROLL, F., b. Aberavon, 6135, Pte., k. in a., F., 30/10/14.

CARPENTER, S., b. Down Ampney, 10838, Pte., k. in a., F., 19/10/14.

CARROLL, J. T., b. Spitalfields, 23902, Pte., k. in a., F., 3/9/16.

CARTER, W., b. S. Oswald, 33975, Pte., d. Italy, 22/9/18.

CASSELLS, R., b. Liverpool, 12154, Pte., k. in a., F., 1/10/17.

CASTREY, A., b. West Bromwich, 5790, Sgt., k. in a., Italy, 3/5/18.

CHALLENGER, D., b. Abertillery, 47245, Pte., d. of w., F., 9/10/17.

CHAMBERLAIN, A., b. Brierley Hill, 8639, L/Cpl., d. of w., F., 20/3/16.

CHAMPION, G. F., b. Cardiff, 4239, Sgt., d. of w., F., 3/9/16, M.M.

CHAPMAN, P. M., e. London, 45692, Pte., k. in a., F., 9/10/17.

CHAPPELL, G., e. Manchester, 53762, Pte., k. in a., F., 30/3/17.

CHARLES, J., b. Barry Port, 5549, Pte., k. in a., F., 16/5/15.

CHECKETT, F. E. A., b. Birmingham, 10724, Pte., k. in a., F., 30/10/14.

CHEERS, S., b. Chester, 10472, Pte., d. of w., F., 19/5/16.

CHESTERTON, E., b. Islington, 6200, Pte., k. in a., F., 16/5/15.

CHICK, W., b. Bridgwater, 6378, Pte., k. in a., F., 16/5/15.

CHILD, J., b. Glossop, 17515, Pte., d. of w., F., 4/10/15.

CHIVERS, A., b. Chadderton, 56577, Pte., d. of w., F., 26/10/17.

CLANCEY, D., b. Cardiff, 10970, Pte., k. in a., F., 22/3/16.

CLARK, F., b. Lymm, 24444, Pte., d. of w., F., 16/3/16.

CLARK, H., b. Stepney, 10799, Pte., d. of w., F., 25/1/15.

CLARKE, A., b. Crewe, 33113, Pte., k. in a., F., 21/7/17.

CLARKE, A. H., b. Coventry, 6253, L/Sgt., k. in a., F., 30/10/14.

CLARKE, C. A., b. Birmingham, 9816, Pte., k. in a., F., 20/10/14.

CLARKE, F., b. Hounslow, 9370, Dmr., k. in a., F., 27/10/14.

CLARKE, G., b. Cardiff, 5114, Pte., k. in a., F., 16/5/15.

CLARKE, W., b. Plymouth, 5307, Pte., d. of w., F., 16/3/16.

CLARKE, W., b. Chester, 5804, Pte., k. in a., F., 16/5/15.

CLAY, A., b. Wolverhampton, 5714, A/Sgt., k. in a., F., 16/7/16.

CLAYTON, J., b. Llandudno, 27665, Pte., k. in a., F., 29/8/16.

CLIFTON, R. A., e. Cardiff, 31692, Pte., k. in a., F., 1/10/17.

CLOWER, A., b. Ripley, 31031, Pte., k. in a., F., 14/5/16.

COHEN, L., e. Liverpool, 54178, Pte., k. in a., F., 22/12/16.

COLCLOUGH, J., b. Tunstall, 24648, Sgt., k. in a., Italy, 27/10/18.

COLE, W., b. Seaforth, 8304, Pte., d. of w., F., 23/10/14.

COLES, F. J., b. Manchester, 11208, Pte., k. in a., F., 21/10/14.

COLLACOTT, R., b. St. Austell, 6082, Pte., k. in a., F., 11/3/15.

COLLIER, G., b. Walsall, 7010, Pte., k. in a., F., 30/10/14.

COLLIER, J. T., b. High Beech, 53773, Pte., k. in a., F., 10/10/17.

COLLINS, J., b. Liverpool, 63596, Pte., k. in a., F., 4/5/17.

COLLINS, W. J., b. Hawarden, 7,921, Pte., k. in a., Italy, 23/10/18.

COMPTON, C. H., b. Mountain Ash, 4950, L/Cpl., k. in a., F., 9/10/17.

COMPTON, F., b. Taunton, 5260, Pte., d. of w., F., 23/3/15.

CONDREY, C., b. Wrexham, 8184, A/Sgt., k. in a., F., 16/5/15.

COOK, C., b. Warwick, 19261, Pte., k. in a., F., 25/9/15.

COOK, F., b. Walsall, 7043, Pte., k. in a., F., 16/5/15.

COOK, W. M., b. London, 10294, Pte., k. in a., F., 20/10/14.

COOPER, C. L., b. London, 10405, Pte., d., F., 31/10/14.

COOPER, F., b. Birmingham, 13380, Pte., k. in a., F., 3/9/16.

CORBETT, J. J., e. London, 28066, Pte., k. in a., F., 27/2/17.

CORNES, W. H., b. Birmingham, 6260, Pte., k. in a., F., 30/10/14.

CORNISH, T., b. Wrexham, 10919, Cpl., d. of w., F., 26/1/15.

COTTER, W. J., b. Aberdare, 10847, Cpl., k. in a., F., 21/10/14.

COULSON, C., b. Llanhilleth, Mon., 17152, Pte., k. in a., F., 25/9/15.

COULSON, W., b. Oswestry, 10297, Pte., d., F., 9/8/15.

COULTHARD, J., b. St. Patrick's, Stockton, 7163, Pte., k. in a., F., 21/10/14.

CRANMER, C. T., b. Black Torington, Devon, 63665, L/Cpl., k. in a., Italy, 31/10/18.

CRAVEN, S., b. Birmingham, 8284, C.Q.M.S., k. in a., F., 30/10/14.

CROFT, T., b. Radcliffe, Lancs, 54162, Pte., k. in a., F., 4/5/17.

CROFT, W. E., b. Worthen, Salop, 6273, Pte., k. in a., F., 16/5/15.

CROOK, T., b. Bolton, 23514, Pte., k. in a., F., 15/5/17.

CROOKS, F., b. Parr, St. Helens, 10985, Pte., k. in a., F., 6/11/14.

CROSS, J., b. Pembridge, Hereford, 6256, Pte., d., Home, 17/2/17.

CROSSLEY, E., b. Aston, Hawarden, 12493, Pte., d. of w., F., 26/2/17.

CROW, F., b. Ardwick, Manchester, 18701, Pte., k. in a., F., 19/7/16.

CROWDER, W. G., b. Birmingham, 53774, Pte., k. in a., F., 4/5/17.

CROWLEY, L., b. Newport, Mon., 4416, Pte., k. in a., F., 22/2/16.

CROWTHER, J. T., b. Clayton-le-Moors, Lancs., 23861, Pte., k. in a., F., 15/5/17.

CUEL, H. S., b. Dublin, 5261, Pte., k. in a., F., 30/10/14.

CULLIFORD, P., b. Llangeinor, Glam., 13860, Pte., k. in a., Italy, 3/5/18.

CURRAN, W. W., b. Swansea, 69200, Pte., k. in a., Italy, 9/8/18.

DALLEY, J. E., b. Birmingham, 8322, Pte., k. in a., F., 21/10/14.

DALRYMPLE, E., b. Workington, 24094, L/Sgt., k. in a., F., 2/9/16.

DANDO, F., b. Bristol, 5588, Pte., k. in a., F., 14/5/17.

DANDY, H., b. Willenhall, Staffs, 9642, C.S.M., k. in a., F., 3/9/16, M.M.

DARCY, J., b. St. Mary's, Chester, 18199, Pte., k. in a., F., 18/7/16.

DARLINGTON, A., b. Openshaw, Lancs, 56620, Pte., d., F., 14/12/16.

DAVIES, A., b. Canton, Cardiff, 10488, Pte., d., F., 12/7/17.

DAVIES, A., b. Wrexham, 10840, Pte., k. in a., F., 31/10/14.

DAVIES, A., b. Birkenhead, 10936, Pte., k. in a., F., 30/10/14.

DAVIES, A., b. Aberdare, 10798, Pte., d., F., 9/11/18.

DAVIES, C., b. Boughton Heath, Cheshire, 10953, Pte., k. in a., F., 16/5/15.

DAVIES, D., b. Abergele, 5718, Pte., k. in a., F., 29/12/14.

DAVIES, D., b. Pontywaith, Glam., 18121, Pte., k. in a., F., 9/10/17, M.M. and Clasp.

DAVIES, D., e. Lampeter, 53958, Pte., k. in a., F., 4/5/17.

DAVIES, D. D., b. Trehafod, Glam., 4632, L/Cpl., k. in a., F., 25/9/15.

DAVIES, D. J., b. Llanwonno, Glam., 9265, Pte., k. in a., F., 16/5/15.

DAVIES, D. S., b. Cefn, Brecknock, 17738, Pte., k. in a., F., 7/10/15.

DAVIES, E., b. Llanbeblig, Carnarvon, 4675, Pte., d. of w., F., 6/11/14.

DAVIES, E., b. Merthyr, 18118, Pte., k. in a., F., 30/4/16.

DAVIES, G., b. Church Stoke, Mont., 9329, Sgt., k. in a., F., 24/7/15.

DAVIES, H., b. Montgomery, 10482, Cpl., k. in a., F., 16/5/15.

DAVIES, H. H., b. Bethesda, Carn., 5809, Pte., k. in a., F., 16/5/15.

DAVIES, I., b. Mardy, Glam., 12180, Pte., k. in a., F., 5/7/16.

DAVIES, I., b. Ferndale, 16477, Pte., k. in a., F., 4/5/17.

DAVIES, J., b. Brymbo, Denbigh, 10872, Pte., k. in a., F., 20/10/14.

DAVIES, J., b. Eglwysbach, Denbigh, A/Cpl., d. of w., F., 15/2/15.

DAVIES, J., b. Aberhosan, Mont., 10507, Cpl., k. in a., F., 25/9/15.

DAVIES, J., b. Ferndale, 11321, A/Cpl., k. in a., F., 26/2/17.

DAVIES, J., b. Liverpool, 36569, Pte., k. in a., F., 27/8/16.

DAVIES, J., b. Bridgend, 75380, Pte., k. in a., F., 27/10/17.

DAVIES, J., b. Abergele, 11069, Pte., k. in a., F., 16/5/15.

DAVIES, J., b. Mold, 5931, Pte., k. in a., F., 16/5/15.

DAVIES, J. W., b. Chester, 11139, Pte., k. in a., F., 4/10/14.

DAVIES, J. W., b. Aberdare, 13438, Pte., k. in a., F., 25/9/15.

DAVIES, O., b. Aberystwyth, 6071, Pte., k. in a., F., 16/5/15.

DAVIES, P. J., b. Prestatyn, 11351, Pte., k. in a., F., 30/1/15.

DAVIES, R., b. Pentre Ystrad, 4873, Pte., d. of w., F., 26/1/15.

DAVIES, R. H., b. Cwmyglo, 40349, Pte., k. in a., F., 3/9/16.

DAVIES, R. J., b. Wrexham, 3126, Pte., d. of w., F., 22/1/15.

DAVIES, R. J., b. Swansea, 10024, Sgt., k. in a., F., 28/8/16.

DAVIES, R. W., b. Wrexham, 4815, Pte., k. in a., F., 16/5/15.

DAVIES, S., b. Ruthin, 15425, L/Cpl., k. in a., F., 3/9/16.

DAVIES, T., b. Merthyr Tydvil, 5750, Pte., k. in a., F., 30/10/14.

DAVIES, T., b. Wrexham, 16931, Pte., k. in a., F., 25/9/15.

DAVIES, T., b. Cwmbwrla, 47248, Pte., d., Italy, 6/11/18.

DAVIES, T. J., b. Abertillery, 19215, L/Cpl., k. in a., F., 5/5/17.

DAVIES, W., b. Monmouth, 6040, Pte., k. in a., F., 30/10/14.

DAVIES, W., b. West Ham, 56621, Pte., d. of w., F., 3/10/17.

DAVIES, W. J., b. Bethesda, 44275, Pte., k. in a., F., 27/5/17.

DAVIES, W. T., b. Dolfrwynog, 53605, Pte., k. in a., F., 30/3/17.

DAVIS, B., b. Stafford, 11345, Pte., k. in a., F., 3/9/16.

DAYUS, F. H., b. Birmingham, 11383, Cpl., k. in a., F., 29/8/16.

DEACON, W. H., b. Leicester, 24370, Pte., k. in a., F., 27/8/16.

DEAN, J., b. Padiham, 39718, A/Sgt., d. of w., Italy, 3/11/18.

DEAN, T. D., b. London, 5289, Pte., k. in a., F., 20/10/14.

DESMOND, J., b. Cwmbran, Mon., 4370, Pte., k. in a., F., 16/5/15.

DEXTER, E., b. Peterborough, 4546, L/Cpl., k. in a., F., 25/9/15.

DIER, R. S., b. Pembroke Dock, 10572, Pte., k. in a., F., 19/10/14.

DILNOTT, W. H., b. Coventry, 8821, Cpl., k. in a., F., 30/6/16.

DINNING, R. C., b. Glasgow, 11033, L/Cpl., d., F., 25/10/18.

DISLEY, W., e. Preston, 55724, Pte., k. in a., F., 26/2/17.

DIXON, W. G., b. Bangor, 55714, L/Cpl., k. in a., F., 2/10/17.

DOBBY, F., b. Leytonstone, 27286, Pte., k. in a., F., 3/9/16.

DOBSON, T., b. Chester, 4499, L/Cpl., k. in a., F., 28/8/16.

DODD, A., b. Chester, 7863, Pte., k. in a., F., 15/6/15.

DODD, W. A., b. London, 27081, Pte., k. in a., F., 4/5/17.

DOLMAN, J., b. Burntwood, Staffs, 24263, Pte., k. in a., F., 29/4/16.

DONOVAN, M., b. Ireland, 19155, Pte., k. in a., F., 11/6/15.

DOOLEY, W. H., b. Westminster, 8460, Pte., k. in a., F., 24/12/14.

DOUBLER, F., b. Roath, 16806, Pte., k. in a., F., 30/9/17.

DOWLING, J., b. Slough, 9866, Pte., k. in a., F., 14/5/17.

DOWNES, J., b. Manchester, 5523, Pte., k. in a., F., 16/5/15.

DRISCOLL, D., b. London, 23915, Pte., d., Italy, 31/10/18.

DUCKERS, T. W., b. Birkenhead, 6650, L/Cpl., k. in a., F., 28/8/16.

DUGDALE, T., b. Liverpool, 4466, Pte., k. in a., F., 5/7/16.

DUGGAN, G., b. Hereford, 54915, Pte., k. in a., F., 26/10/17.

DUKE, T., b. Cork, 17406, Pte., k. in a., F., 25/9/15.

DUNDON, C. J., b. Kirkdale, 19486, Pte., k. in a., F., 25/9/15.

DURKIN, W., b. Chester, 11440, L/Cpl., k. in a., F., 3/9/16.

DUTTON, A. E., b. Weston, Cheshire, 17340, L/Cpl., k. in a., F., 25/9/15.

DUTTON, B., b. Pontnewydd, 5699, Pte., d. of w., Home, 29/12/14.

DUTTON, R., b. Pendleton, 266886, Pte., d. of w., F., 3/10/17.

DYSON, G. H., b. Swansea, 9331, Pte., d. of w., F., 21/11/16.

EATON, S. E., b. Llandudno Junction, 53876, Pte., d., F., 13/1/17.

EBENEZER, J. D., b. Nantcwnlle, 40399, Pte., d. of w., F., 13/1/17.

ECCLES, J. W., b. Birmingham, 9004, Pte., k. in a., F., 20/3/15.

EDMUNDS, W., b. Coventry, 9897, Pte., d. of w., F., 13/11/14.

EDWARDS, A., b. Newport, 4943, Pte., k. in a., F., 16/5/15.

EDWARDS, A. T., b. Aberystwyth, 27022, Pte., k. in a., F., 3/9/16.

EDWARDS, D., b. Bangor, 8408, Pte., k. in a., F., 30/10/14.

EDWARDS, D. J., e. Swansea, 53059, Pte., k. in a., F., 4/5/17.

EDWARDS, E., b. Denbigh, 76913, Pte., k. in a., Italy, 23/10/18.

EDWARDS, H., b. Llantrisant Valley, 12026, Pte., k. in a., F., 28/8/15.

EDWARDS, H. W., b. Conway, 53693, Pte., d. of w., F., 6/5/17.

EDWARDS, P. T., e. Flint, 53904, Pte., k. in a., F., 21/7/17.

EDWARDS, R. E., b. Corwen, 34944, Pte., k. in a., F., 28/8/16.

EDWARDS, R. T., b. Wrexham, 8907, Pte., k. in a., F., 23/5/15.

EDWARDS, R. W., b. Coedpoeth, 3971, Pte., k. in a., F., 30/10/14.

EDWARDS, T., b. Wrexham, 4852, Pte., k. in a., F., 13/3/15.

EDWARDS, T., b. Aberporth, 9448, Pte., k. in a., F., 24/7/15.

EDWARDS, W., b. Brecon, 2681, Cpl., d. of w., Home, 7/10/15.

EDWARDS, W., b. Newton-le-

Willows, 4189, Pte., k. in a., F., 16/5/15.

EDWARDS, W., b. Treharris, 11123, A/Cpl., d., Home, 6/10/18.

EDWARDS, W., b. Holywell, 53889, Pte., k. in a., F., 22/7/17.

EDWARDS, W. H., b. Llanfyllin, 40390, Pte., k. in a., F., 3/9/16.

EDWARDS, W. J., b. Perth, 23176, L/Cpl., k. in a., F., 4/8/17.

EGAN, M., b. Widnes, 235703, Pte., k. in a., F., 1/10/17.

ELLIS, D. J., b. Conway, 6032, Pte., k. in a., F., 16/5/15.

ELLIS, E., b. Denbigh, 5346, Pte., k. in a., F., 3/9/16.

ELLIS, E. P., b. Blaenau Festiniog, 53689, Pte., d. of w., F., 10/1/17.

ELLIS, J., b. Buckley, 5289, Pte., k. in a., F., 16/5/15.

ELLIS, R., b. Oswestry, 8486, Pte., k. in a., F., 7/11/14.

ELLIS, W., b. Llanddeiniolen, 40178, Pte., k. in a., F., 3/9/16.

ELLSON, F., b. Chester, 8201, Pte., k. in a., F., 25/9/15.

ELSON, W., b. Cardiff, Glam., 56987, L/Cpl., k. in a., F., 1/10/17.

ELVIS, J., b. Tylorstown, 5887, Pte., k. in a., F., 25/9/15.

EVANS, E., b. Oswestry, 8589, Pte., k. in a., F., 23/8/15.

EVANS, E., b. Menai Bridge, 53609, Pte., k. in a., F., 12/1/17.

EVANS, E., b. Merthyr, 29510, Pte., d. of w., F., 4/12/10.

EVANS, E., b. Carnarvon, 40342, Pte., k. in a., F., 26/8/16.

EVANS, H. A., b. Birmingham, 9605, Pte., k. in a., F., 16/5/15.

EVANS, J., b. Wrexham, 8932, Pte., d. of w., F., 23/5/15.

EVANS, J., b. Skewen, 18147, L/Cpl., k. in a., F., 3/9/16.

EVANS, J., b. London, 56605, Pte., k. in a., F., 28/8/16.

EVANS, J., b. Pontypool, 16992, Pte., k. in a., F., 25/9/15.

EVANS, J., b. Wrexham, 53690, Pte., d. of w., F., 27/2/17.

EVANS, J. S., b. Denbigh, 4118, Pte., d. of w., F., 1/6/15.

EVANS, R., b. Caio, 37488, Pte., k. in a., F., 21/8/16.

EVANS, R., b. Denbigh, 53692, Pte., k. in a., F., 11/1/17.

EVANS, R. C., b. Oswestry, 5151, Pte., k. in a., F., 16/5/15.

EVANS, R. T., b. Llanstyndwy, 53779, Pte., k. in a., Italy, 3/5/18.

EVANS, S., b. Denbigh, 40842, L/Cpl., k. in a., F., 1/10/17.

EVANS, S. C., b. Newport, 6137, Cpl., d. of w., F., 21/7/15.

EVANS, T., b. Tally Harris, 17757, L/Cpl., d. of w., F., 9/7/16.

EVANS, W., b. Penderyn, 11227, Pte., k. in a., F., 16/5/15.

EVANS, W. A., b. Llanberis, 40432, Pte., k. in a., F., 3/9/16.

EVANS, W. H., b. Merthyr Tydvil, 33528, Pte., d., Italy, 24/7/18.

EVANS, W. H., b. Wrexham, 6419, Pte., k. in a., F., 25/9/15.

EWINGTON, T. G., b. Abercynon, 5191, Pte., k. in a., F., 16/5/15.

EYTON, J. R., b. Wrexham, 10032, Pte., k. in a., F., 20/10/14.

FALLON, J., b. Manchester, 8265, Pte., k. in a., F., 30/10/14.

FARR, T., b. Dowlais, 56601, L/Cpl., k. in a., F., 29/8/16.

FARRELL, G., b. Chester, 5137, Pte., k. in a., F., 11/12/14.

FATHERS, T., b. Oxford, 8144, Pte., k. in a., F., 16/5/15.

FAULKES, L. R., b. Islington, 26828, Pte., d. of w., F., 6/9/16.

FAWCETT, W., b. Tranmere, 8311, Pte., k. in a., F., 30/10/14.

FEAR, S., b. Carmarthen, 33251, Pte., k. in a., F., 3/9/16.

FENTON, J. T., b. Manchester, 33263, Pte., k. in a., F., 3/3/16.

FERGUSON, T., b. Flint, 3670, Pte., k. in a., F., 16/5/15.

FERN, W., b. Llanbeblig, 7083, Pte., k. in a., F., 30/10/14.

FERNES, A., b. Bradford, 235535, Pte., k. in a., F., 1/10/17.

FIELDHOUSE, A., e. Trefynant, 53612, Pte., k. in a., F., 2/10/17.

FILSELL, A., b. Swanwick, 10581, Pte., k. in a., F., 30/10/14.

FINCH, F., b. Miles Platting, 235534, L/Cpl., k. in a., F., 1/10/17.

FINCH, J. C., b. Leamington, 11853, Pte., d. of w., F., 22/1/15.

FISHER, J., b. Wrexham, 5643, Pte., k. in a., F., 25/9/15.

FITZPATRICK, F., b. Liverpool, 10143, Pte., k. in a., F., 20/10/14.

FLETCHER, T., b. Leamington, 6183, Pte., k. in a., F., 30/10/14.

FLINT, W. C., b. Pontypridd, 5107, Pte., k. in a., F., 16/5/15.

FLOOK, F., b. Pontypool, 16988, Pte., k. in a., F., 3/9/16.

FLYNN, P., b. Manchester, 6112, Cpl., k. in a., F., 29/12/14.

FORSYTH, J., b. Liverpool, 10962, Pte., d., F., 25/8/18.

FORTT, W. H., b. Malta, 42201, Pte., k. in a., F., 26/10/17.

FORWARD, P. V., b. St. James', Taunton, 10712, Pte., k. in a., F., 16/5/15.

FOULKES, T., b. Old Colwyn, 53613, Pte., k. in a., F., 4/5/17.

FOWLER, B., b. Bonnymaen, 40019, Pte., d. of w., F., 16/7/16.

FOX, M. A., b. Swansea, 4634, Pte., k. in a., F., 20/10/14.

FOX, W., b. Worcester, 55706, Pte., k. in a., F., 14/5/17.

FRAMPTON, H., b. Cardiff, 10604, Cpl., k. in a., F., 16/5/15.

FRANKLIN, A., b. Lambeth, 11390, Pte., k. in a., F., 16/5/15.

FRANKLIN, G., b. Newport, 17442, Pte., d. of w., Home, 29/11/17, M.M.

FREEBURY, W., b. Wroughton, 18864, Pte., k. in a., F., 3/9/16.

FREEMAN, H., b. Manchester, 5320, Pte., k. in a., F., 16/5/15.

FRENCH, W., b. Rhos, 9964, Pte., d., F., 13/6/15.

FRY, R. E., b. Dublin, 9788, Pte., d. of w., F., 6/11/14.

FURY, W., b. Leigh, Lancs, 17679, Pte., k. in a., F., 21/10/14.

GALE, F., b. Llanhilleth, 17346, Pte., k. in a., F., 26/6/15.

GAPE, D., b. Swansea, 6374, Pte., k. in a., F., 30/10/14.

GARDNER, H., b. Birmingham, 11343, Pte., d. of w., F., 3/1/15.

GARRETT, A., b. Birmingham, 9895, Pte., k. in a., F., 30/10/14.

GAUNT, F., b. Birmingham, 19484, Pte., k. in a., F., 25/9/15.

GEE, O., b. Macclesfield, 9997, L/Cpl., k. in a., F., 25/11/15.

GEORGE, G. F., b. Bengeworth, 7023, Cpl., k. in a., F., 24/10/14.

GEORGE, T., b. Aberdare, 6182, Pte., k. in a., F., 16/5/15.

GERRARD, J. F., b. Chester, 7624, Cpl., k. in a., F., 16/5/15.

GIBBARD, G., b. East Ham, 10433, Pte., k. in a., F., 21/10/14.

GIBSON, J., b. Whitehaven, 24460, L/Cpl., d. of w., F., 23/7/16.

GILES, J. F., b. Birmingham, 11421, Pte., k. in a., F., 16/5/15.

GILLESPIE, J., b. Llandudno, 53816, Pte., d. of w., F., 10/1/17.

GITTINS, A., b. Newtown, 53618, Pte., d. of w., F., 9/12/16.

GITTINS, G., b. Buckley, 10477, Pte., k. in a., F., 20/7/16, M.M.

GLEED, J., b. Penalt, 11669, Pte., k. in a., F., 16/5/15.

GODDARD, J., b. Aberavon, 5413, Pte., k. in a., F., 16/5/15.

GODFREY, F., b. Pontypridd, 5055, Pte., k. in a., F., 13/4/15.

GODWIN, W., b. Cardiff, 4228, Pte., k. in a., F., 20/10/14.

GOLDSTEIN, P., b. Birmingham, 17078, L/Cpl., k. in a., F., 25/9/15.

GOODWIN, J. T., b. Rochdale, 46578, Pte., k. in a., F., 23/7/17.

GOODYEAR, F., b. Coventry, 10149, L/Cpl., k. in a., F., 25/9/15.

GOODYEAR, J., b. St. Helens, 18401, Pte., d. of w., Italy, 12/3/18.

GORDON, J. J. B., b. Stoke, 7121, Pte., k. in a., F., 4/5/17.

GOULDEN, F. L., e. Altrincham, 19380, Pte., k. in a., F., 27/8/16.

GOWER, G. T., b. Islington, 26807, Pte., k. in a., F., 12/1/17.

GRAHAM, A., b. London, 24848, Pte., k. in a., F., 14/7/16.

GRAY, J., b. Mountain Ash, 6191, Pte., k. in a., F., 16/5/15.

GREEN, E. W., b. Birmingham, 4124, Pte., k. in a., F., 4/7/16.

GREEN, F. E., b. Cheltenham, 5963, Pte., k. in a., F., 21/10/14.

GREEN, J., b. Treforest, 56627, Pte., k. in a., F., 3/9/16.

GREEN, J., b. Elwell, Notts, 20986, Pte., k. in a., F., 10/10/17.

GREEN, R., b. Luton, 34816, Pte., d. of w., F., 30/8/16.

GREENALL, E., b. St. Helens, 56583, Pte., k. in a., F., 7/10/17.

GREENWAY, F. W. F., b. Birmingham, 6413, L/Cpl., d., F., 15/12/14.

GRIFFIN, W., b. London, 10464, Pte., d. of w., F., 18/2/15.

GRIFFITH, J., b. Aberffraw, 69187, Pte., k. in a., F., 25/10/18.

GRIFFITHS, D., b. America, 56628, Pte., k. in a., F., 3/9/16.

GRIFFITHS, E., b. Rhosybol, 40813, Pte., k. in a., F., 3/9/16.

GRIFFITHS, G., b. Wrexham, 10916, Pte., d. of w., Home, 31/5/15.

GRIFFITHS, J., e. Wrexham, 53674, Pte., k. in a., F., 12/1/17.

GRIFFITHS, O., b. Denbigh, 53846, Pte., k. in a., F., 25/2/17.

GRIFFITHS, R. B., b. Llanddeiniolen, 40109, Pte., k. in a., F., 24/9/16.

GRIFFITHS, T. H., b. Carnarvon, 53821, Pte., k. in a., F., 4/5/17.

GRIFFITHS, W., b. Mold, 4629, Pte., k. in a., F., 16/5/15.

GRIFFITHS, W., b. Treherbert, 5914, Pte., k. in a., F., 30/10/14.

GRIFFITHS, W., b. Ty Croes, 43909, Pte., d., Italy, 20/4/18.

GRIMSHAW, J., b. Hulme, 66654, Pte., k. in a., F., 27/10/17.

GUERAN, W. G., b. London, 8946, Sgt., k. in a., F., 16/5/15.

GUNN, T. C., b. Leicester, 35464, Pte., d. of w., F., 5/8/16.

GWENALL, P., b. Birmingham, 9918, Pte., k. in a., F., 15/12/14.

HABBERLEY, T. H., b. Barrow, 6334, Pte., k. in a., F., 16/5/15.

HADWEN, C. G., b. Birkdale, 53776, L/Cpl., k. in a., F., 9/10/17.

HAGAN, W., b. Dudley, 6424, Pte., d. of w., F., 27/11/14.

HALL, C. J., b. Christchurch Ashton, 4912, Pte., k. in a., F., 16/5/15.

HALL, J., b. Liverpool, 4621, Pte., k. in a., F., 16/5/15.

HALL, S., b. Whixall, 6308, Pte., k. in a., F., 25/9/15.

HALL, T., b. Hurst, Ashton-under-Lyne, 11180, Pte., k. in a., F., 15/12/14.

HAMER, T. E., b. Newtown, 17285, Pte., k. in a., F., 25/9/15.

HAMLETT, J., b. Ruabon, 53622, Pte., k. in a., F., 30/3/17.

HANNAH, A., e. Queensferry, 53888, Pte., d. of w., F., 4/5/17.

HANNIGAN, W., b. Tredegar, 17356, Pte., d. of w., F., 11/10/15.

HARDING, A., b. Market Drayton, 11472, L/Cpl., k. in a., F., 16/5/15.

HARDING, J., b. Worcester, 9988, L/Sgt., k. in a., F., 28/8/16.

HARDING, W., b. Market Drayton, 11471, Pte., k. in a., F., 16/5/15.

HARLEY, J. S., b. Llandrillo, 5342, Pte., k. in a., F., 28/8/16.

HARRIES, C., b. Llanelly, 17003, Pte., k. in a., F., 21/5/15.

HARRIS, F., b. Clyro, 31819, Pte., k. in a., F., 1/7/16.

HARRIS, G., b. London, 12411, Pte., d. of w., F., 2/1/15.

HARRIS, I., b. Birmingham, 4066, Pte., k. in a., F., 16/5/15.

HARRIS, J., b. Pentre Ystrad, 4526, Pte., k. in a., F., 25/9/15.

HARRISON, J., b. Tarleton, 267200, Pte., k. in a., F., 27/10/17.

HARROD, R., b. Birmingham, 6213, Sgt., k. in a., F., 21/10/14.

HART, W. A., b. Llandudno, 20007, Sgt., k. in a., Italy, 3/5/15.

HASPREY, T., b. Dudley, 6393, Pte., k. in a., F., 30/4/16.

HAWKINS, F. J., b. Luton, 26999, Cpl., d., F., 4/8/17.

HAWKINS, T. S., b. Grangetown, 10087, Pte., k. in a., F., 21/10/14.

HAWTHORN, W., b. Manchester, 5335, Pte., k. in a., F., 27/8/16.

HAYES, J., b. Kingsdale, Cork, 4448, Pte., k. in a., F., 16/5/15.

HAYES, R., b. Llanelly, 17516, Pte., k. in a., F., 7/10/15.

HAYNES, J., b. Barrow, 7855, Pte., k. in a., F., 25/9/15.

HAYTON, J. W., e. Lancaster, 53752, Pte., k. in a., F., 26/2/17.

HAYWARD, J., b. Oswestry, 11538, L/Sgt., k. in a., F., 14/5/17.

HAZLEWOOD, J., b. Birmingham, 6217, L/Cpl., k. in a., F., 11/10/17.

HEADINGTON, J. T., b. Bristol, 5870, Pte., d. of w., F., 25/12/14.

HEALY, D. J., b. Tralee, 6721, Sgt., k. in a., F., 21/10/14.

HEARN, D. H., b. Kennington, 17729, L/Cpl., k. in a., F., 26/2/17.

HEATH, S., b. Sutton-in-Ashfield, 19671, Pte., k. in a., F., 25/9/15.

HEELEY, T., b. Smethwick, 8046, Pte., k. in a., F., 3/10/15.

HEIN, E. C., b. Simla, India, 10453, Sgt., k. in a., M., 22/11/15.

HEMMING, T., b. Birmingham, 10868, Pte., k. in a., F., 30/10/14.

HENDERSON, J., e. Mold, 53909, Pte., k. in a., F., 4/5/17.

HENDERSON, J. T., b. Cumberland, 5395, Pte., k. in a., F., 25/9/15.

HENMAN, A. G., b. Birmingham, 17176, Pte., k. in a., F., 25/9/15.

HENNESSEY, C., b. Dowlais, 10940, Pte., k. in a., F., 30/10/14.

HENRY, J., b. London, 31380, Cpl., k. in a., Italy, 3/5/18, M.M. and Clasp.

HENRY, R., b. Birmingham, 5919, Pte., k. in a., F., 30/10/14.

HENSHALL, A., b. Hanley, 18080, Pte., k. in a., F., 16/5/15.

HEWITT, T., b. Birmingham, 9771, L/Cpl., k. in a., F., 25/9/15.

HEYWARD, A., e. Acrefair, 53627, Pte., k. in a., F., 30/3/17.

HIBBERT, D. J. T., b. London, 57427, L/Cpl., k. in a., F., 3/5/18.

HIGGINBOTTOM, J., b. Newcastle, Staffs, 5292, Pte., k. in a., F., 16/5/15.

HIGGINSON, F., b. Birmingham, 6078, Pte., k. in a., F., 15/12/14.

HILL, E. S., b. Hanley, 17834, Pte., k. in a., F., 25/9/15.

HILL, T., b. Birmingham, 10423, Pte., k. in a., F., 30/10/14.

HILL, W., b. Birmingham, 5861, Pte., k. in a., F., 20/10/14.

HILLIER, W. G., b. Bristol, 9414, Pte., k. in a., F., 10/11/14.

HILLITT, W. F., b. Birmingham, 9745, Pte., k. in a., F., 30/10/14.

HINES, W., b. Leicester, 5488, Pte., k. in a., F., 25/9/15.

HISCOCK, C. H., b. Chepstow, 10417, Pte., k. in a., F., 30/10/14.

HISCOCK, T., b. London, 27364, Pte., k. in a., F., 27/2/17.

HOBSON, A., b. Birmingham, 6014, L/Cpl., k. in a., F., 30/10/14.

HODGETTS, H. F., b. Halifax, 52152, Pte., k. in a., F., 26/10/17.

HODGETTS, J. H., b. Worcester, 10811, L/Cpl., k. in a., F., 4/11/16.

HOGAN, M., b. Dublin, 56609, Pte., k. in a., F., 26/2/17.

HOLDEN, W. S., b. Quetta, India, 7923, Sgt., k. in a., F., 21/10/14.

HOLE, A. J., b. Trinant, 17348, Pte., k. in a., F., 1/5/16.

HOLLAND, T., b. Scholar Green, 39331, Pte., k. in a., F., 16/8/16.

HOLLICK, A., b. Birmingham, 17657, L/Cpl., k. in a., F., 3/9/16.

HOLLYMAN, A., b. Bristol, 235552, Pte., k. in a., F., 26/10/17.

HOLMES, W., b. Homestead, America, 8967, Sgt., k. in a., F., 16/5/15.

HOLT, A. J., b. Bagueley, 17655, Pte., k. in a., F., 25/9/15.

HONEYBOURNE, H., b. Birmingham, 6143, Pte., k. in a., F., 30/10/14.

HOOK, J., b. Atherton, Manchester, 18185, Cpl., k. in a., F., 3/9/16.

HOOPER, H. J., b. Cardiff, 11036, Pte., k. in a., F., 19/10/14.

HOOSON, D., b. Pentre Houghton, 4905, Pte., k. in a., F., 20/10/14.

HOPKINS, J., b. Birmingham, 7775, L/Cpl., k. in a., F., 16/5/15.

HOSKINS, J., b. Redbrook, 6080, Pte., k. in a., F., 28/10/14.

HOSKINS, T. E., b. Whitford, 37890, Pte., k. in a., F., 26/10/17.

HOTCHKISS, R. B., e. Shotton, 53937, Pte., k. in a., F., 3/4/17.

HOWARD, W., b. Newport, 17483, Pte., k. in a., F., 25/9/15.

HOWELLS, A. J. D., b. Pembroke, 17023, Pte., d. of w., F., 4/11/15.

HOWELLS, E. S., b. Barry, 11844, Pte., k. in a., F., 16/5/15.

HUBBARD, G., b. Wallington, 36345, L/Cpl., k. in a., Italy, 8/10/17.

HUBBARD, T., b. Thorpe, 235561, Pte., k. in a., Italy, 24/10/18.

HUGHES, C., b. Stockport, 11347, Cpl., k. in a., F., 25/9/15.

HUGHES, D., b. Taibach, 5409, Pte., k. in a., F., 16/5/15.

HUGHES, D., b. Dyserth, 53706, Pte., d. of w., F., 20/5/17.

HUGHES, E., b. Llandrillo, 25086, Pte., k. in a., F., 10/10/17.

HUGHES, E. J., b. Llandeiniclen, 40135, Pte., k. in a., F., 4/12/16.

HUGHES, E. T., b. Oppenholt, 5815, Pte., d. of w., F., 9/7/16.

HUGHES, G., b. Wrexham, 19209, k. in a., F., 14/7/16.

HUGHES, J., b. Cerrig-y-Druidion, 11933, Pte., k. in a., F., 3/9/16.

HUGHES, J., b. Llangyfelach, 56629, Pte., k. in a., F., 3/9/16.

HUGHES, J., b. Northop, 53629, Pte., k. in a., F., 26/2/17.

HUGHES, J. R., b. Denbigh, 53630, Pte., k. in a., F., 20/7/17.

HUGHES, K., b. Dinas Powis, 57423, Pte., k. in a., F., 1/10/17.

HUGHES, M. H., b. Machynlleth, 10027, Pte., k. in a., F., 19/10/14.

HUGHES, R., b. Llandecwyn, 37788, Pte., d. of w., F., 4/12/16.

HUGHES, R., b. Gwalchmai, 53703, Pte., k. in a., F., 1/10/17.

HUGHES, R. A., b. Oxford, 16817, Sgt., k. in a., F., 25/9/15.

HUGHES, R. W., b. Mold, 6106, Pte., k. in a., F., 16/5/15.

HUGHES, T. J., b. Corwen, 44242, Pte., d. of w., F., 28/2/17.

HUGHES, W., b. Dolgelley, 5940, Pte., k. in a., F., 9/12/14.

HUGHES, W., b. Llandudno, 8254, Pte., k. in a., F., 25/9/15.

HUGHES, W., b. Llangollen, 66836, Pte., d., Home, 7/5/18.

HUGHES, W., e. Carnarvon, 265802, Pte., d. of w., F., 2/10/17.

HUGHES, W. D., b. Tydwiliog, 17304, Pte., k. in a., F., 25/9/15.

HUGHES, W. O., b. Denbigh, 6421, L/Cpl., k. in a., F., 16/5/15.

HULL, W. T., b. Lambeth, 235523, Pte., d. of w., F., 2/10/17.

HULMSTON, J., b. Denbigh, 24635, Pte., k. in a., F., 3/9/16.

HUMPHREYS, C., b. Pontypridd, 5072, Pte., d. of w., F., 19/5/15.

HUMPHREYS, J., b. Dolgelley, 6037, Pte., k. in a., F., 16/5/15.

HUMPHREYS, W., b. Holyhead, 5689, Pte., k. in a., F., 16/5/15.

HUMPHREYS, W. H., b. Jhansi, India, 11277, Cpl., k. in a., F., 3/9/16.

HUNT, A., b. Birmingham, 10763, Pte., k. in a., F., 20/10/14.

HUNT, E. C., b. Heddington, 9185, Pte., k. in a., F., 4/7/17.

HUNT, J. D., b. Trealaw, 4919, Pte., k. in a., F., 4/5/17.

HURLEY, D., b. Merthyr, 6305, Pte., k. in a., F., 16/5/15.

HURLEY, M., b. Swansea, 4846, Pte., k. in a., F., 16/5/15.

HURST, J., e. Swinton, 267245, Pte., k. in a., F., 14/5/17.

HUSKISSON, F., b. Walsall, 6664, Pte., k. in a., F., 10/1/17.

HUSSEY, J., b. Farkel, co. Clare, 6203, Pte., k. in a., F., 16/5/15.

HUTCHINSON, T., b. Liverpool, 6783, Pte., k. in a., F., 25/9/15.

HUYTON, E., b. Hulme, 53823, Pte., d. of w., F., 15/3/17.

IGO, J., b. Manchester, 4393, Pte., k. in a., F., 13/10/15.

ILLSLEY, G., b. Chadsmoor, 18630, Pte., k. in a., F., 27/8/16, M.M.

JACKSON, D., b. Pentre, 11513, Pte., k. in a., F., 30/6/16.

JACKSON, F., b. Manchester, 7040, Cpl., k. in a., F., 16/5/15.

JACKSON, H., b. Ashton, 5028, Pte., k. in a., F., 16/5/15.

JACKSON, H., b. Haile, 235535, Pte., d. of w., Italy, 10/5/18.

JACKSON, J., b. Great Eccleston, 18866, Sgt., k. in a., F., 30/6/16.

JACKSON, J., b. Bollington, 4564, Pte., d. of w., F., 19/12/14.

JACKSON, R., b. Woburn Sands, 27681, Pte., d. of w., F., 12/1/17.

JAMES, C., b. Middleton, 24644, Pte., k. in a., F., 1/7/16.

JAMES, G., b. Middlesboro', 6292, Pte., k. in a., F., 16/5/15.

JAMES, H., b. Flint, 25695, Pte., d., Italy, 12/6/18.

JAMES, S., b. Bath, 17526, Cpl., d. of w., F., 1/4/16.

JAMES, W., b. Birmingham, 9374, Pte., k. in a., F., 30/3/17.

JARMAN, T., b. Liverpool, 31240, Pte., d., Home, 24/12/15.

JARVIS, W., b. Birmingham, 6917, Pte., k. in a., F., 16/5/15.

JASPER, S., b. Llangollen, 6430, Pte., k. in a., F., 1/10/17.

JEAL, R. D., b. Walworth, 10304, Pte., k. in a., F., 21/10/14.

JEFFERY, T. J., b. Newport, Mon., 6892, Pte., k. in a., F., 16/5/15.

JELLICOE, J., b. Newton, Hyde,

4567, Pte., d. of w., F., 26/9/15.

JENKINS, B. D., b. Boncath, 31227, Pte., k. in a., F., 27/2/17, M.M.

JENKINS, F. H., b. London, 10054, Cpl., k. in a., F., 3/9/16.

JENKINS, I., b. Pontypridd, 17276, Pte., d. of w., Home, 13/7/16.

JENKINS, W. E., b. Cwmparc, 67131, Pte., k. in a., F., 9/10/17.

JENNINGS, E., b. Birmingham, 8188, Pte., k. in a., F., 16/5/15.

JENNINGS, W., b. Bangor, 4280, L/Cpl., k. in a., F., 16/5/15.

JOHNS, T. F., b. Cardiff, 56659, Pte., k. in a., F., 3/9/16.

JOHNSON, J., b. Manchester, 42180, Pte., k. in a., F., 10/10/17.

JOHNSON, P., b. Nottingham, 5966, Pte., k. in a., F., 30/10/14.

JONES, A., e. Bangor, 53805, Pte., k. in a., F., 1/10/17.

JONES, A., b. Church Stretton, 56585, Pte., d. of w., F., 3/10/17.

JONES, A. E., b. New Mills, 44260, Pte., k. in a., F., 28/10/17.

JONES, B., b. Pontypridd, 11458, Pte., k. in a., F., 16/5/15.

JONES, C. E., b. Welshpool, 36551, Pte., k. in a., F., 29/6/16.

JONES, D., b. Ruthin, 19315, Pte., k. in a., F., 27/8/16.

JONES, D., b. Tredegar, 47293, L/Cpl., k. in a., Italy, 23/10/18.

JONES, D., b. Llanfyrllandogan, 10960, Pte., k. in a., F., 30/10/14.

JONES, D., b. Denbigh, 18176, Pte., d. of w., F., 24/3/17.

JONES, D. C., b. Denbigh, 43991, Pte., d., F., 14/9/17.

JONES, D. G., b. Rhondda, 13428, Pte., k. in a., F., 28/8/16.

JONES, E., b. Oswestry, 3988, Pte., k. in a., F., 16/5/15.

JONES, E., b. Denbigh, 6465, Pte., k. in a., F., 1/7/16.

JONES, E., b. Denbigh, 8483, Pte., d., F., 4/12/14.

JONES, E., b. Pittsburg, America, 36798, Pte., k. in a., F., 15/5/17.

JONES, E., b. Toxteth, Liverpool, 25337, Pte., k. in a., F., 5/9/16.

JONES, E., b. Llanfihangel, 53768, Pte., k. in a., F., 30/3/17.

JONES, E., b. Denbigh, 6496, Pte., k. in a., F., 23/8/15.

JONES, E., b. Festiniog, 16928, Pte., d. of w., F., 16/7/15.

JONES, E., b. Wrexham, 10434, Pte., k. in a., F., 21/10/14.

JONES, E., b. Dolgelley, 11027, Pte., d. of w., F., 17/5/15.

JONES, E., b. Llanrhaiadr, 17297, Pte., k. in a., F., 5/7/16.

JONES, E. E., b. Llanddeiniolen, 40032, Pte., k. in a., F., 22/10/16.

JONES, E. T., b. Denbigh, 34885, Pte., k. in a., F., 3/9/16.

JONES, E. W., b. Llanddeiniolen, 40132, Pte., k. in a., Italy, 3/5/18.

JONES, F. W., b. Llandudno, 5784, Pte., k. in a., F., 16/5/15.

JONES, G., b. Wem, 7049, Pte., k. in a., F., 30/10/14.

JONES, G., b. Cardiff, 10898, Pte., k. in a., F., 16/5/15.

JONES, G. D., b. Trevigin, 53638, Pte., d. of w., F., 30/3/17.

JONES, G. T., b. Llangar, 28268, Pte., k. in a., F., 28/10/17.

JONES, H., b. Bryngwran, 37234, Pte., k. in a., F., 23/7/17.

JONES, H., b. Holywell, 53748, Pte., d. of w., F., 24/6/17.

JONES, H. G., b. Bangor, 35357, Pte., k. in a., F., 26/2/17.

JONES, H. G., b. Holyhead, 6365, Pte., k. in a., F., 16/5/16.

JONES, H. G., b. Llanfairfechan, 53824, Pte., k. in a., F., 26/2/17.

JONES, I., b. Ruabon, 37394, L/Cpl., k. in a., F., 8/10/17.

JONES, I., b. Llanllyfni, 53859, Pte., k. in a., F., 5/7/17.

JONES, I., b. Abergele, 11126, Pte., k. in a., F., 30/10/14.

JONES, J., b. Rhuddlan, 5097, Pte., k. in a., F., 16/5/15.

JONES, J., b. Denbigh, 4683, Pte., k. in a., F., 18/12/14.

JONES, J., b. Birkenhead, 5669, Pte., d. of w., F., 27/9/15.

JONES, J., b. Wrexham, 5915, Pte., k. in a., F., 30/10/14.

JONES, J., b. Pembroke, 9250, L/Cpl., k. in a., F., 30/10/15.

JONES, J., b. Aberdare, 17798, Pte., k. in a., F., 25/9/15.

JONES, J., b. Denbigh, 19259, Pte., d. of w., F., 4/9/16.

JONES, J., b. Blaina, 19659, Pte., k. in a., F., 3/9/16.

JONES, J., b. Abergele, 39940, Pte., k. in a., F., 3/9/16.

JONES, J., e. Amlwch, Anglesey, 53851, Pte., k. in a., F., 27/2/17.

JONES, J., b. Ferndale, 5074, Pte., k. in a., F., 21/5/15.

JONES, J. C., b. Ruthin, 8580, Pte., k. in a., F., 7/11/14.

JONES, J. D., b. Colwyn, 4345, Pte., k. in a., F., 20/10/14.

JONES, J. D., b. Llanddeiniolen, 40102, Pte., k. in a., F., 3/9/16.

JONES, J. D., b. Llandudno, 15538, L/Cpl., k. in a., F., 30/9/17.

JONES, J. I., b. Menai Bridge, 43595, Pte., k. in a., F., 27/2/17.

JONES, J. R., b. Ruthin, 6338, Pte., k. in a., F., 21/5/15.

JONES, J. R., b. Neston, 10657, Pte., k. in a., F., 16/5/15.

JONES, J. T., b. Shotton, 53715, Pte., k. in a., F., 4/5/17.

JONES, J. T., b. Festiniog, 5352, Pte., d. of w., F., 30/9/15.

JONES, J. W., b. Bwlchgwyn, 32556, Pte., d. of w., F., 2/3/17.

JONES, L., b. Carnarvon, 40217, Pte., k. in a., F., 28/8/16.

JONES, O., b. Llandwrog, 40041, Pte., k. in a., F., 27/2/17.

JONES, O., b. Penmachno, 40067, Pte., k. in a., F., 3/9/16.

JONES, O. R., b. Beaumaris, 6480, Pte., k. in a., F., 16/5/15.

JONES, R., b. Porth, 4522, Pte., k. in a., F., 30/10/14.

JONES, R., b. Llanarmon, 5987, Pte., k. in a., F., 16/5/15.

JONES, R., b. Pwllheli, 53782, Pte., k. in a., F., 1/10/17.

JONES, R., b. Bryncethin, 54165, Pte., k. in a., F., 27/2/17.

JONES, R. E., b. Bangor, 10040, Pte., k. in a., F., 21/10/14.

JONES, R. J., b. Northop, 5708, Pte., k. in a., F., 16/5/15.

JONES, R. R., b. Port Dinorwic, 5562, Pte., d. of w., F., 29/9/15.

JONES, R. T., b. Denbigh, 3459, Pte., k. in a., F., 16/5/15.

JONES, R. W. B., b. Cockett, 29519, L/Cpl., k. in a., F., 29/8/16.

JONES, T., b. Tregarth, 14931, Pte., k. in a., F., 26/10/17.

JONES, T., b. Blaenau Festiniog, 33495, Pte., k. in a., F., 14/7/16.

JONES, T. E., b. Rhyl, 19124, Pte., k. in a., F., 25/9/15.

JONES, T. R., b. Newport, Mon., 16990, L/Cpl., k. in a., F., 28/8/16.

JONES, T. T., b. Waenfawr, 40333, L/Cpl., k. in a., F., 29/8/16.

JONES, T. W. P., b. Cwmavon, 4278, L/Cpl., d. of w., F., 23/3/16.

JONES, W., b. Blaenau Festiniog, 5498, Pte., k. in a., F., 3/9/16.

JONES, W., b. Porth, 6007, Pte., k. in a., F., 16/5/15.

JONES, W., b. Waenfawr, 40372, Pte., k. in a., F., 9/12/16.

JONES, W., b. Aberdaron, 53753, Pte., k. in a., F., 8/1/17.

JONES, W., b. Portmadoc, 53785, Pte., d. of w., F., 1/3/17.

JONES, W., b. Llanberis, 53843, Pte., d. of w., Home, 2/7/17.

JONES, W., b. Rossett, 57441, Pte., k. in a., Italy, 26/7/18.

JONES, W., b. Llanrwst, 40662, Pte., k. in a., F., 31/8/16.

JONES, W. E., b. Treharris,

18265, Pte., k. in a., F., 15/7/16.

JONES, W. E., e. Liverpool, 36495, A/Cpl., d. of w., F., 3/12/16.

JONES, W. G., b. Birmingham, 6766, Cpl., k. in a., F., 19/10/14.

JONES, W. G., b. Groeslon, 40690, Pte., k. in a., F., 14/5/17.

JONES, W. N., b. Cardiff, 15604, Pte., k. in a., F., 1/10/17.

JUKES, A. G. S., b. Burton, 8316, Cpl., d., F., 21/11/14.

JUKES, J., b. Hednesford, 19136, Pte., k. in a., F., 28/6/15.

KANE, J., b. Swansea, 11002, Pte., k. in a., F., 30/10/14.

KEEFE, A., b. Merthyr, 10246, Pte., k. in a., F., 20/10/14.

KELLAWAY, F. E., b. Cardiff, 17694, Pte., k. in a., F., 25/9/15.

KELLAWAY, G. H., b. Bristol, 10973, Pte., k. in a., F., 30/10/14.

KELLY, F., b. Bersham, 4301, Pte., k. in a., F., 19/10/14.

KELLY, G. E., b. Dublin, 10928, Pte., k. in a., F., 20/10/14.

KELLY, J. F., b. Bolton, 10781, Pte., d. of w., F., 18/5/15.

KELLY, R. O., b. Pwllheli, 9258, Pte., d. of w., Home, 22/5/15.

KENDRICK, J., e. Wrexham, 57061, Pte., k. in a., F., 23/7/17.

KERANS, E., b. Seaforth, 267178, Pte., k. in a., F., 4/5/17.

KERKHOFF, W., b. Birmingham, 7899, Pte., d., M., 1/9/16.

KERR, W., b. Silloth, 5319, Pte., d. of w., F., 5/4/16.

KEWLEY, R., b. Everton, 4469, Pte., k. in a., F., 16/5/15.

KEYES, C., b. Salford, 266979, Pte., k. in a., F., 15/5/17.

KING, E. G., b. Gt. Clacton, 35079, Pte., k. in a., F., 3/9/16.

KING, J. W., b. Chiswick, 31345, Pte., d. of w., F., 4/9/16.

KING, W. H., b. Aberaman, 5211, Pte., k. in a., F., 10/3/15.

KIRBY, E. J., b. Merthyr, 17743, Pte., d. of w., F., 22/7/16.

KIRKHAM, J., b. Darwen, 17173, Pte., k. in a., F., 25/9/15.

KIRKHAM, W., b. Northampton, 11313, Cpl., k. in a., F., 16/5/15.

KITSON, A., b. Bloxwich, 18399, L/Cpl., k. in a., F., 27/8/16.

KNIGHT, C. E., b. St. Pancras, London, 56631, Pte., k. in a., F., 28/8/16.

KNIGHT, J., b. Pentre Ystrad, 4662, Pte., k. in a., F., 16/5/15.

LAFFERTY, T., b. Macclesfield, 10950, L/Cpl., k. in a., F., 16/5/15.

LAING, D. J., b. Conway, 10508, Pte., k. in a., F., 7/11/14.

LAKEY, W. J., b. London, 26759, Cpl., k. in a., F., 3/9/16.

LAMB, J., b. Boughton, 4373, Pte., k. in a., F., 16/5/15.

LAMBOURNE, C., b. Atherstone, 10640, Pte., k. in a., F., 30/10/14.

LAMOTHE, S., b. Liverpool, 8802, L/Cpl., k. in a., F., 3/9/16.

LANE, J., b. Weston-super-Mare, 9187, L/Cpl., k. in a., F., 16/5/15.

LANE, J., b. Birmingham, 10727, Pte., k. in a., F., 20/10/14.

LANE, J., b. Merthyr, 11287, Pte., k. in a., F., 25/9/15.

LARGE, S., b. Bridge Trafford, 10770, Pte., k. in a., F., 30/10/14.

LARKING, G., b. Greenwich, 56634, Pte., k. in a., F., 28/8/16.

LARNER, E. F., b. Cirencester, 10841, Pte., k. in a., F., 20/10/14.

LAVENDER, A., b. Worcester, 10189, L/Cpl., d. of w., F., 7/6/16.

LAW, A. J., b. Aberdare, 4691, Pte., k. in a., F., 20/10/14.

LAW, G. F., b. Devonport, 5120, Pte., d., F., 15/2/15.

LAWRENCE, C. L., b. Llanorthwl, 5231, Pte., k. in a., F., 28/11/14.

LAWRENCE, O., e. Swansea, 53962, Pte., d. of w., F., 1/10/16.

LAYTON, D. G., b. Merthyr, 19222, Pte., k. in a., F., 3/9/16.

LEE, D., b. Swansea, 3876, Pte., d. of w., F., 30/1/15.

LEE, G., b. Liverpool, 235709, Pte., k. in a., Italy, 17/4/18.

LEE, H., b. Batley Carr, 53641, Pte., k. in a., F., 1/10/17.

LEE, H. C., e. Stratford, 54333, Pte., k. in a., F., 11/10/17.

LEE, J. W., b. Carlisle, 266758, Pte., k. in a., F., 5/5/17.

LEE, L. P., b. Kidderminster, 10746, Pte., k. in a., F., 19/10/14.

LEE, R. J., b. Plymouth, 7261, Pte., k. in a., F., 16/5/15.

LEEKE, E., b. Ludlow, 10929, A/C.S.M., k. in a., F., 28/10/17.

LEIGH, R., b. Newton-le-Willows, 19654, Pte., k. in a., F., 30/8/16.

LEKMAN, F., b. Liverpool, 7050, L/Cpl., d. of w., F., 18/5/15.

LEWIS, A., b. Bedlinog, 17524, Pte., k. in a., F., 25/9/15.

LEWIS, A. W., b. Birmingham, 10702, L/Cpl., k. in a., F., 30/10/14.

LEWIS, C., b. Pill, Newport, 9348, Pte., d., F., 9/12/14.

LEWIS, D., b. Swansea, 6162, Pte., k. in a., F., 16/5/15.

LEWIS, D., b. Plymouth, U.S.A., 31528, Pte., d., Home, 7/2/16.

LEWIS, D. J., b. Gorseinon, 17318, Sgt., k. in a., F., 28/8/16.

LEWIS, E., b. Gwalchmai, 39190, Pte., k. in a., F., 25/8/16.

LEWIS, E., b. Llanddewi, Mon., 10719, Pte., k. in a., F., 20/10/14.

LEWIS, J., b. Chester, 17186, L/Cpl., k. in a., F., 9/10/17.

LEWIS, J., b. Groeslon, 40641, Pte., k. in a., F., 4/5/17.

LEWIS, R. S., b. London, 10715, Pte., k. in a., F., 30/10/14.

LEWIS, T. S., b. Pontycymmer, 23590, Sgt., k. in a., F., 5/12/16.

LEWIS, W. H., b. Merthyr, 3944, Pte., k. in a., F., 16/5/15.

LEWIS, W. H., b. Liverpool, 40077, Pte., k. in a., F., 3/9/16.

LEWIS, W. J., b. Neath, 10066, Pte., k. in a., F., 16/5/15.

LEYLAND, W., b. Chorley, 53829, Pte., k. in a., F., 26/2/17.

LIGHTFOOT, W., b. Crewe, 16505, Pte., k. in a., F., 18/7/16.

LILLIE, C. W., b. Deptford, 56632, Pte., k. in a., F., 15/5/17.

LINTON, P., b. London, 17557, Pte., d. of w., F., 28/9/15.

LIVESEY, H. H., b. Preston, 53830, Pte., k. in a., F., 4/5/17.

LLEWELLYN, A. W., b. Peterstowe, 19385, Pte., d. of w., F., 20/10/15.

LLEWELLIN, J., b. Liverpool, 53831, Pte., k. in a., F., 26/2/17.

LLOYD, D. O., b. Bodfari, 9444, Sgt., k. in a., F., 25/9/15.

LLOYD, E., b. Rhyl, 10451, Pte., k. in a., F., 21/10/14.

LLOYD, H., b. Llanerfyl, 5777, Pte., k. in a., F., 30/10/14.

LLOYD, J. H., b. Birmingham, 10588, Sgt., k. in a., F., 26/2/17.

LLOYD, R., e. Ryhl, 53916, Pte., k. in a., F., 4/5/17.

LLOYD, T. J., b. Swansea, 31596, Pte., k. in a., F., 3/5/17.

LLOYD, T. R., b. Nantlle, 5729, Pte., d., F., 16/3/15.

LOCKLEY, W., b. Chester, 8899, Pte., k. in a., F., 14/5/17.

LOFTUS, A. E., b. Denbigh, 10476, Pte., k. in a., F., 28/5/16.

LOMAX, P., b. Ashton-in-Makerfield, 31480, L/Cpl., d. of w., F., 20/5/17.

LONG, E., b. Derby, 8876, Pte., k. in a., F., 25/8/15.

LONG, J., b. London, 10730, Pte., k. in a., F., 19/10/14.

LONGLAND, D., b. Hanley, 19761, Pte., k. in a., F., 14/7/16.

LORD, T., b. Bacup, 63306, Pte., k. in a., F., 14/5/17.

LOVETT, F., b. Ashby de-la-Zouch, 56635, Pte., d. of w., F., 29/8/16.

LOWE, G., b. Birmingham, 9235, Pte., d. of w., F., 1/4/16.

LOWE, G. W., b. Birmingham, 8875, Pte., k. in a., F., 13/3/15.

LOWE, W., b. Wrexham, 11135, L/Cpl., k. in a., F., 7/11/14.

LUCAS, P., b. Bridgnorth, 3952, Pte., d., F., 26/2/15.

LUDLAM, W. E., b. South Normanton, 19458, Pte., k. in a., F., 25/9/15.

LURVEY, W., b. Newport, 3824, Cpl., k. in a., F., 16/5/15.

LYNCH, W., b. Liverpool, 10586, Pte., k. in a., F., 16/5/15.

MADDERN, J., b. Trehafod, 5434, Pte., k. in a., F., 25/9/15.

MADDOCKS, A. B., b. Birmingham, 11459, Pte., k. in a., F., 16/5/15.

MADDOCKS, D., b. Liverpool, 10963, Pte., k. in a., F., 30/10/14.

MADDOCKS, W. H., b. Birmingham, 9748, C.S.M., k. in a., F., 25/9/15.

MADINE, W., b. Liverpool, 11059, Pte., d. of w., F., 2/11/14.

MAGGS, R. P. G., b. Gilfach Goch, 36493, Pte., k. in a., F., 3/9/16.

MAHONEY, W., b. Newport, 2637, Pte., k. in a., F., 25/2/17.

MALINS, T. W., b. Alcester, 10332, Pte., k. in a., F., 3/9/16.

MANDY, H. E., b. East Ham, 10406, L/Cpl., d., F., 31/10/14.

MARKHAM, J. H., b. Nottingham, 7077, L/Cpl., k. in a., F., 16/5/15.

MARONEY, J., b. Tredegar, 8723, Pte., k. in a., F., 1/10/17.

MARSH, F., e. Oldham, 36496, Pte., k. in a., F., 27/5/17.

MARSHALL, C., b. London, 27642, Pte., k. in a., F., 3/9/16.

MARSHALL, C. H., b. Smethwick, 9577, Sgt., d. of w., F., 13/2/16, D.C.M.

MARSTON, C., b. Presteign, 9089, Pte., k. in a., F., 19/10/14.

MARTELL, H. W., b. Newport, 10576, L/Cpl., k. in a., F., 26/1/15.

MARTIN, A., b. London, 5169, Sgt., k. in a., F., 19/10/14.

MASH, J., b. Northwich, Cheshire, 4509, Pte., k. in a., F., 30/10/14.

MASON, J., b. Pontypridd, 11447, Pte., k. in a., F., 13/3/15.

MATHERS, G., b. Nottingham, 18403, Pte., k. in a., F., 16/5/15.

MATTHEWS, J., b. Plymouth, 10139, Pte., k. in a., F., 16/5/15.

MATTHEWS, J., b. Coventry, 18602, Pte., d. of w., F., 31/5/16.

MATTHEWS, T., b. Tylorstown, 5283, Pte., k. in a., F., 16/5/15.

MATTHEWS, T., b. Shrewsbury, 6563, Pte., k. in a., F., 30/10/14.

MAYALL, T., b. Birmingham, 23954, Pte., d. of w., F., 12/7/16.

McALLISTER, P. J., b. Liverpool, 30074, Pte., k. in a., F., 3/9/16.

McCARTHY, F. C., b. Birmingham, 33153, L/Cpl., k. in a., F., 10/10/17.

McCARTHY, J., b. Swansea, 3832, Pte., k. in a., F., 16/5/15.

McDONALD, J., b. St. Helens, 46839, Sgt., k. in a., F., 1/10/17.

McDONOUGH, J., b. Liverpool, 11697, Pte., d. of w., F., 14/7/16.

McELROY, G. L., b. Rhyl, 8307, Pte., k. in a., F., 16/5/15.

McGRATH, J., b. Workington, 36522, Pte., k. in a., F., 29/8/16.

McGRATH, J., b. Clonmell, 10660, Pte., k. in a., F., 20/10/14.

McGUIRE, W. J., b. Liverpool, 6079, Pte., k. in a., F., 3/9/16.

McLELLAN, G., b. Bootle, 5884, Pte., k. in a., F., 16/5/15.

McRETH, R., b. Glasgow, 14638, L/Cpl., k. in a., F., 16/5/15.

MELBOURNE, D., b. Orford, 4147, Pte., d. of w., F., 1/3/17.

MELIA, A., b. Gorton, 4444, Pte., k. in a., F., 27/8/16.

MELIA, J., b. Liverpool, 4725, Pte., k. in a., F., 16/5/15.

MERCHANT, T. G., b. Ystrad, 11143, Pte., k. in a., F., 27/10/14.

MEREDITH, E., b. Merthyr Tydvil, 6288, Pte., k. in a., F., 30/10/14.

MERRICK, A., b. Ystradfodwg, 3536, Pte., k. in a., F., 16/5/15.

MESTON, F., b. London, 4356, Pte., d., F., 3/7/15.

MIDDLEHURST, R. C., b. St. Helens, 70116, Pte., k. in a., F., 1/10/17.

MILES, N., b. Neath, 5842, Pte., k. in a., F., 20/10/14.

MILLARD, J. J., b. Liverpool, 10360, Band Sgt., k. in a., F., 30/10/14.

MILLS, J., b. Eastbourne, 17901, Pte., k. in a., F., 25/9/15.

MILLWARD, E. T., b. Birmingham, 9912, Pte., d., F., 21/10/14.

MINCHER, T., b. Birmingham, 19445, Pte., k. in a., F., 25/9/15.

MINOGUE, S., b. India, 6000, L/Cpl., d. of w., F., 3/10/17.

MITCHELL, J. H., b. Birmingham, 6157, A/Cpl., k. in a., F., 30/10/14.

MOGG, A., b. London, 19657, L/Cpl., k. in a., F., 28/3/16.

MONKS, J., b. Bolton, 17903, Pte., k. in a., F., 16/5/15.

MOORES, T., b. Denbigh, 53645, Pte., d. of w., F., 2/7/17.

MORAN, T., b. Birmingham, 10682, Pte., k. in a., F., 20/10/14.

MORGAN, B. R., b. Glyn Neath, 36762, Pte., d. of w., F., 16/8/16.

MORGAN, D. I., b. Merthyr, 56638, Pte., k. in a., F., 2/10/17.

MORGAN, D. O., b. Pembroke, 10180, Pte., k. in a., F., 20/10/14.

MORGAN, E., b. Treorchy, 6286, Pte., k. in a., F., 30/10/14.

MORGAN, G., b. Pontypridd, 10778, Pte., k. in a., F., 20/10/14.

MORGAN, R., b. Newport, 10158, Pte., k. in a., F., 20/10/14.

MORGAN, R., e. Carnarvon, 53802, Pte., k. in a., F., 14/5/17.

MORGAN, T., b. Birmingham, 8176, Pte., k. in a., F., 16/5/15.

MORGAN, T., b. Trecastle, 53971, Pte., d., F., 18/12/16.

MORGANS, J., b. Brecon, 6484, A/Sgt., k. in a., F., 16/5/15.

MORRIS, A., b. Christchurch, 24018, Pte., k. in a., F., 3/9/16.

MORRIS, A., b. Llandebie, 17520, Pte., d. of w., F., 26/5/15.

MORRIS, C., b. Melyn Cryddan, 6072, Pte., d., F., 12/12/14.

MORRIS, D. J., b. Carnarvon, 39817, Pte., k. in a., F., 29/8/16.

MORRIS, E., b. London, 10801, Pte., k. in a., F., 30/10/14.

MORRIS, E., b. Merthyr, 17880, Pte., k. in a., F., 14/7/16.

MORRIS, G., b. London, 27476, Pte., k. in a., F., 28/8/16.

MORRIS, H., b. Bagillt, 53642, Pte., k. in a., F., 27/2/17.

MORRIS, J., b. Glyncorrwg, 6357, Pte., d. of w., F., 23/6/15.

MORRIS, J., b. Glyn, 53644, Pte., k. in a., F., 1/10/17.

MORRIS, I., b. Llanddeiniolen, 40171, Pte., k. in a., F., 3/9/16.

MORRIS, M., b. Wrexham, 37685, Pte., k. in a., F., 19/7/16.

MORRIS, R., b. Llanddeiniolen, 40136, Pte., k. in a., F., 29/8/16.

MORRIS, T. J., b. Ruthin, 17437, Pte., k. in a., F., 25/9/15.

MORRIS, T. J., b. Wigan, 5375, Pte., k. in a., F., 16/5/15.

MORRISON, C. D., b. London, 4013, Pte., d. of w., F., 16/3/16.

MORTIBOY, A., b. Birmingham,

8267, Pte., k. in a., F., 16/5/15.

Moss, J., e. Bolton, 23653, Pte., d. of w., F., 8/1/16.

Moss, H., b. Burnley, 24682, L/Cpl., k. in a., F., 27/8/16.

Mullen, J., b. Manchester, 10573, L/Cpl., d. of w., F., 26/9/15.

Mullock, F., b. Crewe, 4692, L/Cpl., k. in a., F., 16/5/15.

Murphy, L., b. Preston, 235529, Pte., k. in a., F., 2/10/17.

Murray, J., b. Co. Mayo, 3092, Pte., k. in a., F., 16/5/15.

Murray, J., b. Newport, 4426, Pte., k. in a., F., 13/3/15.

Murray, J., b. New South Wales, 36031, Pte., k. in a., F., 27/8/16.

Murray, W., b. Miles Platting, 235538, Pte., d. of w., Italy, 3/5/18.

Nancarrow, R., b. Stockport, 17752, Pte., k. in a., F., 3/9/16.

Nash, J., b. Roscommon, 6005, Pte., k. in a., F., 30/10/14.

Nation, W. E. G., b. Tylorstown, 56639, Pte., k. in a., F., 3/9/16.

Naylor, G., b. Oldham, 7912, Pte., k. in a., F., 16/5/15.

Neal, W., b. Birmingham, 8753, Pte., k. in a., F., 7/11/14.

Neat, S. M., b. Llanelly, 29616, Pte., k. in a., F., 3/9/16.

Needham, S., e. Flint, 53918, Pte., k. in a., F., 14/5/17.

Newbold, A., b. Willenhall, 19631, Pte., k. in a., F., 4/7/16.

Newland, J., b. London, 11216, Pte., k. in a., F., 30/10/14.

Newton, J. A., b. Bordesley, 4731, Pte., k. in a., F., 24/1/15.

Nicholson, A., b. Manchester, 235563, Pte., d., Italy, 8/4/18.

Nicholls, J., b. Colemere, 70119, Pte., k. in a., F., 10/10/17.

Nield, A., b. Chester, 4984, L/Cpl., k. in a., F., 3/9/16.

Nock, W. H., b. Halesowen, 11374, L/Cpl., k. in a., F., 28/8/16.

Norman, F., b. Highbridge, 10446, Sgt., k. in a., F., 7/11/14.

Norman, S. J., b. Brighton, 63730, Pte., k. in a., F., 22/7/17.

Oates, P., b. Pontnewyndd, 17455, Pte., k. in a., F., 25/9/15.

Oates, R., b. Mold, 5221, Pte., d. of w., F., 30/1/15.

O'Brien, A., b. Birkenhead, 4534, Pte., k. in a., F., 15/7/16, M.M.

O'Brien, D., b. Port Talbot, 10200, Pte., k. in a., F., 16/5/15.

O'Brien, R., b. Cardiff, 11242, A/Cpl., k. in a., F., 26/5/16.

O'Brien, W., b. Cardiff, 5165, Pte., k. in a., F., 25/9/15.

O'Gara, A., b. Birmingham, 8438, Pte., d. of w., F., 21/5/15.

Oliver, F., b. Aldershot, 43615, Pte., k. in a., F., 11/1/17.

Oliver, G., b. Wrexham, 9728, A/Sgt., k. in a., F., 3/9/16.

Oliver, M., b. Gresford, 11703, L/Cpl., d. of w., Home, 10/6/15.

Olsen, J., e. Seaforth, 53791, Pte., k. in a., F., 14/5/17.

O'Neil, J., b. Dowlais, 4732, Pte., k. in a., F., 31/12/14.

Ormonde, W., b. Norton Bridge, 5494, Pte., k. in a., F., 16/5/15.

Osborne, A., b. Birmingham, 10468, Pte., k. in a., F., 18/7/15.

O'Shea, M. J., b. Cardiff, 5111, Pte., k. in a., F., 21/12/14.

Overton, E. H., b. Shrewsbury, 56592, Pte., k. in a., F., 1/10/17.

Owen, D., b. Cwmyglo, 40359, Pte., k. in a., F., 11/1/17.

Owen, D. H., b. Llandudno, 25004, Pte., k. in a., F., 3/9/16.

Owen, D. R., b. Llanfairfechan, 6379, Pte., k. in a., F., 16/5/15.

Owen, E., b. Brynsiencyn, 40037, Pte., k. in a., F., 3/9/16.

Owen, E. S., b. Glan Conway, 5649, Pte., k. in a., F., 28/6/15.

Owen, G., b. Festiniog, 20268, Pte., d. of w., F., 19/1/17.

Owen, J., b. Cwmyglo, 40352, Pte., k. in a., F., 3/9/16.

Owen, M., b. Merthyr, 17703, Cpl., k. in a., F., 25/9/15.

Owen, R., b. Anglesey, 6026, Pte., k. in a., F., 28/5/15.

Owen, R., b. Beaumaris, 11171, Pte., k. in a., F., 23/7/17.

Owen, W., b. Penrhiwceiber, 17288, Pte., k. in a., F., 25/9/15.

Owens, D., b. Llanberis, 6406, Pte., k. in a., F., 2/9/16.

Owens, R., b. Liverpool, 53764, L/Cpl., k. in a., F., 9/10/17.

Owens, R. T., b. Ruthin, 7865, Pte., k. in a., F., 16/5/15.

Oxley, W., b. Lytham, 46471, L/Cpl., d., Italy, 9/3/18.

Page, A. J., b. Bristol, 31385, L/Cpl., k. in a., F., 30/3/16.

Page, G., b. London, 22249, Pte., k. in a., F., 18/7/17.

Paget, J., b. Bristol, 9008, A/Cpl., k. in a., F., 2/9/16.

Palmer, J., b. Pontlottyn, 4356, Pte., k. in a., F., 16/1/15.

Palmer, J., b. Birmingham, 18397, Pte., k. in a., F., 29/8/16.

Palmer, J., b. Hoxton, 35265, Pte., k. in a., F., 3/9/16.

Palmer, L. C., b. Cathays, 11103, Pte., k. in a., F., 20/10/14.

Palmer, R., b. Birmingham, 6932, Cpl., k. in a., F., 14/7/16.

Parker, E., b. Birmingham, 9367, L/Cpl., k. in a., F., 16/5/15.

Parker, J., b. Mold, 2762, Pte., k. in a., F., 20/10/14.

Parkes, W. L., b. Derby, 17995, Pte., k. in a., F., 25/10/15.

Parnham, H., b. Derby, 19622, Pte., d. of w., F., 4/11/15.

Parry, H., b. Llanddeiniolen, 40101, Pte., k. in a., F., 3/9/16.

Parry, J., b. Bodfain, 6417, Pte., k. in a., F., 16/5/15.

Parry, J., b. Birmingham, 9808, Pte., k. in a., F., 28/5/16.

Parry, J. E., b. St. Asaph, 53672, Pte., k. in a., F., 14/5/17.

Parry, L., b. Holywell, 57438, Pte., d. of w., F., 28/10/17.

Parry, R., b. Dongelly, 6029, Pte., k. in a., F., 16/5/15.

Parry, W., b. Newport, 11030, Pte., k. in a., F., 30/10/14.

Parry, W. J., b. Carnarvon, 266791, Pte., k. in a., F., 22/7/17.

Parry, W. J., b. Penmorfa, 34788, Pte., k. in a., F., 3/9/16.

Paul, W. J., b. Bristol, 10615, Pte., k. in a., F., 20/10/14.

Penn, J., b. Birmingham, 10871, Pte., k. in a., F., 29/3/16.

Penney, W. J., b. Chester, 10131, Pte., k. in a., F., 19/10/14.

Peploe, W., b. Pontypool, 6003, Pte., k. in a., F., 30/10/14.

Perkins, A., b. Pembroke, 19894, Pte., k. in a., F., 3/9/16.

Perry, S., b. Walsall, 7742, Cpl., k. in a., F., 16/5/15.

Peters, E. A., b. Sutton, 6246, Pte., k. in a., F., 16/11/14.

Peters, E. A., b. Sutton, 10316, Sgt., k. in a., F., 16/5/15.

Peters, W. H., b. Birmingham, 9769, Pte., k. in a., F., 16/5/15.

Pettifer, T. B., b. Dudley, 10241, L/Cpl., k. in a., F., 21/10/14.

Phillips, D. G., b. Hirwain, Aberdare, 4666, Pte., k. in a., F., 16/5/15.

Phillips, H., b. London, 27318, Pte., k. in a., F., 4/5/17, M.M.

Pickering, T., b. Bradwell Grove, 8491, Pte., d., F., 19/6/17.

Pickering, W., b. Bridlington, 34877, Sgt., k. in a., F., 4/5/17, M.M.

Pickford, J., b. Stockport, 11341, Pte., k. in a., F., 16/5/15.

Pierce, J., b. Fulham, 17797, Pte., k. in a., F., 28/6/15.

PIKE, J. H., b. Glyncorrwg, 4645, Pte., d., F., 19/12/17.

PILKINGTON, T., e. Manchester, 54150, Pte., k. in a., F., 14/5/17.

PILLER, P., b. Cardiff, 5144, Pte., k. in a., F., 16/5/15.

PILLING, G., b. Bury, 23811, A/Cpl., k. in a., F., 4/5/17, M.M.

PITMAN, W. J., b. Treharris, 4886, Pte., k. in a., F., 3/9/16.

PLANT, E., b. Hanley, 24570, Pte., k. in a., F., 3/9/16.

POPE, H., b. Blackburn, 7179, Pte., k. in a., F., 30/10/14.

POWELL, D. J., b. Trebanog, 5548, Pte., k. in a., F., 16/5/15.

POWELL, E., e. Abergele, 55715, Pte., k. in a., F., 14/5/17.

POWELL, F., b. Blackwood, 4514, Pte., k. in a., F., 16/5/15.

POWER, F. G., b. Saltney, 53726, Pte., k. in a., F., 27/2/17.

POYNER, G., b. Birmingham, 8147, Cpl., k. in a., F., 16/5/15.

POYNTON, W., b. Wrexham, 53727, Pte., k. in a., F., 15/5/17.

PREECE, G. H., b. Wrexham, 6359, L/Sgt., d. of w., F., 1/9/16.

PREEN, T., b. Birmingham, 6885, Pte., k. in a., F., 10/3/15.

PRESTIDGE, A., b. Bedminster, 5764, Pte., k. in a., F., 16/5/15.

PRIDAY, F. H., b. Gloucester, 10439, Pte., d., F., 26/1/15.

PRIEST, G., b. Bilston, 12693, Pte., d. of w., Home, 19/7/16.

PRICE, D. I., b. Abergwili, 40048, Pte., k. in a., F., 26/2/17.

PRICE, J. P., b. Wrexham, 6429, Sgt., k. in a., F., 16/5/15.

PRICE, P., b. Chester, 4861, Pte., k. in a., F., 27/8/16.

PRICE, T., e. Rhyl, 53926, Pte., d., F., 13/12/16.

PRITCHARD, A., b. Garn Dolbenmaen, 40107, Pte., k. in a., F., 1/9/16.

PRITCHARD, D. W., b. Rhyl, 6109, L/Cpl., k. in a., F., 29/8/16.

PRITCHARD, G., b. Ross, 7093, L/Cpl., k. in a., F., 30/10/14.

PRITCHARD, H., b. Ebbw Vale, 4391, Pte., k. in a., F., 21/10/14.

PRITCHARD, J., b. Rhyl, 3424, Pte., k. in a., F., 28/12/14.

PRITCHARD, J. G., b. Waenfawr, 37974, Pte., k. in a., F., 1/10/17.

PRITCHARD, M. W., b. Llanberis, 40200, Pte., d., F., 7/2/17.

PROBERT, J., b. Oswestry, 6160, Pte., k. in a., F., 25/9/15.

PRODGER, J., b. Bangor, 10063, k. in a., F., 21/10/14.

PROFFITT, J., b. Wrexham, 6111, Pte., k. in a., F., 16/5/15.

PROSSER, F., b. Wigan, 15726, Pte., k. in a., F., 1/7/16.

PRYDDERCH, T. C., b. Coedpoeth, 5633, Pte., d. of w., F., 26/2/17.

PUGH, A., b. Llanwonno, 29647, Pte., k. in a., F., 3/9/16.

PUGH, H., b. Upper Corris, 49296, Pte., d., Italy, 17/1/18.

PUGH, R. J., b. Brecon, 55073, Pte., k. in a., F., 14/5/17.

PULLEN, E. G., b. London, 10793, Pte., k. in a., F., 19/10/14.

PULSFORD, A., b. Treharris, 5258, L/Cpl., k. in a., F., 27/2/17.

PURCELL, J., b. Ruabon, 39704, Pte., k. in a., F., 25/8/16.

PURKISS, A. M., b. Hampstead, 35150, Pte., k. in a., F., 4/9/16.

QUAYLE, W. H., b. I.O.M., 7840, Pte., d., F., 1/11/18.

QUILL, D. J., b. London, 10889, Cpl., k. in a., F., 21/10/14.

QUINN, J., b. Mountain Ash, 10773, Pte., k. in a., F., 21/10/14.

RADY, J. W., b. Manchester, 70313, Pte., d., Italy, 29/10/18.

RAESTER, W., b. Stoke Lacey, 53655, Pte., k. in a., F., 25/2/17.

RAFFERTY, T. A., b. Abergavenny, 27982, Pte., k. in a., F., 27/8/16.

RAIL, D. S., b. Hayle, 10707, L/Cpl., k. in a., F., 16/5/15.

RANDLE, G., b. Nuneaton, 11854, L/Cpl., k. in a., F., 16/5/15.

RATHBONE, R., b. Saltney, 4521, Pte., k. in a., F., 26/1/15.

RAVENHILL, E. N., b. Birmingham, 9682, Pte., d. of w., Home, 15/11/14.

RAWLINS, W., b. Sale, 17670, Pte., d. of w., F., 7/9/16.

REES, D. J., b. Swansea, 10000, Pte., k. in a., F., 21/10/14.

REES, E., b. Cardiff, 11782, Pte., k. in a., F., 11/3/15.

REES, J., b. Burry, 5297, L/Cpl., k. in a., F., 25/9/15.

REES, O., b. Ferndale, 14886, Pte., k. in a., F., 16/5/15.

REES, R., b. Treherbert, 4518, Pte., k. in a., F., 30/4/16.

REES, R., b. Ferndale, 4930, Pte., k. in a., F., 30/10/14.

REID, C. R. S., e. Cardiff, 70388, Pte., d. of w., F., 28/10/17.

REYNOLDS, W., b. Shrewsbury, 7888, Cpl., k. in a., F., 30/10/14.

RICE, W., b. Swansea, 4971, Pte., k. in a., F., 14/5/16.

RICHARDS, D. J., b. Pontypridd, 9302, Pte., k. in a., F., 21/10/14.

RICHARDS, H. G., b. Bangor, 37674, Pte., k. in a., F., 3/9/16.

RICHARDS, J., b. Merthyr, 17894, Pte., d. of w., Home, 20/6/15.

RICHARDS, T., b. Birmingham,

RICHARDSON, A., b. Manchester, 10554, Pte., k. in a., F., 20/10/14.

RICHES, C., b. London, 5158, Pte., k. in a., F., 30/10/14.

RICHINGS, P. J., b. Bristol, 24516, Pte., k. in a., F., 30/6/16.

RICKETTS, H. J., b. Birmingham, 9758, Sgt., k. in a., F., 30/4/16.

RIGBY, A. T., b. Gloucester, 10852, Pte., k. in a., F., 4/5/17.

RIGBY, L., b. Birkenhead, 7192, Pte., k. in a., F., 21/10/14.

RILEY, E., b. Crewe, 3839, Pte., k. in a., F., 23/11/14.

RILEY, E., b. Cardiff, 5112, Pte., k. in a., F., 26/8/15.

RILEY, J., b. Liverpool, 6845, Pte., k. in a., F., 16/5/15.

RILEY, W., b. Leeds, 48962, L/Cpl., d. of w., F., 29/10/17.

ROBERTS, A. J., b. Aberystwyth, 4367, Pte., d. of w., F., 2/5/16.

ROBERTS, C., b. St. Asaph, 9062, Pte., k. in a., F., 30/10/14.

ROBERTS, E., b. Penmorfa, 53850, Pte., d. of w., F., 20/5/17.

ROBERTS, E., e. Colwyn Bay, 53920, Pte., k. in a., F., 30/9/16.

ROBERTS, E., b. Nevin, 5348, Pte., k. in a., F., 16/5/15.

ROBERTS, E. E., b. Conway, 53732, Pte., k. in a., F., 5/5/17.

ROBERTS, E. O., b. Nevin, 40327, Pte., k. in a., F., 3/9/16.

ROBERTS, G. R., b. Llanbeblig, 4676, Pte., k. in a., F., 30/10/14.

ROBERTS, H., b. Aberffraw, 25750, Pte., k. in a., F., 5/7/16.

ROBERTS, H., b. Llysfaen, 37764, Pte., k. in a., F., 14/7/16.

ROBERTS, I., b. Ruthin, 8678, Pte., k. in a., F., 16/5/15.

ROBERTS, J., b. Llanrwst, 9603, Pte., d. of w., F., 30/1/15.

ROBERTS, J., b. Wrexham, 11172, L/Cpl., k. in a., F., 25/9/15.

ROBERTS, J. F., b. Birmingham, 11480, Pte., k. in a., F., 5/5/17.

ROBERTS, J. G., b. Festiniog, 6445, Pte., k. in a., F., 16/5/15.

ROBERTS, J. O., b. Cerrig-y-Druidion, 34936, Pte., k. in a., F., 28/8/16.

ROBERTS, J. R., b. Carnarvon, 6358, Pte., k. in a., F., 16/5/15.

ROBERTS, J. V., b. Bootle, 36635, Pte., k. in a., F., 18/7/16.

ROBERTS, R., b. Festiniog, 19081, Pte., k. in a., F., 25/9/15.

ROBERTS, R., b. Whitworth, 266952, Pte., d. of w., Home, 20/6/17.

ROBERTS, R. G., b. Llanllyfni,

40482, Pte., k. in a., F., 11/1/17.

ROBERTS, R. T., b. Penmaenmawr, 40444, Pte., k. in a., F., 11/1/17.

ROBERTS, T., b. Mold, 5818, A/Cpl., k. in a., F., 16/5/15.

ROBERTS, T., b. Chester, 11262, Pte., d. of w., F., 19/3/15.

ROBERTS, T., b. Pontypridd, 21028, Pte., k. in a., F., 7/3/16.

ROBERTS, T. J., e. Higher Shotton, 53921, L/Cpl., k. in a., F., 9/12/16.

ROBERTS, W., e. Carnarvon, 19532, Pte., k. in a., F., 3/9/16.

ROBERTS, W., b. Bangor, 53834, Pte., k. in a., F., 2/11/16.

ROBERTS, W. E., b. Llanddeiniolen, 40175, Pte., k. in a., F., 27/8/16.

ROBERTS, W. O., b. Conway, 4368, Pte., d. of w., F., 28/5/16.

ROBERTS, W. O., b. Denbigh, 5331, Sgt., d., F., 15/11/18.

ROBERTS, W. P., b. Rhyl, 11603, L/Sgt., d., Italy, 26/10/18.

ROBINSON, H., b. Swansea, 11196, Pte., d. of w., F., 2/12/14.

ROBLETT, E., b. Hoddesdon, 10809, Sgt., d. of w., F., 14/7/16.

ROGERS, A., b. Oswestry, 12096, Pte., k. in a., F., 25/9/15.

ROGERS, C. F., b. Oswestry, 9315, Cpl., k. in a., F., 30/10/14.

ROGERS, F. M., b. Shrewsbury, 10867, L/Cpl., k. in a., F., 25/9/15.

ROGERS, G., b. Bristol, 9065, Pte., k. in a., F., 16/5/15.

ROGERS, S., b. Chirk, 53740, L/Cpl., d. of w., F., 8/10/17.

ROGERS, T., b. High Ercall, 235650, Pte., k. in a., F., 9/10/17.

ROSE, D., b. Birmingham, 10751, L/Sgt., k. in a., F., 21/10/14.

ROSE, S., b. Bedwas, 43617, L/Cpl., k. in a., F., 14/5/17.

ROSSER, A. E., b. Neath, 6073, Pte., k. in a., F., 16/5/15.

ROWLANDS, C., b. Chester, 56596, Pte., k. in a., F., 1/10/17.

ROWLANDS, H., b. Holyhead, 10536, Pte., k. in a., F., 26/1/15.

ROWLANDS, J., b. Mold, 6461, Pte., k. in a., F., 16/5/15.

ROWLEY, S. E., b. Newport, 9714, Cpl., k. in a., F., 16/5/15.

RUSHTON, A. W., b. Rugeley, 18143, L/Cpl., k. in a., Italy, 25/4/18.

RUSHTON, F. G., b. Birmingham, 9692, Pte., k. in a., F., 16/5/15.

RUSSELL, C., b. Ludlow, 7751, L/Cpl., k. in a., F., 16/5/15.

RUSSELL, J., b. Birmingham,

IV—20

5087, Pte., k. in a., F., 30/1/15.

RYDER, A. E., b. Birmingham, 6742, Pte., d. of w., F., 7/11/14.

RYLANCE, H., b. Liverpool, 17923, Pte., k. in a., F., 9/4/16.

SAGER, W., b. Shawforth, 52067, Pte., d. of w., F., 28/2/17.

SALMON, D., b. Pembroke, 31204, Pte., k. in a., F., 6/2/16.

SALMON, E., b. Pembroke, 31203, Pte., d. of w., F., 7/2/16.

SAMUEL, J., b. Ynysybwl, 17453, Pte., k. in a., F., 25/9/15.

SANDERSON, G., b. Carlisle, 23547, Cpl., k. in a., F., 3/9/16.

SANFORD, G. F., b. Newcastle, 10135, Pte., k. in a., F., 30/10/14.

SANT, J., b. Chester, 6583, Pte., k. in a., F., 19/10/14.

SATTERTHWAITE, J., b. Birmingham, 9845, Pte., k. in a., F., 30/10/14.

SAUNDERS, L. J., b. Farringdon, 10837, Cpl., k. in a., F., 16/5/15.

SCARLET, J. T., b. Boney Hay, 18330, Pte., k. in a., F., 3/9/16.

SCOTT, E., b. Little Somerford, 10519, Pte., k. in a., F., 25/9/15.

SCOTT, F., b. Manchester, 5389, Pte., k. in a., F., 16/5/15.

SCOTT, J. E., b. Nantwich, 3863, Pte., k. in a., F., 16/5/15.

SCOTT, W. J., b. London, 10787, Pte., k. in a., F., 30/10/14.

SCRAGG, W., b. Birmingham, 9636, Pte., k. in a., F., 30/10/14.

SELDON, J., b. Exeter, 10861, Pte., k. in a., F., 20/10/14.

SELWYN, E., b. Newland, 33333, Pte., k. in a., F., 5/7/16.

SENNAR, R., b. Pwllheli, 11020, Pte., k. in a., F., 21/10/14.

SHARMAN, G. A., b. Lowestoft, 5197, Cpl., d. of w., F., 5/3/15.

SHATWELL, W., b. Bollington, 4505, Pte., k. in a., F., 16/5/15.

SHAW, C., b. Ennis, Co. Clare, 10587, Pte., k. in a., F., 13/3/15.

SHEASBY, G. R., b. Alderminster, 11851, L/Cpl., k. in a., F., 29/8/16, D.C.M.

SHEPHERD, G. S., b. Birmingham, 9500, L/Cpl., k. in a., F., 24/5/15.

SHEPPARD, T., b. Bridgwater, 69171, Pte., d., F., 22/11/17.

SHERWOOD, A., b. Swindon, 7776, Pte., k. in a., F., 16/5/15.

SHOOTER, F., b. Low Moor, 24002, Pte., k. in a., F., 10/4/16.

SHROPSHIRE, W. J., b. Llanfechain, 53659, Pte., d. of w., F., 5/12/16.

SILVERS, H., b. Dudley, 18346, Pte., k. in a., F., 25/9/15.

SIMCOCK, G., b. Hanley, 24650, Pte., k. in a., F., 10/10/17, M.M.

SIMNETT, J., b. Burton-on-Trent, 18939, Pte., k. in a., F., 25/9/15.

SIMONS, W., b. Coventry, 10119, Pte., d., Home, 2/2/17.

SIMS, F. J., b. London, 26748, Pte., k. in a., F., 14/5/17.

SKELLY, W., b. Wrexham, 5322, Pte., d. of w., Italy, 15/11/18, M.M.

SMALE, F., b. Braunton, 5905, Pte., k. in a., F., 7/11/14.

SMALLWOOD, A. H., b. Hanley, 8301, A/Sgt., k. in a., F., 13/3/15.

SMEDLEY, G. H., b. Boston, 235571, Pte., k. in a., F., 8/10/17.

SMITH, A., b. Birmingham, 9721, L/Sgt., d., Italy, 31/3/18, M.M.

SMITH, A., b. Newton, 10178, L/Cpl., k. in a., F., 21/10/14.

SMITH, A. H., b. Bristol, 13386, L/Cpl., d. of w., F., 27/9/15.

SMITH, F., b. Salford, 7224, C.S.M., k. in a., F., 1/10/17, D.C.M.

SMITH, G., b. Everton, 5391, Pte., d. of w., F., 26/5/15.

SMITH, G., b. Ferndale, 70399, Pte., d. of w., F., 31/10/17.

SMITH, S., b. Newport, 4240, Pte., k. in a., F., 10/3/15.

SMITH, T. C., b. Bedminster, 11346, Pte., k. in a., F., 16/5/15.

SMITH, V., e. Seaforth, 53952, Pte., d., F., 12/2/17.

SMITH, W., b. Liverpool, 7827, Pte., k. in a., F., 10/3/15.

SNAPE, F., b. All Saints, 10193, Sgt., k. in a., F., 28/5/15.

SNEAD, H., b. Heigham, 24660, Sgt., k. in a., F., 1/10/17.

SNELL, E., b. Ebbw Vale, 9942, Pte., k. in a., F., 30/10/14.

SOUTHERN, R. H., b. Over Hulton, 52468, Pte., k. in a., F., 1/10/17.

SPEAKMAN, C., b. Stoke, 8334, Pte., d. of w., F., 21/5/15.

SPEED, J. E., b. Hope, 9982, Pte., k. in a., F., 21/10/14.

SPEKE, H., b. Worcester, 70386, Pte., d. of w., F., 30/10/17.

SPENCER, T. B., e. St. Helens, 70125, Pte., d. of w., F., 10/10/17.

SPICER, R., b. St. Asaph, 11394, Pte., k. in a., F., 16/5/15.

SPILLER, C., b. Broughton, 70327, Pte., k. in a., F., 26/10/17.

SPILSBURY, S. G., b. Barrow-in-Furness, 5956, Pte., k. in a., F., 29/10/14.

SPOONER, J. C., b. Hockley, 11479, Sgt., k. in a., F., 26/2/17.

STAGG, A., b. Spon End, 10224, Sgt., d. of w., F., 17/5/15.

STANTON, W., b. Stockport, 11164, A/Sgt., k. in a., F., 16/5/15.

STARKLEY, J. W., b. London, 9902, Pte., k. in a., F., 7/11/14.

STEPHENS, A. J., b. Kingston-on-Thames, 9456, C.M.S., k. in a., F., 25/9/15.

STEPHENS, J., b. Briton Ferry, 17002, Pte., d. of w., F., 26/2/17.

STEPTO, C. P., b. London, 27424, Pte., d. of w., F., 4/9/16.

STEVENS, E., b. Birmingham, 6853, Sgt., d., F., 7/1/16.

STEWART, C., b. Castlebar, Co. Mayo, 10280, Pte., k. in a., F., 21/10/14.

STINCHCOMBE, E., b. Bristol, 6022, Pte., k. in a., F., 16/5/15.

STOCK, D. J., b. Swansea, 56644, Pte., k. in a., F., 3/9/16.

STOKES, J., b. Birmingham, 11588, Pte., k. in a., F., 21/5/15.

STOTT, W., b. Facit, 267252, Pte., k. in a., F., 9/10/17.

STOVOLD, W. M., b. St. Giles, London, 7731, Pte., d. of w., F., 6/11/14.

STRACHAN, W. H., b. Cardiff, 56643, Pte., k. in a., F., 27/8/16.

STUART, T., b. London, 36138, Pte., k. in a., F., 29/8/16.

STUBLEY, G., b. Birmingham, 8148, Pte., k. in a., F., 10/7/16.

STUCKEY, A. B., b. Bristol, 235539, Pte., k. in a., F., 9/10/17.

SULLIVAN, P., b. Dowlais, 10704, Pte., k. in a., F., 30/10/14.

SULLIVAN, R., b. Bantry, Co. Cork, 5733, Pte., k. in a., F., 15/5/17.

SULLIVAN, W., b. Fermanagh, 4016, C.Q.M.S., k. in a., F., 30/10/14.

SUSSEMILCH, H., b. London, 8742, Cpl., k. in a., F., 30/10/14.

SUTTON, J., b. Birmingham, 10352, Pte., k. in a., F., 16/5/15.

SUTTON, L., b. Chester, 4584, Pte., k. in a., F., 16/5/15.

SYVRET, H., b. Guernsey, C.I., 4935, Pte., k. in a., F., 16/5/15.

TABER, A. E., b. Duddeston, 11589, Pte., k. in a., F., 16/5/15.

TALLENTS, W., e. Manchester, 53949, Pte., k. in a., F., 10/1/17.

TAME, T., b. Cardiff, 2085, Pte., k. in a., F., 16/5/15.

TANDY, F. E., b. Warwick, 18601, Pte., k. in a., F., 25/9/15.

TARRY, J. G., b. Birmingham, 5857, Pte., k. in a., F., 16/5/15.

TASKER, J., b. Glossop, 52364, Pte., k. in a., F., 27/10/17.

TAYLOR, G., b. Birmingham, 17292, Pte., k. in a., F., 25/9/15.

TAYLOR, H., b. Wolverhampton, 6566, Pte., k. in a., F., 16/5/15.

TAYLOR, H., b. Oldham, 52441, Pte., d. of w., F., 6/3/17.

TAYLOR, J. H., b. Birmingham, 5277, Cpl., k. in a., F., 14/5/17, M.M.

TAYLOR, P., b. Topsham, 42497, Pte., k. in a., F., 27/10/18.

TAYLOR, R. A., b. Stratford-on-Avon, 10611, Pte., k. in a., F., 30/10/14.

TAYLOR, T. C., b. Monmouth, 17039, L/Cpl., k. in a., F., 5/7/16.

TAYLOR, W., b. Birmingham, 10198, Pte., k. in a., F., 27/8/16.

TEAGUE, G., b. Birkenhead, 5713, Pte., d. of w., F., 17/5/15.

TERRINGTON, F., b. Llandyfodwg, 13695, Cpl., d. of w., Italy, 30/3/18, D.C.M.

THOMAS, A. S., b. Bristol, 9483, Cpl., k. in a., F., 30/10/14.

THOMAS, C., b. Birkenhead, 7172, Pte., d. of w., F., 9/10/15.

THOMAS, E., b. Merthyr, 18119, Pte., k. in a., F., 25/9/15.

THOMAS, E., b. Penmaenmawr, 40464, Pte., d. of w., F., 5/4/17.

THOMAS, E., b. Llangunnock, 70418, Pte., k. in a., F., 26/10/17.

THOMAS, F., b. Bagillt, 5825, Pte., k. in a., F., 16/5/15.

THOMAS, G., b. Tylorstown, 5206, Pte., k. in a., F., 16/5/15.

THOMAS, H., b. Swansea, 11166, Pte., k. in a., F., 30/10/14.

THOMAS, H., b. Pembroke, 6284, Pte., k. in a., F., 16/5/15.

THOMAS, H., b. Glanadda, 53836, Pte., d. of w., F., 19/5/17.

THOMAS, J., e. Shotton, 53947, Pte., k. in a., F., 11/1/17.

THOMAS, J. P., b. Llanbeblig, 11112, Pte., k. in a., F., 21/10/14.

THOMAS, J. P., b. Pwllheli, 40410, Pte., d. of w., F., 10/1/17.

THOMAS, P., b. Hyde, 37760, Pte., d. of w., F., 29/11/16.

THOMAS, P. T., b. Carnarvon, 53757, Pte., k. in a., F., 6/10/16.

THOMAS, R., b. Llanddeiniolen, 40124, Pte., k. in a., F., 28/8/16.

THOMAS, S., b. Radnor, 235655, Pte., k. in a., F., 9/10/17.

THOMAS, T., b. Neath, 17950, Pte., d. of w., Home, 5/10/15.

THOMAS, W., e. Colwyn Bay, 53923, Pte., k. in a., F., 4/5/17.

THOMAS, W., b. Ferndale, 10626, Pte., k. in a., F., 30/10/14.

THOMAS, W. H., b. Carmarthen, 13518, Pte., k. in a., F., 14/7/16.

THOMPSON, A., b. Wavertree, 55160, Pte., d., Home, 31/10/17.

THOMPSON, J., b. Rock Ferry, 4756, A/Sgt., k. in a., F., 15/5/17.

THOMPSON, S. R., b. Pendleton, 5898, Pte., k. in a., F., 30/10/14.

THORNBOROUGH, A. E., b. London, 10769, Sgt., k. in a., F., 14/7/16, M.M.

THORNE, G., b. Bristol, 17735, Pte., k. in a., F., 25/9/15.

TIMMS, T., b. Salford, 10982, Pte., k. in a., F., 21/10/14.

TINMAN, G. H., b. Rhyl, 4250, Pte., k. in a., F., 7/1/15.

TOWNSEND, B., b. Wattstown, 12310, Pte., k. in a., F., 16/5/15.

TRAVERS, J., b. Merthyr, 53980, Pte., d. of w., F., 31/3/17.

TREMBLE, W. C., b. Oxford, 17015, Pte., k. in a., F., 3/9/16.

TRIMNEL, J. A., b. Bristol, 9981, Pte., d. of w., F., 14/3/15.

TUDOR, H. J., b. Abertillery, 29634, Pte., k. in a., F., 3/9/16.

TUNKS, W., b. Chester, 11315, Pte., k. in a., F., 25/9/15.

TURNER, V. L., b. Church Stretton, 70102, Pte., d., Italy, 20/10/18.

TYLER, A. C., b. Birmingham, 9976, Pte., k. in a., F., 21/10/14.

TYMON, R., b. Aspull, 17032, Pte., d., Italy, 21/5/18.

UNDERWOOD, E., b. Bromsberrow, 17902, Pte., k. in a., F., 25/9/15.

VANN, H., b. Birmingham, 9190, Pte., k. in a., F., 29/8/16.

VARLEY, W., b. Middleton, 52090, Pte., d. of w., F., 14/3/17.

VAUGHAN, A., b. Newport, 6175, Pte., d. of w., F., 26/5/15.

VAUGHAN, A., b. Pontypridd, 4577, Pte., k. in a., F., 6/2/16.

VAUGHAN, T., b. Rhosllaner-chrugog, 10864, Pte., k. in a., F., 6/7/15.

VERNALS, J., b. Birmingham, 10284, Pte., k. in a., F., 25/10/14.

VILES, A. F., b. Ferndale, 10341, L/Cpl., d., Italy, 2/9/18.

VINCENT, A., b. Southwark, 27042, Pte., d. of w., F., 18/10/17.

VINCENT, W. J., b. Birmingham, 19128, Pte., k. in a., F., 16/7/15.

WADE, C., b. Pontefract, 10887, Pte., k. in a., F., 16/5/15.

WAGSTAFF, G., b. Coventry, 8057, Pte., k. in a., F., 16/5/15.

WAIGHT, E., b. Birmingham, 8095, Pte., d. of w., F., 24/10/14.

WAINWRIGHT, A., b. Crewe, 9267, Sgt., k. in a., F., 29/8/16.

WALDEN, W., b. Croydon, 23393, Sgt., k. in a., F., 4/5/17.

WALKDEN, J., b. Manchester, 10992, Pte., k. in a., F., 7/11/14.

WALKER, F. E., b. Stoke Newington, 20588, Cpl., k. in a., F., 2/9/18.

WALKER, G., b. Hanley, 10951, Pte., k. in a., F., 24/10/14.

WALKER, J., b. Winsford, 17333, Pte., k. in a., F., 25/9/15.

WALKER, J. S., b. Highgate, 5926, Pte., d. of w., F., 26/9/15.

WALKER, L., b. Farnworth, 18893, Pte., k. in a., F., 25/9/15.

WALKER, T., e. Pontypool, 70441, Pte., k. in a., Italy, 17/4/18.

WALLACE, E., b. Blakesley, 37910, Pte., k. in a., F., 15/7/16.

WARD, C. E., b. Islington, 11066, Pte., k. in a., F., 16/5/15.

WARD, R., e. Deptford, 56651, Pte., k. in a., F., 14/5/17.

WARD, T., b. Chester, 4375, Cpl., k. in a., F., 21/5/15.

WARDLE, R., b. Leigh, 18348, Pte., k. in a., F., 25/9/15.

WARE, A. G., b. Neath, Glam., 17063, Pte., k. in a., F., 25/9/15.

WARE, J., b. London, 10432, Pte., k. in a., F., 21/10/14.

WARNER, W. W., b. Birmingham, 8285, C.S.M., k. in a., F., 25/9/15.

WARREN, F., b. Evesham, 10403, L/Cpl., k. in a., F., 30/10/14.

WATKINS, D. W., b. Cwmgorse, 37701, Pte., k. in a., F., 14/7/16.

WATKINS, G., b. Merthyr, 16729, Cpl., k. in a., F., 28/6/15.

WATKINS, G. I., b. Bristol, 56650, Pte., k. in a., F., 15/5/17.

WATSON, F. A., b. Rugby, 36900, A/Cpl., k. in a., F., 3/9/16.

WATSON, H., b. East Bridgeford, 19464, Pte., k. in a., F., 5/7/16.

WATSON, J. G., b. Woolwich, 10073, Sgt., k. in a., F., 11/11/15.

WATTS, F., b. Dorchester, 5846, A/Sgt., k. in a., F., 15/5/15.

WEAVER, W. J., b. Tinsley Bond, 19745, Pte., d., Italy, 11/6/18.

WEBBER, J., b. Liverpool, 7611, Pte., k. in a., F., 30/10/14.

WEBSTER, C. F., b. Halesowen, 11264, Cpl., k. in a., F., 16/5/15.

WEBSTER, J. A., b. Wolverhampton, 5960, Pte., k. in a., F., 16/5/15.

WELCH, S., b. Hawarden, 5696, Pte., k. in a., F., 16/5/15.

WELLS, W., b. Chester, 6823, Pte., k. in a., F., 30/10/14.

WELSH, M., b. Liverpool, 6699, Pte., k. in a., F., 21/10/14.

WELSH, R., b. Flint, 26389, Pte., k. in a., F., 1/10/17.

WEST, J. O., b. Liverpool, 235570, Pte., k. in a., F., 1/10/17.

WESTON, J., b. Wellington, Salop, 24878, Pte., k. in a., F., 25/9/15.

WESTWOOD, F. C., b. Leamington, 53668, Pte., k. in a., F., 4/12/16.

WESTWOOD, J. T., b. Wolverhampton, 6718, Pte., k. in a., F., 27/10/14.

WHARRAD, T., b. Redditch, 6101, Pte., k. in a., F., 11/3/15.

WHEATLEY, R. T., b. Manchester, 52216, Pte., k. in a., F., 14/5/17.

WHEELER, H. H., b. Cardiff, 10790, L/Cpl., k. in a., F., 3/9/16.

WHEELER, J. R., b. Brecon, 5280, Pte., k. in a., F., 16/5/15.

WHITBREAD, W., b. Wrexham, 10677, C.S.M., k. in a., F., 14/5/17, D.C.M. and M.M.

WHITCOMBE, C., b. Aberdare, 17825, Pte., k. in a., F., 25/9/15.

WHITE, F. C., b. Birmingham, 6946, L/Cpl., k. in a., F., 16/5/15.

WHITE, G. M., e. Michaels, Hereford, 55722, L/Cpl., k. in a., F., 3/5/18.

WHITE, R., b. Birmingham, 9069, Pte., d., 19/6/17.

WHITE, W. J., b. Gresford, 19294, Pte., k. in a., F., 25/9/15.

WHITEHEAD, E., b. Heafrey, 52722, Pte., d. of w., F., 10/5/17.

WHITEHOUSE, G., b. Pelsall, 17505, Pte., k. in a., F., 3/9/16.

WHITNEY, T., b. Arva, Co. Cavan, 6222, Pte., k. in a., F., 16/5/15.

WICKETT, J., b. Birmingham, 10791, Pte., k. in a., F., 25/9/15.

WILBOURN, A., b. Deptford, 56652, Pte., k. in a., F., 3/9/16.

WILBRAHAM, G., b. Woodchurch, 315394, Pte., d. of w., Home, 20/11/17.

WILD, W. K., b. Rochdale, 52064, Pte., k. in a., F., 4/5/17.

WILDING, J., b. Wrexham, 8883, L/Cpl., k. in a., F., 25/9/15.

WILKINS, J., b. Stapleton, 17527, L/Cpl., k. in a., F., 25/9/15.

WILKINSON, A., b. Llanbeblig, 265470, Pte., k. in a., F., 4/5/17.

WILKINSON, F., b. Ramsbottom, 52670, Pte., k. in a., F., 4/5/17.

WILKINSON, J., b. Farnworth, 70346, Pte., k. in a., F., 26/10/17.

WILLIAMS, A., b. Llangrove, 53981, Pte., k. in a., F., 4/5/17.

WILLIAMS, C. B., b. Swansea, 5811, A/L/Cpl., k. in a., F., 16/5/15.

WILLIAMS, D., b. Ferndale, 4613, Pte., k. in a., F., 16/5/15.

WILLIAMS, D., b. Denbigh, 6491, Pte., d. of w., F., 24/5/15.

WILLIAMS, D., b. Trecastle, 53982, Pte., k. in a., F., 26/2/17.

WILLIAMS, D. O., b. Wrexham, 24420, Pte., k. in a., F., 29/8/16.

WILLIAMS, E., b. Abertillery, 4789, Pte., d. of w., F., 14/1/15.

WILLIAMS, E., b. Watts Town, 5428, Pte., k. in a., F., 16/5/15.

WILLIAMS, H., b. Penygroes, 11783, Pte., k. in a., F., 15/7/16.

WILLIAMS, H., b. Bethesda, 13273, Pte., k. in a., F., 2/10/17.

WILLIAMS, H., e. Wrexham, 40902, Pte., d., Home, 2/2/18.

WILLIAMS, H. M., b. Waenfawr, 40439, Pte., k. in a., F., 27/8/16.

WILLIAMS, I., b. Newport, 1238, Pte., k. in a., F., 25/9/15.

WILLIAMS, I., b. Festiniog, 66821, Pte., d. of w., F., 21/11/17.

WILLIAMS, J., b. Swansea, 5977, Pte., k. in a., F., 16/5/15.

WILLIAMS, J., b. Denbigh, 6475, Pte., k. in a., F., 25/9/15.

WILLIAMS, J., e. Bethesda, 53801, Pte., k. in a., F., 4/5/17.

WILLIAMS, J., b. Manchester, 70440, Pte., k. in a., Italy, 3/5/18.

WILLIAMS, J. A., b. Aldershot, 11295, Pte., k. in a., F., 29/8/16.

WILLIAMS, J. D., b. Ruabon, 15916, Pte., k. in a., F., 26/10/17.

WILLIAMS, J. G., b. Harlech, 49800, Pte., k. in a., F., 15/5/17.

WILLIAMS, J. H., b. Talybont, 6349, Pte., k. in a., F., 5/7/16.

WILLIAMS, J. R., b. Holywell, 10258, Pte., k. in a., F., 16/5/15.

WILLIAMS, J. R., b. Trawsfyndd, 18459, Pte., d. of w., F., 29/5/16.

WILLIAMS, J. T., b. Cork, Ireland, 55721, Pte., k. in a., F., 26/2/17.

WILLIAMS, M., b. Arthog, 6253, Pte., k. in a., F., 9/3/15.

WILLIAMS, M., b. Llanberis, 40430, Pte., k. in a., F., 26/2/17.

WILLIAMS, O. G., b. Pwllheli, 53671, Pte., k. in a., F., 25/5/17.

WILLIAMS, O. J., b. Llanrhyddlad, 53745, Pte., d. of w., Italy, 6/4/18.

WILLIAMS, O. R., b. Carnarvon, 5799, Pte., k. in a., F., 16/5/15.

WILLIAMS, P. T., b. Cwmbran, 5172, Cpl., d. of w., F., 12/10/17.

WILLIAMS, R., b. Denbigh, 6013, Pte., k. in a., F., 16/5/15.

WILLIAMS, R., e. Liverpool, 37170, A/Sgt., k. in a., F., 29/8/16.

WILLIAMS, R., b. Holyhead, 44366, Pte., k. in a., F., 26/10/17.

WILLIAMS, R., b. Liverpool, 5977, Pte., k. in a., F., 16/5/15.

WILLIAMS, R., b. Carnarvon, 40402, Pte., d., F., 13/1/17.

WILLIAMS, R., b. Llanberis, 40477, Pte., k. in a., F., 1/9/16.

WILLIAMS, R. J., b. Bodfari, 17796, Pte., k. in a., F., 5/9/16.

WILLIAMS, T., b. Llanfabon, 17436, Pte., k. in a., F., 25/9/15.

WILLIAMS, T., b. Mountain Ash, 19096, Pte., k. in a., F., 3/9/16.

WILLIAMS, T., b. Llanddeiniolen, 40128, Pte., k. in a., F., 28/8/16.

WILLIAMS, T. G., b. Dolbenham, 45157, Pte., k. in a., F., 4/5/17.

WILLIAMS, T. W., b. Digbeth, Warwick, 5164, Pte., k. in a., F., 28/11/14.

WILLIAMS, W., b. Pontypridd, 5313, Pte., k. in a., F., 18/7/16.

WILLIAMS, W., b. Holt, 53666, Pte., d. of w., F., 5/6/17.

WILLIAMS, W. C., b. Denbigh, 6189, Pte., d. of w., F., 28/11/14.

WILLIAMS, W. E., b. Ebenezer, 53840, Pte., k. in a., F., 27/10/17.

WILLIAMS, W. R., b. Bangor, 12293, Pte., k. in a., F., 3/9/16.

WILLIAMS, W. R., b. Llanllyfni, 21126, Pte., d. of w., F., 22/1/17.

WILSHAW, A., b. Hanley, 19150, Pte., k. in a., F., 25/9/15.

WILSON, J. A., b. Liverpool, 5659, Pte., k. in a., F., 12/3/15.

WINROE, R., e. Ormskirk, 53800, Pte., k. in a., F., 4/5/17.

WINROW, J., b. Liverpool, 33027, Pte., k. in a., F., 18/11/15.

WITTON, J., b. Charetown, 17702, Pte., k. in a., F., 2/9/16.

WOOD, T., b. Stretton, 5532, Pte., k. in a., F., 30/4/16.

WOODCOCK, J., b. Runcorn, 17341, Pte., k. in a., F., 25/9/15.

WOODFORD, J., b. Birmingham, 9956, Pte., k. in a., F., 30/10/14.

WOODHOUSE, C. T., b. Newport, 4639, Pte., d., F., 4/10/15.

WOODHOUSE, R., b. Burnley, 24103, Pte., k. in a., F., 8/11/15.

WOOLRICH, W., b. Wolverhampton, 8204, Pte., k. in a., F., 13/3/15.

WORRALL, P., b. Hollins, 266898, Pte., d. of w., Italy, 9/8/18.

WORSFORD, W., b. Guildford, 6557, Pte., k. in a., F., 19/10/14.

WYMAN, C., b. Barking, 10900, Pte., d., F., 3/11/15.

WYNNE, P., b. Liverpool, 10892, Pte., d., F., 19/6/15.

YATES, C., b. Monmouth, 5889, Pte., k. in a., F., 30/10/14.

YEOMANS, A., b. Gloucester, 14814, Pte., k. in a., F., 16/5/15.

ZEILER, M., b. Neath, 29566, L/Cpl., k. in a., F., 14/5/17.

2nd BATTALION

AIREY, R. C., b. Lancaster, 73298, Pte., k. in a., F., 1/9/18.

AKERS, R., b. London, 24661, L/Cpl., k. in a., F., 23/4/18.

ALDEN, S. F., b. Birmingham, 6814, Pte., k. in a., F., 3/11/16.

ALLAN, J., b. Greenock, 9548, L/Cpl., d. of w., F., 17/6/15.

ALLCOCK, G., b. Stratford-on-Avon, 11067, L/Cpl., k. in a., F., 4/11/14.

ALLEN, A. H., b. Cardiff, 11093, Pte., k. in a., F., 30/10/14.

ALLEN, W., b. Haslington, 37245, Pte., k. in a., F., 20/7/16.

ALMOND, F., b. Darwen, 17172, Pte., k. in a., F., 20/7/16.

AMOS, J., b. Rhyl, 203161, Sgt., k. in a., F., 26/9/17.

ANDREWS, C. F., b. Winchester, 56517, Pte., k. in a., F., 26/9/17.

ANDREWS, J., b. Boughton, 4849, Pte., k. in a., F., 26/9/17.

ANKERS, H., e. Wrexham, 200816, L/Cpl., k. in a., F., 2/9/18.

ANSON, T., b. Birkenhead, 7607, L/Cpl., k. in a., F., 30/5/16.

ARCHER, W., b. Cowbridge, 18485, Pte., k. in a., F., 27/8/18.

ARKELL, A. E., b. Birmingham, 8417, L/Cpl., d. of w., F., 3/9/18.

ARMSTRONG, W., b. Newton-le-Willows, 202559, Pte., k. in a., F., 8/10/18.

ASHWORTH, H., b. Bacup, 15507, Sgt., d. of w., F., 6/7/16.

ASHWORTH, W., b. Manchester, 29068, Pte., k. in a., F., 13/9/18.

ASTILL, W., b. Coventry, 15118, Pte., k. in a., F., 8/2/16.

ASTON, S., b. Swansea, 56177, Pte., k. in a., F., 27/5/17.

ATKINS, E. J., e. Barry, 54071, Pte., d. of w., F., 12/2/17.

ATKINSON, A., b. Liverpool, 73299, Pte., k. in a., F., 22/4/18.

ATKINSON, F., b. Cardiff, 37934, Pte., k. in a., F., 23/4/17.

AUSTWICK, J., b. Todmorden, 7149, Pte., k. in a., F., 1/11/14.

BABB, F. R., b. Birmingham, 10443, Pte., k. in a., F., 14/9/15.

BAGGOTT, C. A., b. Bridgend, 74952, Pte., d. of w., F., 12/3/18.

BAILEY, W., b. Burnley, 201813, Pte., k. in a., F., 26/9/17.

BAILEY, W. H., b. Manchester, 66629, Pte., k. in a., F., 26/8/18.

BAKER, H., b. Pontypridd, 93708, Pte., d. of w., F., 9/10/18.

BAKER, J., b. Sheffield, 33322, Pte., k. in a., F., 1/9/18.

BALE, J. W., b. Rugby, 9339, Sgt., k. in a., F., 22/6/16, D.C.M.

BALL, D. F., b. Neath, 26425, Cpl., k. in a., F., 1/9/18.

BALL, G., b. Plymouth, 11148, Pte., k. in a., F., 31/10/14.

BALTON, W., b. Oldham, 52214, Pte., k. in a., F., 27/5/17.

BARLOW, S., b. Malpas, 9453, Pte., k. in a., F., 30/10/14.

BARNES, C. H., b. Cadoxton, Glam., 10678, Pte., d. of w., F., 3/11/14.

BARON, W., b. Blackpool, 8108, L/Cpl., d. of w., F., 13/12/15.

BARRATT, J. R., b. Stockport, 11340, Pte., d. of w., F., 22/9/15.

BARRETT, E. L., b. Colytown, Devon, 10390, Cpl., d. of w., F., 15/9/18, D.C.M.

BARTON, A., b. Warrington, 77755, Pte., k. in a., F., 24/8/18.

BARTON, T., b. Blackburn, 56178, Pte., k. in a., F., 27/5/17.

BASS, H., b. Birmingham, 9318, L/Cpl., d., Home, 24/7/16.

BATEMAN, F., b. Kilkenny, 56719, L/Cpl., d. of w., F., 26/10/16.

BATES, H., b. Walsall, 7812, Pte., k. in a., F., 17/2/17.

BATH, E., b. Stockport, 8279, Pte., k. in a., F., 25/9/15.

BATTYE, A., b. Tintwistle, Cheshire, 56257, Pte., k. in a., F., 27/5/17.

BAXTER, A. N., b. West Bromwich, 10330, Pte., k. in a., F., 27/10/14.

BAYLISS, A. W., b. Birmingham, 31199, Pte., k. in a., F., 22/6/16.

BEAGAN, J., b. Manchester, 63167, Pte., k. in a., F., 27/5/17.

BEASLEY, E., b. Leeds, 91125, Pte., k. in a., F., 15/10/18.

BEATON, C. H., b. Arthur's Bridge, Somerset, 30288, Pte., k. in a., F., 19/8/16.

BEDDER, L. C., b. Cardiff, 11818, Pte., k. in a., F., 15/3/15.

BEDDOES, E. T., b. Sutton Coldfield, 17775, Pte., k. in a., F., 5/7/16.

BEDDOES, W. A., b. Ludlow, Salop, 7639, Pte., k. in a., F., 28/6/15.

BELL, A. K., e. Manchester, 73308, Pte., k. in a., F., 12/7/18.

BELL, F., b. Birmingham, 6386, C.Q.M.S., d. of w., F., 29/9/15.

BELSHAW, R., b. Gorton, 37206, L/Cpl., k. in a., F., 23/4/17.

BENNETT, C., b. Clayton, 73312, Pte., k. in a., F., 1/9/18.

BENNETT, J., b. Stockport, 9384, Cpl., d., Home, 1/9/16, M.M.

BENNETT, R., b. Blackburn, 73306, Pte., k. in a., F., 1/9/18.

BENTLEY, J. J., b. Arthog, 54545, Pte., k. in a., F., 16/4/17.

BERRY, E., b. Burnley, 201639, Pte., k. in a., F., 26/9/17.

BERRY, W. E. J., b. Bridgwater, 11327, Pte., d. of w., F., 9/12/14.

BETHELL, E. F., b. Newport, 70558, Pte., k. in a., F., 20/9/18.

BEVAN, A. G., b. Swansea, 10309, Cpl., k. in a., F., 20/9/18.

BIGGS, G., e. Rhosymedre, 54068, Pte., k. in a., F., 5/11/16.

BIGGS, W. J., b. Rotherhithe, 56214, Pte., k. in a., F., 1/9/18.

BIGNELL, C. H., b. Wrexham, 55174, Pte., d. of w., F., 29/4/17.

BILLINGS, W. G., b. Neath, 55564, Pte., k. in a., F., 26/9/17.

BISHOP, W. T., b. Hopton-Wafers, 73303, Pte., d. of w., F., 24/10/18.

BLACKTIN, H. C., b. Wrexham, 9910, Sgt., k. in a., F., 30/10/16.

BLAIR, W., b. Aspatria, 71945, Pte., k. in a., F., 8/10/18.

BLAYLOCK, W., b. Blackpool, 55102, Pte., k. in a., F., 8/3/17.

BLAYNEY, E. O., b. Trefeglwys, 203531, Pte., k. in a., F., 1/9/18.

BLOOR, A., b. Tunstall, 23938, Pte., k. in a., F., 22/6/16.

BOLTON, W., b. Birmingham, 9561, Pte., d. of w., F., 12/7/15.

BOND, J., b. Lydiate, 266868, Pte., k. in a., F., 27/5/17.

BOOT, W. W., b. Birmingham, 9090, Pte., k. in a., F., 25/9/15.

BOOTH, J., e. Newport, 88777, Pte., k. in a., F., 4/11/18.

BOOTH, T., b. Roorkie, India, 10255, Pte., k. in a., F., 5/6/15.

BOSTOCK, M. L., b. Whitchurch, 17336, L/Cpl., k. in a., F., 25/9/15.

BOSWELL, W. H., b. Birmingham, 6739, Pte., k. in a., F., 20/9/15.

BOURNE, E., b. Llanfair-Caereinion, 55170, Pte., k. in a., F., 26/11/17.

BOWEN, F. W., b. Flint, 9452, Sgt., k. in a., F., 14/11/14.

BOWEN, J., b. Llanboidy, 59427, Pte., k. in a., F., 12/9/18.

BOWEN, T. F., b. Treharris, 73230, Pte., k. in a., F., 8/1/18.

BOWER, L., b. Bradford, 46420, Cpl., d. of w., F., 22/6/18.

BOWERS, G., b. Eccleshall, Stafford, 7000, Pte., k. in a., F., 20/7/16.

BOYES, J., b. Holywell, 54605, Pte., k. in a., F., 7/3/17.

BRADLEY, H., b. Flint, 12800, Pte., d. of w., F., 30/4/17.

BRADLEY, H., b. Birkenhead, 70274, Pte., k. in a., F., 19/10/17.

BRADLEY, L. J., e. Welshpool, 55175, Pte., k. in a., F., 20/4/17.

BRADSHAW, T., b. Northmoore, 7930, Pte., k. in a., F., 7/11/14.

BRADY, A., b. Stockport, 53005, Pte., k. in a., F., 26/9/17.

BRADY, W., b. Wrexham, 7239, Pte., d. of w., F., 18/7/16.

BRAMHALL, S., b. Dukinfield, Cheshire, 8437, Pte., k. in a., F., 18/10/18.

BRAZENHALL, H., b. Birmingham, 9571, Pte., d. of w., Home, 26/6/18.

BRIDGMAN, H. S., b. St. Dominic, Cornwall, 56522, Pte., k. in a., F., 26/9/17.

BRIGGS, A., b. Stepney, 27058, Pte., k. in a., F., 5/11/16.

BRISTOW, T., b. Overton-on-Dee, 55176, Pte., k. in a., F., 23/4/17.

BRITAM, A., b. Manchester, 267250, Pte., k. in a., F., 26/9/17.

BRITTON, A. S., b. Panteg, 89278, Pte., k. in a., F., 4/11/18.

BROMLEY, G. W., b. Bethnal Green, 27532, Pte., k. in a., F., 23/4/17.

BROOKER-CAREY, C., b. Colne,

46446, Pte., k. in a., F., 30/11/17.

BROOKS, R. G., b. Abergavenny, 8624, Pte., k. in a., F., 20/7/16.

BROWN, B., b. Abertillery, 59601, Pte., k. in a., F., 19/5/18.

BROWN, G., b. Pimlico, 10325, Dmr., k. in a., F., 19/10/17.

BROWN, G. A., b. Roath, 10628, Pte., d. of w., F., 2/1/15.

BROWNBILL, A., b. Liverpool, 72460, Pte., d. of w., F., 5/9/18.

BROWNING, C. G., b. Birmingham, 8727, Pte., k. in a., F., 4/11/14.

BRUIN, W., b. Bethnal Green, 24461, Pte., d. of w., F., 7/11/16.

BUCK, A., b. Nottingham, 11436, Pte., d., At Sea, 3/8/18.

BUFFEY, W., e. Wrexham, 54065, Pte., d. of w., F., 23/8/17.

BUNN, G., b. Hereford, 202724, Pte., k. in a., F., 20/5/18.

BURD, R. C., b. Newtown, 57042, Pte., k. in a., F., 13/9/18.

BURGESS, E. B., b. Swansea, 55558, Pte., k. in a., F., 10/10/17.

BURGESS, W. V., b. Widnes, 7826, Pte., d. of w., F., 26/11/14.

BURROWS, W. T., e. Ogmore Vale, 89211, Pte., d. of w., F., 4/11/18.

BURTENSHAW, F., b. London, 9277, L/Cpl., k. in a., F., 25/8/18.

BUTCHER, S., b. Oswestry, 11478, k. in a., F., 19/10/17.

BUTLER, F. S., b. Buckhurst Hill, Essex, 56206, Pte., k. in a., F., 18/8/17.

BYE, D., b. Bristol, 7079, Cpl., k. in a., F., 23/4/17.

CADMAN, B., b. Rotherham, 6015, Pte., k. in a., F., 18/7/16.

CADY, S. J., b. Pontypridd, 201602, Pte., d. of w., F., 29/9/17.

CARGILL, T., b. Ilkeston, 72012, Pte., k. in a., F., 16/10/18.

CARNEY, T., b. St. Chads, Warwick, 37417, Pte., k. in a., F., 23/4/17.

CARRIGAN, J., e. Wrexham, 54073, Pte., k. in a., F., 27/10/16.

CARTER, E., b. Runcorn, 7146, Pte., k. in a., F., 16/4/15.

CARTER, J., b. Cardiff, 8931, Pte., k. in a., F., 22/6/16.

CARTER, W., b. Wolverhampton, 5873, Pte., k. in a., F., 7/11/14.

CAVILL, A. J., b. Mardy, 88832, Pte., k. in a., F., 27/10/18.

CAWTHRAY, H., b. York, 77965, Pte., k. in a., F., 13/9/18.

CECIL, F., b. Abersychan, 69473, Pte., d. of w., F., 15/9/18.

CHADDERTON, H. S., b. Ashton-under-Lyne, 52440, Pte., k. in a., F., 27/5/17.

CHADWICK, W., b. U.S.A., 76371, Pte., d. of w., F., 15/9/18.

CHALINOR, S., b. Birkenhead, 7052, Pte., k. in a., F., 6/8/15.

CHAMBERS, W. A., e. Lewisham, 70261, Pte., d. of w., Home, 8/6/18.

CHAPLIN, J. H., b. Birmingham, 36881, Pte., k. in a., F., 20/5/17.

CHAPMAN, F., e. Holborn, 27979, Pte., k. in a., F., 8/10/18.

CHARLES, R., e. Oswestry, 291522, Pte., k. in a., F., 27/5/17.

CHATFIELD, E., b. Chester, 10108, L/Cpl., k. in a., F., 20/9/15.

CHATTERTON, G., b. Colne, 201869, Pte., d. of w., F., 19/7/18.

CHATWIN, W., b. Birmingham, 9181, Pte., k. in a., F., 22/6/16.

CHISHOLM, J. R., b. Coventry, 9733, Pte., k. in a., F., 2/1/16.

CHRISTOPHER, H., b. Heskin, 93378, Pte., d. of w., F., 2/9/18.

CLARKE, E., b. Beswick, 19862, Pte., k. in a., F., 27/1/16.

CLARKE, H., b. Ruthin, 12220, Pte., k. in a., F., 22/6/16.

CLARKE, J. J., b. Liverpool, 93361, Pte., k. in a., F., 24/8/18.

CLARKE, R. T., b. Brecon, 11115, Pte., k. in a., F., 22/6/16.

CLAYTON, A. J., b. New Tredegar, 73710, Pte., k. in a., F., 9/5/18.

CLEMENTS, W. T., b. Grays, Essex, 55894, Pte., k. in a., F., 21/3/18.

CLIFFORD, P., b. Salford, 63948, Pte., d. of w., F., 28/4/17.

COATES, E. J., b. Blagdon, 31036, L/Cpl., k. in a., F., 28/11/17.

COCKS, T. C., b. Brixton, 10717, Pte., k. in a., F., 21/10/17.

COHEN, E., b. London, 8755, L/Cpl., k. in a., F., 22/8/16.

COHEN, M., b. Manchester, 63170, Pte., k. in a., F., 27/5/17.

COKER, W., b. Birmingham, 7955, Pte., k. in a., F., 24/10/16.

COLE, T. J., b. Penderry, Glam., 73244, Pte., k. in a., F., 1/9/18.

COLLIER, F., b. Panteg, Mon., 18350, Pte., k. in a., F., 27/5/17.

COLLINSON, J., b. Blackburn, 201747, Pte., k. in a., F., 12/3/18.

COMERFORD, G., b. Birmingham, 9116, Pte., d., Home, 26/3/15.

CONDICK, E., b. Westleigh, Devon, 9639, Pte., k. in a., F., 27/10/14.

CONNOLLY, J., b. Manchester, 5990, Pte., k. in a., F., 14/6/15.

COOKE, J., b. Blackburn, 73357, Pte., d. of w., F., 6/6/18.

COOKE, J. W. B., b. Ruthin, 54114, Pte., k. in a., F., 24/10/16.

COOKE, P., b. Worsley, 93367, Pte., k. in a., F., 1/9/18.

COOPER, E., b. Manchester, 73330, Pte., k. in a., F., 30/11/17.

CORBETT, F., b. Birmingham, 6673, Pte., d. of w., F., 22/9/15.

COSTELLO, F., b. Salford, 8276, Pte., k. in a., F., 7/11/14.

COULTAS, G., b. Filey, 59709, Pte., k. in a., F., 25/11/17.

COULTON, J. R., b. Liverpool, 72008, Pte., k. in a., F., 13/9/18.

COURTNEY, E., b. Roath, 9353, Sgt., k. in a., F., 26/9/17, M.M.

COX, G. H., b. Birmingham, 8112, L/Cpl., d. of w., F., 20/6/15.

COX, J., b. Bolton, 31022, Pte., k. in a., F., 20/7/16.

CRAIG, H., b. Guisborough, 31032, L/Cpl., k. in a., F., 20/7/16.

CRAIG, J. H., b. Dublin, 18392, Pte., k. in a., F., 26/9/17.

CREWE, S. H., b. Camden Town, 56201, Pte., k. in a., F., 26/9/17.

CRIPPS, H. G., b. Reading, 12065, Pte., k. in a., F., 20/7/16.

CRITCHLEY, W., b. Liverpool, 66201, Pte., k. in a., F., 25/8/16.

CRUMPTON, A. H., b. St. James, Hereford, 31030, Pte., k. in a., F., 20/7/16.

CUTCLIFFE, E. J., b. Amroth, 57136, Pte., d., F., 5/10/18.

DALY, J., e. Birkenhead, 55604, Pte., k. in a., F., 23/4/18.

DANIELS, D., b. Pontardawe, 37629, Pte., k. in a., F., 27/10/16.

DARLINGTON, F., b. Oldham, 56180, Pte., d. of w., F., 2/9/18.

DAVENPORT, A., b. Sandbach Heath, 8409, Sgt., k. in a., F., 7/11/14.

DAVENPORT, E. E., b. Southam, 9708, A/Cpl., k. in a., F., 29/4/15.

DAVID, B., b. Neath, 55568, Pte., k. in a., F., 27/5/17.

DAVIES, A., b. Neath, 375556, Pte., d. of w., Home, 9/9/19.

DAVIES, A. E., b. Llanidloes, 54607, Pte., k. in a., F., 27/5/17.

DAVIES, A. J., b. Bromsberrow, 56722, L/Cpl., k. in a., F., 5/3/17.

DAVIES, A. R., b. Waunfawr, 55547, Pte., d. of w., Home, 25/2/17.

DAVIES, A. V., b. Liverpool, 73337, Pte., k. in a., F., 26/8/18.

DAVIES, D., e. Llandudno, 36634, Pte., k. in a., F., 26/8/18.

DAVIES, E., b. Merthyr Tydvil, 75080, Pte., k. in a., F., 28/8/18.

DAVIES, F., b. Pembroke Dock, 39740, Pte., k. in a., F., 30/11/17.

DAVIES, F. W., b. Birmingham, 8227, Pte., k. in a., F., 25/10/14.

DAVIES, G., e. Claypit Yazor, 55185, Pte., k. in a., F., 16/4/17.

DAVIES, G., b. Wigan, 73250, Pte., k. in a., F., 1/9/18.

DAVIES, G., b. Bow, London, 89402, Pte., d. of w., Home, 19/11/18.

DAVIES, G. O., b. Llanberis, 54589, Pte., k. in a., F., 28/11/17.

DAVIES, G. T., b. Liverpool, 73339, Pte., d. of w., F., 17/4/18.

DAVIES, H., b. Gwersyllt, 6601, Pte., k. in a., F., 19/8/16.

DAVIES, H. F., b. Rhyl, 11165, Pte., d. of w., F., 26/3/18.

DAVIES, J., b. Breconshire, 77481, Pte., k. in a., F., 24/8/18.

DAVIES, J., b. Llandinam, 29459, Pte., k. in a., F., 1/9/18.

DAVIES, J., b. St. Asaph, 60969, Pte., d. of w., F., 14/3/18.

DAVIES, J. E., b. Llanelidan, 73248, Pte., k. in a., F., 28/11/17.

DAVIES, J. R., b. Aberystwyth, 8546, Pte., k. in a., F., 15/3/16.

DAVIES, J. T., b. Machynlleth, 73249, Pte., d. of w., F., 25/4/18.

DAVIES, J. W., b. Llangoed, 61072, Pte., k. in a., F., 20/1/18.

DAVIES, J. W., b. Smethwick, 11980, L/Sgt., k. in a., F., 23/4/17.

DAVIES, M., b. Llandudno, 61350, Pte., k. in a., F., 28/11/17.

DAVIES, O. G. W., b. Shrewsbury, 93642, L/Cpl., k. in a., F., 3/11/18.

DAVIES, P., b. Sheffield, 17014, Pte., k. in a., F., 5/2/16.

DAVIES, R. B., b. Blaenau Festiniog, 61200, Pte., k. in a., F., 23/8/18.

DAVIES, T., b. Llanberis, 11024, Pte., k. in a., F., 7/11/14.

DAVIES, T. J., b. Tylorstown, 4474, Pte., k. in a., F., 22/6/16.

DAVIES, T. J., b. Rhiwlas, 18036, Pte., k. in a., F., 23/8/18.

DAVIES, T. W., b. Liverpool, 10364, Pte., d. of w., F., 8/4/16.

DAVIES, W., b. Ystradgodwy, 5540, Pte., k. in a., F., 27/5/17, M.M.

DAVIES, W., b. Gwersyllt, 16903, Pte., k. in a., F., 21/5/16.

DAVIES, W., b. Penywain, 19897, Pte., k. in a., F., 26/9/17.

DAVIES, W., b. Llandudno, 26208, Pte., d. of w., F., 3/8/17.

DAVIES, W., b. Llanfigan, 37119, L/Cpl., k. in a., F., 22/6/16.

DAVIES, W., b. Cwmbychan, 39991, Pte., k. in a., F., 26/9/17.

DAVIES, W., b. Llanegryn, 61189, Pte., k. in a., F., 18/10/18.

DAVIES, W. J., b. Abercarn, 11200, Pte., k. in a., F., 26/8/18.

DAVIES, W. K., b. Wrexham, 200385, Pte., k. in a., F., 27/5/17.

DAVIS, T., b. Birmingham, 6749, Pte., d. of w., F., 17/5/15.

DAVISON, A., b. Stoke-on-Trent, 29211, Pte., k. in a., F., 3/5/18.

DAWSON, A., b. Nelson, 31467, Pte., k. in a., F., 7/11/16.

DEAN, S., b. Warrington, 8338, Pte., k. in a., F., 25/9/15.

DEAN, S., b. Mold, 39026, Pte., k. in a., F., 27/5/17.

DEARN, W., b. Smethwick, 7679, A/Sgt., k. in a., F., 11/1/15.

DEEMINGS, G., b. Atherstone, 9542, Pte., k. in a., F., 22/6/16.

DERRY, H., b. Burntwood, 36329, Pte., k. in a., F., 22/6/16.

DICKENSON, J., b. Leek, 23794, Pte., k. in a., F., 20/7/16.

DIKE, F., b. Trowbridge, 10606, Pte., k. in a., F., 30/10/14.

DOLLIN, W. P., b. Bristol, 88762, Pte., k. in a., F., 27/10/18.

DOLMAN, A., b. Shrewsbury, 8181, Pte., k. in a., F., 25/9/15.

DONEGAN, T., b. Clonmel, Tipperary, 33254, Pte., d., Home, 20/3/18.

DOOLEY, A., b. Cerney, 3976, L/Cpl., k. in a., F., 21/8/16.

DOUBLEDAY, J., b. Ardwick, 20631, Pte., k. in a., F., 4/11/18.

DOUGLAS, G., b. Kidderminster, 9618, Pte., d. of w., F., 4/11/14.

DOWNES, J., b. Whitchurch, 10340, Cpl., k. in a., F., 18/7/16.

DOYLE, W., b. Manchester, 29136, Pte., d. of w., F., 14/7/18.

DRAPER, H. S., b. Kingsthorpe, 202318, Pte., k. in a., F., 27/5/17.

DRINKWATER, I. C., b. Cardiff, 235365, Sgt., k. in a., F., 28/11/17.

DRISCOLL, E., b. Cardiff, 39579, Pte., k. in a., F., 23/4/16.

DULEY, A., b. Aston, 11147, Pte., k. in a., F., 20/7/16.

DUNNE, B., b. Liverpool, 7800, L/Cpl., d. of w., F., 11/1/15.

DYSON, A., b. Sheffield, 56254, Pte., k. in a., F., 19/5/18.

EARNSHAW, T., b. Sheffield, 31052, L/Cpl., k. in a., F., 25/4/16.

EATON, J., b. Llandyssil, 55197, Pte., d. of w., F., 25/4/17.

EBBRELL, T., b. Rockferry, 56240, Pte., k. in a., F., 26/9/17.

EDGE, E. G., b. Llangeinor, 20660, L/Cpl., k. in a., F., 1/9/18.

EDMONDS, J., b. Birmingham, 9368, Pte., k. in a., F., 8/11/14.

EDMUNDS, J. S., b. Pontypridd, 56677, Pte., k. in a., F., 25/11/17.

EDMUNDSON, J., b. Burnley, 70159, Pte., k. in a., F., 21/8/18.

EDSON, G., b. Pinxton, 19624, Pte., k. in a., F., 22/6/16.

EDWARDS, E., b. Llanfyllin, 33434, L/Cpl., k. in a., F., 17/5/16.

EDWARDS, E., b. Hanley, 36744, Pte., k. in a., F., 5/11/16.

EDWARDS, E., b. Merthyr, 19797, Pte., d. of w., F., 23/1/16.

EDWARDS, E. E., b. Llanycil, 4838, Sgt., d., F., 18/5/15.

EDWARDS, F., b. St. Asaph, 12233, Pte., d., F., 14/12/14.

EDWARDS, G., b. Llanelidan, 89445, Pte., k. in a., F., 18/10/18.

EDWARDS, G. O., e. Liverpool, 36863, Pte., k. in a., F., 17/5/16.

EDWARDS, H. R., b. Llandysilio, 55609, Pte., k. in a., F., 21/5/17.

EDWARDS, J., b. Penmaenmawr, 8998, Pte., k. in a., F., 25/9/15.

EDWARDS, R. J., b. Lixwm, 73721, Pte., k. in a., F., 1/9/18.

EDWARDS, W., b. Carmarthen, 5484, Pte., k. in a., F., 22/6/16.

EDWARDS, W., b. Ffynnongroew, 39993, Pte., k. in a., F., 13/10/17.

EDWARDS, W. J., b. Penrhos, 38150, Pte., k. in a., F., 22/8/16.

EDWIN, T., b. Birmingham, 6240, Sgt., k. in a., F., 13/6/15.

ELCOCKS, R., b. Wellington, Salop, 7772, Pte., d. of w., Home, 26/6/15.

ELKS, G. H., b. Burton-on-Trent, 18940, Pte., d. of w., F., 19/5/18.

ELLIOTT, G., b. Cwmcarn, 17721, Pte., d. of w., F., 1/1/17.

ELLIOTT, S., b. Trinity, Blackburn, 8309, L/Sgt., d. of w., Home, 18/9/16, M.M.

ELLIS, D. T., b. Llanfair-caereinion, 55193, Pte., d. of w., F., 11/10/17.

ELLIS, T. J., e. Treflach, 55192, Pte., d., F., 22/2/17.

ELSTON, J., b. Seacombe, 6913, Pte., k. in a., F., 23/5/15.

EMANUEL, D., b. Briton Ferry, 16679, L/Cpl., k. in a., F., 25/9/15.

ENSOR, H., b. Stratford-on-Avon, 9025, Pte., k. in a., F., 22/6/16.

ESSEX, A. E., b. Birmingham, 8067, Pte., d. of w., F., 4/11/14.

EVANS, A., b. Mardy, 5429, Pte., k. in a., F., 23/4/17.

EVANS, A. M., b. Manchester, 29659, Pte., k. in a., F., 26/9/17.

EVANS, D., b. Tongwynlais, 20614, Pte., k. in a., F., 24/4/18.

EVANS, E., b. Birmingham, 6828, Pte., d., F., 23/10/14.

EVANS, E., b. Rhosddu, 31815, Pte., k. in a., F., 20/7/16.

EVANS, E., b. Rhydymain, 291469, Pte., k. in a., F., 27/5/17.

EVANS, E. D., b. Oswestry, 292592, Pte., k. in a., F., 27/5/17.

EVANS, E. J., b. Llangynog, 6360, Pte., k. in a., F., 22/6/16.

EVANS, F., e. Whitchurch, Salop, 55195, Pte., k. in a., F., 23/4/17.

EVANS, F. H., b. Smethwick, 9644, Pte., d. of w., F., 26/7/16, M.M.

EVANS, H., b. Birmingham, 9662, Sgt., d. of w., F., 5/11/16.

EVANS, H., b. Llanwnnog, 55201, Pte., k. in a., F., 23/4/17.

EVANS, J., b. Newcastle, Stafford, 7065, Cpl., k. in a., F., 22/6/16.

EVANS, J., e. Wrexham, 55608, Pte., k. in a., F., 23/4/17.

EVANS, J., b. Walkden, 59495, Pte., k. in a., F., 26/9/17.

EVANS, J., b. Llandilo, 9132, Pte., d. of w., F., 29/1/16.

EVANS, J., e. Welshpool, 55202, Pte., k. in a., F., 30/8/18.

EVANS, J. A., b. Carrog, 56181, Pte., d. of w., Home, 2/10/18.

EVANS, J. G., b. Newtown, 55200, L/Cpl., k. in a., F., 25/11/17.

EVANS, J. T., b. Llandilo, 29508, L/Sgt., d. of w., F., 7/11/16.

EVANS, L., b. Bangor, 28998, Pte., k. in a., F., 12/7/18.

EVANS, L., b. Wrexham, 39061, Pte., k. in a., F., 27/10/16.

EVANS, R., b. Welshpool, 54117, Pte., k. in a., F., 27/5/17.

EVANS, R., e. Ruabon, 200980, Pte., k. in a., F., 27/5/17.

EVANS, R. C. W., b. Nantgaredig, 68854, Pte., d. of w., F., 3/12/18.

EVANS, R. H., b. Llandwrog, 60917, Pte., k. in a., F., 26/9/17.

EVANS, W., b. Oswestry, 10114, Pte., k. in a., F., 25/9/15.

EVANS, W., b. Oswestry, 66315, Pte., k. in a., F., 22/8/17.

EVANS, W., b. Mold, 6009, Pte., k. in a., F., 7/9/15.

EVANS, W., b. Atherstone, 9610, Pte., k. in a., F., 16/2/16.

EVANS, W., e. Hereford, 55206, Pte., k. in a., F., 23/4/17.

EVASON, J., b. Liverpool, 73361, Pte., k. in a., F., 24/4/18.

EYTON, J. J., b. Wrexham, 36130, Pte., k. in a., F., 26/9/17.

FACER, J., b. Leicester, 56232, Pte., k. in a., F., 27/5/17.

FAIRBURN, J. R. W., b. Limehouse, 26840, Pte., d., F., 28/12/16.

FARR, T., e. Llandudno, 55208, Pte., k. in a., F., 23/4/17.

FARRELL, D., b. Coventry, 8799, Pte., k. in a., F., 15/7/16.

FARRELL, J., b. Chester, 7969, Pte., k. in a., F., 25/10/14.

FAULKNER, F. T., b. Cheltenham, 6395, Pte., k. in a., F., 22/6/16.

FAULKNER, J., b. Liverpool, 73377, Pte., d. of w., F., 22/4/18.

FEBER, W., b. Bacup, 201488, Pte., d. of w., F., 27/9/17.

FERRINGTON, A. E., b. Crewe, 202757, Pte., k. in a., F., 28/11/17.

FIDLER, J. W., e. Poulton, Ches., 55612, Pte., k. in a., F., 8/10/18.

FIELD, C., b. Birmingham, 8114, Pte., k. in a., F., 14/11/14.

FIRTH, E., b. Portsmouth, 9114, Pte., k. in a., F., 25/9/15.

FITTON, J. T., b. Haslingden, 23964, Pte., k. in a., F., 16/9/16.

FLINT, G., b. Birmingham, 36665, Pte., k. in a., F., 27/5/17.

FOOTE, W., b. Roath, 9247, L/Sgt., k. in a., F., 2/1/16.

FORD, R. H., b. Manchester, 36553, Pte., k. in a., F., 19/8/16.

FOULKES, T., b. Conway, 73263, Pte., k. in a., F., 25/4/18.

FOWLER, E. J., b. Bradford, 48871, Pte., k. in a., F., 23/4/17.

FOWLER, J., b. Blackburn, 73363, Pte., k. in a., F., 31/8/18.

FOWLER, R. A., b. Welton, 56546, Pte., k. in a., F., 26/8/18.

FOX, H., b. Buckley, 89364, Pte., k. in a., F., 27/10/18.

FOX, H., b. Birmingham, 10424, L/Cpl., d. of w., F., 24/4/17.

FOX, R., b. Cheltenham, 8891, Pte., d. of w., F., 30/11/17.

FRADLEY, J., b. Birmingham, 36417, Pte., k. in a., F., 22/6/16.

FRANCIS, W., b. Tunstall, 20580, Sgt., k. in a., F., 30/1/17.

FRENCH, J., b. St. Helens, 56204, L/Sgt., k. in a., F., 25/11/17.

FULLWOOD, J. B., b. Wolverhampton, 29991, Pte., k. in a., F., 3/9/18.

FURZER, F. T., b. London, 26515, Pte., d. of w., F., 28/10/16.

GANNON, M. P., b. Newcastle, Staffs, 28336, Pte., d. of w., F., 26/8/18.

GARDNER, A. E., b. Blackfriars, 28129, Pte., k. in a., F., 8/10/18.

GARRATT, J. E., b. Birmingham, 9404, L/Cpl., k. in a., F., 16/5/15.

GARTH, A., b. Shaw, Lancs., 73415, Pte., k. in a., F., 1/9/18.

GARTH, A. E., b. Salop, 41759, Pte., k. in a., F., 27/5/17.

GAZEY, G., b. Birmingham, 36625, Pte., k. in a., F., 20/6/16.

GEORGE, A. E., b. Tutbury, 8649, Pte., k. in a., F., 10/3/15.

GILLIBRAND, T., b. Osbaldeston, 73508, Pte., d. of w., F., 21/6/18.

GILLIGAN, R. T., b. Birmingham, 6788, Pte., k. in a., F., 16/5/15.

GLEEDE, K. C., b. King's Stanley, 73366, Cpl., k. in a., F., 16/10/18.

GLOVER, J., b. Malling, 73360, Pte., k. in a., F., 28/11/17.

GOLBY, J. F., b. Birmingham, 9699, L/Cpl., k. in a., F., 20/7/16.

GOLLEDGE, J. D., b. Trealaw, 4593, L/Cpl., d. of w., F., 30/8/16.

GORMAN, A. W., b. Plymouth, 9749, L/Sgt., k. in a., F., 27/5/17.

GORMAN, F. L., b. Ballymot, Sligo, 55572, Pte., d., F., 21/4/18.

GOUGH, A., b. Ledbury North, 55214, Pte., k. in a., F., 22/5/17.

GOZZARD, B., b. Hammerwich, 14042, Pte., d. of w., F., 20/5/15.

GRAHAM, W., b. Southampton, 38819, Pte., d., F., 12/11/16.

GRAINGER, W., b. Shalton, 8380, Cpl., k. in a., F., 5/2/16.

GRAY, C. W., b. Brixton, 27936, Sgt., k. in a., F., 4/11/18, M.M.

GRAY, J., b. Cardiff, 73273, Pte., k. in a., F., 8/10/18.

GRAY, R. I., b. Cardiff, 73266, Pte., k. in a., F., 28/11/17.

GRAY, S., b. Birmingham, 6142, Pte., k. in a., F., 25/9/15.

GREEN, G., b. Worplesdon, 8922, Pte., k. in a., F., 14/9/15.

GREENHALGH, T. H., b. Bolton, 19742, Pte., k. in a., F., 25/9/15.

GREGORY, E., b. Cardigan, 73271, Pte., k. in a., F., 28/11/17.

GRIFFITHS, G. E., b. Llanllechid, 18380, Pte., k. in a., F., 27/5/17.

GRIFFITHS, J., b. Llechryd, 73269, Pte., k. in a., F., 2/7/18.

GRIFFITHS, J. A., e. Penygroes, 73265, Pte., k. in a., F., 28/11/17.

GRIFFITHS, R., b. Conway, 73270, Pte., k. in a., F., 28/11/17.

GRIFFITHS, T., e. Carnarvon, 55035, Pte., k. in a., F., 23/4/17.

GRIFFITHS, W., b. Pembroke, 73267, Pte., k. in a., F., 28/11/17.

GRIFFITHS, W., e. Llanberis, 44195, Pte., k. in a., F., 15/5/17.

GRIFFITHS, W. J., b. Llanrwst, 5220, Pte., k. in a., F., 25/9/15.

GRIGG, T. W., b. Wednesbury, 6803, Pte., k. in a., F., 12/12/14.

GRIMMETT, T., b. Birmingham, 8917, Pte., k. in a., F., 21/1/16.

GRISTOCK, F., e. Cardiff, 54083, Pte., d. of w., F., 5/6/17.

GROCOTT, F., b. Market Drayton, 7797, Pte., k. in a., F., 1/11/14.

GUEST, I., b. Castleford, 57158, Pte., k. in a., F., 21/6/18, M.M.

HALCROW, G. W., b. Southport, 75421, Pte., k. in a., F., 1/9/18.

HALL, C., b. Froghall, 37351, Pte., k. in a., F., 20/7/16.

HALL, T., b. Oldham, 24215, L/Cpl., k. in a., F., 26/8/18.

HALL, W. T., e. Welshpool, 55228, Pte., k. in a., F., 30/11/17.

HALLMARK, D., b. Winsford, 39849, Pte., k. in a., F., 23/4/17.

HAM, W., b. Cardiff, 11238, Pte., k. in a., F., 26/10/14.

HAMER, F. G., e. Downton, 55226, Pte., k. in a., F., 23/4/17.

HAMPSON, A., b. St. Helens, 56242, Pte., k. in a., F., 27/5/17.

HAMPSON, W., b. Liverpool, 7108, Pte., d., Home, 10/12/14.

HANCOCK, J., b. Swansea, 6586, L/Cpl., k. in a., F., 20/7/16.

HAND, S., b. Birmingham, 9155, Pte., d., F., 11/7/15.

HANDLEY, J., b. Salford, 37329, L/Cpl., k. in a., F., 5/11/16.

HANDLEY, R., b. Seaforth, 73402, Pte., k. in a., F., 1/12/17.

HANDLEY, S., b. Gloucester, 6636, L/Sgt., k. in a., F., 6/11/14.

HANNABY, R., b. Conway, 9587, L/Cpl., k. in a., F., 25/9/15.

HARDESS, A., b. Cardiff, 75154, Pte., d. of w., F., 13/9/18.

HARE, H., b. Cardiff, 37561, Pte., k. in a., F., 23/4/17.

HARPER, H. J., b. Birmingham, 11234, L/Cpl., d. of w., F., 31/8/18.

HARRIS, A., b. Wolverhampton, 6930, Pte., k. in a., F., 25/9/15.

HARRIS, A. J., b. Deolali, India, 11291, Sgt., d., F., 15/6/18.

HARRIS, C. A., b. Birmingham, 9440, Pte., k. in a., F., 19/5/18.

HARRIS, D., b. Willenhall, 36925, L/Cpl., k. in a., F., 23/4/17.

HARRIS, J. H., b. Neath, 37070, Pte., d., F., 23/12/16.

HARRISON, A. V., b. Timarn, New Zealand, 23445, Pte., d. of w., F., 2/9/18.

HARRISON, T., b. Wigan, 73567, Pte., d. of w., F., 5/12/18.

HART, W. E., b. Rainford, 73398, Pte., d. of w., F., 25/4/18.

HARTLEY, E., b. Hope, Flint, 33296, Pte., k. in a., F., 20/7/16.

HARTLEY, T., e. Ashton-under-Lyne, 242859, Pte., d. of w., F., 2/9/18.

HARVEY, A., b. West Derby, 5974, Pte., k. in a., F., 28/2/15.

HARVEY, A. V., b. Birmingham, 10329, Sgt., k. in a., F., 25/9/15.

HATELY, E. P., b. Homerton, 35471, Cpl., k. in a., F., 12/7/18.

HAWKINS, B., b. Sheffield, 12121, Pte., k. in a., F., 27/5/17.

HAWORTH, W. C., b. Blackburn, 73397, Pte., k. in a., F., 28/11/17.

HAYCOCKS, J., b. Wrexham, 8149, Pte., d. of w., F., 10/6/15.

HAYDEN, T., b. Kilbride, Co. Wicklow, 38565, Pte., k. in a., F., 19/8/16.

HAYES, W. J., b. Tyrone, 56536, Pte., k. in a., F., 26/9/17.

HEALD, W. G., b. Leeds, 29612, L/Cpl., k. in a., F., 23/4/17.

HEALEY, E., b. Reading, 8725, L/Cpl., k. in a., F., 26/10/14.

HEARD, A. E., b. Birmingham, 10622, Pte., k. in a., F., 21/5/16.

HEATH, A. H., b. Hockley, 8630, Pte., k. in a., F., 22/6/16.

HEATH, G., b. Swindon, 38563, Pte., k. in a., F., 5/11/16.

HEATH, W. E., b. Bolton, 19750, Pte., k. in a., F., 20/7/16.

HEATON, R., b. Miles Platting, 56183, Pte., k. in a., F., 27/6/17.

HELLYN, F., b. Wrexham, 5309, L/Cpl., k. in a., F., 5/11/16.

HENNEY, F., b. Atherstone, 37117, Pte., k. in a., F., 6/7/16.

HERBERT, G. W., b. London, 35366, Pte., k. in a., F., 20/8/16.

HERD, R. E., b. Oxford, 60638, Pte., k. in a., F., 26/9/17.

HERON, J., b. Liverpool, 73405, Pte., k. in a., F., 22/4/18.

HEYS, F., b. Blackburn, 73394, Pte., k. in a., F., 29/11/17.

HICKINSON, St. A., b. Bamford, 56560, Pte., k. in a., F., 26/9/17.

HIGGIN, W. H. H., b. Rochdale, 9031, Pte., d., Home, 11/5/15.

HIGGINS, E., b. Cardiff, 24654, Pte., k. in a., F., 15/11/15.

HIGGINS, G., b. Birmingham, 8784, Pte., k. in a., F., 22/10/14.

HIGGINS, J., b. Glasgow, 36283, Pte., d. of w., F., 7/7/16.

HIGHAM, J., e. Manchester, 28949, Pte., k. in a., F., 27/5/17.

HIGSON, H., b. Nelson, 201805, Pte., k. in a., F., 1/9/18.

HILL, F. J., b. Westbury-on-Tryn, 8963, Pte., k. in a., F., 4/11/14.

HILL, T., b. Birmingham, 8357, Pte., k. in a., F., 30/1/15.

HILTON, C., b. Chequerbent, 38761, Pte., k. in a., F., 20/8/16.

HILTON, F., b. Leigh, 29243, L/Cpl., d. of w., F., 25/4/18.

HINKS, F., b. Birmingham, 11233, Sgt., k. in a., F., 27/10/18.

HOBRIN, J. F., b. London, 22947, Pte., d. of w., F., 8/10/17.

HODGES, H., b. Ledbury, 47390, Pte., d. of w., F., 6/5/18.

HODGES, H. G. W., b. Southam, 36922, L/Cpl., k. in a., F., 20/7/16.

HOGBEN, W. W., b. Sandgate, 11053, L/Sgt., d. of w., Home, 15/10/17, D.C.M.

HOLDEN, A., b. Haslington, 66586, Pte., k. in a., F., 25/11/17.

HOLDSWORTH, J., b. Burnley, 201986, Pte., k. in a., F., 28/11/17.

HOLLINGSWORTH, T. A., b. London, 27073, L/Cpl., k. in a., F., 23/4/17.

HOLT, H., b. Bolton, 201785, Pte., d. of w., F., 7/11/17.

HOLT, W., b. Manchester, 73390, Pte., k. in a., F., 24/8/18.

HONEYBOURNE, T., b. Birmingham, 11076, Pte., k. in a., F., 20/6/15.

HOOPER, F. H., b. Penarth, 73277, Pte., d. of w., F., 30/11/17.

HOPE, J., b. Cubbington, 7696, Pte., k. in a., F., 25/9/15.

HOPKINS, A. O., b. Pontypool, 37570, Pte., d. of w., Home, 16/4/17.

HOPKINS, W., b. Woollos, 6410, Pte., k. in a., F., 5/2/16.

HOPLEY, J. T., b. Tilston, 36673, Pte., k. in a., F., 22/6/16.

HOSKINS, A., b. Tunstall, 23941, Pte., k. in a., F., 23/4/17.

HOWE, A., b. St. Athan, 73742, Pte., d. of w., F., 16/7/18.

HOWELLS, W. J., b. Merthyr Tydfil, 54086, Pte., k. in a., F., 26/9/17.

HUGHES, D., b. Llandecwyn, 20297, Pte., k. in a., F., 4/11/18.

HUGHES, D., e. Wanstead, 55223, Pte., d. of w., F., 28/9/17.

HUGHES, E., b. Higher Tranmere,

8398, Cpl., k. in a., F., 22/6/16.

HUGHES, E. W., b. Cardiff, 235371, Pte., k. in a., F., 26/9/17.

HUGHES, G. L., b. Corwen, 68452, Pte., k. in a., F., 26/9/17.

HUGHES, H., e. Wrexham, 54596, L/Cpl., k. in a., F., 27/5/17.

HUGHES, H., b. Birkenhead, 16924, Pte., k. in a., F., 27/5/17.

HUGHES, J., b. Bodorgan, 55009, L/Cpl., k. in a., F., 25/8/18.

HUGHES, J., e. Wrexham, 200911, Pte., k. in a., F., 27/5/17.

HUGHES, J. E., b. Newton Heath, 36677, Pte., d. of w., F., 8/11/16.

HUGHES, P., b. Merthyr, 8669, Pte., d. of w., F., 30/4/15.

HUGHES, R., b. Maentwrog, 8849, Pte., k. in a., F., 22/8/16.

HUGHES, T., b. Wrexham, 9094, Pte., k. in a., F., 26/1/15.

HUGHES, T., b. Worthen, 9836, Sgt., k. in a., F., 23/4/17, D.C.M., M.M.

HUGHES, T., b. Buckley, 40470, Pte., k. in a., F., 19/8/16.

HUGHES, W., b. Capel Curig, 54616, Pte., d., F., 22/4/17.

HUGHES, W. H., b. Llandrog, 40629, Pte., k. in a., F., 26/10/16.

HUGHES, W. M., b. Llanddeiniolen, 44185, Pte., k. in a., F., 26/9/17.

HUGHES, W. O., b. Liverpool, 73408, Pte., d. of w., F., 27/8/18.

HUGHES, W. R., b. Llanglydwen, 10117, Pte., k. in a., F., 22/6/16.

HULBERT, T., b. Bristol, 6773, Pte., k. in a., F., 16/5/15.

HUMPHREY, J. T., b. Llandwrog, 54559, Pte., k. in a., F., 8/3/17.

HUMPHREYS, E. B., b. Machynlleth, 73279, Pte., k. in a., F., 28/11/17.

HUMPHREYS, W., b. Llanfihangel, 61030, L/Cpl., k. in a., F., 13/9/18.

HUNSTONE, J., b. Hulme, 64007, Pte., k. in a., F., 1/9/18.

HUNT, A., b. Warrington, 202547, Pte., k. in a., F., 26/9/17.

HUNT, A., b. Bristol, 9194, Pte., d., Home, 26/5/15.

HURST, R. W., b. Salford, 73416, Pte., k. in a., F., 24/4/18.

HUTCHINS, A., b. Marlborough, 5511, Pte., k. in a., F., 22/6/16.

IBBERSON, A., b. Worsboro' Dale, 56235, Pte., k. in a., F., 27/5/17.

IBBOTSON, C., b. Ashton-under-Lyne, 8391, Sgt., k. in a., F., 28/11/17, M.M.

INGHAM, G., b. Newcastle, Staffs,

56551, Pte., k. in a., F., 26/9/17.

INGHAM, J., b. Stalybridge, 46367, Pte., k. in a., F., 1/7/18.

ISON, J., b. Walsall, 9732, Pte., d. of w., F., 17/9/15.

JACKSON, H., b. Baguley, 56247, Pte., k. in a., F., 27/5/17.

JAMES, B., b. Chepstow, 5575, Pte., k. in a., F., 19/4/16.

JAMES, E. T., b. London, 17068, L/Cpl., k. in a., F., 24/9/17.

JAMES, W., e. Ogmore Vale, 89172, Pte., k. in a., F., 23/10/18.

JAMES, W. J., b. Tylorstown, Glam., 56730, Pte., d. of w., F., 1/12/17.

JANKINSON, J., b. Chester, 10703, Pte., k. in a., F., 9/5/15.

JARMAN, E. G., b. London, 22841, Pte., d. of w., F., 2/5/17.

JARVIS, T., e. Welshpool, 55234, L/Cpl., k. in a., F., 28/11/17.

JENKINS, A. E., b. Cheltenham, 8813, Pte., k. in a., F., 23/4/17, M.M.

JENKINS, D. W., b. Aberystwyth, 11289, Pte., k. in a., F., 4/7/16.

JENKINS, G., b. Llantrisant, 7242, Pte., k. in a., F., 25/10/14.

JOHN, D., e. Swansea, 56732, Pte., d. of w., F., 17/3/18.

JOHNSON, C. E., b. Overton, 10500, Pte., k. in a., F., 26/10/14.

JOHNSON, C., b. Crewe, 46465, L/Cpl., k. in a., F., 20/8/17.

JOHNSTON, T., b. Liverpool, 8823, Pte., k. in a., F., 20/3/15.

JOHNSTON, W., b. Hyde, 24343, Pte., k. in a., F., 6/7/16.

JONES, A., b. Bwlchgwyn, 10319, Pte., d., F., 11/7/15.

JONES, A., b. Aldershot, 8390, Pte., k. in a., F., 25/9/15.

JONES, A. L., b. Liverpool, 202851, L/Sgt. d. of w., F., 2/7/18.

JONES, A. T., b. Llanasa, 55036, Pte., k. in a., F., 19/12/16.

JONES, B. L., b. Colwyn Bay, 6048, Pte., k. in a., F., 20/7/16.

JONES, D., e. Holywell, 55013, Pte., k. in a., F., 23/4/17.

JONES, D., e. Dolgelly, 25546, Pte., d., F., 7/2/17.

JONES, D., b. Llanddewiber, 40302, Pte., k. in a., F., 19/8/16.

JONES, D. E., b. Llanemolen, 40307, Pte., d., F., 22/9/16.

JONES, D. G., b. Llanechel, 60946, Pte., k. in a., F., 26/9/17.

JONES, D. H., b. Margam, 235372, Pte., k. in a., F., 25/4/18.

JONES, D. T., b. Llanuwchllyn, 61078, Pte., k. in a., F., 8/1/18.

JONES, E., b. Tregeiriog, 39148, Pte., k. in a., F., 3/11/16.

JONES, E., b. Colwyn Bay, 6637, Pte., d., F. 21/4/18.

JONES, E., b. Bangor, 204091, Pte., k. in a., F., 1/9/18.

JONES, E., e. Wrexham, 54056, Pte., k. in a., F., 27/10/16.

JONES, E., b. Aberaman, 77354, Pte., k. in a., F., 24/8/18.

JONES, E. G., b. Pwllheli, 11209, Sgt., d., F., 22/2/17, M.M.

JONES, E. H., b. Eglwys, 37908, Pte., k. in a., F., 21/8/16.

JONES, E. M., b. Llan-fair-Caereinion, 37105, Pte., k. in a., F., 19/8/16.

JONES, E. M., b. Bridgend, 8556, Pte., k. in a., F., 22/6/16.

JONES, E. O., e. Willesden Green, 201385, Pte., k. in a., F., 27/5/17.

JONES, E. O., b. Waenfawr, 68477, Pte., k. in a., F., 9/1/18.

JONES, E. T., e. London, 34785, Pte., k. in a., F., 13/9/18.

JONES, E. W., b. Ellesmere, 11333, Cpl., d., F., 6/7/16, M.M.

JONES, E. W., b. Bala, 39192, Pte., d. of w., Home, 12/1/17.

JONES, G. E., b. Waenfawr, 40309, Pte., d. of w., F., 28/10/16.

JONES, G. J., b. Birkenhead, 8945, Cpl., k. in a., F., 6/11/14.

JONES, H., b. Llanelian, 33101, Pte., k. in a., F., 16/7/16.

JONES, H., b. Llanfwrog, 8481, Pte., d., F., 1/3/15.

JONES, H., b. Llanfair, P.G., 10168, Pte., k. in a., F., 16/9/15.

JONES, H., b. Barnsley, 19430, Cpl., k. in a., F., 26/9/17.

JONES, H., b. Shotton, 54564, Pte., k. in a., F., 26/9/17.

JONES, H. J., b. Bristol, 70198, Pte., k. in a., F., 1/9/18.

JONES, I., b. Llanrwst, 9061, Pte., k. in a., F., 25/9/15.

JONES, I. J., b. Tirbach, 37532, Pte., k. in a., F., 3/9/18.

JONES, J., b. Llanfihangel, 54128, Pte., k. in a., F., 5/11/16.

JONES, J., b. Llandulas, 31230, Pte., k. in a., F., 30/10/16.

JONES, J., b. Llanddoget, 89551, Pte., d. of w., F., 16/10/18.

JONES, J., e. Llanelly, 235388, Pte., k. in a., F., 1/9/18.

JONES, J., b. Llanymynech, 17036, L/Cpl., k. in a., F., 20/7/16.

JONES, J., b. Rhuddlan, 54599, Pte., d. of w., F., 23/5/17.

JONES, J. E., b. Llandysilio, 37826, L/Cpl., k. in a., F., 5/11/16.

JONES, J. H., b. London, 17145, L/Cpl., d. of w., F., 8/3/17.

JONES, J. H., b. Liverpool, 68487, Pte., k. in a., F., 1/9/18.

JONES, J. M., b. Llandegai, 37814, Pte., k. in a., F., 22/8/16.

JONES, J. P., b. Dolwyddelen,

70083, Pte., k. in a., F., 1/9/18.

JONES, J. R., b. Tregaron, 27998, Pte., k. in a., F., 27/5/17.

JONES, J. T., b. Abergele, Denbigh, 8252, Pte., d. of w., F., 31/10/14.

JONES, J. T., b. Llanfihangel, 55230, Pte., k. in a., F., 27/5/17.

JONES, M. L., b. Tonypandy, 18535, Pte., k. in a., F., 5/11/16.

JONES, O., b. Festiniog, 20224, Pte., k. in a., F., 8/8/16.

JONES, R., b. Coedpoeth, 33094, Pte., k. in a., F., 27/5/17.

JONES, R., b. Llanllyfni, 89357, Pte., k. in a., F., 16/10/18.

JONES, R., b. Mostyn, 8443, Pte., k. in a., F., 25/9/15.

JONES, R., b. Bodorgan, 266622, Pte., k. in a., F., 27/5/17.

JONES, R. C., b. Willesden, 34857, Cpl., d. of w., F., 8/11/16.

JONES, R. E., e. Carnarvon, 55012, Pte., k. in a., F., 12/7/18.

JONES, R. H., b. Waenfawr, 40337, Pte., k. in a., F., 27/5/17.

JONES, R. J., b. Gellifor, 29849, Pte., k. in a., F., 20/8/16.

JONES, R. S., b. Llangar, 28269, Pte., d. of w., F., 20/9/18.

JONES, R. T., b. Llansaintffraid, 75923, Pte., k. in a., F., 18/10/18.

JONES, T., b. Marchwell, 8159, Pte., d. of w., F., 12/11/14.

JONES, T., b. Rhyl, 39844, Pte., k. in a., F., 26/9/17.

JONES, T., b. Llanbister, 55244, Pte., k. in a., F., 24/9/17.

JONES, T., b. Penygroes, 56248, Pte., k. in a., F., 27/5/17.

JONES, T., b. Criccieth, 266595, Pte., d., F., 1/10/17.

JONES, T. D., b. Llandefalle, 55251, Pte., k. in a., F., 23/4/17.

JONES, T. G., b. Swansea, 235387, Pte., k. in a., F., 28/11/17.

JONES, T. I., b. Swansea, 73286, Pte., k. in a., F., 12/9/18.

JONES, T. J., b. Llangammarch, 73285, Pte., k. in a., F., 28/11/17.

JONES, T. P., b. Llysfaen, 87014, Pte., k. in a., F., 13/9/18.

JONES, W., b. Cwmavon, 5464, Pte., k. in a., F., 27/5/17.

JONES, W., b. Bodedern, 6487, Pte., k. in a., F., 16/5/15.

JONES, W., b. Mochdre, 43853, Pte., k. in a., F., 27/5/17.

JONES, W., e. Llanfyllin, 55239, Pte., d. of w., F., 19/10/17.

JONES, W., e. Welshpool, 55256, Pte., k. in a., F., 23/4/17.

JONES, W., e. Barrow, 93756, Pte., k. in a., F., 8/10/18.

JONES, W. E., b. Liverpool, 11038, Pte., k. in a., F., 12/3/15.

JONES, W. G., b. Gwern-cae-

Athraw, 36666, Pte., k. in a.,
F., 20/7/16.

JONES, W. G., b. Pistill, 61097,
Pte., d., Home, 3/3/18.

JONES, W. H., b. Ladywood,
11179, Pte., d. of w., F.,
20/11/15.

JONES, W. P., b. Denbigh, 29653,
Pte., d. of w., F., 27/4/17.

KEEPAX, W., b. Birmingham,
10172, Pte., k. in a., F.,
26/10/14.

KELLY, J., b. Liverpool, 6846,
A/Cpl., k. in a., F., 4/2/15.

KELLY, R., b. Blaengarw, 37550,
Pte., k. in a., F., 27/5/17.

KEOHAN, W., b. Merthyr, 14853,
Pte., k. in a., F., 13/3/18.

KERSHAW, F. V., b. Manchester,
66302, Pte., d. of w., F.,
25/11/17.

KESPER, C., b. Wrexham, 8372,
Cpl., k. in a., F., 25/10/14.

KILVERT, C., e. Llansantffraid,
Mon., 201039, Pte., k. in a.,
F., 27/5/17.

KING, A. G., b. Steynton, 39646,
Pte., k. in a., F., 27/5/17.

KINGSTON, H., b. Blaengarw,
54095, Pte., k. in a., F.,
5/11/16.

KNIGHT, S., b. Smethwick, 7759,
L/Cpl., k. in a., F., 7/11/14.

KYNASTON, J., b. Dolgelley, 9114,
Pte., k. in a., F., 23/10/14.

LACEY, A., b. Bootle, 8303, Pte.,
d. of w., F., 20/5/16.

LAFFERTY, H., b. Prestbury,
10530, Pte., k. in a., F.,
5/11/14.

LAMPITT, L., b. Birmingham,
11191, Pte., k. in a., F.,
5/4/16.

LANE, J., b. Birmingham, 8817,
Pte., k. in a., F., 24/10/14.

LANGFORD, S., b. Much Wenlock,
8397, Sgt., d. of w., F.,
24/10/14.

LANGLEY, W., b. Mold, 240482,
Sgt., k. in a., F., 19/4/18.

LANGTON, A. E., b. Daventry,
9035, Pte., k. in a., F.,
22/6/16.

LANHAM, G., b. Felstead, 56013,
Pte., k. in a., F., 27/10/18.

LARGE, R. A., b. Southampton,
75682, Pte., d. of w., F.,
21/10/18.

LAURIE, A., b. Birmingham, 8150,
C.S.M., k. in a., F., 23/9/15.

LAWLEY, T., b. West Bromwich,
7741, Pte., k. in a., F.,
28/10/14.

LEACH, G. G., b. Cardiff, 11306,
Pte., k. in a., F., 16/5/15.

LEACH, W., b. Nantwich, 19481,
Pte., k. in a., F., 1/9/18.

LEAKER, E. G., b. Bristol, 9511,
Pte., d. of w., Home, 20/11/14.

LEE, F., b. London, 60244, Pte.,
k. in a., F., 22/6/17.

LEECH, J., b. Shifnal, 7862, Sgt.,
k. in a., F., 29/9/16.

LEECH, J. F., b. Timperley,

201811, Pte., k. in a., F.,
3/9/18.

LEES, H. B., b. Worksop, 9291,
Pte., k. in a., F., 20/7/16,
M.M.

LEES, J. H., b. Macclesfield,
66620, Pte., d. of w., F.,
24/8/18.

LEES, J. W., b. St. George's,
56221, Pte., d. of w., F.,
23/5/17.

LEMARE, W. H., b. Cardiff, 73760,
Pte., d., F., 5/8/18.

LENTON, J., b. Balsall Heath,
5051, Pte., k. in a., F.,
20/7/16.

LEWIS, D., b. Ynysybwl, 11280,
Pte., k. in a., F., 22/6/16.

LEWIS, E., b. Llanelly, 202542,
Pte., d. of w., F., 18/5/18.

LEWIS, E., b. Gwersyllt, 78393,
Pte., d. of w., Home, 24/9/18.

LEWIS, G., b. Llanwono, 14712,
L/Cpl., k. in a., F., 7/3/17.

LEWIS, H., b. Pen-y-Sarn, 24646,
Pte., k. in a., F., 22/4/18.

LEWIS, J., e. Pontypridd, 235389,
Pte., d. of w., F., 22/4/18.

LEWIS, R. J., b. Llangwyllog,
40066, Pte., d. of w., F.,
22/8/16.

LEWIS, W. H., b. Ystrad, 5586,
Pte., d. of w., F., 20/7/16.

LEYSTON, E. T., b. Pontypridd,
56520, Pte., k. in a., F.,
1/9/18.

LINDSAY, E., b. Bermondsey,
56693, Pte., d. of w., F.,
1/2/17.

LLEWELYN, J., b. Cwmavon,
18611, Pte., k. in a., F.,
5/11/16.

LLOYD, A., b. Clunbury, 31068,
L/Cpl., k. in a., F., 26/9/17.

LLOYD, F. C., b. Bristol, 9842,
Pte., k. in a., F., 4/11/14.

LLOYD, J., b. Ystradgynlais,
38216, Pte., k. in a., F.,
19/8/16.

LLOYD, R., b. Llanrug, 87229,
Pte., k. in a., F., 21/10/18.

LLOYD, T., e. Wrexham, 200852,
Pte., d. of w., F., 23/9/17.

LLOYD, T. E., b. Guilsfield, 9950,
Dmr., k. in a., F., 22/6/17.

LLOYD, W., b. Newtown, 54568,
Pte., k. in a., F., 26/9/17.

LLOYD, W. A., b. Stoke, 75424,
Pte., d. of w., 9/5/18.

LLOYD, W. H., b. Caerwys,
89462, Pte., d. of w., F.,
14/10/18.

LONG, J., b. Merthyr, Glam.,
56695, Pte., k. in a., F.,
23/4/17.

LOVATT, J., b. Longton, 6429,
Pte., k. in a., F., 26/7/16.

LOVELL, S., b. Bristol, 9415,
Cpl., k. in a., F., 14/9/15.

LOWE, E., b. Treharris, 11088,
Pte., k. in a., F., 25/10/14.

LOWE, H., b. Stafford, 73431,
Pte., k. in a., F., 25/11/17.

LOWNDES, W., b. Burton, 6332,
Pte., d. of w., F., 2/1/15.

LUCAS, J. B., b. Knighton, 38105,
Pte., k. in a., F., 5/11/16.

LUDLOW, E. T., b. Hampton
Fields, 15698, Pte., d. of w.,
F., 4/11/18.

MACKERNESS, C., b. Halling,
9391, L/Sgt., k. in a., F.,
25/11/17.

MAGGS, H. J., b. Bedminster,
9180, Pte., d. of w., F.,
22/8/16.

MAHONEY, W., b. Bristol, 9510,
Pte., k. in a., F., 22/6/16.

MALLORY, E., b. Kennington,
6648, Sgt., k. in a., F.,
15/3/15.

MALYON, A. H., b. London, 14153,
Pte., k. in a., F., 6/7/16.

MARCHANT, C., e. Edenbridge,
56213, Pte., d. of w., F.,
13/9/18.

MARKE, H., b. London, 8683,
C.S.M., k. in a., F., 23/4/17,
M.M.

MARSH, F., b. Brookthorpe,
54384, Pte., k. in a., F.,
12/9/18.

MASON, C. H., b. Birmingham,
7981, Pte., k. in a., F.,
20/7/16.

MASON, J., b. Willesden, 60556,
L/Cpl., k. in a., F., 1/9/18.

MATTHEWS, G. D., b. Hastings,
9430, Pte., k. in a., F.,
14/9/15.

MATTHEWS, H., b. West Cowes,
11449, Pte., d. of w., F.,
12/7/15.

MATTHEWS, T. E., b. Holywell,
6376, Pte., k. in a., F.,
30/6/15.

MAUNTON, E. T., b. St. Mary's,
2909, Sgt., k. in a., F.,
29/10/14.

MAY, J. E., b. London, 10966,
Dmr., k. in a., F., 2/11/14.

MAYCOCK, H. G., b. London,
235367, Sgt., k. in a., F.,
26/9/17.

MAYNARD, H., b. Littleborough,
77745, Pte., k. in a., F.,
1/9/18.

MAYNAID, R., e. Carmarthen,
202630, Pte., k. in a., F.,
25/8/18.

McCROHON, J. V., b. Birmingham,
9726, A/Sgt., k. in a., F.,
20/7/16.

McCULLOCK, P., b. North Shields,
38273, Pte., d. of w., F.,
6/11/16.

McCUTCHEON, G., b. Shank Hill,
Co. Antrim, 60241, Pte., k. in
a., F., 22/6/17.

McHUGH, H., b. Stockport,
10556, Pte., k. in a., F.,
20/7/16.

McLOUGHLIN, L. T., b. Birkenhead, 12890, Pte., k. in a., F.,
22/6/16.

McNULTY, P., b. Birkenhead,

7602, Pte., k. in a., F., 19/11/14.

MEDLAND, W. G., b. Exbourne, 94461, Pte., d. of w., F., 7/11/18.

MEHERS, L., b. Wigan, 56255, Pte., d. of w., F., 28/5/17.

MELLOR, S., b. Llanynys, 24524, Pte., k. in a., F., 22/9/15.

METCALF, W., b. Stoneyholme, 7227, Pte., k. in a., F., 28/10/14.

MIDDLETON, G., b. London, 10201, Pte., k. in a., F., 30/5/15.

MIDDLETON, W., b. Tibberton, 201530, Pte., k. in a., F., 13/10/17.

MILES, G., b. Newbury, 10412, L/Cpl., k. in a., F., 23/4/17.

MILES, W. S., b. Ashton-under-Hill, 9596, Pte., k. in a., F., 3/11/14.

MILLER, W., b. Warrington, 56238, Pte., d. of w., F., 1/6/17.

MILLINGTON, C., b. Merthyr, 54455, Pte., k. in a., F., 23/4/17.

MILLS, W. J., b. Leicester, 8337, Sgt., k. in a., F., 2/7/18.

MINERS, A., b. Swansea, 5575, C.S.M., k. in a., F., 20/7/16, M.M.

MITCHELL, P. G., b. Gt. Malvern, 9120, L/Cpl., k. in a., F., 20/8/16.

MOIR, M., b. Accrington, 201655, Pte., d., F., 5/10/17.

MOODY, A. J., b. Slaithwaite, 13070, Pte., d. of w., F., 25/11/17.

MOORE, R., b. Goole, 202155, Pte., k. in a., F., 1/9/18.

MOORE, W., b. Merthyr, 6004, Pte., k. in a., F., 20/5/15.

MORGAN, D., b. Dumbarton, 11778, Pte., k. in a., F., 6/7/16.

MORGAN, E. J., b. Aberdare, 31546, Pte., k. in a., F., 19/7/16.

MORGAN, H., b. Ruyton-Eleven-Towns, 54603, Pte., k. in a., F., 27/5/17.

MORGAN, H., b. Workington, 39830, Cpl., k. in a., F., 26/8/18.

MORGAN, M., b. Fishguard, 45153, Pte., k. in a., F., 26/11/17.

MORGAN, S., b. Shrewsbury, 8325, Pte., k. in a., F., 27/5/17.

MORRIS, A. J., b. Cardiff, 9113, Pte., k. in a., F., 25/9/15.

MORRIS, E. L., b. Rhiwlas, 6053, L/Cpl., k. in a., F., 22/6/16.

MORRIS, G. W., b. Peterborough, 36732, L/Sgt., d. of w., F., 28/5/17.

MORRIS, J., b. Bullington, 8804, Pte., k. in a., F., 18/7/16.

MORRIS, T., b. Liverpool, 24076, Pte., k. in a., F., 5/2/16.

MORRIS, W., b. Ebw Vale, 38787, Pte., d. of w., F., 20/8/16.

MOSS, H., b. Handbridge, 10227, L/Cpl., d. of w., F., 28/7/16, D.C.M.

MOSSOP, E., b. Mosser, 36911, Pte., k. in a., F., 20/7/16.

MOTTERSHEAD, A., b. Hyde, 10216, Pte., k. in a., F., 14/9/15.

MOULD, H., b. Cobridge, 24573, Cpl., k. in a., F., 26/9/17.

MOUNTENEY, A., b. Stockport, 8083, Pte., k. in a., F., 25/9/15.

MOUNTFORD, J., b. Leicester, 9041, Cpl., k. in a., F., 5/2/16.

MULES, A. G., b. Penarth, 235382, Pte., k. in a., F., 26/9/17.

MULLEY, G., b. Middleton, 61216, Pte., k. in a., F., 26/9/17.

MURRAY, J., b. Glasgow, 27217, L/Cpl., k. in a., F., 6/7/16.

MURRAY, J., b. Wigan, 38825, Pte., k. in a., F., 5/11/16.

MYLAN, M., b. Swansea, 8553, Pte., k. in a., F., 20/7/16.

NAPPER, B., b. London, 56541, Pte., k. in a., F., 1/9/18.

NASH, C., b. Knowbury, 73445, Pte., d. of w., F., 24/8/18.

NASH, E. H., b. Canterbury, 4638, Pte., d. of w., F., 29/7/16.

NEAL, J., b. Wolverhampton, 9138, Pte., k. in a., F., 25/9/15.

NEKREWS, D., b. Swansea, 17367, Pte., k. in a., F., 5/2/16.

NELMES, W. T., b. Aberaman, 93767, Pte., d. of w., F., 28/10/18.

NELSON, C., b. Coventry, 8138, Pte., k. in a., F., 27/10/14.

NESMITH, A., b. Birmingham, 8682, Pte., k. in a., F., 22/6/16, M.M.

NETTLETON, H., b. Stockport, 46180, Pte., k. in a., F., 28/11/17.

NEWBROOK, S., b. Whitchurch, 10275, Sgt., k. in a., F., 25/4/16.

NEWELL, D., b. Pwllheli, 265378, Pte., k. in a., F., 1/9/18.

NEWMAN, E. H., b. Birmingham, 9160, L/Cpl., k. in a., F., 2/6/16.

NICHOLLS, E., b. Cardiff, 8565, Pte., d. of w., F., 5/12/14.

NICHOLLS, G., b. Barnes, 56205, L/Cpl., k. in a., F., 25/11/17.

NICKLIN, A., b. Reans, 9604, Pte., k. in a., F., 25/9/15.

NIELD, J. J. C., b. Barrow-in-Furness, 24384, Pte., k. in a., F., 20/7/16.

NIXON, P., b. Hanley, 24375, Pte., k. in a., F., 27/1/16.

NOBES, J., b. Birkenhead, 24236, Pte., d. of w., F., 27/6/16.

NOLAN, T., b. Durham, 7144, A/Cpl., k. in a., F., 16/5/15.

NORMAN, A. E., b. Shrewsbury, 73446, Pte., k. in a., F., 28/11/17.

NORTON, A., b. Birmingham, 8215, Pte., k. in a., F., 25/10/14.

NORTON, W. H., e. Manchester, 33381, Pte., d., F., 22/2/17.

OAKES, S., b. Widnes, 56244, Pte., d. of w., F., 9/6/17.

O'BRIEN, P., b. Ballyguiry, Co. Waterford, 24636, Pte., k. in a., F., 13/8/16.

OBRIEN, W. T., b. Rhondda, 56701, Pte., d. of w., F., 10/11/18.

O'NEILL, J., b. Newport, 73784, Pte., k. in a., F., 3/9/18.

OSBORNE, G. W. J., b. London, 9632, Pte., k. in a., F., 26/10/14.

OSMOND, F., b. London, 9586, L/Cpl., k. in a., F., 27/5/17.

OWEN, D., b. Abererch, 36267, Pte., k. in a., F., 8/10/18.

OWEN, D. R., b. Conway, 55016, Pte., k. in a., F., 27/5/17.

OWEN, E. R., b. Llanberis, 8544, Pte., d. of w., F., 8/7/16.

OWEN, F. R., b. Maenan, 29610, Pte., k. in a., F., 27/5/17.

OWEN, G., b. Llanddaniel, 267298, Pte., d. of w., F., 20/5/18.

OWEN, H., b. Carnarvon, 20109, Pte., d. of w., Home, 15/11/16.

OWEN, H., b. Bryngwran, 7701, k. in a., F., 25/9/15.

OWENS, A., b. Wrexham, 19791, Pte., d. of w., F., 5/11/16.

OWENS, F., b. Liverpool, 31251, Pte., k. in a., F., 20/7/16.

OWENS, J., b. Carmarthen, 45184, Pte., k. in a., F., 26/9/17.

OWENS, T., b. Widnes, 63988, Pte., d. of w., F., 3/9/18.

OWENS, W., b. Chester, 7615, L/Sgt., k. in a., F., 10/12/17.

OWENS, W. H., b. Windsor, 10514, Pte., d. of w., F., 20/6/15.

PADDOCK, C., b. Ellesmere, 200084, Pte., k. in a., F., 22/6/17.

PAGE, N., b. Darlaston, 12945, Pte., k. in a., F., 3/11/18.

PALMER, W., b. London, 6166, Pte., k. in a., F., 20/7/16.

PANE, E., b. London, 24158, Pte., k. in a., F., 22/6/16.

PARDOE, E. J., b. Birmingham, 9773, Cpl., k. in a., F., 10/11/14.

PARDOE, W., b. Birmingham, 9417, L/Cpl., k. in a., F., 25/9/15.

PARKER, A., b. Birmingham, 36450, Pte., k. in a., F., 23/4/17.

PARKER, T., b. Bradford, 52656, Pte., k. in a., F., 26/9/17.

PARKER, T. H., b. Rugeley, 36892, A/Cpl., k. in a., F., 6/11/16.

PARKINSON, G., b. Moreton, 39802, Pte., d., F., 12/11/16.

PARMAN, W., b. Birmingham, 8665, A/Cpl., k. in a., F., 20/7/16.

PARNELL, R. B., e. Merthyr,

54101, Pte., k. in a., F., 27/5/17.

PARRY, A., b. Llanrwst, 203173, Pte., k. in a., F., 21/3/18.

PARRY, E., b. Holyhead, 49874, Pte., k. in a., F., 26/9/17.

PARRY, I. J., b. Llanwouno, 10767, Pte., k. in a., F., 24/10/14.

PARRY, J., b. Rhyl, 16262, Pte., k. in a., F., 27/5/17.

PARRY, J. H., b. Toxteth, 78340, Pte., d. of w., F., 21/10/18.

PARRY, J. S., b. Pendleton, 78266, Pte., k. in a., F., 8/10/18.

PARRY, J. W., b. Rhuddlan, 5287, Pte., k. in a., F., 5/2/16.

PARRY, N. J., b. Chester, 10567, Sgt., k. in a., F., 27/5/17.

PARRY, R., b. Penmaenmawr, 55017, Cpl., k. in a., F., 27/5/17.

PARRY, W., b. Ewlon, 5711, Pte., k. in a., F., 20/7/16.

PARRY, W., b. Hanley, 9631, Pte., k. in a., F., 22/6/16.

PARSONS, O., b. Highbridge, 5632, C.Q.M.S., k. in a., F., 26/10/14.

PATTERSON, D., b. Inverness, 204222, Pte., k. in a., F., 21/6/18.

PATTISON, P., b. Llynelly, 8731, C.S.M., k. in a., F., 22/6/16, D.C.M.

PAYNE, G., b. Birmingham, 9594, Pte., d., Home, 10/2/17.

PAYNE, J. R., b. Brierfield, 201839, Pte., d. of w., F., 2/7/18.

PEARSON, F., e. London, 45798, Pte., d. of w., F., 6/5/18.

PEARSON, H., b. West Bromwich, 5710, Pte., d., Home, 5/3/18.

PEMBERTON, W., b. Leigh, 24128, Pte., d. of w., F., 24/4/17.

PENDLETON, G., b. Treharris, 11102, Pte., k. in a., F., 5/2/15.

PENNINGTON, F., b. Sheffield, 7279, Pte., k. in a., F., 25/10/14.

PENNY, D. E., b. Cardiff, 36875, Sgt., k. in a., F., 27/5/17.

PERCIVAL, S. J., b. Handsworth, 9814, Cpl., k. in a., F., 25/9/15.

PERKS, A. G., b. Birmingham, 36505, Cpl., d. of w., F., 31/8/18, M.M.

PERKS, W., b. Birmingham, 9088, Pte., k. in a., F., 26/10/14.

PERRY, G., b. Worcester, 36475, Pte., k. in a., F., 22/6/16.

PETERS, B., b. Llandegla, 201066, Pte., k. in a., F., 18/10/18.

PHILLIPS, F., b. Chester, 201408, Pte., k. in a., F., 9/1/17.

PHILLIPS, W., b. Waenllyd, 93735, Pte., k. in a., F., 8/10/18.

PICKUP, A., b. Burnley, 7931, Pte., d. of w., Home, 11/9/16.

PIKE, S. E., b. Berkhamsted, 36589, Pte., d. of w., Home, 5/9/16.

PITKEATHLY, F. J., b. Rotherhithe, 60255, Pte., k. in a., F., 21/10/17.

PLANT, A., b. Dawley, 56191, Pte., k. in a., F., 25/11/17.

PLUMBLEY, H., b. Liverpool, 17926, Pte., k. in a., F., 22/6/16.

POOLE, H. V., b. London, 45767, Pte., d. of w., F., 21/6/18.

POTTER, W. J., b. London, 22657, Pte., d. of w., F., 22/9/18.

POTTS, D., b. Warrington, 31243, Pte., k. in a., F., 9/4/16.

POTTS, W., b. Tunstall, 23960, Pte., k. in a., F., 22/6/16.

POWELL, G., b. Cardiff, 38640, Cpl., k. in a., F., 25/11/17.

POWELL, W. H., b. Mountain Ash, 93732, Pte., k. in a., F., 8/10/18.

PRETTY, D., b. Bradley Green, 36660, Pte., k. in a., F., 20/7/16.

PRICE, A. E., b. Hallow, 88620, Pte., k. in a., F., 16/10/18.

PRICE, B., b. Newbridge-on-Wye, 9204, Pte., k. in a., F., 22/6/16.

PRICE, C., b. Felinfoel, 31167, Pte., k. in a., F., 20/7/16.

PRICE, C. H., b. Gloucester, 9512, Pte., k. in a., F., 29/10/14.

PRICE, E., b. Cardiff, 9263, L/Cpl., d. of w., F., 24/1/15.

PRICE, E. S., b. Shrewsbury, 10286, Dmr., k. in a., F., 25/9/15.

PRICE, H., b. Brymbo, 8495, Pte., d. of w., F., 20/7/16, M.M.

PRICE, J., b. Ruthin, 37678, Pte., d. of w., F., 30/5/17.

PRICE, J., b. Mainstone, 61376, Pte., k. in a., F., 1/9/18.

PRICE, T., b. Birmingham, 8297, Pte., k. in a., F., 26/10/14.

PRICE, W., b. Ynishir, 56846, Pte., d. of w., F., 9/1/18.

PRITCHARD, J., b. Llanbeblig, 9681, Pte., d. of w., F., 23/7/16.

PROBERT, W. H., b. Birmingham, 9560, Pte., k. in a., F., 25/10/14.

PROPERT, F., b. Wingfield, 31198, L/Cpl., d. of w., F., 24/7/16.

PUFFETT, R., b. Banbury, 9084, Pte., k. in a., F., 10/7/15.

PUGH, J., b. Wrexham, 5367, Pte., d. of w., F., 12/11/16.

PUGH, L., b. Wrexham, 56222, Pte., k. in a., F., 27/5/17.

PUGH, R., b. Nelson, 61330, Pte., k. in a., F., 26/9/17.

PURCELL, T. H., b. Pontypool, 56190, Pte., d. of w., F., 12/6/17.

PURCELL, W., b. Welshpool, 7187, d. of w., F., 9/4/15.

PYATT, J. W., b. Tamworth, 9536, L/Cpl., k. in a., F., 22/6/16.

QUINEY, H., b. Stratford-on-Avon, 10756, Pte., d. of w., F., 21/7/16.

QUINN, A., b. Bristol, 12395, Pte., k. in a., F., 27/1/16.

RATCLIFFE, W., b. Northwood, 17830, Cpl., k. in a., F., 24/10/16.

RAY, T. J., b. Llanelly, 77577, Pte., k. in a., F., 1/9/18.

REANEY, G. E., b. Wolverhampton, 8423, Pte., k. in a., F., 25/9/15.

REES, D. J., b. Merthyr, 17827, Pte., k. in a., F., 20/7/16.

REES, R., b. Cardiff, 17713, Pte., d. of w., F., 3/8/16.

REID, F. W., b. Birmingham, 6326, Pte., k. in a., F., 16/5/15.

RHODEN, J. C., b. Wolverhampton, 6299, Sgt., k. in a., F., 28/11/17.

RICE, G., b. Coventry, 7944, Pte., k. in a., F., 23/2/15.

RICHARDS, B. T., b. Ferndale, 88600, Pte., k. in a., F., 16/10/18.

RICHARDS, R. J., b. Bala, 89572, Pte., k. in a., F., 18/10/18.

RICHARDS, T. E., b. Llanllwchaern, 73800, Pte., d. of w., F., 4/9/18.

RICHARDS, W. O., b. St. David's, 11444, Pte., k. in a., F., 18/7/16.

RICKETTS, E. W., b. Worcester, 9349, Pte., k. in a., F., 26/4/15.

RIDING, T., b. Liverpool, 9652, Pte., d. of w., F., 24/6/16.

RIGBY, W., b. Wilmslow, 31313, L/Cpl., d. of w., F., 8/11/16.

RILEY, J. W., b. Heaviley, 4664, Pte., d. of w., F., 9/11/16.

RINGER, H. T. F., b. London, 28073, Pte., d. of w., F., 9/10/18.

RIVINGTON, T., b. Birkenhead, 7197, Pte., d. of w., F., 17/5/15.

ROBERTS, C., b. Birmingham, 60242, Pte., d. of w., F., 1/12/17.

ROBERTS, C., b. Ruthin, 4218, Pte., k. in a., F., 1/9/18.

ROBERTS, D., b. Corwen, 37093, Pte., k. in a., F., 22/6/16.

ROBERTS, D., b. Corwen, 39741, Pte., k. in a., F., 30/10/17.

ROBERTS, D. D., b. Pontyberem, 13420, Pte., k. in a., F., 26/9/17.

ROBERTS, E., b. Llanenddwyn, 17503, Pte., k. in a., F., 23/4/17.

ROBERTS, E., b. Flint, 12821, Pte., k. in a., F., 22/6/16.

ROBERTS, E., b. Corwen, 37092, Pte., k. in a., F., 20/7/16.

ROBERTS, E., b. Dolgelly, 15100, Cpl., k. in a., F., 6/7/16.

ROBERTS, E. T., b. Hope, 37618, L/Cpl., k. in a., F., 3/11/16.

ROBERTS, G. R., b. Bethesda, 56706, Pte., d. of w., F., 31/10/16.

ROBERTS, H., b. Dolbenmaen, 40065, Pte., k. in a., F., 20/8/16.

ROBERTS, J., b. Denbigh, 55004, Pte., k. in a., F., 27/5/17.

ROBERTS, J., b. Ruthin, 4149, Pte., k. in a., F., 19/7/16.

ROBERTS, J., b. Mold, 12298, Pte., k. in a., F., 20/7/16.

ROBERTS, J. L., b. Blaenau Festiniog, 39702, Pte., k. in a., F., 5/11/16.

ROBERTS, J. S., b. Bangor, 37761, Pte., k. in a., F., 17/8/17.

ROBERTS, L., b. Llandudno, 6679, Pte., k. in a., F., 9/9/14.

ROBERTS, R. E., b. Groeslon, 40238, Pte., k. in a., F., 26/10/16.

ROBERTS, R. H., b. Llanrwst, 11198, Pte., k. in a., F., 20/6/15.

ROBERTS, T. C., b. Flint, 5926, Pte., d. of w., F., 10/6/18.

ROBERTS, W., e. Llanberis, 54108, Cpl., d. of w., F., 27/4/18.

ROBERTS, W. H., b. Cardiff, 94469, Pte., k. in a., F., 4/11/18.

ROBINSON, W., b. Newton Heath, 8764, Cpl., k. in a., F., 20/7/16.

ROGERS, G. T., b. Bristol, 8490, Sgt., k. in a., F., 20/7/16.

ROGERS, P., e. Wrexham, 54109, Pte., k. in a., F., 5/11/16.

ROGERS, W., b. Tixall, 9319, Pte., k. in a., F., 7/11/14.

ROGERS, W., b. Manchester, 71892, Pte., d. of w., F., 2/9/18.

ROOM, W., b. Birmingham, 60245, Pte., k. in a., F., 22/6/17.

ROSE, A. H., b. Handsworth, 36502, Pte., d. of w., F., 18/7/16.

ROSE, F. H. W., b. Birmingham, 8174, Pte., k. in a., F., 30/10/14.

ROSE, S., b. Runcorn, 8229, Pte., d. of w., F., 8/6/15.

ROSSI, J., e. Manchester, 93773, Pte., d. of w., F., 20/10/18.

ROUND, J., b. Birmingham, 9686, Pte., d. of w., F., 9/7/16.

ROWE, F. S., e. Birmingham, 36792, Pte., k. in a., F., 6/7/16.

ROWLAND, O., b. Hammersmith, 30121, Pte., k. in a., F., 5/11/16.

ROWLANDS, H., b. Llanrug, 40186, Pte., d., Home, 3/3/17.

ROWLANDS, J., b. Sandbach, 9083, Sgt., k. in a., F., 25/10/14.

SALISBURY, E., b. Chester, 7967, Pte., k. in a., F., 14/8/16, D.C.M.

SALT, B. T., b. Oakamoor, 23888, Pte., k. in a., F., 22/6/16.

SAMPSON, H., b. Mile End, 24462, L/Cpl., d. of w., F., 6/2/16.

SAMUEL, A., e. Llanelly, 75208, Pte., k. in a., F., 1/9/18.

SAMUEL, C. H., b. Morriston, 36721, Pte., k. in a., F., 22/6/16.

SARGANT, W., b. Birmingham, 9882, Pte., k. in a., F., 5/2/16.

SEFTON, B. B., b. Oldham, 73479, Pte., k. in a., F., 28/11/17.

SELBY, A. J. F., e. Portsmouth, 235818, Pte., k. in a., F., 30/6/18.

SEPHTON, J., b. St. Helens, 36294, Pte., k. in a., F., 22/6/16.

SEWELL, E. W., b. Liverpool, 31425, L/Sgt., k. in a., F., 21/8/16.

SEXTON, G., b. Aberdare, 38662, Pte., k. in a., F., 5/3/17.

SHACKLETON, E., b. Burnley, 201797, Pte., k. in a., F., 26/9/17.

SHAW, T., b. Stafford, 5348, Pte., k. in a., F., 25/9/15.

SHAW, U., b. Stalybridge, 39330, Pte., d. of w., F., 30/10/16.

SHEARER, W., b. Wrexham, 24395, Pte., k. in a., F., 27/5/17.

SHEPPARD, H., b. Swansea, 11307, L/Cpl., k. in a., F., 24/4/16.

SHEPPARD, S. E., b. Bath, 8543, Pte., d. of w., F., 6/11/16.

SHUTE, J. R., b. Portishead, 88679, Pte., k. in a., F., 4/11/18.

SIMMONS, W. H., b. London, 8843, L/Cpl., d. of w., F., 29/10/14.

SIMPSON, H., b. Clitheroe, 73468, Pte., k. in a., F., 8/10/18.

SIMPSON, W., b. Colne, 201770, Pte., k. in a., F., 1/12/17.

SIMPSON, W. T., b. Birmingham, 5264, Pte., k. in a., F., 2/6/16.

SINCLAIR, A. E., b. London, 24229, Pte., d. of w., F., 19/2/17.

SINGLETON, C. J., b. Bamberbridge, 201853, Pte., k. in a., F., 26/9/17.

SLATER, E., b. Kidsgrove, 6657, Pte., k. in a., F., 24/4/16.

SMART, S., b. Fenton, 13645, L/Cpl., d. of w., F., 5/11/16.

SMITH, A. E., b. Atherstone, 12429, Pte., k. in a., F., 20/9/15.

SMITH, C. H., b. Pelton, 11305, Pte., k. in a., F., 25/9/15.

SMITH, D., b. Bentley, 23207, Pte., k. in a., F., 25/9/15.

SMITH, H., b. Elms Stirchley, 54880, Pte., d., F., 28/6/18.

SMITH, J., b. Newbridge, 38246, Pte., k. in a., F., 3/11/16.

SMITH, S., b. Abertillery, 93738, Pte., k. in a., F., 16/10/18.

SMITH, S., b. Sheffield, 60259, Pte., k. in a., F., 1/9/18.

SMITH, W. H., b. Box, 5514, Sgt., k. in a., F., 21/8/16.

SMITH, W. T., b. Merthyr, 8517, L/Cpl., d. of w., F., 16/3/15.

SPACKMAN, F. H., b. Mile End,

24432, Pte., d. of w., F., 30/4/16.

SPEED, R., b. Hawarden, 8389, A/Sgt., k. in a., F., 30/10/14.

SPENCER, A., b. Cardiff, 38261, Pte., d. of w., F., 23/12/16.

SPENCER, C. H., b. Birmingham, 11960, Cpl., d. of w., F., 30/10/16.

SPENCER, H., b. Highgate, London, 26642, Pte., k. in a., F., 27/5/17.

SPENCER, J. A., b. Dowlais, 56707, Pte., d. of w., F., 11/11/16.

SPIERS, B., b. Oswestry, 10474, L/Cpl., k. in a., F., 20/7/16.

SPROSTON, G., b. Christchurch, 37062, Pte., k. in a., F., 27/5/17.

STAIT, A., b. Birmingham, 8911, Pte., k. in a., F., 22/6/16.

STAIT, F., b. Birmingham, 9108, Pte., k. in a., F., 11/7/15.

STANSFIELD, H., b. Accrington, 201660, Pte., k. in a., F., 21/10/17.

STARKEY, J. H., b. Buglawton, 392298, Pte., k. in a., F., 13/3/18.

STEAD, R., b. Wyre Tenbury, 9529, L/Cpl., k. in a., F., 26/10/14.

STENSON, A., b. Birmingham, 8328, Pte., d. of w., F., 7/12/14.

STEPHENS, B., b. Birmingham, 36507, Pte., k. in a., F., 20/7/16.

STEPHENS, D. E., b. Whitchurch, 56744, Pte., d., F., 20/11/16.

STEPHENS, J. A., b. Cardiff, 6455, Cpl., k. in a., F., 16/5/15.

STEPHENS, P. J., b. Chepstow, 56225, L/Cpl., d. of w., F., 28/5/17.

STEVENS, J., b. Cardiff, 56713, Cpl., d. of w., F., 4/11/18.

STEVENS, P. J., b. Stroud, 6860, Pte., k. in a., F., 25/1/15.

STEVENS, W., b. Lizard, 31218, Pte., k. in a., F., 20/7/16.

STILLWELL, A. E., b. London, 73472, Pte., k. in a., F., 10/3/18.

STOCK, B., b. Cardiff, 24377, Pte., k. in a., F., 20/7/16.

STOCKWELL, W. H., b. Birmingham, 10945, Sgt., k. in a., F., 19/8/16, M.M.

STOKES, J., b. Aberdare, 5980, L/Cpl., k. in a., F., 29/4/16.

STONE, W. H., b. Birmingham, 8293, Pte., d. of w., F., 20/7/15.

STONEHOUSE, T., b. Prescott, 4715, L/Cpl., k. in a., F., 6/7/16.

STOTT, E., b. High Crompton, 73469, Pte., d., F., 21/6/18.

STOTT, W. M., b. Burnley, 73817, Pte., k. in a., F., 2/9/18.

STREFFORD, T., b. Motherwell,

89365, Pte., d. of w., F., 15/11/18.

STRETCH, J., b. Newton, 63687, Pte., d. of w., F., 6/5/18.

STROUD, C., e. Monmouth, 6238, Pte., k. in a., F., 25/9/15.

STURK, W. D., b. London, 22150, Pte., k. in a., F., 27/5/17.

SWIFT, J., b. Liverpool, 7223, L/Cpl., k. in a., F., 23/4/17.

SWIFT, T., b. London, 27491, Pte., k. in a., F., 3/11/16.

TATTON, A., b. Leek, 11120, Pte., k. in a., F., 20/7/16.

TAYLOR, A., b. Evesham, 8381, Sgt., d. of w., F., 28/9/17.

TAYLOR, D. L., b. Aberdare, 56748, Pte., d. of w., F., 8/11/16.

TAYLOR, E., b. Birchley Heath, 9676, L/Cpl., d. of w., F., 24/8/16.

TAYLOR, J., b. Birmingham, 6816, Pte., k. in a., F., 16/5/17.

TAYLOR, P. E., b. Feering, 55883, Pte., k. in a., F., 28/11/17.

TAYLOR, R. T., b. Liverpool, 37834, Pte., d. of w., F., 8/11/16.

TAYLOR, T. J., b. Penrhiwceiber, 53835, Pte., d. of w., Home, 24/2/19.

TAYLOR, W. J., b. Bristol, 9186, Pte., k. in a., F., 20/7/16.

THOMAS, A., b. Newport, 4586, L/Cpl., k. in a., F., 25/7/15.

THOMAS, C. P., b. Bagillt, 16004, Pte., k. in a., F., 12/7/18.

THOMAS, D., b. Llanfestiniog, 26395, Pte., k. in a., F., 4/11/18.

THOMAS, F., b. London, 6385, C.S.M., k. in a., F., 19/8/16, M.M.

THOMAS, G., b. Hanley, 9628, L/Cpl., d. of w., F., 7/11/16.

THOMAS, H., b. Aberffraw, 21270, Pte., k. in a., F., 9/1/18.

THOMAS, H., e. Bangor, 55022, Pte., k. in a., F., 26/9/17.

THOMAS, H., b. Carnarvon, 89331, Pte., k. in a., F., 4/11/18.

THOMAS, J., b. Pantlossie, 16328, Pte., k. in a., F., 1/9/18.

THOMAS, J. R., b. Talycafn, 40262, Pte., k. in a., F., 26/9/17.

THOMAS, L. J., b. Llansamlet, 75162, Pte., k. in a., F., 12/9/18.

THOMAS, R., b. Llanbedr, 61005, Pte., k. in a., F., 26/9/17.

THOMAS, S., b. Stoke-on-Trent, 24665, Pte., d. of w., F., 20/8/16.

THOMAS, S., b. Holyhead, 5867, Pte., d. of w., F., 10/8/15.

THOMAS, T., b. Bangor, 63595, Pte., k. in a., F., 25/11/17.

THOMAS, W., b. Newport, 6893, Pte., d. of w., F., 22/5/15.

THOMPSON, A., b. Kilnhurst,

30260, Sgt., k. in a., F., 2/7/18.

THOMPSON, J., b. Leeds, 37058, Pte., d. of w., F., 25/4/17.

THOMPSON, P. W. G., b. Birmingham, 9091, Pte., d., F., 16/2/15.

THOMPSON, R., b. Stockport, 39173, Pte., k. in a., F., 21/8/16.

THORBURN, W. B., b. Manchester, 62688, Pte., k. in a., F., 26/9/17.

THORMAN, A. H., b. Chester, 10496, L/Cpl., k. in a., F., 26/10/14.

THORNILEY, J., b. Steeton Moor, 41565, Pte., k. in a., F., 1/9/18.

THRELFALL, W. H., e. Burnley, 201800, Pte., k. in a., F., 24/8/18.

TINLEY, F., b. Liverpool, 6020, Pte., k. in a., F., 22/6/16.

TINTON, A., b. Barry, 4622, Sgt., k. in a., F., 23/4/17.

TOMKINS, F., b. Pontypool, 44098, Pte., d. of w., F., 8/10/18.

TOMLIN, H., b. Bristol, 10922, Pte., k. in a., F., 27/5/17.

TOMLINSON, A., b. Handsworth, 37052, Pte., k. in a., F., 6/7/16.

TOMLINSON, J., b. Buckley, 36966, Pte., k. in a., F., 20/8/16.

TONGE, E. J., b. Llanfihangel, 77457, Pte., k. in a., F., 1/9/18.

TONGUE, P., b. Bolton, 63573, Pte., k. in a., F., 26/9/17.

TOOTHILL, W., b. Bury, 18863, Sgt., d. of w., F., 18/10/18.

TOZER, R. C., b. Torquay, 11410, Pte., k. in a., F., 13/11/14.

TRACEY, B., b. Birmingham, 10154, L/Cpl., k. in a., F., 29/12/15.

TRENHOLM, A. E., b. Stockton, 31534, L/Cpl., d. of w., F., 2/7/18, M.M.

TRIPPIER, J., b. Booth, 63048, Pte., k. in a., F., 27/5/17.

TURRALL, W. F., b. Birmingham, 11424, Sgt., k. in a., F., 3/5/18, M.M.

TWIGG, G., b. Birmingham, 6886, A/C.S.M., k. in a., F., 20/8/16.

TYDD, J. T., b. Tattenhall, 8629, Pte., k. in a., F., 3/11/14.

VALE, F., b. Birmingham, 9690, Pte., k. in a., F., 22/6/16.

VICKERS, P., b. Holywell, 61192, Pte., k. in a., F., 22/4/18.

VYSE, M., b. Luton, 10344, Pte., d. of w., F., 20/7/16, M.M.

WALKER, C. A., b. Newton-le-Willows, 6623, A/Sgt., k. in a., F., 26/9/17.

WALKER, S., b. Hoole Chester, 8457, Pte., k. in a., F., 22/6/16.

WALKER, W., b. Liverpool,

36960, Pte., k. in a., F., 26/9/17.

WALTON, J., b. Bilston, 8427, L/Cpl., d. of w., F., 30/4/18.

WALTON, J. H., b. Liverpool, 36908, Pte., k. in a., F., 20/7/16.

WALTON, S., b. Llanbradach, 5556, Pte., k. in a., F., 18/7/16.

WARBURTON, R., b. Warrington, 24077, Pte., k. in a., F., 14/3/16.

WARD, B., b. Crossmaglen, 39846, Pte., d. of w., F., 24/4/17.

WARD, J. W., b. Chester, 9280, Pte., k. in a., F., 25/9/15.

WARD, R., b. Jarrow, 56556, Pte., k. in a., F., 30/11/17.

WARDELL, W. A., b. Birmingham, 8312, Pte., k. in a., F., 25/9/15.

WARDEN, J., b. Preston, 5985, Sgt., k. in a., F., 22/8/16.

WARDLE, J., b. Broadbottom, 24344, Pte., d. of w., F., 7/7/16.

WARHURST, A. L., b. Manchester, 62771, Pte., k. in a., F., 3/9/18.

WARRY, W., b. Ilminster, 5580, k. in a., F., 19/2/16.

WATERHOUSE, J., e. Manchester, 266827, Pte., k. in a., F., 21/6/18.

WATERWORTH, D., b. Baxenden, 93348, Pte., k. in a., F., 1/9/18.

WATHEN, J., b. Bedwellty, 8521, Sgt., k. in a., F., 10/11/14.

WATKINS, S. C., b. Treforest, 5225, Pte., k. in a., F., 20/7/16.

WATSON, W. B., b. Carlisle, 70202, L/Cpl., k. in a., F., 1/9/18.

WEAVER, W., b. Birmingham, 8318, Pte., k. in a., F., 13/7/15.

WEBB, J. J., b. Barry, 36715, L/Cpl., k. in a., F., 22/6/16.

WEBSTER, G., b. Hanley, 6214, Sgt., k. in a., F., 23/8/17.

WEEDON, G., b. Davenham, 8165, L/Cpl., k. in a., F., 16/5/15.

WEIR, T., b. Liverpool, 8805, L/Cpl., k. in a., F., 24/10/16.

WESTACOTT, A., b. Bristol, 9361, L/Cpl, k. in a., F., 1/9/18, D.C.M.

WESTMORE, A. T., b. London, 56228, Pte., k. in a., F., 27/5/17.

WETTON, E., b. Birmingham, 9670, Pte., k. in a., F., 26/10/14.

WHERLEY, G. F., b. Penarth, 31174, A/Sgt., k. in a., F., 22/12/16.

WHITE, J., b. London, 8514, Pte., k. in a., F., 22/6/16.

WHITE, T., b. Holt, 76106, Pte., k. in a., F., 1/9/18.

WHITEHEAD, J. E., b. Preston,

73490, Pte., d. of w., F., 8/9/18.

WHITTAKER, J., b. Burnley, 201877, Pte., k. in a., F., 26/9/17.

WILKINSON, T. H., b. Christchurch, 8222, L/Sgt., k. in a., F., 26/9/17.

WILLIAMS, A., b. Treorchy, 56750, Pte., d. of w., F., 3/5/17.

WILLIAMS, A., b. Oswestry, 4143, Pte., k. in a., F., 13/9/18.

WILLIAMS, A., b. Birmingham, 7663, Pte., k. in a., F., 29/4/15.

WILLIAMS, A., b. Birmingham, 7948, Pte., k. in a., F., 2/1/16.

WILLIAMS, D., b. Swansea, 66969, Pte., k. in a., F., 12/7/18.

WILLIAMS, D., b. Towyn, 6381, Pte., k. in a., F., 25/9/15.

WILLIAMS, D. O., b. Gwalchmai, 5358, Sgt., k. in a., F., 6/11/16.

WILLIAMS, E., b. Llanidloes, 15884, L/Cpl., k. in a., F., 26/11/17.

WILLIAMS, G., e. Wrexham, 54060, Pte., k. in a., F., 26/11/17.

WILLIAMS, G., b. Abererch, 40630, Pte., k. in a., F., 30/10/16.

WILLIAMS, H., b. Beaumaris, 7719, Pte., k. in a., F., 27/4/15.

WILLIAMS, H. L., e. Blaenanerch, 11875, Pte., k. in a., F., 22/4/18.

WILLIAMS, H. R., b. Llandudno, 16429, Pte., d. of w., F., 26/11/17.

WILLIAMS, I., b. Bettws-in-Rhos, 40266, Pte., k. in a., F., 20/8/16.

WILLIAMS, J., b. Colwyn Bay, 54585, Pte., d. of w., F., 26/2/17.

WILLIAMS, J., b. Cemaes Bay, 203522, Pte., d. of w., F., 13/10/18.

WILLIAMS, J., b. Ruabon, 54368, Pte., k. in a., F., 1/9/18.

WILLIAMS, J., b. Conway, 8242, Sgt., k. in a., F., 25/4/16.

WILLIAMS, J. H., b. Kerry, 37686, Pte., k. in a., F., 19/10/17.

WILLIAMS, J. R., b. Llandegai, 12592, Pte., k. in a., F., 23/4/17.

WILLIAMS, M. J., b. Madley, 73494, Pte., k. in a., F., 28/11/17.

WILLIAMS, R., b. Llandwrog, 14462, Pte., k. in a., F., 21/10/18.

WILLIAMS, R., b. Aberystwyth, 35499, Pte., k. in a., F., 5/11/16.

WILLIAMS, R., b. Wrexham, 40246, Pte., k. in a., F., 26/10/16.

WILLIAMS, R., e. Llanrug, Carn.,

54147, Pte., d. of w., F., 7/11/16.

WILLIAMS, R., b. Criccieth, 37104, Pte., k. in a., F., 6/11/16.

WILLIAMS, R., b. Darwen, 60820, Pte., k. in a., F., 13/10/17.

WILLIAMS, R. D., b. Carnarvon, 69252, Pte., d. of w., F., 5/1/18.

WILLIAMS, T., b. Beaumaris, 11146, L/Cpl., k. in a., F., 22/6/16, M.M.

WILLIAMS, T., b. Wrexham, 200343, Pte., d. of w., F., 9/10/18.

WILLIAMS, T. G. G., b. Liverpool, 40044, Pte., k. in a., F., 19/8/16.

WILLIAMS, T. J., b. Aberdare, 73224, Pte., d. of w., F., 17/9/18.

WILLIAMS, W., b. Bodfari, 14925, Pte., d. of w., F., 29/1/17.

WILLIAMS, W., b. Waenfawr, 54583, Pte., d. of w., F., 2/10/17.

WILLIAMS, W., b. Llanymynech, 54672, Pte., k. in a., F., 16/10/18.

WILLIAMS, W., b. Llanuwchllyn, 60926, Pte., d. of w., F., 21/9/18.

WILLIAMS, W. D., b. Treherbert, 11091, Pte., k. in a., F., 24/6/15.

WILLIAMS, W. J., b. Pontypridd, 5731, Pte., k. in a., F., 13/3/15.

WILLIAMSON, R., b. Boston, 56563, L/Cpl., k. in a., F., 27/10/18.

WILLOCK, A., b. Sheriffhales, 8053, Pte., k. in a., F., 25/9/15.

WILLS, W. C., b. Cardiff, 10996, Pte., d., F., 1/11/14.

WILSON, C., b. Liverpool, 73492, Pte., k. in a., F., 22/4/18.

WILTON, W. F., b. Adderbury, 4602, Sgt., d., F., 26/12/15.

WINSLADE, W., b. Kirkdale, 45107, Pte., k. in a., F., 1/9/18.

WITHINGTON, W. H., b. Birmingham, 7816, Pte., d. of w., F., 4/1/16.

WOOD, J., b. Blackburn, 73499, Pte., k. in a., F., 27/10/18.

WOODFINE, G. H., b. Wrexham, 55024, Pte., k. in a., F., 27/5/17.

WOODIER, W., b. Northwich, 8092, Pte., d. of w., F., 2/11/14.

WOODMAN, W., b. St. Giles, 35248, Pte., k. in a., F., 27/5/17.

WOODS, E. W., b. London, 28057, L/Cpl., k. in a., F., 27/5/17.

WOOLLEY, J. L., b. Newtown, 290088, Pte., k. in a., F., 20/5/17.

WRENCH, J., b. Cheadle, 56246, Pte., d. of w., F., 11/6/17.

WYLLIE, J., b. Bangor, 5317, Pte., k. in a., F., 22/6/16, M.M.

YOUNG, E., b. Ushaw Moor, 55772, Pte., d., F., 3/11/18.

YOUNG, G. E., b. Bedminster, 9514, Pte., k. in a., F., 22/6/16.

YOUNG, G. H., b. Langton, 56233, Pte., k. in a., F., 25/11/17.

ZORIAN, J., b. Salford, 60589, Pte., d. of w., F., 13/10/17.

3rd BATTALION

BANNISTER, P., b. St. Helens, 24548, Pte., d., Home, 8/3/17.

BARNES, W. H., b. Walsall, 13947, Pte., d., Home, 13/7/18.

BOWEN, S. R., b. Llandilo, 14168, Pte., d., Home, 14/2/17.

BUTSON, G. G., b. Bristol, 9489, Pte., d., Home, 3/5/16.

COOK, G., b. London, 21672, L/Sgt., d., Home, 4/11/18.

CROFT, G. E. J., b. Woodford, 22058, Sgt., d., Home, 2/11/18.

CROMPTON, E., b. Garstang, 48963, Pte., d., Home, 30/7/16.

DAVIES, E., b. Bwlch, 11745, A/Sgt., d., At Sea, 15/4/17.

DAVIES, R., b. Llansilin, 61101, Pte., d., Home, 18/2/17.

DAVIES, W., b. Denbigh, 36032, Pte., d., Home, 23/9/16.

DAVIES, W. O., b. Llandysilio, 37827, Pte., d., Home, 6/6/18.

EDWARDS, J. M., e. Bootle, 49108, Pte., d., Home, 12/12/16.

EEDE, B. A., b. London, 44813, Pte., d., Home, 17/12/16.

EVANS, J., b. Birmingham, 5968, Pte., d., Home, 24/2/17.

FELL, N., b. Langwith, 19867, Sgt., d., M., 10/8/18.

FISHWICK, W. H., b. Ruyton-Eleven-Towns, 49068, Sgt., d., At Sea, 10/10/18.

FLATMAN, W., b. Doniplace, 55161, Cpl., k. in a., West Africa, 10/4/18.

FOULKES, D. R., b. Llanbrynmair, 90278, d., Home, 12/7/18.

FRANCIS, E., b. Llangadfan, 61081, Pte., d., Home, 8/3/17.

GERRARD, W., b. Leigh, 14002, Sgt., d., Home, 5/4/17.

GILL, R., b. Dunster, 6087, Pte., d., Home, 6/9/15.

GITTINS, J., b. Llangyniew, 91703, Pte., d., Home, 1/7/18.

GREEN, J., b. Holt, 61100, Pte., d., Home, 15/2/17.

HALL, R. H., b. Manchester, 6326, Pte., d., At Sea, 10/10/18.

HILLIARD, S., e. Wrexham, 19420, Pte., d., Home, 4/11/18.

HOOPER, J., b. Whittlewoods, 24446, Pte., d., Home, 16/10/15.

HUGHES, J., e. Llandudno, 3316, Pte., d., Home, 6/5/16.

JARWOOD, F. R. F., b. Dartmouth, 4404, Pte., d., Home, 12/2/17.

JONES, C., b. Corwen, 19118, Pte., d., Home, 24/2/15.

JONES, E., b. Blaenau Festiniog, 267886, Pte., d., Home, 5/11/18.

JONES, H., b. Llanrhaiadr, 201115, Pte., d., Home, 5/11/18.

JONES, H. E., b. Colwyn Bay, 92328, Pte., d., Home, 2/8/18.

JONES, H. P., b. Denbigh, 92268, Pte., d., Home, 6/7/18.

JONES, J., b. Mostyn, 4718, Pte., d., Home, 4/9/14.

JONES, J. F., b. Ffrith, 5637, Pte., d., Home, 14/1/15.

JONES, R., e. Bangor, 74314, Pte., d., At Sea, 10/10/18.

KING, C. W., b. Penarth, 15307, Pte., d., Home, 9/4/16.

LEESE, J., b. Fenton, 17762, Pte., d., Home, 2/1/15.

MANDRY, T., b. Treharris, 88599, Pte., d., Home, 4/8/18.

MARSH, J. R., e. Pontypridd, 88783, Pte., d., Home, 4/11/18.

McFADDEN, J., b. Dromore, 13248, Sgt., d., Home, 27/9/16.

MORGAN, A., b. Risca, 31166, L/Cpl., d., Home, 1/1/16.

OWEN, J. E., b. Ellesmere, 61033, Pte., d., Home, 10/7/17.

PALMER, W. G., b. Rossett, 5358, Pte., d., Home, 9/3/16.

POTTS, E., b. Crewe, 17210, Pte., d., Home, 5/3/15.

PRICE, A., b. Llanblodwel, 203104, Pte., d., Home, 10/11/18.

PRICE, W., b. Llanrug, 61155, Pte., d., Home, 18/6/17.

RILEY, T., b. Pontypridd, 19709, Pte., d., Home, 6/11/18.

RODEN, F., b. Market Drayton, 23519, Pte., d., Home, 25/5/15.

ROWLANDS, D., b. Llanfihangel, 61116, Pte., d., At Sea, 10/10/18.

ROWLANDS, O., e. Wrexham, 92069, Pte., d., Home, 17/7/18.

SMITH, C., b. Birkenhead, 73031, Pte., d., Home, 6/11/18.

SMITH, J., b. Preston, 52457, Pte., d., Home, 10/3/17.

SNELSON, T., b. Lostock, 70644, Pte., d., Home, 2/11/18.

THOMAS, D. J., b. Bala, 61022, Pte., d., Home, 20/2/17.

THOMAS, E., b. Llanrwst, 92077, Pte., d., At Sea, 10/10/18.

THOMAS, E., b. Pontddu, 61036, Pte., d., Home, 18/1/18.

WALKER, C., b. Worcester, 88703, Pte., d., Home, 3/6/18.

WATTS, H. W., b. London, 60005, Sgt., d., Home, 21/1/18.

WILCOCK, J., b. Liverpool, 19305, Pte., d., Home, 2/9/18.

WILLIAMS, E., b. Aberdare, 11842, Pte., d., Home, 12/10/14.

WILLIAMS, G. R., b. Llanddeinio-len, 60931, Pte., d., Home, 22/2/17.

WILLIAMS, T. J., b. Eglwysbach, 20668, Pte., d., At Sea, 15/4/17.

WILSHAW, A., b. Hanley, 18070, Pte., d., Home, 6/1/15.

WRIGHT, C., b. Cronton, 75393, Pte., d., Home, 11/10/17.

8th BATTALION

ACKLAND, R. D., b. Tenby, 19653, Pte., k. in a., G., 6/1/16.

ADDISON, R., b. London, 24358, Pte., k. in a., M., 25/1/17.

AMOS, S., b. Bedminster, 12695, L/Cpl., k. in a., M., 9/4/16.

ARNOLD, B., b. Cardiff, 33045, Pte., d. of w., G., 13/11/15.

ARNOLD, G., b. Swansea, 30432, A/Cpl., d., I., 19/7/18.

ARTINGSTALL, A., b. Ashton-under-Lyne, 20907, Pte., d. of w., M., 29/4/18.

ASPEY, R. G., b. Hollinsgreen, 37143, Pte., d., I., 1/10/18.

BADDELEY, W. A., b. Newcastle, 30007, Pte., k. in a., M., 13/4/17.

BAILEY, B., b. Walthamstow, 30130, Pte., k. in a., M., 25/1/17.

BAILEY, I., b. Halnerend, 18354, Pte., k. in a., M., 9/4/16.

BARDSLEY, J., b. Stockport, 39285, Pte., d., M., 12/5/17.

BARKER, G. W., b. Wolverhampton, 12329, Pte., d. of w., G., 26/9/15.

BARNBROOK, J., b. Brierley Hill, Staffs, 12674, Cpl., d. of w., Malta, 29/8/15.

BARNES, A., b. Birmingham, 6127, Pte., d., I., 1/10/18.

BARRON, J., b. Kilmacthomas, 11756, Pte., k. in a., G., 7/8/15.

BARRY, W., b. Cardiff, 18122, Pte., k. in a., G., 19/8/15.

BASSETT, T., b. Garnant, 12389, Pte., d., M., 22/6/18.

BATE, E., b. Runcorn, 17339, Pte., k. in a., G., 2/12/15.

BEAUMONT, M., b. Leeds, 30182, Pte., d. of w., M., 16/2/17.

BELLIS, J., b. Flint, 12583, A/Cpl., d., M., 22/7/16.

BERNEY, P., b. Wexford, 12418, A/Cpl., k. in a., G., 7/1/16.

BERRY, W. T., b. Llanbadarn, 31062, Pte., d., At Sea, 4/12/15.

BEVAN, W., b. Morriston, 11763, Pte., k. in a., G., 16/8/15.

BICKERTON, W., b. Burslem, 23692, Pte., d., M., 2/7/16.

BODENHAM, R., b. Cardiff, 5535, Cpl., d., M., 28/9/18.

BOWYER, B., b. Hanley, 24080, Pte., d., M., 26/5/16.

BROADBENT, H., b. Halifax, 23991, A/Cpl., k. in a., M., 16/2/17.

BROCKBANK, S. W., b. Clifton, 41748, Pte., d. of w., M., 18/2/17.

BROCKLEY, J., b. Ashton-under-Lyne, 12133, Pte., k. in a., G., 9/8/15.

BRODRICK, D., b. Aberavon, 5414, Pte., d., At Sea, 7/12/15.

BROSTALL, T., b. Liverpool, 11882, Pte., k. in a., G., 7/8/15.

BRYAN, S., b. Mold, 11623, Pte., k. in a., G., 8/8/15.

BUCK, W., b. Merthyr, 69617, Pte., d., I., 21/7/18.

BUCKLEY, W. E., b. Chasetown, 37357, Pte., d., M., 10/10/18.

BULL, T., b. Swansea, 12869, Pte., k. in a., G., 7/1/16.

BULLOCK, H., b. Hanley, 11509, Pte., k. in a., G., 28/8/15.

BUNKELL, F. J., b. London, 30104, Pte., d., M., 12/7/16.

BURLAND, E., b. Ystrad, 5730, Pte., d. of w., M., 15/2/17.

BUTLER, S., b. Kenilworth, 11951, Pte., d. of w., At Sea, 25/8/15.

BUTLER, W., b. West Bromwich, 23592, Pte., d. of w., I., 8/5/16.

BYWATERS, W., b. Headland, 37108, Pte., d. of w., M., 29/4/18.

CAMPLING, T., b. Middlesbrough, 49072, Sgt., d. of w., M., 30/4/18. M.M.

CAPPELL, M., b. Bridgend, 19896, Pte., k. in a., M., 9/4/16.

CARD, W. T., b. Stockstead, 63068, Pte., d., M., 17/10/17.

CARMAN, E. H., b. Norwich, 31344, Pte., d., M., 7/5/16.

CASTLE, F., b. St. Albans, 31634, Pte., d. of w., M., 10/2/17.

CHADWICK, A., b. Heckmondwyke, 30195, Pte., k. in a., M., 16/2/17.

CLAYTON, R., b. Ashton-under Lyne, 11566, Cpl., d. of w., M., 2/5/18.

CLEGG, J., b. Macclesfield, 39272, Pte., d., M., 16/7/17.

COATES, A., b. Tunstall, 24581, Pte., d., M., 29/6/16.

COLLIER, S., b. Burton-on-Trent, 30010, Pte., d., M., 17/1/17.

COOK, W., b. Lower Gornal, 36400, L/Cpl., d., I., 15/9/18.

COOKE, W., b. Stockport, 46173, Pte., k. in a., M., 25/1/17.

COOMBS, F. J., b. Ogmore Vale, 12516, Pte., k. in a., G., 7/8/15.

COSTELLO, W., b. Flint, 11682, Pte., k. in a., M., 3/2/17.

CRAWFORD, T. J., b. Chester, 9241, Pte., k. in a., M., 9/4/16.

CULLIP, S. G., b. Putney, 30136, Pte., d. of w., M., 16/2/17.

CURTIS, S., b. Coed-Franc, 31261, Pte., k. in a., M., 1/2/17.

DABINETT, J., b. Shepton Beauchamp, 11879, Pte., k. in a., G., 27/7/15.

DAFFERN, J. T., b. Birmingham, 35520, Pte., d. of w., M., 17/2/17.

DAVIDSON, J., b. Wolverhampton, 13823, Pte., d. of w., Home, 25/9/15.

DAVIES, A., b. Bersham, 12550, Pte., d., E., 23/10/15.

DAVIES, B. F., b. Llangammerch, 24361, Pte., k. in a., M., 3/2/17.

DAVIES, C., b. Llanelly, 14733, Pte., d., I., 25/9/18.

DAVIES, C. J., b. Bethnal Green, 24453, Pte., d. of w., At Sea, 8/12/15.

DAVIES, D., b. Larne, 13369, Pte., d. of w., I., 10/5/16.

DAVIES, G., b. Hope, 30303, A/L/Sgt., k. in a., M., 20/12/16.

DAVIES, H., b. Lampeter, 12687, Pte., d., G., 11/8/15.

DAVIES, H., b. Llangynhafal, 37672, Pte., d., I., 4/8/16.

DAVIES, H., b. Neath, 39007, Pte., d. of w., M., 19/4/17.

DAVIES, J., b. Ystrad Effrod, 12035, L/Cpl., d. of w., Home, 4/9/15.

DAVIES, J., b. Llancynnid, 19379, Pte., k. in a., M., 25/1/17.

DAVIES, J., b. Bettwsynrhos, 36609, Pte., d., M., 23/6/16.

DAVIES, J. R., b. Abergele, 5364, C.S.M., d., M., 20/11/16.

DAVIES, L., b. Cardigan, 12176, Pte., k. in a., G., 16/8/15.

DAVIES, L., b. Llanegwad, 12225, Pte., d., M., 9/5/16.

DAVIES, M., b. Cerrig-y-Druidion, 203716, Pte., d., Home, 11/6/18.

DAVIES, R. M., b. Treherbert, 6634, Pte., k. in a., M., 9/4/16.

DAVIES, R. P., b. Llandulas, 36718, Pte., d., M., 28/6/16.

DAVIES, S., b. Merthyr, 12818, Pte., k. in a., G., 7/8/15.

DAY, C. H., b. Gloucester, 24487, Pte., d. of w., E., 15/1/16.

DAY, G. W., b. Cheadle, 23768, Pte., k. in a., M., 11/4/17.

DICKERSON, F. J., b. Burton-on-Trent, 30016, Pte., k. in a., M., 14/1/17.

DODD, J., b. Eastham, 12449, Pte., d., Malta, 19/10/15.

DOOLEY, W., b. Cerney, Wrexham, 12155, Pte., d., Home, 21/11/14.

DOWDING, G. A., b. Chadsmore, 24822, Pte., d., M., 1/6/16.

DOYLE, E., b. Wrexham, 12074, Pte., d., I., 8/6/17.

DREWITT, F. J., b. Kington Langley, 24098, Pte., k. in a., M., 9/4/16.

DUDLEY, T., b. Crewe, 33106, Pte., k. in a., M. 25/1/17.

DUNKLEY, W. C., b. Northampton,

12554, Pte., k. in a., M., 5/4/16.

DUTTON, W. J., b. Wrexham, 12556, Pte., d., E., 4/10/15.

DWYER, T., b. Dublin, 11722, Pte., d., M., 20/7/15.

EARLE, J., b. Trowbridge, 24025, Pte., d. of w., G., 18/8/15.

EDDIES, J., b. Whitchurch, 12319, Pte., k. in a., G., 11/8/15.

EDWARDS, A., b. Boddelwiddan, 16261, Pte., d., I., 24/6/18.

EDWARDS, W., b. Aberdare, 17951, Pte., k. in a., M., 7/4/16.

EDWARDS, W. J., b. Ystrad, 20411, Pte., k. in a., M., 9/4/16.

ELLIOT, A. F., b. Beeley, 31108, Pte., d., M., 27/4/16.

ELLIS, H. T., b. Mountain Ash, 11952, Pte., k. in a., M., 9/4/16.

ELLIS, W., b. Chester, 5838, Pte., d. of w., G., 21/8/15.

EMERY, F., b. Fenton, 30017, Pte., d. of w., M., 18/2/17.

ENOCH, E. W., b. Workington, 31519, P., d., At Sea, 6/11/15.

EVANS, A., b. Llangystinin, 12396, Pte., d., G., 17/8/15.

EVANS, C. S., b. Newtown, 290668, Pte., d., I., 13/7/18.

EVANS, E., b. Cefn-Mawr, 70017, Pte., d., I., 30/7/18.

EVANS, E., b. Criccieth, 37057, Pte., d. of w., M., 19/2/17.

EVANS, G., b. Ammanford, 12242, Pte., d. of w., E., 17/9/15.

EVANS, G., b. Welshpool, 12582, Pte., d. of w., G., 7/10/15.

EVANS, H., b. Penygroes, 40440, Pte., k. in a., M., 13/4/17.

EVANS, J., b. Llangunnock, 12150, Pte., k. in a., G., 16/8/15.

EVANS, J., b. Rhyl, 30323, Pte., d., M., 29/5/17.

EVANS, P., b. Llandegai, 12246, Pte., k. in a., M., 5/4/16.

EVANS, T., b. Ystradyfodwy, 12500, Pte., d. of w., M., 17/2/17.

EVANS, T. I., b. Glynceinog, 11468, Cpl., k. in a., M., 22/4/16.

EVERETT, E. N., b. Upper Stratton, 37870, Pte., d., M., 13/10/16.

EVERITT, S., b. Ardsley, 30208, Pte., d. of w., M., 15/1/17.

EVESON, H., b. Old Swinford, 36465, Pte., k. in a., M., 3/2/17.

FLETCHER, F., b. Longton, 32537, Pte., d., M., 5/7/16.

FLETCHER, P., b. Hoyland, 30214, Pte., d. of w., M., 12/4/17.

FOLEY, W., b. Dudley, 30019, Pte., k. in a., M., 25/1/17.

FORSTER, F., b. Tunstall, 24842, Pte., k. in a., M., 9/4/16.

FOSTER, C., b. Rochdale, 23775, Pte., k. in a., M., 13/1/17.

FOSTER, H., b. Sheffield, 30212, Pte., d. of w., M., 17/2/17.

FREETH, A., b. Wednesbury,

11516, Sgt., d. of w., M., 18/4/16.

GANDY, T., b. Northwich, 30449, Pte., k. in a., M., 3/2/17.

GARDNER, V. A., b. Gt. Yarmouth, 28839, Pte., d., M., 11/7/16.

GARNER, T., b. Eglwys Bach, 12237, L/Cpl., k. in a., M., 5/4/16.

GELL, A. H., b. Aberdare, 19942, Pte., k. in a., G., 7/8/15.

GILBERT, W. B., b. London, 30159, Pte., d. of w., M., 25/1/17.

GITTINS, H., b. Llandrinio, 12567, Pte., d. of w., M., 28/3/17.

GLENDENNING, A., b. Briton Ferry, 11526, Pte., k. in a., G., 7/8/15.

GOFF, G., b. Orrell, Bootle, 30087, Pte., d. of w., M., 26/1/17.

GORDON, T. I., b. Longton, 30021, Pte., d. of w., M., 21/1/17.

GOTT, W., b. Ripon, 46322, Pte., k. in a., M., 16/2/17.

GREEN, L., b. Failsworth, 36182, Pte., d. of w., M., 7/4/17.

GREGORY, W., b. Church, 2823, Pte., d. of w., M., 18/12/16.

GRICE, T., b. Walsall, 24586, Pte., d., M., 19/9/16.

GRIFFITHS, A., b. Hawarden, 12637, Pte., k. in a., M., 5/4/16.

GRIFFITHS, R. T., b. Dyserth, 12117, Cpl., d., G., 14/11/16.

GRIFFITHS, T. J., b. Ffynnon Grdew, 30384, Pte., d., M., 8/1/18.

GRIFFITHS, W. S., b. Clydach Vale, 5681, Pte., d. of w., M., 5/4/16.

GRIFFITHS, W. W., b. Birkenhead, 30326, Pte., d. of w., M., 16/2/17.

GROTTICK, P. C., b. Bow, 31556, Sgt., k. in a., M., 9/4/16.

GROVES, G., b. Higher Peover, 39296, Pte., d., M., 22/12/17.

HACKETT, P. C., b. Longton, 23564, Pte., d. of w., M., 19/4/16.

HALL, J., b. Hyde, 39292, Pte., d. of w., M., 18/2/17.

HALLAM, J., b. Manchester, 29019, Pte., d., M. 23/6/16.

HAMMOND, A. E., b. London, 24067, Pte., k. in a., M., 5/4/16.

HAMPSON, W., b. Hindley, 31314, Pte., k. in a., M., 5/4/16.

HARDING, J. C., b. London, 11884, Pte., k. in a., G., 7/8/15.

HARLEY, L., b. Abercarn, 31521, Pte., d. of w., Malta, 22/10/15.

HARNEY, G., b. Manchester, 12376, Pte., k. in a., G., 6/8/15.

HARRATT, J., b. Brown Hills, 30029, Pte., d. of w., M., 25/2/17.

HASSALL, J., b. Tunstall, 12082, Pte., k. in a., M., 25/1/17.

HAYMAN, W., b. Nantymoel, 4895, Pte., k. in a., M., 25/1/17.

HAYWARD, E. J., b. Dawley, 24532, A/Cpl., d., M., 24/12/17.

HEAL, S. G., b. Bideford, 204340, Pte., d., I., 29/7/18.

HENDERSON, T., b. Edinburgh, 13764, Pte., d. of w., At Sea, 18/8/15.

HENNESSEY, M. P., b. Wrexham, 10957, Sgt., k. in a., M., 5/4/16.

HIBBERSON, T., b. Sheffield, 31522, Pte., k. in a., M., 9/4/16.

HICKINBOTHAM, A., b. Cannock, 19746, Pte., k. in a., G., 7/8/15.

HIGGINBOTHAM, J., b. Stockport, 30435, Pte., k. in a., M., 13/4/17.

HILDITCH, F., b. Fulham, 31618, Pte., d. of w., M., 8/4/16.

HILL, W. H., b. Burslem, 24601, Pte., k. in a., M., 9/4/16.

HOBBS, W., b. Cardiff, 37810, Pte., d., M., 15/7/16.

HODGE, T., b. Wellington, 31541, Sgt., k. in a., M., 15/2/17.

HODGES, T., b. Wellow, 19988, Pte., d., Home, 7/2/16.

HOLLAND, J., b. Northwich, 48840, Pte., d. of w., M., 25/1/17.

HOOK, B., b. Hoxton, 24041, Pte., d. of w., Home, 31/10/16.

HOOSEN, T. J., b. Northop, 11849, Pte., k. in a., G., 4/10/15.

HOPKINS, A., b. Neath, 12146, Cpl., k. in a., M., 25/1/17.

HOTEN, A., b. Pinxton, 33184, Pte., k. in a., M., 11/4/17.

HOWELLS, A., b. Penarth, 12309, Pte., d. of w., M., 20/2/17.

HUDSON, W. T., b. Chester, 46113, Pte., k. in a., M., 20/12/16.

HUGHES, A., b. Aberdare, 37704, Pte., d., I., 8/8/17.

HUGHES, E., b. Llanasa, 25039, Pte., k. in a., M., 5/4/16.

HUGHES, E. D., b. Penmaenmawr, 36280, Pte., d., M., 23/6/16.

HUGHES, H., b. Holyhead, 13110, Pte., k. in a., G., 29/8/15.

HUGHES, J. R., b. Llanrwst, 11913, Pte., k. in a., G., 11/11/15.

HUGHES, J. T., b. Bodfari, 12009, Cpl., k. in a., M., 13/4/17.

HUGHES, R. J., b. Holyhead, 13175, Pte., k. in a., G., 7/8/15.

HUGHES, S., b. Kidwelly, 12535, Pte., d. of w., Home, 12/3/18.

HUGHES, T., b. Llanelly, 12226, Pte., k. in a., G., 12/8/15.

HUGHES, W., b. Amlwch, 12152, Pte., d. of w., G., 8/1/16.

HUMFRAYS, R., b. Scarborough, 49090, Pte., k. in a., M., 25/1/17.

HUMPHREYS, T. J., b. Holyhead, 44418, Pte., d., M., 23/7/17.

HUTCHINGS, A. E., b. Penarth, 12312, Pte., k. in a., G., 7/1/16.

HUYTON, W., b. Hanley, 23632, Pte., d., M., 16/6/16.

HYDE, J. A., b. Oakengates, 12453, Cpl., k. in a., M., 9/4/16.

IBALL, A., b. Buckley, 11456, Pte., k. in a., M., 5/4/16.

INGHAM, A. J., b. Liverpool, 31604, Pte., d., M., 8/6/16.

INSKIP, J., b. Longton, 8371, C.S.M., d., I., 7/7/16.

ISHERWOOD, S. W., b. Radford, 46168, Pte., k. in a., M., 25/1/17.

IZZARD, C., b. Birmingham, 12717, Pte., d., E., 7/10/15.

JACOBS, G., b. Whitland, 12338, L/Cpl., d. of w., M., 26/1/17.

JAMES, J., b. Maesteg, 11950, Pte., k. in a., G., 19/10/15.

JARMAN, W., b. Penywrath, 23822, Pte., k. in a., M., 9/4/16.

JENKINS, B., b. Llangennech, 69634, Pte., d., I., 15/10/18.

JENKINS, S., b. Llanelly, 13391, Pte., k. in a., G., 12/8/15.

JENKINS, W., b. Ammanford, 13255, Pte., d., At Sea, 18/8/15.

JENKINS, W. E., b. Bedminster, 31614, Pte., d. of w., M., 13/4/17.

JOHNSON, E., b. Manchester, 30373, Pte., k. in a., M., 15/2/17.

JOHNSON, H. M., b. Bethnal Green, 31309, Pte., d., At Sea, 4/12/15.

JONES, A., b. Gwytherin, 39327, Pte., d., M., 23/7/17.

JONES, A. V., b. Margam, 31542, Pte., d., Malta, 28/9/15.

JONES, C., b. Festiniog, 267994, Pte., d., M., 3/8/18.

JONES, D., b. Llanarthney, 13131, Pte., d. of w., G., 17/8/15.

JONES, E. J., b. Denbigh, 24101, Pte., d., M., 19/6/18.

JONES, E. J., b. Eglwyssilan, 24767, Pte., d., E., 23/12/15.

JONES, F., b. Penmachno, 36832, Pte., k. in a., M., 15/2/17.

JONES, G. W., b. Cardiff, 43779, Pte., k. in a., M., 25/1/17.

JONES, H., b. Llanwenllwyfo, 12629, Pte., k. in a., G., 15/10/15.

JONES, H., b. Bangor, 11710, Pte., d. of w., G., 17/8/15.

JONES, H., b. Penrhyndeudraeth, 12328, Pte., k. in a., G., 22/9/15.

JONES, I., b. Northop, 12051, Pte., k. in a., G., 12/8/15.

JONES, J., b. Barry, 12363, Pte., d., Home, 22/6/15.

JONES, J., b. Flint, 60786, Pte., d., M., 22/7/17.

JONES, J., b. Wrexham, 49853, Pte., d. of w., M., 29/4/18.

JONES, J. E., b. Llangollen, 11658, Pte., d. of w., E., 14/8/15.

JONES, J. F., b. Hawarden, 12772, L/Cpl., k. in a., G., 22/8/15.

JONES, J. R., b. Llandewi, 25403, Pte., d., At Sea, 2/11/15.

JONES, L., b. Conway, 31505, Pte., d. of w., M., 26/1/17.

JONES, M., b. Swansea, 16821, Pte., k. in a., M., 9/4/16.

JONES, N. G., b. Carnarvon, 266711, Pte., d. of w., Home, 19/7/18.

JONES, R., b. Buckley, 12436, L/Cpl., k. in a., M., 9/4/16.

JONES, R., b. Rhoscolyn, 13345, Pte., d., E., 2/12/15.

JONES, R., b. Carnarvon, 19923, Pte., k. in a., G., 2/1/16.

JONES, R., b. Gwyddelwern, 25088, Pte., d. of w., Malta, 23/1/16.

JONES, R. J., b. Llanddulas, 36335, L/Cpl., d., M., 13/7/16.

JONES, S., b. Taillwydon, 5756, Pte., k. in a., M., 9/4/16.

JONES, T., b. Gainsborough, 5462, L/Cpl., d. of w., I., 13/3/17.

JONES, T., b. Welshpool, 13271, Pte., d., G., 30/11/15.

JONES, T., e. Llandudno, 20386, Pte., d., I., 30/10/18.

JONES, V., b. Bala, 40062, Pte., k. in a., M., 25/1/17.

JONES, W., b. Connah's Quay, 11544, L/Cpl., k. in a., M., 11/4/17.

JONES, W., b. Bodwrog, 12119, Pte., d. of w., M., 25/4/16.

JONES, W., b. Wrexham, 17760, Pte., d., At Sea, 27/8/15.

JONES, W., b. Bath, 31605, Pte., d. of w., G., 5/1/16.

JONES, W., b. Capelgormon, 69263, Pte., d., I., 2/10/18.

JONES, W., b. Macclesfield, 30441, Pte., k. in a., M., 25/1/17.

JONES, W. J., b. Northop, 5841, Pte., d. of w., At Sea, 12/8/15.

JUDGE, J., b. Oldbury, 35506, Pte., k. in a., M., 15/2/17.

JUKES, J. W., b. Birmingham, 5227, Pte., d., M., 21/6/16.

JUTSON, T., b. Great Bridge, 12464, Pte., d., At Sea, 1/9/15.

KEEN, S., b. Warrington, 13512, Pte., d., At Sea. 19/7/16.

KELLY, T., b. Bolton. 23689, Pte., k. in a., M., 15/2/17.

KINGHAM, H. J., b. London, 31639, Pte., d., I., 20/6/16.

KITSON, W. H., b. Doncaster, 30230, Pte., d., M., 20/11/16.

KNIGHT, J. E., b. Wellingborough, 31606, Pte., k. in a., G., 7/1/16.

LANGLEY, J., b. Leeswood, 11768, Pte., d., Malta, 21/8/15.

LEA, J. E., b. Wrexham, 31067, Pte., k. in a., M., 25/1/17.

LEDDY, B., b. Dewsbury, 11533, Pte., k. in a., G., 10/8/15.

LEGG, A., b. Penarth, 12496, Pte., d. of w., G., 16/8/15.

LEIGHTON, J., b. Tunstall, 30038, Pte., d., M., 2/5/16.

LEWIS, J., b. Caerwen, 12089, Pte., d., E., 21/10/15.

LEWIS, M., e. Aberdare, 24492, Pte., k. in a., M., 5/4/16.

LEWIS, T. E., b. Llangurig, 5058, Pte., k. in a., M., 9/4/16.

LLOYD, D. J., b. Northop, 12080, L/Cpl., d. of w., Home, 2/9/15.

LLOYD, W., e. Wrexham, 49845, Pte., d., M., 2/11/17.

LONGSTAFF, J. C., b. Kingston-on-Thames, 31624, L/Cpl., k. in a., M., 5/4/16.

LOVELOCK, L., e. Mold, 30400, Pte., k. in a., M., 15/2/17.

LUCK, C. H., b. Manchester, 11718, Cpl., k. in a., M., 5/4/16.

LYNCH, F., b. Manchester, 30399, L/Cpl., d., M., 20/8/18.

MAIDMENT, G., b. Pimlico, 30167, Pte., d., M., 30/7/16.

MANNING, M., b. Liverpool, 11512, L/Sgt., d. of w., G., 24/8/15.

MARTIN, G., b. Flint, 32511, Pte., d., M., 10/6/16.

MARTIN, T., b. Blackburn, 30076, Pte., k. in a., M., 25/1/17.

MASON, T. W., b. Rawcliffe, 30241, Pte., d., M., 25/7/17.

MATHIAS, S. E., b. Cardiff, 11942, Pte., d., Home, 13/9/15.

MATTHEWS, A., b. Vardre, 5693, Pte., d. of w., M., 15/2/17.

MATTHEWS, A. W., b. Sedgeley, 12706, Pte., k. in a., G., 11/8/15.

MATTHEWS, P. W., b. Tonypandy, 4619, Cpl., k. in a., G., 8/1/16.

MAYO, W., b. London, 12189, Pte., k. in a., M., 5/4/16.

McDONAGH, J., b. Lochglyne, 12284, Sgt., d. of w., I., 12/3/17.

MacDONALD, J., b. Rosskeen, 18683, Pte., k. in a., M., 3/2/17.

McGOVAN, H., b. Bath, 12203, Sgt., d. of w., G., 17/8/15.

MEREDITH, E. H., b. Raglan, 18274, Pte., d. of w., M., 9/4/16.

MERRITT, F., b. London, 24043, Pte., d. of w., G., 21/7/15.

MIDGHALL, J., b. Garston, 17927, Pte., k. in a., M., 25/1/17.

MONK, L. G., b. London, 23764, Pte., d., Malta, 29/12/15.

MORAN, P., b. Liverpool, 11820, Pte., k. in a., M., 9/4/16.

MORGAN, C., b. Coleford, 5594, Pte., d., M., 7/10/18.

MORGAN, D. J., b. Kidwelly, 12532, Pte., d., At Sea, 30/10/15.

MORGAN, J., b. Pembroke, 13329, Pte., d., M., 21/6/16.

MORGAN, J. E., b. Llandovery, 12430, Pte., k. in a., G., 11/8/15.

MORRIS, A. E., b. Llanelly, 11661, Sgt., k. in a., M., 5/4/16.

MORRIS, A. E., b. Denbigh, 40790, L/Cpl., k. in a., M., 15/2/17.

MORRIS, R., b. Flint, 11895, Pte., k. in a., G., 7/8/15.

MORRIS, R., b. Ruabon, 30307, L/Cpl., k. in a., M., 15/2/17.

MORRIS, W., b. Cwmavon, 12087, Pte., k. in a., G., 12/8/15.

MORTON, D. C., b. Aberdare, 53105, Pte., k. in a., M., 29/4/18.

MOTTERSHEAD, A., b. Over Peover, 48842, Pte., k. in a., M., 18/1/17.

MULLINEX, H., b. Middlewood, 19929, L/Cpl., k. in a., G., 24/7/15.

NASH, S., b. Bristol, 24014, Pte., d. of w., G., 16/8/15.

NAVIN, A., b. Dublin, 5506, Pte., d., M., 21/4/17.

NEVE, T. B., b. London, 31607, Pte., k. in a., M., 5/4/16.

NEWNS, S., b. Oswestry, 12321, Sgt., d., Malta, 22/11/15.

NICHOLAS, F. R., b. Leominster, 37083, Pte., d., M., 28/8/16.

NICHOLS, P., b. Hawarden, 11536, Pte., d., G., 20/10/15.

NORTON, T., b. Orcop, 18463, L/Cpl., d. of w., G., 13/8/15.

O'NEILL, D., b. Mycross, 11514, Pte., k. in a., G., 10/8/15.

O'NEILL, J., b. Middlesbrough, 49078, L/Sgt., k. in a., M., 15/2/17.

O'SULLIVAN, P., b. Castle Lyons, 31529, Pte., k. in a., M., 9/4/16.

OTTLEY, W. R., b. London, 12468, Pte., d. of w., At Sea, 13/8/15.

OWEN, J., b. Llandudno, 49240, Pte., d., M., 26/10/17.

OWEN, J. H., b. Abergele, 12477, Pte., k. in a., G., 16/8/15.

OWEN, N., b. Northop, 11667, L/Cpl., k. in a., G., 21/9/15.

OWEN, R., b. Llansadwrn, 25067, Pte., k. in a., G., 7/1/16.

OWEN, R., b. Llangynwyd, 12086, Sgt., k. in a., M., 9/4/16.

OWEN, T., e. Holyhead, 266720, Pte., d. of w., M., 29/4/18.

OWEN, W., b. Llansadwrn, 49843, Pte., d., M., 26/9/17.

OWEN, W., b. Llandudno, 60667, Pte., d., M., 30/10/17.

PARRY, E. E., b. Denbigh, 12003, Sgt., k. in a., M., 5/4/16.

PARSON, J., b. Cardiff, 69910, Pte., d., I., 5/10/18.

PARSONS, J., b. Llanfair, 13841, L/Cpl., k. in a., M., 9/4/16.

PATTISON, S., b. Newcastle, 31709, Pte., k. in a., G., 5/1/16.

PAUL, H. S., b. Barry, 31625, L/Cpl., k. in a., M., 5/4/16.

PEARCE, F., b. Penley, 12263, Pte., d., G., 5/12/15.

PETERS, J., b. Connah's Quay, 12650, L/Cpl., d., M., 27/5/16.

PHILLIPS, C. C., b. Bedwellty, 18789, Pte., k. in a., M., 25/1/17.

PHILLIPS, J., b. Wingate, 31510, Pte., k. in a., G., 8/11/15.

PLANT, E., b. Wrexham, 30349, L/Cpl., d., I., 24/9/18.

PLATT, F., b. Penley, 5668, Pte., d. of w. M., 16/2/17.

POWELL, G. E., e. Llandudno, 21168, Pte., k. in a., M., 25/1/17.

POWELL, H. J., b. Blaeneu, 15378, Pte., d. of w., M., 26/1/17.

PREECE, A., b. Kingston, 6551, Pte., k. in a., M., 9/4/16.

PRESTON, A., b. Batley, 30246, Pte., d., M., 10/8/16.

PRICE, F. G., b. Hanwood, 9288, A/C.S.M., d. of w., At Sea, 12/1/16.

PRICE, G. R., b. Aberdare, 31547, Pte., d., G., 16/9/16.

PRICE, H., b. Pennsylvania, 5609, Cpl., k. in a., M., 9/4/16.

PRICE, S., b. Wolverhampton, 12664, Pte., d., G., 1/12/15.

PRIDDLE, A. W., b. Rimpton, 31626, Pte., k. in a., G., 20/9/15.

PRITCHARD, D. E., b. Rhyl, 45889, Pte., k. in a., M., 25/1/17.

PRITCHARD, J., b. Derby, 19459, Pte., k. in a., G., 17/8/15.

PRITCHARD, P., b. Liverpool, 18474, Pte., d., G., 11/12/15.

PROBERT, W., b. Ebbw Vale, 12730, Pte., d. of w., M., 13/4/16.

PROFFITT, F., b. Stockport, 19774, Pte., d. of w., M., 29/4/16.

PROSSER, R., b. Llanwonno, 31278, Pte., k. in a., G., 2/1/16.

PRYTHERCH, T. R., b. Bangor, 20689, Pte., d., M., 17/7/17.

PUGH, A. T., b. Rhostyllen, 11647, Pte., d., M., 16/5/16.

PUGH, B., b. Fenton, 18008, Pte., d., G., 1/12/15.

RADFORD, S., b. Cadoxton, 19635, Pte., d. of w., M., 10/8/15.

REECE, W., b. Birkenhead, 12114, Pte., k. in a., M., 12/5/16.

REES, H. J., b. Llangeinwyr, 12130, L/Sgt., k. in a., M., 25/1/17.

REES, I., b. Pontlottyn, 12422, Pte., d. of w., G., 29/9/15.

REES, R., b. Coity, 31608, Pte., d., G., 3/10/15.

RENSHAW, H., b. Harpurhey, 46306, Pte., d., M., 11/7/17.

RICHARDS, A. E., b. Llandudno, 266684, Pte., d., M., 25/6/18.

RICHARDS, E. T., b. Aberystwyth, 31548, Pte., d., E., 4/11/15.

RICHARDS, J. T., b. Llangollen, 6112, Pte., k. in a., G., 24/7/15.

RICHARDS, L., b. Llantrisant, 18897, Pte., d., At Sea, 12/10/15.

RIGBY, A., b. Liverpool, 30068, Pte., d. of w., M., 2/5/16.

RIGBY, W., b. Bolton, 19461, Sgt., d., M., 9/9/16.

ROBERTS, H., b. Wrexham, 69298, Pte., d., At Sea, 30/10/17.

ROBERTS, H., b. Llandysilio, 1166, Pte., d., G., 29/7/15.

ROBERTS, I. H., b. Llysfaen, 11835, Pte., k. in a., M., 3/2/17.

ROBERTS, J., b. Brymbo, 31382, Pte., d. of w., M., 9/4/16.

ROBERTS, J., b. Portmadoc, 267423, Pte., k. in a., M., 29/4/18.

ROBERTS, J. G., b. Llangefni, 29541, Pte., k. in a., M., 15/2/17.

ROBERTS, J. H., b. Leicester, 49080, Cpl., k. in a., M., 15/2/17.

ROBERTS, J. T., b. Wigan, 24401, Pte., d. of w., G., 5/1/16.

ROBERTS, M., b. Penllech, 49237, Pte., d., M., 25/9/18.

ROBERTS, O., b. Anglesey, 21217, Pte., d., M., 23/7/17.

ROBERTS, R., b. Dinas Mawddwy, 13478, Pte., d. of w., At Sea, 21/8/15.

ROBERTS, R., b. Chirk, 36285, Pte., d., M., 10/7/16.

ROBERTS, T., b. Penmorfa, 5754, Pte., k. in a., G., 25/10/15.

ROBERTS, W., b. Manchester, 12016, Pte., k. in a., M., 4/4/16.

ROBERTS, W., b. Beddgelert, 12513, Pte., k. in a., M., 5/4/16.

ROBERTS, W., e. Rhyl, 30428, Pte., d., M., 23/7/17.

ROBINSON, C., b. Oldham, 31338, Pte., k. in a., G., 4/12/15.

ROGERS, D., b. Fenton, 12785, L/Cpl., d. of w., G., 7/8/15.

ROGERS, E., b. Stoke-on-Trent, 12786, Pte., d. of w., At Sea, 8/8/15.

RONAN, W., b. Manning, 11759, Pte., k. in a., M., 5/5/16.

ROOK, S., b. Mitcham, 30268, Pte., d. of w., M., 16/2/17.

ROURKE, F., b. Ashton-under-Lyne, 36929, Pte., k. in a., M., 16/2/17.

ROWLAND, R., b. Llangibby, 31532, Pte., k. in a., G., 31/8/15.

ROWLINSON, W., b. Lawston, 12552, Pte., k. in a., G., 7/10/15.

RUDGE, W. F., b. Llandudno, 5728, Pte., d., M., 8/8/16.

SAMPSON, D., b. Blaenrhondda, 15054, L/Cpl., d., M., 24/6/17.

SAMUELS, J., b. Ruabon, 24165, Pte., d., M., 27/6/16.

SANDREY, G., b. Pontypridd, 12306, Pte., d. of w., M., 16/2/17.

SAUNDERS, B. J., b. Treorchy, 11760, Pte., k. in a., G., 10/8/15.

SAUNDERS, S., b. High Wycombe, 22560, Pte., d., M., 21/7/17.

SEDDON, A., b. Haydock, 24549, Pte., d., M., 8/6/18.

SEETON, T., e. Cranbrook, 30172, Pte., k. in a., M., 16/2/17.

SEVERNS, Z., b. Bilston, 11523, Cpl., d. of w., M., 23/4/17.

SEWELL, F. J., b. Barry, 37855, Pte., d. of w., M., 26/1/17.

SHARPLES, H., b. Blakenhall, 12703, Pte., d. of w., M., 27/4/16.

SHIRTCLIFF, O., b. Harworth, 12485, Pte., d., Malta, 5/1/16.

SIMPKINS, E., b. West Bromwich, 19448, Pte., d. of w., At Sea, 10/10/15.

SLATER, B., b. Ogmore Vale, 16046, Pte., d. of w., At Sea, 20/7/15.

SLATER, E., b. Holywell, 11606, Pte., k. in a., G., 7/8/15.

SMITH, C. P., b. Cardiff, 5129, Pte., k. in a., M., 9/4/16.

SMITH, E., b. Glanamman, 12223, Pte., k. in a., G., 11/8/15.

SMITH, F., b. Fenton, 24596, Pte., k. in a., M., 14/2/17.

SMITH, W., b. Newton, 24185, Pte., k. in a., M., 11/4/17.

SMITH, W. J., b. Hawarden, 12684, Pte., k. in a., G., 23/8/15.

SOMERFIELD, C., b. Bloxwich, 6598, Pte., d. of w., M., 16/4/16.

SPEAR, S., b. Penarth, 12499, Pte., d. of w., M., 16/2/17.

STAGG, J. H., b. Shepton Mallet, 31171, Pte., k. in a., M., 11/4/17.

STANLEY, J., b. Flint, 5379, Pte., d. of w., M., 25/1/17.

STEWART, C., b. Markinch, 24588, Pte., d. of w., M., 22/4/16.

STITT, J., b. Liverpool, 11084, Pte., d. of w., M., 6/4/16.

STOCKS, B., b. Pinxton, 19677, Pte., k. in a., G., 11/8/15.

STOCKTON, J., b. Croxton Green, 19381, Pte., d. of w., M., 21/4/16.

STRANGWARD, O., e. Pontefract, 30285, Pte., k. in a., M., 13/4/17.

STUCKEY, R. A., b. Ealing, 28733, Pte., d., M., 27/7/17.

TABER, A., b. Birmingham, 24641, Pte., d. of w., M., 20/12/16.

TAYLOR, A., b. Tredegar, 11747, Pte., d. of w., Malta, 13/8/15.

TAYLOR, A. H., b. Borough, 26723, Pte., k. in a., M., 15/1/17.

TAYLOR, W., e. Mold, 30411, Pte., k. in a., M., 21/1/17.

THOMAS, E. H., b. Eglwysilan, 18157, Pte., d., M., 12/6/16.

THOMAS, H., b. Llangadfan, 12200, Pte., k. in a., G., 16/8/15.

THOMAS, J., b. Pontypridd, 11874, Pte., d., M., 28/5/16.

THOMAS, W., b. Borsdale Wood, 31341, Pte., k. in a., G., 7/1/16.

THOMAS, W., b. Taffs Well, 49825, Pte., d., M., 5/8/17.

THOMAS, W. J., b. Penclwdd, 12961, Pte., d., M., 11/7/16.

THORNTON, W. J., b. Tipton, 44403, Pte., d., M., 9/7/17.

THORPE, R. G., b. Stretton Audley, 11473, Sgt., k. in a., G., 17/8/15.

TOOLE, W., b. Tunstall, 31086, L/Cpl., k. in a., M., 5/4/16.

TRESIDER, J. H., b. Aston, 35524, Pte., d., M., 20/7/16.

TURNER, E., b. Quadham, 30125, Pte., d. of w., M., 25/1/17.

TURNER, G. F., b. Mansfield, 24082, Pte., d. of w., M., 24/2/17.

VAUGHAN, J. H., b. Llanbedr, 39055, Pte., d. of w., M., 9/5/17.

VICARAGE, H. J., b. Swansea, 36680, Pte., d., M., 16/8/16.

WADE, J., b. Stalybridge, 28811, Pte., k. in a., G., 11/11/15.

WAITE, H., b. Poplar, 49100, L/Cpl., k. in a., M., 25/1/17.

WALKER, A., b. London, 19919, Pte., k. in a., M., 15/2/17.

WALKER, G., b. London, 11540, Pte., k. in a., M., 9/4/16.

WARD, A., b. Rochford, 19634, Pte., k. in a., M., 9/4/16.

WATTS, J. E., b. Connah's Quay, 11611, Pte., k. in a., G., 19/8/15.

WEST, S., b. Aberystwyth, 18358, Pte., d., M., 1/7/16.

WHITE, T. V., b. Camden Town, 30281, Pte., d. of w., M., 20/12/16.

WHITEWOOD, H., b. Middlesbrough, 12387, k. in a., G., 15/8/15.

WHITLEY, J., b. Mold, 30359, Pte., d. of w., M., 25/1/17.

WIFFEN, J. H., b. Haverhill, 11930, Sgt., k. in a., G., 7/8/15.

WILCOXON, H., b. Thornton-le-Moore, 12098, Pte., d. of w., G., 6/1/16.

WILLIAMS, A. C., b. London, 24099, Pte., d. of w., At Sea, 10/8/15.

WILLIAMS, A. C., b. Gwytherin, 12238, Pte., k. in a., G., 20/8/15.

WILLIAMS, C., b. Mansfield, 12524, L/Cpl., k. in a., M., 15/2/17.

WILLIAMS, D., b. St. Dogmael's, 17227, Pte., k. in a., M., 25/1/17.

WILLIAMS, D. G., b. Llanelly, 12525, Pte., k. in a., G., 11/8/15.

WILLIAMS, D. L., b. Pwllheli, 12272, Cpl., d. of w., G., 22/7/15.

WILLIAMS, E., b. Wrexham,

31080, Pte., k. in a., G., 5/1/16.

WILLIAMS, E. S. L., b. Denbigh, 11577, Sgt., d. of w., At Sea, 8/8/15.

WILLIAMS, G., b. Llangollen, 11715, Pte.. d., Home, 7/12/14.

WILLIAMS, H. L., b. Llanyche, 19414. Pte., k. in a., M., 9/4/16.

WILLIAMS, J., b. Penygraig, 24753, Pte., k. in a., M., 5/4/16.

WILLIAMS, J., b. Bethesda, 12543, Pte., k. in a., M., 9/4/16.

WILLIAMS, J., b. Llanllechio, 60759, Pte., d. of w., M., 30/4/18.

WILLIAMS, J. L., b. Liverpool, 11985, Pte., k. in a., G., 7/8/15.

WILLIAMS, N., b. Margam, 31273, Pte., d. of w., M., 8/4/16.

WILLIAMS, R., b. West Bromwich, 11525, Cpl., k. in a., G., 11/8/15.

WILLIAMS, R. O., b. Wrexham, 49854, Pte., k. in a., M., 29/4/18.

WILLIAMS, W., b. Wrexham, 12324, Pte., d. of w., At Sea, 17/8/15.

WILLIAMS, W. B., b. Pontlliw, 11910, Sgt., k. in a., G., 7/8/15.

WILLIAMS, W. H., b. Blaenau Festiniog, 291540, Pte., d., At Sea, 15/4/17.

WILLIAMS, W. J., b. Bangor, 12289, Pte., d. of w., M., 15/4/16.

WILSON, J., b. Burton-on-Trent, 28846, Pte., k. in a., G., 12/11/15.

WILSON, J. T., b. Norwich, 30070, Pte., d., M., 20/5/16.

WRIGHT, J., b. Deeping St. James, 11850, Cpl., d. of w., M., 2/3/17.

WRIGHT, T. B., b. Stafford, 12368, Sgt., k. in a., M., 9/4/16.

YOUNG, W. P. A., b. Trowbridge, 24048, Pte., k. in a., G., 3/11/15.

9th BATTALION

ACKROYD, E., b. Halifax, 12837, Pte., d. of w., F., 27/9/15.

ADAMS, T., b. Liverpool, 15937, Pte., k. in a., F., 25/9/15.

ALLEN, F., b. Longton, 46242, Cpl., k. in a., F., 3/11/16.

ALLMAN, G., b. Chester, 74551, Pte., k. in a., F., 14/6/18.

ALSOP, T., b. Preston, 15358, Pte., d. of w., F., 9/4/16.

ANGEL, G. T., b. London, 26585, Pte., k. in a., F., 20/9/17.

APPLEBY, H., b. London, 17548, Pte., d., 6/9/18.

ARDEN, H. E., b. Bethnal Green,

45725, Pte., k. in a., F., 7/6/17.

ATHERTON, G., b. Widnes, 16531, Pte., k. in a., F., 11/11/16.

ATTWOOD, J. C., b. West Bromwich, 12956, Sgt., k. in a., F., 25/9/15.

AUBREY, B. H., b. Briton Ferry, 36970, L/Cpl., d. of w., F., 14/5/18.

AVERY, F., b. Birmingham, 23101, Pte., d. of w., F., 7/10/15.

BAKER, T. J., b. Ebbw Vale, 54194, Pte., k. in a., F., 4/11/16.

BAMFORTH, J., b. Ashton-under-Lyne, 238060, Pte., k. in a., F., 7/5/18.

BANKS, J., b. Heywood, 52089, Pte., d., F., 24/6/18.

BARGUSS, H., b. Witney, 12210, Pte., k. in a., F., 25/9/15.

BARLOW, J. H., b. Hollinwood, 33425, Pte., k. in a., F., 3/7/16.

BARNES, R. H., b. Blackburn, 70504, Pte., k. in a., F., 14/6/18.

BARRETT, F. E., b. Leeds, 9674, L/Cpl., d. of w., F., 18/8/16.

BARTON, G. H., b. St. Helens, 75144, Pte., k. in a., F., 28/5/18.

BARTON, W., b. Southport, 13844, Pte., k. in a., F., 22/3/16.

BARTON, W., b. Hadlow, 56301, Pte., k. in a., F., 14/6/18.

BASSETT, J., b. Darwonno, 15020, Pte., k. in a., F., 22/3/18, M.M.

BATES, E., b. Stoke-on-Trent, 24591, Pte., k. in a., F., 20/9/17.

BATTERSBY, J., b. Manchester, 19314, Pte., k. in a., F., 3/7/16.

BAYLEY, W., b. Burton, 13712, Pte., k. in a., F., 22/3/18.

BEALE, A. E., e. Abertillery, 57920, Pte., d., F., 3/11/18.

BEDDOE, D. T., b. Bedwellty, 54195, Pte., k. in a., F., 22/3/18, M.M.

BELL, J., b. Neston, 75896, Pte., k. in a., F., 22/3/18.

BELLAMY, W. H., b. Daventry, 56349, Pte., k. in a., F., 23/10/17.

BELLIS, P., b. Hope, 12713, L/Sgt., d. of w., F., 25/9/15.

BENNETT, B. T., b. Bristol, 14819, Pte., k. in a., F., 14/6/18.

BENNETT, W. G., e. Reading, 56296, Pte., d., Home, 30/8/17.

BETTS, G. W., b. Peckham, 27796, Pte., k. in a., F., 30/5/18.

BEYNON, A., b. Llanelly, 13165, Pte., k. in a., F., 25/9/15.

BIBBY, T., b. Wigan, 52738, Pte., k. in a., F., 20/9/17.

BIRCHALL, H., b. Stockport, 33065, Cpl., k. in a., F., 22/3/18.

BISCOE, R. W. L., b. London,

56294, Pte., d. of w., F., 13/6/17.

BITHELL, H., b. Flint, 13452, Pte., k. in a., F., 20/11/16.

BLAKE, T., b. Cardiff, 31943, Pte., k. in a., F., 3/7/16.

BLOORE, J., b. Llandegla, 31500, Pte., k. in a., F., 3/7/16.

BOLEYN, E., b. Balsall Heath, 23160, L/Cpl., k. in a, F., 25/9/15.

BOLLAND, R., b. Wolverhampton. 235702, Pte., d. of w., F., 12/6/18.

BOLTON, H. W., b. Clerkenwell. 22111, Pte., k. in a., F., 20/11/16.

BOND, T., b. Westcott, 34048, Pte., k. in a., F., 14/6/18.

BOND, W., b. Birkdale, 266815, Pte., k. in a., F., 20/9/17.

BONSALL, H., b. Chelmorton, 33463, L/Sgt., k. in a.. F., 4/1/18, M.M.

BOWCOTT, F., e. Newport, 57930, Sgt., k. in a., F., 30/5/18.

BOWEN, A., b. Brithdir, 33498, Pte., k. in a., F., 7/6/17.

BOWEN, C. A., b. Llanelly, 13437, Pte., d. of w., F., 25/8/16.

BOWEN, J. V., b. Cardiff, 77415, Pte., k. in a., F., 20/10/18.

BOWLES, T., b. Witney, 23899, Pte., k. in a., F., 7/2/16.

BOWLEY, H., b. Criccieth, 37056, Pte., k. in a., F., 5/9/16.

BRADLEY, G., b. Clunbury, 70104, Pte., d. of w., F., 13/5/18.

BRADLEY, J., b. Shipston-on-Stour, 36423, Pte., k. in a., F., 20/11/16.

BRADLEY, R., b. Stanton Hill, 31788, Cpl., d. of w., F., 18/12/17.

BRENNAN, J., b. Portsmouth, 27864, Sgt., d., Home, 10/10/18.

BRENNAN, M. P., b. Leyton, 29845, Pte., k. in a., F., 20/11/16.

BRETTELL, B., b. Lye, 11751, Pte., d. of w., F., 3/7/16.

BROWN, A., b. Wrexham, 19995, Pte., k. in a., F., 23/10/18.

BROWN, H. G., b. Ford, 46261, Pte., k. in a., F., 2/11/16.

BROWN, J. H., e. Birkenhead, 57743, Pte., d. of w., F., 24/9/18.

BRYAN, J., b. Wrexham, 4343, Pte., k. in a., F., 13/2/17.

BURKHILL, J., b. Birkenhead, 315490, Pte., k. in a., F., 20/10/18.

BURNETT, F., b. Whitchurch, 57944, Pte., d. of w., F., 18/4/18.

BURNS, W. A., b. Gorton, 266833, Pte., k. in a., F., 22/3/18.

BURRIDGE, F., b. Shepton Mallet, 57479, Pte., d., F., 6/1/19.

BURROWS, J., b. Hawarden, 12828, Pte., k. in a., F., 25/9/15.

BURT, A., b. Stone, 33236, Pte., k. in a., F., 1/5/17.

BUTTER, R. H., e. Southwald, 55167, Pte., k. in a., F., 29/4/18.

BYATT, F., b. Burslem, 6430, Sgt., k. in a., F., 25/9/15.

CADWALLADER, C., b. Ellesmere Port, 56414, Pte., k. in a., F., 20/9/17.

CAMPDEN, W., b. Moxley, 46221, Pte., d. of w., F., 7/4/17.

CAPLE, H., b. Bridgwater, 16100, L/Cpl., k. in a., F., 25/9/15.

CARR, J., e. Wrexham, 54278, Pte., k. in a., F., 28/10/16.

CARTER, B., b. Birmingham, 46457, Cpl., k. in a., F., 22/3/18.

CASWELL, W., b. Birmingham, 16498, Pte., k. in a., F., 3/7/16.

CATLOW, A., b. Nelson, 46994, Pte., k. in a., F., 31/7/17.

CAWLEY, W. J., b. Huddersfield, 59746, Cpl., k. in a., F., 23/10/18.

CHAMPION, A. S., b. Stanningley, 36065, k. in a., F., 3/11/16.

CHAPMAN, J., b. London, 53999, Pte., k. in a., F., 10/6/18.

CHAPPELL, G. H., b. Kilburn, 21953, L/Cpl., k. in a., F., 18/4/18.

CHATHAM, J. B., b. Holt, 60999, Pte., d. of w., Home, 1/5/18.

CHESTER, C., b. Armthorpe, 46275, L/Sgt., d. of w., F., 16/11/17.

CHESTER, W. J., b. Somerton, 54292, Pte., d. of w., F., 2/10/17.

CHESTERS, C., b. Coppenhall, 8199, Pte., k. in a., F., 31/7/17.

CLAGUE, J., b. Douglas, 235078, Pte., k. in a., F., 31/7/17.

CLARK, W. E., b. London, 23098, Pte., k. in a., F., 25/9/15.

CLAYTON, W., b. Lincoln, 31035, Pte., k. in a., F., 3/7/16.

CLOUGH, J., b. Clayton-le-Moors, Lancs., 24191, k. in a., F., 1/4/16.

CLUTTON, F., b. Wrexham, 17290, L/Cpl., k. in a., F., 22/3/18.

COLE, L., b. Launceston, 75300, Pte., k. in a., F., 18/4/18.

CONDUIT, G., b. Bridgwater, 5512, Pte., k. in a., F., 18/4/18.

CONNAH, R., b. Bistre, 15788, L/Cpl., k. in a., F., 20/11/16.

COOK, F. A., b. Usk, 57959, Pte., k. in a., F., 14/6/18.

COOPER, F., b. Walsall, 24195, Pte., k. in a., F., 3/7/16.

COOPER, J., b. Chadlington, 235069, Pte., k. in a., F., 7/6/17.

COPE, A., b. Hyde, 31647, Pte., k. in a., F., 2/9/16.

COPSON, A., e. London, 235166, Pte., k. in a., F., 28/5/18.

COTTAM, A., b. Chorley, 52479, L/Cpl., k. in a., F., 22/3/18.

COUPER, F. W., b. Llanblethian, 56305, Pte., k. in a., F., 7/6/17.

CRAWFORD, C., b. Liverpool, 36237, L/Cpl., k. in a., F., 5/6/17.

CRITCHLEY, E., b. Manchester, 52413, Pte., k. in a., F., 31/7/17.

CROFT, H. C., b. Upton Park, 43777, Pte., d., F., 7/8/18.

CROMAN, A. B., b. Birkenhead, 52295, Pte., k. in a., F., 19/7/17.

CULLEN, D., b. Prescot, 14747, Pte., k. in a., F., 25/7/16.

CULLIFORD, J. J., b. Somerton, 13203, Pte., k. in a., F., 31/7/17.

DANIELS, L. F., b. Manchester, 315316, Pte., k. in a., F., 22/3/18.

DAVENPORT, H., b. Stourbridge, 9006, Cpl., k. in a., F., 3/7/16.

DAVID, E. M., b. Pyle, 18763, Pte., d. of w., F., 7/11/18.

DAVIES, B. H., b. Liverpool, 36281, Pte., k. in a., F., 3/7/16.

DAVIES, D., b. Colwyn Bay, 13484, Pte., k. in a., F., 22/3/18, D.C.M.

DAVIES, D., b. Aberystwyth, 15886, Pte., d. of w., F., 8/2/16.

DAVIES, D. T., b. Tredegar, 54200, Pte., d. of w., F., 8/4/17.

DAVIES, E., b. Blaenau Festiniog, 19965, L/Cpl., d. of w., F., 10/1/16.

DAVIES, E. G., b. Denbigh, 23048, Pte., k. in a., F., 25/9/15.

DAVIES, E. I., b. Rhondda, 16398, Pte., k. in a., F., 25/9/15.

DAVIES, H., b. Llanelly, 13151, Pte., k. in a., F., 25/9/15.

DAVIES, H. J., b. Llanelly, 14222, Pte., d. of w., F., 4/10/18.

DAVIES, J., b. Llandudno, 16596, Pte., k. in a., F., 25/9/15.

DAVIES, J., b. Merthyr, 23127, Pte., k. in a., F., 7/6/17.

DAVIES, J., b. Cefn Mawr, 23188, L/Cpl., d. of w., F., 14/6/17.

DAVIES, J., b. Narbeth, 54297, Pte., k. in a., F., 7/6/17.

DAVIES, J., b. Salford, 75880, Pte., d. of w., F., 27/3/18.

DAVIES, J., b. Llanfair, P.G., 15879, Pte., k. in a., F., 25/9/15.

DAVIES, J. E., b. Mardy, 19177, Pte., k. in a., F., 3/7/16.

DAVIES, J. P., b. Llanfair, 203821, Pte., k. in a., F., 14/6/18.

DAVIES, R., b. Wrexham, 12949, Pte., k. in a., F., 25/9/15.

DAVIES, R. I., b. Swansea, 16604, Pte., d. of w., F., 5/10/15.

DAVIES, T., b. Cerrig-y-druidion, 13205, Pte., k. in a., F., 25/9/15.

DAVIES, T., b. Hednesford, 13716, Pte., d. of w., F., 21/11/16.

DAVIES, T., b. Dihewid Aberayron, 13736, Cpl., k. in a., F., 3/7/16.

DAVIES, T., b. Barmouth, 37132, Pte., k. in a., F., 15/6/17.

DAVIES, T. G., b. Pembroke, 57511, k. in a., F., 14/6/18.

DAVIES, W., b. Cardiff, 13565, L/Cpl., d. of w., F., 5/7/17.

DAVIES, W. J., b. Pontyberem, 235210, L/Cpl., k. in a., F., 29/4/18.

DENNIS, J., b. Pontypool, 16878, Pte., d. of w., F., 20/10/18.

DENTETH, S., b. Crewe, 57003, Sgt., k. in a., F., 18/4/18.

DENTON, G. E., b. London, 27324, Pte., k. in a., F., 13/3/16.

DEVINE, R., b. Liverpool, 31831, L/Cpl., k. in a., F., 2/7/16.

DIXON, T., b. Leigh, 46243, L/Cpl., d. of w., F., 6/7/16.

DOBINSON, R., b. Dalston, 242948, Pte., d. of w., F., 2/6/18.

DONOVAN, J., b. Rhondda, 29013, Pte., d. of w., F., 5/11/16.

DRIVER, W. B., b. Wrexham, 57937, Pte., k. in a., F., 28/5/18.

DUCKWORTH, H., b. Blackburn, 52381, Pte., k. in a., F., 31/7/17.

DUNNING, F., b. Newport, 54201, Pte., k. in a., F., 31/7/17.

DYKES, W., b. Crewe, 37246, Sgt., k. in a., F., 18/4/18.

EDGE, S., b. Ogmore Vale, 13693, Cpl., k. in a., F., 25/9/15.

EDMONDS, P. L., b. London, 35157, Pte., d. of w., F., 25/10/17.

EDWARDS, A., b. Nantyglo, 55403, L/Cpl., k. in a., F., 28/5/18.

EDWARDS, D. J., b. Bridgend, 12994, L/Sgt., k. in a., F., 25/9/15.

EDWARDS, E., b. Porth, 16504, Pte., d. of w., F., 11/7/16.

EDWARDS, E. C., b. Beckenham, 13689, Pte., k. in a., F., 18/4/18.

EDWARDS, J., b. Llanerchymedd, 39314, Pte., d. of w., F., 5/10/17.

EDWARDS, J. R., b. Hubberstone, 23080, Pte., k. in a., F., 25/9/15.

EDWARDS, R., b. London, 46231, d., F., 27/11/16.

EDWARDS, W. H., b. Ferndale, 5407, Pte., k. in a., F., 7/11/18.

ELLIS, J., b. Jarrow-on-Tyne, 46472, L/Cpl., k. in a., F., 20/9/17.

ELLIS, J., b. Tyldesley, 23903, Pte., d., F., 8/2/16.

ELLIS, J., b. Carnarvon, 265911, Pte., k. in a., F., 9/5/18.

EMERY, W., b. Smethwick, 23129, Pte., k. in a., F., 29/7/16.

ENGLAND, W., b. Warrington, 13641. Pte., k. in a., F., 25/9/15.

ENGLISH, J., b. Moona, 235130, Pte., d. of w., F., 30/5/17.

ETHERINGTON, H., b. Burnley, 47026, Pte., k. in a., F., 14/6/18.

EVANS, A., b. Trimsaran, 12878, Pte., k. in a., F., 25/9/15.

EVANS, A., b. Knighton, 54274, Pte., k. in a., F., 31/7/17.

EVANS, A. D., b. Berriew, 33079, Pte., k. in a., F., 20/12/15.

EVANS, C., b. Penally, 8439, Sgt., d. of w., F., 3/11/16.

EVANS, D. H., b. Llanbrynmain, 203536, Pte., d., F., 15/10/18.

EVANS, D. J., b. Briton Ferry, 16877, Sgt., k. in a., F., 18/4/18.

EVANS, E., b. Wrexham, 44114, Pte., k. in a., F., 18/4/18.

EVANS, G., b. Amlwch, 15792, Pte., d. of w., F., 21/10/18.

EVANS, G., b. Swansea, 66928, Pte., k. in a., F., 14/6/18.

EVANS, H., b. Warrington, 13285, Cpl., k. in a., F., 21/2/16.

EVANS, J., b. Brynamman, 13485, Cpl., k. in a., F., 29/4/18, M.M.

EVANS, J., b. Bistre Buckley, 16461, Pte., k. in a., F., 25/9/15.

EVANS, J., b. Bootle, 235094, Pte., k. in a., F., 5/8/17.

EVANS, J. J., b. Exlyzally, 31376, Pte., k. in a., F., 7/12/15.

EVANS, J. L., b. Barmouth, 37306, Pte., k. in a., F., 21/11/16.

EVANS, R., b. Llanrug, 23071, Pte., k. in a., F., 25/9/15.

EVANS, S. J., b. Charminster, 16331, Pte., k. in a., F., 25/9/15.

EVANS, T., b. Llanelly, 12866, Pte., k. in a., F., 3/7/16.

EVANS, T. H., b. Merthyr, 16368, Pte., k. in a., F., 25/9/15.

EVANS, T. L. C., b. Brymbo, 21170, Pte., k. in a., F., 20/9/17.

EVANS, T. R., b. Blaenau Festiniog, 20815, L/Cpl., k. in a., F., 20/9/17, M.M.

EVANS, W., b. Llanfair, 203557, Pte., d. of w., F., 22/10/18.

FARRAR, H., e. Nelson, 201909, Pte., d. of w., F., 4/10/18.

FELLOWS, W., b. Hednesford, 12763, Pte., k. in a., F., 20/11/16.

FENTON, C., b. Chirk, 13412, C.S.M., k. in a., F., 25/9/15.

FISHER, G. H., b. Llantilio Crossenny, 54204, Pte., d. of w., F., 30/5/18, D.C.M.

FITTON, J. T., b. Haslingden, 23964, Pte., k. in a., F., 16/9/16.

FITZGIBBON, V. H., b. Aberystwyth, 11078, Pte., k. in a., F., 18/4/18.

FLINT, H. G., b. Bath, 75889, Pte., d., F., 27/11/18.

FORSHAW, W., b. Southport, 64591, Pte., k. in a., F., 14/6/18.

FOSSE, G. H., b. Holyhead, 75955, Pte., k. in a., F., 6/11/18.

FOSTER, H., b. Prescot, 74606, Pte., k. in a., F., 18/4/18.

FOSTER, J., b. Walsall Wood, 13722, Pte., d. of w., F., 26/9/15.

FOX, P. A., b. Bury, 47034, Pte., d. of w., F., 8/6/17.

FRANCIS, J., b. Llanelly, 15581, L/Cpl., k. in a., F., 15/6/17.

FREDERICK, J., b. St. Mary's Hill, 16276, Pte., k. in a., F., 25/9/15.

FRENCH, G. H., b. Leicester, 1992, Pte., k. in a., F., 25/9/15.

FRISBY, W. A., e. Chelmsford, 55863, Pte., k. in a., F., 11/10/17.

GALLOP, W., e. Bournemouth, 60156, Pte., k. in a., F., 1/5/18.

GAMAGE, E. A., b. Swansea, 204712, Pte., k. in a., F., 23/10/18.

GARDNER, J., b. Rugeley, 13604, Pte., k. in a., F., 25/9/15.

GIBBONS, F., b. Worcester, 44374, Pte., k. in a., F., 22/3/18.

GILLETT, H., b. London, 21974, Pte., k. in a., F., 18/4/18.

GILLIGAN, J., b. Liverpool, 235148, Pte., k. in a., F., 28/5/18.

GLADWIN, W., e. Hereford, 204367, Pte., k. in a., F., 22/3/18.

GLOVER, A., b. Liverpool, 57926, Pte., k. in a., F., 18/4/18.

GODSELL, F., b. Cheltenham, 11995, Pte., k. in a., F., 3/7/16.

GOLDING-HANN, G., b. Kerridge, 54208, Pte., k. in a., F., 13/6/17.

GOLDSBY, H., b. London, 12854, Sgt., k. in a., F., 27/7/16, M.M.

GOUGH, W., b. Cardiff, 31110, Pte., k. in a., F., 20/12/15.

GRAHAM, A., b. Liverpool, 66853, Pte., k. in a., F., 14/6/18.

GRAHAM, W., b. Lennaxton, 267598, Pte., k. in a., F., 22/3/18.

GRANT, M. W., b. Liverpool, 235693, Pte., k. in a., F., 31/7/17.

GREEN, A., b. South Normanton, 24188, Pte., k. in a., F., 3/7/16.

GREEN, J., b. Cardiff, 54309, Pte., d., F., 3/11/18.

GRIFFITHS, A., b. Buckley, 11939, Pte., d. of w., F., 20/9/17.

GRIFFITHS, D., b. Llandyssil, 12967, Pte., k. in a., F., 22/3/18.

GRIFFITHS, E., b. Tilstock, 12802, Pte., k. in a., F., 23/8/16.

GRIFFITHS, E., b. Northop, 12942, L/Cpl., k. in a., F., 22/3/18.

GRIFFITHS, E. O., b. Llanberis, 40428, Pte., k. in a., F., 29/4/18.

GRIFFITHS, J., b. Pwllheli, 21020, Pte., k. in a., F., 22/3/18.

GRIFFITHS, R., e. Llanelly, 57935, Pte., d., F., 24/7/18.

GRIFFITHS, W., e. Flint, 240650, Pte., k. in a., F., 22/3/18.

GRIFFITHS, W. H., b. Cardiff, 57916, Pte., d., F., 21/10/18.

GROVES, J., b. Weaverham, 23919, Pte., d. of w., F., 9/7/16.

GUNNING, J., b. Liverpool, 60204, Pte., d. of w., F., 28/10/17.

GUNTER, F. S., b. Rhydyfelyn, 16325, Pte., k. in a., F., 25/9/15.

GUNTER, W., b. Briton Ferry, 16891, Pte., k. in a., F., 31/7/17.

HADLEY, T., b. Oldbury, 23106, Pte., k. in a., F., 25/9/15.

HAGGER, C. H., b. Stepney, 57946, L/Cpl., k. in a., F., 18/4/18.

HALL, C., b. Newcastle, 23971, Pte., k. in a., F., 18/2/16.

HALL, H. E., b. West Bromwich, 60430, L/Cpl., k. in a., F., 29/4/18.

HAMBLY, E. G., b. Parkham, 54314, Pte., d. of w., F., 20/10/18.

HAMNER, W., b. Salford, 47063, Pte., k. in a., F., 22/3/18.

HAMPSON, E., b. Ashton-under-Lyne, 52562, Pte., k. in a., F., 28/5/18.

HAMPSON, S., b. Wigan, 29253, Pte., k. in a., F., 18/12/17.

HANCOCK, J., b. Yeovil, 37947, Pte., d. of w., F., 6/6/18.

HANKS, A. E. G., b. Portskewett, 54358, Pte., k. in a., F., 12/9/18.

HANN, W., e. Abergavenny, 54210, Pte., d. of w., F., 7/6/17.

HARDON, J. E., b. Stalybridge, 33018, Pte., d. of w., F., 8/7/16.

HARDY, C. J., b. Blakewell, 33004, Pte., k. in a., F., 25/9/15.

HARES, H. E., b. Shepton Mallet, 75094, Pte., d., F., 15/10/18.

HARRIES, T., b. Llanelly, 13164, Pte., k. in a., F., 3/7/16.

HARRIS, E., e. Mountain Ash, 57910, L/Cpl., d. of w., F., 24/4/18.

HARRIS, T., b. Wolverhampton, 12823, Pte., k. in a., F., 12/5/17.

HARRIS, W. E., e. St. Helens, 13423, Pte., k. in a., F., 30/7/16.

HARRISON, J., b. Bolton, 14980, Pte., k. in a., F., 22/3/18.

HARRISON, J., b. Chester, 75874, Cpl., k. in a., F., 22/3/18.

HARROP, C. P., b. Wrexham, 29590, L/Cpl., k. in a., F., 27/10/16.

HARWOOD, H., b. Darwen, 60278, L/Cpl., d. of w., F., 22/6/17.

HASLAM, F., b. Ramsbottom, 13225, Cpl., k. in a., F., 25/9/15.

HAWKINS, A. L., b. Great Doddington, 56350, Pte., k. in a., F., 5/6/17.

HEALEY, W., b. Reading, 10633, Pte., k. in a., F., 31/7/17.

HEMMING, C., b. Panteg, 204382, Pte., d. of w., F., 24/3/18.

HENSHAW, T., b. Llanelly, 13179, Pte., k. in a., F., 25/9/15.

HEPWORTH, E., b. Manchester, 266946, Pte., k. in a., F., 22/3/18.

HERBERT, D., b. Rochdale, 57951, Pte., k. in a., F., 18/4/18.

HERRIDGE, G. J., b. London, 22063, Cpl., k. in a., F., 16/6/17.

HESS, G., b. Liverpool, 235117, Pte., k. in a., F., 31/7/17.

HIER, T., b. Newport, 6443, L/Cpl., k. in a., F., 16/9/16.

HIGGINS, J. E., b. India, 52227, Pte., k. in a., F., 18/12/17.

HIGHAM, M. R., b. Longton, 52459, Pte., d. of w., F., 19/9/17.

HIGHTON, H., b. Blackburn, 43757, Cpl., k. in a., F., 22/3/18.

HIGSON, W., b. Pendleton, 52588, Pte., k. in a., F., 31/7/17.

HILL, A., b. Kempsel, 57273, Pte., d. of w., Home, 4/11/18.

HILL, F., b. Hednesford, 13706, Pte., k. in a., F., 7/7/16.

HILL, J., b. Manchester, 18491, Pte., k. in a., F., 18/4/18.

HILL, J., b. Stockport, 58429, Pte., d. of w., F., 3/10/18.

HILL, P., b. Bourne, 56302, Pte., d. of w., F., 16/6/17.

HILL, W., b. Leeds, 13459, Pte., k. in a., F., 25/9/15.

HILLIAR, W. G., b. Bermondsey, 26596, Pte., d. of w., F., 9/6/17.

HILTON, A., b. Burslem, 16568, L/Cpl., k. in a., F., 25/9/15.

HINDLE, R., b. Blackburn, 57674, Pte., k. in a., F., 7/11/18.

HINDLEY, H., b. Leigh, 28564, Pte., k. in a., F., 22/3/18.

HOGAN, C., b. Liverpool, 24064, Pte., k. in a., F., 22/3/18.

HOLDEN, C., b. Accrington, 67270, Pte., k. in a., F., 8/5/18.

HOOPER, T., b. Camborne, 13325, L/Cpl., k. in a., F., 3/7/16, M.M.

HOPKINS, W., b. Liverpool, 52245, Pte., k. in a., F., 22/3/18.

HOPPER, A. H., b. Llanidloes, 16570, L/Sgt., d., F., 26/10/18.

HOPWOOD, J., b. Coedpath, Denbigh, 17222, Pte., k. in a., F., 22/3/18.

HORSEMAN, A., b. Bristol, 13376, Pte., k. in a., F., 2/7/16.

HOUGHTON, A., b. Dalmarnock, 16588, Sgt., d. of w., F., 3/4/16.

HOWCROFT, W., e. Bradford, 56103, Pte., d. of w., F., 5/11/18.

HOWE, F. W., e. Barry, 69214, Pte., k. in a., F., 22/3/18.

HOWELLS, T., b. Plasmarl, 16519, Pte., k. in a., F., 20/11/16.

HOWELLS, T., b. Swansea, 12868, Pte., k. in a., F., 25/9/15.

HUGHES, D., b. Penycae, 200408, Pte., d. of w., F., 24/10/18, M.M. and Clasp.

HUGHES, E. G., b. Tremadoc, 10253, L/Cpl., k. in a., F., 28/10/16.

HUGHES, E. W., b. Broughton, 15745, Pte., k. in a., F., 25/9/15.

HUGHES, I., b. Loughor, 19975, Pte., d. of w., F., 24/9/15.

HUGHES, J. D., b. Llandudno, 61221, Pte., k. in a., F., 18/4/18.

HUGHES, J. L., b. Holywell, 29866, Pte., k. in a., F., 12/8/16.

HUGHES, J. T., b. Llangyfelach, 16327, L/Sgt., k. in a., F., 25/9/15.

HUGHES, R., b. Llangollen, 15817, Pte., k. in a., F., 17/11/16.

HUGHES, R., b. Tycroes, 265927, Pte., k. in a., F., 22/3/18.

HUGHES, T., b. Rynys Valley, 39137, Pte., k. in a., F., 31/8/16.

HUGHES, T. J., b. Llandilo, 13198, L/Cpl., k. in a., F., 3/7/16.

HUGHES, T. O., b. Flint, 13633, Sgt., k. in a., F., 25/9/15.

HUGHES, W., e. Wrexham, 200706, Pte., d. of w., Home, 4/12/18.

HUGHES, W. O., b. Llangollen, 16824, Pte., k. in a., F., 25/9/15.

HUGHES, W. W., b. Blaenau Festiniog, 316830, Pte., k. in a., F., 30/9/18.

HULME, R., b. St. Helens, 47055, Pte., d. of w., F., 29/3/18.

HUMPHREYS, T., b. Flint, 76087, Pte., k. in a., F., 7/11/18.

HUMPHRIES, J., b. Old Hill, 46211, Pte., k. in a., F., 22/3/18.

HUNTLEY, E. R., b. Aberdare, 16686, Pte., k. in a., F., 25/9/15.

HURLEY, T., b. Ebbw Vale, 54188, Pte., k. in a., F., 14/6/18.

HUXLEY, H., b. Wrexham, 19397, Cpl., k. in a., F., 12/5/17.

IBALL, T., b. Hawarden, 19526, Pte., k. in a., F., 24/10/17.

INGRAM, S., b. Workington, 33080, Pte., d., F., 7/2/16.

JENKINS, D. J., b. Aberdare, 12877, Pte., k. in a., F., 25/9/15.

JENKINS, F., b. Dafen, 12903, L/Sgt., d. of w., F., 8/5/18.

JENKINS, W. E., b. Wrexham, 24200, Pte., k. in a., F., 3/7/16.

JOHN, A., b. Ferndale, 5401, Pte., k. in a., F., 7/6/17.

JOHN, G., b. Llanwnda, 54323, Pte., k. in a., F., 3/11/16.

JOHN, T. H., b. Llangyfelach, 202670, Pte., k. in a., F., 18/4/18.

JOHNSON, J. E., b. Dewsbury, 202135, Pte., d. of w., F., 24/10/18.

JOHNSTON, T. W., b. Dundee, 60283, Pte., d. of w., F., 26/3/18.

JONES, A., b. Birmingham, 23075, Pte., d., F. 25/9/15.

JONES, B., b. Northop Hall, 26077, Pte., k. in a., F., 22/3/18.

JONES, D., b. Corwen, 73163, Pte., d., F., 28/6/18.

JONES, D., b. Ystradmeurig, 31421, Pte., k. in a., F., 27/10/16.

JONES, D. T., b. Llanmochllyn, 203970, Pte., d. of w., F., 15/4/18.

JONES, E., b. Llanrws, 13488, Pte., k. in a., F., 25/9/15.

JONES, E., b. Bolton, 19789, Cpl., k. in a., F., 7/6/17.

JONES, E., b. Garthbeibio, 204033, Pte., d. of w., F., 30/11/17.

JONES, E. M., b. London, 22574, Pte., k. in a., F., 18/4/18.

JONES, E. O., b. Clydach, 54320, L/Cpl., k. in a., F., 28/10/16.

JONES, F., b. Pentrevolas, 68486, Pte., d., F., 20/8/18.

JONES, F., b. Manchester, 12838, Pte., d. of w., F., 25/9/15.

JONES, F. G., b. Pontypool, 12822, Pte., k. in a., F., 25/9/15.

JONES, G. H., b. Birmingham, 36403, Pte., k. in a., F., 3/7/16.

JONES, H., b. Lambeth, 23586, L/Cpl., k. in a., F., 12/5/17.

JONES, H., b. Llanbeulan, 203964, Pte., d., F., 4/6/18.

JONES, I., b. Wyrley, 13717, Pte., k. in a., F., 25/7/16.

JONES, J., b. Llanfair-or-llwyn, 12902, Pte., k. in a., F., 25/9/15.

JONES, J., b. Abercynon, 13022, Pte., k. in a., F., 25/9/15.

JONES, J., b. Cemmaes, 23419, Pte., k. in a., F., 30/5/18.

JONES, J., b. Wrexham, 24671, L/Cpl., k. in a., F., 10/8/16.

Jones, J., b. Conway, 36136, Pte., k. in a., F., 12/5/17.

Jones, J. D., b. Llanrwst, 13097, Pte., k. in a., F., 25/9/15.

Jones, J. G., b. Llanrwst, 37963, L/Cpl., d. of w., F., 5/11/16.

Jones, J. H., b. Barmouth, 16672, Pte., k. in a., F., 25/9/15.

Jones, J. O., b. Merioneth, 204092, Pte., k. in a., F., 9/5/18.

Jones, J. O., b. Rhyl, 204315, Pte., d. of w., F., 30/9/18.

Jones, J. P., b. Aberdaron, 204003, Pte., k. in a., F., 18/4/18.

Jones, J. R., b. Yspytty, 203668, Pte., k. in a., F., 20/9/17.

Jones, J. W., b. Sellattyn, 15465, Pte., k. in a., F., 30/9/18.

Jones, J. W., e. Shrewsbury, 38107, Pte., d. of w., F., 3/8/17.

Jones, L., b. Redwharf Bay, 203606, Pte., k. in a., F., 23/10/17.

Jones, O. E., b. Bangor, 33105, Pte., k. in a., F., 22/7/16.

Jones, P., b. Machynlleth, 15055, Pte., d. of w., F., 15/6/18.

Jones, R., e. Carnarvon, 54620, Pte., d. of w., Home, 24/12/17.

Jones, R. G., b. Gwersyllt, 13440, L/Cpl., k. in a., F., 25/9/15.

Jones, R. H., b. Fishguard, 57513, Pte., k. in a., F., 20/10/18.

Jones, R. T., e. Ruthin, 54506, Pte., k. in a., F., 8/5/18.

Jones, S., b. Manchester, 56343, Pte., k. in a., F., 5/6/17.

Jones, T., b. Llanrhaiadr, 13185, Pte., d., F., 28/5/18.

Jones, T., b. Llanelly, 13367, Pte., k. in a., F., 31/7/17, M.M. and Clasp.

Jones, T. J., b. Coed Penmaen, 12349, L/Cpl., d. of w., F., 28/5/18.

Jones, W., b. Llanfyllin, 13664, Sgt., k. in a., F., 3/7/16.

Jones, W., b. Criccieth, 15887, Pte., k. in a., F., 25/9/15.

Jones, W., b. Llangefni, 54173, Pte., k. in a., F., 7/4/17.

Jones, W. A., b. Bodedern, 203592, Pte., k. in a., F., 22/3/18.

Jones, W. A., b. Llanguike, 13241, Pte., k. in a., F., 25/9/15.

Jones, W. D., b. Penmaenmawr, 54263, Pte., k. in a., F., 28/10/16.

Jones, W. H., b. Glanamman, 13195, L/Cpl., d. of w., F., 7/4/17.

Jones, W. T., b. Llanrwst, 44308, Pte., d. of w., F., 18/6/17.

Jones, W. W., b. Pontypridd, 16326, Pte., k. in a., F., 25/9/15.

Jordan, P., b. St. Helens, 13400, Pte., d. of w., F., 15/11/16.

Julien, R., b. Pontefract, 12997, Cpl., d. of w., F., 28/9/15.

Kay, H., e. Bury, 57949, Pte., d., F., 31/5/18.

Keeling, F., b. Salford, 16712, Pte., k. in a., F., 30/10/16.

Kelly, J., b. Limerick, 23109, Pte., d. of w., F., 17/3/16.

Kelsall, J. S., b. Wilmslow, 75904, Pte., d. of w., F., 2/5/18.

King, G. D., b. Oxford, 13523, L/Cpl., d. of w., F., 27/9/15.

King, G. E., e. Cardiff, 60511, Pte., d., F., 30/6/18.

Kingdon, A. R., b. Porthcawl, 75494, Pte., k. in a., F., 14/6/18.

Kingsbury, R. T., b. London, 31997, Pte., k. in a., F., 20/11/16.

Kirby, J. E., b. London, 5524, L/Cpl., d. of w., F., 28/7/16.

Knibbs, F., b. Chipping Norton, 13086, L/Cpl., d. of w., F., 28/9/15.

Knott, C., b. Manchester, 52211, Pte., d. of w., F., 17/6/17.

Labram, F., b. Grendon, 56332, Pte., k. in a., F., 31/7/17.

Langan, J., b. Rochdale, 57685, Pte., k. in a., F., 30/9/18.

Larman, J. R., b. London, 44767, Pte., k. in a., F., 20/10/18.

Latham, T., b. Northop, 23399, L/Cpl., k. in a., F., 12/5/17.

Ledsham, L., b. Boughton, 12891, Pte., k. in a., F., 25/9/15.

Lee, W. L., b. Llanelly, 29867, Pte., k. in a., F., 26/10/16.

Leonard, J., b. Garndiffaith, 19967, Pte., k. in a., F., 25/9/15.

Lewis, B., b. Landore, 13685, L/Cpl., k. in a., F., 3/7/16.

Lewis, E., b. Cwmavon, 37874, Pte., k. in a., F., 3/10/17.

Lewis, E., b. Ilfracombe, 18745, L/Cpl., d., F., 29/7/18.

Lewis, H., b. Llantarnam, 42067, Pte., k. in a., F., 23/10/18.

Lewis, H. C., b. Llangellech, 63175, Pte., d. of w., F., 8/10/17.

Lewis, H. G. W., b. Halifax, 235133, Pte., k. in a., F., 31/7/17.

Lewis, J., b. Buckley, 12957, L/Cpl., k. in a., F., 3/7/16.

Lewis, L., b. Ferndale, 57955, Pte., k. in a., F., 18/4/18.

Leyland, T., e. Bolton, 52466, Pte., d., F., 2/4/18.

Line, G., b. Burnside, 39182, Pte., k. in a., F., 4/11/17.

Linfoot, T. H., b. Manchester, 63889, Pte., k. in a., F., 22/3/18.

Linthwaite, A. E., b. Birmingham, 31711, Pte., k. in a., F., 4/3/16.

Little, T., b. Hanley Castle, 46248, L/Cpl., d. of w., F., 30/10/16.

Livesey, E., b. Oldham, 204753, Pte., d., F., 6/1/19.

Llewellyn, F. A., e. Newport, 54220, Pte., d. of w., F., 11/4/18.

Lloyd, J. T., b. Stafford, 6294, A/Sgt., d., Home, 13/5/15.

Lloyd, T., b. Chester, 12889, Sgt., k. in a., F., 15/6/17.

Lloyd, W., b. Wrexham, 12925, Pte., k. in a., F., 25/9/15.

Lloyd, W. J., b. Cardiff, 54329, Pte., d. of w., F., 13/11/16.

Locke, F., b. London, 21561, Pte., k. in a., F., 5/8/17.

Lockwood, A. C., b. Leytonstone, 22116, Pte., d., F., 14/4/18.

Logan, W., b. Bristol, 55745, Cpl., k. in a., F., 25/9/15.

Lord, C., b. Shaw, 57919, Pte., k. in a., F., 18/4/18.

Lord, J. A., b. Bolton, 57684, Pte., k. in a., F., 7/11/18.

Lyle, W., b. Llanwonno, 6504, Pte., k. in a., F., 18/4/18.

Lynch, T., b. Liverpool, 47104, Pte., k. in a., F., 3/8/17.

Lynch, W., b. Relton, 13014, Pte., k. in a., F., 7/2/16.

Major, T. R., b. Kendal, 70480, Pte., k. in a., F., 22/3/18.

Mannely, F., b. Towyn, 23217, Pte., d. of w., F., 21/9/17.

Marland, P., e. Hyde, 33001, Cpl., k. in a., F., 14/6/18.

Marner, C., b. Greenwich, 13087, Pte., k. in a., F., 25/9/15.

Marquis, F., b. Liverpool, 63178, Pte., d. of w., F., 20/7/17.

Marsh, A., b. Preston, 42511, Pte., k. in a., F., 30/9/18.

Martin, E. T., e. Oswestry, 75576, Pte., d. of w., F., 28/4/18.

Martin, L., b. Walsall, 23074, Pte., k. in a., F., 25/9/15.

Mason, T. M., b. West Hartlepool, 24919, Cpl., k. in a., F., 3/7/16.

Massey, W., b. Stretford, 46212, Pte., d. of w., F., 8/7/16.

Matthews, G. W., b. Hanley, 23534, Cpl., k. in a., F., 31/7/17.

May, M., b. Streamstown, 46866, Pte., k. in a., F., 31/7/17.

McCarthy, J., b. Pontypridd, 20877, Pte., k. in a., F., 20/9/17.

McDade, C., b. Falkirk, 10420, Pte., k. in a., F., 15/9/18.

Meadon, E., b. Newcastle-under-Lyme, 19956, Pte., k. in a., F., 16/9/15.

Middlebrook, S. A., b. London, 24631, Pte., k. in a., F., 22/3/18.

Millington, J., b. Northop, 13315, Pte., k. in a., F., 25/9/15.

Mills, A., b. Chichester, 21649, Sgt., d. of w., F., 20/3/19.

Mills, J., b. Rochdale, 55123, L/Cpl., k. in a., F., 20/9/17.

MILLS, W., b. Halling, 15933, Pte., k. in a., F., 25/9/15.

MITCHELL, F., b. Morriston, 14355, Pte., k. in a., F., 18/4/18.

MOLYNEUX, J., b. Salford, 203991, Pte., k. in a., F., 20/10/18.

MOON, S. A., b. Morden, 56169, Pte., k. in a., F., 2/5/18.

MOORCROFT, H., b. Kirkdale, 23073, Pte., k. in a., F., 25/9/15.

MOORE, F., b. Norton Canes, 7048, Sgt., k. in a., F., 24/7/16.

MORAN, M., b. Oldham, 74990, Pte., k. in a., F., 14/6/18.

MORGAN, D., b. Abergavenny, 57947, Pte., d., F., 22/6/18.

MORGAN, G. L., b. Gorseinon, 75544, Pte., k. in a., F., 14/6/18.

MORGANS, W., b. Carmarthen, 13359, Cpl., k. in a., F., 29/4/18.

MORRIS, A., b. Liverpool, 52990, Pte., k. in a., F., 28/5/18.

MORRIS, D., b. Eglwysbach, 203719, Pte., k. in a., F., 14/6/18.

MORRIS, H., b. Clynderwen, 39645, Pte., d., F., 5/4/17.

MORRIS, J., b. Whitworth, 52086, Pte., d., F., 19/2/17.

MORRIS, J., b. Swansea, 15004, Pte., k. in a., F., 22/3/18.

MORRIS, J. J., e. Carmarthen, 268205, Pte., d. of w., F., 29/4/18.

MORRIS, P., b. Oswestry, 16708, Pte., k. in a., F., 7/11/15.

MORRIS, W., b. Llanselin, 23091, Pte., k. in a., F., 25/9/15.

MORT, H., b. Manchester, 70486, Pte., d. of w., F., 7/5/18.

MOTTRAM, J., b. Dukinfield, 39291, Pte., k. in a., F., 22/7/16.

MULROY, T., b. Golden Hill, 46481, Pte., k. in a., F., 8/4/18.

MUNRO, Ian, b. London, 60288, Pte., k. in a., F., 14/6/18.

MURPHY, C., b. Tipperary, 12528, Pte., d. of w., F., 17/8/18.

MURPHY, T., b. Weston, 17331, L/Cpl., k. in a., F., 22/3/18.

MURRAY, J. A., b. Newcastle-on-Tyne, 46230, Pte., k. in a., F., 22/3/18.

NEWBY, J. A., b. Cyston, 69447, Pte., k. in a., F., 1/5/18.

NORMAN, R., b. Totley, 60282, Pte., k. in a., F., 22/3/18.

NORMANTON, J., e. Wrexham, 54282, Pte., d., F., 1/9/18.

O'BRIEN, P., e. Colwyn Bay, 57929, Cpl., d. of w., F., 12/4/18.

O'BRIEN, T., b. Kilmurrybricam, 13264, Pte., k. in a., F., 8/11/15.

O'NEILL, J., b. Liverpool, 242254, Pte., d., F., 20/10/18.

O'NEILL, M., e. Cardiff, 54340, Cpl., k. in a., F., 18/4/18.

OSLER, B., b. Mostyn, 13296, Pte., k. in a., F., 28/5/17.

OWEN, J. G., b. Llangean, 203337, Pte., d., F., 20/10/18.

OWEN, J. H., b. Welshpool, 204310, Pte., k. in a., F., 14/6/18.

OWEN, J. R., b. Bangor, 13035, L/Cpl., k. in a., F., 25/9/15.

OWEN, R., e. Dolgelly, 268071, Pte., k. in a., F., 6/11/18.

OWEN, S., b. West Derby, 33028, Cpl., k. in a., F., 7/6/17.

OWEN, T., b. Newborough, 33098, Pte., k. in a., F., 1/5/18.

OWEN, W. S., b. Llanerchymedd, 70183, Pte., d. of w., F., 9/5/18.

PALING, A., b. Manchester, 12988, Sgt., d., F., 7/2/16.

PALMER, H., b. Birmingham, 6789, Sgt., k. in a., F., 3/7/16.

PAPA, A., b. Hackney, 45006, L/Sgt., k. in a., F., 14/6/18.

PARKER, G., b. Liverpool, 13350, L/Sgt., k. in a., F., 25/9/15.

PARKER, L., b. Helperby, 47147, Pte., k. in a., F., 31/7/17.

PARRY, E., b. Llanelly, 13178, Pte., k. in a., F., 25/9/15.

PARRY, H. M., e. Talysarn, 54578, Pte., d., F., 7/8/18.

PARRY, J., b. Northop, 13309, Pte., k. in a., F., 25/9/15.

PARRY, J., b. Gaerwen, 29181, Pte., d. of w., F., 8/6/17.

PARRY, J., b. Wrexham, 5655, Pte., d. of w., F., 4/12/15.

PARRY, R. M., b. Birkenhead, 68458, Pte., k. in a., F., 29/4/18.

PARRY, W., b. Port Madoc, 202762, Pte., k. in a., F., 14/6/18.

PARRY, W. H., b. Mostyn, 75503, Pte., k. in a., F., 18/4/18.

PARTINGTON, W., b. Bolton, 52598, Pte., k. in a., F., 12/5/17.

PASH, A., b. London, 28080, L/Cpl., k. in a., F., 30/9/18.

PATE, W., b. Burnley, 67186, Pte., k. in a., F., 14/6/18.

PAYNE, C., b. Stourport, 13085, Pte., k. in a., F., 25/9/15.

PEARCE, A. L., b. Camberwell, 45048, Pte., d., F., 16/11/18.

PEARSON, S., b. London, 13274, Pte., k. in a., F., 25/9/15.

PENLINGTON, C. B., b. Wrexham, 37978, Pte., k. in a., F., 2/11/16.

PENNYFATHER, H. E., b. Walthamstow, 27353, Pte., d., F., 24/3/18.

PERRY, J., b. Corely, 12759, Pte., k. in a., F., 25/9/15.

PETTIE, J. E., b. Giggleswick, 47145, Pte., k. in a., F., 22/3/18.

PHILLIPS, F., b. Uxbridge, 52771, Pte., k. in a., F., 30/5/18.

PHILLIPS, J. J., b. Oswestry, 200900, Sgt., k. in a., F., 23/10/18.

PICTON, S., b. Pembroke Dock, 235511, Pte., k. in a., F., 18/4/18.

PIERCY, G., b. Soughton, 15397, Pte., k. in a., F., 30/9/18.

PIKE, A. E., b. St. Pancras, 60281, Pte., k. in a., F., 23/10/17.

PINFOLD, A. G. V., b. Cleckheaton, 57924, Pte., k. in a., F., 29/4/18.

PLATT, T., b. Wrexham, 23111, Cpl., k. in a., F., 30/9/18.

POWELL, E., b. Loughor, 16676, Pte., k. in a., F., 23/11/15.

POWELL, E., e. Abergavenny, 54228, L/Cpl., k. in a., F., 31/7/17.

POWELL, F., b. Crewe, 39240, Pte., k. in a., F., 3/5/17.

POWELL, J. A., e. Llandrindod Wells, 55626, Pte., d. of w., F., 7/11/18.

POXON, E., b. West Bromwich, 8069, Pte., k. in a., F., 23/7/16.

PRICE, D., b. Dowlais, 23070, Pte., d. of w., F., 30/9/15.

PRICE, J. A., e. Llanbister, 235762, Pte., k. in a., F., 18/4/18.

PRICE, M., b. Llanddewy, 16349, L/Cpl., k. in a., F., 25/9/15.

PRICE, S., b. Pontypool, 23084, Pte., d. of w., F., 27/9/15.

PRITCHARD, D. W., b. Treharris, 16332, Pte., k. in a., F., 7/7/16.

PROSSER, T., e. Abergavenny, 54230, Pte., d. of w., F., 12/5/17.

PUCKETT, A., b. Pritchfield, 54344, Pte., k. in a., F., 20/10/16.

PUGH, E. J., b. Mold, 42448, Pte., d., F., 2/3/18.

PUGH, T., b. Newtown, 19271, Pte., d. of w., F., 1/10/17.

PULLEN, G., e. Wrexham, 200708, Pte., k. in a., F., 7/6/17. D.C.M.

PURCELL, T., b. Bermuda, 46264, Pte., k. in a., F., 20/9/17.

PURDY, F. D., b. Lambeth, 21727, Pte., k. in a., F., 29/4/18.

PYE, E., b. Mellor, 47146, Pte., k. in a., F., 22/3/18.

RADFORD, H., b. Longdon, 13708, Pte., k. in a., F., 3/7/16.

REDMORE, F. J., e. Newport, 73194, Pte., d., F., 30/10/18.

REED, W. J., b. Sunderland, 7221, C.S.M., k. in a., F., 25/9/15.

REEKS, J., b. Tiverton, 13319, Pte., k. in a., F., 25/9/15.

REES, B. G., e. Neath, 73200, Pte., k. in a., F., 22/3/18.

REES, E., b. Bwlchewym, 73644, Pte., k. in a., F., 4/1/18.

REES, L. T., b. Loughor, 19976, Pte., k. in a., F., 7/7/16.

REES, R. D., b. Neath, 20943,

Pte., d. of w., F., 15/11/18, D.C.M.

REES, T., b. Burry Port, 13157, Pte., k. in a., F., 25/9/15.

REEVE, W. G., b. Woolwich, 291663, Pte., k. in a., F., 22/3/18.

REEVES, J., b. Bettisfield, 12935, Pte., k. in a., F., 25/9/15.

REID, W., b. Marylebone, 235124, Pte., d. of w., Home, 21/10/17.

RENNIE, J., b. Calliestown, 235114, Pte., d. of w., F., 22/9/17.

RICHARDS, I. E., b. Briton Ferry, 70588, Pte., d., F., 4/11/18.

RILEY, M., b. Blackburn, 70495, Pte., k. in a., F., 18/4/18.

RITCHIE, H., e. Glasgow, 75696, Pte., k. in a., F., 22/3/18.

ROBERTS, A., b. West Bromwich, 23907, Pte., k. in a., F., 3/7/16.

ROBERTS, E., b. Bethel, 40354, Pte., d., F., 3/11/18.

ROBERTS, E., b. Broughton, 39627, Pte., k. in a., F., 30/9/18.

ROBERTS, E. G., b. Flint, 5396, Pte., d. of w., F., 31/1/18.

ROBERTS, G., b. Rhyl, 202465, Pte., d. of w., F., 15/6/18.

ROBERTS, J., b. Blaenau Festiniog, 13670, Pte., k. in a., F., 3/7/16.

ROBERTS, J., b. Aberffraw, 39050, Pte., d. of w., F., 21/9/17.

ROBERTS, J., e. Cardiff, 73203, Pte., d., F., 31/5/18.

ROBERTS, J., b. Rhos, 69287, Pte., d. of w., F., 3/5/18.

ROBERTS, J. A., b. Weston Rhyn, 23088, Pte., k. in a., F., 25/9/15.

ROBERTS, J. D., b. Wrexham, 36784, L/Cpl., k. in a., F., 31/3/16.

ROBERTS, J. H., b. Llangefni, 11683, Pte., k. in a., F., 3/7/16.

ROBERTS, J. H., b. Liverpool, 235141, Pte., k. in a., F., 20/9/17.

ROBERTS, J. L., b. Llandrillo-yn-Rhos, 29387, Pte., d. of w., F., 12/4/18.

ROBERTS, J. O., b. Rhosybol, 12609, Pte., k. in a., F., 25/9/15.

ROBERTS, R., b. Llansantfraid, 13033, Pte., k. in a., F., 3/7/16.

ROBERTS, T., b. Port Donorwic, 54967, Pte., d., F., 27/10/18.

ROBERTS, T. J., b. Blaenau Festiniog, 43688, Pte., k. in a., F., 14/6/18.

ROBERTS, W., b. Hawarden, 16019, Pte., k. in a., F., 2/10/15.

ROBERTS, W., b. Flint, 31871, Pte., k. in a., F., 7/7/16.

ROBERTS, W., e. Wrexham, 201885, Pte., d. of w., F., 19/4/18.

ROBERTS, W. H., e. St. Helens, 20947, Pte., k. in a., F., 31/7/17.

ROBERTS, W. J., b. Bagillt, 13640, Pte., k. in a., F., 5/9/15.

ROBERTS, W. L., b. Hawarden, 12944, Pte., k. in a., F., 25/9/15.

ROBINSON, E. G., b. Macclesfield, 57906, Pte., d., F., 22/9/18.

RODDY, T., e. Hednesford, 31990, Pte., d., F., 8/7/18.

RODEN, W. C., b. Hereford, 69636, Pte., k. in a., F., 14/6/18.

RODGERS, F., b. Northwinfield, 10060, Pte., d., F., 22/8/17.

ROGERS, A., b. Manchester, 70497, Pte., k. in a., F., 18/4/18.

ROSENBERG, S., b. Birmingham, 47156, Pte., k. in a., F., 8/5/18.

ROSS, M., b. London, 27683, Sgt., k. in a., F., 16/8/18.

ROWE, E. J., b. Newton, 73196, Pte., k. in a., F., 14/6/18.

ROWE, J. O., b. Neath, 9705, Cpl., d., F., 21/8/16.

ROWLANDS, D. J., b. Ystrad, 73202, Pte., k. in a., F., 4/1/18.

RUNDLE, W., b. Holborn, 22505, Pte., d. of w., F., 1/5/18.

RYDER, A., b. Sandbach, 33489, Pte., d. of w., F., 9/7/16.

RYELL, R., b. London, 46272, Cpl., d., F., 24/5/18.

SAVAGE, F., b. West Bromwich, 12954, Pte., k. in a., F., 25/9/15.

SAVAGE, M. G., b. Bethnal Green, 26655, Pte., d. of w., F., 1/10/18.

SCOTT, C. W., b. Manchester, 242858, Pte., k. in a., F., 30/9/18.

SEED, R., b. Church, 58323, Pte., k. in a., F., 23/10/18.

SEEFUS, J. F., b. Liverpool, 244/3, Pte., d. of w., Home, 21/1/16.

SHARP, C. A., b. South Warnborough, 22303, Pte., d., F., 17/10/18.

SHARPLES, J., b. Clitheroe, 47168, Pte., k. in a., F., 31/7/17.

SHEPHERD, A., b. Notting Hill, 26622, Pte., k. in a., F., 21/10/18.

SHERRATT, G. H., b. Chell, 56114, Pte., k. in a., F., 28/5/18.

SHILLAM, J., b. Winchcombe, 15946, L/Cpl., k. in a., F., 25/9/15.

SHIMMIN, R. C., b. Foxdale, 235096, Pte., k. in a., F., 20/9/17.

SILVERMAN, D., b. Manchester, 73651, Pte., k. in a., F., 28/1/18.

SIMCOX, J., b. West Bromwich, 23161, Pte., k. in a., F., 25/9/15.

SIMMS, A., b. Blythe Bridge, 24541, L/Cpl., k. in a., F., 25/9/15.

SLATE, A. T., b. Bethnal Green, 34707, Pte., k. in a., F., 30/9/18.

SLATER, A., b. Blackburn, 57905, Pte., d., F., 2/11/18.

SLEIGH, F., b. Manchester, 66117, Pte., k. in a., F., 19/9/17.

SLINGER, E., b. Leeds, 202190, Pte., d. of w., F., 5/6/18.

SMETHURST, W. P., b. Blackburn, 19368, Pte., k. in a., F., 8/6/17.

SMITH, E., b. Newport, 73207, Pte., d., F., 21/7/18.

SMITH, E. W., b. Colne, 56471, Pte., d., F., 30/10/18.

SMITH, J., e. Kinmel Park, 45268, Pte., k. in a., F., 29/4/18.

SMITH, J., b. Belfast, 16380, Pte., d. of w., F., 24/7/17.

SMITH, T., b. Coventry, 6379, L/Cpl., k. in a., F., 11/8/16.

SMITH, T., b. Kippax, 46253, Pte., k. in a., F., 3/10/17.

SMITH, W., b. Atherstone, 11821, Pte., k. in a., F., 31/7/17.

SPENCER, G. H., b. Llantrissant, 16661, Pte., k. in a., F., 25/9/15.

SPILLER, A., b. Penarth, 12497, L/Cpl., d. of w., F., 28/10/16.

SPILSBURY, S. P., b. Bowden, 23118, L/Cpl., k. in a., F., 7/7/16.

STEPHENS, W. J., b. Wernfarm, 13032, Pte., k. in a., F., 25/9/15.

STEVENS, S., b. West Bromwich, 31112, Pte., k. in a., F., 3/7/16.

STEVENS, W. T., b. Llantwit, 16749, L/Cpl., k. in a., F., 18/4/18.

STEVENSON, R. A., b. Salford, 31147, Pte., k. in a., F., 20/10/18.

STOCKTON, T., b. Liverpool, 57712, Pte., k. in a., F., 20/10/18.

STONEBRIDGE, W., e. Brecon, 55657, Pte., k. in a., F., 8/5/18.

STOPHER, G. A., b. Tidal Basin, 46266, Pte., k. in a., F., 22/3/18.

SUGARS, A., b. Kentish Town, 26576, Pte., k. in a., F., 27/3/18.

SULLIVAN, E. A. S., b. Highbury, 21973, Pte., k. in a., F., 23/10/18.

SUTLEFF, H., b. Denver, 56355, Pte., k. in a., F., 8/6/17.

SWAINSON, J., b. Liverpool, 36558, Pte., k. in a., F., 7/6/17.

SWANN, N., b. Dukinfield, 267109, Pte., k. in a., F., 6/11/18.

SWEET, C., e. Atherstone, 69126, Pte., d. of w., F., 5/5/18.

TACK, H., b. Aylesbury, 13293, Sgt., k. in a., F., 10/8/16.

TATUM, G., b. Mold, 12959, Pte., k. in a., F., 25/9/15.

TAYLOR, H., b. Warrington, 75096, Pte., d., F., 28/4/18.

TAYLOR, J., b. St. Helens, 12094, L/Cpl., k. in a., F., 7/7/16.

TAYLOR, J., b. Dowlais, 18956, Pte., k. in a., F., 7/6/17.

TAYLOR, W. C., b. Kensworth, 56366, Pte., d. of w., F., 20/9/17.

TERRY, A., b. Birmingham, 46281, Pte., k. in a., F., 16/9/16.

THOMAS, A., b. Tonypandy, 5590, Pte., d. of w., F., 1/8/16.

THOMAS, D. J., b. Blaenporth, 12968, Pte., d. of w., F., 10/8/16.

THOMAS, G. B., b. Burry Port, 75091, Pte., d., Home, 29/10/18.

THOMAS, H., b. Llamsamlet, 37952, Cpl., k. in a., F., 30/10/16.

THOMAS, J., b. Holywell, 6201, L/Sgt., k. in a., F., 25/9/15.

THOMAS, J., b. Llanrwst, 16791, Pte., k. in a., F., 25/9/15.

THOMAS, J., b. Moss, 23869, Pte., d., F., 8/9/18.

THOMAS, J., b. Cefn Cribbwr, 70071, Pte., k. in a., F., 18/4/18.

THOMAS, L. J., b. Llangennech, 57964, Pte., d. of w., F., 1/5/18.

THOMAS, R. E., b. Neath, 61313, Pte., k. in a., F., 20/9/17.

THOMAS, R. O., b. Llanfachreth, 20915, L/Cpl., d., F., 29/8/18.

THOMAS, W., b. Cilybebyll, 29525, Sgt., k. in a., F., 16/9/18.

THOMAS, W. M., b. Llanglydwen, 73210, Pte., d. of w., F., 26/3/18.

THOMPSON, J., b. Manchester, 70505, Pte., d. of w., F., 18/4/18.

THOMPSON, W., b. Rhostyllyn, 12635, Pte., d. of w., F., 1/10/15.

THORNE, A. J., b. Cardiff, 267949, Pte., k. in a., F., 30/5/18.

THORNTON, G. H., b. Nelson, 67044, Pte., k. in a., F., 20/10/18.

THORNTON, J., b. Newcastle, 23942, Pte., k. in a., F., 3/7/16.

TIBBS, W., b. Ynistawe, 56747, Pte., k. in a., F., 7/11/18.

TIERNEY, J., b. Liverpool, 73661, Pte., d. of w., F., 31/5/18.

TOMKINS, J., b. Worcester, 12775, Pte., k. in a., F., 25/9/15.

TOMLINSON, E., b. Cannock, 14517, Pte., k. in a., F., 25/7/16.

TOMLINSON, J. H., b. Manchester, 63047, Pte., k. in a., F., 7/6/17.

TOOTELL, W. E., b. Chorley, 73656, Pte., d. of w., F., 8/1/18.

TOOTH, J., b. Mansfield, 23607, Pte., k. in a., F., 20/10/18.

TOZER, J., b. Holywell, 12732, L/Cpl., k. in a., F., 25/9/15.

TUCKER, W., b. Bankyfelin, 13208, A/Cpl., k. in a., F., 11/11/16.

TURNER, A., b. Brighton, 68797, Cpl., k. in a., F., 22/3/18.

TURNER, F. G., b. Cambridge, 56335, Pte., k. in a., F., 14/6/18.

TURNER, G., b. Liverpool, 315750, Pte., k. in a., F., 7/11/18.

TURNER, J., b. Sydney Bridge, 12708, Pte., k. in a., F., 12/5/17.

TURNER, J., b. Southport, 64573, Pte., d., F., 22/3/18.

UNSWORTH, G., b. Liverpool, 73668, Pte., k. in a., F., 30/9/18.

VALENTINE, T., e. Northampton, 60413, Pte., d. of w., F., 15/6/17.

VARLEY, R., b. Stockport, 315162, Pte., k. in a., F., 21/10/18.

VARNDELL, C. C. T., e. Clapham, 70586, Pte., d. of w., F., 16/7/18.

VASEY, T., b. Bolton, 23116, Pte., d. of w., F., 19/10/15.

VATER, A., b. Aberdare, 19782, L/Cpl., k. in a., F., 29/9/17.

VAUGHAN, R., b. Llanrhaiadr, 5744, Pte., k. in a., F., 25/9/15.

VENNER, H. M., b. Rhondda, 16395, Pte., k. in a., F., 2/7/16.

VICKERY, G. V., b. Tidenham, 54247, Pte., d. of w., F., 29/4/18.

VOWLES, H., b. West Bromwich, 5268, Pte., k. in a., F., 3/7/16.

WAINMAN, H., b. Birmingham, 70583, Pte., d. of w., F., 13/5/18.

WALKER, F., b. Chester, 12590, Pte., k. in a., F., 25/9/15.

WALKER, R., b. Rochdale, 33044, Pte., k. in a., F., 22/3/18.

WALL, A. T., b. Cardiff, 24429, Pte., d. of w., F., 7/11/18.

WARD, A., b. Birmingham, 11672, Sgt., k. in a., F., 3/7/16.

WARD, W., b. Liverpool, 13276, L/Cpl., k. in a., F., 31/7/17.

WASLEY, W., b. Wigan, 24062, Pte., d. of w., F., 12/6/18.

WATKINS, J., b. Talgarth, 15944, Pte., d. of w., F., 26/3/16.

WATKINS, J. H., e. Brecon, 88870, Pte., d. of w., F., 26/11/18.

WATTS, E., b. Cardiff, 69501, Pte., k. in a., F., 18/4/18.

WEAVER, F., b. Warwick, 23094, Pte., k. in a., F., 25/9/15.

WEEKS, F., b. Rhondda, 15703, L/Sgt., d. of w., F., 20/10/18, M.M.

WELLS, J. R., b. Birmingham,

6604, Sgt., d. of w., F., 29/9/15.

WESCOMBE, F., e. Pontypridd, 70593, Sgt., k. in a., F., 18/4/18.

WEST, C., b. Llansamlet, 15939, Cpl., k. in a., F., 3/7/16.

WHITE, H. A., b. Upton, 202425, Pte., k. in a., F., 16/8/18.

WHITHAM, C. S. W., b. Manchester, 63891, Pte., k. in a., F., 22/7/17.

WHITHAM, V. L., b. Holt, 75100, Pte., d. of w., F., 19/9/18.

WHITLEY, J., b. Mostyn, 13302, Pte., k. in a., F., 11/11/16.

WHITTAKER, W., e. Oldham, 60239, Pte., k. in a., F., 22/3/18.

WIDDUP, W. I., b. Liverpool, 70512, Pte., d. of w., F., 30/6/18.

WIGGIN, F. T., b. Llandaff, 73221, Pte., k. in a., F., 8/1/18.

WILKINS, T., b. Llanelly, 13136, Pte., k. in a., F., 25/9/15.

WILLIAMS, A., b. Kinnerley, 31901, Pte., k. in a., F., 12/1/17.

WILLIAMS, A., b. Rhostyllen, 44309, Pte., k. in a., F., 23/3/18.

WILLIAMS, A., b. Llanrug, 13021, Pte., d. of w., F., 27/9/15.

WILLIAMS, B., b. Newland, 33331, Pte., d., F., 14/10/18.

WILLIAMS, C., b. Twynyrodyn, 73220, Pte., k. in a., F., 7/11/18.

WILLIAMS, D., b. Pent Blech, 44244, Pte., k. in a., F., 18/4/18.

WILLIAMS, D., b. Manchester, 57157, Pte., k. in a., F., 14/6/18.

WILLIAMS, D., b. Merthyr, 70080, Pte., d., F., 16/9/18.

WILLIAMS, D. J., b. Burry Port, 13385, Pte., k. in a., F., 25/9/15.

WILLIAMS, E., b. Hanley, 36054, Pte., k. in a., F., 3/7/16.

WILLIAMS, E. B., b. Mold, 77302, Pte., d. of w., F., 25/10/18.

WILLIAMS, G., b. Llanelly, 11966, Pte., k. in a., F., 3/7/16.

WILLIAMS, G., b. Deganwy, 15198, Cpl., k. in a., F., 5/10/17.

WILLIAMS, G., b. Abertillery, 54250, L/Cpl., d. of w., F., 20/9/17.

WILLIAMS, H., b. Vroncysyllte, 24633, Pte., k. in a., F., 3/7/16.

WILLIAMS, H., b. Pembroke, 13570, Sgt., k. in a., F., 3/7/16.

WILLIAMS, H., b. Llangefni, 20302, Pte., k. in a., F., 7/6/17.

WILLIAMS, H. E., b. Llandudno,

49983, Pte., k. in a., F., 22/3/18.

WILLIAMS, J., b. Liverpool, 13237, Pte., k. in a., F., 2/6/18.

WILLIAMS, J., b. Abertillery, 47336, Pte., d. of w., F., 31/7/17.

WILLIAMS, J., b. Llanfihangel, 74846, Pte., d. of w., Home, 23/5/18.

WILLIAMS, J. E., e. Merthyr, 57912, Pte., k. in a., F., 14/6/18.

WILLIAMS, J. O., b. Liverpool, 13104, Cpl., k. in a., F., 25/9/15.

WILLIAMS, J. R., b. Llandudno, 13282, Sgt., k. in a., F., 25/10/16.

WILLIAMS, M., b. Bedlinog, 15948, Pte., d. of w., Home, 3/10/15.

WILLIAMS, R. E., b. Conway, 12734, Pte., k. in a., F., 25/9/15.

WILLIAMS, S., b. Llanelly, 13163, Cpl., d. of w., Home, 20/10/15.

WILLIAMS, T., b. Pontypridd, 13727, Pte., k. in a., F., 3/7/16.

WILLIAMS, T., b. Mountain Ash, 75543, Pte., k. in a., F., 18/4/18.

WILLIAMS, T. A., b. Merthyr, 38737, Pte., d. of w., F., 23/4/18.

WILLIAMS, T. E., b. Wrexham, 23115, Pte., k. in a., F., 3/7/16.

WILLIAMS, W. J., e. Mountain Ash', 73218, Pte., k. in a., F., 8/5/18.

WILLMOTT, W., b. London, 13569, Pte., k. in a., F., 11/11/16.

WOOD, J., b. Crewe, 15940, Pte., k. in a., F., 25/9/15.

WOODWARD, W., b. Stockport, 316789, Pte., k. in a., F., 14/6/18.

WORSNOP, C., b. Preston, 242935, Pte., k. in a., F., 14/6/18.

WRIGHT, D. R., b. Cefn, 36388, Pte., k. in a., F., 29/4/18.

YATES, A., b. Manchester, 4948, Pte., k. in a., F., 1/9/16.

YATES, A., b. Blackburn, 47213, Pte., k. in a., F., 11/10/17.

10th BATTALION

ABEL, W., b. Birmingham, 13243, Pte., k. in a., F., 13/11/16.

ABERCROMBY, F., e. Wrexham, 57032, L/Sgt., k. in a., F., 8/4/17.

ACKERS, P., b. Altcar, 51438, Pte., k. in a., F., 26/9/17.

ALDERMAN, T., b. Kingston, 38813, Pte., k. in a., F., 16/8/16.

ALLEN, F., b. Ellesmere, 54697, Pte., k. in a., F., 13/11/16.

ALLOTT, J., e. Stockport, 54898, Pte., d., F., 25/1/17.

ANDREWS, W., b. Chadsley, 16917, Pte., k. in a., F., 13/11/16.

ANTHONY, I., b. Ammanford, 12897, Pte., k. in a., F., 16/8/16.

ALSOP, T., b. Preston, 15358, Pte., d. of w., F., 9/4/16.

ARDERN, J., b. Stockport, 54696, Pte., k. in a., F., 17/6/17.

ARTER, R. H. T., b. Deptford, 60224, Pte., k. in a., F., 14/6/17.

ARTHEY, F., b. Ardleigh, 56044, Pte., k. in a., F., 11/4/17.

ARTHURS, S. J., b. London, 15509, Pte., k. in a., F., 20/7/16.

ASBURY, R. J., b. Birmingham, 60355, Pte., k. in a., F., 4/8/17.

ASHBY, G., b. Tysoe, 27782, L/Cpl., k. in a., F., 16/8/16.

ASHES, V., b. Pendleton, 55553, Pte., k. in a., F., 8/4/17.

ATHERTON, E., b. Towyn, 32515, Pte., k. in a., F., 16/8/16.

ATKINSON, G., b. Pennington, 39533, Pte., k. in a., F., 26/9/17.

BAGSHALL, W., b. Anerley, 22231, Pte., k. in a., F., 13/11/16.

BAILEY, E., b. Sheffield, 60477, Pte., k. in a., F., 28/9/17.

BAILEY, F., b. Mow Cop, 60196, Pte., k. in a., F., 16/6/17.

BAILEY, S., b. Briton Ferry, 15825, Pte., k. in a., F., 13/11/16.

BALL, J., e. Burslem, 28589, Pte., k. in a., F., 26/9/17.

BALLARD, J. R., b. Liverpool, 15175, Pte., k. in a., F., 16/8/16, M.M.

BARLOW, H., b. Whitchurch, 54705, Pte., k. in a., F., 13/11/16.

BARLOW, J., b. Wishaw, 38158, Pte., k. in a., F., 16/8/16.

BARLOW, W., b. Manchester, 62875, Pte., k. in a., F., 26/9/17.

BARNETT, F., b. Burslem, 23458, Pte., k. in a., F., 3/1/16.

BARRETT, T., b. Bristol, 70165, Pte., d., F., 24/10/17.

BARRY, G., b. London, 57414, Pte., d., Home, 23/10/17.

BARTON, T., b. Llanasa, 14914, L/Sgt., k. in a., F., 16/8/16.

BASSETT, A., b. Ystradfodwg, 15201, Pte., k. in a., F., 17/2/16.

BAXTER, C. W., b. Wrexham, 61260, Pte., k. in a., F., 26/9/17.

BEDDOW, E., b. Upton Magna, 54709, Pte., k. in a., F., 13/11/16.

BEHRENS, C. J., b. Bolton, 52217, Pte., k. in a., F., 29/4/17.

BELLIS, S., b. Oakenholt, 18360, Pte., k. in a., F., 16/8/16.

BENJAMIN, T., b. Llantwit, 15028, Pte., k. in a., F., 27/4/17.

BENNETT, W., b. Old Ford, 56005, Pte., k. in a., F., 27/4/17.

BERRY, A., b. Altrincham, 54703, Pte., k. in a., F., 13/11/16.

BEVAN, A. G. H., b. Little Dean, 54999, Pte., k. in a., F., 30/4/17.

BEVAN, D. C., b. Newtown, 54698, Pte., k. in a., F., 13/11/16.

BEVAN, H., b. Bagillt, 15715, Pte., k. in a., F., 2/3/16.

BEYNON, E., b. Gower, 60298, Pte., d. of w., F., 18/6/17.

BIRCHALL, G. W., b. St. Luke's, 24779, Pte., k. in a., F., 20/7/16.

BLUNT, C. F., e. Birmingham, 36480, Pte., k. in a., F., 11/4/17.

BODYCOMBE, E. L., b. Neath Abbey, 54704, Pte., k. in a., F., 13/11/16.

BOLDERSTON, J., e. Wrexham, 57021, Pte., k. in a., F., 13/11/16.

BOLGER, J., e. Bury, 202855, Pte., k. in a., F., 26/9/17.

BONE, S., b. Blackpool, 36940, Pte., k. in a., F., 16/8/16.

BOOTH, J., b. Stalybridge, 63520, Pte., k. in a., F., 27/9/17.

BOWKER, H., b. Sharrow, 12192, Pte., k. in a., F., 20/7/16.

BRADSHAW, J., b. Westhead, 266867, Pte., d. of w., F., 16/6/17.

BRADSHAW, J., e. Market Drayton, 54902, Pte., k. in a., F., 8/4/17.

BRADY, T., b. London, 10636, Pte., k. in a., F., 2/3/16.

BRANCH, W., b. Bideford, 18351, Pte., k. in a., F., 16/8/16.

BREAKWELL, H., b. Wolverhampton, 60434, Pte., k. in a., F., 26/9/17.

BREWER, J., b. Chatham Green, 56041, Pte., k. in a., F., 13/6/17.

BRIDGES, T., b. Leithrim, 6323, Pte., d. of w., F., 18/5/16.

BRIDLE, W. J., b. Moreton, 15413, Sgt., k. in a., F., 13/11/16.

BRINDLEY, T. F., b. Fenton, 31816, Pte., k. in a., F., 20/7/16.

BROOKES, T., b. Manchester, 54700, Pte., k. in a., F., 13/11/16.

BROOKS, A., b. Bermondsey, 35185, Pte., k. in a., F., 19/8/16.

BROUGHTON, H., b. Wednesbury, 12736, Pte., k. in a., F., 16/8/16.

BROWN, E. J., b. Walford, 54903, L/Cpl., k. in a., F., 11/4/17.

BROWN, F., b. Burton-on-Trent,

24272, Sgt., k. in a., F., 27/9/17.

BROWN, J., b. Thurmaston, 60431, Pte., k. in a., F., 26/9/17.

BROWN, R. J., b. Cadoxton, 60516, Pte., k. in a., F., 27/9/17.

BROWN, W., b. Cardiff, 235730, Pte., k. in a., F., 26/9/17.

BRYANT, F. A., b. London, 27234, Pte., d. of w., F., 25/11/15.

BULLEN, C. W., b. St. Luke's, 34820, Pte., k. in a., F., 16/8/16.

BULLOCK, C., b. Wednesbury, 8263, Pte., k. in a., F., 20/7/16.

BUNNETT, T. J., b. Hope, 15087, Pte., k. in a., F., 16/1/16.

BURGESS, H., b. Denton, 15342, Pte., k. in a., F., 20/7/16.

BURGESS, J., b. Kippax, 17772, Pte., k. in a., F., 20/7/16.

BUTLERTON, H., b. Broughton, 33219, Pte., k. in a., F., 16/8/16.

BUTTERFIELD, J., e. Ulverston, 55040, Pte., d. of w., F., 12/4/17.

BUTTLE, W., b. Norwich, 56010, Pte., k. in a., F., 16/6/17.

BWYE, F. H., b. Penarth, 12365, Pte., k. in a., F., 17/6/17.

CAMPBELL, J., b. Chester, 16238, Pte., k. in a., F., 17/2/16.

CAMPION, R. H., b. Burton-on-Trent, 23310, Pte., k. in a., F., 20/7/16.

CAPEY, E., b. Burslem, 18300, Pte., k. in a., F., 19/10/14.

CARBERRY, T., b. Liverpool, 33673, Pte., k. in a., F., 13/11/16.

CARROLL, J., b. Penrhyndeudraeth, 15383, Pte., k. in a., F., 20/7/16.

CARTWRIGHT, J., b. Wigan, 24407, Pte., k. in a., F., 20/7/16.

CATHERALL, E., b. Bistre, 15787, L/Sgt., k. in a., F., 17/2/16.

CATLING, G. C., b. Manchester, 55555, Pte., k. in a., F., 11/4/17.

CHAMBERLAIN, H., b. Grantham, 60428, Pte., k. in a., F., 26/9/17.

CHAMBERS, W., b. Soughton, 15400, Cpl., d. of w., F., 27/6/17.

CHANNON, S. G., b. Ottery St. Mary, 60358, Pte., k. in a., F., 16/6/17.

CHAPLIN, T. G., b. Willesborough, 60354, Pte., k. in a., F., 16/6/17.

CHAPMAN, A., b. Bollington, 60308, Pte., d. of w., F., 15/6/17.

CHESTERS, G. L., b. Salford, 11054, L/Cpl., d. of w., F., 14/8/17.

CHEW, C. A., b. Ruabon, 201368, Pte., d. of w., F., 14/5/17.

CHORLTON, E., e. Welshpool, 54394, Pte., d., F., 18/5/17.

CLARK, J., b. Plattbridge, Lancs, 15522, A/C.S.M., k. in a., F., 16/8/16.

CLARKE, T., b. Bury, 60299, Pte., k. in a., F., 18/6/17.

CLAYTON, J., b. Westleigh, 19968, Pte., k. in a., F., 19/8/16.

CLAYTON, W. H., b. Brymbo, 15801, Pte., d. of w., F., 8/8/16.

CLEWES, W., b. Manchester, 38835, Pte., k. in a., F., 16/8/16.

CLUTTON, J., b. Wrexham, 57076, Pte., k. in a., F., 13/11/16.

COCKAYNE, A. H., b. Liverpool, 66209, Pte., k. in a., F., 26/9/17.

COLBERT, B., b. Shoreditch, 34584, Pte., k. in a., F., 26/9/17.

COLCLOUGH, J., b. Tunstall, 23493, Pte., k. in a., F., 22/11/15.

COLLINS, W., b. London, 16114, Pte., k. in a., F., 3/3/16.

COLLINS, W. J., b. Clyst St. Mary, 54843, Pte., d. of w., F., 24/11/16.

COLOHAN, T., b. Chester, 8901, Pte., k. in a., F., 20/7/16.

COOK, F., b. Kilburn, 23465, Pte., k. in a., F., 19/8/16.

COOPER, A. W., b. Little Dewchurch, 54909, Cpl., d., F., 17/12/16.

COOPER, F. C., b. Norwich, 60448, Pte., k. in a., F., 26/9/17.

CORDIER, H. J., b. Cwmbran, 34303, Cpl., k. in a., F., 13/11/16.

CORKER, H. R., b. Leeds, 12476, Pte., k. in a., F., 17/2/16.

CORNWELL, A. W., b. London, 34987, Pte., k. in a., F., 11/4/17.

CORNWELL, F. C., b. Tottenham, 56034, Pte., d. of w., Home, 17/7/17.

COSTELLO, P., b. Flint, 14917, Pte., k. in a., F., 16/8/16.

COSTER, H. W., b. Canonbury, 35042, Pte., d. of w., F., 27/8/16.

COX, J. W., b. Birmingham, 36426, Pte., k. in a., F., 16/8/16.

CRABTREE, J., e. Wallasey, 56992, Pte., d. of w., F., 29/11/16.

CROFTS, E. E., b. London, 21878, Pte., d., F., 23/6/18.

CROOK, H., b. Birtle, 14305, Pte., d. of w., F., 20/7/16.

CROSS, A., b. West Bergholt, 56011, L/Cpl., k. in a., F., 11/4/17.

CROW, A., b. Chipping Norton, 9804, Pte., k. in a., F., 2/3/16.

CULLING, J. H., b. Gosport, 12261, Pte., d. of w., F., 18/2/16.

CUMMINGS, A., e. Manchester, 54707, Pte., d., F., 13/1/17.

DADE, J., b. Nottingham, 15459, Pte., d. of w., F., 21/8/16.

DALE, W., b. London, 22169, Pte., k. in a., F., 13/11/16.

DALLISON, B., b. South Streatham, 15664, L/Cpl., k. in a., F., 3/3/16.

DANIEL, J., b. Clydach Vale, 15142, Pte., d. of w., F., 18/2/16.

DANIELS, P. C., b. King's Stanley, 16242, L/Cpl., k. in a., F., 1/4/16.

DANIELS, W., b. Wigan, 33965, Pte., k. in a., F., 26/9/17.

DAVEY, W. B., b. Soughton, 15404, A/Cpl., k. in a., F., 3/3/16.

DAVIES, A., b. Wolverhampton, 34335, Pte., k. in a., F., 20/9/17.

DAVIES, A., b. Nantgarw, 18525, Pte., k. in a., F., 16/8/16.

DAVIES, B., b. Flint, 15183, L/Cpl., k. in a., F., 19/2/16.

DAVIES, D., b. Llanbadarn, 45139, Pte., k. in a., F., 30/4/17.

DAVIES, E., b. Llanrhaiadr-yn-Mochant, 23153, Pte., k. in a., F., 15/7/17.

DAVIES, E. D., b. Rhondda, 35434, Pte., d. of w., F., 25/8/16.

DAVIES, H., e. Blaenau Festiniog, 291212, Pte., k. in a., F., 11/5/17.

DAVIES, H. G., b. Llandudno, 40571, Pte., k. in a., F., 16/8/16.

DAVIES, H. T., b. Abergele, 16023, L/Cpl., d. of w., F., 26/2/16.

DAVIES, J., b. Cheltenham, 40086, Pte., k. in a., F., 20/7/16.

DAVIES, J. L., b. Liverpool, 40459, L/Cpl., k. in a., F., 20/7/16.

DAVIES, J. M., b. Llandrindod Wells, 38513, Pte., k. in a., F., 16/8/16.

DAVIES, J. R., b. Llandulais, 15470, Pte., d. of w., F., 20/2/16.

DAVIES, R. O., b. Manchester, 17688, Cpl., k. in a., F., 20/7/16.

DAVIES, S., b. Morriston, 15045, Pte., k. in a., F., 13/11/16.

DAVIES, S. T., b. Llandrillo, 15147, Pte., k. in a., F., 16/8/16.

DAVIES, T. E., b. Hackney, 45030, Pte., k. in a., F., 5/5/17.

DAVIES, T. F., b. London, 16117, Pte., k. in a., F., 20/7/16.

DAVIES, T. O., b. Exdale, 15502, Pte., d. of w., F., 18/2/16.

DAVIES, W., b. Rhondda, 20365, Pte., k. in a., F., 16/8/16.

DAVIES, W., b. Newport, 38177, Pte., k. in a., F., 19/8/16.

DAVIES, W. E., b. Llanrwst, 49028, Pte., k. in a., F., 14/6/17.

DAVIES, W. H., b. Llandegla, 15316, Pte., k. in a., F., 2/3/16.

DAVIES, W. J., b. Llanrug, 40387, Pte., k. in a., F., 19/8/16.

DAVIES, W. T., b. Crynant, 19254, Pte., k. in a., F., 13/11/16.

DEAN, J., b. Rhyl, 54841, Pte., k. in a., F., 8/4/17.

DEAN, J. T., b. Stockport, 33313, Pte., k. in a., F., 20/7/16.

DEAN, W. C., b. London, 26626, Pte., k. in a., F., 20/7/16.

DEARDEN, J. T., e. Wrexham, 57068, Pte., d., F., 21/11/16.

DEEN, W. A., b. Merthyr, 33685, L/Cpl., k. in a., F., 20/7/16.

DEVEREUX, L., b. Tewkesbury, 15131, Pte., k. in a., F., 2/3/16.

DICKINSON, E. C., b. Brereton, 60228, L/Cpl., d. of w., F., 27/9/17.

DITCHFIELD, E., e. Wrexham, 54459, Pte., k. in a., F., 13/11/16.

DIVER, F., b. Chorlton-on-Medlock, 15516, Sgt., k. in a., F., 20/7/16.

DOMINY, S. W., b. London, 27219, Pte., k. in a., F., 20/7/16.

DONOVAN, J., b. Milford, 10543, Pte., k. in a., F., 13/11/16.

DOOLEY, H., b. Plymouth, 14017, Sgt., k. in a., F., 16/8/16.

DOWDLE, G., b. Ilfracombe, 38180, Pte., k. in a., F., 16/8/16.

DOWLING, P., b. Kilkenny, 34197, Pte., d. of w., F., 27/9/17.

DOWNING, T., b. Cannock, 36575, Pte., k. in a., F., 16/8/16.

DRISCOLL, M., b. Cardiff, 15312, A/Cpl., k. in a., F., 16/8/16.

DUDLEY, H., b. Barmouth, 23191, L/Cpl., k. in a., F., 30/4/16.

DUNFORD, C. H., b. Wedmore, 7842, L/Cpl., k. in a., F., 20/7/16.

DUNKLEY, W., b. Kidderminster, 13603, Pte., k. in a., F., 11/4/17.

DUNN, J., b. Cardiff, 54919, Pte., k. in a., F., 27/9/17.

DUNNICLIFFE, W. H., b. Staunton Harold, 56018, Pte., k. in a., F., 27/9/17.

DURBIN, S. L., b. Bristol, 33682, Pte., k. in a., F., 20/7/16.

DYER, J., b. Yarpole, 31899, Pte., k. in a., F., 16/8/16.

EARLY, H., b. London, 35072, Pte., k. in a., F., 13/11/16.

EDGE, W., e. Wrexham, 57072, Pte., k. in a., F., 13/11/16.

EDMONDS, H. C., b. London, 54462, Pte., k. in a., F., 14/6/17.

EDMONDS, T., b. Stockport, 31318, Pte., d. of w., F., 9/1/17.

EDWARDS, A., b. Rhos, 15461, Pte., d., F., 3/11/15.

EDWARDS, A., b. Tilstock, 54923, Pte., d., F., 4/2/17.

EDWARDS, C. W., b. Twerton, 60488, Pte., k. in a., F., 26/9/17.

EDWARDS, D. E., b. Llanon, 16149, Pte., k. in a., F., 20/7/16.

EDWARDS, E., b. Rhosesmor, 36977, Pte., k. in a., F., 16/8/16.

EDWARDS, F., b. Ruabon, 54440, Pte., k. in a., F., 13/11/16.

EDWARDS, F., b. Eaton, 54922, Pte., k. in a., F., 11/4/17.

EDWARDS, J. M., b. Porth, 38057, Pte., k. in a., F., 16/8/16.

EDWARDS, J. R., b. London, 27774, Pte., d. of w., F., 28/11/16.

EDWARDS, R., e. Wrexham, 57004, Pte., k. in a., F., 26/9/17.

EDWARDS, R., b. Gwernymynydd, 54713, Pte., k. in a., F., 13/11/16.

EEDE, L. H., b. London, 15002, Pte., k. in a., F., 15/10/15.

ELLIS, A., b. Birmingham, 36915, Pte., d., F., 14/12/16.

ELLIS, H. O., b. Cwmyglo, 40367, Cpl., k. in a., F., 13/11/16.

ELLIS, O., b. Llandegai, 61233, Pte., k. in a., F., 27/9/17.

ELLIS, T. F., b. Wrexham, 15266, Cpl., k. in a., F., 20/7/16.

ENDERSBY, A., b. Streatham, 26666, Pte., k. in a., F., 13/11/16.

EVANS, C., e. Wrexham, 56990, Pte., k. in a., F., 13/11/16.

EVANS, C. C., b. Birmingham, 36320, Pte., k. in a., F., 13/11/16.

EVANS, D., b. Conwil Caio, 37321, Pte., k. in a., F., 19/8/16.

EVANS, D., b. Swansea, 14961, Pte., k. in a., F., 13/11/16.

EVANS, D. J., b. Ferndale, 37950, L/Cpl., k. in a., F., 16/8/16.

EVANS, E., b. Trefriw, 15289, Pte., k. in a., F., 13/11/16.

EVANS, I., b. Swansea, 15039, Pte., k. in a., F., 30/3/16.

EVANS, J., b. Blaenau Festiniog, 16309, Pte., k. in a., F., 19/2/16.

EVANS, J., b. Whixall, 54920, Pte., k. in a., F., 30/4/17.

EVANS, J. E., b. Mold, 15693, Pte., k. in a., F., 13/11/16.

EVANS, J. G., b. Cellan, 13009, L/Cpl., k. in a., F., 20/7/16.

EVANS, J. J., b. Rhondda, 31348, Pte., d. of w., F., 4/6/18.

EVANS, J. W., b. Glyn, 19388, Pte., d. of w., F., 30/9/17.

EVANS, O. E., b. Garn, 44268, Pte., d. of w., F., 20/10/17.

EVANS, P., b. Flint, 15720, Pte., k. in a., F., 20/7/16.

EVANS, R., e. London, 40151, L/Cpl., k. in a., F., 20/7/16.

EVANS, R., b. Rhyl, 39082, A/L/Cpl., k. in a., F., 16/8/16.

EVANS, R., e. Welshpool, 54398, Pte., k. in a., F., 13/11/16.

EVANS, R. M., b. London, 15089, Cpl., k. in a., F., 9/12/15.

EVANS, S., e. Llandudno, 40849, Sgt., k. in a., F., 8/4/17.

EVANS, T., b. Llandudno, 15529, Pte., k. in a., F., 17/2/16.

EVANS, T. D., b. Llanelly, 15578, Pte., d. of w., F., 9/3/16.

EVANS, W., b. Llanrwst, 15290, Pte., k. in a., F., 2/1/16.

EVANS, W. J., b. Mardy, 15125, L/Sgt., k. in a., F., 15/3/16.

EVANS, W. J., b. Ferndale, 15438, Pte., k. in a., F., 20/7/16.

EVANS, W. R., b. Llanelly, 235034, Pte., k. in a., F., 19/4/17.

EVERSON, S., b. London, 36056, Pte., k. in a., F., 4/1/17.

EYNON, A. V., b. Pembroke, 15052, Pte., d. of w., F., 30/9/17.

FALLOWS, L., b. Newton, 31159, Pte., k. in a., F., 17/2/16.

FEARNS, T., b. Oakamoor, 23455, Pte., k. in a., F., 16/8/16.

FELL, T., b. Hyde, 54718, Pte., k. in a., F., 13/11/16.

FINDLAY, G. D., b. Tullynessle, 12958, Pte., d., Home, 20/10/14.

FISHER, J. T., b. London, 27347, Pte., k. in a., F., 30/4/16.

FLEET, A., b. Tarporley, 54719, Pte., k. in a., F., 13/11/16.

FLETCHER, J. H., b. Liverpool, 60468, Pte., k. in a., F., 26/9/17.

FORSTER, H. W., b. London, 27074, Pte., k. in a., F., 28/2/17.

FORSTER, J. W., b. Silverdale, 54399, Pte., d., F., 9/4/17.

FROST, F., b. Chadwell Heath, 56047, Pte., k. in a., F., 11/4/17.

GALLAGHAN, P., b. Co. Armagh, 23280, Pte., k. in a., F., 19/8/16.

GAM, S., b. Ratcliffe, Middlesex, 27288, Pte., k. in a., F., 17/10/15.

GATSCIEAS, S., b. Bristol, 70171, Pte., k. in a., F., 26/9/17.

GEORGE, T., b. Swansea, 38089, Sgt., k. in a., F., 16/8/16.

GIBBS, W. J., b. Sunderland, 60386, Pte., k. in a., F., 16/6/17.

GITSON, F. A., b. Bristol, 235022, Pte., k. in a., F., 27/4/17.

GOODWIN, J. E., b. Wrexham, 15141, Pte., d. of w., F., 1/5/16.

GOULD, A., b. London, 17364, L/Cpl., k. in a., F., 26/9/17.

GOULD, W. R., b. Bristol, 235023, Pte., k. in a., F., 2/5/17.

GOWER, H., b. Highgate, 34957, Pte., k. in a., F., 25/9/17.

GREEN, T., b. Swadlincote, 23220, Pte., k. in a., F., 20/7/16.

GREENWOOD, H. T., b. London, 27184, Pte., k. in a., F., 16/8/16.

GREENWOOD, J., b. St. Mark's, 18695, Pte., d., F., 13/3/17.

GRIFFITHS, D., b. Pontardawe,

13977, Pte., k. in a., F., 24/8/18.

GRIFFITHS, D. R., b. Llwynypia, 15005, Sgt., k. in a., F., 26/9/17.

GRIFFITHS, E., b. Barmouth, 39912, Pte., k. in a., F., 13/11/16.

GRIFFITHS, E., b. Mold, 16048, Sgt., k. in a., F., 19/8/16.

GRIFFITHS, O., b. Newborough, 15182, Pte., d. of w., F., 11/7/16.

GRIFFITHS, O., b. Holyhead, 21419, Pte., k. in a., F., 26/9/17.

GRIFFITHS, R. E., b. Bala, 54721, Pte., d., F., 28/4/17.

GRIFFITHS, T., b. Picton, 15115, Pte., k. in a., F., 3/3/16.

GRIFFITHS, W. E., b. Cefn, 60991, Pte., k. in a., F., 26/9/17.

GROOM, W., b. St. John's, 10199, Pte., k. in a., F., 27/4/17.

HAMBLET, A., e. Wrexham, 54944, Pte., k. in a., F., 26/9/17.

HAMPSON, J., b. Hadfield, 17767, Pte., k. in a., F., 29/3/18.

HANKINS, H., b. Cardiff, 56690, Pte., k. in a., F., 26/9/17.

HARE, H. S., b. Barton-on-Humber, 60375, Pte., d. of w., F., 25/6/17.

HARRHY, F., b. Llanhennick, 24424, Pte., d. of w., F., 5/1/16.

HARRIES, T., b. Roath, 11943, Pte., k. in a., F., 30/4/16.

HARRIS, D. W., b. Llanfair, 54728, Pte., k. in a., F., 13/11/16.

HARRIS, H. C., b. London, 23728, Cpl., d. of w., Home, 23/1/17.

HARRIS, J., b. Ogmore Vale, 14526, Pte., k. in a., F., 29/4/17.

HARRIS, L., b. Leek, 23487, Pte., k. in a., F., 13/11/16.

HARRY, W., b. Tavistock, 60423, Pte., k. in a., F., 27/9/17.

HAYHURST, W., b. Ramsbottom, 266988, Pte., k. in a., F., 30/4/17.

HEALEY, J., b. Darwen, 33535, Pte., k. in a., F., 16/8/16.

HEARNE, A., b. Chesham, 23296, Pte., k. in a., F., 26/9/17.

HEATH, E., b. Fenton, 23494, Pte., k. in a., F., 16/8/16.

HEIGHWAY, W. H., b. Llanbedrog, 44270, Pte., k. in a., F., 26/9/17.

HENSHAW, R., e. Wrexham, 57019, Pte., d. of w., F., 18/11/16.

HESTER, M., b. Ballenaheglish, 15447, Pte., k. in a., F., 30/4/16.

HETHERINGTON, W. G., e. Wrexham, 54846, Pte., k. in a., F., 28/11/16.

HEWETT, A. V., b. Cardiff, 60340, Pte., k. in a., F., 14/6/17.

HIGGINS, C., b. Stanton, 55052, Pte., k. in a., F., 14/6/17.

HIGGINSON, C. J., b. Shrewsbury, 15078, Pte., d. of w., F., 20/12/15.

HIGHAM, F., b. Hyde, 48841, Pte., d., F., 25/12/18.

HILL, A., b. Hyde, 39765, Pte., k. in a., F., 16/8/16.

HILL, A., b. Ditton, 60367, Pte., k. in a., F., 17/6/17.

HILL, J., b. Newbridge, 33548, L/Cpl., k. in a., F., 26/9/17.

HILL, J., b. Windlebury, 24810, Pte., k. in a., F., 20/7/16.

HOARE, W., b. Camberwell, 22532, Pte., d. of w., F., 14/11/16.

HOBSON, W. J., b. Llandudno, 15532, Pte., k. in a., F., 30/3/16.

HOCKHAM, B., b. Clapham, 15053, Pte., k. in a., F., 19/12/15.

HOLLAND, E., b. Derby, 23436, Pte., k. in a., F., 20/7/16.

HOLLINGSWORTH, E., b. Rhyl, 15197, Pte., k. in a., F., 13/11/16.

HOLLINGSWORTH, S., b. Rhyl, 15731, Pte., k. in a., F., 19/2/16.

HOLLINS, H., b. Rugeley, 19121, Sgt., k. in a., F., 30/4/16.

HOOSON, G., b. Gresford, 13839, Pte., k. in a., F., 23/11/15.

HORNBY, G., b. Garstang, 15334, Pte., k. in a., F., 2/3/16.

HORTON, F. V., b. Coventry, 36238, Pte., k. in a., F., 30/4/16.

HOWARTH, W., b. Leigh, 33224, L/Cpl., k. in a., F., 26/9/17.

HOWCROFT, E., b. Manchester, 33971, Pte., k. in a., F., 16/8/16.

HOWELLS, W. E., b. Stockton, 54928, Pte., k. in a., F., 26/9/17.

HOWLEY, S., b. Clydach Vale, 19711, Pte., k. in a., F., 28/11/16.

HUGHES, H., b. Penygarnedd, 15464, Pte., k. in a., F., 16/8/16.

HUGHES, H., b. Llanddona, 15501, Pte., k. in a., F., 20/7/16.

HUGHES, J., b. Swansea, 15036, Pte., d. of w., F., 1/5/16.

HUGHES, J., b. Anglesey, 54402, Pte., k. in a., F., 13/11/16.

HUGHES, J. C., b. Cardiff, 26595, L/Sgt., d. of w., F., 3/10/16.

HUGHES, M. W., b. Llandeiniolen, 8943, L/Cpl., d. of w., F., 19/8/16.

HUGHES, P., b. Ruabon, 15492, Sgt., d. of w., F., 1/10/17.

HUGHES, R., b. Rhos, 24488, Pte., k. in a., F., 16/8/16.

HUGHES, R., b. Gwffylliog, 39326, Pte., k. in a., F., 16/8/16.

HUGHES, R., b. Llandegar, 33348, Pte., k. in a., F., 16/8/16.

HUGHES, R. J. G., b. Conway, 21578, L/Cpl., d. of w., F., 25/8/16.

HUGHES, T., b. Trigle, 72892, Pte., k. in a., F., 26/9/17.

HUGHES, W. T., b. Dyserth, 54727, Pte., k. in a., F., 13/11/16.

HUMPHREYS, A., e. Wrexham, 57017, L/Cpl., k. in a., F., 11/4/17.

HUMPHREYS, R., e. Carnarvon, 54723, Pte., k. in a., F., 13/11/16.

HUMPHRIES, J., b. Sedgeley, 15472, Pte., k. in a., F., 21/12/15.

HUNT, H. F., b. Birmingham, 29656, Pte., d., F., 25/2/17.

HURLEY, D., b. St. Woollos, 33741, Pte., k. in a., F., 26/9/17.

HUSSEY, H., b. St. Mary's, 24891, Cpl., k. in a., F., 16/8/16, M.M.

IRESON, J. W., b. Dukinfield, 54994, Pte., d., F., 22/12/16.

JACKLIN, L., b. Rusholme, 238088, Pte., d. of w., F., 8/12/17.

JACKSON, E., b. Northop, 15785, Sgt., k. in a., F., 20/7/16.

JACKSON, L., b. Liversedge, 54993, Pte., k. in a., F., 26/9/17.

JAMES, J. R., b. Dolgelly, 35441, Pte., k. in a., F., 28/11/16.

JAMES, W. E., b. Dolgelly, 35371, L/Cpl., k. in a., F., 16/8/16.

JENKINS, J., b. Bristol, 11111, Pte., d. of w., F., 11/4/17.

JENKINS, J. T., b. Treharris, 16024, A/Sgt., k. in a., F., 20/7/16.

JENKINS, R. J., b. Cefn, 33994, L/Cpl., k. in a., F., 21/4/18.

JENNINGS, T., b. Rhyl, 12522, Pte., k. in a., F., 11/4/17.

JOHNSON, E., b. Gresford, 44387, Pte., d. of w., F., 7/5/17.

JOHNSON, E. J., b. London, 27227, Pte., d. of w., F., 26/1/16.

JOHNSON, J., b. Wrexham, 5664, Pte., k. in a., F., 20/7/16.

JOHNSON, M. J., e. Dumfries, 60429, Pte., k. in a., F., 1/10/18.

JOHNSON, W. H., b. Hurst, 12381, Pte., d. of w., F., 19/11/16.

JONES, A., e. Welshpool, 54410, Pte., k. in a., F., 13/11/16.

JONES, A. J., b. Bridgnorth, 70289, Pte., d. of w., F., 5/11/17.

JONES, C., b. Brynamman, 15338, Pte., d. of w., F., 22/2/16.

JONES, D., b. Llanelly, 15199, Pte., k. in a., F., 17/2/16.

JONES, D., b. Llangeniew, 20698, Pte., k. in a., F., 11/4/17.

JONES, D. D., b. Llanrug, 16176, Pte., d. of w., F., 5/3/16.

JONES, D. H. A., b. Llangollen,

39311, L/Cpl., k. in a., F., 14/5/17.
JONES, D. W., e. Welshpool, 54411, Pte., k. in a., F., 13/11/16.
JONES, E., b. Oswestry, 10487, Pte., d. of w., F., 9/10/17.
JONES, E. H., b. Llanberis, 40096, L/Cpl., k. in a., F., 13/11/16.
JONES, F. W., b. London, 22180, Pte., k. in a., F., 20/7/16.
JONES, G., b. Coity, 16051, A/C.S.M., k. in a., F., 20/7/16.
JONES, G. P., b. Weston Rhyn, 36826, Pte., k. in a., F., 20/7/16.
JONES, G. T., b. Ruabon, 14656, Pte., d. of w., F., 29/9/17.
JONES, H., b. Flint, 39944, Cpl., k. in a., F., 18/6/17.
JONES, H., e. Carnarvon, 265653, Pte., k. in a., F., 26/9/17.
JONES, I. G., b. Ton Pentre, 5031, Pte., d. of w., F., 2/5/16.
JONES, J., b. Wrexham, 12636, Pte., k. in a., F., 13/11/16.
JONES, J., b. Carnarvon, 15471, Pte., d. of w., F., 19/8/16.
JONES, J., b. Newchurch, 23413, Pte., d. of w., F., 4/4/16.
JONES, J., b. Llangadfan, 54445, Pte., d. of w., F., 13/5/17.
JONES, J. H., b. Flint, 14649, Pte., d. of w., F., 27/8/16.
JONES, J. H., b. Flint, 54732, Pte., k. in a., F., 14/5/17.
JONES, J. P., b. Bagillt, 15243, Pte., k. in a., F., 2/3/16.
JONES, J. R., b. Church Stoke, 55651, Pte., k. in a., F., 21/8/18.
JONES, L., e. Rhyl, 16829, Pte., k. in a., F., 16/8/16.
JONES, L. R., b. Corris, 54738, Pte., k. in a., F., 13/11/16.
JONES, O., b. Bodorgan, 40925, Pte., d., F., 2/3/17.
JONES, O., b. Bodwrog. 44349, Pte., d. of w., F., 27/6/17.
JONES, O. E., b. London, 70156, L/Cpl., k. in a., F., 29/11/17.
JONES, R., b. Llandwrog, 12979, Sgt., k. in a., F., 13/5/17.
JONES, R., e. Colwyn Bay, 54735, L/Cpl., k. in a., F., 11/5/17.
JONES, R., b. Bryncrug, 15160, L/Cpl., d. of w., F., 6/1/16.
JONES, R., b. Denbigh, 44000, Pte., d. of w., F., 13/5/17.
JONES, R. D., b. Llanwrda, 60322, Pte., k. in a., F., 14/6/17.
JONES, R. E., b. Llanfairfechan, 15488, Pte., d. of w., F., 14/9/16.
JONES, R. H., b. Festiniog, 54737, Pte., k. in a., F., 13/11/16.
JONES, R. J., b. Llandegai, 54945, Pte., k. in a., F., 26/9/17.
JONES, R. P., b. Tregarth, 15228, Pte., d., F., 13/5/16.
JONES, R. W., b. Penisarwaen, 60323, Pte., d. of w., F., 15/6/17.

JONES, S., b. Rhos, 44292, Pte., d. of w., F., 14/4/17.
JONES, S. E., b. Hanley, 23495, Pte., k. in a., F., 16/8/16.
JONES, T., b. Llanfechell, 14991, Pte., k. in a., F., 3/3/16.
JONES, T., b. Bryncroes, 15370, Pte., k. in a., F., 3/3/16.
JONES, T., b. Llandovery, 15640, Pte., k. in a., F., 16/8/16.
JONES, T., b. Brynmawr, 33746, Pte., k. in a., F., 14/5/17.
JONES, T., b. Festiniog, 70149, Pte., k. in a., F., 26/9/17.
JONES, T. A., b. Wrexham, 31377, Pte., k. in a., F., 20/7/16.
JONES, T. C., b. Llanrug, 40366, Pte., k. in a., F., 20/7/16.
JONES, T. S., b. Birkenhead, 44130, Pte., k. in a., F., 8/4/17.
JONES, W., b. Blaenau Festiniog, 23480, L/Cpl., k. in a., F., 20/7/16.
JONES, W., e. Carnarvon, 25181, Pte., k. in a., F., 20/7/16.
JONES, W., b. Bomere Heath, 235038, Pte., d. of w., F., 3/5/17.
JONES, W., b. Llanelly, 235049, Pte., k. in a., F., 26/9/17.
JONES, W. A., e. Welshpool, 54409, Pte., d., F., 17/11/16.
JONES, W. H., b. Wrexham, 54733, Pte., k. in a., F., 13/11/16.
JONES, W. J., b. Aberdare, 15025, Pte., k. in a., F., 16/8/16.
JONES, W. T., b. Bagillt, 15722, Sgt., k. in a., F., 16/8/16, D.C.M.
KELLY, T., e. Wrexham, 57031, Pte., d. of w., F., 19/6/17.
KELLETT, T. H., b. Rhondda, 33609, Pte., d. of w., F., 24/7/16.
KENNEDY, T., b. Sligo, 12417, Pte., k. in a., F., 19/8/16.
KERSHAW, E., b. New Hey, 31244, Pte., k. in a., F., 16/8/16.
KIMBER, W., b. Bedwelty, 33558, Pte., k. in a., F., 26/9/17.
KERFOOT, J. W., b. Leigh, 37148, Pte., d. of w., F., 23/5/17.
KIRKMAN, W. B., b. Halifax, 60324, Pte., k. in a., F., 26/9/17.
KNIGHT, B., b. Lydney, 23303, Pte., k. in a., F., 3/3/16.
KNOWLES, T. R., b. Denbigh, 29615, Cpl., k. in a., F., 13/11/16.
LADD, J. E., b. Moylegrove, 235040, Pte., d. of w., F., 15/6/17.
LALLIMONT, E. W., e. Wrexham, 57055, Pte., k. in a., F., 13/11/16.
LAMB, J., b. Fulham, 60482, Pte., k. in a., F., 26/9/17.
LAMBERT, G., e. Harrow, 54414, Pte., k. in a., F., 13/11/16.

LANE, J. H., b. Horwich, 15357, Pte., k. in a., F., 13/11/16.
LATHAM, A., b. Berrynarbor, 60341, Pte., k. in a., F., 26/9/17.
LATIMER, F. G., b. London, 21677, L/Cpl., k. in a., F., 19/8/16.
LEE, R. C., b. Madeley, 54413, Pte., k. in a., F., 13/11/16.
LEES, F., b. Oldham, 29988, Pte., k. in a., F., 16/8/16.
LEES, T., b. Oldham, 23798, Pte., k. in a., F., 26/11/17.
LEESE, J., b. Tunstall, 36036, Pte., k. in a., F., 16/8/16.
LEWIS, B., b. Ynysmudw, 23233, Pte., k. in a., F., 28/4/17.
LEWIS, B. W., b. Cadoxton, 16334, Pte., k. in a., F., 19/8/16.
LEWIS, D. J., b. Llanelly, 5732, Sgt., k. in a., F., 20/7/16.
LEWIS, G. A., b. Croydon, 34826, L/Cpl., k. in a., F., 21/10/17.
LEWIS, J., b. Aberaman, 34175, Pte., k. in a., F., 16/8/16.
LEWIS, J., b. Penrhiwfer, 33560, Pte., d. of w., F., 28/7/16.
LEWIS, L. L., b. Dulais, 20809, L/Cpl., k. in a., F., 16/8/16.
LEWIS, P., b. Mold, 55065, Pte., d. of w., F., 15/5/17.
LEWIS, T., b. Aberdare, 19801, Pte., k. in a., F., 28/2/17.
LEWIS, W., b. Cardiff, 14230, Pte., k. in a., F., 11/4/17.
LEWIS, W., b. Cefn-Mawr, 25406, Pte., k. in a., F., 25/5/18.
LEWIS, W., b. Anglesey, 40947, Pte., k. in a., F., 8/4/17.
LINDLEY, R., b. Kearsley, 23358, Pte., k. in a., F., 17/2/16.
LINDSAY, A. F., b. Finchley, 34649, Pte., k. in a., F., 20/7/16.
LINEY, F., b. Aston, 60380, Pte., k. in a., F., 26/9/17.
LINHAM, G. J., b. Bristol, 235027, Pte., k. in a., F., 14/5/17.
LINHAM, J., b. Cadoxton, 15668, Pte., k. in a., F., 27/7/16.
LLEWELYN, D., b. Pontypridd, 15127, Pte., k. in a., F., 2/3/16.
LLEWELLYN, T. J., b. Pembroke, 16277, Pte., k. in a., F., 2/3/16.
LLOYD, B., b. Rhos, 15597, Pte., d. of w., F., 11/6/18.
LLOYD, E. E., b. Llantysilio, 26088, Pte., d. of w., F., 4/10/17.
LLOYD, E., b. Denbigh, 39066, Pte., k. in a., F., 11/4/17.
LLOYD, J. W., b. Stockport, 54250, Pte., k. in a., F., 13/11/16.
LLOYD, W. J., b. Halkyn, 235042, Pte., k. in a., F., 17/6/17.
LOFTUS, R. J., b. Denbigh, 3167, Sgt., k. in a., F., 19/1/16.
LONSDALE, R. S., b. Highbury, 35324, Pte., k. in a., F., 27/4/17.
LUCAS, F. A., b. Clerkenwell,

34705, Pte., k. in a., F., 22/4/18.

LUXFORD, E., b. Rhymney, 60202, Pte., k. in a., F., 26/9/17.

LYNCH, M., b. Tibochine, 9442, Pte., d. of w., F., 20/4/17.

LYNCH, T., b. Sligo, 23213, Pte., k. in a., F., 28/11/15.

MACDONALD, W., b. Liverpool, 14166, Pte., d. of w., F., 3/5/16.

MALONEY, E., b. Swansea, 15654, Pte., k. in a., F., 20/7/16.

MALONEY, M., b. Stockport, 36145, Pte., d. of w., F., 22/4/17.

MANLEY, J. W., b. Mold, 15153, Pte., d. of w., Home, 21/7/16.

MANNING, W. H., b. Trehafod, 16049, Pte., k. in a., F., 19/8/16.

MARKHAM, C. J., b. Everton, 44278, Pte., k. in a., F., 14/6/17.

MARROW, D., b. Northop, 15187, Pte., k. in a., F., 24/1/16.

MARSHALL, E., b. Worcester, 235028, Pte., k. in a., F., 14/5/17.

MARSTON, S., b. Oldbury, 12781, Pte., k. in a., F., 17/2/16.

MARTIN, W., b. Newport, 54861, Pte., k. in a., F., 8/4/17.

MASKREY, C., b. Wolstanton, 23553, Pte., k. in a., F., 13/5/17.

MASON, H. J. R., b. Liverpool, 15186, Pte., k. in a., F., 19/11/16.

MASON, S. R., b. Sedgeley, 15249, Pte., d. of w., F., 20/12/15.

MATTHEWS, R., b. Manchester, 60385, Pte., k. in a., F., 26/9/17.

MAYO, H., b. Pendleton, 266976, Pte., k. in a., F., 18/7/17.

MCCANDLISH, H., b. Gorton, 37205, Pte., k. in a., F., 8/4/17.

MCFARLANE, J., b. Stockport, 15346, Pte., k. in a., F., 13/11/16.

MCINTEE, J., b. St. Helens, 32548, Pte., k. in a., F., 16/6/17.

MCLEA, E., b. Roath, 235729, A/L/Cpl., k. in a., F., 13/4/18.

MELIA, A., b. Ashton, 15329, Pte., d. of w., F., 30/4/16.

MEREDITH, J., b. Llanyre, 55068, Pte., k. in a., F., 28/2/17.

MESSENGER, W., b. Curthwaite, 48930, Pte., k. in a., F., 16/6/17.

MICHAELS, M., e. Stepney, 54958, Pte., d. of w., F., 3/1/17.

MILLINGTON, W., b. Buckley, 16291, Pte., d. of w., F., 17/2/16.

MOON, G., b. Llandaff, 35405, Pte., k. in a., F., 16/8/16.

MOORE, W. H., b. Sale, 17319, Sgt., k. in a., F., 16/8/16.

MORGAN, C., b. Rhymney, 33776, Pte., k. in a., F., 20/7/16.

MORGAN, J., b. Swansea, 31306, L/Cpl., k. in a., F., 20/7/16.

MORGAN, W., b. Newtown, 54416, Pte., k. in a., F., 13/11/16.

MORRIS, B. M., b. Blaknell, 23486, Pte., k. in a., F., 2/3/16.

MORRIS, D. I., b. Capel Garmon, 15275, Pte., k. in a., F., 30/3/16.

MORRIS, H., b. Llangerniew, 15216, Pte., k. in a., F., 16/8/16.

MORRIS, I. J., b. Blackyn, 36976, Pte., k. in a., F., 20/7/16.

MORRIS, J. P., b. Liverpool, 37288, Pte., k. in a., F., 16/8/16.

MORRIS, O. H., e. Wrexham, 57050, Pte., k. in a., F., 16/6/17.

MORRIS, T., b. Hirnant, 54484, Pte., k. in a., F., 10/4/17.

MOSES, O. D., b. Pontypool, 23186, Pte., k. in a., F., 15/5/17.

MOUNTFORD, F. H., e. Newcastle, 54422, Pte., k. in a., F., 13/11/16.

MULLIN, J. H., b. Everton, 18267, Cpl., k. in a., F., 9/7/16.

MUMFORD, J., b. Dukinfield, 60312, Pte., k. in a., F., 26/9/17.

MURPHY, C., b. Crewe, 8190, Cpl., k. in a., F., 13/11/16.

MURPHY, G., b. London, 22800, Cpl., k. in a., F., 16/8/16.

NEAVE, W., b. Hackford, 16755, Pte., k. in a., F., 20/7/16.

NEWBOLD, W. F., e. Wrexham, 57054, Pte., k. in a., F., 13/11/16.

NEWTON, C., b. London, 57092, Pte., k. in a., F., 29/4/17.

NICHOLAS, H. J., b. Briton Ferry, 17567, Pte., k. in a., F., 16/8/16.

NIXON, T., b. Amlwch, 15056, Pte., k. in a., F., 16/8/16.

NORTHWOOD, C., b. Pleasley, 23687, Pte., d. of w., F., 25/2/16.

OATES, A., b. Sheffield, 36462, Pte., k. in a., F., 15/6/17.

O'BRIEN, D., b. Cwmbran, 5131, Pte., k. in a., F., 24/1/16.

O'BRIEN, P., b. Tuam, 15451, Pte., k. in a., F., 3/3/16.

O'DONNELL, J., b. Preston, 60389, Pte., d. of w., F., 3/10/17.

O'DONNELL, J. J., b. Dublin, 15541, Pte., k. in a., F., 13/11/16.

O'GRADY, J., b. Sligo, 60491, Pte., k. in a., F., 26/9/17.

O'GRADY, W., b. Abergavenny, 34135, Pte., d. of w., F., 30/9/17.

O'NEILL, C., b. Edge Hill, Liverpool, 235810, Cpl., d. of w., F., 22/12/17.

OSBORN, J., b. Llantrisant, 15047, Pte., k. in a., F., 22/1/16.

OSBOURNE, J., b. Eakring, 14913, Pte., k. in a., F., 27/4/17.

OWEN, E., b. Carnarvon, 26184, Pte., k. in a., F., 20/7/16.

OWEN, H., b. Llangefni, 14237, Pte., k. in a., F., 20/7/16.

OWEN, I., b. Llandebie, 17521, k. in a., F., 2/3/16.

OWEN, R., b. Llanfair, 15251, Pte., k. in a., F., 27/11/15.

OWEN, T. O., b. Eglwysbach, 37787, Pte., k. in a., F., 28/2/17.

OWENS, J., b. Tregarth, 15227, Pte., d., F., 30/12/18.

OWENS, O., b. Llanfflewyn, 31857, Pte., k. in a., F., 1/2/16.

OWENS, P., b. Rhuddlan, 39135, Pte., d. of w., F., 25/8/16.

OWENS, T. E., b. Bridgwater, 23444, Pte., k. in a., F., 13/11/16.

PARBUTT, T., b. Skegby, 23279, Pte., k. in a., F., 27/4/17.

PARKER, J. A., e. Hounslow, 46250, Pte., k. in a., F., 29/11/17.

PARKER, S. A., e. Liverpool, 55074, Cpl., k. in a., F., 11/4/17.

PARR, J., b. Briton Ferry, 15572, Pte., k. in a., F., 18/2/16.

PARRY, J., b. Mold, 16025, Pte., d. of w., F., 24/10/15.

PARRY, J., e. Wrexham, 56997, Sgt., k. in a., F., 1/5/17.

PARRY, W., b. Bangor, 54427, Pte., k. in a., F., 13/11/16.

PARRY, W. P., b. Dolbenmaen, 40315, Pte., k. in a., F., 20/7/16.

PEARMAN, W. R., b. Roydon, 56030, Pte., k. in a., F., 11/4/17.

PENNEY, T., b. Bristol, 15157, Pte., d. of w., F., 30/4/16.

PERKINS, W. G., b. Pembroke, 23031, Pte., k. in a., F., 13/11/16.

PETTINGER, H., b. Southampton, 60418, Pte., k. in a., F., 17/6/17.

PETTIT, H. V., b. Finedon, 39779, Pte., k. in a., F., 16/8/16.

PHILLBRICK, W. E., b. London, 23916, Pte., k. in a., F., 16/8/16.

PHILLIPS, A., b. Landrino, 15303, Pte., k. in a., F., 30/3/16.

PHILLIPS, D., b. Celmaenllyd, 40214, A/Cpl., k. in a., F., 16/8/16.

PHILLIPS, R. N., b. Mold, 15405, Sgt., d. of w., F., 10/4/17.

PHILLPOT, J. W., b. London, 26578, Pte., d. of w., F., 21/7/16.

PIERCE, E., b. Penybont, 60216, Pte., d. of w., F., 16/6/17.

PIERCE, G. F., b. Weston Rhyn,

15364, Pte., k. in a., F., 20/7/16.

PIERCY, L., b. Hawarden, 44032, Pte., k. in a., F., 26/9/17.

PIPER, H. V., b. Gosport, 56024, Pte., d. of w., Home, 11/5/17.

PLASTER, A., b. Bedwelty, 33799, Pte., k. in a., F., 20/7/16.

PLEVIN, P., b. Chester, 43978, Sgt., k. in a., F., 26/9/17.

POLIN, E. A., b. Conway, 15483, L/Cpl., k. in a., F., 20/7/16.

POWELL, G. M., e. Pontardawe, 235043, Pte., k. in a., F., 27/4/17.

POWELL, N., b. Gwaelod-y-Garth, 19286, Pte., d. of w., F., 13/12/17.

PRICE, E., b. Glanavon, 16055, Pte., k. in a., F., 19/2/16.

PRICE, W. L., b. Beddoe, 55075, Pte., d. of w., F., 11/4/17.

PRITCHARD, E., b. Bethesda, 14930, Pte., k. in a., F., 14/5/16.

PRITCHARD, J. E., b. Llandudno, 5806, Pte., k. in a., F., 13/11/16.

PRITCHARD, J. H., b. Brymbo, 10290, Pte., k. in a., F., 29/11/17.

PRITCHARD, S., b. Holyhead, 55647, Pte., k. in a., F., 8/4/17.

PRITCHARD, W. J., b. Llanllyfni, 29579, Pte., k. in a., F., 20/7/16.

PROSSER, H. G., b. Bodenham, 15729, Cpl., k. in a., F., 11/4/17.

PROSSER, T. A., e. Neath, 34141, Pte., k. in a., F., 20/7/16.

PUFFER, J., b. Birmingham, 36664, Pte., k. in a., F., 20/7/16.

PYE, J. F., b. London, 28166, L/Cpl., k. in a., F., 8/4/18.

QUARTERMAIN, E. E., b. London, 70144, L/Cpl., k. in a., F., 26/9/17.

RACKSTRAW, A. V., b. Birmingham, 15656, Cpl., d. of w., F., 16/3/16.

RAYNOR, P., b. Coldhurst, 33819, Pte., k. in a., F., 11/4/17.

REARDON, M., b. Pontlottyn, 16199, Pte., k. in a., F., 19/2/16.

REED, G. J., b. Cinderford, 15700, Cpl., k. in a., F., 2/3/16.

REED, J., b. Liverpool, 54968, Pte., k. in a., F., 8/4/17.

REED, J. W., b. Briton Ferry, 31233, Pte., d. of w., F., 29/9/17.

REES, E., b. Llantrisant, 15048, Pte., d. of w., F., 10/4/17.

REES, J. D., b. Llandebie, 13188, Pte., k. in a., F., 20/7/16.

REES, R., b. Merthyr, 54965, Pte., k. in a., F., 8/1/17.

REEVES, R., b. Ellesmere, 241717, Pte., k. in a., F., 14/6/17.

REYNOLDS, D., b. Neath, 25767, Pte., d. of w., F., 4/5/17.

REYNOLDS, J. A., e. Wrexham, 54438, Pte., k. in a., F., 28/4/17.

REYNOLDS, W., b. Llanwit, 201255, Pte., k. in a., F., 26/9/17.

RICHARDS, G., e. Wrexham, 56768, Pte., k. in a., F., 13/11/16.

RICHARDS, W. J., b. Ynyscanhairn, 16284, Pte., d. of w., Home, 16/10/16.

ROBERTS, D., e. Denbigh, 56777, Pte., d. of w., F., 18/11/16.

ROBERTS, E., b. Denbigh, 15313, C.S.M., d. of w., F., 30/7/16, M.M.

ROBERTS, E. T., b. Llangollen, 15824, Pte., d. of w., F., 14/4/17.

ROBERTS, G., b. Capel Curig, 15371, Pte., k. in a., F., 3/3/16.

ROBERTS, H., b. Blaenau Festiniog, 40954, Pte., d. of w., Home, 7/5/18.

ROBERTS, H. P., b. London, 60424, Pte., d. of w., F., 21/7/17.

ROBERTS, I. J., b. Ruabon, 26100, Pte., k. in a., F., 19/8/16.

ROBERTS, J., b. Llanwonno, 14986, Pte., k. in a., F., 17/12/15.

ROBERTS, J., b. Llanddeiniolen, 40167, Pte., k. in a., F., 20/7/16.

ROBERTS, J. E., e. Bournemouth, 23754, Cpl., k. in a., F., 17/2/16.

ROBERTS, J. H., b. Wrexham, 24906, Pte., k. in a., F., 30/11/16.

ROBERTS, L. C., b. Frome, 34033, Pte., k. in a., F., 13/11/16.

ROBERTS, O., b. Bettws-y-coed, 40142, Pte., k. in a., F., 20/7/16.

ROBERTS, P. A., b. Walford, 54964, Pte., k. in a., F., 26/9/17.

ROBERTS, R., b. Llangristiolus, 15670, Pte., k. in a., F., 17/2/16.

ROBERTS, R., b. Oswestry, 28541, Pte., k. in a., F., 13/11/16.

ROBERTS, R. J., b. Tydweiliog, 15372, A/Sgt., k. in a., F., 20/7/16.

ROBERTS, T., b. Llaneugrad, 36333, Cpl., k. in a., F., 13/11/16.

ROBERTS, T., e. Wrexham, 39154, Pte., k. in a., F., 11/4/17.

ROBERTS, W., b. Cerrigceinwen, 12015, Pte., k. in a., F., 13/11/16.

ROBERTS, W., b. Llanwnda, 15073, Pte., k. in a., F., 16/8/16.

ROBERTS, W., b. Caerhûn, 20914, Pte., k. in a., F., 16/6/17.

ROBERTS, W. J., e. Wrexham, 56762, Pte., k. in a., F., 18/6/17.

ROBERTS, W. T., b. Bangor, 14971, Pte., k. in a., F., 3/3/16.

ROBERTS, W. V., b. Aberdare, 23452, Pte., k. in a., F., 17/2/16.

ROBINSON, J., b. Burntwood, 23281, A/Cpl., d. of w., F., 17/2/16.

ROGERS, H., b. Eglwyseg, 18328, Pte., k. in a., F., 3/3/16.

ROGERS, P., b. Chiddon, 36663, Pte., k. in a., F., 20/7/16.

ROGERS, T., b. Mold, 15179, Pte., d. of w., F., 17/2/16.

ROLFE, J., b. London, 22762, Pte., k. in a., F., 19/8/16.

ROSTANCE, J. H., b. Burton, 36343, L/Cpl., k. in a., F., 20/7/16.

ROWLANDS, E., b. Llanddeiniolen, 40179, Pte., k. in a., F., 27/4/17.

ROWLANDS, F., b. Machynlleth, 60215, Pte., k. in a., F., 13/4/18.

ROWLANDS, J., b. Mold, 70152, L/Sgt., k. in a., F., 26/11/17.

ROWLANDS, J., b. Weston Rhyn, 36825, Pte., k. in a., F., 16/8/16.

ROWLANDS, R. O., b. Buckley, 15088, A/Sgt., k. in a., F., 17/2/16.

ROWLEY, W., b. Walsall, 8780, Sgt., k. in a., F., 24/9/17.

RUDD, A., b. Frizington, 15625, Pte., d., F., 30/10/18.

RYAN, E. M., e. Bridgend, 25905, Pte., k. in a., F., 11/4/17.

SALTWELL, R. J., b. Fyfield, 26780, Cpl., k. in a., F., 16/8/16.

SANDERS, G., b. Gunnislake, 15015, Pte., k. in a., F., 16/8/16.

SAUNDERS, C., b. Hadnall, 15406, Sgt., k. in a., F., 26/9/17.

SAUNDERS, S. T. W., b. Ipswich, 34121, Pte., k. in a., F., 20/7/16.

SCHOFIELD, W., b. Heywood, 55133, Pte., k. in a., F., 17/2/17.

SCHOLES, J., b. Oldham, 39261, Pte., k. in a., F., 16/8/16.

SEAGER, G., b. Southwark, 35100, Pte., k. in a., F., 13/11/16.

SETCHFIELD, H., b. Cardiff, 70186, Pte., k. in a., F., 26/9/17.

SHAW, J., b. London, 9983, Pte., k. in a., F., 20/7/16.

SHEPHERD, C., b. Chester, 9741, L/Cpl., k. in a., F., 20/7/16.

SHEPLEY, C., b. Macclesfield, 36266, Pte., k. in a., F., 30/4/16.

SHEPPARD, W. J., b. London, 27046, Pte., k. in a., F., 30/4/17.

SHIERS, G., b. Chester, 60504, Pte., d. of w., F., 13/10/17.

SHUKER, S., b. Bishops Castle,

60419, Pte., d. of w., F., 16/6/17.

SIDEBOTTOM, A., b. Chester, 55081, Pte., d. of w., F., 15/6/17.

SIDES, D., b. Oswestry, 26252, Pte., k. in a., F., 16/8/16.

SIEGAL, N., b. London, 35358, Pte., k. in a., F., 16/8/16.

SIGLEY, F., b. Leek, 23189, Pte., k. in a., F., 30/4/16.

SIMISTER, J. E., b. Salford, 267074, Pte., k. in a., F., 18/6/17.

SIMS, D. H., b. Glamorgan, 14190, Pte., d. of w., F., 1/5/16.

SLATER, S. J., b. Birmingham, 36581, Pte., k. in a., F., 14/6/17.

SMALLMAN, R., b. Walsall, 55083, Pte., k. in a., F., 28/2/17.

SMITH, A., b. Llanhilleth, 17530, Sgt., d. of w., F., 8/5/17.

SMITH, A. G., b. Holyhead, 36379, L/Cpl., k. in a., F., 13/11/16.

SMITH, H., b. Burslem, 28306, Pte., k. in a., F., 4/8/17.

SMITH, J., b. Silverdale, 15278, L/Sgt., k. in a., F., 20/7/16.

SMITH, T., b. Burry Port, 15665, Pte., k. in a., F., 16/8/16.

SMITH, T., b. Colne Engaine, 56035, Pte., k. in a., F., 27/2/17.

SMITH, W. W., b. Roath, 33585, Pte., k. in a., F., 17/8/16.

SPEED, J., b. Ellesmere, 36209, Pte., k. in a., F., 13/11/16.

SPENCER, T., b. Derby, 23276, Pte., k. in a., F., 19/2/16.

SPROSTON, A., b. Colwyn Bay, 23059, Sgt., k. in a., F., 16/8/16.

STAINTON, W., b. Beetham, 15549, L/Cpl., k. in a., F., 7/12/15.

STANDRING, S., b. Oldham, 63738, Pte., d., F., 20/6/17.

STANT, W., e. Wrexham, 56766, Pte., k. in a., F., 14/6/17.

STEVENS, H., b. Denton, 15279, Pte., d. of w., F., 1/12/17.

STEWART, T., b. Neyland, 15416, Pte., k. in a., F., 17/2/16.

STILTON, R., b. London, 34598, Pte., k. in a., F., 20/7/16.

STOKER, J., b. Mold, 54695, Pte., k. in a., F., 13/11/16.

STONE, W. G., b. London, 33881, L/Cpl., k. in a., F., 28/2/17.

STOOKES, H., b. Dawlish, 13956, Pte., k. in a., F., 17/2/16.

STOTT, J., b. Parr, 15592, Pte., k. in a., F., 20/7/16.

STRODE, E., b. Caldicott, 15178, Pte., d. of w., F., 29/4/17.

SUTTON, W., b. Bedminster, 54881, Pte., k. in a., F., 26/9/17.

SWANCOTT, G. J., e. Knighton, 54431, Pte., k. in a., F., 13/11/16.

TANNER, A. E., e. Welshpool,

54433, Pte., k. in a., F., 13/11/16.

TAYLOR, C., b. Cross Keys, 33843, Pte., d. of w., F., 29/9/17.

THOMAS, A., b. Llanddeiniolen, 40174, Pte., k. in a., F., 20/7/16.

THOMAS, A. C., b. Milford Haven, 12285, Pte., k. in a., F., 20/7/16.

THOMAS, C., b. Wrexham, 23114, Pte., k. in a., F., 16/8/16.

THOMAS, E., b. Pontycymmer, 17709, Sgt., k. in a., F., 16/8/16.

THOMAS, E. R., b. Rhondda, 29236, Pte., k. in a., F., 26/9/17.

THOMAS, F., b. Glossop, 54888, Pte., d. of w., F., 1/3/17.

THOMAS, G., b. Dowlais, 15680, Pte., k. in a., F., 2/3/16.

THOMAS, G., b. Liverpool, 55672, Cpl., d. of w., F., 5/6/17.

THOMAS, H., e. Welshpool, 54434, Pte., d., F., 18/11/16.

THOMAS, J. J., b. Swansea, 24404, Pte., k. in a., F., 19/2/16.

THOMAS, J. R., b. Pontyberem, 33875, Pte., k. in a., F., 27/9/17.

THOMAS, L., b. Pentir, 14936, Pte., k. in a., F., 13/11/16.

THOMAS, L., b. Rhydclafdy, 49816, Pte., k. in a., F., 16/6/17.

THOMAS, R., b. Llanerfyl, 55649, Pte., k. in a., F., 26/9/17.

THOMAS, W., b. Bagillt, 69365, Pte., d., Home, 14/1/18.

THOMAS, W. E., b. Llanelly, 12043, Pte., k. in a., F., 16/8/16.

THOMPSON, F., b. Oldham, 24125, Pte., k. in a., F., 28/2/17.

THORP, D. E., e. Wrexham, 56761, Pte., k. in a., F., 13/11/16.

TIMMS, H., b. Selston, 23221, Pte., k. in a., F., 17/2/16.

TINSLEY, G., b. Etruria, 23496, Pte., k. in a., F., 30/3/16.

TOOHEY, M., b. Widnes, 5373, L/Cpl., k. in a., F., 16/8/16.

TRIPPIER, H., b. Haslingden, 60409, Pte., k. in a., F., 16/6/17.

TRIVETT, J. E., b. Llandudno, 15291, Cpl., k. in a., F., 13/11/16.

TUDOR, J., b. Ffrith, 43990, Pte., k. in a., F., 28/2/17.

TUNE, C., b. Billericay, 21866, Cpl., d. of w., F., 6/12/16.

TUNLEY, J. A., b. Radnorshire, 54887, Pte., k. in a., F., 11/4/17.

TURNER, J. R. M., b. London, 27366, Pte., k. in a., F., 16/8/16.

TURRELL, E. W., b. Lowestoft, 55085, Pte., k. in a., F., 14/6/17.

VAUGHAN, A. C., b. Kivernol,

53111, Pte., k. in a., F., 26/9/17.

VERNON, W., b. Liverpool, 39277, Pte., k. in a., F., 19/8/16.

VOST, T., b. Millington, 39754, Pte., k. in a., F., 13/9/16.

VYNE, J. S., b. Kempston, 24913, Pte., d. of w., F., 29/9/17.

WAINWRIGHT, E. J., b. Hawarden, 20787, Pte., d. of w., Home, 5/2/17.

WAINWRIGHT, P. W., b. Montford Bridge, 17701, Pte., k. in a., F., 13/11/16.

WALKER, F., b. Kettlebrook, 9534, L/St., k. in a., F., 16/8/16.

WALLEY, V. L., b. Burslem, 54437, Pte., k. in a., F., 13/11/16.

WALTERS, B., b. Cwmbran, 26058, Pte., k. in a., F., 20/7/16.

WALTERS, D., b. Wattstown, 5192, Cpl., k. in a., F., 13/11/16.

WALTERS, T., b. Briton Ferry, 15619, Pte., k. in a., F., 20/7/16.

WARD, W., b. Shrewsbury, 39282, Pte., k. in a., F., 16/8/16.

WATSON, H., b. Isle of Ely, 15433, Sgt., k. in a., F., 11/4/17.

WAY, E. W., b. Bradpole, 55091, Pte., d. of w., F., 28/2/17.

WHEELER, F. R., b. London, 56037, Pte., d. of w., F., 30/9/17.

WHITE, A. H., b. E. Harringfield, 56031, Pte., k. in a., F., 8/4/17.

WHITE, T., b. Wolverhampton, 16317, Pte., d. of w., F., 29/3/16.

WHITE, T., b. London, 35137, Pte., k. in a., F., 13/4/18.

WHITEHEAD, M., b. Derby, 33905, Sgt., k. in a., F., 26/9/17.

WHITTINGHAM, H. S., e. Welshpool, 54448, Sgt., k. in a., F., 27/9/17.

WHYBRA, D. E., e. London, 35496, Pte., k. in a., F., 16/8/16.

WICKLAND, G. T., b. Tenby, 15511, A/L/Sgt., k. in a., F., 16/8/16.

WILCOX, E. J., b. Gwynnerton, 54446, Pte., k. in a., F., 14/10/16.

WILDE, J. H., e. Cefn, 200759, Pte., k. in a., F., 26/9/17.

WILDRIDGE, W., b. Liverpool, 36120, Pte., k. in a., F., 20/7/16.

WILKES, A. E., b. Holyhead, 16259, L/Cpl., k. in a., F., 19/2/16.

WILKINSON, A. E. C., b. Bangor, 43959, Pte., k. in a., F., 28/2/17.

WILKINSON, J., b. Preston, 40725, Pte., k. in a., F., 29/4/17.

WILLCOCK, S., b. Hope, 21495, Pte., k. in a., F., 16/8/16.

WILLEY, A., b. Llanidloes, 55565, Pte., d. of w., F., 12/4/17.

WILLIAMS, C. A., b. Bettws-y-Coed, 15301, Pte., k. in a., F., 19/2/16.

WILLIAMS, D., b. Pentir, 15225, Pte., d., F., 2/4/16.

WILLIAMS, D. E., e. Wrexham, 56767, Pte., k. in a., F., 13/11/16.

WILLIAMS, E., b. Aberdare, 16179, Pte., d. of w., F., 7/10/17.

WILLIAMS, E., b. Llanerchymedd, 15129, Pte., k. in a., F., 13/11/16.

WILLIAMS, E. J., b. Troedyrhiw, 34045, Pte., d. of w., F., 26/9/17.

WILLIAMS, E. J., b. Llanfairfechan, 15474, Pte., k. in a., F., 30/3/16.

WILLIAMS, E. O., b. Birkenhead, 15340, Pte., d. of w., F., 19/12/15.

WILLIAMS, E. T., b. Llanbeblig, 18370, Pte., k. in a., F., 20/7/16.

WILLIAMS, F. W., b. Jullandar, 14972, Pte., k. in a., F., 16/8/16.

WILLIAMS, G. H., b. Soughton, 15403, L/Cpl., d. of w., F., 30/4/16.

WILLIAMS, H., b. Tremadoc, 15262, Pte., k. in a., F., 21/8/18.

WILLIAMS, H. P., b. Llanllechid, 21173, Pte., k. in a., F., 16/8/16.

WILLIAMS, I., b. Nevin, 37608, Pte., k. in a., F., 18/8/16.

WILLIAMS, I., b. Eglwysbach, 49819, Pte., d. of w., Home, 21/5/17.

WILLIAMS, J., b. Talywain, 15143, Pte., k. in a., F., 16/8/16.

WILLIAMS, J., b. Llangristiolus, 24288, Pte., k. in a., F., 16/8/16.

WILLIAMS, J., b. Aberystwyth, 15132, Pte., k. in a., F., 3/3/16.

WILLIAMS, J. H., b. Varteg, 15017, Pte., d. of w., F., 3/11/16.

WILLIAMS, J. L., b. Newcastle Emlyn, 34847, Pte., k. in a., F., 16/8/16.

WILLIAMS, L. J., b. Penrhos, 15613, Cpl., d. of w., F., 22/12/15.

WILLIAMS, M., b. Llanddeiniolen, 40161, Pte., k. in a., F., 11/4/17.

WILLIAMS, M., b. Holywell, 14672, A/Cpl., k. in a., F., 20/7/16.

WILLIAMS, M., b. Llanarmon, 15367, Pte., k. in a., F., 16/8/16.

WILLIAMS, P., b. Glan Conway, 13553, Pte., k. in a., F., 18/8/16.

WILLIAMS, P., b. Towyn, 17603, Pte., k. in a., F., 16/8/16.

WILLIAMS, R., b. Brynsiencyn, 15443, Pte., k. in a., F., 20/7/16.

WILLIAMS, R., b. Abergele, 16297, L/Cpl., k. in a., F., 20/7/16.

WILLIAMS, R., b. Llaneedwen, 49861, Pte., k. in a., F., 26/9/17.

WILLIAMS, R. R., b. Llanerchymedd, 44208, Pte., d. of w., F., 11/4/17.

WILLIAMS, S. L. F., b. Deganwy, 44137, Pte., k. in a., F., 26/9/17.

WILLIAMS, T., b. Gwersyllt, 54260, Pte., k. in a., F., 13/11/16.

WILLIAMS, T. J., e. Llanrwst, 54436, Pte., k. in a., F., 13/11/16.

WILLIAMS, T. N., b. Carnarvon, 37780, Pte., d. of w., Home, 4/8/16.

WILLIAMS, W., b. Llanerchymedd, 15000, Pte., d. of w., F., 30/1/16.

WILLIAMS, W., b. Ystradyfodwg, 15058, Pte., k. in a., F., 16/8/16.

WILLIAMS, W., b. Bala, 43934, Pte., d. of w., F., 20/6/17.

WILLIAMS, W. H., b. Llanreyor, 15377, Pte., d. of w., F., 18/2/16.

WILSON, G., b. Cardiff, 23266, Pte., k. in a., F., 12/9/16.

WILSON, T. G., b. Henham, 56002, Sgt., k. in a., F., 17/6/17.

WINDSOR, J., b. Dalston, 34951, Pte., k. in a., F., 14/10/16.

WRIGHT, G., b. Birmingham, 15086, L/Cpl., k. in a., F., 17/6/17.

WRIGHT, J., b. Oldham, 60377, Pte., k. in a., F., 17/6/17.

WRIGHT, J., b. Birkenhead, 23155, Pte., k. in a., F., 30/4/17.

WRIGHT, R. F., b. Peterborough, 56033, Pte., k. in a., F., 27/4/17.

WRITER, T., b. London, 54982, Pte., d. of w., F., 1/12/16.

WROE, W., b. St. Helens, 56783, Pte., k. in a., F., 10/5/17.

WYNNE, R. A., b. Denbigh, 4697, Pte., k. in a., F., 20/7/16, M.M.

11th BATTALION

ADAMS, W. H., b. Pontypridd, 13994, Pte., d. of w., S., 30/9/18.

ALABASTER, J., e. London, 68898, Pte., k. in a., Se., 6/5/18.

ALLEN, G., b. Cardiff, 268010, Pte., k. in a., Se., 18/9/18.

ANDERSON, A., e. London, 205228, Pte., k. in a., Se., 18/9/18.

BELLIS, T., b. Oakenholt, 267730, Pte., k. in a., Se., 18/9/18.

BLAKE, W. H., b. Windsor, 68900, Cpl., k. in a., Se., 18/9/18.

BOWLER, W., b. Chadderton, 77061, Pte., k. in a., Se., 13/9/18.

BRAIDE, W., b. Warrington, 13644, Sgt., d. of w., S., 16/9/18.

BRASSINGTON, J., b. Ewloe, 69835, Pte., k. in a., Se., 18/9/18.

BROOKS, R. S., b. Bolton, 204957, Pte., k. in a., Se., 18/9/18.

BROWN, T., b. St. Helens, 13988, L/Cpl., k. in a., Se., 2/11/16.

CAUSER, T., b. Walsall, 14287, Pte., d., S., 30/12/16.

CLAYTON, E. L., b. Kennington, 34853, Cpl., k. in a., Se., 18/9/18.

CLEWS, J. T., b. Walsall, 14170, Pte., k. in a., Se., 15/9/18.

CONROY, J., b. St. Helens, 13856, Pte., d. of w., S., 5/11/16.

CORBY, J. E., b. Empingham, 13769, L/Cpl., k. in a., S., 15/11/17.

CORRIE, H. C., b. Leeds, 205247, Pte., k. in a., Se., 18/9/18.

COUPER, J., b. Llanblethian, 14033, Pte., k. in a., Se., 20/3/17.

CROWTHER, J. S., b. Huddersfield, 75607, Pte., k. in a., Se., 18/9/18.

DALE, E., b. Mowcop, 28952, Pte., d., S., 26/12/17.

DALY, P., b. Dublin, 77026, Pte., k. in a., Se., 18/9/18.

DANIEL, R., b. Llandebie, 14149, L/Sgt., k. in a., Se., 18/9/18.

DAVIES, E., b. Llanefydd, 40237, Pte., d. of w., S., 20/9/18.

DAVIES, J. E., e. Rhyl, 41802, Pte., d. of w., Malta, 22/10/18.

DAVIES, T., b. Crosshands, 68852, L/Cpl., k. in a., Se., 31/7/17.

DEEBLE, A., b. Burnley, 204886, Pte., k. in a., Se., 18/9/18.

DIXON, J., b. Swansea, 14201, L/Sgt., d. of w., S., 22/9/18.

DONE, J., b. Salford, 68947, Pte., d. of w., S., 28/2/18.

DOUGLAS, T., b. Llanasa, 203259, Pte., k. in a., Se., 18/9/18.

DUNN, R., b. Ashington, 77024, Pte., k. in a., Se., 18/9/18.

EDEN, J., b. Kineton, 14091, Pte., d. of w., F., 19/10/15.

EDWARDS, E., b. Llansilin, 30452, Pte., d. of w., S., 11/6/18.

EDWARDS, J. A., b. Wrexham, 69748, Pte., d. of w., S., 18/9/18.

ELLIS, D., b. Bettws-Gwerful-Goch, 30453, Pte., k. in a., S., 10/6/18.

ELSON, T., b. Newcastle, 96705, Pte., k. in a., Se., 18/9/18.

EVANS, A. G., b. Aberdaron, 43551, Pte., k. in a., Se., 28/10/16.

EVANS, D. S., b. Swansea, 14490, Pte., k. in a., Se., 14/5/18.

EVANS, E., b. Pontypridd, 13788, L/Cpl., k. in a., Se., 18/9/18.

EVANS, G., b. Blaenau Festiniog, 14472, Pte., d., S., 6/9/17.

EVANS, J., b. Leigh, 14378, Pte., d. of w., S., 7/8/17.

EVANS, J. T., b. Norton Canes, 13952, Pte., d., S., 30/3/18.

EVANS, J. T., b. Gowerton, 14304, Pte., d., Home, 2/12/14.

EVANS, R., b. Llandaefewr, 13921, Pte., k. in a., Se., 28/6/18.

EVANS, S. M., b. Llangeneck, 21553, Pte., k. in a., Se., 18/9/18.

FEASEY, D., b. Birmingham, 14155, Sgt., d., Home, 7/10/14.

FEREDAY, E., b. Upton-on-Severn, 96727, Pte., d., S., 1/10/18.

FITTON, W., b. Ashton-under-Lyne, 14812, Pte., d. of w., S., 18/12/17.

FITZGIBBON, J., b. Cardiff, 69716, Pte., k. in a., Se., 18/9/18.

FOSTER, H., b. Coventry, 68904, Pte., k. in a., Se., 18/9/18.

FOSTER, W., b. Presteign, 30489, Pte., d., S., 30/10/16.

FOULKES, O., b. Llanelian, 203538, Pte., d., Malta, 19/10/18.

FOWLES, W., b. Ruabon, 25446, Pte., k. in a., Se., 18/9/18.

GADD, E., b. Mardy, 14300, Pte., k. in a., Se., 6/5/18.

GIFFORD, P., b. Croxley Green, 96730, Pte., k. in a., Se., 18/9/18.

GOSTELLER, G., b. Liverpool, 66856, Pte., d. of w., S., 20/9/18.

GRIFFITHS, T., b. Llanllyfni, 39909, Pte., d., S., 24/6/17.

GRIMES, M., b. Liverpool, 77067, Pte., k. in a., Se., 18/9/18.

HALL, S. E., b. Llanrwst, 14530, Pte., k. in a., Se., 18/9/18.

HALLIWELL, J., b. Atherton, 77065, Pte., k. in a., Se., 18/9/18.

HAMILTON, R., b. Prescot, 13848, Cpl., d. of w., S., 23/9/18.

HANEY, J., b. Skipton, 14051, Cpl., d., Malta, 26/8/18.

HANKEY, A., b. Chester, 14433, Pte., d., Home, 3/12/14.

HARRIS, B. T., b. Swansea, 242235, Pte., d., S., 7/6/18.

HARRISON, J., b. Mottram, 46133, Pte., d. of w., S., 12/5/18.

HARTLEY, W., b. Battersea, 68996, Pte., k. in a., Se., 26/6/18.

HARWOOD, S., b. Llantrisant, 14682, Cpl., k. in a., Se., 18/9/18.

HASTINGS, W. H., b. Stratford, 68979, Pte., k. in a., Se., 18/9/18.

HAW, E., b. London, 14261, Pte., k. in a., Se., 18/9/18.

HAYWARD, I., b. Pontypool, 13986, Pte., d. of w., S., 5/11/16.

HIGGINBOTHAM, H., b. Stockport, 56463, Pte., k. in a., Se., 18/9/18.

HINTON, A., b. Merthyr, 31409, Pte., k. in a., Se., 18/9/18.

HODDART, D., b. Blaenau Festiniog, 14459, Pte., d., S., 26/9/18.

HOPKINS, R. A., b. Llangeinor, 13836, Pte., k. in a., S., 18/9/18.

HOWELLS, G. A., e. Welshpool, 30305, Pte., k. in a., Se., 18/9/18.

HOWSON, R., b. Blackburn, 14062, Pte., d., S., 25/9/18.

HUGHES, T. J., b. Llandudno, 14881, Pte., k. in a., Se., 28/10/16.

HUGHES, W. R., b. Llanhelig, 14540, Sgt., k. in a., Se., 20/11/16.

HUGHES, W. T., b. Waenfawr, 69840, Pte., d., Se., 30/9/18.

HUMPHREYS, T. M., e. Caerphilly, 75640, Pte., k. in a., Se., 18/9/18.

HUMPHRIES, J., b. Machynlleth, 27908, Pte., k. in a., Se., 18/9/18.

HUNTER, R., b. Rochdale, 75618, Pte., k. in a., S., 18/9/18.

HURLOW, A. A., e. Carmarthen, 68869, Pte., k. in a., Se., 19/2/17.

JAMES, D., e. Neath, 19253, Pte., k. in a., Se., 18/9/18.

JAMES, T. B., b. Llansamlet, 13791, Pte., d. of w., S., 7/10/18.

JAMES, W., b. Llangynwed, 14702, Pte., k. in a., Se., 18/9/18.

JENKINS, G., b. Ferndale, 69847, Pte., k. in a., Se., 18/9/18.

JENKINS, T., b. Llantrisant, 14680, L/Cpl., d. of w., Se., 21/9/18.

JERVIS, W. A., b. Farnworth, 14067, Pte., d. of w., S., 8/11/16.

JOHN, B., b. Williamstown, 14791, Pte., d. of w., S., 26/9/18.

JOHNSON, W. H., b. Liverpool, 14573, Pte., d., F., 5/10/15.

JONES, D., b. Llannon, 14124, Pte., k. in a., Se., 18/9/18.

JONES, D., b. Pontygwaith, 14689, Pte., d., Se., 6/11/16.

JONES, D., b. Denbigh, 24782, Pte., k. in a., Se., 18/9/18.

JONES, E., b. Malpas, 14064, Pte., d., Home, 18/6/18.

JONES, J., b. Llanidloes, 14009, Sgt., k. in a., Se., 15/9/18.

JONES, J., b. Stockport, 235344, Pte., k. in a., Se., 6/5/18.

JONES, L., b. Capeldydydd, 37634, Pte., k. in a., Se., 18/9/18.

JONES, R. M., b. Tal-y-llyn, 75630, Pte., k. in a., Se., 28/6/18.

JONES, T., b. Cefn Coed, 68993, Pte., k. in a., Se., 18/9/18.

JONES, T. J., b. Llantrisant, 14030, Pte., d. of w., S., 7/11/16.

JONES, T. W., b. Treharris, 14984, Pte., k. in a., S., 18/9/18.

JONES, W., b. Llantrisant, 14706, Sgt., k. in a., Se., 18/9/18.

JONES, W. J., b. Rhondda, 13968, Pte., k. in a., Se., 6/5/18.

KELLY, C., b. New York, 46123, L/Cpl., k. in a., Se., 18/9/18.

KEYLOCK, A., e. Knighton, 46127, Pte., d., S., 29/9/18.

LAWES, A. C., b. Windsor, 205237, Pte., k. in a., Se., 18/9/18.

LEWIS, D., b. Llanwonno, 68995, Pte., d. of w., S., 30/6/18.

LEWIS, G. W., b. Llanblethian, 14039, Pte., d. of w., Se., 24/9/18.

LEWIS, R., b. Pontardawe, 44262, Pte., k. in a., Se., 18/9/18.

LEWIS, W. G., b. Llanelly, 14134, Pte., k. in a., Se., 15/8/17.

LUDLAM, W., b. Heywood, 14571, L/Cpl., k. in a., Se., 18/9/18.

MAKIN, F., b. Macclesfield, 46228, L/Cpl., d. of w., S., 25/9/18.

MEE, J., b. Derby, 35528, Pte., k. in a., Se., 21/2/17.

MERCER, A., b. St. Helens, 13939, L/Cpl., k. in a., Se., 18/9/18.

MOLYNEUX, D., b. St. Helens, 13881, L/Cpl., d. of w., S., 15/9/16.

MORGAN, D. C., b. Llantarnam, 13780, Pte., k. in a., Se., 18/9/18.

MORRIS, H., b. Llanddeiniolen, 40126, Pte., d. of w., S., 12/6/17.

MORTON, J., b. Brighouse, 13802, Cpl., k. in a., Se., 20/3/17.

MULLIN, J., b. Liverpool, 14081, L/Cpl., k. in a., Se., 15/9/18.

NELLIST, C. W., b. Pudsey, 24333, Sgt., k. in a., Se., 2/5/17.

NESTER, T., b. Hulme, 77054, Pte., k. in a., Se., 18/9/18.

OWEN, E., b. Llanfair P.G., 14858, Pte., d., S., 16/12/17.

OWEN, G., b. Chasetown, 14320, Pte., d. of w., S., 27/9/18.

OWENS, B. T., b. Haverfordwest, 15151, C.S.M., k. in a., S., 18/9/18.

PARRY, E. W., b. Llanllyfni, 14446, Pte., k. in a., Se., 18/9/18.

PEMBERTON, H., b. Warrington, 14063, Pte., k. in a., Se., 18/9/18.

PEPPERRELL, E. G., b. London, 68901, L/Cpl., d., Malta, 30/9/18.

PETERS, M., b. Hope, 15109, Pte., d., Se., 7/9/18, M.M.

PETTIFOR, J. W., b. Chesterfield, 15481, Sgt., k. in a., Se., 6/5/18.

PILKINGTON, J., b. Bolton, 77036, Pte., k. in a., Se., 18/9/18.

PLANT, A. W., b. Horwich, 77073, L/Cpl., k. in a., Se., 18/9/18.

POTTER, J., b. Formby, 267123, Pte., k. in a., Se., 18/9/18.

PRINCE, T. H., b. Rhosddu, 267856, Pte., d. of w., S., 26/9/18.

PRITCHARD, H., b. Llangefni, 14538, Pte., d. of w., S., 4/10/18.

PRYDDERCH, H., b. Dolwyddelen, 20233, Pte., k. in a., Se., 18/9/18.

PYE, W., b. Market Drayton, 46683, Pte., k. in a., Se., 18/9/18.

REES, D., b. Clydach Vale, 14892, Pte., d. of w., S., 19/9/18.

REES, D. R., e. Carmarthen, 68878, Pte., k. in a., Se., 18/9/18.

RICHARDS D. J., b. St. Peter's, 39507, Pte., k. in a., Se., 18/9/18.

RICHARDS, P., b. Pontypridd, 14312, Pte., k. in a., Se., 14/9/16.

ROBERTS, A. H., b. Cardiff, 45858, Pte., d., Se., 19/11/18.

ROBERTS, D., b. Bethesda, 23510, L/Cpl., d. of w., S., 15/5/18.

ROBERTS, E. J., b. Gyffin, 265245, Pte., k. in a., Se., 18/9/18.

ROBERTS, E., b. Llandebie, 14342, Sgt., k. in a., Se., 18/9/18.

ROBERTS, E., b. Amlwch, 12369, Pte., k. in a., Se., 18/9/18.

ROBERTS, W., b. Cowbridge, 14208, Sgt., k. in a., Se., 18/9/18.

ROBERTS, W., b. Walsall, 204645, Pte., k. in a., Se., 19/9/18.

ROSCALEER, S., b. Widnes, 14104, Pte., d. of w., S., 15/9/16.

ROSSER, D., b. Ferndale, 14566, Pte., k. in a., F., 18/9/15.

RYDER, J., b. Liverpool, 18664, Pte., k. in a., Se., 18/9/18.

SANSOM, W. R., b. Kingston-on-Thames, 41567, Pte., k. in a., Se., 18/9/18.

SHARP, V. F., b. Wargrave, 31855, Pte., k. in a., Se., 28/9/17.

SHARPLES, S., b. Pendleton, 77080, Pte., k. in a., Se., 18/9/18.

SIMMONDS, H. J., b. Walworth, 96724, Pte., k. in a., Se., 18/9/18.

SLEVIN, E., b. St. Helens, 13904, Sgt., d. of w., S., 15/9/18.

SMITH, R., b. Tonypandy, 68959, Pte., d. of w., S., 11/3/18.

SNELSON, E., b. Middlewich, 13903, Sgt., d., Home, 4/9/18.

SWAINSBURY, L., b. London, 27455, Pte., d., S., 4/9/17.

THOMAS, D. W., b. Morriston, 69739, Pte., k. in a., Se., 18/9/18.

THOMAS, J., b. Llanelly, 14956, Sgt., d., Home, 3/9/15.

THOMAS, O., b. Neath, 20371, Pte., d. of w., S., 9/5/17.

THOMPSON, J. O., b. Llandudno, 14536, Sgt., d. of w., S., 28/6/18.

THORNE, H. T., b. London, 77083, Pte., d., S., 25/9/18.

TURNER, J., b. Leeds, 77056, Pte., k. in a., Se., 18/9/18.

TURNER, T., b. Whitechapel, 26607, Pte., k. in a., Se., 21/7/17.

WAKELIN, C. J., b. London, 11237, Pte., k. in a., Se., 21/7/17.

WALTERS, E., b. Llanelly, 68890, Pte., k. in a., Se., 6/5/18.

WALTERS, F., b. Surbiton, 96720, Pte., k. in a., Se., 18/9/18.

WATKINS, D., b. Ferndale, 36146, Pte., k. in a., Se., 18/9/18.

WAY, A., b. Merthyr, 24865, Pte., d. of w., F., 23/9/15.

WEBSTER, D. J., b. Cefn Cribbwr, 14634, Pte., d., S., 19/9/16.

WILLIAMS, F., b. London, 68967, Pte., d. of w., S., 21/9/18.

WILLIAMS, I., b. Login, 13924, Pte., d., S., 29/3/16.

WILLIAMS, J., b. Trefnant, 205222, Pte., k. in a., Se., 18/9/18.

WILLIAMS, J., e. Wrexham, 205223, Pte., k. in a., Se., 14/9/18.

WILLIAMS, L., b. Ruthin, 204976, Pte., d. of w., S., 10/10/18.

WILLIAMS, R. H., b. Gloucester, 13778, Sgt., d. of w., S., 10/7/18.

WILLIAMS, W., b. Blaenau Festiniog, 14842, Pte., d. of w., S., 22/2/17.

WILLIAMS, W., b. Holyhead, 44043, Pte., k. in a., S., 18/9/18.

WILLIAMS, W. E., b. Llandegai, 203757, Pte., k. in a., Se., 18/9/18.

WILLIAMS, W. H., b. Blaenau Festiniog, 20209, Pte., d., S., 18/8/17.

WILLIAMSON, A., b. Llantrisant, 14787, Pte., d. of w., S., 22/12/17.

WOODBINE, R., b. Llanfairfechan, 21057, L/Cpl., k. in a., Se., 20/3/17.

WYNNE, W. J., b. Llanenddwyn, 36612, Pte., d. of w., S., 18/9/18.

12th BATTALION

CAMPBELL, W., b. Blackburn, 52465, Pte., d., Home, 7/8/18.

CARNEY, J., b. Carrick Castle, 6480, Pte., d., Home, 15/7/16.

CHAMBERS, C., b. Manchester, 55875, Pte., d., Home, 9/11/18.

DEARDEN, T., b. St. Helens, 55618, Pte., d., Home, 15/10/18.

DUTTON, O. G., b. Northwich, 55647, Pte., d., Home, 26/10/18.

EASTWOOD, J., b. Blackpool, 55444, Pte., d., Home, 21/10/18.

GARDNER, W. H., e. Carlisle, 22782, Pte., d., Home, 18/5/18.

HANNA, H., b. Manchester, 54306, L/Cpl., d., At Sea, 10/10/18.

HOLMES, A., b. Leyland, 55446, Pte., d., Home, 8/10/18.

HORAN, T., b. Lancaster, 55399, Pte., d., Home, 5/10/18.

JACKSON, F., b. Sale, 55593, Pte., d., Home, 21/10/18.

JONES, D., b. Denbigh, 19868, Pte., d., F., 11/9/15.

JONES, E., b. Salford, 55627, Pte., d., Home, 18/10/18.

JONES, J., e. Menai Bridge, 37823, Pte., d., Home, 20/3/16.

KERFOOT, S., b. Northwich, 53009, Pte., d., Home, 26/4/18.

KERSHAW, W. H., e. Rhyl, 48961, Pte., d., Home, 30/6/18.

SINGLETON, J., b. Burnley, 55415, Pte., d., Home, 8/10/18.

SINGLETON, S., e. Manchester, 53238, Pte., d., At Sea, 10/10/18.

SMALL, F., b. Bolton, 55572, Pte., d., Home, 20/10/18.

TAYLOR, T. A., b. Yarkhill, 21064, Pte., d., Home, 6/1/17.

THOMPSON, J., b. Altrincham, 39774, Pte., d., Home, 13/5/16.

TYLDSLEY, W., b. Warrington, 23441, Pte., d., Home, 15/6/18.

WARBURTON, T., b. Kimbolton, 23986, Pte., d., Home, 14/2/18.

WESTWELL, H., b. Leigh, 53990, Pte., d., Home, 3/7/18.

WILSON, R., b. Gt. Harwood, 55909, Pte., d., Home, 5/11/18.

13th BATTALION

ABBOTT, F., b. Neath, 19828, Pte., k. in a., F., 21/6/18.

ABBOTT, H. E., b. Liverpool, 238168, Pte., d. of w., F., 16/9/18.

ADAM, J., b. Inverurie, 60227, L/Cpl., k. in a., F., 22/4/18.

ALLSOP, H., b. Sutton-in-Ashfield, 23642, Pte., k. in a., F., 8/10/18.

ANDERSON, B., b. Nottingham, 72860, Pte., k. in a., F., 27/8/18.

ANDREWS, H., b. Manchester, 24979, Sgt., d. of w., Home, 9/12/17.

ANDREWS, W., e. Cardiff, 89228, Pte., k. in a., F., 4/11/18.

ARIEL, D. J., b. Llanwonno, 18162, Pte., d. of w., F., 11/3/18.

ARMSTRONG, C., b. London, 27511, Pte., k. in a., F., 11/4/17.

ARNOLD, J., b. Stockport, 39198, Pte., k. in a., F., 23/8/18.

ATKINSON, T. E., b. Bowners, 46377, Pte., k. in a., F., 28/8/18.

BACON, S. A., b. London, 34759, Pte., d. of w., F., 27/8/18.

BALLINGER, J., b. Manchester, 73534, Pte., k. in a., F., 8/10/18.

BARKER, G. R., b. Manchester, 58058, Pte., k. in a., F., 28/8/18.

BARKER, W. G., b. Glyn Neath, 61373, Pte., k. in a., F., 22/4/18.

BARLOW, E. I., b. Rhos, 52185, Pte., d. of w., F., 26/8/18.

BARLOW, R. A., b. Manchester, 31124, Pte., k. in a., F., 10/7/16.

BATER, W., b. Swansea, 23625, Pte., k. in a., F., 9/3/18.

BAYLISS, B., b. Newport, 58510, Pte., k. in a., F., 27/8/18.

BEECH, Z., b. Llanbradach, 57957, Pte., k. in a., F., 28/8/18.

BILLING, A., b. London, 72865, Pte., k. in a., F., 29/7/17.

BIRCH, J., b. Great Bardfield, 22783, Pte., k. in a., F., 18/2/17.

BIRLEY, J. H., b. Sheffield, 56088, Pte., k. in a., F., 1/8/17.

BISHOP, C. H., b. Malmesbury, 235317, Pte., k. in a., F., 1/9/18.

BLACK, W. R., b. Llanfair P.G., 16223, L/Sgt., k. in a., F., 14/11/17.

BLUCK, J., b. Birmingham, 69815, Pte., d. of w., F., 25/4/18.

BOOTH, A. G., b. Devonport, 44395, L/Cpl., k. in a., F., 26/8/18.

BOSLEY, A., b. Clotton, 241996, Pte., d. of w., F., 11/5/18.

BOWDEN, A., b. Cardiff, 267950, Pte., k. in a., F., 22/4/18.

BOWKER, A., b. Stalybridge, 21082, Pte., d. of w., F., 29/8/16.

BOWKER, R., e. Manchester, 52543, Pte., k. in a., F., 8/10/18.

BRADBURY, G. A., b. Longton, 60361, Pte., k. in a., F., 28/8/18.

BRAY, W., b. St. Swinthin's, 60251, Pte., d. of w., F., 2/9/18.

BREDEN, C., b. Walton, 14438, Pte., d. of w., Home, 30/9/17.

BREEN, J. E., b. Tattenhall, 55265, L/Cpl., d. of w., F., 20/6/17.

BRIGGS, G., b. London, 26654, Pte., k. in a., F., 10/7/16.

BRIGGS, H. F., b. Liverpool, 23781, Pte., k. in a., F., 27/8/18.

BROCK, J. E., b. Briton Ferry, 19827, Pte., k. in a., F., 18/3/16.

BROWN, E. T., b. St. Asaph, 16561, Pte., k. in a., F., 20/3/16.

BROWN, W. S., b. Pentre, 18769, Sgt., d. of w., F., 19/9/18.

BUCKLEY, W., b. Leeds, 72806, Pte., d. of w., F., 26/8/17.

BURFORD, C., b. Manchester, 43540, Sgt., k. in a., F., 10/5/18.

BURY, H., e. Darwen, 46976, Pte., k. in a., F., 22/4/18.

BUTLER, G. W., b. London, 53992, Pte., k. in a., F., 8/10/18.

CALLAN, J. J., b. Carlisle, 18013, A/Cpl., d. of w., F., 15/2/17.

CANNELL, E. S., b. Douglas, I.O.M., 64593, Pte., k. in a., F., 2/9/18.

CAREY, E., b. Mullengar, 37299, Pte., d. of w., F., 23/4/18.

CARRADICE, J., b. Kendal, 48942, Pte., k. in a., F., 3/8/17.

CARROLL, M., b. Burnley, 46759, L/Cpl., k. in a., F., 2/9/17.

CASEMORE, H. H., b. London, 34774, Pte., k. in a., F., 23/8/17.

CATLOW, H., b. Denton, 52566, L/Cpl., d. of w., F., 3/5/18.

CHANTLER, H. P., b. Cheadle, 72874, Pte., k. in a., F., 27/8/18.

CHECKETT, A. H., b. Hay, 15894, Pte., k. in a., F., 27/7/17.

CHUBB, M., b. Zeal, Wilts, 235319, Pte., d. of w., F., 30/7/17.

CLEARY, J. F., b. Manchester, 24212, Pte., k. in a., F., 31/7/17.

CLEARY, W., b. Manchester, 31131, Pte., k. in a., F., 28/2/16.

COGDALE, E. W., b. Leyton, 27499, Pte., k. in a., F., 10/7/16.

COLE, A. W., b. Llandyfodwg, 16358, Sgt., k. in a., F., 22/4/18.

COLEMAN, C. E., b. Folkestone, 22789, Pte., k. in a., F., 22/7/16.

CONNOLLY, P. H., b. Frodsham, 55266, Pte., k. in a., F., 22/4/18.

COOPER, S., b. Hawarden, 17236, Pte., k. in a., F., 22/4/18.

CORNISH, E., b. Cardiff, 14488, L/Cpl., k. in a., F., 22/4/18, M.M.

COZENS, F. W., b. London, 56054, Pte., d. of w., F., 3/5/17.

CROWTHER, J., b. Middleton, 52058, Pte., k. in a., F., 22/4/18.

CULLEN, R., b. Longsight, 46332, L/Cpl., k. in a., F., 29/7/17.

CUTTS, A., b. Sutton-in-Ashfield, 23702, Pte., d., F., 14/4/16.

DAGG, J. S., b. Cardiff, 75305, Pte., d. of w., F., 2/9/18.

DALLORZA, J., b. Liverpool, 51459, Pte., k. in a., F., 10/3/18.

DAVIES, A., b. Brynteg, 16939, Pte., k. in a., F., 21/2/16.

DAVIES, B. G., b. Briton Ferry, 17066, Pte., d. of w., F., 23/9/18.

DAVIES, B. H., b. Ystradyfodwe, 17800, Cpl., k. in a., F., 22/4/18.

DAVIES, C., b. St. Pancras, 35216, Pte., k. in a., F., 10/3/18.

DAVIES, D., b. Pennal, 19376, Pte., k. in a., F., 25/1/16.

DAVIES, D., b. Llanrhystyd, 21306, Pte., d. of w., F., 24/4/18.

DAVIES, F., b. Wrexham, 15847, Cpl., d. of w., F., 2/8/17.

DAVIES, G., b. Crewe, 16557, Pte., k. in a., F., 22/4/18.

DAVIES, M., b. Cefn, 16983, Cpl., k. in a., F., 30/5/16.

DAVIES, J., b. Denbigh, 16772, L/Cpl., k. in a., F., 22/4/18.

DAVIES, J., b. Wrexham, 39053, L/Cpl., k. in a., F., 31/7/17.

DAVIES, J. L., b. Ebbw Vale, 31161, Cpl., d. of w., F., 31/7/17, V.C.

DAVIES, J. M., b. London, 26831, L/Sgt., k. in a., F., 22/4/18.

DAVIES, M. H., b. Aberavon, 42187, Pte., k. in a., F., 31/7/17.

DAVIES, R. E., b. Gronant, 16798, Cpl., k. in a., F., 21/6/18.

DAVIES, T. E., b. Llanidloes, 57459, Pte., k. in a., F., 14/11/17.

DAVIES, T. O., b. Trefriw, 26071, Pte., k. in a., F., 9/4/17.

DAVIES, W. B., b. Llanbeblig, 17230, Pte., d. of w., F., 8/2/17.

DAVIES, W. V., e. Blaenau Festiniog, 55267, Pte., k. in a., F., 26/8/18.

DAVISON, W. M., b. Dudley, 242054, Pte., k. in a., F., 29/8/18.

DE BONNAIRE, S. S., b. London, 56019, L/Cpl., k. in a., F., 23/8/18.

DENTON, A., b. Accrington, 24217, Pte., k. in a., F., 10/7/16.

DENYER, J. E., b. Southwark, 45155, Pte., k. in a., F., 19/9/18.

DEROME, F., b. Kendal, 58080, Pte., k. in a., F., 19/9/18.

DICKIE, G. M., b. Barony, 56529, Pte., d. of w., F., 24/4/18.

DICKSON, J., b. Shankhill, 72877, Pte., k. in a., F., 31/7/17.

DINCLEY, G. A., b. Liverpool, 66200, Pte., k. in a., F., 26/8/18.

DIX, G., b. Newport, 70061, Pte., d., F., 3/11/18.

DOOLEY, J., b. Wexford, 66298, Pte., k. in a., F., 31/7/17.

DOUGLAS, G. T., b. Skeffling, 56230, Pte., d. of w., F., 22/9/18.

DOWLER, J., b. Salford, 46559, Pte., k. in a., F., 22/4/18.

DOWNEY, J., b. Scotchwood, 235450, Pte., k. in a., F., 22/4/18.

DRIVER, J., b. Hyde, 46189, Pte., k. in a., F., 19/9/18.

DUFFY, F. J., b. London, 21746, Pte., k. in a., F., 22/4/18.

DUGGAN, S., e. Gladestry, 55189, Pte., k. in a., F., 22/4/18.

DUXBURY, W., b. Mellor, 46330, L/Cpl., d. of w., F., 26/8/18.

EDDY, E. S. L., b. Pontypridd, 19705, Pte., k. in a., F., 22/4/18.

EDMUNDSON, F., b. Oldham, 63585, Pte., k. in a., F., 31/7/17.

EDSER, E., b. Whitchurch, 75753, Pte., d. of w., F., 20/9/18.

EDWARDS, D., b. Mountain Ash, 58083, Pte., k. in a., F., 27/8/18.

EDWARDS, E., b. Colwyn Bay, 17420, Pte., d. of w., F., 19/6/16.

EDWARDS, E., b. Blaenau Festiniog, 75546, Pte., k. in a., F., 22/4/18.

EDWARDS, G., e. Blaenau Festiniog, 55279, Pte., d. of w., F., 22/6/17.

EDWARDS, J. A., b. Bangor, 205534, Pte., k. in a., F., 8/10/18.

EDWARDS, P. S. A., b. Bristol, 235313, Pte., k. in a., F., 31/7/17.

EDWARDS, W., e. Carnarvon, 55273, Pte., k. in a., F., 23/8/18.

ELLIS, E., b. Nantglyn, 16909, Pte., k. in a., F., 10/7/16.

ELSTONE, T. C., b. Cardiff, 58081, Pte., k. in a., F., 8/10/18.

EVANS, A. E., b. Llandudno, 16068, A/Cpl., k. in a., F., 10/7/16.

EVANS, D., b. Bethesda, 55275, Pte., k. in a., F., 22/4/18.

EVANS, E., b. Gwersyllt, 16807, L/Cpl., k. in a., F., 22/4/18.

EVANS, E., b. Tennesia, 17099, Pte., d. of w., F., 10/7/16.

EVANS, E., b. Tregaron, 69143, Pte., k. in a., F., 7/4/18.

EVANS, G., b. Wroxeter, 46333, Pte., k. in a., F., 23/8/18.

EVANS, G. J., b. Llanrhaiadr, 37967, Pte., k. in a., F., 15/6/17.

EVANS, J., b. Amlwch, 203981, Pte., k. in a., F., 22/4/18.

EVANS, J., b. Rhesycae, 61203, Pte., k. in a., F., 22/4/18.

EVANS, J. E., b. Llandyssil, 55278, Pte., d. of w., F., 1/5/17.

EVANS, J. G., b. Ferndale, 89239, Pte., k. in a., F., 4/11/18.

EVANS, O., b. Pontypool, 42224, Pte., k. in a., F., 22/4/18.

EVANS, R., b. Rhyl, 16950, Pte., k. in a., F., 5/3/16.

EVANS, R. L., b. Berriew, 25377, Cpl., d., F., 22/2/16.

EVANS, T., b. Dolgelly, 89615, Pte., d. of w., F., 29/10/18.

EVANS, W., b. Rhyl, 16834, L/Cpl., d., F., 4/11/18.

EVANS, W. D., b. Tredegar, 44770, Pte., k. in a., F., 22/6/17.

EVANS, W. R., b. Kerry, 55282, Pte., k. in a., F., 23/8/18.

EVERALL, B. J., b. Lydbury, 55277, Pte., d. of w., Home, 13/11/17.

FIELD, W. H., b. Manchester, 58085, Pte., k. in a., F., 1/9/18.

FISHER, J. A., b. London, 27087, Pte., k. in a., F., 24/4/17.

FLETCHER, J., b. London, 26950, Pte., d. of w., F., 26/2/17.

FOX, W. J., b. Cadoxton, 31426, Pte., k. in a., F., 10/7/16.

FRANCIS, E. R., b. Wolverhampton, 58087, Pte., k. in a., F., 16/9/17.

GAINE, J., b. Holyhead, 18200, Pte., d. of w., F., 2/6/16.

GARRATT, E. E., b. Liverpool, 15987, Pte., d. of w., F., 11/7/16.

GASKELL, H., b. Upholland, 46787, Pte., k. in a., F., 10/3/18.

GASTON, H., b. Lindfield, 56209, Pte., k. in a., F., 20/10/18.

GITTENS, A., b. Manchester, 24985, L/Cpl., k. in a., F., 4/11/18.

GRANDFIELD, W. H., b. Neath, 17594, Pte., d. of w., F., 3/10/16.

GRATRIX, J., b. Sale, 72883, Pte., d. of w., F., 10/5/18.

GREEN, F., b. Manchester, 31440, Pte., k. in a., F., 10/7/16.

GREEN, H., b. Rothley, 56085, Pte., d., F., 3/7/17.

GREEN, J., b. Merthyr, 76426, Pte., d. of w., F., 1/9/18.

GREENHALGH, J., b. Mold, 16492, Pte., k. in a., F., 24/7/16.

GRIFFITHS, D. W., b. Aberayron, 45141, Pte., d. of w., F., 19/3/18.

GRIFFITHS, J., b. Rhyl, 17402, Pte., k. in a., F., 7/12/16.

GRIFFITHS, J. T., b. Ruabon, 15902, Pte., d. of w., F., 16/7/16.

GRIFFITHS, R. O., b. Pengongl, 203697, Pte., k. in a., F., 22/4/18.

GRIFFITHS, W., b. Ruabon, 16907, L/Cpl., d. of w., F., 8/7/16.

GROSSMITH, A. E. H., b. London, 23581, Pte., d., F., 19/4/16.

HALL, T., b. Weaste, 46798, Pte., d. of w., F., 3/8/17.

HALE, W., b. Chalford, 14795, Pte., d. of w., Home, 30/10/18.

HAMBLETON, A., b. London, 27186, Pte., d. of w., F., 24/8/18.

HAMBLING, B. G., b. Clayton-le-Moors, 23145, Pte., k. in a., F., 22/4/18.

HAMER, R., e. Oldham, 46806, Pte., k. in a., F., 9/3/18.

HAMILTON, C., b. King's Cross, 34596, Pte., k. in a., F., 10/3/18.

HANGER, W. H., b. Stepney, 22272, Pte., k. in a., F., 22/4/18.

HANSON, C., b. Margam, 37595, Pte., k. in a., F., 18/2/17.

HARDING, W. A., b. London, 26978, L/Cpl., d. of w., F., 13/7/16.

HARPER, W. R., b. Birmingham, 235490, Pte., d. of w., F., 5/11/18.

HARRIES, J., b. Llandebie, 40951, Pte., d. of w., F., 6/5/18.

HARRISON, J. A., b. Broughton, 24760, Pte., k. in a., F., 27/8/16.

HATTON, J., b. St. Helens, 19848, Pte., d. of w., F., 8/7/16.

HAWKINS, J., b. Fenton, 317257, Pte., k. in a., F., 16/9/18.

HAYES, E. W., b. Bethnal Green, 26651, Pte., d. of w., F., 14/7/16.

HENSHAW, J. W., b. Lowton, 24211, Pte., d. of w., F., 27/3/18.

HEVEY, W., b. St. Helens, 16070, Pte., k. in a., F., 10/7/16.

HIGGINBOTHAM, G., b. Stockport, 54925, Pte., k. in a., F., 23/8/18.

HIGGINBOTTOM, H., b. Ashton-under-Lyne, 87585, Pte., k. in a., F., 8/10/18.

HILTON, R., b. Manchester, 24305, Pte., k. in a., F., 29/9/16.

HINTON, H., b. Warrington, 18901, Pte., k. in a., F., 17/6/17.

HOBSON, J., b. Llandudno, 44142, Pte., k. in a., F., 22/6/17.

HOGBEN, H. E., b. Elmstead, 55150, Pte., k. in a., F., 28/8/18.

HOLDEN, H., e. Birkenhead, 70249, Pte., d., Home, 26/6/18.

HOLMES, A., b. Bentham, 266954, Pte., k. in a., F., 27/8/18.

HOSLER, R., b. Ince, 64567, Pte., d. of w., F., 23/8/18.

HOTCHKISS, S., b. Swansea, 17433, Pte., k. in a., F., 26/8/18.

HOUGH, R. G., b. Marchwiel, 16799, Pte., k. in a., F., 2/8/17.

HOWARTH, J. P., e. Manchester, 24926, L/Cpl., k. in a., F., 3/4/17.

HOWELL, D. b. Crewe, 58521, Pte., k. in a., F., 8/10/18.

HOWELLS, J. T., e. Neath, 17967, Pte., d. of w., F., 4/8/17.

HUDSON, J., b. Suton Wyndham, 60422, Pte., k. in a., F., 23/8/18.

HUGALL, A. E., b. Barnsbury,

45009, Pte., k. in a., F., 22/4/18, M.M.

HUGHES, B. V., b. Blaenau Festiniog, 23640, Pte., k. in a., F., 18/2/18.

HUGHES, D. H., e. Carnarvon, 21246, Sgt., k. in a., F., 22/4/18, M.M.

HUGHES, E., b. Bagillt, 316685, Pte., k. in a., F., 22/4/18.

HUGHES, E. J., b. Bangor, 17262, Pte., d. of w., F., 12/7/16.

HUGHES, J. E., b. Llanfwrog, 17490, Pte., k. in a., F., 11/7/16.

HUGHES, R., b. Portmadoc, 19602, Pte., k. in a., F., 21/6/17.

HUGHES, R. E., b. Llangollen, 16600, C.S.M., k. in a., F., 22/4/18.

HUGHES, U., b. Beaumaris, 17371, Pte., k. in a., F., 10/7/16.

HUGHES, W., b. Rhyl, 21707, Pte., d. of w., F., 23/9/18.

HUGHES, W., b. Bangor, 53833, Pte., k. in a., F., 7/11/18.

HULBERT, A., b. Pontypridd, 88827, Pte., d. of w., F., 21/10/18.

HUMPHREYS, W. E., b. Llancwm, 76395, Pte., k. in a., F., 12/9/18.

HUNT, J. W. H., b. Islington, 34736, Pte., k. in a., F., 11/7/16.

HUTSON, G. C. H., b. Lambeth, 96148, Pte., k. in a., F., 21/10/18.

IRVINE, J., b. Govan, 72839, Pte., k. in a., F., 31/7/17.

ISAAC, G. H., b. Ogmore Vale, 89142, Pte., k. in a., F., 6/11/18.

JACKSON, J. R., b. Fleetwood, 55055, Pte., k. in a., F., 22/4/18.

JACQUES, F., b. Birmingham, 16376, Pte., k. in a., F., 13/10/16.

JAMES, H. I., b. Stockton-on-Tees, 21816, Sgt., k. in a., F., 19/9/18.

JAMES, W., b. Kidwelly, 31684, Pte., k. in a., F., 31/7/17.

JAMES, W. J., b. Nantymoel, 72837, Pte., k. in a., F., 31/7/17.

JAMESON, A., b. Wigan, 52299, Pte., k. in a., F., 22/4/18.

JEREMIAH, B. J., b. Ystradyfodng, 17619, Pte., k. in a., F., 30/5/16.

JERVIS, R., b. Llanllechid, 17869, Pte., d. of w., F., 20/1/16.

JOHNSTON, R., b. Carlisle, 91569, Pte., k. in a., F., 8/10/18.

JONES, A., e. Wrexham, 56993, Cpl., d. of w., F., 23/8/18.

JONES, A., b. Aberbeeg, 72809, Pte., k. in a., F., 9/10/18.

JONES, A. M., b. Llandeinider, 17283, Pte., d. of w., F., 11/7/16.

JONES, D. J., b. Ruabon, 15903, Pte., k. in a., F., 19/9/18, M.M.

JONES, E., b. Gwersyllt, 16775, Pte., k. in a., F., 5/7/16.

JONES, E., e. Carnarvon, 54825, Pte., k. in a., F., 22/6/17.

JONES, G., b. Abererch, 16091, Pte., k. in a., F., 10/7/16.

JONES, G., b. Rhostryfan, 40701, Pte., k. in a., F., 22/4/18.

JONES, H., b. Llanenghli, 18151, Pte., k. in a., F., 7/6/16.

JONES, H., b. Morville, 67076, Pte., k. in a., F., 29/8/18.

JONES, H. J., b. Liverpool, 16590, Pte., k. in a., F., 15/5/16.

JONES, J., b. Llangollen, 16159, Pte., k. in a., F., 31/7/17.

JONES, J., b. Bettws, 20186, Pte., d. of w., F., 28/2/17.

JONES, J., e. Wrexham, 55296, Pte., k. in a., F., 2/9/18.

JONES, J. A., b. Newcastle Emlyn, 59656, Pte., k. in a., F., 8/10/18.

JONES, J., b. St. Asaph, 28360, Pte., k. in a., F., 8/8/18.

JONES, J., e. Newport, 89021, Pte., k. in a., F., 4/11/18.

JONES, J. F., b. Ruabon, 16943, Pte., k. in a., F., 7/7/16.

JONES, J. H., b. Machynlleth, 23041, Cpl., k. in a., F., 18/2/16.

JONES, J. H., b. Dolgelly, 49882, Pte., d. of w., F., 27/8/18.

JONES, J. J., b. Abergele, 17108, A/Sgt., k. in a., F., 10/7/16.

JONES, M., b. Kidwelly, 24316, Pte., k. in a., F., 22/4/18.

JONES, O., b. Blaenau Festiniog, 16873, Pte., k. in a., F., 17/6/17.

JONES, O. T., b. Llanfair, 37018, L/Cpl., k. in a., F., 22/4/18.

JONES, P. E., b. Llangedwyn, 37688, Pte., k. in a., F., 1/8/17.

JONES, P. J., b. Llanbrynmair, 36998, L/Cpl., k. in a., F., 23/8/18.

JONES, P. T., b. Broughton, 77139, Pte., k. in a., F., 8/10/18.

JONES, R., b. Ruabon, 17006, L/Cpl., d. of w., F., 2/3/16.

JONES, R., b. Rhondda, 17094, Pte., k. in a., F., 1/4/17.

JONES, R., b. Llandinam, 18061, Pte., k. in a., F., 7/11/18.

JONES, R. A., b. Bala, 23403, Pte., k. in a., F., 1/9/16.

JONES, R. H., b. Bettws G.G., 17978, L/Cpl., d. of w., F., 8/10/18.

JONES, R. J., e. Welshpool, 235756, Pte., k. in a., F., 26/8/18.

JONES, S., b. Neath, 17590, Pte., d. of w., F., 21/12/15.

JONES, T., b. Rhyl, 16560, Pte., k. in a., F., 17/6/17.

JONES, T. J., b. Llandwrog, 54824, Pte., d., F., 14/5/17.

JONES, T. L., b. Llanddewi Bregi, 16523, Pte., d. of w., F., 11/7/16.

JONES, T. O., b. Denbigh, 16632, Pte., k. in a., F., 27/8/18.

JONES, T. W., b. Denbigh, 15956, Pte., k. in a., F., 10/7/16.

JONES, W., b. Oswestry, 16527, L/Cpl., k. in a., F., 23/9/16.

JONES, W., b. Southport, 20280, Pte., d. of w., F., 12/7/16.

JONES, W. C., b. Rhyl, 16293, Pte., k. in a., F., 14/5/16.

JONES, W. D., b. Llantwit Lower, 18028, Pte., k. in a., F., 31/7/17.

JUKES, W., b. Birmingham, 43862, L/Cpl., d. of w., F., 26/4/18.

KERLEY, J. W., b. Salford, 60379, Pte., d. of w., F., 23/4/18.

KILGANNON, M., b. Sale, 54815, Pte., k. in a., F., 31/7/17.

KINSON, A., b. Gloucester, 54324, Pte., k. in a., F., 10/3/18.

KIRBY, A. W., b. Seacombe, 70291, Pte., k. in a., F., 28/8/18.

KOLLER, J. O., b. London, 52354, Pte., d. of w., F., 24/8/18.

LATCHFORD, N., b. Leigh, 15771, Sgt., k. in a., F., 22/4/18.

LATHROPE, J., b. Pendleton, 29034, Pte., d. of w., F., 23/10/18.

LAWRENCE, R. G., b. Stoke, 34536, Pte., d., F., 25/9/16.

LAWSON, B., b. Dublin, 58118, Pte., k. in a., F., 27/8/18.

LEAH, E. F., b. Mordiford, 18023, L/Cpl., k. in a., F., 22/4/18.

LEARY, T., b. Ashton-under-Lyne, 23662, Pte., d. of w., F., 31/7/17.

LEE, E., e. Welshpool, 235758, L/Cpl., k. in a., F., 26/8/18.

LEES, G. W., b. London, 20085, L/Cpl., k. in a., F., 3/7/18.

LEWIS, D., b. Neath, 19832, Pte., d. of w., Home, 31/7/16.

LEWIS, D. D., b. Cwmbellan, 24929, Pte., k. in a., F., 18/2/16.

LEWIS, D. T., e. Neath, 89234, Pte., k. in a., F., 8/11/18.

LEWIS, E. C., b. Ystrad, 91483, Pte., d. of w., F., 25/9/18.

LEWIS, R., b. Rhondda, 16271, L/Cpl., k. in a., F., 10/3/18.

LEWIS, W. D., b. Carmarthen, 6353, Pte., k. in a., F., 9/5/18.

LITTLER, A., b. Gresford, 315093, Cpl., k. in a., F., 3/9/18.

LLOYD, H., b. Pembroke, 17580, Pte., k. in a., F., 22/4/18.

LLOYD, R., b. Wrexham, 23368, Pte., k. in a., F., 10/7/16.

LLOYD, R. J., b. Newport, 88763, Pte., k. in a., F., 20/10/18.

LONGHURST, W., b. Oswestry, 55261, Pte., k. in a., F., 22/4/18.

LOVETT, H. E., b. Liverpool, 316023, Pte., k. in a., F., 29/8/18.

LUCAS, R. H., b. Manchester,

31363, Pte., d. of w., F., F., 5/5/16.

LUXTON, S., b. London, 60217, Pte., k. in a., F., 8/10/18.

LYE, G., b. Manchester, 58120, Pte., d. of w., F., 24/8/18.

LYTHGOE, N., b. Rhosddu, 15864, Pte., d. of w., F., 20/1/16.

MADDOCKS, S., b. Broughton, 24761, Pte., k. in a., F., 23/8/18.

MAGUIRE, J. A., b. London, 27327, Cpl., k. in a., F., 30/5/16.

MARSDEN, W. A. S., b. Manchester, 58131, Pte., k. in a., F., 26/8/18.

MARSH, A., b. Manchester, 31138, Pte., d. of w., F., 7/4/16.

MARTIN, J., b. Breage, 16769, Pte., k. in a., F., 29/10/16.

MARTINS, J., e. Croydon, 44807, Pte., k. in a., F., 22/4/18.

MASSEY, H., b. Mossley, 315101, Pte., k. in a., F., 23/8/18.

MATHER, T. S., b. Wallasey, 57972, Pte., k. in a., F., 26/8/18.

MATHIAS, J., b. London, 17169, Pte., k. in a., F., 10/7/16.

MATTHEWS, J., b. Ruabon, 28669, Pte., k. in a., F., 22/4/18.

MAYNE, W., b. Liverpool, 57971, Pte., d. of w., F., 21/10/18.

McCORMACK, G. A., b. London, 27473, Pte., d. of w., F., 22/2/16.

McDONALD, W., b. London, 22043, Cpl., d. of w., F., 6/5/18.

McGILL, W., b. Manchester, 57974, Pte., k. in a., F., 27/8/18.

McKAY, J., b. Edinburgh, 19688, Pte., k. in a., F., 22/4/18.

McLOUGHLIN, J., b. Liverpool, 77848, Pte., d. of w., F., 22/9/18.

MEEK, C. W. S., b. Scarborough, 267716, Pte., k. in a., F., 8/10/18.

MELSON, E. L., b. Stratford, 44769, Pte., k. in a., F., 9/5/18.

MIDDLETON, J. E., b. Pool Quay, 93511, Pte., d. of w., F., 10/9/18.

MILLER, C. E., b. Cardiff, 57970, Pte., d. of w., F., 16/9/18.

MILLIGAN, H., b. Blackburn, 43756, Pte., d. of w., F., 3/8/17.

MITCHELL, S., b. Caerau, 88629, Pte., k. in a., F., 8/10/18.

MOLYNEUX, G., b. Tyldesley, 53646, Pte., k. in a., F., 10/3/18.

MONKS, W., b. Warrington, 23254, Cpl., k. in a., F., 7/7/16.

MOORCROFT, A., b. Preston, 57975, Pte., k. in a., F., 27/8/18.

MOORE, R., b. Wrexham, 16727, Sgt., k. in a., F., 12/10/16.

MORGAN, D. W., b. Dulais Higher,

18020, Pte., d. of w., F., 10/7/16.

MORGAN, J. T., b. Pontypridd, 88784, Pte., k. in a., F., 20/10/18.

MORGAN, R. E., b. Carno, 203679, Pte., d. of w., F., 28/8/18.

MORGAN, W. B. B., b. Llansamlet, 292052, Pte., k. in a., F., 29/8/18.

MORRIS, A., b. Coity, 37393, Pte., k. in a., F., 24/4/17.

MORRIS, E., b. West Bromwich, 75245, Pte., k. in a., F., 8/10/18.

MORRIS, E., b. Ruabon, 15913, Pte., k. in a., F., 27/8/16.

MORRIS, I. W., b. Connahs Quay. 36692, Pte., k. in a., F., 31/7/17.

MORRIS, J. E., b. Ruabon, 16467, L/Cpl., d. of w., F., 11/7/16.

MORRIS, R. W., b. Llanynys, 17610, Pte., k. in a., F., 31/7/17.

MORRIS, T., b. Rhyl, 17261, Sgt., k. in a., F., 4/11/18.

MORRIS, W. G., b. Dolwyddelan, 54830, L/Cpl., k. in a., F., 22/4/18.

MOSES, S., b. Durham, 202365, L/Cpl., k. in a., F., 28/8/18.

MULCRONE, J., b. Oldham, 58127, Pte., k. in a., F., 31/8/18.

NATION, S. G., b. Taunton, 23737, L/Cpl., k. in a., F., 22/4/18.

NICHOLLS, J., b. London, 28163, Cpl., d. of w., F., 29/4/18.

NORTON, B. W., b. Hull, 56065, Pte., k. in a., F., 31/7/17.

NURSE, F. A., b. Rainhill, 23313, Pte., k. in a., F., 30/5/16.

NUTT, H. T., b. London, 88859, Pte., k. in a., F., 21/10/18.

OGDEN, J. H., b. Manchester, 23782, Pte., k. in a., F., 11/12/16.

OLIVER, W., b. Manchester, 43469, L/Cpl., k. in a., F., 23/8/18.

ORMESHER, T. M., b. Blowick, 46881, Pte., d. of w., F., 30/5/18.

OWEN, H., b. Llanidan, 16423, Pte., d., Home, 28/4/16.

OWEN, H., b. Talysarn, 54575, Pte., d. of w., F., 4/11/18.

OWEN, L., b. Llandudno, 203798, Pte., k. in a., F., 19/9/18.

PAILTHORPE, F., b. Hyde, 57986, Pte., k. in a., F., 26/8/18.

PARK, J. W., b. Chipping, 58149, Pte., k. in a., F., 26/8/18.

PARKER, J. E., b. Manchester, 15845, Pte., d. of w., F., 31/1/16.

PARKER, T. D. M., b. Liverpool, 17535, Pte., d. of w., F., 22/5/17.

PARKES, W., b. Four Crosses, 49889, Pte., d. of w., F., 29/8/18.

PARKHOUSE, D., b. Briton Ferry,

17168, Pte., k. in a., F., 23/8/17.

PARRY, E., b. Llanerchymedd, 17546, Pte., d. of w., F., 2/6/16.

PARRY, E., b. Rhos Goch, 61115, Pte., k. in a., F., 4/9/17.

PARRY, T., b. Llanfairfechan, 16426, Pte., d. of w., F., 5/8/17.

PEARCE, J., b. London, 28008, Pte., k. in a., F., 25/3/18.

PEARSON, G. W., b. Hazel Slade, 13601, Sgt., k. in a., F., 20/10/18.

PEATE, S., b. Bordesley, 23930, Pte., d. of w., F., 22/4/16.

PENNINGTON, T. H., b. Walkden, 57982, Pte., k. in a., F., 8/10/18.

PHILLIPS, H. E., b. Tregynon, 43746, Pte., d. of w., F., 25/4/18.

PHILLIPS, P., b. Ruabon, 15921, Pte., k. in a., F., 6/10/16.

PHILLIPS, T., b. Goldburn, 58146, Pte., d. of w., F., 10/6/18.

PHILLIPS, T., b. Berriew, 60950, Pte., k. in a., F., 22/4/18.

PHILLIPS, W. H., b. Gravesend, 56051, Pte., k. in a., F., 26/6/17.

PIPER, F., b. Bacup, 33476, Pte., d. of w., F., 20/1/16.

PRESCOTT, J. B., e. Manchester, 57980, Pte., k. in a., F., 10/5/18.

PRESCOTT, W., b. Ruabon, 15926, Pte., k. in a., F., 25/1/16.

PRICE, A., b. Towyn, 16083, Pte., d. of w., F., 13/10/16.

PRICE, E., b. Holywell, 17244, L/Cpl., d. of w., F., 22/4/16.

PRICE, J. E., b. Rhayader, 39644, Pte., k. in a., F., 1/8/17.

PRIDDING, J., e. Wrexham, 54643, Pte., d. of w., F., 6/2/17.

PROCTOR, S., b. Manchester, 57983, Pte., k. in a., F., 31/8/18.

PROTHEROE, D. W., b. Tonna, 19842, Pte., k. in a., F., 4/3/16.

PRUETT, J., b. Wrexham, 33321, Pte., d. of w., F., 25/3/18.

QUIGLEY, W. J., b. Liverpool, 16550, Pte., k. in a., F., 8/4/17.

RADDON, E. S., b. London, 27994, Pte., k. in a., F., 23/8/18.

RANICAR, J. W., b. Crewe, 235453, Pte., k. in a., F., 22/4/18.

RAYNER, A., b. Manchester, 57989, Pte., d., F., 18/6/18.

REES, E., b. Merthyr, 60203, Pte., k. in a., F., 22/4/18.

REES, G. T., e. Porth, 58000, Pte., d. of w., F., 23/10/18.

REES, T., b. Abererch, 16093, Sgt., k. in a., F., 22/4/18.

REES, T. H. E., b. Swansea, 16172, Sgt., k. in a., F., 22/4/18.

REES, W. N., e. Newport, 88803, Pte., k. in a., F., 4/11/18.

REGAN, J., b. Wigan, 58538, L/Cpl., k. in a., F., 8/10/18.

RICE, T., b. Dublin, 45587, Pte., k. in a., F., 19/9/18.

RICHARDS, D., b. Llandyssul, 16642, Pte., d. of w., F., 1/7/17.

RICHARDS, R. C., b. Cardigan, 93541, Pte., k. in a., F., 1/9/18.

RICHARDS, R. D., b. Llanrhaiadr, 235764, Pte., k. in a., F., 9/3/18.

RICHARDSON, R. W., b. Hull, 16185, Pte., k. in a., F., 11/7/16.

RIMMER, L., b. Southport, 60125, Pte., k. in a., F., 22/4/18.

ROBERTS, A., b. Milnsbridge, 23090, Sgt., d. of w., F., 31/5/18.

ROBERTS, A., b. Wrexham, 54649, Pte., k. in a., F., 22/4/18.

ROBERTS, A. D., b. Whitchurch, 61204, Pte., k. in a., F., 9/8/18.

ROBERTS, D., b. Cerrig-y-Druidion, 34886, Pte., k. in a., F., 18/6/17.

ROBERTS, D. P., b. St. Asaph, 17253, L/Cpl., d. of w., F., 26/8/18.

ROBERTS, F., b. Moss, 17239, Pte., k. in a., F., 12/10/16.

ROBERTS, G., b. Wrexham, 19471, Sgt., k. in a., F., 9/2/17.

ROBERTS, G., e. Carnarvon, 54655, Pte., k. in a., F., 26/6/17.

ROBERTS, J., b. Ruabon, 15919, Pte., k. in a., F., 11/7/16.

ROBERTS, J., b. Colwyn Bay, 27964, L/Cpl., k. in a., F., 30/5/16.

ROBERTS, L. D., b. London, 15867, Pte., d. of w., F., 5/6/16.

ROBERTS, L. J., b. Carnarvon, 54579, Pte., k. in a., F., 10/3/18.

ROBERTS, O., b. Llandudno, 205066, Pte., k. in a., F., 22/4/18.

ROBERTS, P. J., b. Wrexham, 57993, Pte., k. in a., F., 26/8/18.

ROBERTS, R., b. Llangynhafal, 54646, Pte., k. in a., F., 6/12/16.

ROBERTS, R. O., b. Liverpool, 73809, Pte., k. in a., F., 23/8/18.

ROBERTS, T., b. Llangollen, 17396, L/Cpl., d. of w., Home, 22/4/17.

ROBERTS, T., b. Anglesey, 54652, Pte., d. of w., F., 1/8/17.

ROBERTS, T. E., b. Talyllyn, 31298, L/Cpl., k. in a., F., 10/7/16.

ROBERTS, T. J., b. Manchester, 24975, Pte., k. in a., F., 10/7/16.

ROBERTS, T. J., b. Llanberis, 40210, Pte., k. in a., F., 22/4/18.

ROBERTS, T. S., b. Llysfaen, 36843, Pte., k. in a., F., 21/4/16.

ROBERTS, W., b. Colwyn Bay, 16069, Pte., k. in a., F., 1/8/17.

ROBERTS, W., b. Llanbedr, 61283, Pte., d. of w., F., 15/5/18.

ROBERTS, W. J., b. Bangor, 54647, Pte., k. in a., F., 23/6/17.

ROBERTS, W. O., b. Denbigh, 54657, A/Cpl., k. in a., F., 22/4/18.

ROBINS, A. E., b. Whitchurch, 61480, Pte., d. of w., F., 24/8/18.

ROBINSON, C., e. London, 235191, Pte., d. of w., F., 10/10/18.

ROBINSON, P. J., b. Liverpool, 58152, Pte., k. in a., F., 28/8/18.

RODBURNE, W. H., b. Stratton, 235320, Pte., k. in a., F., 2/9/17.

ROOM, W. J., b. Dunstable, 45604, Pte., d. of w., F., 25/3/18.

ROSE, W. H., b. Hurdsfield, 92717, Pte., k. in a., F., 16/9/18.

ROTHENBURG, H., b. Hull, 54787, Pte., k. in a., F., 22/4/18.

ROWLAND, W. H., b. Ruabon, 16566, Cpl., k. in a., F., 29/7/17.

ROYLE, G. A., b. Manchester, 58004, Pte., d. of w., F., 12/9/18.

RUGG, W. S., b. Bath, 235315, Pte., d. of w., F., 23/4/18.

RUTTER, A. H., b. Bridgnorth, 58002, Pte., d. of w., Home, 4/6/19.

RUTTER, F., b. Cardiff, 72866, Pte., k. in a., F., 22/4/18.

RYDER, R., b. Pontypridd, 61429, Pte., k. in a., F., 28/8/18.

SALISBURY, H., e. Wrexham, 54658, Pte., d. of w., F., 10/12/16.

SALISBURY, R. P., b. Cardiff, 58621, Pte., k. in a., F., 27/8/18.

SALUSBURY, J. E., b. Denbigh, 16440, A/C.Q.M.S., k. in a., F., 23/4/18.

SAUNDERS, E., b. Altrincham, 54816, Pte., k. in a., F., 22/4/18.

SAVAGE, A. J., b. Croydon, 22062, Pte., k. in a., F., 22/4/18.

SAVEGAR, C., b. Beanswood, 19684, Pte., k. in a., F., 16/3/17.

SAW, H. G., b. Princes Risborough, 34948, L/Cpl., k. in a., F., 31/7/17.

SCHOFIELD, W., b. Manchester, 31727, Pte., d. of w., F., 21/2/17.

SCHOLES, F., b. Waterfoot, 58010, Pte., k. in a., F., 8/10/18.

SEARLE, W., b. London, 91626, Pte., d. of w., F., 18/9/18.

SEDDON, A., b. Bolton, 63137, Pte., k. in a., F., 8/10/18.

SEYMOUR, F. W., b. Broseley, 63489, Pte., k. in a., F., 31/7/17.

SEYMOUR, W. G., b. High Wycombe, 58540, Pte., k. in a., F., 23/8/18.

SHARP, S., b. Wargrave, 19267, Pte., k. in a., F., 11/4/16.

SHARPLES, L. L., b. Liverpool, 58164, Pte., k. in a., F., 26/8/18.

SHAW, A., b. Blackburn, 24299, Pte., k. in a., F., 27/2/16.

SHELDON, C., b. Oswestry, 33281, Pte., d. of w., F., 25/4/16.

SHEPHERD, W., b. Burnley, 201693, Pte., k. in a., F., 19/9/18.

SHEPPARD, J. H., b. London, 26869, Pte., d. of w., Home, 27/9/16.

SHEPPERD, J. H., b. Neath, 18768, Pte., k. in a., F., 24/4/17.

SHOTTON, W., b. Amblecot, 56128, Pte., k. in a., F., 22/4/18, M.M.

SHUTT, A., b. Wolverhampton, 89271, Pte., d. of w., F., 21/10/18.

SIGLEY, H., b. Manchester, 58158, Pte., k. in a., F., 19/9/18.

SMITH, C., b. London, 45527, Pte., k. in a., F., 2/9/18.

SMITH, F., b. St. Helens, 45525, Pte., d. of w., F., 23/10/18.

SMITH, F. R., b. Elwick, 317003, Pte., k. in a., F., 27/8/18.

SMITH, J., b. Blackburn, 33347, Pte., d. of w., F., 4/2/17.

SMITH, J. H. A., b. London, 58011, Pte., k. in a., F., 27/8/18.

SMITH, P. H., b. London, 45557, Pte., k. in a., F., 29/8/18.

SMITH, R. J. L., b. Llandudno, 16067, Pte., d. of w., F., 30/7/17.

SOUTHERN, R. H., b. Bolton, 291667, Pte., k. in a., F., 26/8/18.

SPEED, H. S., b. Hoole, 238104, Pte., k. in a., F., 31/8/18.

SPEIGHT, W., b. Dewsbury, 18163, Pte., k. in a., F., 6/7/16.

SPEIGHT, W. W., b. Carlton, 72810, Pte., k. in a., F., 1/8/17.

SPENCER, F., b. Warrington, 92721, Pte., k. in a., F., 8/10/18.

SPRINGER, E. R., b. Barbadoes, 27894, Pte., k. in a., F., 2/6/16.

STEVENSON, F., b. Derby, 56080, Pte., d. of w., F., 8/10/18.

STOCK, A., b. Caerphilly, 57465, A/Sgt., d. of w., F., 23/4/18.

STONE, H. I., b. Talywain, 91420, Pte., d. of w., F., 1/9/18.

STONE, J. E., b. Salford, 58160, Pte., d. of w., F., 18/9/18.

STOOK, T., b. Newbridge, 58022, Pte., d. of w., F., 17/9/18.

SUTCLIFFE, H., b. Oldham, 235458, Pte., k. in a., F., 3/7/18.

SWARBRICK, W., b. Preston, 58163, Pte., k. in a., F., 28/8/18.

TANNER, A., b. Dalston, 27828, Pte., d. of w., F., 12/7/16.

TARLING, A., b. Blanfort, 61420, Pte., k. in a., F., 10/3/18.

TARRY, J. G., b. London, 56074, Cpl., d. of w., F., 28/8/18.

TAVERNOR, A., b. Salford, 42355, Pte., d. of w., F., 4/5/18.

TAYLOR, D. G., b. Swansea, 76425, Pte., k. in a., F., 19/9/18.

TAYLOR, G. E., b. Ross, 92723, Pte., k. in a., F., 3/9/18.

TAYLOR, H., b. Middleton, 42356, Pte., k. in a., F., 4/9/17.

TAYLOR, J., b. Manchester, 58026, Pte., k. in a., F., 9/8/18.

THOMAS, A., b. Rhosymedre, 15857, Sgt., d., F., 1/4/17.

THOMAS, D., b. Taibach, 19933, L/Cpl., k. in a., F., 18/2/16.

THOMAS, D., e. Carnarvon, 54662, Pte., k. in a., F., 23/8/18.

THOMAS, E. O., b. Llangefni, 55418, Pte., d. of w., Home, 17/5/18.

THOMAS, F. J., b. Briton Ferry, 17595, L/Cpl., d. of w., F., 10/7/16.

THOMAS, H. J., b. Rhondda, 18057, Pte., k. in a., F., 10/7/16.

THOMAS, J., b. Briton Ferry, 17167, L/Sgt., k. in a., F., 10/7/16.

THOMAS, J., b. Ruabon, 16013, Pte., d. of w., F., 10/7/16.

THOMAS, J. E., b. Bolton, 39726, Pte., k. in a., F., 23/8/18.

THOMAS, J. W. C., b. Hackney Weir, 22164, L/Cpl., k. in a., F., 5/11/18.

THOMAS, M. H., b. Blaina, 88830, Pte., d. of w., F., 29/10/18.

THOMAS, O., b. Blaenavon, 88896, Pte., d. of w., F., 16/11/18.

THOMAS, T., b. Ponkey, 17116, Cpl., k. in a., F., 22/4/18.

THOMAS, T., b. Pwllheli, 54835, Pte., k. in a., F., 1/4/17.

THOMAS, W., b. Llysfaen, 54664, Pte., k. in a., F., 27/8/18.

THOMAS, W., b. Bootle, 58024, Pte., k. in a., F., 23/8/18.

THOMAS, W. P., b. Llanrug, 78054, Pte., d. of w., F., 30/9/18.

THOMPSON, A., b. Tingley, 16594, Sgt., k. in a., F., 7/6/16.

THOMPSON, E., b. Lancaster, 93515, Pte., k. in a., F., 1/9/18.

THORNE, A., b. Maesteg, 292209, Pte., d. of w., F., 24/8/17.

TONGE, P., e. Wrexham, 24794, Pte., k. in a., F., 31/7/17.

TOPPING, H., b. Huddersfield, 17929, L/Cpl., k. in a., F., 22/4/18.

TRAVERS, D., b. St. Helens, 45515, Pte., k. in a., F., 22/4/18.

TROW, T. H., b. Salford, 24122, Cpl., k. in a., F., 12/5/16.

TURNER, E., b. Ruabon, 15909, Pte., k. in a., F., 31/7/17.

TURNER, W. J., b. Welshpool, 89612, Pte., d. of w., F., 17/11/18.

TURTINGTON, J., b. Blackburn, 46924, Pte., k. in a., F., 30/8/18.

TUTE, S., b. Manchester, 58168, Pte., k. in a., F., 8/10/18.

TYLER, H. J., b. Swansea, 16592, Pte., k. in a., F., 10/7/16.

VOWLES, O., b. Hailsea, 15606, Pte., d. of w., F., 24/8/18.

WALLING, J. L., b. Preston Patrick, 58032, Pte., k. in a., F., 23/8/18.

WALTHO, A., b. Armitage, 18640, Cpl., d. of w., F., 6/8/17.

WALTON, S., b. Bromley, 22476, Pte., k. in a., F., 10/7/16.

WARBURTON, E., b. Birkenhead, 91036, Pte., d. of w., F., 9/11/18.

WARE, E. E., b. Nottingham, 56082, L/Cpl., k. in a., F., 8/10/18.

WARREN, W., b. Cardiff, 38700, Pte., k. in a., F., 22/4/18, M.M.

WATKINS, A., b. Lyonshall, 92729, Pte., k. in a., F., 2/9/18.

WATKINS, C., b. Pontypridd, 88702, Pte., k. in a., F., 4/11/18.

WATKINS, F. N., b. St. Asaph, 17137, Pte., k. in a., F., 26/6/17.

WATKINS, J. E., b. Wrexham, 17126, Pte., k. in a., F., 13/1/16.

WATKINS, L. W., b. Tredegar, 89006, Pte., d. of w., F., 4/11/18.

WATKINSON, H., b. Liverpool, 16774, L/Cpl., k. in a., F., 27/8/16.

WATSON, W., b. Manchester, 24310, Pte., d., F., 10/11/18.

WEED, W., b. Sutton Bridge, 16913, L/Cpl., k. in a., F., 10/7/16.

WELSH, W. W. J., b. Seacombe, 66247, Pte., k. in a., F., 31/7/17.

WESTAWAY, W., b. Pontypridd, 69956, Pte., k. in a., F., 1/9/18.

WHITE, C., b. Tilshead, 235309, Cpl., d. of w., F., 27/7/17.

WHITE, R. J., e. London, 44398, Sgt., k. in a., F., 26/8/18.

WHITE, T., b. Waterfoot, 204563, Pte., k. in a., F., 26/8/18.

WHITEHEAD, A., b. Mold, 15858, Cpl., k. in a., F., 10/7/16.

WHITEHURST, C., b. Cardiff, 23589, Pte., d. of w., F., 17/5/18.

WHITSON, H., b. Whitehaven, 58180, Pte., d. of w., F., 29/8/18.

WHITTAKER, A., b. Burnley, 58044, Pte., k. in a., F., 23/8/18.

WHYMAN, J. W., b. Manchester, 56091, Pte., k. in a., F., 8/10/18.

WILCOCK, W., b. Hawarden, 17382, Pte., k. in a., F., 31/7/17.

WILLIAMS, A., b. Bridgend, 17102, Pte., d. of w., F., 12/7/16.

WILLIAMS, B., b. Mold, 16493, Cpl., k. in a., F., 10/7/16.

WILLIAMS, D., b. Llandegar, 16844, Pte., d., Home, 10/5/15.

WILLIAMS, E., b. Abergele, 17613, Pte., k. in a., F., 10/7/16.

WILLIAMS, E., b. Llangristiolus, 28342, Pte., k. in a., F., 20/10/18.

WILLIAMS, E., b. Penegroes, 45167, L/Cpl., d. of w., Home, 11/10/18, D.C.M.

WILLIAMS, E., b. Brymbo, 16938, Pte., k. in a., F., 6/12/16.

WILLIAMS, E., b. Ysbylty, 37238, L/Cpl., d. of w., F., 13/11/17.

WILLIAMS, E., b. Holyhead, 89453, Pte., k. in a., F., 20/10/18.

WILLIAMS, E. H., b. Ellesmere Port, 17419, Pte., k. in a., F., 10/7/16.

WILLIAMS, H., b. Ruabon, 16979, Pte., k. in a., F., 20/2/16.

WILLIAMS, H. D., b. Cynwyd, 40791, Pte., k. in a., F., 23/8/18.

WILLIAMS, J., b. Pentraeth, 37465, L/Cpl., d. of w., F., 24/4/18.

WILLIAMS, J. L., e. Hanley, 61183, Pte., k. in a., F., 2/9/17.

WILLIAMS, J. L., b. Gyffin, Carn., 77222, Pte., k. in a., F., 29/8/18.

WILLIAMS, J. R., b. Llanllechid, 19845, Pte., k. in a., F., 23/8/18.

WILLIAMS, J. T., b. Ruabon, 28286, Pte., k. in a., F., 22/4/18.

WILLIAMS, L., b. Rhyl, 16442, Pte., k. in a., F., 10/7/16.

WILLIAMS, L., b. Glyn Ceiriog, 18899, Pte., k. in a., F., 12/5/17.

WILLIAMS, M. L., b. Denbigh, 23367, Pte., k. in a., F., 10/7/16.

WILLIAMS, O., b. Anglesey, 31354, Pte., d. of w., F., 28/8/16.

WILLIAMS, P., b. Beaumaris, 17370, Pte., k. in a., F., 10/7/16.

WILLIAMS, R., b. Llandegfan, 17231, Pte., k. in a., F., 30/5/16.

WILLIAMS, R., b. Corwen, 61038, Pte., k. in a., F., 22/4/18.

WILLIAMS, R. O., b. Llanddeiniolen, 40172, Pte., k. in a., F., 22/4/18.

WILLIAMS, T. J., b. Neath, 18029, Pte., k. in a., F., 10/7/16.

WILLIAMS, T. J., b. Llanfairtalhaiarn, 60966, Pte., k. in a., F., 22/4/18.

WILLIAMS, W. M., b. Dyserth, 58030, Pte., k. in a., F., 27/8/18.

WILLIAMS, W. O., b. Prestatyn, 37165, Pte., k. in a., F., 31/7/17.

WILLIAMSON, R. W., b. Ludworth, 93530, Pte., k. in a., F., 29/8/18.

WILLS, J., b. Warrington, 93522, Pte., d. of w., F., 30/9/18.

WILMAN, B., b. Salford, 58171, Pte., k. in a., F., 29/8/18.

WILSON, A., b. Norwich, 27375, Pte., k. in a., F., 22/4/18.

WILSON, E., b. Swansea, 33594, Pte., k. in a., F., 27/8/18.

WINTON, D., e. Hawarden, 241012, Pte., k. in a., F., 1/9/18.

WOLFE, S., b. London, 235296, Pte., d. of w., F., 1/8/17.

WOLVERSON, E., b. Sedgeley, 17392, Cpl., d. of w., F., 1/8/17.

WOOD, F., b. London, 26660, Pte., k. in a., F., 26/8/16.

WOOD, J., b. Manchester, 58043, Pte., k. in a., F., 11/9/18.

WORTHY, W. F., b. Newport, 93518, Pte., k. in a., F., 1/9/18.

WRENCH, S., b. Guilden, 58036, Pte., k. in a., F., 23/8/18.

WRIDE, W. J., b. Rhondda, 267953, Pte., d. of w., F., 28/8/18.

WRIGHT, A. S., b. Grantham, 58028, Pte., d. of w., F., 4/9/18.

WRIGHT, H. A., b. Salford, 58034, Pte., d. of w., F., 28/8/18.

WRIGHT, W. C. M., b. Newport, 43928, L/Cpl., d. of w., F., 16/9/18.

WYATT, J., b. Ruabon, 17412, Pte., k. in a., F., 10/7/16.

YAPP, T. C., b. Blaenavon, 88759, Pte., k. in a., F., 8/10/18.

YOUNG, T. A., b. Hale, 45672, Pte., k. in a., F., 29/8/18.

14th BATTALION

ADDIS, J. W., b. Llanfwrog, 21064, Pte., d. of w., F., 7/7/16.

ADDIS, W. J., b. Townhope, 235585, Pte., k. in a., F., 29/12/17.

AIMES, C., b. Accrington, 20887, Pte., k. in a., F., 22/4/16.

ALDERSON, H. T., b. Llanfair P.G., 21215, Pte., d., F., 7/6/17.

ANKERS, J. H., b. Chester, 66100, Pte., k. in a., F., 23/8/18.

ANTHONY, W. R., b. Wrexham, 39969, Pte., d. of w., F., 1/2/17.

ARCHIBALD, E., b. Rhosddu, 11469, Pte., k. in a., F., 7/3/18.

ASHTON, W., b. St. Helens, 20924, Pte., k. in a., F., 10/7/16.

ASHWORTH, H., b. Heywood, 80201, Pte., d. of w., F., 7/10/18.

ASPIN, G., b. Blackburn, 21017, Pte., k. in a., F., 5/9/17.

ATKINS, B., b. Pontypridd, 21409, Pte., k. in a., F., 6/7/16.

AWBERY, G. W., e. Birkenhead, 75946, Pte., k. in a., F., 22/4/18.

BALDERSTON, J., b. Ulverston, 58223, Pte., k. in a., F., 28/8/18.

BARNETT, J., b. Hartshill, 21067, Sgt., d. of w., F., 23/4/18.

BEAUCHAMP, T., b. Edinburgh, 67682, Pte., k. in a., F., 22/4/18.

BEAUMONT, W., b. Dukinfield, 56400, Pte., k. in a., F., 18/9/18.

BEDDOES, A., b. Dudley, 241797, Pte., k. in a., F., 22/4/18.

BELLIS, J., b. Bagillt, 20527, Pte., k. in a., F., 14/2/17.

BENNETT, D., b. Llanelly, 94375, Pte., k. in a., F., 6/11/18.

BENNETT, W. J., b. Connahs Quay, 20707, L/Cpl., k. in a., F., 10/7/16.

BENTLEY, F., b. Glossop, 55320, Pte., k. in a., F., 18/2/17.

BENYON, W., b. Parr, 13609, Pte., k. in a., F., 2/9/17.

BIRCH, W., b. Wolverhampton, 266983, Pte., d. of w., F., 1/9/17.

BITHELL, T., b. Mostyn, 20852, Pte., k. in a., F., 5/6/16.

BLACKBURN, R., b. Seaforth, 75949, Pte., k. in a., F., 22/4/18.

BLACKWELL, P. H., b. Ffynnon Groew, 20532, Cpl., k. in a., F., 10/7/16.

BOOME, C. H., b. London, 21992, Pte., d. of w., F., 8/10/18.

BOREHAM, P., b. Bethnal Green, 34746, Pte., k. in a., F., 10/7/16.

BOULTON, W. J., b. Cardiff, 80207, Pte., k. in a., F., 18/9/18.

BRADFORD, J. C., b. London, 26805, Pte., k. in a., F., 6/7/16.

BRAMMER, J., b. Smallthorne,

30008, Pte., d. of w., Home, 18/6/18.

BREES, D., b. Mallwyd, 55318, Pte., k. in a., F., 18/2/17.

BROCK, J. I., b. Tregarth, 267871, Pte., k. in a., F., 2/9/17.

BROWN, F., b. Astely Bridge, 58222, Pte., k. in a., F., 28/8/18.

BROWN, J., b. Liverpool, 58220, Pte., k. in a., F., 27/8/18.

BROWN, R., b. Glasgow, 29065, Pte., d. of w., F., 23/4/18.

BROWN, W., b. Devonport, 80208, Pte., k. in a., F., 18/9/18, M.M.

BURGESS, C., b. Clitheroe, 73320, Pte., d., F., 9/6/18.

BURGESS, E., b. Cardiff, 13387, L/Cpl., k. in a., F., 23/8/18.

BUSHELL, A., b. Liverpool, 315200, Pte., k. in a., F., 22/4/18.

BUTCHERS, T., b. Llanelly, 20133, Pte., k. in a., F., 10/7/16.

CALDON, P. W., b. Cardiff, 75302, Pte., k. in a., F., 26/8/18.

CALLOW, J., b. Bolton, 20104, L/Cpl., k. in a., F., 8/7/16.

CANN, P. C., b. Liverpool, 80218, Pte., k. in a., F., 18/9/18.

CARR, R. S., b. Cheadle, 56381, Pte., k. in a., F., 22/4/18.

CARTER, L., b. Warrington, 240472, A/Sgt., k. in a., F., 22/4/18.

CARTER, P., b. Cardiff, 77319, Pte., d. of w., F., 4/11/18.

CARTER, R., b. Burton, 39657, Pte., k. in a., F., 7/12/17.

CHASE, E., b. Whitchurch, 55325, Pte., k. in a., F., 15/6/17.

CHATER, S. F., b. Dalston, 34842, Pte., k. in a., F., 2/9/17.

CHATHAM, S., b. Llanelly, 18801, Sgt., k. in a., F., 20/10/18.

CHESTERS, R., b. Little Drayton, 93314, Pte., d. of w., F., 21/10/18.

CHESWORTH, A., b. Haydock, 20918, Pte., k. in a., F., 10/7/16.

CHICK, A., b. Penarth, 58226, Pte., k. in a., F., 27/8/18.

CLARKE, R., b. Bridgend, 20417, Pte., k. in a., F., 6/7/16.

CLITHEROE, F., b. Burnley, 58238, Pte., k. in a., F., 18/9/18.

CLOUGH, H., b. Salford, 73333, Pte., k. in a., F., 18/9/18.

COGHLIN, W. H., b. Swansea, 292194, Pte., d. of w., F., 1/11/18.

COLKETT, H. T., b. Custom House, 34763, Pte., k. in a., F., 6/7/16.

COLLETT, C. R., b. Wisbech, 55856, Pte., k. in a., F., 2/9/18.

COLLIER, J., b. Ardwick, 58230, Pte., k. in a., F., 18/9/18.

COLYER, A. E., b. London, 34949, Pte., k. in a., F., 6/7/16.

COLYER, G., b. London, 34883, Pte., k. in a., F., 6/7/16.

COOK, G., b. London, 27333, L/Cpl., k. in a., F., 2/9/17.

COOK, P. W., b. Halstead, 55853, Pte., d. of w., F., 18/9/18.

COOKE, B., b. Middlewich, 88401, Pte., k. in a., F., 6/10/18.

COOKE, W. J., b. Glam., 20778, Pte., k. in a., F., 10/7/16.

COOKSON, J. L., b. Preston, 52595, Pte., d. of w., F., 20/10/18, D.C.M.

COOPER, F., b. West Kirby, 20515, Pte., k. in a., F., 8/10/18.

COOPER, R. P., b. London, 27893, Pte., k. in a., F., 22/4/18.

COOPER, S. J., b. London, 34852, Pte., k. in a., F., 6/7/16.

CORDWELL, G. W., b. London, 55858, Pte., k. in a., F., 24/6/17.

COTTRELL, J., b. Ashton-under-Lyne, 21256, Pte., k. in a., F., 5/6/16.

COULBURN, G. H. F., b. West Houghton, 75941, Pte., k. in a., F., 22/4/18.

COULDEN, T. R., b. London, 27034, Pte., d. of w., F., 28/12/16.

COULSON, H., b. London, 34750, Pte., d. of w., F., 12/7/16.

COX, E., b. Davenham, 56377, Pte., k. in a., F., 24/7/17.

CRAY, A. E., b. London, 22849, L/Sgt., k. in a., F., 22/4/18.

CRESSWELL, G., b. Merthyr, 315425, Pte., k. in a., F., 18/9/18.

CROCOMBE, S., e. Flint, 240807, Pte., k. in a., F., 2/9/17.

CROSSMAN, F., b. The Hythe, 55824, Pte., k. in a., F., 22/4/18.

CROUCH, C., b. Stockwell, 60265, Pte., d. of w., F., 3/8/17.

CROUCH, W., b. King's Cross, 34581, Pte., d., F., 27/6/17.

CUFF, J., b. Preston, 291623, L/Cpl., d. of w., F., 28/10/18.

CUNCLIFFE, R., b. Billings, 20094, L/Cpl., k. in a., F., 7/5/16.

CUNNIFF, J., b. Oldham, 58235, Pte., k. in a., F., 25/6/18.

DALE, R., b. Bagillt, 20847, Pte., k. in a., F., 2/3/16.

DALLIMERE, A. V., b. Cardiff, 58202, Sgt., d. of w., F., 13/10/18, M.M.

DANE, H., b. Crewe, 23257, Cpl., k. in a., F., 26/8/18.

DANIELS, G. H., b. London, 26938, Pte., k. in a., F., 10/7/16.

DANIELS, R., b. Seacombe, 20797, Pte., k. in a., F., 10/7/16.

DARBYSHIRE, W., b. Pilkington, 55327, Pte., k. in a., F., 15/6/17.

DAVIES, C., b. Hawarden, 20796, Pte., k. in a., F., 6/5/16.

DAVIES, D. B., b. Gwernogle, 94368, Pte., d. of w., F., 10/11/18.

DAVIES, D. H., b. Dinorwic, 40370, Pte., k. in a., F., 31/7/17.

DAVIES, E., b. Cardiff, 56869, L/Cpl., d. of w., F., 3/5/17.

DAVIES, E. L., b. Neath, 20842, L/Sgt., k. in a., F., 18/2/17.

DAVIES, E. T., e. Welshpool, 55329, Pte., k. in a., F., 18/2/17.

DAVIES, F. W., b. Newtown, 235330, Pte., k. in a., F., 22/4/18.

DAVIES, G., b. Llandudno, 20018, Sgt., k. in a., F., 6/7/16.

DAVIES, G., b. Broughton, 78090, Pte., d. of w., F., 8/10/18.

DAVIES, G., b. Trefriw, 21119, Pte., k. in a., F., 6/7/16.

DAVIES, I., b. Aberdare, 235616, Pte., k. in a., F., 23/8/18.

DAVIES, J. J., b. Church, 20387, Pte., k. in a., F., 10/7/16.

DAVIES, M. H., b. London, 21595, Pte., k. in a., F., 29/12/17.

DAVIES, M. O., e. Wrexham, 57073, Pte., k. in a., F., 28/8/18.

DAVIES, M. R., b. Llanwrda, 58397, Pte., k. in a., F., 24/8/18.

DAVIES, T., b. Llanrug, 37037, Pte., k. in a., F., 10/7/16.

DAVIES, T. A., b. Denbigh, 315043, Sgt., k. in a., F., 18/9/18.

DAVIES, W. L., b. Coity, 20662, Pte., k. in a., F., 17/5/16.

DAVIES, W. M., b. Blaenau Festiniog, 55330, Pte., k. in a., F., 21/1/17.

DAVIES, W. T., b. Penbangk, 27401, Pte., k. in a., F., 8/11/17.

DAVIES, T. G., b. London, 21873, Pte., k. in a., F., 1/9/16.

DEAKIN, W. A., b. Salford, 37035, Pte., k. in a., F., 9/7/16.

DENHAM, J., e. Shaw, 58243, Pte., d. of w., F., 7/10/18.

DICKENS, P. R., b. Walthamstow, 44998, Pte., k. in a., F., 30/8/18.

DICKINSON, W., e. Manchester, 58244, Pte., d. of w., F., 24/8/18.

DOUBLEDAY, C., b. Saltney, 4279, Pte., k. in a., F., 18/2/17.

DOYLE, J. T., b. Manchester, 292264, Pte., k. in a., F., 22/4/18.

DUGDALE, S., b. Brierfield, 58245, Pte., k. in a., F., 24/8/18.

DUGGAN, J., b. London, 21923, Pte., k. in a., F., 31/10/16.

DUNFORD, W. H., b. Dowlais Top, 80221, Pte., k. in a., F., 5/10/18.

DUNKS, C., b. London, 27513, Pte., k. in a., F., 23/8/18.

EASTHAM, W., b. Blackburn, 20882, Pte., k. in a., F., 18/2/17.

EDGE, S., e. Wrexham, 57047, Cpl., k. in a., F., 6/11/18, M.M.

EDWARDS, A., b. Oswestry, 55334, Pte., k. in a., F., 18/2/17.

EDWARDS, G. D., b. Llanllechio, 37335, L/Sgt., d. of w., F., 2/5/18.

EDWARDS, J. W., b. Llangwm, 21160, Pte., d. of w., F., 11/7/16.

EDWARDS, R., b. Bangor, 55339, Pte., k. in a., F., 24/2/17.

EGDEN, H. L., b. Salford, 291628, Pte., d. of w., F., 2/9/17.

EGERTON, H. E., b. Whitford, 21305, C.S.M., k. in a., F., 26/8/18.

ELLIS, E. T., b. Minera, 87475, Pte., k. in a., F., 20/10/18.

ELLIS, J. S., b. Bala, 21166, Pte., k. in a., F., 6/7/16.

EVANS, A., b. Llanarmon, 61026, Pte., d., F., 25/10/18.

EVANS, A. E., b. Neath, 20859, Pte., d. of w., F., 8/7/16.

EVANS, A. E., b. Mold, 20743, Pte., k. in a., F., 27/2/16.

EVANS, D., b. Ogmore Vale, 20183, Sgt., k. in a., F., 4/11/18.

EVANS, D. I., b. Cwmparc, 80225, Pte., k. in a., F., 18/9/18.

EVANS, D. J., b. Ebbw Vale, 94394, Pte., k. in a., F., 5/11/18.

EVANS, E. T., e. Flint, 240879, Pte., k. in a., F., 6/11/18.

EVANS, H. A., b. Liverpool, 63444, Pte., d. of w., F., 2/8/17.

EVANS, H. P., b. Derwenlas, 235410, Pte., k. in a., F., 4/8/17.

EVANS, J. H., b. Gowerton, 292314, Pte., k. in a., F., 26/8/18.

EVANS, J. L., b. Ruthin, 37656, Pte., d. of w., F., 7/9/18.

EVANS, R. H., b. Llanwrug, 21105, A/Sgt., k. in a., F., 24/7/17.

EVANS, R. J., b. Llannwchllyn, 21290, Pte., d. of w., Home, 8/9/10.

EVANS, R. T., b. Bagillt, 20717, L/Cpl., k. in a., F., 10/7/16.

EVANS, T., b. Penygroes, 20066, Pte., k. in a., F., 10/7/16.

EVANS, T. B., b. Merthyr, 34080, Pte., d., F., 19/8/17.

EVANS, W., b. Swansea, 56870, L/Cpl., k. in a., F., 18/2/17.

FARR, D. J., b. Rhondda, 21287, Pte., k. in a., F., 6/7/16.

FARRAGE, G., b. Coed-Ffranc, 20873, Sgt., k. in a., F., 12/4/16.

FARRINGTON, W., b. Manchester, 31428, Pte., k. in a., F., 5/8/17.

FARTHING, A., b. London, 34833, Pte., k. in a., F., 18/2/17.

FELLOWS, E., b. Delamere, 55342, Pte., d. of w., F., 27/8/18.

FENN, A. R., b. Fressingfield, 55945, Pte., k. in a., F., 15/6/17.

FENNAH, J., b. Hawarden, 21016, Pte., d. of w., F., 10/7/16.

FIELD, H. J., b. Walthamstow, 26841, Pte., d. of w., F., 7/7/16.

FINNEY, C., b. Forden, 55341, Pte., k. in a., F., 28/8/18.

FISHER, A., b. Audenshaw, 21458, Pte., k. in a., F., 3/5/16.

FITCHEN, H., b. London, 28159, Pte., k. in a., F., 20/4/18.

FITZGIBBONS, J., b. London, 22135, Pte., k. in a., F., 24/6/17.

FLANNIGAN, J. H., b. Maryport, 315051, Pte., k. in a., F., F., 18/9/18.

FLAXINGTON, J., b. Bradford, 33274, L/Cpl., d. of w., F., 3/5/18.

FLITCROFT, C., b. Bolton, 73958, Pte., d., Home, 3/12/17.

FORD, R. F., b. Clitheroe, 46780, Pte., k. in a., F., 23/8/18.

FORMSTONE, J., b. Gresford, 60782, Pte., k. in a., F., 9/5/18.

FOWLER, C. G., b. St. Peter's, 80231, Pte., k. in a., F., 18/9/18.

FOX, G., b. London, 36685, Pte., k. in a., F., 26/7/17.

FOX, P., b. Flint, 20565, Pte., d. of w., Home, 16/7/17.

FRAMPTON, A., b. Portsmouth, 54256, Sgt., k. in a., F., 4/8/17.

FRANCIS, G., b. St. Helens, 28413, Pte., k. in a., F., 23/8/18.

FRANCIS, J. T., b. Burton Wood, 60069, Pte., k. in a., F., 31/7/17.

FRENCH, J. W., b. London, 56378, Pte., k. in a., F., 22/4/18.

FROST, J., b. Wimbish, 55862, Cpl., k. in a., F., 21/6/18.

GABRIEL, A. E., b. Warrington, 20656, L/Cpl., k. in a., F., 2/9/17.

GATLEY, H., b. Llandudno, 20039, Pte., k. in a., F., 7/10/16.

GONNING, W. A., b. London, 27771, Pte., k. in a., F., 10/7/16.

GRANTHAM, H., b. Wilmslow, 55350, Pte., d. of w., F., 24/4/18.

GREEN, A. J., e. London, 24827, Pte., k. in a., F., 24/6/17.

GREENHALGH, E., b. Church, 20897, Pte., d. of w., F., 26/4/18.

GRIFFITH, E., b. Bryncroes, 21330, Pte., k. in a., F., 9/7/16.

GRIFFITHS, C. T., b. Warrington,

315239, Pte., k. in a., F., 20/9/18.

GRIFFITHS, E., b. Ponkey, 69817, Pte., k. in a., F., 26/8/18.

GRIFFITHS, G., b. Ystradfelltae, 21222, Pte., k. in a., F., 31/8/17.

GRIFFITHS, G., b. Rhoshirwaen, 61134, Pte., k. in a., F., 22/4/18.

GRIFFITHS, H. P., b. Bangor, 20752, Pte., d. of w., F., 19/6/16.

GRIFFITHS, J., b. Liverpool, 49885, Pte., k. in a., F., 18/9/18.

GRIFFITHS, J., e. Tonypandy, 19087, Pte., k. in a., F., 23/7/17.

GRIFFITHS, M. H., b. Mold, 21488, Pte., k. in a., F., 25/2/17.

GRIFFITHS, R., b. Almamynytho, 20817, Pte., k. in a., F., 10/7/16.

GRIFFITHS, R. R., b. Croesor, 21080, L/Cpl., k. in a., F., 31/1/17.

GRIFFITHS, T., b. Llanfaelog, 33290, Pte., d., F., 18/11/16.

GRIFFITHS, W., b. Rhydbach, 20488, Pte., k. in a., F., 10/7/16.

GRIFFITHS, W. D., b. Fishguard, 33986, Pte., d. of w., F., 30/8/17.

GRIFFITHS, W. J., b. Dolgelly, 39515, Pte., k. in a., F., 2/9/17.

GRIFFITHS, W. T., b. Brymbo, 87471, Pte., k. in a., F., 7/10/18.

GROVES, T., b. Pontypridd, 19512, Pte., k. in a., F., 10/7/16.

GUILFOYLE, J., b. Clayton-le-Moors, 20398, Pte., d., F., 30/5/16.

GUNNER, G., b. Cardiff, 56875, Pte., k. in a., F., 2/9/17.

HALL, W., b. Greenock, 25383, Pte., k. in a., F., 10/7/16, M.M.

HALLARD, A. W., b. Manchester, 33343, L/Cpl., d. of w., F., 1/9/18.

HAMPSHIRE, J., b. Wakefield, 63440, Pte., k. in a., F., 4/8/17.

HANDLEY, T. W., b. Glazeley, 241749, Pte., k. in a., F., 26/8/18.

HANSFORD, W. G. W., b. London, 27835, Pte., k. in a., F., 9/7/16.

HARDMAN, A., b. St. Helens, 20919, L/Cpl., d., F., 1/6/16.

HARRIS, R., b. Llandudno, 20454, Pte., k. in a., F., 2/9/17.

HATT, W. H., b. London, 34608, Pte., k. in a., F., 5/6/16.

HAWKINS, J. A., b. Treforest, 20965, Pte., d. of w., F., 9/7/16.

HAYES, W. V., b. Chester, 44131, Pte., k. in a., F., 21/6/18.

HAYWARD, A., b. Pontypridd, 20783, Pte., k. in a., F., 5/6/16.

HAYWARD, E. H., b. Cardiff, 56879, Pte., k. in a., F., 18/9/18.

HAYWARD, S., b. Cowbridge, 20893, L/Cpl., k. in a., F., 24/6/17.

HEMMING, F. W. E., b. London, 55953, Pte., k. in a., F., 18/9/18.

HILL, A. S., b. London, 27463, Pte., k. in a., F., 10/7/16.

HINDLEY, E., b. Newton, 29091, Pte., k. in a., F., 18/9/18.

HOBBS, S. R., b. Neath, 26911, Pte., k. in a., F., 9/7/16.

HODGE, V. L., b. Manchester, 241687, Pte., k. in a., F., 31/7/17.

HODSKINSON, H., b. Burwardsley, 56372, Pte., k. in a., F., 22/4/18.

HOLLIDAY, T. H., b. Ivegell, 46809, L/Cpl., k. in a., F., 22/4/18.

HOLMES, B., b. Dalton, 241683, Pte., d. of w., F., 5/8/17.

HOPSON, W., b. Leytonstone, 35179, Pte., k. in a., F., 10/7/16.

HOURIHAN, J., b. London, 34613, Pte., k. in a., F., 5/6/16.

HOUSTON, A., b. Ventnor, 20008, Pte., d., Home, 18/5/15.

HOWELLS, W. H., b. Llantwit Major, 20895, C.S.M., k. in a., F., 3/3/16.

HUGHES, D. W., e. Queen's Ferry, 241045, Pte., k. in a., F., 25/8/18.

HUGHES, H. T., b. Ynyscynhowrn, 21245, Pte., k. in a., F., 10/7/16.

HUGHES, J., b. Bethesda, 59675, Pte., d. of w., F., 13/5/18.

HUGHES, J., b. Cefn Mawr, 23371, Cpl., k. in a., F., 18/9/18.

HUGHES, J. N., b. Wrexham, 21342, Pte., d. of w., Home, 21/7/16.

HUGHES, J. R., b. Gwersylt, 88487, Pte., k. in a., F., 5/10/18.

HUGHES, L. C., b. Ponkey, 87412, Pte., d. of w., F., 8/10/18.

HUGHES, N. M., b. Shrewsbury, 56569, Pte., k. in a., F., 29/12/17.

HUGHES, R. J., b. Mochdre, 20024, Cpl., k. in a., F., 18/9/18.

HUGHES, R. S., b. Holywell, 20723, Pte., d., F., 10/2/16.

HUGHES, T. B., b. Gilfynydd, 20765, Pte., k. in a., F., 2/3/16.

HUGHES, W., b. Llanfathan, 18104, Pte., d. of w., F., 5/2/16.

HUGHES, W. J., b. Newport, 18184, Pte., k. in a., F., 10/12/16.

HUTT, H. D., b. Llandudno, 20131, L/Cpl., k. in a., F., 26/8/18.

INGRAM, G. E. H., b. Brighton, 22874, Pte., k. in a., F., 22/4/18.

IRELAND, J., b. Kirkham, 71797, Pte., d. of w., F., 16/10/18.

JACKSON, J. L., b. Bacup, 67778, L/Cpl., d. of w., F., 24/8/18.

JACKSON, S., b. Lower Peover, 75894, Pte., d., F., 4/7/18.

JACKSON, W. F., b. Newport, 235617, Pte., k. in a., F., 2/9/17.

JAMES, J., b. Mold, 21045, A/Cpl., k. in a., F., 10/7/16.

JAMES, T. R., b. Widnes, 21070, Cpl., k. in a., F., 2/3/16.

JENKINS, J., b. Pontrhydyfin, 17579, Pte., k. in a., F., 6/7/16.

JENKINS, T., b. Crynant, 21181, Cpl., d. of w., F., 28/8/18.

JOHN, D. B., b. Briton Ferry, 19835, Sgt., k. in a., F., 10/7/16.

JOHNSON, H., b. Leeds, 35553, Pte., k. in a., F., 18/9/18.

JOHNSON, W., b. Hope, 55355, Pte., k. in a., F., 18/2/17.

JONES, A. D., b. Llandudno Junction, 36799, L/Cpl., d. of w., F., 11/7/16.

JONES, C., b. Gwersyllt, 16781, Pte., k. in a., F., 13/10/18.

JONES, C., b. Gwersyllt, 23134, Pte., k. in a., F., 18/2/17.

JONES, C., b. Rhosnessney, 88553, Pte., k. in a., F., 7/10/18.

JONES, D. E., b. Manchester, 20699, Pte., k. in a., F., 10/7/16.

JONES, D. G., e. Neath, 89145, Pte., d., F., 29/10/18.

JONES, D. R., b. Llanberis, 21103, Pte., k. in a., F., 10/7/16.

JONES, E., e. Wrexham, 61338, Pte., k. in a., F., 4/8/17.

JONES, E., b. Wrexham, 37192, Pte., d. of w., F., 12/8/16.

JONES, E., b. Connah's Quay, 20589, Cpl., d. of w., F., 23/4/18, D.C.M., M.M. and Clasp.

JONES, E. O., b. Llandudno, 20163, Pte., k. in a., F., 5/6/16.

JONES, H., b. Manchester, 66631, Pte., k. in a., F., 2/9/17.

JONES, H., b. Llanrwst, 21037, L/Cpl., k. in a., F., 6/4/17.

JONES, H., b. Llandudno, 20092, Pte., k. in a., F., 2/9/17.

JONES, H., b. Bagillt, 20984, Pte., k. in a., F., 25/2/17.

JONES, H. D., b. Berriew, 73292, Pte., k. in a., F., 18/9/18.

JONES, H. J., b. Criccieth, 20583, Pte., k. in a., F., 24/12/15.

JONES, J., b. Llandudno, 20032, Pte., d. of w., F., 25/10/18.

JONES, J., b. Festiniog, 20274, Pte., k. in a., F., 31/1/17.

JONES, J. H., b. Ponkey, 87409, Pte., k. in a., F., 8/11/18.

JONES, J. H., e. Colwyn Bay, 240917, Pte., k. in a., F., 29/8/18.

JONES, J. M., b. Conway, 21375, Pte., k. in a., F., 18/3/16.

JONES, L., b. Llanrhyddlad, 21258, Pte., k. in a., F., 15/6/17.

JONES, L., b. Denbigh, 21392, Pte., k. in a., F., 6/7/16.

JONES, M. C., b. Wigan, 87488, Pte., d. of w., F., 15/10/18.

JONES, O. R., b. Holyhead, 20571, L/Cpl., k. in a., F., 20/3/16.

JONES, P., b. Trevor, 20977, L/Cpl., k. in a., F., 10/7/16.

JONES, P., b. Cefn, 54766, Pte., k. in a., F., 25/2/17.

JONES, R., b. Machen, 21124, Pte., k. in a., F., 6/5/16.

JONES, R., b. Mold, 21184, Pte., k. in a., F., 13/9/16.

JONES, R., b. Llanberis, 21102, Pte., k. in a., F., 23/8/18.

JONES, R., b. Bootle, 20006, Pte., k. in a., F., 19/3/16.

JONES, R., b. Pembrey, 20187, Pte., k. in a., F., 11/7/16.

JONES, R., b. Corwen, 20824, Pte., k. in a., F., 6/7/16.

JONES, R., b. Beaumaris, 24719, Pte., k. in a., F., 5/10/16.

JONES, R. D., b. Bangor, 21139, L/Cpl., k. in a., F., 25/7/16.

JONES, R. E., b. Machynlleth, 20432, Pte., d. of w., F., 24/12/15.

JONES, R. R., b. Blaenau Festiniog, 55359, Pte., k. in a., F., 19/2/17.

JONES, R. W., b. Llanllyfni, 20220, Pte., d. of w., F., 9/7/16.

JONES, S., b. Rhos, 87408, Pte., k. in a., F., 8/11/18.

JONES, T., b. Bettws-yn-Rhos, 5460, A/Cpl., k. in a., F., 28/8/18.

JONES, T., b. Llangar, 20378, Pte., d. of w., F., 5/6/16.

JONES, T. C., b. Bagillt, 21235, Pte., k. in a., F., 10/7/16, M.M.

JONES, T. H., b. Llanberis, 49870, Pte., k. in a., F., 21/6/18.

JONES, T. K., b. Llangastennin, 20335, Pte., k. in a., F., 6/7/16.

JONES, W., b. Llandegfan, 20931, Pte., k. in a., F., 10/7/16.

JONES, W., e. Colwyn Bay, 241150, L/Cpl., k. in a., F., 26/8/18.

JONES, W., b. Llandovery, 292188, Pte., k. in a., F., 26/8/18.

JONES, W. A., b. Llandefeilog, 56883, Pte., k. in a., F., 1/10/16.

JONES, W. E., b. London, 28015, L/Cpl., k. in a., F., 22/4/18.

JONES, W. R., b. Llangristrolus, 20973, Pte., k. in a., F., 31/7/17.

JONES, W. R., b. Towyn, 291187, Pte., k. in a., F., 31/8/17.

JONES, W. T., b. Carnarvon, 29639, Pte., k. in a., F., 20/10/18.

KAY, H., b. Darwen, 33150, L/Cpl. k. in a., F., 28/12/17.

KEEN, W., b. Longton, 17992, Pte., k. in a., F., 7/10/16.

KENIFICK, R. J., b. Aberavon, 94407, Pte., k. in a., F., 2/11/18.

KENYON, R., b. Cefn Mawr, 88384, Pte., k. in a., F., 8/10/18.

KENYON, W., b. Wigan, 67175, Pte., k. in a., F., 31/7/17.

KER, R. J., b. Liverpool, 66324, Pte., k. in a., F., 6/10/18.

KING, G., b. Pencoed, 21081, Pte., k. in a., F., 2/3/16.

KIRKMAN, W., b. Bolton, 20677, Pte., d. of w., F., 1/9/17.

KNIGHT, W., b. North Weald, 55869, Pte., k. in a., F., 23/8/18.

LANCELOTTE, C., b. Chester, 56396, Pte., k. in a., F., 4/8/17.

LANG, J., b. Blackburn, 20443, Sgt., k. in a., F., 18/9/18.

LATHAM, R., b. Connah's Quay, 20706, L/Sgt., d. of w., F., 5/10/18.

LAVIN, A., b. Ashton-under-Lyne, 55298, Pte., d. of w., F., 23/4/18.

LEAKE, S., b. Hanley, 17907, Pte., k. in a., F., 23/8/18.

LEAKER, A. E., b. Locking, 235607, Pte., k. in a., F., 3/12/17.

LEAMAN, S., b. Dawlish, 21134, Pte., k. in a., F., 6/10/18.

LEAR, W., b. Longton, 56106, L/Cpl., d. of w., F., 9/6/18.

LEATHERS, A., b. S. Elm, 55839, Pte., k. in a., F., 22/4/18.

LESLIE, A. J., b. Mitcham, 27420, Pte., d. of w., F., 1/8/17.

LEWIS, E., b. Machynlleth, 55299, Pte., d. of w., F., 24/2/17.

LEWIS, E., b. Llanwnnog, 291026, Pte., k. in a., F., 8/10/18.

LEWIS, J., b. Woking, 34910, Pte., k. in a., F., 11/4/16.

LEWIS, J. H., b. Carnarvon, 37349, Pte., k. in a., F., 9/7/16.

LEWIS, T., b. Llanfairynghornwy, 20513, Pte., k. in a., F., 6/7/16.

LEWIS, W., b. Llenfechell, 20476, Pte., k. in a., F., 9/7/16.

LING, O., b. Blaina, 20663, Pte., k. in a., F., 4/9/18.

LIVERMORE, S., b. Southminster, 55870, Pte., k. in a., F., 28/8/18.

LLOYD, A., b. Penmynydd, 291946, Pte., d. of w., F., 12/10/18.

LLOYD, J., b. Dolgelly, 20188, Cpl., k. in a., F., 1/9/17.

LLOYD, M., b. Llangefysant, 61528, Pte., k. in a., F., 28/8/18.

LOMAX, J. S., b. Atherton, 21430, Pte., d. of w., F., 7/7/16.

LOMBARDINE, A., b. Cardiff, 56891, Pte., d. of w., F., 21/1/17.

LOVE, S., b. Penarth, 20781, Pte., k. in a., F., 22/4/18.

LOVELESS, E., b. Bristol, 20199, L/Cpl., k. in a., F., 23/8/18.

LOWE, L., b. Ashton-under-Lyne, 20836, Pte., k. in a., F., 9/7/16.

LUNT, C., b. Weston, 20141, Pte., d. of w., F., 19/7/16.

MACKINTOSH, S., b. Walton, 66910, Pte., k. in a., F., 25/8/18.

MADDOCKS, W., b. Birkenhead, 18945, Pte., k. in a., F., 20/10/18.

MADLEY, A., b. Lydbrook, 75370, Pte., k. in a., F., 26/8/18.

MAINWARING, W. J., b. Swansea, 15038, Pte., d. of w., F., 26/8/18.

MAKIN, J., b. Dukinfield, 25979, Pte., k. in a., F., 23/8/18.

MANNINGS, J. C., b. Stoke Newington, 35211, Pte., d. of w., F., 16/7/16.

MARTIN, G. W. J., b. Swanscombe, 34813, Pte., k. in a., F., 10/7/16.

MASCALL, F., b. Radwinter, 55838, Pte., d. of w., F., 18/8/17.

MASSEY, T. J., b. Queen's Ferry, 20143, Pte., k. in a., F., 10/7/16.

MATHER, J., b. Lancaster, 204837, Pte., k. in a., F., 26/8/18.

McGRATH, D., b. Accrington, 60587, Pte., k. in a., F., 22/4/18.

McHALE, H., b. Llanrwst, 20603, Pte., k. in a., F., 18/9/18, D.C.M.

McHUGH, J., b. Rochdale, 28944, Pte., d. F., 11/4/18.

MEPHAM, S. A., b. Barry Dock, 78033, Pte., k. in a., F., 13/10/18.

MESSHAM, E., b. Hawarden, 20126, Pte., k. in a., F., 31/8/18.

METCALFE, W. I., b. London, 34535, Pte., k. in a., F., 10/7/16.

MOORE, G. L., b. Hasbury, 20648, L/Cpl., k. in a., F., 10/7/16.

MOORE, P., b. Cardiff, 56893, Pte., d. of w., F., 25/2/17.

MORGAN, B., b. Merthyr, 78140, Pte., k. in a., F., 10/10/18.

MORGAN, D. W., b. Llanwnnog, 21302, L/Sgt., k. in a., F., 10/7/16.

MORGAN, E. L., b. Rhayader, 61488, Pte., k. in a., F., 31/7/17.

MORGAN, O., b. Bagillt, 20524, Cpl., d. of w., F., 8/7/17.

MORGAN, R. T., b. Llanberis, 21479, Pte., k. in a., F., 2/5/17.

MORGANS, W. J., b. Burry Port, 73779, Pte., k. in a., F., 7/10/18.

MORLEY, D., b. London, 34618, Pte., k. in a., F., 9/7/16.

MORRIS, A., b. Pontgoch, 18043, Pte., k. in a., F., 26/8/18.

MORRIS, E., b. Nantybwch, 77442, Pte., k. in a., F., 18/9/18.

MORRIS, J., b. Bishop's Castle, 55069, Pte., k. in a., F., 22/4/18.

MORRIS, M., b. Llanrug, 21128, Pte., k. in a., F., 31/1/17.

MORRIS, R., b. Colwyn, 21957, Pte., k. in a., F., 1/9/16.

MORRIS, T., b. Bagillt, 20982, Pte., k. in a., F., 29/12/17.

MORTON, J., b. Greenock, 21429, L/Sgt., k. in a., F., 31/7/17.

MOSS, W., b. Walton-on-Naze, 55889, Pte., k. in a., F., 22/4/18.

MOSTYN, T., b. Coedpoeth, 89751, Pte., d. of w., F., 6/11/18.

MOUNTFIELD, J. G., b. Manchester, 75620, Pte., d. of w., F., 23/4/18.

MOYER, F. D., b. Peterborough, 27678, Cpl., k. in a., F., 10/7/16.

MULLINEUX, C. E., b. Wybunbury, 315106, Pte., k. in a., F., 23/8/18.

MYCOCK, W., b. Congleton, 56374, L/Cpl., d. of w., F., 15/8/17.

MYHILL, W. G., b. London, 22035, L/Cpl., k. in a., F., 18/9/18, D.C.M.

NASH, R., b. London, 27885, Sgt., d. of w., Home, 13/11/16.

NAVIN, J., b. Glossop, 20652, Cpl., k. in a., F., 2/9/17.

NEWMAN, A. C., b. Bath, 56896, Sgt., k. in a., F., 24/7/17.

NEWMAN, R. R. G., b. London, 8500, C.S.M., k. in a., F., 19/9/18.

NICKLIN, J., b. Portobello, 87453, Pte., k. in a., F., 8/10/18.

NORBURY, R., b. Toft, 56395, Pte., k. in a., F., 8/1/18.

NORRY, G. R., b. Billingsley, 60072, Pte., k. in a., F., 28/8/18.

OCKWELL, H. T., b. Sugwas Pool, 75759, L/Cpl., k. in a., F., 13/10/18, M.M.

OGLEY, A., e. Douglas, 66193, Pte., k. in a., F., 24/7/17.

OLDHAM, C., b. Hazel Grove, 55364, Pte., d. of w., F., 26/12/18.

OWEN, A., b. Llanddeiniolen, 73183, Pte., k. in a., F., 18/9/18.

OWEN, E. G., b. Towyn, 20738, Pte., d. of w., F., 23/6/16.

OWEN, E. M., b. Ceidio, 20901, Cpl., d. of w., F., 10/4/16.

OWEN, H., b. Nantwich, 48867, Pte., k. in a., F., 24/6/17.

OWEN, J. O., b. Llanberis, 21002, Pte., d. of w., Home, 12/11/16.

OWEN, J. R., b. Llandudno, 20016, Pte., k. in a., F., 10/7/16.

OWEN, R., b. Liverpool, 43925, Pte., k. in a., F., 18/9/18.

OWEN, W. J., b. Ynyscynhaiarn, 21469, L/Cpl., k. in a., F., 9/7/16.

OWENS, H., b. London, 27164, Pte., k. in a., F., 9/7/16.

OWENS, L. R., b. Rhos-on-Sea, 73182, Pte., d. of w., F., 2/9/18.

PALIN, J. W., b. Liverpool, 47594, L/Cpl., k. in a., F., 18/2/17.

PARKER, F., b. Wigan, 24415, L/Cpl., k. in a., F., 10/7/16.

PARRY, D., b. Rhyl, 20441, Pte., k. in a., F., 19/3/16.

PARRY, D. P., b. Llanbeblig, 54961, Pte., k. in a., F., 24/8/18.

PARRY, E., b. Llanfair P.G., 20639, Pte., k. in a., F., 25/2/17.

PARRY, E. R., b. Ynyscynhaiarn, 21740, Pte., k. in a., F., 18/9/18.

PARRY, J., b. Ponkey, 87421, Pte., d. of w., F., 6/10/18.

PASCOE, W., b. London, 36196, Pte., k. in a., F., 2/9/17.

PEAKE, T., b. Tunstall, 20850, Pte., d. of w., F., 19/12/15.

PEARCE, F., b. Hatfield Peveril, 26860, Pte., k. in a., F., 10/7/16.

PEARCE, J., b. Chirk, 18386, L/Sgt., k. in a., F., 18/2/17.

PEARCE, W. C., b. Swansea, 76443, Pte., d. of w., F., 8/10/18.

PERKINS, N. L., b. Tylorstown, 33179, Pte., d. of w., F., 7/6/16.

PHILLIPS, E. A., b. Llangedwyn, 54481, Pte., d. of w., F., 27/8/18.

PICKUP, J., b. Burnley, 60052, Pte., d. of w., Home, 29/8/17.

PLANT, J., b. Liverpool, 46357, Pte., k. in a., F., 4/8/17.

POCOCK, C., b. Burrow Bridge, 20876, Pte., k. in a., F., 5/6/16.

POPE, E. E., b. Lowestoft, 55877, L/Sgt., d. of w., F., 13/10/18.

POWELL, W., e. Brecon, 235398, Pte., k. in a., F., 8/5/18.

PRESTON, J., b. Stockport, 203423, Sgt., d. of w., F., 11/10/18.

PRICE, R., b. Neath, 20868, Pte., k. in a., F., 7/10/18.

PRITCHARD, G., b. Llanddaniel, 43628, Pte., d. of w., F., 27/8/17.

PRITCHARD, H., e. Carnarvon, 53792, Pte., d. of w., F., 24/8/18.

PRITCHARD, J., b. Bethesda, 15689, Pte., d. of w., F., 2/11/16, M.M.

PRITCHARD, L., b. Ynyscynhaiarn, 21451, L/Cpl., k. in a., F., 9/7/16.

PRITCHARD, R. O., e. Carnarvon, 53872, Pte., k. in a., F., 26/8/18.

POYNER, J., b. Ullingswick, 66904, Pte., k. in a., F., 29/12/17.

PULLEN, A., b. West Mersea, 55876, Pte., k. in a., F., 23/8/18, M.M.

RAWLING, J., b. Llandudno, 20152, C.Q.M.S., d. of w., F., 21/6/18.

RAWLINGS, E. J., b. London, 27443, L/Cpl., k. in a., F., 1/9/16.

READ, J., b. Blackburn, 20967, Pte., k. in a., F., 2/9/17.

REES, H., b. Tal-y-Llyn, 15515, Pte., k. in a., F., 31/10/16.

REES, J., b. Abergwynolwyn, 204750, Pte., d. of w., F., 24/4/18.

REES, R. W., b. Cwmpark, 20367, Pte., k. in a., F., 10/7/16.

REYNOLDS, W. J., b. London, 26711, Pte., k. in a., F., 10/7/16.

RICHARDS, D. L., b. Treddol, 46064, Pte., d. of w., F., 27/10/16.

RICHARDS, M., b. Newport, 56900, Pte., k. in a., F., 25/2/17.

RICHARDS, W. T., b. Llanwrtyd Wells, 22259, Cpl., k. in a., F., 24/7/17.

ROACH, J., b. Liverpool, 41656, Pte., k. in a., F., 18/9/18.

ROBERTS, D., b. Dolwyddelan, 20253, Pte., k. in a., F., 6/7/16.

ROBERTS, F., b. Bala, 34609, Pte., k. in a., F., 9/7/16.

ROBERTS, G., b. Chirk, 19676, Pte., k. in a., F., 2/3/16.

ROBERTS, H., b. Bethesda, 21138, Pte., k. in a., F., 7/2/16.

ROBERTS, I., b. Abergele, 20138, Pte., k. in a., F., 7/6/16.

ROBERTS, I., b. Oswestry, 60745, Pte., k. in a., F., 2/9/17.

ROBERTS, J., b. Penycae, 88496, Pte., k. in a., F., 5/11/18.

ROBERTS, J. O., b. Penmaenmawr, 41531, Pte., k. in a., F., 25/2/17.

ROBERTS, J. R., b. Penmaenmawr, 21386, L/Cpl., k. in a., F., 24/2/17, M.M.

ROBERTS, L., b. Llandudno, 21378, Pte., k. in a., F., 6/10/18.

ROBERTS, L., b. Pontcysyllte, 43627, Pte., k. in a., F., 6/4/17.

ROBERTS, L. H., b. Conway, 16084, Pte., d. of w., F., 14/11/16.

ROBERTS, M., b. Chirk, 88424, Pte., k. in a., F., 8/10/18.

ROBERTS, M., b. Llanfair, 21268, Pte., d., Home, 18/11/15.

ROBERTS, M., e. Blaenau Festiniog, 55304, Pte., k. in a., F., 9/2/17.

ROBERTS, P., b. Llanelian, 21255, Pte., d. of w., F., 19/7/16.

ROBERTS, R. R., b. Llanfwrog, 21480, A/Cpl., d. of w., F., 7/7/16.

ROBERTS, W., b. Llaneilian, 20058, Pte., k. in a., F., 18/9/18.

ROBERTS, W., e. Welshpool, 55315, Pte., k. in a., F., 25/2/17.

ROBINS, W. C., b. Hawarden, 17387, Cpl., k. in a., F., 18/9/18.

ROONEY, P., b. Preston, 94494, Pte., k. in a., F., 4/11/18.

ROSSER, E., b. Pentre, 20970, Pte., k. in a., F., 6/7/16.

ROWLANDS, D., b. Gwalchmai, 69707, Pte., k. in a., F., 30/8/18.

ROWLANDS, W. J., b. Llanfair P.G., 21199, L/Cpl., k. in a., F., 6/7/16.

RULE, G. E., b. Cardiff, 35218, Pte., k. in a., F., 4/8/17.

SALISBURY, T., b. Pwllheli, 266529, Pte., k. in a., F., 6/10/18.

SAUNDERS, P. G., b. Bristol, 89040, Pte., d. of w., F., 18/12/16.

SERVANT, J. E., b. London, 27803, Pte., d. of w., F., 5/6/16.

SHAPLAND, A. R., b. Goodleigh, 37549, Pte., k. in a., F., 20/9/17.

SHARLAND, C., b. Exeter, 93703, Pte., k. in a., F., 18/9/18.

SHARP, T., b. Manchester, 41781, Pe., k. in a., F., 25/2/17.

SHAW, J. G., b. Liverpool, 24490, Pte., k. in a., F., 28/6/17.

SIMS, M. V., b. Glyn Neath, 20844, A/Sgt., d. of w., F., 12/7/16.

SINCLAIR, J., b. Manchester, 31879, L/Cpl., k. in a., F., 24/6/17.

SKIMING, J., b. Liverpool, 43880, Pte., k. in a., F., 18/9/18.

SMITH, H., b. Carshalton, 26436, Cpl., d. of w., F., 23/4/18.

SMITH, H. G., e. London, 43606, L/Cpl., k. in a., F., 24/8/18.

SMITH, J. I., b. Connah's Quay, 18240, Pte., k. in a., F., 19/2/17.

SMITH, W. S., b. Stroud, 21613, L/Cpl., k. in a., F., 18/9/18.

SOAR, S., b. Sutton-in-Ashfield, 21151, Cpl., k. in a., F., 2/9/17, M.M.

SPELLER, W. H., b. Stratford, 26657, L/Cpl., k. in a., F., 23/8/18.

START, J., e. Macclesfield, 56401, Pte., k. in a., F., 6/10/18.

STEADMAN, J., b. Cwm, 93704, Pte., k. in a., F., 18/9/18.

STEWART, H., b. Barking, 34564, Pte., d. of w., Home, 29/6/16.

STODDARD, H., e. Altrincham, 56410, Pte., k. in a., F., 7/10/18.

STODDART, E. D., b. Festiniog, 20212, Pte., k. in a., F., 31/7/17.

SUCKLEY, G., b. Ffrwd, 33309, Pte., k. in a., F., 6/5/16.

SYKES, H., b. Marshcapel, 55880, Pte., k. in a., F., 4/8/17.

TABERNER, P., b. Pemberton, 20772, L/Cpl., k. in a., F., 25/2/16.

TALBOT, P., b. Penkridge, 20531, Sgt., k. in a., F., 24/7/17.

TAYLOR, B., b. Pinxton, 21031, A/Sgt., k. in a., F., 30/1/16.

TAYLOR, C., e. Penygroes, 88602, Pte., k. in a., F., 8/11/18.

TAYLOR, J., b. Skelmersdale, 21108, Pte., k. in a., F., 26/8/18.

TERRATT, W., b. Merthyr, 55719, Pte., d., F., 23/10/18.

THOMAS, A., b. Old Colwyn, 20484, Pte., k. in a., F., 10/7/16.

THOMAS, D., b. Festiniog, 20464, Pte., k. in a., F., 10/7/16.

THOMAS, E., b. Cardiff, 56908, L/Sgt., k. in a., F., 4/8/17, M.M.

THOMAS, E., b. Wellington, 41545, Pte., k. in a., F., 23/7/17.

THOMAS, J., b. Llanguike, 21078, Pte., k. in a., F., 2/8/17.

THOMAS, J., b. Porth, 21136, Pte., d. of w., F., 29/8/18.

THOMAS, R., b. Bryngwran, 21262, Pte., k. in a., F., 9/7/16.

THOMAS, R., b. Rhosybol, 20515, L/Cpl., k. in a., F., 24/6/17.

THOMAS, R. O., b. Bronrhiw, 40494, Pte., d. of w., F., 7/1/18.

THOMAS, R. T., b. Dolwyddelan, 44277, Pte., k. in a., F., 18/9/18.

THOMAS, S., b. Coed Franc, 37571, Pte., k. in a., F., 4/8/17.

THOMAS, T. H., b. Aberystwyth, 54257, Cpl., d. of w., F., 21/6/18.

THOMAS, W., b. Stokesay, 75276, Pte., k. in a., F., 26/8/18.

THOMAS, W., b. Birmingham, 20804, L/Cpl., k. in a., F., 17/3/16.

THOMAS, W., b. Cwmyglo, 20950, Pte., k. in a., F., 10/7/16.

THOMPSON, J., b. Church Aston, 6548, Pte., d. of w., F., 7/10/16.

THOMPSTONE, S., b. Manchester, 21068, L/Cpl., k. in a., F., 20/10/18, M.M.

THOMSON, D., b. Shadwell, 26717, Pte., k. in a., F., 18/2/17.

THORN, H. H., b. Cardiff, 241783, Pte., k. in a., F., 26/7/17.

THURSTON, L., b. Stoke Newington, 27248, Pte., k. in a., F., 20/10/18.

TILLOTSON, A., b. Leeds, 80169, Pte., k. in a., F., 18/9/18.

TIPTON, C. E., b. Stanton Lacey, 56564, Pte., d. of w., Home, 10/6/18.

TONKINS, T., b. Ynishir, 21161, L/Cpl., k. in a., F., 10/7/16.

TORR, J. H., b. Macclesfield, 235462, Sgt., k. in a., F., 13/10/18.

TOWNSEND, G. H., e. Ogmore Vale, 89118, Pte., d. of w., F., 5/11/18.

TUCKER, S., b. Martock, 22383, R.S.M., d. of w., F., 8/9/18, M.C.

TURNER, A. P., b. Manchester, 42360, Pte., d. of w., F., 19/10/18.

TURNER, D., b. Walsall Wood, 20821, Pte., d. of w., F., 6/10/18.

TURVEY, W. F., b. Gloucester, 235063, Pte., d. of w., F., 26/6/17.

VALENTINE, J. E., b. Penycae, 87333, Pte., k. in a., F., 20/10/18.

VARLEY, G., b. Padiham, 20102, Pte., k. in a., F., 4/8/17.

VAUGHAN, C., b. Brynmawr, 61464, Pte., d. of w., F., 30/12/17.

VAUX, E., e. Pontypool, 88980, Pte., k. in a., F., 4/11/18.

WALKER, J. M., b. Millom, 93993, Cpl., k. in a., F., 4/11/18.

WALKER, W. E., e. Shotton, 89419, Pte., k. in a., F., 5/11/18.

WALTERS, L., b. Llandilo, 75524, Pte., k. in a., F., 21/10/18.

WALTERS, T., b. Hucknall, 20530, Pte., k. in a., F., 6/7/16.

WARMAN, E. G., b. London, 26992, Pte., d. of w., F., 24/6/17.

WARREN, H., b. St. Helens, 75525, Pte., k. in a., F., 8/11/18.

WATKINS, L., b. Ferndale, 21218, Pte., d. of w., F., 4/11/18.

WEBB, G., b. Kingstown, 235402, L/Cpl., k. in a., F., 8/10/18.

WELLS, G. S., b. Hunslet, 31373, Pte., k. in a., F., 2/9/17.

WELLS, H. H., b. Leeds, 31372, Pte., d. of w., F., 21/3/17.

WELLS, W., b. Rochester, 24557, Pte., k. in a., F., 29/12/17.

WHALLEY, H., b. Blackburn, 75767, Pte., d. of w., F., 8/6/18.

WHITE, J., b. Warrington, 315301, Pte., d. of w., F., 16/3/18.

WHITTAKER, A., b. Birmingham, 17443, Sgt., k. in a., F., 22/4/18.

WHITTAKER, W. K., b. Manchester, 54370, Pte., k. in a., F., 31/10/18.

WHITTINGTON, H., e. Newport, 89274, Pte., k. in a., F., 4/11/18.

WILES, A. J., b. Ipswich, 27949, Pte., d. of w., F., 10/7/16.

WILLCOCK, W., b. St. Helens, 75954, Pte., d. of w., F., 18/9/18.

WILLIAMS, A., b. Gwersyllt, 87300, Pte., k. in a., F., 13/10/18.

WILLIAMS, C., e. Colwyn Bay, 241137, Pte., k. in a., F., 4/11/18.

WILLIAMS, D., b. Yspytty Ifan, 36849, Pte., k. in a., F., 10/7/16.

WILLIAMS, D. G., b. Bargoed, 61432, Pte., k. in a., F., 31/8/17.

WILLIAMS, E., b. Penymynydd, 19193, Pte., k. in a., F., 21/2/16.

WILLIAMS, E., b. Llaniestyn, 21323, Pte., k. in a., F., 6/7/16.

WILLIAMS, E. J., b. Llanberis, 21104, Pte., k. in a., F., 24/4/16.

WILLIAMS, E. P., b. Denio, 20394, Pte., k. in a., F., 10/7/16.

WILLIAMS, F., e. Chester, 93305, Pte., k. in a., F., 18/9/18.

WILLIAMS, G., b. Newport, 73214, Pte., k. in a., F., 26/8/18.

WILLIAMS, H., b. London, 26848, Pte., d. of w., F., 26/3/16.

WILLIAMS, J., b. Llanfair P.G., 20933, Pte., k. in a., F., 22/4/18.

WILLIAMS, J., b. Pwllheli, 43749, Pte., k. in a., F., 23/3/18.

WILLIAMS, J., e. Mold, 60752, Pte., k. in a., F., 18/9/18.

WILLIAMS, J. E., b. Conway, 20346, Sgt., k. in a., F., 15/6/17.

WILLIAMS, J. F., b. Cwm-y-Glo, 40371, Pte., d. of w., F., 20/10/18.

WILLIAMS, L., e. Llandudno, 21343, Cpl., d., Home, 16/2/17.

WILLIAMS, L., b. Llanerchymedd, 21047, Pte., d., F., 22/4/16.

WILLIAMS, M., b. Broughton, 87321, Pte., k. in a., F., 8/11/18.

WILLIAMS, O. T., e. Liverpool, 37190, Pte., k. in a., F., 25/2/17.

WILLIAMS, R., b. Llanor, 21462, Pte., k. in a., F., 10/7/16.

WILLIAMS, R., b. Ruabon, 28321, Pte., k. in a., F., 8/11/17.

WILLIAMS, R., b. Beddgelert, 317032, Pte., d. of w., F., 18/3/18.

WILLIAMS, R. J., b. Llanelly, 56653, Pte., d., F., 18/7/18.

WILLIAMS, R. J., b. Llanfairfechan, 21010, Pte., d., F., 23/2/16.

WILLIAMS, R. J., e. Conway, 60804, Pte., k. in a., F., 23/7/17.

WILLIAMS, T., b. Cemmaes Bay, 267316, Pte., d. of w., F., 8/11/18.

WILLIAMS, T., b. Llanerchymedd, 21121, Pte., k. in a., F., 6/7/16.

WILLIAMS, T. E., b. Corwen, 19401, Pte., d. of w., F., 18/2/17.

WILLIAMS, T. J., b. Porth, 78136, Pte., k. in a., F., 4/8/17.

WILLIAMS, W. E., b. Bistre, 20957, Pte., k. in a., F., 9/7/16.

WILLIAMS, W. H., b. Bistre, 21239, Pte., d., Home, 24/5/15.

WILLIAMS, W. J., b. Bethesda, 76121, Pte., d. of w., F., 5/10/18.

WILLIAMS, W. O., b. Cerrigceinwen, 21387, Pte., k. in a., F., 10/7/16.

WILLOUGHBY, T., b. London, 26027, Pte., d. of w., F., 28/1/17.

WILSON, G., b. Burnbank, 20675, Pte., k. in a., F., 10/7/16.

WILSON, H., b. Putney, 34970, Pte., k. in a., F., 10/7/16.

WINDSOR, S., b. Stretford, 60060, Pte., k. in a., F., 4/8/17.

WOODS, J., b. Liverpool, 56413, Pte., k. in a., F., 4/8/17.

WORSLEY, J. H., b. Lymm, 46430, Pte., d. of w., F., 6/8/17.

WORTHY, E., b. Putney, 31595, Pte., d. of w., Home, 14/11/18.

YOUNG, T., b. London, 22889, Pte., k. in a., F., 10/7/16.

15th BATTALION

ADAMS, T., b. Cardington, 60121, Pte., k. in a., F., 27/7/17.

AKKER, J. T., b. Burnley, 291608, Pte., k. in a., F., 4/8/17.

ALLEN, K. B., b. Hampstead, 22051, Pte., k. in a., F., 23/3/16.

ALLEN, T. R., b. Abertillery, 21767, L/Cpl., k. in a., F., 6/5/17.

AMEY, J. S., b. Redhill, 53868, Pte., d., F., 20/2/17.

ANDREWS, W. A., b. Haggerston, 27585, Pte., d. of w., F., 13/7/16.

ARMSTRONG, A. J., e. London, 235162, Pte., k. in a., F., 4/8/17.

ASHTON, E., e. Bury, 203984, Pte., d. of w., F., 28/7/17.

BAIRD, J. C., b. Connah's Quay, 19535, Pte., k. in a., F., 31/7/17.

BAKER, A., b. Coseley, 56119, Pte., k. in a., F., 27/7/17.

BARKER, S. E., e. London, 235163, Pte., k. in a., F., 31/7/17.

BARNES, J., b. London, 235277, Pte., k. in a., F., 27/7/17.

BARNETT, G., b. Hindley, 59439, Pte., k. in a., F., 27/7/17.

BARRATT, G. H., e. Gresford, 202525, Pte., k. in a., F., 4/8/17.

BARRETT, R., b. Stepney, 22122, Pte., k. in a., F., 31/7/17.

BARTHOLOMEW, D., b. Islington, 22872, Pte., k. in a., F., 14/1/16.

BATES, T. H., b. Nantwich, 60141, Pte., k. in a., F., 4/8/17.

BATES, J., b. London, 28136, Pte., d. of w., F., 13/7/16.

BEECH, J. E., b. Rhyl, 22194, Pte., k. in a., F., 22/7/16.

BELL, J., b. Higher Broughton, 60117, Pte., k. in a., F., 27/7/17.

BENNETT, A. C., b. Woodlands, 53988, Pte., d. of w., F., 13/10/16.

BENTLEY, T., b. Hixon, 56094, Pte., k. in a., F., 14/5/17.

BERRY, A., b. Waltham Cross, 55904, Pte., k. in a., F., 4/8/17.

BEVAN, F., b. Hereford, 21602, Pte., k. in a., F., 25/5/17.

BIRD, H., b. London, 22206, Pte., d. of w., F., 13/4/16.

BISHOP, H. J., e. London, 22123, Pte., d. of w., F., 15/6/17.

BOLTON, G. W., b. Rochdale, 60111, Pte., k. in a., F., 27/7/17.

BOWEN, S. T., b. Liverpool, 44086, Pte., k. in a., F., 10/4/17.

BRADSHAW, J., b. Waterhouse, 22801, C.S.M., d. of w., F., 10/4/17.

BURDEN, E. G., b. Portland, 53989, Pte., d. of w., F., 11/10/17.

BUSH, W., b. London, 21869, Pte., k. in a., F., 11/7/16.

BUTCHER, A., b. London, 27282, Pte., k. in a., F., 27/7/17.

CAKEWELL, G., e. Walsall, 56145, Pte., k. in a., F., 14/5/17.

CAUCUTT, W. G., b. London, 22366, Pte., k. in a., F., 10/7/16.

CHURCH, H. E., b. London, 21796, Pte., d. of w., F., 19/3/16.

CLARKE, A., b. Manchester, 23577, Pte., k. in a., F., 10/7/16.

COLLINS, G., b. Cambridge, 28079, Pte., k. in a., F., 6/7/16.

COLLINS, T., b. London, 21975, Sgt., k. in a., F., 10/7/16.

COOPER, A. H., b. Finsbury, 22978, Pte., k. in a., F., 10/7/16.

CORDINGLEY, P., b. Windhill, 56122, Pte., k. in a., F., 4/8/17.

COSLETT, A., b. Cadoxton, 241852, Pte., k. in a., F., 4/8/17.

COULSON, A., e. Accrington, 60143, Pte., k. in a., F., 25/7/17.

COULSON, F. A. J., b. London, 21877, Pte., k. in a., F., 4/8/17.

COURTNEY, J. H., b. London, 22780, Pte., d. of w., F., 12/1/16.

COX, S. D., e. London, 235167, Pte., k. in a., F., 4/8/17.

DAVIES, D. O. D., b. Llanidloes, 37611, Pte., k. in a., F., 27/7/17.

DAVIES, E., b. Rhos, 25587, Pte., k. in a., F., 10/7/16.

DAVIES, E. J., b. Dulbba, 22639, Pte., k. in a., F., 10/7/16.

DAVIES, I., b. Llanwrtyd Wells, 54784, Pte., k. in a., F., 25/7/17.

DAVIES, P. B., b. Llanelly, 22836, Pte., k. in a., F., 10/7/16.

DAVIES, R. V., b. Llandudno, 56806, Pte., k. in a., F., 31/7/17.

DAVIES, S. C., e. Swansea, 291726, Pte., k. in a., F., 31/7/17.

DAVIES, T. H., b. Abergwynolwyn, 290490, Pte., k. in a., F., 27/7/17.

DAVIES, W., b. Northophall, 60597, Pte., k. in a., F., 4/9/17.

DAVIES, W. T. H., b. Llanfihangel, 21820, Cpl., k. in a., F., 11/7/16.

DAVIS, A. A., b. York, 27996, L/Cpl., k. in a., F., 2/10/16.

DAVIS, A. E., b. Finchingfield, 55908, Pte., k. in a., F., 17/6/17.

DAVIS, H. O., b. London, 22029, Pte., d. of w., F., 16/7/16.

DAWKINS, W., e. Morriston, 291727, Pte., k. in a., F., 27/7/17.

DEAN, W. G., b. Wimborne, 54001, Pte., k. in a., F., 3/10/16.

DODD, M. H., b. London, 21606, Pte., d. of w., F., 14/6/17.

DONGWORTH, J. T., b. London, 22273, Pte., d. of w., F., 21/12/15.

DONOGHUE, J. H., b. London, 21660, Pte., k. in a., F., 11/7/16.

DOWNS, I., b. Bilston, 22507, Pte., d. of w., F., 13/5/16, M.M.

DRISCOLL, W., b. London, 22534, Pte., k. in a., F., 10/7/16.

DYER, J. W. A., b. London, 22294, Pte., d. of w., F., 25/6/17.

EDMONDSON, J., e. Wrexham, 54785, Pte., k. in a., F., 4/8/17.

EDWARDS, I., e. London, 22368, L/Cpl., k. in a., F., 27/7/17.

EDWARDS, O., b. Llangollen, 291798, Pte., k. in a., F., 27/7/17.

ELLIS, D., b. Llanbeblig, 55691, Pte., k. in a., F., 27/7/17.

ELLIS, R., b. Manchester, 62773, Pte., k. in a., F., 17/11/17.

ELLISON, P., e. London, 235170, Pte., k. in a., F., 4/8/17.

EMERY, F., b. London, 37298, Pte., k. in a., F., 5/7/16.

EMMETT, F. W., b. Stalybridge, 55398, Pte., k. in a., F., 21/1/17.

EVANS, A. C., b. London, 21620, Pte., k. in a., F., 31/10/16.

EVANS, E., b. Trawsfynydd, 61117, Pte., k. in a., F., 4/8/17.

EVANS, J., b. Barmouth, 11998, Pte., k. in a., F., 4/8/17.

EVANS, J. H., b. Bolton, 38530, Pte., k. in a., F., 27/6/17.

EVANS, R., b. Groeslon, 55396, Pte., k. in a., F., 28/7/17.

EVANS, T. H., b. Cefn Mawr, 33163, L/Cpl., d. of w., Home, 7/9/17.

EVERETT, F. J., b. London, 21556, Pte., d. of w., F., 15/5/16.

FEWINS, F., b. London, 54005, Pte., d. of w., F., 10/2/17.

FINCH, F., b. London, 21651, Pte., d. of w., F., 4/9/16.

FITTALL, A. J., b. London, 22721, Pte., d., Home, 19/8/15.

GIBBS, O., b. London, 21662, Sgt., k. in a., F., 10/7/16.

GILBEY, W., b. Bishop's Stortford, 55948, L/Cpl., k. in a., F., 4/8/17.

GOODWIN, E., b. Haddon, 22307, Pte., k. in a., F., 3/10/16.

GREAVES, S., b. Manchester, 292687, Pte., k. in a., F., 4/8/17.

GRIFFITHS, D. J., b. Aberhosan, 203975, Pte., d. of w., F., 25/5/18.

GRIFFITHS, W., b. Nevin, 20090, Pte., k. in a., F., 27/7/17.

GROVE, L., b. Watford, 22034, Pte., k. in a., F., 8/5/16.

GURNER, W. H., b. Rhosddu, 4851, Pte., k. in a., F., 27/7/17.

GUY, J. W., b. Sheffield, 22884, Sgt., k. in a., F., 4/8/17.

HACKETT, J., b. Longton, 61185, Pte., k. in a., F., 27/7/17.

HAGUE, J. J., b. Newton Moor, 28582, Pte., k. in a., F., 31/7/17.

HANKEY, T., b. Northwich, 235476, Pte., k. in a., F., 16/3/18.

HARDING, F. L., b. London, 21644, Pte., d., F., 6/10/18.

HARRIS, H. J., b. London, 22954, Pte., k. in a., F., 7/7/16.

HART, W. G., b. Birmingham, 33468, Pte., k. in a., F., 20/8/17.

HARVEY, A., b. Cardiff, 56815, Pte., k. in a., F., 26/10/16.
HATHWAY, R. B., b. London, 22244, Pte., d. of w., F., 15/7/16.
HAYWARD, J., b. Manchester, 22656, Pte., d., Home, 31/8/15.
HILL, A. G., b. Walthamstow, 26653, Pte., d. of w., F., 11/4/16.
HILL, G., b. Northleigh, 55696, Pte., d. of w., F., 27/8/17.
HILL, M., b. London, 22698, Pte., k. in a., F., 4/8/17.
HILL, R., b. Port Talbot, 19901, Cpl., k. in a., F., 27/11/17.
HILL, S. J., b. London, 22282, Pte., d., F., 31/8/16.
HILLS, W., b. Southminster, 55952, Pte., k. in a., F., 28/7/17.
HODSOLL, A. A., b. Stratford, 22155, Sgt., d. of w., F., 6/9/16.
HOLDEN, T. H., b. Rochdale, 60114, Pte., d. of w., F., 3/8/17.
HOOD, S., b. Pembroke, 22038, Pte., k. in a., F., 8/5/16.
HOOK, F. G., b. Brixton, 28140, Pte., k. in a., F., 8/1/16.
HOOKWAY, E., b. Cardiff, 12498, Pte., k. in a., F., 4/8/17.
HOWELLS, H. S., b. London, 21977, Pte., d. of w., Home, 20/7/16.
HUGHES, J., b. Cefn Mawr, 33160, Pte., k. in a., F., 10/7/16.
HUGHES, J., e. Liverpool, 22453, L/Cpl., d. of w., F., 5/2/17.
HUGHSTON, T., b. Chester, 70250, Pte., k. in a., F., 29/9/17.
INGMAN, A., b. Denbigh, 21583, Pte., k. in a., F., 4/9/17.
JENNINGS, T. F., b. London, 22547, Pte., k. in a., F., 28/1/16.
JONES, E., b. Llanddona, 54794, Pte., d. of w., F., 15/6/17.
JONES, E., b. Liverpool, 54797, Pte., k. in a., F., 27/7/17.
JONES, E. G., b. Aberystwyth, 22360, Pte., d. of w., F., 8/5/16.
JONES, E. J., e. Queen's Ferry, 55908, Pte., k. in a., F., 4/8/17.
JONES, F., b. Bettws, Mont., 61311, Pte., k. in a., F., 4/8/17.
JONES, I. J. L., b. London, 21713, Pte., k. in a., F., 8/5/16.
JONES, J. I., b. London, 21596, Pte., k. in a., F., 4/9/16.
JONES, R., b. Llanidloes, 54795, Pte., k. in a., F., 15/6/17.
JONES, R. W., b. Walworth, 21588, Pte., k. in a., F., 11/7/16.
JONES, T. A., b. Dodleston, 37044, Pte., k. in a., F., 10/7/16.
JONES, T. P., b. Wrexham, 56824, Pte., k. in a., F., 1/9/16.

JONES, W., b. Bagillt, 203255, Pte., k. in a., F., 31/7/17.
JONES, W., b. Llanelly, 21569, Pte., k. in a., F., 7/7/16.
JONES, W., e. Wrexham, 54792, Pte., k. in a., F., 27/7/17.
JONES, W., b. Trawsfynydd, 55685, Pte., k. in a., F., 4/8/17.
JONES, W., b. Wrexham, 241930, Pte., d. of w., F., 5/8/17.
JONES, W., b. Dyffryn, 290597, Pte., k. in a., F., 27/7/17.
JONES, W. M., b. Margam, 55684, Pte., k. in a., F., 4/8/17.
JONES, W. P., b. London, 21505, Pte., k. in a., F., 29/1/16.
JUDD, S. C., b. Bermondsey, 22957, Pte., k. in a., F., 6/7/16.
KIMMER, J., e. Seaforth, 53809, Pte., k. in a., F., 4/8/17.
KING, S. J., b. London, 28101, Pte., k. in a., F., 7/7/16.
KRIGER, F., b. London, 28169, Pte., k. in a., F., 22/4/16.
KYFFIN, C. L., e. Gresford, 202533, Pte., k. in a., F., 27/7/17.
LANGDON, F., b. London, 21815, Pte., k. in a., F., 12/10/16, M.M.
LEADBEATTER, J. V., b. London, 21979, Pte., k. in a., F., 7/7/16.
LEAVER, W., b. Bradford-on-Avon, 291958, Pte., k. in a., F., 25/7/17.
LEE, J. W., b. Huddersfield, 25705, Pte., k. in a., F., 27/7/17.
LENDON, A. L., b. London, 28196, Pte., d., Home, 10/11/17.
LLOYD, E. S., e. Stafford, 33399, A/Cpl., k. in a., F., 26/4/18.
LLOYD, W., e. Flint, 54746, Pte., k. in a., F., 6/2/17.
LOCKWOOD, C. E., b. London, 22347, Pte., d. of w., F., 13/7/16.
MACRO, W. H., b. London, 21730, Cpl., d. of w., F., 1/11/16.
MADDEN, T., b. London, 22472, Pte., k. in a., F., 7/7/16.
MARLINSKI, B., b. London, 22878, Pte., k. in a., F., 11/7/16.
MARSH, A., b. London, 28048, Pte., k. in a., F., 25/2/16.
MARTIN, A., e. Blackpool, 24999, Pte., k. in a., F., 10/7/16.
MATTHEWS, S., b. Penzance, 28141, Pte., d., F., 23/9/16.
MAYHEW, E. E., b. Islington, 28130, Pte., k. in a., F., 5/10/16.
McCONNELL, E. J., b. Brixton, 21807, Pte., d., F., 17/6/16.
MEALEY, H., b. London, 22335, Pte., k. in a., F., 10/4/16.
MEYNELL, E. G., b. London, 28178, Pte., k. in a., F., 6/7/16.
MILLETT, L., e. London, 235184, Pte., k. in a., F., 4/8/17.

MORGAN, O., b. Kingston-on-Thames, 22535, Pte., k. in a., F., 27/7/17.
MORGAN, T., b. Cefn, 54800, Pte., d. of w., F., 25/6/17.
MORGAN, W. G., b. Swansea, 292553, Pte., k. in a., F., 4/9/17.
MORRIS, E., b. Ainsworth, 61020, Pte., d. of w., F., 26/7/17.
MORRIS, W. M., b. Barking, 21813, Pte., d. of w., F., 23/8/17.
MULLINGS, T. A., b. Walthamstow, 22794, Pte., k. in a., F., 8/7/16.
MUNN, R. O., b. Highbury, 34742, Pte., k. in a., F., 27/9/16.
NICE, H. T., b. Stanway, 55917, Pte., k. in a., F., 27/7/17.
NIPE, W. A., b. London, 22655, Pte., k. in a., F., 6/7/16.
NORMAN, S. J., b. Clerkenwell, 22054, Sgt., k. in a., F., 28/7/17.
OAKLEY, A., b. Pendlebury, 55709, Pte., k. in a., F., 4/8/17.
OWEN, J. B., b. Holyhead, 60787, Pte., k. in a., F., 27/7/17.
OWEN, T. H., b. Bangor, 21551, Pte., k. in a., F., 1/3/16.
PALMER, F., b. Oxford, 28154, Pte., d. of w., F., 14/10/16.
PARK, T. H., b. London, 22941, Pte., k. in a., F., 3/6/16.
PARKINGTON, S. A., b. Stanton, 22193, Pte., k. in a., F., 11/1/16.
PARRY, A., b. Holywell, 54747, Pte., d. of w., F., 7/8/17.
PARRY, G., b. Cemmaes, 55996, Pte., k. in a., F., 31/7/17.
PARRY, W. A., e. Wrexham, 55412, Pte., k. in a., F., 27/7/17.
PATTISON, W., b. Stockport, 235413, Sgt., k. in a., F., 4/9/17.
PATTRICK, F., b. Brightlingsea, 55925, Pte., k. in a., F., 8/10/17.
PAWSON, W., e. Bradford, 235187, Pte., k. in a., F., 4/8/17.
PERCIVAL, W., b. Wrexham, 55687, Pte., k. in a., F., 4/8/17.
PESCOTT, A. H., b. London, 21674, Pte., k. in a., F., 10/7/16.
PICKETT, F. G., b. High Wycombe, 35274, Pte., k. in a., F., 10/7/16.
PIERSON, F., e. Midhurst, 60130, Pte., k. in a., F., 4/8/17.
PINLESS, F., e. Preston, 55425, Pte., k. in a., F., 27/7/17.
POWELL, C. H., b. London, 21900, Pte., d. of w., F., 28/9/16.
PRATER, P., b. Llangynfd, 21526, Sgt., k. in a., F., 26/5/16.
PRICE, F. E., e. Newport, 54801, Pte., k. in a., F., 27/7/17.
PUGH, T. R., e. Holborn, 22213, L/Cpl., k. in a., F., 10/7/16.

QUARRELL, F., b. Birlingham, 56832, Pte., d. of w., F., 18/6/17.

RANGELEY, A., b. Hayfield, 235434, L/Cpl., d. of w., F., 6/9/17.

REEVES, W., b. Lampton, 60133, Pte., k. in a., F., 27/7/17.

REYNOLDS, T. H., b. Rugby, 235287, Pte., d. of w., F., 12/8/17.

RICHARDS, T. W., b. Whitchurch, 56833, Pte., k. in a., F., 20/1/17.

RICHTER, W. H., e. London, 235189, Pte., k. in a., F., 27/7/17.

ROBERTS, O., b. Abererch, 61010, Pte., k. in a., F., 25/7/17.

ROBERTS, O., b. Llangaffo, 61123, Pte., k. in a., F., 25/7/17.

ROBERTS, W., b. Llanfyllin, 61051, Pte., k. in a., F., 25/7/17.

ROBERTSON, A., b. London, 35086, Pte., k. in a., F., 10/7/16.

ROBINSON, C., b. Milnrow, 54483, Pte., k. in a., F., 31/7/17.

ROGERS, J. B., b. Bargoed, 21560, Pte., k. in a., F., 10/7/16.

ROPER, J., b. London, 55924, Pte., d. of w., F., 17/6/17.

ROSE, W., b. Birmingham, 235288, Pte., k. in a., F., 6/12/17.

ROWLAND, J. E., b. Hoxton, 21972, Pte., k. in a., F., 6/9/16.

SALWAY, A. J., b. London, 22937, Pte., k. in a., F., 10/7/16.

SAWYER, E., e. London, 235192, Pte., k. in a., F., 4/8/17.

SCUDDER, F. W., e. Deptford, 235193, Pte., k. in a., F., 4/8/17.

SHELDRICK, F., b. London, 27981, L/Cpl., k. in a., F., 27/7/17.

SHEPPARD, H. C. W., b. Salisbury, 21998, Pte., k. in a., F., 10/7/16.

SIMPSON, A. W., b. London, 22350, Pte., d. of w., F., 21/12/15.

SLOUGH, A., b. Boxmoor, 21726, Pte., k. in a., F., 11/7/16.

SMITH, J. A., b. Radford, 291956, Pte., k. in a., F., 27/7/17.

SMITH, T., b. London, 26551, Pte., k. in a., F., 31/7/17.

SOLOMONS, C., b. London, 34657, Pte., d. of w., F., 14/10/17.

STANSFIELD, F., b. Walsden, 56149, Pte., k. in a., F., 4/8/17.

STANWAY, H., b. St. Helen's, 55967, Pte., k. in a., F., 14/5/17.

STARBROOK, J. A., b. Hoxton, 28109, Pte., k. in a., F., 5/10/16.

STEPHENS, W., b. Carew, 60122, Pte., k. in a., F., 27/7/17.

STEVENS, T. H., b. Edmonton, 21863, Cpl., k. in a., F., 3/6/16.

STEWART, L. G., b. Limavady, 55992, L/Cpl., k. in a., F., 27/7/17.

STOCKS, T., b. London, 28156, Pte., k. in a., F., 10/7/16.

STOKES, R., b. London, 21645, Pte., k. in a., F., 4/8/17.

STOTT, F., b. West Rainton, 57149, Cpl., k. in a., F., 27/7/17.

SWINGLER, J. W. F., b. Peshawar, 8923, L/Sgt., k. in a., F., 6/5/17.

TANCOCK, E. W., b. London, 22576, Pte., k. in a., F., 5/7/16.

TASSELL, A. J., b. London, 22340, Cpl., d. of w., F., 20/3/16.

THOMAS, D., b. Machynlleth, 61307, Pte., k. in a., F., 27/7/17.

THOMAS, E., b. Nant Budul, 54764, Pte., k. in a., F., 17/6/17.

THOMAS, H. R., b. Newtown, 291007, Cpl., k. in a., F., 27/7/17.

THOMAS, J., b. Connah's Quay, 55414, Pte., k. in a., F., 27/7/17.

THOMAS, M., b. Ruabon, 16981, Pte., k. in a., F., 10/7/16.

THOMAS, R., b. Barmouth, 291046, Pte., k. in a., F., 27/7/17.

THOMAS, T. A., b. Llangollen, 21520, Pte., k. in a., F., 21/8/16.

THOMAS, W., b. Meliden, 54760, Pte., k. in a., F., 2/12/16.

THURGILL, A., b. Clapton, 22991, Pte., k. in a., F., 19/3/16.

TITMUSS, F. H., b. London, 27043, Pte., k. in a., F., 14/5/16.

VARNALS, E., b. Tottenham, 22027, Pte., d. of w., F., 13/7/16.

WADE, D., b. Camberwell, 22324, Pte., k. in a., F., 10/4/16.

WATKINS, C. H., b. Abersychan, 56800, L/Cpl., d. of w., F., 15/10/16.

WATKINS, G. W., e. Newport, 21198, Pte., k. in a., F., 12/4/17.

WEATHERMAN, W., b. Macclesfield, 292390, Pte., k. in a., F., 28/7/17.

WEBSTER, C., b. London, 22963, Pte., d. of w., Home, 24/7/16.

WEBSTER, W., b. Church Stoke, 45773, Pte., k. in a., F., 25/7/17.

WELLS, P., b. Huddersfield, 56136, Pte., k. in a., F., 27/7/17.

WHITE, F. P., b. London, 22332, Pte., k. in a., F., 28/6/17.

WHITE, H., b. Manchester, 60128, Pte., k. in a., F., 4/8/17.

WHITE, R., b. Plymouth, 56844, Pte., k. in a., F., 31/7/17.

WHITTOME, H. J., b. London, 22675, Pte., k. in a., F., 8/1/16.

WILKINS, G., b. Llanfyllin, 21552, Cpl., k. in a., F., 5/7/16.

WILLIAMS, C., b. Exeter, 22887, Pte., k. in a., F., 17/6/17.

WILLIAMS, E. V., b. Hornsey, 21524, Pte., d. of w., F., 9/2/16.

WILLIAMS, J. V., b. Penzance, 18382, Pte., k. in a., F., 4/9/17.

WILLIAMS, O., b. Caergeiliog, 56838, Pte., k. in a., F., 27/6/17.

WILLIAMS, P. R., b. Llanwrtyd, 22895, L/Cpl., k. in a., F., 10/7/16.

WILLIAMS, R., b. Llandudno, 22589, L/Cpl., k. in a., F., 2/9/17, D.C.M.

WILLIAMS, R. I., b. Colwyn Bay, 54769, Pte., k. in a., F., 10/4/17.

WILLIAMS, R. J., b. Aberllefenny, 291579, Pte., k. in a., F., 4/8/17.

WILLIAMS, S. J., b. Aberystwyth, 22175, Cpl., k. in a., F., 4/8/17.

WILLIAMS, S. P., e. Blaenau Festiniog, 54774, Pte., d., F., 8/1/17.

WILLIAMS, T., b. Denbigh, 201148, Pte., k. in a., F., 31/7/17.

WILLIAMS, T., b. Newtown, 241873, Pte., k. in a., F., 4/8/17.

WILLIAMS, W., b. Williamstown, 13424, Pte., d. of w., F., 20/2/17.

WILLIAMS, W., b. Saltney, 55421, Pte., d., F., 10/2/18.

WILLIAMS, W., b. Machynlleth, 290125, Sgt., k. in a., F., 27/7/17.

WILLIAMS, W., b. Tremadoc, 291802, Pte., k. in a., F., 4/8/17.

WILLIAMS, W., b. Cerrigceinwen, 291952, Pte., k. in a., F., 7/1/18.

WILLIS, T. H., b. London, 22412, Pte., k. in a., F., 11/4/16.

WILMAN, C. L., b. London, 21615, Pte., k. in a., F., 10/7/16.

WILSON, F. M., b. London, 22240, Sgt., d., F., 23/1/18.

WILSON, W. W., b. St. Pancras, 35214, Pte., d. of w., F., 11/7/16.

WOODWARD, G. W. J., b. Swindon, 56509, Pte., d. of w., F., 2/8/17.

WRAGG, J., b. Huddersfield, 56158, Pte., d. of w., F., 28/12/17.

WYATT, V. A. W., b. Stroud, 61494, Pte., k. in a., F., 2/9/17.

YATES, G. W., b. Burton-on-Trent, 56118, Pte., k. in a., F., 17/6/17.

16th BATTALION

ALLAN, H., b. Preston, 73512, Pte., k. in a., F., 22/4/18.

ANDREWS, G. T., b. Braybourne, 55728, Pte., k. in a., F., 26/8/18.

ANTROBUS, T., b. Buckley, 87139, Pte., k. in a., F., 18/9/18.

ASHFIELD, J. C., b. Shifnal, 56499, Pte., d. of w., F., 8/10/17.

ASHWORTH, C., e. Wrexham, 54520, L/Cpl., k. in a., F., 31/7/17.

ASTON, S., b. Birmingham, 93988, Pte., k. in a., F., 8/10/18.

ATKINS, H., b. London, 26648, A/Sgt., k. in a., F., 11/7/16.

ATKINSON, W. J., b. Stockton, 235441, Sgt., k. in a., F., 24/8/18.

ATTWOOD, J. G., b. Wolverhampton, 241200, Sgt., d., F., 29/10/18.

BAILEY, F. C., b. Rotherhithe, 55794, Pte., k. in a., F., 26/12/17.

BAILEY, G., b. Pontypridd, 18918, Pte., k. in a., F., 22/4/18.

BAINTON, H. Q., b. Atwick, 55807, Pte., d. of w., Home, 14/5/18.

BAKER, F., b. Hadley, 60768, Pte., d. of w., F., 21/9/17.

BAKER, H., b. Moss Green, 19434, Cpl., k. in a., F., 10/7/16.

BALDWIN, A., b. Burnley, 58385, Pte., k. in a., F., 27/8/18.

BALL, G. R., b. Bexley, 34895, Pte., k. in a., F., 2/8/17.

BANN, J. E., e. Macclesfield, 76753, Pte., k. in a., F., 8/10/18.

BANNER, G., b. Widnes, 58366, Pte., k. in a., F., 3/9/18.

BARCLAY, J., b. Tonypandy, 18492, Pte., k. in a., F., 12/3/17.

BARNES, J., b. Withnell, 19417, L/Cpl., k. in a., F., 15/3/18.

BARRETT, H., b. Heywood, 19505, Pte., k. in a., F., 10/7/16.

BATCHELOR, A. E., b. Springbourne, 45264, Pte., k. in a., F., 31/7/17.

BATE, W. J., b. Pembroke, 89263, Pte., k. in a., F., 2/11/18.

BEE, W., b. Salwick, 58383, Pte., d. of w., F., 3/9/18.

BEECH, H., e. Stockport, 235326, Pte., d. of w., F., 23/4/18.

BEECH, J., b. Tunstall, 28964, Cpl., d. of w., F., 23/4/18.

BENNETT, J., e. Southport, 58381, Pte., k. in a., F., 18/9/18.

BENNETT, J. E., b. Ponkey, 87223, Pte., k. in a., F., 8/10/18.

BENTLEY, J., b. Wybunbury, 56439, Pte., k. in a., F., 18/9/18.

BESWICK, H., b. Chester, 235324, Pte., k. in a., F., 31/7/17.

BEVAN, G., b. Glyn, 19731, Pte., k. in a., F., 1/9/17.

BIDGOOD, J. A., b. London, 34830, Pte., d. of w., F., 2/8/17.

BILLS, F. H., b. Neath, 18251, Pte., k. in a., F., 11/7/16.

BIRD, J. W., b. Heigham, 77613, Pte., d. of w., F., 6/11/18.

BLACK, S., b. Leigh, 73525, Pte., k. in a., F., 15/3/18.

BLACKMORE, G. A. J., b. Cheltenham, 60187, Pte., k. in a., F., 22/4/18.

BOARDMAN, T., b. Blackpool, 73520, Pte., k. in a., F., 15/3/18.

BOND, T. C., b. Pentredwr, 88396, Pte., k. in a., F., 4/11/18.

BONNETT, W., b. Walton-at-Stone, 235190, Pte., k. in a., F., 31/7/17.

BOTTOMLEY, A., b. Blackburn, 19849, Pte., k. in a., F., 31/7/17.

BOWDEN, J., b. Bridport, 53991, Pte., d. of w., F., 5/5/18.

BOWRY, W., b. London, 57654, Pte., k. in a., F., 26/8/18.

BRADLEY, J. H., b. Wellington, 58384, Pte., k. in a., F., 24/8/18.

BRATT, P., b. Chester, 70242, Pte., d. of w., F., 17/5/18.

BRENNAN, J., b. Kirkham, 93919, Pte., k. in a., F., 8/10/18.

BRIGHTON, A. M. M., b. Ditchingham, 56445, Sgt., k. in a., F., 22/4/18.

BROWN, A. G., b. London, 21858, Pte., k. in a., F., 22/4/18.

BROWN, C. W., b. Southampton, 31457, Pte., k. in a., F., 14/6/17.

BROWN, E., b. Melverley, 56450, Pte., k. in a., F., 22/4/18.

BROWN, J. E., b. Cardiff, 93920, Pte., d. of w., F., 8/10/18.

BROWN, W., e. Liverpool, 19039, Pte., k. in a., F., 11/7/16.

BUCHAN, E., b. Oldham, 73524, Pte., k. in a., F., 15/3/18.

BUCKLEY, H., b. Witton, 77607, Pte., d. of w., F., 4/9/18.

BURGESS, H., b. London, 60161, Pte., k. in a., F., 31/7/17.

BURGWIN, C. E., b. Shrewsbury, 56476, Pte., d. of w., F., 5/8/17.

BURN, P., b. Brampton, 73519, Pte., k. in a., F., 22/4/18.

BUTLER, L. W., b. London, 93922, Pte., d. of w., F., 8/10/18.

BUTTERWORTH, J. R., e. Ashton-under-Lyne, 52142, Pte., k. in a., F., 12/4/18.

CALVERT, J., b. Blackburn, 70240, Cpl., k. in a., F., 22/4/18.

CAREY, W. J., b. Blackwood, 93925, Pte., k. in a., F., 8/11/18.

CARR, G., b. Flint, 19408, C.S.M., d. of w., F., 18/7/16.

CARTER, G. S., b. London, 27414, Sgt., k. in a., F., 2/12/16.

CARVER, E. C., b. Faversham, 55765, Pte., k. in a., F., 29/7/17.

CASSIDY, J. T., b. London, 27742, Pte., k. in a., F., 5/5/18.

CESHION, J., b. Cardiff, 36642, Pte., k. in a., F., 11/7/16.

CHADWICK, G., b. Blackburn, 33152, Pte., k. in a., F., 18/9/18.

CHAPLIN, T. G., b. Wepton, 23178, Pte., d., Home, 8/1/17.

CHARE, L., b. Birmingham, 61248, Pte., k. in a., F., 22/4/18.

CHICK, T., e. Cardiff, 38857, Pte., k. in a., F., 8/10/18.

CHURCHILL, W. T., e. Neath, 23053, Pte., d., F., 28/10/18.

CLARKE, A. T., b. Birmingham, 15530, Pte., k. in a., F., 3/7/18.

CLARKE, V. B., b. Barbadoes, 27895, Pte., k. in a., F., 31/7/17.

COACHWORTH, T., b. Herne Hill, 55751, Pte., k. in a., F., 18/9/18.

COATES, J., e. Gateshead, 60170, Pte., k. in a., F., 2/8/17.

COLE, L. E. F., e. London, 73537, Pte., d. of w., F., 23/9/18.

COLLINSON, H., b. Hyde, 62778, L/Cpl., k. in a., F., 30/8/18.

COOKE, T., b. Liverpool, 73513, Pte., k. in a., F., 8/10/18.

COPE, H., b. Liverpool, 29351, Pte., k. in a., F., 21/10/18.

COPP, B., e. Neath, 19030, Pte., k. in a., F., 7/2/16.

CORBETT, J. L., b. Patricroft, 235328, Pte., k. in a., F., 9/11/17.

CORBETT, W. G., b. Wythington, 55457, Pte., k. in a., F., 15/3/18.

CORFIELD, V. G., b. Coreley, 202707, Pte., k. in a., F., 22/4/18.

COULSON, A. J., b. Llanhilleth, 93924, Pte., k. in a., F., 4/11/18.

COUSINS, G., e. Hertford, 235200, Pte., k. in a., F., 15/3/18.

COWDEROY, C., b. Birkenhead, 56443, Pte., k. in a., F., 31/7/17.

COWDERY, W., b. Abertillery, 61479, Pte., d. of w., F., 18/5/18.

COX, A. R., b. London, 27488, Pte., k. in a., F., 11/7/16.

COX, H., b. Coventry, 94219, Pte., d. of w., F., 10/11/18.

COXON, H. V., b. Alton, 58393, Pte., k. in a., F., 4/11/18.

CROWTHER, F. E., b. London, 27196, Pte., k. in a., F., 10/7/16.

CRUMP, E. J., b. London, 21772, Pte., k. in a., F., 22/4/18.

CURRY, M., b. Accrington, 73557, Pte., k. in a., F., 1/9/18.

DAVIES, D., b. Pen-y-cae, 18329, Pte., d. of w., F., 3/9/18.

DAVIES, D. J., b. Ystradgynlais, 93951, Pte., k. in a., F., 8/10/18.

DAVIES, D. M., b. Kidwelly, 18624, L/Cpl., d. of w., Home, 7/8/17.

DAVIES, E., b. Dowlais, 93405, Pte., k. in a., F., 18/9/18.

DAVIES, E. O., e. Llanelly, 19042, L/Sgt., k. in a., F., 11/7/16.

DAVIES, H., b. Yspytty-ifan, 37011, Pte., k. in a., F., 10/7/16.

DAVIES, J., b. Abergele, 15239, Pte., k. in a., F., 15/3/18.

DAVIES, J., b. Llanerchymedd, 203580, Pte., d. of w., F., 7/5/18.

DAVIES, J. C., b. Talgarth, 55432, Pte., k. in a., F., 22/4/18.

DAVIES, J. D., b. Llanfynydd, 87006, Pte., d. of w., F., 26/10/18.

DAVIES, J. O. V., b. Oswestry, 23756, Pte., k. in a., F., 10/7/16.

DAVIES, L., b. Garn, 87703, Pte., k. in a., F., 4/11/18.

DAVIES, L., b. Blaina, 78124, Pte., d. of w., F., 7/11/18.

DAVIES, R. E., b. Llandudno, 33291, Pte., k. in a., F., 31/7/17.

DAVIES, R. R., b. Wrexham, 18293, d. of w., F., 7/12/16.

DAVIES, S. F., b. Liverpool, 37228, Pte., k. in a., F., 10/7/16.

DAVIES, T., b. Ellesmere, 24658, Cpl., k. in a., F., 26/8/18.

DAVIES, T., b. Cwmllynfell, 88592, Pte., k. in a., F., 4/11/18.

DAVIES, T., b. Llanarth, 203818, Pte., k. in a., F., 27/8/18.

DAVIES, W., b. Llanrhos, 37176, L/Cpl., k. in a., F., 22/4/18.

DAVIES, W. H., b. Broughton, 87157, Pte., k. in a., F., 18/9/18.

DAVISON, F., b. Bistre, 18369, Pte., k. in a., F., 19/6/17.

DAWES, A. E., e. Hertford, 235202, Pte., k. in a., F., 31/7/17.

DAWSON, J., b. Glossop, 73544, Pte., k. in a., F., 8/10/18.

DEAN, T., b. Crawford Village, 266845, Pte., d. of w., F., 20/5/18.

DENNIS, N. A., b. London, 34770, Pte., k. in a., F., 11/7/16.

DENTON, G., b. Flint, 19112, Sgt., d. of w., F., 8/3/16.

DIGGLE, N. S., b. Manchester, 52541, Pte., k. in a., F., 31/7/17.

DOLAN, G. E., b. Liverpool, 55965, Pte., k. in a., F., 18/9/18.

DONE, P., b. Weston Point, 58344, Pte., k. in a., F., 18/9/18.

DOWDEN, W., b. Newport, 59689, Pte., d. of w., F., 26/6/17.

DREW, D. M., b. Clydach Vale, 76693, Pte., k. in a., F., 4/11/18.

DREW, P., b. Bristol, 94229, Pte., k. in a., F., 3/11/18.

DUGGAN, J., b. London, 93956, Pte., k. in a., F., 8/10/18.

DYKINS, H., b. Holywell, 19109, L/Cpl., k. in a., F., 11/7/16.

EAMES, E. A., b. London, 27740, Pte., k. in a., F., 8/10/18.

EATON, J. B., b. Buenos Ayres, 23177, Pte., k. in a., F., 11/7/16.

EDGE, N. E., b. Cheadle, 19181, Pte., k. in a., F., 11/7/16.

EDWARDS, A. R., e. Wrexham, 36828, Pte., k. in a., F., 22/4/18.

EDWARDS, C., b. Ruabon, 23046, C.Q.M.S., k. in a., F., 22/6/17.

EDWARDS, E., b. Rhyl, 17649, Pte., k. in a., F., 25/2/17.

EDWARDS, E. R., b. Gravesend, 46361, Pte., d. of w., F., 1/8/17.

EDWARDS, E. W., b. Ruabon, 37340, Pte., k. in a., F., 11/7/16.

EDWARDS, F., b. Garndiffath, 94232, Pte., k. in a., F., 3/11/18.

EDWARDS, F., b. Llangollen, 37710, Pte., k. in a., F., 27/8/18.

EDWARDS, G., b. Manchester, 28520, Pte., k. in a., F., 12/4/18.

EDWARDS, H., b. Llanfair P.G., 37281, Pte., d. of w., F., 25/2/17.

EDWARDS, H. O., b. Bwlchgwyn, 87005, Pte., k. in a., F., 8/10/18.

EDWARDS, J., b. Morriston, 18836, L/Cpl., d. of w., F., 7/7/16.

EDWARDS, J. B., e. Liverpool, 52986, Pte., k. in a., F., 18/9/18.

EDWARDS, P., b. Gwersyllt, 87158, Pte., k. in a., F., 18/9/18.

EDWARDS, R. O., b. Llanerchy-medd, 23287, Cpl., k. in a., F., 26/8/18.

EDWARDS, R. W., b. London, 235204, Pte., k. in a., F., 31/7/17.

EDWARDS, T., b. Mold, 18447, Sgt., k. in a., F., 31/7/17, D.C.M.

EDWARDS, W., b. Rhondda, 19618, Pte., k. in a., F., 30/5/16.

EDWARDS, W., b. Accrington, 16487, Pte., k. in a., F., 11/7/16.

EDWARDS, W., b. Llangollen, 17771, L/Cpl., k. in a., F., 31/7/17.

ELEY, S. G., b. Tiddickstone Higher, 94233, Pte., d. of w., F., 30/10/18.

ELIAS, G., b. Neath, 58249, Sgt., k. in a., F., 26/8/18.

ELLIOTT, A. E., b. London, 22496, Pte., k. in a., F., 22/4/18.

ELLIS, G. J., b. Wrexham, 36638, Pte., k. in a., F., 11/7/16.

ELLIS, J., b. Accrington, 204516, Pte., k. in a., F., 4/11/18.

ELLIS, S., b. Hawarden, 19527, Pte., d. of w., F., 11/3/16.

ELLIS, T., b. Birmingham, 27970, L/Cpl., k. in a., F., 11/7/16.

EVANS, A. P., b. Aberystwyth, 78181, Pte., k. in a., F., 4/11/18.

EVANS, C. T., b. Carnarvon, 44140, Pte., k. in a., F., 24/8/18.

EVANS, D., b. Llangeitho, 34784, Pte., k. in a., F., 11/7/16.

EVANS, D., b. Cwmavon, 18610, Sgt., d. of w., F., 24/4/18.

EVANS, D., b. Newchurch, 55430, Cpl., k. in a., F., 30/7/17.

EVANS, D. B., b. Dowlais, 18795, Cpl., k. in a., F., 9/4/17.

EVANS, E., b. Llanfair, 39185, Cpl., k. in a., F., 19/9/17.

EVANS, E. J., b. Old Colwyn, 36640, Pte., k. in a., F., 10/7/16.

EVANS, F., b. Leeds, 87145, Pte., d. of w., F., 29/10/18.

EVANS, H., b. Llanllwni, 55453, Pte., k. in a., F., 31/7/17.

EVANS, H. T., b. Dolgelly, 204457, Pte., k. in a., F., 19/9/17.

EVANS, J., b. Cynwyd, 23330, Pte., k. in a., F., 11/7/16.

EVANS, J., b. Brymbo, 40198, Pte., k. in a., F., 30/7/17.

EVANS, J. T., b. Amlwch, 23877, Cpl., k. in a., F., 18/9/18.

EVANS, J. W., b. Cribyn, 31405, Pte., d. of w., F., 22/3/16.

EVANS, P., b. Dowlais, 18947, L/Cpl., k. in a., F., 2/12/16.

EVANS, R. G., b. Llanllyfni, 203739, Pte., k. in a., F., 22/4/18.

EVANS, R. J., b. Llanymys, 19278, Pte., k. in a., F., 10/7/16.

EVANS, W., b. Ystreu, 18974, Pte., k. in a., F., 6/7/16.

EVANS, W., b. Huthwaite, 19343, L/Cpl., k. in a., F., 11/7/16.

EVENSON, T., b. Whitchurch, 56451, Pte., k. in a., F., 22/4/18.

FAIRCLOUGH, W., b. Heath Charnock, 73553, Pte., k. in a., F., 16/5/18.

FELTON, F. J., b. London, 235206, Pte., k. in a., F., 31/7/17.

FERGUSSON, T., b. Whitchurch, 18665, A/Cpl., k. in a., F., 11/7/16.

FISHER, W. A., b. Broughton, 18876, Pte., k. in a., F., 8/10/18.

FLETCHER, A. A., e. Hertford, 235205, Pte., k. in a., F., 31/7/17.

FLINT, A., b. London, 31475, Pte., d., F., 14/1/17.

FLINT, H., b. Hadfield, 241706, Pte., k. in a., F., 18/9/18.

FOLLETT, T. W., b. Taffs Well, 18975, Pte., d. of w., F., 13/1/16.

FOLLOWS, J., b. Ashton-under-Lyne, 73554, Pte., k. in a., F., 22/4/18.

FOSTER, A., b. Godalming, 55753, Pte., k. in a., F., 31/7/17.

FOWLER, J., b. Nottingham, 93961, Pte., k. in a., F., 8/10/18.

FOX, W., b. Buckley, 18783, Pte., d. of w., F., 7/3/16.

FRANCIS, J. R., b. Wrexham, 39093, Pte., d., F., 4/8/17.

FRASER, R., b. Liverpool, 73555, Pte., k. in a., F., 15/3/18.

FRETWELL, R., b. Barnsley, 23148, Pte. k. in a., F., 11/7/16.

FRY, W. H., b. Pirbright, 55742, Pte., k. in a., F., 18/9/18.

GALLEN, R. A. L., b. Capel Garmon, 19599, Pte., k. in a., F., 11/4/16.

GALLIMORE, A. E., b. Sandbach, 63946, Pte., k. in a., F., 15/3/18.

GARDNER, W., b. Carnforth, 56460, Pte., k. in a., F., 21/7/17.

GAYLER, F. V., b. London, 34953, Pte., k. in a., F., 10/7/16.

GEAR, G., e. Manchester, 31741, Pte., k. in a., F., 11/7/16.

GENNER, A. T., b. Bitterley, 37169, Pte., k. in a., F., 14/6/17.

GEORGE, H. E., b. London, 21586, A/Cpl., k. in a., F., 22/4/18.

GERRARD, A., e. Llangefni, 18599, Pte., d. of w., F., 4/9/18.

GIBSON, S., b. Winsford, 77620, Pte., d. of w., F., 26/6/18.

GILLON, M., b. Liverpool, 11987, Pte., d., F., 25/12/16.

GLADDIS, F. R., e. Andover, 60162, Pte., k. in a., F., 17/3/18.

GODFREY, C., b. Merthyr Tydvil, 56507, Cpl., k. in a., F., 22/4/18.

GOLDSMITH, R., b. London, 26592, L/Cpl., k. in a., F., 19/9/17.

GORST, J., b. Chester, 60178, Pte., k. in a., F., 4/8/17.

GOTHERRIDGE, T. H., b. Mansfield, 58267, Pte., k. in a., F., 8/7/18.

GOUGH, S., b. Pontypridd, 31422, Pte., k. in a., F., 6/10/16.

GOULDING, J., b. Chorley, 93401, Pte., k. in a., F., 26/8/18.

GRAHAM, G., b. London, 35311, Pte., k. in a., F., 10/7/16.

GRAINEY, T., b. Rhyl, 29640, Pte., k. in a., F., 18/9/18.

GRANGER, A. L., b. King's Lynn,

55791, Pte., d. of w., F., 2/8/17.

GREEN, J. T., b. Westhoughton, 58268, Pte., d. of w., F., 30/12/18.

GREGORY, L., b. London, 55797, Pte., k. in a., F., 4/8/17.

GRIFFIN, T. V., b. Bootle, 55707, Pte., k. in a., F., 16/6/18.

GRIFFITHS, E. T., b. Llanenwyn, 19232, L/Cpl., k. in a., F., 24/8/18, M.M.

GRIFFITHS, G., b. Brymbo, 6641, Pte., k. in a., F., 31/7/17.

GRIFFITHS, J., b. Meliden, 58345, Pte., k. in a., F., 4/11/18.

GRIFFITHS, J., b. Haydock, 70239, Sgt., d., F., 31/10/18.

GRIFFITHS, R., b. Shrewsbury, 18825, C.S.M., d., Home, 24/4/16.

GRIFFITHS, S., b. Bodorgan, 24709, L/Cpl., k. in a., F., 30/7/17.

GRIFFITHS, S., e. Tonypandy, 19050, Pte., k. in a., F., 11/7/16.

GRIFFITHS, T., e. Tonypandy, 89188, Pte., k. in a., F., 4/11/18.

GRIFFITHS, T. N., b. Johnstown, 24874, Pte., k. in a., F., 30/8/17.

GRIMSHAW, R., b. Darwen, 56453, Pte., d. of w., F., 23/7/17.

GROVES, R. H., e. Wrexham, 54502, Pte., k. in a., F., 2/8/17.

HAMER, H., b. Wrexham, 36362, Pte., k. in a., F., 11/7/16.

HAMER, W. C., b. Cardiff, 55437, Pte., k. in a., F., 18/9/18.

HAMMONDS, A., b. Stalybridge, 235337, Pte., k. in a., F., 2/9/18.

HAMPSON, R., b. Hyde, 315240, Pte., k. in a., F., 30/8/18.

HAMS, F. J., b. Manchester, 235341, Pte., k. in a., F., 22/4/18.

HANKEY, R. E., b. Preesall-fylde, 58277, Pte., k. in a., F., 8/10/18.

HANNAN, C., b. Irlam, 267175, Pte., k. in a., F., 19/9/17.

HARRIS, A., b. Hereford, 93968, Pte., k. in a., F., 21/10/18.

HARRIS, D., b. Bedlinog, 19369, Pte., d., Home, 15/12/15.

HARRIS, E., b. Ynyscytaiarn, 36383, Pte., d. of w., F., 6/7/16.

HARRIS, W. C., b. Rudry, 19275, Pte., k. in a., F., 30/1/16.

HART, C., b. Wigan, 58284, Pte., k. in a., F., 4/11/18.

HARVEY, W., b. Nevendon, 55951, Pte., k. in a., F., 8/10/18.

HAWKINS, W. S., b. Cardiff, 18409, Pte., k. in a., F., 18/9/18.

HEAP, J., b. Singapore, 58276, Pte., k. in a., F., 24/8/18.

HEARD, A. A., b. London, 26735, Pte., k. in a., F., 22/4/18.

HEARNE, T., b. Clydach, 55051, Pte., k. in a., F., 15/3/18.

HEATON, H., b. Hollinwood, 33011, Pte., k. in a., F., 11/7/16.

HESKEY, W. T., b. Kynerrsley, 56446, Pte., k. in a., F., 31/7/17.

HEWITT, A., b. Connah's Quay, 18243, Pte., k. in a., F., 11/7/16.

HIBBERT, E., b. Bradford, 267503, Pte., k. in a., F., 19/9/17.

HICKMAN, T., e. Tonypandy, 19048, Cpl., k. in a., F., 11/7/16.

HILL, F., b. London, 73570, L/Cpl., k. in a., F., 8/10/18.

HISCOCK, H. J., e. London, 60158, Pte., k. in a., F., 22/4/18.

HOLDER, J. W., b. London, 55757, Pte., k. in a., F., 17/6/17.

HOLGATE, W. L., b. Darwen, 18983, L/Cpl., k. in a., F., 11/7/16.

HOLLINS, P., b. Ashley, 54522, Pte., d. of w., F., 12/11/16.

HOLME, A., b. Seaforth, 36282, Pte., k. in a., F., 8/10/18.

HOLMES, E., e. Wrexham, 54505, Pte., k. in a., F., 2/8/17.

HOLT, L. S., e. Rhosymedre, 200738, Sgt., k. in a., F., 22/4/18.

HOOSE, H., b. Overton, 18596, Cpl., k. in a., F., 11/7/16.

HOPE, C., b. Coed Poeth, 87136, L/Cpl., k. in a., F., 4/11/18.

HOPKINS, H. R., b. Newport, 10563, Sgt., k. in a., F., 18/9/18.

HORNE, H., b. Manchester, 38332, Pte., k. in a., F., 14/3/17.

HORROCKS, G., b. Harpurhey, 58281, Pte., k. in a., F., 29/8/18.

HOWARD, J. J. H., b. Aberystwyth, 19963, L/Cpl., d. of w., F., 12/7/16.

HUGHES, E., b. Abergele, 18688, Pte., d. of w., F., 11/4/16.

HUGHES, E., b. Romiley, 235340, Pte., k. in a., F., 31/7/17.

HUGHES, E., b. Mold, 267494, Pte., k. in a., F., 19/9/17.

HUGHES, E. E., b. London, 34979, Pte., k. in a., F., 11/7/16.

HUGHES, E. O., b. Llanbeblig, 265780, Pte., k. in a., F., 16/6/18.

HUGHES, E. S., b. Greenfield, 203257, Pte., k. in a., F., 19/9/17.

HUGHES, G., b. Llanllechid, 23560, Pte., k. in a., F., 10/7/16.

HUGHES, H., b. Flint, 28463, Sgt., k. in a., F., 8/10/18.

HUGHES, H., b. Llandwrog, 40129, Pte., k. in a., F., 25/2/17.

o

Hughes, H. T., b. Trawsfynydd, 69871, Pte., d. of w., F., 3/9/18.

Hughes, M., b. Llanengan, 18416, Pte., k. in a., F., 19/2/16.

Hughes, R., b. Bettws-y-Coed, 18245, A/Cpl., k. in a., F., 11/7/16.

Hughes, R. C., b. Llangefni, 59677, Pte., k. in a., F., 21/7/17.

Hughes, T., b. Carnarvon, 25025, Pte., k. in a., F., 22/4/18.

Hughes, W., b. Llandegai, 18178, Pte., k. in a., F., 11/12/15.

Hughes, W. H., e. Tonypandy, 19035, Pte., d. of w., F., 15/7/17.

Hughes, W. M., b. Carnarvon, 265896, Cpl., k. in a., F., 22/4/18.

Humphreys, H., b. Wellington, 19872, Pte., k. in a., F., 10/1/16.

Humphries, D., b. Senghenydd, 19362, Pte., k. in a., F., 11/7/16.

Hunt, J., b. Burnley, 77621, Pte., k. in a., F., 26/8/18.

Hussey, F. J., b. Cwmaman, 86986, Pte., k. in a., F., 8/10/18.

Iball, L., b. Buckley, 23739, L/Sgt., k. in a., F., 19/9/17.

Ingram, J., b. Llanfair, 56818, Pte., d., F., 15/4/18.

Jackson, J., b. Burnley, 60045, Pte., k. in a., F., 16/5/18.

James, C., b. Ynyscynhaiar, 315545, Pte., k. in a., F., 28/10/17.

James, G., b. Maenclochog, 55440, Pte., k. in a., F., 30/7/17.

James, J., b. Ystradgynlais, 93969, Pte., k. in a., F., 5/10/18.

James, R., b. Merthyr, 57152, Pte., k. in a., F., 22/4/18.

James, T., b. Pennal, 23391, Pte., d. of w., Home, 23/7/16.

Jarvis, J. H., b. Hereford, 58358, Pte., k. in a., F., 28/8/18.

Jeffries, E. G., b. Tirphil, 94205, Pte., d. of w., F., 19/11/18.

Jenkins, S. G., b. Llangynwyd, 31143, Pte., k. in a., F., 19/2/16.

Jenkins, T. J., b. Pontrhydfendigaid, 45179, Pte., k. in a., F., 31/7/17.

Jenkins, W. H., b. Treherbert, 78101, Pte., k. in a., F., 4/11/18.

Jennings, F., b. Langford, 72264, Pte., d. of w., F., 1/9/18.

John, W., b. Tenby, 55464, Pte., k. in a., F., 15/1/17.

Johnson, C. R., b. Wolverhampton, 93975, Pte., d. of w., F., 9/10/18.

Johnson, J., b. Wrexham, 18179, Sgt., k. in a., F., 2/12/16.

Johnson, W., b. Bradford, 19239, Sgt., k. in a., F., 11/7/16.

Jones, A., b. Llanrwst, 37469, Pte., d. of w., Home, 4/9/16.

Jones, A. E., b. Glantraeth, 24743, Pte., k. in a., F., 11/7/16.

Jones, C., b. Cardiff, 201532, A/Cpl., d. of w., F., 5/11/18.

Jones, C. O., b. Wrexham, 17803, Pte., k. in a., F., 4/11/18.

Jones, D., b. Amlwch, 23344, Pte., k. in a., F., 22/4/18.

Jones, D. J., b. Denio, 40272, Pte., k. in a., F., 22/6/18.

Jones, D. S., b. Rudry, 18663, Pte., k. in a., F., 11/7/16.

Jones, D. W., b. Corwen, 19959, Pte., k. in a., F., 22/4/18.

Jones, E., e. Wrexham, 19058, Pte., d. of w., F., 21/7/16.

Jones, E., b. Blaenau Festiniog, 49034, Pte., d. of w., F., 4/8/17.

Jones, E., b. Hanwood, 40036, Pte., d. of w., F., 3/10/16.

Jones, F. G., e. Wrexham, 19055, Pte., k. in a., F., 11/7/16.

Jones, G., b. Llanbeblig, 19353, Pte., k. in a., F., 10/7/16.

Jones, G. H., b. Beaumaris, 37510, Pte., k. in a., F., 14/6/17.

Jones, G. O., b. Brymbo, 87487, Pte., k. in a., F., 8/10/18.

Jones, H. P., b. Acrefair, 88314, Pte., k. in a., F., 4/11/18.

Jones, I., b. Pontllanfraith, 18835, Pte., d. of w., F., 15/7/16.

Jones, J., b. Birkenhead, 203904, Pte., d. of w., F., 14/11/18.

Jones, J., b. Llanrhaiadr, 19078, L/Cpl., k. in a., F., 11/7/16.

Jones, J., b. Llanelidan, 23268, Pte., d. of w., F., 12/7/16.

Jones, J., b. Pen-y-fford, 24116, Pte., k. in a., F., 10/7/16.

Jones, J., b. Llanengan, 53826, Pte., k. in a., F., 21/7/17.

Jones, J., b. Blaenau Festiniog, 93935, Pte., k. in a., F., 8/10/18.

Jones, J., b. Llanfaglan, 204088, Pte., k. in a., F., 22/4/18.

Jones, J., b. Farndon, 19469, A/Sgt., d. of w., F., 14/7/16.

Jones, J., b. Wigan, 202540, Pte., k. in a., F., 3/8/17.

Jones, J. G., b. Llysfaen, 18886, Pte., d. of w., F., 11/7/16.

Jones, J. H., b. Valley, R.S.O., 19138, Pte., k. in a., F., 10/1/16.

Jones, J. H., b. Penrhyn, 19141, L/Cpl., k. in a., F., 17/12/15.

Jones, J. P., b. Merthyr, 18949, Pte., k. in a., F., 11/7/16.

Jones, K., b. Rhayader, 24881, Cpl., k. in a., F., 17/7/16.

Jones, L., b. Glynceiriog, 18756, L/Cpl., d. of w., F., 17/2/17.

Jones, L., b. Rhos, 37714, Pte., k. in a., F., 31/7/17.

Jones, L., e. Llandilo, 202827, L/Cpl., k. in a., F., 8/10/18.

Jones, L. E., b. Llanfair, 17935, Sgt., d. of w., E., 7/11/17.

Jones, P., b. Holywell, 36845, L/Sgt., k. in a., F., 22/4/18.

Jones, R., b. Troedyrhiw, 267952, Pte., d. of w., F., 12/6/18.

Jones, R., b. Cordana, 37251, Pte., d. of w., F., 11/7/16.

Jones, R., b. Newborough, 43798, Pte., d. of w., F., 30/8/18.

Jones, R., b. Llanrhyddlad, 11625, Pte., d. of w., F., 17/2/17.

Jones, R., b. Llanwnnog, 93936, Pte., k. in a., F., 8/10/18.

Jones, R., b. Portmadoc, 203567, L/Cpl., k. in a., F., 8/10/18.

Jones, R., b. Gwalchmai, 203763, Pte., k. in a., F., 22/4/18.

Jones, R. E., b. Llanidloes, 23247, Pte., k. in a., F., 21/2/16.

Jones, R. E., b. Mold, 76039, Pte., d. of w., F., 9/10/18.

Jones, R. G., b. Amlwch, 24707, Pte., k. in a., F., 27/2/17.

Jones, R. O., b. Deudraeth, 19146, Pte., k. in a., F., 9/6/16.

Jones, R. T., b. Bwlchgwyn, 200550, Pte., d. of w., F., 13/11/18.

Jones, R. W., b. Ebenezer, 20317, L/Cpl., k. in a., F., 21/2/16.

Jones, S., b. Hawarden, 36047, Pte., k. in a., F., 10/7/16.

Jones, T., b. Cwmdandwr, 17197, Pte., k. in a., F., 18/9/18.

Jones, T., e. Liverpool, 60163, Pte., k. in a., F., 30/7/17.

Jones, T. C., e. Caergwrle, 87227, Pte., k. in a., F., 8/10/18.

Jones, T. G., b. Cwm, 16434, Cpl., k. in a., F., 15/3/18.

Jones, T. S., b. Merthyr, 18579, Pte., k. in a., F., 8/4/17.

Jones, W., b. Llansilin, 19389, Pte., k. in a., F., 10/7/16.

Jones, W., b. Derwen, 17980, Pte., k. in a., F., 11/7/16.

Jones, W., e. Bangor, 61016, Pte., k. in a., F., 18/9/18.

Jones, W. E., b. Ruabon, 36627, L/Cpl., k. in a., F., 18/9/18.

Jones, W. H., b. Rhosgadfan, 40811, Pte., d. of w., F., 10/10/16.

Jones, W. J., b. Penrhyndeudraeth, 19228, Pte., k. in a., F., 11/7/16.

Kelly, W., b. Liverpool, 63534, Pte., d. of w., Home, 23/9/18.

Kelsall, C., b. Glossop, 18981, Pte., k. in a., F., 6/7/16.

Kempshall, I. R. A. J., b. Capel, 55738, Pte., k. in a., F., 15/3/18.

Kerrigan, W., b. Manchester, 28894, Pte., k. in a., F., 22/4/18.

Kirkham, T., b. Wrexham, 55544, Pte., d., F., 28/4/18.

KNIGHT, G. H., b. Guildford, 55761, Pte., d. of w., F., 31/7/17.

KNIGHT, J., b. Buckley, 19530, Pte., d. of w., F., 4/8/17.

KNOWLES, F., b. Aberavon, 19563, Pte., k. in a., F., 11/7/16.

KNOWLES, W. J., b. Bacup, 56464, Pte., d. of w., F., 20/9/17.

LAKELAND, L., b. Burnley, 201860, Pte., k. in a., F., 4/11/18.

LAKELAND, W., b. Preston, 58294, Pte., d. of w., F., 31/8/18.

LANCELOTTE, C. W., e. Wrexham, 267775, Pte., d. of w., F., 21/9/17.

LANGFORD, G. T., b. Llantrisant, 18543, Cpl., k. in a., F., 22/4/18.

LANGLEY, W., b. London, 26516, L/Cpl., d. of w., F., 17/7/16.

LANGSTAFF, H., b. Blackburn, 31718, Pte., d. of w., Home, 21/10/16.

LAYCOCK, F., b. Colne, 5465, Pte., d. of w., F., 12/8/17.

LEIGH, J. H., b. Pontypridd, 19244, Pte., d. of w., F., 24/8/18.

LEWIS, A. E., b. Ogmore Vale, 87544, Pte., k. in a., F., 8/10/18.

LEWIS, D., e. Pontypridd, 19028, Pte., k. in a., F., 10/7/16.

LEWIS, J., b. Liverpool, 77653, Pte., k. in a., F., 30/8/18.

LEWIS, L., b. Llantrisant, 13701, C.S.M., k. in a., F., 8/10/18.

LEWIS, R., b. Holyhead, 23346, Pte., k. in a., F., 11/7/16.

LEWIS, T., b. Chirk, 24143, Pte., k. in a., F., 11/7/16.

LEWIS, W., e. Cardiff, 77916, Pte., k. in a., F., 20/10/18.

LINFORD, T., b. Preston, 201684, Cpl., d. of w., F., 13/11/18.

LIPPIATT, A. J., b. Almondsbury, 18718, Pte., k. in a., F., 1/9/17.

LLOYD, A., b. Adderley Green, 25724, Pte., d. of w., Home, 12/8/17.

LLOYD, A., b. Llangunton, 94139, Pte., k. in a., F., 4/11/18.

LLOYD, J., b. Carthbeibio, 24751, Pte., d., F., 14/11/16.

LLOYD, W., b. Llanfair, 61111, Pte., d. of w., F., 23/4/18.

LONGDEN, J. F., e. Manchester, 73430, Pte., k. in a., F., 8/10/18.

LOWE, R., b. Lincoln, 70384, Pte., d. of w., Home, 2/5/18.

LOWRIE, V. C., b. London, 27460, Pte., k. in a., F., 1/9/17.

LOYNS, J. C., b. Birkenhead, 70301, Pte., k. in a., F., 3/9/18.

LUCAS, J., b. Liverpool, 70022, Pte., k. in a., F., 4/11/18.

McDONALD, F., b. Burnley, 201685, Pte., d. of w., F., 24/4/18.

MADDOCK, S. A., b. Stoke-on-Trent, 56466, Pte., k. in a., F., 31/7/17.

MAJOR, G., b. London, 26837, Pte., k. in a., F., 22/4/18.

MANSELL, J. R. B., b. Devonport, 54017, Pte., d. of w., F., 21/9/17.

MARTIN, W. A., b. Wrexham, 54572, L/Cpl., k. in a., F., 20/4/17.

MASON, D., b. Aberystwyth, 23354, Pte., k. in a., F., 11/7/16.

MASON, L. L., b. Manchester, 31655, Pte., k. in a., F., 11/7/16.

MASSEY, T., b. Wilmslow, 36756, Pte., k. in a., F., 11/11/16.

MATTHEWS, D. T., b. Treherbert, 18431, Sgt., k. in a., F., 22/4/18.

MATTINSON, J. G., e. Carlisle, 58305, Pte., k. in a., F., 18/5/18.

MAYBURY, I., b. Nantybar, 86987, L/Cpl., k. in a., F., 8/10/18.

MAYGER, E. A., b. London, 55770, Pte., d. of w., F., 8/10/17.

McCARTHY, W., b. Brithdir, 40091, Pte., d., F., 23/10/18.

McKOWN, D., b. Shaw, 24815, L/Sgt., k. in a., F., 31/7/17.

MELVIN, E. J., b. London, 35132, L/Cpl., k. in a., F., 22/4/18.

MESSHAM, P., b. Hawarden, 21494, Pte., k. in a., F., 23/8/16.

MILES, E., b. Ystrad, 19178, Pte., k. in a., F., 11/7/16.

MILLS, A., b. Llanidloes, 5596, Sgt., k. in a., F., 31/7/17.

MITCHAM, C. H., b. London, 54016, Pte., k. in a., F., 3/9/18.

MITCHELL, R., b. Burnley, 58304, Pte., k. in a., F., 26/8/18.

MOLYNEUX, E. C., b. Nannerch, 44236, Pte., k. in a., F., 18/9/18.

MORGAN, J., b. Burnley, 87846, Pte., k. in a., F., 18/9/18.

MORGAN, J., b. Crynant, 23562, Pte., k. in a., F., 10/7/16.

MORGAN, J. H., b. Newtown, 235846, Sgt., d. of w., F., 21/11/18.

MORGAN, J. O., b. Llanllechid, 60697, Pte., k. in a., F., 2/8/17.

MORGAN, T., b. Glyn, 73176, Pte., k. in a., F., 8/10/18.

MORGAN, T. J., b. Blaenau Festiniog, 36767, Pte., k. in a., F., 11/7/16.

MORGANS, T., b. Treherbert, 18961, Pte., k. in a., F., 11/7/16.

MORRIS, F., b. Blackpool, 58302, Pte., k. in a., F., 26/8/18.

MORRIS, J., b. Barmouth, 34960, Pte., k. in a., F., 11/7/16.

MORRIS, J. R., b. Castle Caereinion, 89537, Pte., d. of w., Home, 27/11/18.

MORRIS, O., b. Liverpool, 40890, Pte., d. of w., F., 9/7/18.

MORRIS, R. E., e. Denbigh, 54510, Pte., k. in a., F., 17/6/17.

MORTON, A. E., b. Leicester, 27114, Pte., k. in a., F., 19/4/16.

MOSES, T., b. Swansea, 36761, Pte., k. in a., F., 11/12/16.

MURPHY, C., b. Cork, 35055, Pte., k. in a., F., 18/9/18, M.M.

NEWMAN, A. J., b. London, 27871, Cpl., k. in a., F., 4/11/18.

NICHOLAS, T. E., b. Hawarden, 18585, Sgt., k. in a., F., 22/4/18.

NICHOLLS, J., b. London, 55815, Pte., k. in a., F., 2/8/17.

NICHOLSON, H., b. Leeds, 60164, Pte., k. in a., F., 8/7/18.

NORFOLK, C., b. Woodford, 35088, Pte., k. in a., F., 19/5/18.

O'BRIEN, T., e. Tonypandy, 23243, Pte., k. in a., F., 11/7/16.

O'NEILL, P., b. Roscommon, 267502, Pte., k. in a., F., 19/9/17.

OWEN, D. P., b. Llanberis, 40042, Pte., d. of w., F., 24/8/18.

OWEN, E. J., b. London, 21892, L/Cpl., d. of w., F., 26/8/18.

OWEN, F., e. Flint, 55380, Pte., k. in a., F., 22/4/18.

OWEN, G., b. Gryngoch, 203627, Pte., k. in a., F., 22/4/18.

OWEN, H. H., e. Carnarvon, 53765, Pte., k. in a., F., 22/4/18.

OWEN, J., b. Pentraeth, 24717, Pte., k. in a., F., 21/2/16.

OWEN, R., b. Llanddaniel, 43754, Pte., k. in a., F., 3/9/18.

OWEN, W., b. Brynguran, 24736, Pte., k. in a., F., 11/7/16.

OWEN, W., e. Wrexham, 60731, L/Cpl., k. in a., F., 8/10/18.

OWEN, W. J., e. Llanrwst, 18676, Pte., k. in a., F., 10/7/16.

OWENS, R. D., b. Whitford, 18455, Pte., k. in a., F., 29/10/16.

PARDOE, J., b. Ombersley, 56488, Pte., k. in a., F., 22/4/18.

PARFITT, D. J., b. Egham, 55740, Pte., d. of w., F., 28/2/18.

PARKER, R., b. Caton, 48901, L/Cpl., k. in a., F., 8/10/18.

PARR, H. S., e. Wrexham, 54511, Pte., k. in a., F., 8/10/18.

PARRY, J., e. Buckley, 18820, Pte., k. in a., F., 31/7/17.

PARRY, T., b. Llanfair P.G., 23003, L/Cpl., k. in a., F., 18/9/18.

PARRY, T. J., b. Ruthin, 17965, Pte., d. of w., F., 14/9/18.

PARRY, W. G., b. Colwyn, 77595, Pte., k. in a., F., 8/7/18.

PATE, E. J., b. Rhondda, 23274, Pte., d. of w., F., 7/7/16.

PEARCE, C., b. Chirk, 88362, Pte., k. in a., F., 6/10/18.

PEARCE, H., b. Doncaster, 24771, L/Cpl., d. of w., F., 24/4/18.

PELL, G., b. Alderley Edge, 77633, Pte., k. in a., F., 26/8/18.

PERKINS, F., b. Manchester, 19588, L/Cpl., k. in a., F., 11/7/16.

PERRIN, P. P., b. Broughton, 87414, Pte., d. of w., F., 8/10/18.

PERRY, W., b. Warwick, 44206, Pte., k. in a., F., 15/3/18.

PHELPS, G., b. Bristol, 73692, Cpl., k. in a., F., 22/4/18.

PHELPS, H., b. Cardiff, 54497, Pte., k. in a., F., 22/4/18.

PHILLIPS, F., b. Whitchurch, 23058, Pte., k. in a., F., 11/7/16.

PHILLIPS, S. I., b. Glynceriog, 18073, Pte., k. in a., F., 31/5/16.

PHILLIPS, W. A., b. Whitchurch, 18078, Pte., k. in a., F., 11/7/16.

PIERCE, R. W., b. Barry, 10639, Pte., k. in a., F., 15/3/18.

PLUNKETT, G., e. Tonypandy, 89220, Pte., k. in a., F., 4/11/18.

PRESTON, R., b. Wigan, 58308, Pte., k. in a., F., 24/8/18.

PRICE, C., b. Walton, 23351, Pte., d., F., 10/2/16.

PRICE, J. J., b. Aberystwyth, 77449, Pte., k. in a., F., 22/10/18.

PRICE, S., b. Aberdare, 201253, Pte., k. in a., F., 1/9/17.

PRIESTLEY, A., b. Marsden, 19871, Pte., k. in a., F., 11/7/16.

PRINCE, W., e. Wrexham, 205288, Sgt., k. in a., F., 18/9/18.

PRITCHARD, J., b. Talysarn, 89531, Pte., k. in a., F., 20/10/18.

PRITCHARD, R. M., b. Bangor, 37971, Pte., k. in a., F., 29/8/16.

PRITCHARD, W., b. Newtown, 19252, Pte., k. in a., F., 11/7/16.

PRITCHARD, W. J., b. Pwllheli, 40856, Pte., k. in a., F., 14/2/17.

PROSSER, D., e. Neath, 37004, Pte., k. in a., F., 30/8/16.

PROTHERO, G. R., b. Pontypridd, 18922, Sgt., d. of w., F., 7/2/17, M.M.

PRYCE, W. R., b. Llantarnam, 18421, Pte., k. in a., F., 10/7/16.

PUGH, J., b. Bersham, 87239, Pte., k. in a., F., 8/10/18.

PUGH, T. S., b. Blaenau Festiniog, 19575, L/Cpl., k. in a., F., 6/7/16.

PUGH, W., e. Wrexham, 54512, Pte., d., F., 19/12/16.

PURDIE, H., b. Kilbirnie, 60165, Pte., d. of w., F., 16/3/18.

PYPER, R. W., b. Belfast, 37187, Pte., k. in a., F., 12/5/16.

QUY, E. W., b. Sydenham, 26907, L/Sgt., d. of w., F., 20/6/18.

RADCLIFFE, E. V., b. Cardiff, 40939, Pte., k. in a., F., 22/4/18.

RAVENHILL, G., b. Birmingham, 4087, Cpl., k. in a., F., 24/8/18.

RAYMENT, A. H., b. Stockport, 235360, Pte., k. in a., F., 30/8/18.

REED, T. W., b. Chapel-en-le-Frith, 17854, Pte., k. in a., F., 11/7/16.

REES, C. J., b. Barry, 58539, Pte., k. in a., F., 26/8/18.

REES, G., b. Pembroke, 55444, Pte., k. in a., F., 22/6/17.

REES, J., b. Ruabon, 25305, L/Cpl., k. in a., F., 8/11/18.

REGAN, P., b. Cardiff, 38647, Pte., k. in a., F., 22/4/18.

RICHARDS, W., b. Rhyl, 16701, Pte., k. in a., F., 11/7/16.

RIDDLE, W. G. C., b. Thornbury, 93906, Pte., k. in a., F., 8/10/18.

RIDGWELL, T. J., b. London, 28543, L/Cpl., d., Home, 28/9/16.

RIDING, H. A., b. Nelson, 58317, Pte., k. in a., F., 18/9/18.

RILEY, R., b. Lancaster, 53013, Pte., k. in a., F., 26/8/18.

RILEY, T., e. Glossop, 292355, Pte., k. in a., F., 25/8/18.

ROBERTS, C., e. Queensferry, 201116, L/Cpl., d. of w., F., 9/10/18.

ROBERTS, D. J., b. Wrexham, 23612, L/Cpl., k. in a., F., 11/7/16.

ROBERTS, E. J., b. Pentir, 18451, L/Sgt., k. in a., F., 22/4/18.

ROBERTS, F., b. Bethesda, 19165, Cpl., d. of w., F., 12/7/16.

ROBERTS, H., b. Ruabon, 36628, Pte., k. in a., F., 12/8/17.

ROBERTS, J., b. Llanllechid, 18367, Pte., k. in a., F., 11/7/16.

ROBERTS, J., b. Connah's Quay, 18881, L/Cpl., k. in a., F., 24/8/18.

ROBERTS, J., e. Wrexham, 19066, Pte., d. of w., F., 27/8/18.

ROBERTS, J. N., b. Liverpool, 267844, Pte., k. in a., F., 26/8/18.

ROBERTS, J. W., b. Wrexham, 18319, Pte., d. of w., F., 3/10/16.

ROBERTS, N. C., b. Shrewsbury, 58312, Pte., k. in a., F., 26/8/18.

ROBERTS, R., b. Llanwnda, 19105, Pte., k. in a., F., 9/4/17.

ROBERTS, R., e. Llandudno, 54513, Pte., k. in a., F., 2/8/17.

ROBERTS, R., b. Gwytherin, 19377, L/Cpl., d., F., 9/10/18, M.M. and Clasp.

ROBERTS, R., b. Corwen, 203746, Pte., k. in a., F., 8/10/18.

ROBERTS, T., b. Aberfan, 75328, Pte., k. in a., F., 18/9/18.

ROBERTS, T. R., b. Llandegai, 18453, Pte., d., F., 17/2/17.

ROBERTS, W., b. Bootle, 18393, Pte., k. in a., F., 22/8/16.

ROBERTS, W., e. Colwyn, 40646, Pte., d. of w., F., 24/4/18.

RODEN, J., b. Hanley, 23773, Pte., d. of w., F., 10/10/18.

ROGERS, D., e. Wrexham, 93418, Pte., d. of w., F., 4/9/18.

ROGERS, J. W., b. Canada, 54348, Pte., k. in a., F., 31/7/17.

ROGERSON, R., b. Preston, 58313, Pte., k. in a., F., 8/11/18.

ROSE, J. P., b. Bugsworth, 86923, Pte., k. in a., F., 8/11/18.

ROSE, W. J., b. Swansea, 11363, Pte., k. in a., F., 29/7/17.

ROWLANDS, D., e. Carnarvon, 265564, Pte., k. in a., F., 22/4/18.

ROWLANDS, E. D., b. Aberystwyth, 19964, L/Cpl., d., F., 31/10/18.

ROWLANDS, J., b. Whitford, 5301, Pte., k. in a., F., 4/3/17.

ROYLE, W. H., b. Worsley, 74995, Pte., k. in a., F., 4/11/18.

RUTTER, G., b. Holme, 235359, Pte., d. of w., F., 4/5/18.

RYLANDS, F. H., b. Penrith, 93939, Pte., d. of w., F., 9/10/18.

SANDERS, A. J., b. Wrafton, 93828, Sgt., d. of w., F., 20/10/18.

SANFORD, R. H., e. London, 60910, Pte., k. in a., F., 22/4/18.

SANGER, A. J., b. London, 44839, Pte., k. in a., F., 19/9/17.

SAVAGE, J. F., b. Bangor, 31725, Pte., d., Home, 6/11/15.

SCHOFIELD, A., b. Openshaw, 19906, Pte., k. in a., F., 11/7/16.

SCHOFIELD, C., b. Rochdale, 58320, Pte., d. of w., Home, 7/10/18.

SCOULAR, W., b. Leith, 21621, L/Sgt., k. in a., F., 22/4/18.

SEALE, W. H., b. Southport, 66906, Pte., d. of w., F., 27/8/18.

SEAWARD, R. A., b. London, 22189, Sgt., k. in a., F., 22/4/18.

SHARPE, H., b. Gloucester, 203357, Pte., k. in a., F., 15/3/18.

SHAW, H., e. Leek, 54530, Pte., k. in a., F., 22/6/17.

SHENTON, W. L., b. Luton, 18731, A/Sgt., k. in a., F., 31/7/17.

SHEPHERD, C. B., b. Ferrybridge, 60135, Pte., k. in a., F., 10/5/18.

SHERIFF, R. E., b. Welshpool, 58321, Pte., d. of w., F., 20/6/18.

SHERLOCK, G. E., e. Wrexham, 54514, Pte., d., F., 27/10/17.
SHORROCK, F., b. Leeds, 67074, Pte., k. in a., F., 18/9/18.
SHORT, C., b. London, 26662, Pte., k. in a., F., 31/7/17.
SHUKER, S., b. Shifnal, 56501, Pte., k. in a., F., 31/7/17.
SIDDALL, S., b. Manchester, 46664, Pte., k. in a., F., 22/4/18.
SIDDONS, H., b. Manchester, 204609, Pte., k. in a., F., 24/8/18.
SIFLEET, G. E., b. Llandudno, 19019, Pte., k. in a., F., 27/2/16.
SKINNER, C. D., b. Cardiff, 78325, Pte., k. in a., F., 4/11/18.
SLATCHER, C., b. Knowbury, 267670, Pte., k. in a., F., 22/4/18.
SLATER, G., b. Lomyleigh, 235362, Pte., d. of w., F., 7/10/17.
SMART, R., b. Bolton, 242873, Pte., k. in a., F., 20/10/18.
SMITH, A., b. Buckley, 18471, Pte., k. in a., F., 22/6/17.
SMITH, A. J., b. Rawtenstall, 87854, Pte., k. in a., F., 18/9/18.
SMITH, A. W., e. Stockport, 58329, Pte., k. in a., F., 17/5/18.
SMITH, B., b. Romiley, 56440, Pte., k. in a., F., 31/7/17.
SMITH, E., b. Esclusham, 200223, Pte., k. in a., F., 22/4/18.
SMITH, H., b. Shaw, 31464, Pte., k. in a., F., 11/7/16.
SMITH, S. C., e. London, 54026, Pte., d. of w., F., 8/10/16.
SMITH, S. F., b. London, 34768, Pte., k. in a., F., 11/7/16.
SMITH, T., b. London, 22988, Pte., k. in a., F., 4/11/18.
SMITH, W. H., b. Fenton, 28977, Pte., k. in a., F., 19/9/17.
SNAPE, H., e. Seaforth, 345766, Pte., k. in a., F., 4/11/18.
SPEAR, T. J., b. Trevthin, 78292, Pte., k. in a., F., 22/10/18.
SPURGEON, W. A., b. Maldon, 36190, Pte., k. in a., F., 30/9/16.
STANLEY, L. J., e. London, 22979, Pte., d. of w., F., 2/9/18.
STEVENSON, K. J., b. London, 23258, Pte., d. of w., F., 26/8/18.
STREET, C., b. Woodville, 36530, Pte., d. of w., F., 24/7/17.
SUGDEN, J., b. Castleford, 56489, Pte., d. of w., F., 7/9/17.
SULLIVAN, E., b. London, 35108, Pte., k. in a., F., 11/7/16.
TAYLOR, C., b. Royton, 91523, Pte., k. in a., F., 4/11/18.
TAYLOR, J., b. Manchester, 29007, Pte., k. in a., F., 8/10/18.
TAYLOR, J., b. Liverpool, 235364, Pte., k. in a., F., 18/9/18.

THOMAS, A., b. Broughton, 200387, Pte., k. in a., F., 4/11/18.
THOMAS, A., b. Bretton, 39320, Pte., k. in a., F., 10/12/17.
THOMAS, C., b. Treforest, 18519, L/Cpl., k. in a., F., 1/9/17.
THOMAS, G. A., b. Rhyl, 19137, Pte., k. in a., F., 10/1/16.
THOMAS, G. J., b. Colwyn Bay, 39897, Cpl., d. of w., F., 16/3/18.
THOMAS, H., b. Liverpool, 55970, Pte., k. in a., F., 22/4/18.
THOMAS, H., b. Carnarvon, 68740, Pte., k. in a., F., 26/12/17.
THOMAS, I., b. Penmaenmawr, 54490, Pte., d., F., 14/12/16.
THOMAS, J. F., b. Ruthin, 31325, Pte., k. in a., F., 11/7/16.
THOMAS, T., b. Pontypridd, 19093, Pte., k. in a., F., 11/7/16.
THOMAS, W. B., b. Bangor, 44831, Pte., k. in a., F., 18/9/18.
THOMAS, W. I., b. Swansea, 19681, Pte., k. in a., F., 31/5/16.
THOMAS, W. J., b. Pontardawe, 54058, L/Cpl., k. in a., F., 22/4/18, M.M.
TIBBS, J. H., b. Blaenavon, 94178, Pte., d. of w., F., 5/11/18.
TIMMS, J., e. Llangefni, 28754, Pte., k. in a., F., 1/9/18.
TOVEY, B., b. Merthyr Vale, 18920, Pte., k. in a., F., 11/7/16.
TROAKES, W. J., b. Newport, 18963, Cpl., k. in a., F., 18/2/16.
TROW, H., b. Bolton, 58330, Pte., k. in a., F., 4/11/18.
TUNNAH, H., b. Weston Rhyn, 88375, Pte., k. in a., F., 4/11/18.
TURNER, G. H., b. London, 21703, Pte., d. of w., F., 25/4/18.
TWEEDALL, T., b. Hyde, 77645, Pte., k. in a., F., 26/8/18.
VARDY, W. B., b. South Shields, 54665, Pte., k. in a., F., 23/2/17.
VAUGHAN, G., b. Westbury, 18680, L/Cpl., k. in a., F., 11/7/16.
WALKER, C. S., b. London, 18674, A/Sgt., d. of w., F., 17/12/16.
WALKER, E., b. Mottram-London-dale, 16591, Pte., k. in a., F., 24/8/18.
WALLACE, J., b. Neath, 86997, Pte., d. of w., F., 9/10/18.
WALTON, J., b. Avenbury, 18552, Pte., k. in a., F., 10/7/16.
WARBURTON, W., b. Bolton, 54119, Pte., d. of w., F., 12/4/18.
WARD, A. H., e. London, 26733, Pte., k. in a., F., 31/7/17.
WARD, H., b. London, 21792, L/Sgt., d. of w., F., 12/4/18.

WARD, T., e. Cardiff, 93421, Pte., d. of w., F., 1/9/18.
WARREN, A., b. Plymouth, 93826, Sgt., k. in a., F., 8/10/18.
WATSON, Z., b. Ystrad, 19255, Pte., k. in a., F., 11/7/16.
WESTALL, W. G., e. Tonypandy, 89109, Pte., k. in a., F., 4/11/18.
WESTON, A. H., b. Wrexham, 23197, Pte., k. in a., F., 11/7/16.
WHEELER, J., b. Wooburn, 18166, L/Cpl., k. in a., F., 17/6/17.
WHEELER, R. D., b. London, 22479, L/Sgt., k. in a., F., 22/4/18.
WHITE, F., b. Yeovil, 30299, Pte., k. in a., F., 2/8/17.
WHITTAL, E., b. Worthen, 203528, Pte., d. of w., F., 10/11/17.
WICKENDEN, J. W., b. London, 54035, Pte., d. of w., F., 25/2/17.
WIGLEY, T., b. Hawarden, 43814, Pte., k. in a., F., 30/8/18.
WITTS, A. H., b. Mansfield, 24223, Pte., k. in a., F., 10/7/16.
WILLIAMS, A., b. Llanstephan, 55462, Pte., k. in a., F., 8/10/18.
WILLIAMS, A. P., b. Llangefni, 19999, Pte., k. in a., F., 11/7/16.
WILLIAMS, A. W., b. Rhos, 203330, Pte., k. in a., F., 22/4/18.
WILLIAMS, C., b. Mold, 36982, Pte., k. in a., F., 11/7/16.
WILLIAMS, D., b. Blaenau Festiniog, 54518, Pte., k. in a., F., 25/2/17.
WILLIAMS, D. M., b. Maentwrog, 20223, Pte., k. in a., F., 31/7/17.
WILLIAMS, E., b. Llanmorgan, 203693, Pte., k. in a., F., 22/4/18.
WILLIAMS, E., b. Landore, 19810, Pte., k. in a., F., 27/2/16.
WILLIAMS, G., b. Llandilo Fawr, 31406, Pte., k. in a., F., 23/5/16.
WILLIAMS, G., b. Llandrillo, 23023, Pte., d. of w., F., 6/7/16.
WILLIAMS, G. H., b. Kington, 56477, Pte., k. in a., F., 2/8/17.
WILLIAMS, G. O., b. Blaenau Festiniog, 19163, A/Cpl., k. in a., F., 11/7/16.
WILLIAMS, G. W., b. London, 43584, L/Cpl., d. of w., F., 25/4/18.
WILLIAMS, H., b. Llanddona, 54670, Pte., k. in a., F., 24/4/17.
WILLIAMS, H. R., b. Llandegai, 18804, Pte., k. in a., F., 11/7/16.

WILLIAMS, J., b. Llanrhaiadr, 54685, Pte., k. in a., F., 9/4/17.

WILLIAMS, J. B. P., b. West Indies, 19981, Pte., k. in a., F., 25/6/17.

WILLIAMS, J. M., b. Llanllyfni, 18577, A/Cpl., d. of w., F., 3/12/16.

WILLIAMS, O., b. Llanllechid, 204089, Pte., d. of w., F., 3/5/18.

WILLIAMS, P., b. Llanfair, 204282, Pte., k. in a., F., 1/9/18.

WILLIAMS, R., b. Llanllyfni, 18576, Pte., d. of w., F., 1/3/16.

WILLIAMS, R., b. Llanllyfni, 54673, Pte., k. in a., F., 26/8/18.

WILLIAMS, R., b. Ifton Heath, 88395, Pte., k. in a., F., 6/10/18.

WILLIAMS, R., b. Llynfaes, 25752, Pte., k. in a., F., 21/6/18.

WILLIAMS, R. B., b. Waenfawr, 70097, Pte., k. in a., F., 22/4/18.

WILLIAMS, R. H., b. Dulais Lower, 18250, Pte., d. of w., F., 10/7/16.

WILLIAMS, R. H., e. Llandudno, 25121, Pte., k. in a., F., 2/8/17.

WILLIAMS, S., b. Wrexham, 18322, Pte., k. in a., F., 11/7/16.

WILLIAMS, S., b. Meliden, 36645, Pte., k. in a., F., 11/7/16.

WILLIAMS, S., b. Cilybebyll, 23028, Pte., k. in a., F., 11/7/16.

WILLIAMS, T., b. Tattenhall, 23062, Pte., d. of w., F., 2/8/17.

WILLIAMS, T., b. Glyneath Higher, 18253, Pte., k. in a., F., 11/7/16.

WILLIAMS, T. D., e. Carnarvon, 54671, Pte., d. of w., F., 27/6/17.

WILLIAMS, T. G., b. Bangor, 54687, Pte., k. in a., F., 2/8/17.

WILLIAMS, T. P., b. Glanogwen, 15743, Pte., k. in a., F., 27/8/18.

WILLIAMS, W., b. Holywell, 14645, Pte., k. in a., F., 17/5/18.

WILLIAMS, W., b. Bala, 204283, Pte., k. in a., F., 22/4/18.

WILLIAMS, W. H., b. Llangoed, 21523, L/Cpl., k. in a., F., 11/7/16.

WILLIAMS, W. J., b. Bethesda, 19085, Pte., k. in a., F., 10/7/16.

WILLIAMS, W. J., b. Penmaenmawr, 316014, Pte., d. of w., F., 27/8/18.

WILLIAMS, W. R., b. Pen-y-groes, 203762, Pte., k. in a., F., 22/4/18.

WILLIAMSON, H., b. Bistre, 18498, L/Cpl., k. in a., F., 31/7/17.

WILLIAMSON, J. A., b. Ashby-de-la-Zouch, 54688, Pte., k. in a., F., 6/12/16.

WILSON, G., b. Blackburn, 18908, Cpl., k. in a., F., 11/7/16.

WILSON, H. W., e. Liverpool, 204519, Pte., k. in a., F., 26/8/18.

WILSON, J., e. Royton, 66945, Pte., k. in a., F., 22/4/18.

WINSTONE, T., b. Ebbw Vale, 204588, Pte., k. in a., F., 26/8/18.

WINTER, H. H., b. London, 27848, Pte., k. in a., F., 1/9/17.

WOOD, S. J., b. London, 22827, Cpl., k. in a., F., 18/9/18.

WOOLRICH, W., e. Wrexham, 19056, Pte., k. in a., F., 11/7/16.

WOOTTON, A., b. Gwersyllt, 235051, Pte., k. in a., F., 17/5/18.

YENERALSKY, R., b. London, 54031, Pte., k. in a., F., 31/7/17.

YOUD, W. A., b. Hope, 18618, Pte., d. of w., Home, 21/10/18.

YOUNG, A., b. Trefnant, 23802, Pte., k. in a., F., 24/1/16.

17th BATTALION

ACKLAND, S., b. Swansea, 75295, Pte., k. in a., F., 6/8/18.

ADSHEAD, H., b. Altrincham, 72834, Pte., k. in a., F., 31/7/17.

ALTON, T., b. Nuneaton, 9609, Cpl., k. in a., F., 12/11/17.

ANDERSON, A. W. G., b. London, 267911, Pte., k. in a., F., 31/7/17.

ANDERSON, R. F., b. Wincham, 46499, Pte., d. of w., F., 28/2/17.

ARCHER, F. S., b. Romford, 56017, Pte., k. in a., F., 22/4/18.

ARNOLD, A. E., b. Liverpool, 66790, Pte., k. in a., F., 8/3/18.

ASHBY, T., b. Kettering, 56329, Pte., d. of w., F., 23/9/18.

ASHTON, J., b. Nantwich, 60575, Pte., k. in a., F., 31/7/17.

AUSTIN, H., b. Wombridge, 60573, Pte., k. in a., F., 31/7/17.

BAKER, B., b. Salford, 46489, Pte., k. in a., F., 13/9/18.

BALL, A., b. Congleton, 267020, Pte., d. of w., F., 26/8/17.

BALL, F., b. Newport, 47235, Pte., k. in a., F., 26/8/17.

BANNISTER, H. A., b. London, 22010, Pte., k. in a., F., 6/9/18.

BARBER, E. R. C., b. London, 59722, Pte., k. in a., F., 28/2/17.

BARNETT, H. E., b. London, 27570, Cpl., d. of w., F., 31/7/17.

BARTLETT, W., b. London, 235264, Pte., k. in a., F., 8/10/18.

BASTIANO, D. D., b. Swansea, 25671, A/Cpl., d. of w., F., 1/8/17.

BATEMAN, L. S., b. Rochdale, 67836, Pte., k. in a., F., 1/5/18.

BEAVAN, G. C., b. London, 27292, Pte., k. in a., F., 10/7/16.

BELLIS, A., b. Ruabon, 36371, L/Cpl., k. in a., F., 31/7/17.

BELLIS, H., b. Flint, 25526, L/Cpl., k. in a., F., 12/7/16.

BENNETT, A. W., b. Stroud, 93566, Pte., d. of w., F., 12/9/18.

BENNETT, C. E., b. Market Drayton, 315950, Pte., k. in a., F., 23/11/17.

BENTLEY, W. D., b. Hanley, 60530, Pte., k. in a., F., 31/7/17.

BERKSHIRE, C. R., b. London, 27766, Pte., k. in a., F., 31/7/17.

BERRINGTON, L. W., b. Fleur-de-Lis, 93682, Pte., d. of w., F., 9/11/18.

BETTS, A., b. Skegby, 26196, Pte., k. in a., F., 12/7/16.

BEVAN, B. G., b. Lydney, 25139, Pte., d. of w., F., 22/7/16.

BLEACKLEY, S. L., b. Heywood, 267174, Pte., d. of w., F., 31/7/17.

BOOTH, J. T., b. Marple, 48839, Pte., k. in a., F., 31/7/17.

BOURTON, A. H., b. Abersychan, 93565, Pte., d. of w., F., 2/9/18.

BOZIER, R., e. Hertford, 235224, Pte., k. in a., F., 30/8/18.

BRADSHAW, E., b. Colne, 59660, Pte., d. of w., Home, 7/2/18.

BRADWELL, T. A., b. Bishop Auckland, 26079, Pte., k. in a., F., 29/8/17.

BRAMFIELD, J. J., b. Queensferry, 25937, Pte., d. of w., F., 25/3/16.

BRISCOE, E. E., b. Bedford, 26247, Pte., d. of w., F., 11/10/17.

BROOK, J. T., b. Hailsham, 60572, Pte., k. in a., F., 31/7/17.

BROWN, E., b. Bridgnorth, 315201, Pte., k. in a., F., 1/5/18.

BROWN, R., b. Newport, 49106, A/Sgt., k. in a., F., 4/9/18.

BULGER, M., b. Liverpool, 66859, Pte., d. of w., F., 29/8/18.

BUNCE, C. W., b. London, 35013, Pte., k. in a., F., 31/7/17.

BURKE, J. P., b. Wolverhampton, 60553, Pte., d. of w., Home, 21/8/17.

BURROWS, D., b. Nelson, 93833, Pte., k. in a., F., 8/10/18.

BURWOOD, R., b. London, 27374, Pte., d. of w., F., 11/5/16.

BYRNE, R. P., b. Guildford, 26964, Pte., d. of w., F., 13/9/18.

CAKEBREAD, C. E., e. Hertford, 235226, Pte., k. in a., F., 30/8/18.

CALDER, F., b. Liverpool, 70281, Pte., k. in a., F., 28/10/18.

CAREY, W., b. Blaina, 93835, Pte., d. of w., F., 8/10/18.

CARPENTER, W., b. Risca, 93548, Pte., k. in a., F., 8/10/18.

CARR, T. J., b. London, 27277, L/Cpl., k. in a., F., 14/2/17.

CARTER, H. F., b. Poulton, 93551, Pte., k. in a., F., 8/10/18.

CARTER, J., b. Blackburn, 26303, L/Cpl., k. in a., F., 15/2/16.

CARTER, T. J., b. Cwmbran, 93568, Pte., k. in a., F., 4/9/18.

CARTWRIGHT, T., e. Wrexham, 26031, Pte., d. of w., Home, 7/5/19.

CATMAR, S. M., b. London, 27924, Pte., k. in a., F., 9/7/16.

CHAPMAN, C. S., e. Hertford, 235227, Pte., k. in a., F., 4/7/18.

CHASTELL, F. G., e. Hertford, 235228, Pte., k. in a., F., 31/7/17.

CLARKE, G., b. London, 27204, Pte., k. in a., F., 8/10/18.

CLARKE, W., b. Newport, 77251, Pte., k. in a., F., 13/8/18.

CLEARY, P., b. Co. Wexford, 25457, Pte., k. in a., F., 9/7/16.

CLEVER, A., b. Bristol, 25845, Pte., d., F., 18/8/16.

CLIVE, W., b. Whitchurch, 60523, Pte., d. of w., F., 16/8/17.

COLEGATE, F., b. London, 54048, Pte., d. of w., Home, 14/8/17.

COLLINS, C. E., e. London, 59747, Sgt., d. of w., Home, 24/12/18, M.M.

COUSINS, H. P., b. Liverpool, 37161, Pte., k. in a., F., 10/7/16.

COX, B. C., b. Cambridge, 202304, Pte., k. in a., F., 29/10/18.

CRAWLEY, M., e. Hertford, 235230, Pte., k. in a., F., 1/9/18.

CUDWORTH, T., b. Machynlleth, 61305, Pte., k. in a., F., 1/9/18.

CULVERWELL, E., b. Egremont, 58405, Pte., k. in a., F., 3/9/18.

CYPLES, E., b. Burslem, 36113, Pte., k. in a., F., 24/4/18.

DAMMERY, R., b. Pendlebury, 267156, Pte., k. in a., F., 10/3/18.

DANIEL, W. E., b. Holsworthy, 60552, Pte., k. in a., F., 31/7/17.

DARCH, W., b. Barnstaple, 59662, Pte., k. in a., F., 31/7/17.

DARLINGTON, T., b. Pant Rhos, 26001, Pte., k. in a., F., 27/7/16.

DAVIES, D., b. Corwen, 35349, Pte., k. in a., F., 9/7/16.

DAVIES, D. R., b. Merioneth, 25465, Pte., k. in a., F., 29/10/18.

DAVIES, D. W., b. Llanrfith, 59699, Pte., k. in a., F., 31/7/17.

DAVIES, E. C., b. Dinas Mawddwy, 61052, Pte., k. in a., F., 8/10/18.

DAVIES, G. C., b. Gelli Rhondda, 56676, Pte., k. in a., F., 2/5/18.

DAVIES, J., b. Wrexham, 36795, Pte., d. of w., F., 24/7/16.

DAVIES, M., b. Caergwrle, 59748, Pte., k. in a., F., 8/10/18.

DAVIES, R. O., b. Coedpoeth, 25167, A/Cpl., k. in a., F., 29/8/17, D.C.M.

DAVIES, S., b. Neath Higher, 19726, Pte., d., F., 1/9/18, M.M.

DAVIES, T., b. Birchgrove, 26315, Pte., k. in a., F., 25/8/16.

DAVIES, T. E., b. Adwy Bersham, 25970, Pte., k. in a., F., 25/2/17.

DAVIES, T. R., b. Lampeter, 24748, L/Cpl., k. in a., F., 12/7/16.

DAVIES, W., b. Penrhyndeudraeth, 201432, Pte., k. in a., F., 1/9/18.

DAVIES, W. H., b. Llantysilio, 25971, Pte., d. of w., Home, 20/7/16.

DEAN, R. A., b. Mardy, 76021, Pte., k. in a., F., 1/5/18.

DENNIS, E., b. Cefntwrch, 27948, Pte., d. of w., F., 19/5/16.

DIGGLE, H., b. Manchester, 25163, Sgt., k. in a., F., 7/7/16.

DOBSON, S. E., b. Hampton Hill, 59684, Pte., d. of w., F., 6/9/18.

DOWTHWAITE, R., b. Penruddock, 235421, Pte., k. in a., F., 8/10/18.

DUCATEL, J. C., b. London, 34501, Pte., d. of w., F., 30/10/18.

DUCKWORTH, J., e. Ashton-under-Lyne, 67031, Pte., d. of w., F., 8/10/18.

DUERDON, J., b. Padiham, 33217, Pte., k. in a., F., 9/4/18.

DUNN, W., b. Ashton-under-Lyne, 25600, Pte., k. in a., F., 8/10/18.

DURRANS, J., b. Waterhead, 25803, Pte., k. in a., F., 12/7/16.

EARP, F. R., b. Egremont, 52937, Pte., d. of w., F., 2/9/18.

EATON, J., b. Longton, 29319, Pte., d. of w., F., 3/9/18.

EDMUNDS, J., b. Birmingham, 33601, L/Cpl., k. in a., F., 4/11/18.

EDMUNDS, J. E., b. Blaenavon, 235630, Pte., k. in a., F., 22/6/18.

EDWARDS, A., b. Bredbury, 67820, Pte., k. in a., F., 30/8/18.

EDWARDS, C., b. Dalston, 54049, Pte., k. in a., F., 31/7/17.

EDWARDS, J., b. Longton, 25955, Pte., k. in a., F., 31/7/17.

EDWARDS, J. D., b. Corwen, 34942, Pte., k. in a., F., 10/7/16.

EDWARDS, O., b. Brynguran, 25783, Pte., k. in a., F., 9/7/16.

EDWARDS, P., b. Cefn-mawr, 93656, Pte., d. of w., F., 28/9/18.

EDWARDS, R., b. Merthyr, 71452, Pte., k. in a., F., 6/8/18.

EDWARDS, R. L., b. Festiniog, 26276, Pte., k. in a., F., 13/5/16.

EDWARDS, S., b. Llandudno, 54376, L/Cpl., k. in a., F., 29/10/18.

EDWARDS, W. A., b. Pentre, 55695, Pte., d. of w., F., 26/4/18.

ELLIS, G., b. Woodville, 70381, L/Cpl., k. in a., F., 8/10/18.

ELLIS, J., b. Buckley, 25673, Pte., k. in a., F., 31/7/17.

ELVEY, G., b. Stanstard, 26232, L/Cpl., k. in a., F., 7/7/16.

EMMERICH, A. E., e. Hastings, 235485, Pte., k. in a., F., 30/8/18.

EVANS, A., b. Farnworth, 18442, Pte., d. of w., F., 1/9/18.

EVANS, A., b. Nettleton, 94111, Pte., d. of w., F., 29/10/18.

EVANS, D. H., b. Pentre Voelas, 33276, Cpl., k. in a., F., 31/7/17.

EVANS, E., b. Llangollen, 25407, Pte., d. of w., F., 2/8/17.

EVANS, E., b. Neath Abbey, 25061, d., Pte., F., 27/11/16.

EVANS, E. H., b. Northop, 26515, Pte., k. in a., F., 12/7/16.

EVANS, I., b. Porth, 72519, Pte., d., F., 3/11/18.

EVANS, J., b. Ruabon, 25193, Pte., k. in a., F., 31/7/17.

EVANS, J., b. Llanddeusant, 33284, Pte., k. in a., F., 20/1/16.

EVANS, J. H., b. Bala, 26421, Pte., k. in a., F., 27/5/17.

EVANS, N. W., b. Wrexham, 26309, Pte., k. in a., F., 28/8/17.

EVANS, O., b. Bethel, 56933, Pte., k. in a., F., 23/12/16.

EVANS, O., b. Llanberis Pass, 68456, Pte., k. in a., F., 15/10/18.

EVANS, R. W., b. Bersham, 26034, Sgt., k. in a., F., 1/5/18.

EVANS, S., e. Pontypridd, 19029, Pte., k. in a., F., 10/9/18.

EVANS, U., b. Port Talbot, 94235, Pte., k. in a., F., 28/10/18.

EVANS, W., b. Dowlais, 93847, Pte., k. in a., F., 5/10/18.

EVANS, W. C., b. Bettws, 13217, Pte., k. in a., F., 31/7/17.

EVANS, W. I. D., e. Newport, 93846, Pte., k. in a., F., 8/10/18.

EVANS, W. J., b. Llanfair P.G., 53877, Pte., d. of w., F., 24/8/17.

FARRELL, L., b. Liverpool, 46615, Pte., d. of w., F., 22/8/18.

FAULKNER, G., b. London, 21074, L/Cpl., k. in a., F., 13/4/18.

FELGATE, J., b. London, 28083, Pte., k. in a., F., 28/10/18.

FEWTRELL, W. F., b. Wrockwardine Wood, 25728, Pte., k. in a., F., 21/8/16.

FIELD, W. E., e. Watford, 202327, Pte., k. in a., F., 27/4/18.

FINNIGAN, W., b. Wrexham, 25092, Pte., k. in a., F., 9/7/16.

FISHER, F. H., b. Winchester, 75371, Cpl., k. in a., F., 8/10/18.

FLETCHER, J., b. Rogerstone, 93657, Pte., k. in a., F., 12/9/18.

FOLWELL, P., b. Canterbury, 56164, Pte., k. in a., F., 31/7/17.

FOOTE, A. W., b. London, 59710, Pte., k. in a., F., 8/10/18.

FORD, G. C., b. Shrewsbury, 315964, Pte., k. in a., F., 1/5/18.

FORRESTER, W., b. Wrexham, 83570, Pte., k. in a., F., 4/9/18.

FOULKES, A., b. Conway, 25817, Pte., d. of w., F., 20/7/16.

FRANCIS, E. W., b. Llandinam, 37196, Pte., k. in a., F., 17/9/16.

FRAYLING, A., b. Cardiff, 93563, Pte., k. in a., F., 15/10/18.

FURLEY, S., b. Oldham, 60555, Pte., k. in a., F., 31/7/17.

FURNESS, W. J. E., b. London, 27772, Pte., k. in a., F., 9/7/16.

GARDNER, A., b. London, 94240, Pte., d. of w., F., 29/10/18.

GARWOOD, G. H., b. London, 45568, Pte., k. in a., F., 30/8/18.

GEORGE, W. H., b. Cardiff, 267906, Pte., k. in a., F., 29/8/17.

GIBSON, W., b. Gresford, 25827, Pte., k. in a., F., 6/9/18.

GIDDENS, W., b. London, 59713, Pte., k. in a., F., 31/7/17.

GLADDING, E., e. Hertford, 234231, Pte., d. of w., F., 9/8/17.

GLINN, W. E., b. Tenby, 235691, Pte., d. of w., F., 9/9/18.

GOFF, G. B., b. Strumpshaw, 202337, Pte., d. of w., F., 26/3/17.

GOODLAND, H. T., b. Cardiff, 54046, Pte., d. of w., F., 3/9/18.

GREEN, A. H., b. London, 22341, Sgt., k. in a., F., 14/5/18.

GRIFFITH, W. E. O., b. Bangor, 26402, Pte., k. in a., F., 10/7/16.

GRIFFITHS, D., b. Wrexham, 25301, Pte., k. in a., F., 23/12/16.

GRIFFITHS, D., b. Tremeirchion, 25420, Sgt., k. in a., F., 12/7/16.

GRIFFITHS, E. H., b. Carnarvon, 265716, Pte., k. in a., F., 31/7/17.

GRIFFITHS, E. J., b. Buckley, 24332, Sgt., k. in a., F., 20/10/17.

GRIFFITHS, G. E., b. Machynlleth, 77493, Pte., k. in a., F., 3/9/18.

GRIFFITHS, H., b. Seven Sisters, 26217, Pte., k. in a., F., 18/8/17.

GRIFFITHS, J. E., b. Mold, 69279, Pte., k. in a., F., 17/3/18.

GRIFFITHS, J. O., b. Newborough, 25669, Pte., k. in a., F., 19/1/16.

GRIFFITHS, O. A., b. Llanbeblig, 56922, Pte., k. in a., F., 29/8/17.

GRIFFITHS, T. D., b. Aberdare, 59757, Pte., k. in a., F., 13/4/18.

GRIFFITHS, W., e. Wrexham, 55675, Pte., k. in a., F., 31/7/17.

GRIGGS, F., b. London, 26746, Pte., k. in a., F., 20/4/18.

GUIVER, S., b. West Hartlepool, 25732, Pte., d. of w., F., 19/1/16.

HALE, G. W., b. Treorchy, 93851, Pte., k. in a., F., 8/10/18.

HALE, O., b. Blakeney, 93681, Pte., k. in a., F., 16/10/18.

HANSON, J. T., e. Liverpool, 56482, Pte., k. in a., F., 24/11/17.

HARDY, W. J., b. Birmingham, 25756, L/Cpl., d. of w., F., 13/7/16.

HARMAN, R., b. Newcastle-on-Tyne, 69402, Pte., d. of w., F., 25/8/18.

HAYDOCK, T., b. Farnworth, 73587, Pte., k. in a., F., 29/10/18.

HEAD, W. H., b. North Mimms, 235652, Pte., k. in a., F., 8/12/17.

HEAP, E., b. Colne, 73588, Pte., d. of w., F., 6/9/18.

HELLINGS, A. E., b. Ystrad Rhondda, 60159, Pte., k. in a., F., 7/8/18.

HENRY, J., b. Wolverhampton, 93606, Pte., k. in a., F., 28/10/18.

HENRY, R., b. Manchester, 27717, Pte., k. in a., F., 10/7/16.

HENRY, T., b. Liverpool, 36636, Pte., d. of w., F., 15/9/16.

HESTER, C. E., e. Hertford, 235234, Pte., k. in a., F., 31/7/17.

HEWITT, J. E., b. West Derby, 25417, Pte., d. of w., F., 17/3/18.

HEYWOOD, J. E., b. Manchester, 73572, Pte., k. in a., F., 1/5/18.

HIBBERT, A., b. Oldham, 73414, Pte., k. in a., F., 6/9/18.

HIGGINSON, A., b. Bamberbridge, 25341, Pte., k. in a., F., 25/8/17.

HILL, J., b. Warrington, 25334, Cpl., k. in a., F., 25/8/16.

HILTON, W., b. Besses o' the Barn, 73583, Pte., k. in a., F., 28/10/18.

HITCHCOCK, B. N., b. London, 11247, Pte., k. in a., F., 8/10/18.

HOARE, D., e. Wrexham, 54443, Pte., k. in a., F., 18/6/18.

HOBBY, D. W., b. Hereford, 93666, Pte., k. in a., F., 8/10/18.

HOBSON, S., b. Macclesfield, 60593, Pte., k. in a., F., 8/10/18.

HODDY, L., b. London, 27702, Pte., k. in a., F., 29/8/17.

HOLDEN, A., b. Blackburn, 93658, Pte., k. in a., F., 29/10/18.

HOLDER, W., b. Carnforth, 93659, Pte., k. in a., F., 4/11/18.

HOLT, S., b. Bootle, 75040, Pte., k. in a., F., 3/9/17.

HOOPER, W., b. Birkenhead, 70471, Pte., k. in a., F., 29/6/18.

HOPKINS, G., b. Resolven, 93577, Pte., k. in a., F., 3/9/18.

HOPWOOD, J. I., b. Pen-y-groes, 73573, Pte., k. in a., F., 4/11/18, M.M.

HOWARD, A. T., b. Liverpool, 204715, Pte., d. of w., F., 8/10/18.

HOWARTH, N., b. Colne, 59659, Pte., k. in a., F., 9/5/18.

HUGHES, A. J., b. Penmaenmawr, 59733, Pte., k. in a., F., 31/7/17.

HUGHES, E., b. Corwen, 34938, Pte., d. of w., F., 21/7/16.

HUGHES, E., e. Fenton, 25745, Pte., d. of w., F., 11/7/16.

HUGHES, J., b. Waenfawr, 25861, Pte., d. of w., F., 15/9/17.

HUGHES, J., e. Carnarvon, 265591, Pte., k. in a., F., 31/8/18, M.M.

HUGHES, J. E., b. Flint, 25646, Pte., d. of w., F., 20/1/16.

HUGHES, J. H., b. Llanystumdwy, 37278, Pte., k. in a., F., 9/7/16.

HUGHES, L., b. Corwen, 25949, Pte., k. in a., F., 27/7/16.

HUGHES, M. W., b. Rhyl, 73581, Pte., k. in a., F., 21/4/18.

HUGHES, O., b. Llandoyfna, 43638, Pte., k. in a., F., 5/8/17.

HUGHES, R., b. Llanddeiniolen, 25157, Pte., k. in a., F., 9/7/16.

HUGHES, R., b. Llangrestiolus, 44345, Pte., k. in a., F., 8/10/18.

HUGHES, R., e. Carnarvon, 23022, Pte., d. of w., F., 24/8/18.

HUGHES, W., b. Holywell, 26433, Pte., d. of w., F., 20/5/16.

ISAAC, J. B., b. Williamstown, 61572, Pte., k. in a., F., 28/9/17.

JACKSON, C. E., b. Manchester, 204717, Pte., d. of w., F., 21/4/18.

JACKSON, H., b. Crook, 73597, Pte., k. in a., F., 19/5/18.

JAMES, A. B., b. Sandhurst, 56168, Pte., k. in a., F., 31/7/17.

JAMES, J., b. Abercanaid, 93862, Pte., k. in a., F., 8/10/18.

JAMES, L., b. Cwmbach, 93863, Pte., k. in a., F., 8/10/18.

JEFFREYS, J. N., b. Hendon, 22041, Pte., k. in a., F., 8/10/18.

JENKINS, D. B., b. Carmarthen, 26423, Pte., k. in a., F., 17/3/18.

JENKINS, H. T., b. Cwmavon, 26197, Pte., k. in a., F., 10/7/16.

JENKINS, M. R., b. Llannon, 94253, Pte., k. in a., F., 4/11/18.

JENKINS, W. H., b. Dowlais, 69572, Pte., d. of w., F., 9/9/18.

JOHN, D., b. Neath, 26283, Pte., k. in a., F., 8/6/16.

JOHN, R., b. Trelaw, 5596, Pte., Pte., k. in a., F., 19/5/18.

JOHNSON, F. A. A., b. Leeds, 73603, Pte., k. in a., F., 1/5/18.

JOHNSON, G., b. Hyde, 24123, Pte., d. of w., F., 7/5/18.

JOHNSON, W., b. Longton, 25868, L/Cpl., k. in a., F., 22/7/16.

JONES, A., b. Llandudno, 36497, Pte., k. in a., F., 31/7/17.

JONES, C., b. Abertillery, 94259, Pte., k. in a., F., 29/10/18.

JONES, C. E., b. Ruabon, 25444, Pte., k. in a., F., 12/7/16.

JONES, D., b. Bangor, 56927, Pte., k. in a., F., 31/7/17.

JONES, D. D., b. Festiniog, 25252, Pte., d. of w., F., 4/8/16.

JONES, D. E., b. Carmarthen, 27118, Sgt., k. in a., F., 8/10/18.

JONES, D. J., e. Brecon, 93609, Pte., d. of w., F., 2/9/18.

JONES, D. J., b. New Tredegar,

94261, Pte., d. of w., F., 29/10/18.

JONES, E., b. Montgomery, 93865, Pte., k. in a., F., 8/10/18.

JONES, E., b. Maentwrog, 26112, Pte., k. in a., F., 29/8/17.

JONES, E. J., b. Peny-cae, 26051, Cpl., k. in a., F., 8/10/18.

JONES, F. A., b. Chester, 69809, Pte., k. in a., F., 8/10/18.

JONES, G. R., b. Llanbeblig, 18566, A/Cpl., d. of w., F., 25/9/18.

JONES, H., b. Resolven, 26343, Pte., k. in a., F., 9/7/16.

JONES, H., b. Aberffraw, 203726, Pte., k. in a., F., 27/6/18.

JONES, H. R., b. Dowlais, 26299, Pte., k. in a., F., 5/6/17.

JONES, H. W., b. Llanberis, 26048, Pte., k. in a., F., 31/7/17.

JONES, I. S., b. Tai-nant, 25942, Pte., d. of w., F., 29/3/18.

JONES, J., b. Nevern, 204719, Pte., d. of w., F., 3/3/18.

JONES, J., b. Wrexham, 25987, Pte., d. of w., F., 18/5/16.

JONES, J., b. Old Colwyn, 36838, Pte., d. of w., F., 11/7/16.

JONES, J., b. Carnarvon, 56926, Pte., k. in a., F., 31/7/17.

JONES, J. L., b. Carnarvon, 43590, Pte., k. in a., F., 12/11/17.

JONES, J. P., b. Llanddewi, 77271, Pte., k. in a., F., 2/9/18.

JONES, J. R., b. Llanasa, 26433, Pte., k. in a., F., 10/7/16.

JONES, J. T., b. Rhos, 77514, Pte., k. in a., F., 3/9/18.

JONES, J. W., b. Festiniog, 25215, Pte., d. of w., F., 15/7/16.

JONES, J. W., b. Llanganhafal, 23269, Pte., k. in a., F., 9/7/16.

JONES, M., b. Festiniog, 25269, Pte., k. in a., F., 29/8/17.

JONES, N. B., b. Blaenau Festiniog, 29509, Pte., k. in a., F., 30/8/18.

JONES, O., b. Penmaen, 43917, Pte., k. in a., F., 31/7/17.

JONES, R., b. Liverpool, 37172, Pte., k. in a., F., 9/7/16.

JONES, R., b. Glyndyfrdwy, 268072, Pte., k. in a., F., 1/5/18.

JONES, R., b. Mynytho, 43648, Pte., k. in a., F., 10/5/18.

JONES, R. A., b. Troedyrhiw, 93611, Pte., d. of w., F., 22/10/18.

JONES, R. H., b. Hawarden, 77269, Pte., k. in a., F., 30/8/18.

JONES, R. H., b. Colwyn Bay, 61540, Pte., k. in a., F., 28/9/17.

JONES, R. L., b. Llanerchymedd, 69260, Pte., k. in a., F., 1/9/18.

JONES, R. R., b. Llanddensant, 36813, Pte., k. in a., F., 24/8/16.

JONES, R. R., e. Llanrhaiadr, 71917, Pte., k. in a., F., 24/8/18.

JONES, R. S., b. Bettws-y-coed, 26066, Pte., k. in a., F., 23/12/16.

JONES, S., b. Weston-Rhyn, 200490, A/Sgt., k. in a., F., 4/11/18.

JONES, S. E., b. Dowlais, 83582, Pte., k. in a., F., 8/10/18.

JONES, T., b. Festiniog, 25290, Pte., k. in a., F., 31/7/17.

JONES, T., b. Rhosllanerchrugog, 26336, Pte., k. in a., F., 10/7/16.

JONES, T., b. Llanfor, 29606, Pte., d. of w., Home, 27/8/16.

JONES, T. H., b. Aberdare, 77275, Pte., k. in a., F., 2/9/18.

JONES, T. H., b. Mold, 26030, Pte., k. in a., F., 6/3/16.

JONES, W., b. Kidsgrove, 25846, Cpl., k. in a., F., 25/4/18.

JONES, W., b. Llandegfan, 25965, Pte., d., F., 31/5/15.

JONES, W., b. London, 27296, Pte., k. in a., F., 12/7/16.

JONES, W., b. Abersoch, 43653, Pte., k. in a., F., 5/10/18.

JONES, W., b. Llanddyfan, 61109, Pte., k. in a., F., 2/5/18.

JONES, W., b. Newborough, 265831, Pte., k. in a., F., 13/5/18.

JONES, W. A., b. Festiniog, 26127, Pte., k. in a., F., 18/4/16.

JONES, W. D., b. Llanfairfechan, 43820, Pte., k. in a., F., 31/7/17.

JONES, W. E., b. Llanrwst, 25244, L/Cpl., k. in a., F., 12/7/16.

JONES, W. E., b. Festiniog, 25214, L/Cpl., k. in a., F., 13/2/17.

JORDAN, J., b. Birkenhead, 60583, Pte., k. in a., F., 16/8/17.

KAY, A., b. Manchester, 62818, Pte., d. of w., F., 5/3/18.

KELLY, W., b. Liverpool, 25704, L/Cpl., d. of w., F., 26/7/16.

KERRY, J. W., b. Coity, 25349, Pte., d., F., 15/2/17.

LARGE, W., b. Wrexham, 43874, Pte., k. in a., F., 21/6/17.

LATTER, C. H., b. London, 28081, Pte., k. in a., F., 8/10/18.

LAWN, T., b. Rochdale, 26253, Pte., k. in a., F., 29/8/17.

LEAKEY, A., b. London, 26853, Pte., d. of w., F., 16/8/16.

LEE, W. J., b. London, 27671, Pte., k. in a., F., 12/5/16.

LEONARD, J., e. Flint, 240952, Pte., k. in a., F., 31/7/17.

LEVINE, W., b. London, 27494, Pte., k. in a., F., 7/9/16.

LEWIS, A. L., b. Seven Sisters, 26220, Pte., k. in a., F., 8/6/16.

LEWIS, J., e. Brecon, 55470, Cpl., k. in a., F., 29/10/18.

LEWIS, R., b. Gwalchmai, 25733, Pte., d., Home, 26/9/15.

LEWIS, S. O., b. Morriston, 26317, Pte., k. in a., F., 9/7/16.

LEWIS, W., b. Aberdare, 25388, Pte., k. in a., F., 10/7/16.

LEWIS, W. E., b. Neath, 93591, Pte., k. in a., F., 6/9/18.

LINARD, J., b. Kingsland, 27249, L/Cpl., k. in a., F., 12/7/16.

LIPTROTT, J. S., b. Liverpool, 58414, Pte., k. in a., F., 3/9/18.

LISLE, J., b. Oldham, 25023, Pte., d., Home, 27/4/17.

LLOYD, E. I., b. Liverpool, 24100, Pte., d. of w., F., 21/8/17.

LLOYD, G., b. Colwall, 93622, Pte., k. in a., F., 8/10/18.

LLOYD, H. M., b. Trawsfynndd, 69272, Pte., d. of w., F., 31/8/18.

LLOYD, J., e. Bettws-y-coed, 52345, Pte., k. in a., F., 29/10/18.

LLOYD, R., b. Festiniog, 26122, Pte., k. in a., F., 28/8/17.

LOCK, H., b. Liverpool, 41659, Pte., d. of w., F., 26/11/16.

LOCKE, W., b. Somerton, 24224, Pte., k. in a., F., 10/7/16.

LONGTON, E., b. Blackburn, 93430, Pte., k. in a., F., 30/8/18.

LOVELL, A., b. Bristol, 93629, Pte., d. of w., F., 3/9/18.

LOWERY, J., b. North Shields, 45545, Pte., d. of w., F., 3/3/18.

LUKE, J. E., b. Gronant, 204143, Pte., k. in a., F., 28/8/17.

MACDONALD, W., b. Manchester, 26096, Pte., d. of w., F., 1/8/17.

MADDOCK, W. F., b. Hope, 25562, Cpl., k. in a., F., 9/7/16.

MADDOX, W., b. Llanelly, 93873, Pte., k. in a., F., 4/11/18.

MAGNESS, A. G., b. Wellington, 59767, Cpl., k. in a., F., 6/10/18.

MARCH, S. R., b. Portslade, 72840, Pte., d. of w., F., 1/9/18.

MARTIN, H., b. Armagh, 46201, Pte., k. in a., F., 8/10/18.

MARTIN, H., b. Hastings, 94265, Pte., k. in a., F., 4/11/18.

MASON, F., b. Ruarddean, 94266, Pte., k. in a., F., 4/11/18.

MASON, J. W., b. Earley, 67506, Pte., k. in a., F., 8/3/18.

MATHER, J. E., b. Pendleton, 60342, Pte., k. in a., F., 24/9/17.

MATHIAS, W. A., b. Brymbo, 26017, Pte., d., F., 23/10/18.

MATTHEWS, G. H., b. Bushbury, 31478, Pte., k. in a., F., 20/10/17.

MATTHEWS, W. H., b. Cromffrw-doer, 94056, Pte., k. in a., F., 4/11/18.

MAW, H. S., b. Labrourne, 35118, Pte., k. in a., F., 9/7/16.

McTIERNON, J. M., b. Birken-head, 46493, Pte., d. of w., F., 5/5/18.

MEE, J. I., b. Liverpool, 267883, Pte., k. in a., F., 28/8/17.

MEREDITH, E., b. Tonypandy, 94061, Pte., k. in a., F., 29/10/18.

MEREDITH, W., b. Welshpool, 290179, Pte., d. of w., F., 13/4/18.

MEREDITH, W. H., b. Ruabon, 25786, A/Cpl., k. in a., F., 9/10/16.

MIDDLETON, J., b. Knutton, 25436, Pte., d. of w., F., 6/2/16.

MILLS, A., b. Thornhaugh, 55477, Pte., k. in a., F., 31/7/17.

MILLS, E. V., b. Aberavon, 59762, A/Cpl., k. in a., F., 29/3/18.

MITTON, A., b. Salford, 267117, Pte., k. in a., F., 1/5/18.

MOORE, G., b. Abertillery, 94150, Pte., k. in a., F., 30/10/18.

MOORE, T., b. Liverpool, 8124, Pte., d. of w., F., 25/8/18.

MORGAN, C., b. Tonyrefail, 94157, Pte., k. in a., F., 29/10/18.

MORGAN, J. H., e. Welshpool, 55525, Pte., k. in a., F., 6/3/18.

MORGAN, L., b. Pentrych, 93635, Pte., k. in a., F., 12/9/18.

MORRIS, G., e. Welshpool, 55474, Pte., k. in a., F., 31/7/17.

MORRIS, G. L., b. Trawsfynydd, 26450, Pte., k. in a., F., 3/3/16.

MORRIS, J., b. Corwen, 25557, Pte., k. in a., F., 12/7/16.

MORRIS, M. H., e. Welshpool, 55475, Pte., k. in a., F., 23/8/18.

MORRIS, P., b. Llangollen, 201374, Pte., k. in a., F., 1/9/18.

MORRIS, R., b. Llanfyllin, 55472, Pte., d., F., 3/3/18.

MORRIS, R., b. Llanrhaidr, 291069, Pte., k. in a., E., 26/3/17.

MORRIS, T., b. Merioneth, 25278, Pte., k. in a., F., 12/5/16.

MORRIS, T., b. Dowlais, 93588, Pte., d. of w., F., 14/9/18.

MURPHY, T., b. Liverpool, 58416, Pte., k. in a., F., 30/8/18.

MYTTON, T., b. Knighton, 55484, Pte., k. in a., F., 9/6/18.

NASH, E., b. Whitchurch, 25175, Cpl., k. in a., F., 12/7/16.

NICHOLAS, W., b. Liverpool, 18943, Pte., k. in a., F., 17/2/17.

NORMAN, H., e. Hertford, 235247, Pte., k. in a., F., 28/8/17.

OATES, H. B., b. Crooks, 93668, Pte., d. of w., F., 8/9/18.

ODDEN, G., b. London, 27593, Pte., k. in a., F., 7/7/16.

OLIVER, T. T., b. Rhondda, 31652, L/Cpl., d. of w., F., 3/8/17, M.M.

O'NEILL, T., b. Llansamlet, 37005, Pte., k. in a., F., 9/7/16.

ONSLOW, D., b. Rhos, 26159, Pte., d. of w., F., 7/6/16.

O'SHEA, J., b. London, 27865, L/Cpl., k. in a., F., 9/7/16.

OWEN, E., b. Llangoed, 72826, L/Cpl., d. of w., F., 21/9/18.

OWEN, E. A., b. Castle Caereinion, 55485, Pte., k. in a., F., 13/3/17.

OWEN, G., b. Festiniog, 25242, Pte., k. in a., F., 10/7/16.

OWEN, J., b. Criccieth, 59698, Pte., k. in a., F., 19/5/18.

OWEN, O. E., b. Bettws-y-coed, 25015, Pte., d. of w., Home, 29/7/16.

OWEN, R., b. Festiniog, 25208, Sgt., d. of w., F., 17/9/18.

OWEN, R., b. Llandegfan, 49013, Pte., k. in a., F., 6/9/18.

OWEN, R. G., e. Pwllheli, 25046, Pte., d., Home, 3/12/15.

OWEN, T. J., b. Festiniog, 20221, Pte., k. in a., F., 1/5/18.

OWEN, W., b. Llanerchymedd, 25900, Pte., k. in a., F., 31/7/17.

OWENS, J., b. Four Crosses, 36604, Pte., k. in a., F., 10/7/16.

PANKS, R. F., b. London, 59719, Pte., k. in a., F., 4/11/18.

PARDELL, J., b. Manchester, 55491, Sgt., d. of w., F., 2/11/18.

PARIS, A. W., e. Wrexham, 55549, L/Sgt., d. of w., F., 31/7/17.

PARSONS, F., b. London, 54038, Pte., k. in a., F., 31/7/17.

PARSONS, W., b. Holyhead, 25514, Pte., k. in a., F., 25/8/16.

PASHLEY, P., b. Mexborough, 60497, Pte., d. of w., F., 7/9/18.

PEARSON, F., b. Writtle, 60559, Pte., k. in a., F., 31/7/17.

PENNINGTON, W. J., b. Bootle, 37325, Pte., k. in a., F., 10/7/16.

PERKIN, C. E., b. Golden Hill, 57147, Pte., k. in a., F., 1/9/18.

PERKS, J. F., b. Wylde Green, 36884, Pte., k. in a., F., 30/8/18.

PERRIN, T. H., b. Broughton, 26025, Pte., k. in a., F., 13/5/16.

PHILIPS, E. W., b. Nunney, 60558, Pte., k. in a., F., 31/7/17.

PHILLIPS, R., b. Briton Ferry, 26422, Sgt., k. in a., F., 30/8/18, D.C.M.

PHILLIPS, W., b. Pembroke, 27695, Pte., k. in a., F., 10/7/16.

PHILLIPS, W. P., b. Birkenhead, 58417, Pte., d. of w., F., 30/8/18.

PICKFORD, R., b. Marple, 235430, Pte., k. in a., F., 8/10/18.

PIERCE, A. E., e. Welshpool, 55494, Pte., d., F., 1/11/18.

PINNINGTON, F., b. Liverpool, 19405, Pte., d. of w., F., 13/7/18.

POOLE, A., e. Welshpool, 55495, Pte., k. in a., F., 31/7/17.

POVAH, T., e. Flint, 240788, Cpl., k. in a., F., 19/5/18.

POWELL, J. H., b. Overton, 25522, Sgt., d. of w., F., 11/7/16.

POWELL, W., e. Welshpool, 55489, Pte., k. in a., F., 13/5/18.

POWYS, G. J., e. Birkenhead, 93902, Pte., k. in a., F., 8/10/18.

PRICE, F. H., b. Seaforth, 60532, Pte., k. in a., F., 31/7/17.

PRITCHARD, H., b. Cwmpenmachno, 26075, Pte., k. in a., F., 12/7/16.

PRITCHARD, O., e. Llangefni, 25511, Pte., k. in a., F., 2/12/16.

PRITCHARD, W. H., b. Llandudno, 25519, Pte., k. in a., F., 15/4/16.

PROBERT, A., e. New Radnor, 55502, Pte., d. of w., F., 20/6/18.

PULMAN, W. G., b. Neath, 26210, Pte., d. of w., F., 19/7/16.

RAMSELL, H. C., e. Welshpool, 55503, Pte., d. of w., F., 24/8/17.

REED, T., b. Ruabon, 25196, L/Cpl., k. in a., F., 7/7/16.

REES, A., b. Griffithstown, 204462, Pte., d. of w., F., 30/8/18.

REEVES, W., b. Hordley, 55504, Pte., d. of w., F., 31/5/18.

RICHARDS, G., e. Porth, 77289, Pte., k. in a., F., 8/10/18.

RIGBY, E., b. Birkdale, 267139, Pte., k. in a., F., 31/7/17.

RIX, H. C., b. Heywood, 28782, Pte., k. in a., F., 12/9/18.

ROACH, T. E., b. St. Clears, 94283, Pte., k. in a., F., 29/10/18.

ROBERTS, B., b. Llandegai, 204316, Pte., k. in a., F., 4/11/18.

ROBERTS, D., b. Corwen, 26246, Pte., k. in a., F., 31/7/17.

ROBERTS, D., b. Trawsfynydd, 94087, Pte., k. in a., F., 29/10/18.

ROBERTS, H., b. Penalt, 55541, Pte., d. of w., F., 23/11/18.

ROBERTS, H., b. Rhiw, 25001, Pte., k. in a., F., 31/7/17.

ROBERTS, J., b. Broughton, 26032, Pte., k. in a., F., 6/7/16.

ROBERTS, J., b. Llanbedrgoch, 26349, Pte., k. in a., F., 12/7/16.

ROBERTS, J., b. Plu. Bodwrog, 26307, Pte., k. in a., F., 9/7/16.

ROBERTS, J., b. Llanengan, 60971, Pte., k. in a., F., 4/11/18.

ROBERTS, J. E., b. Aber, 25115, Pte., k. in a., F., 12/7/16.

ROBERTS, P., b. Llandrillo, 25800, Pte., k. in a., F., 3/4/16.

ROBERTS, R., b. Llysfaen, 25544, Pte., k. in a., F., 4/3/16.

ROBERTS, R. H., b. Beddgelert, 25938, Pte., k. in a., F., 27/7/16.

ROBERTS, S. A. L., b. Gloucester, 73198, Pte., d. of w., F., 2/9/18.

ROBERTS, T., b. Gaerwen, 25530, Pte., k. in a., F., 21/4/16.

ROBERTS, T. H., b. Llandudno, 34674, Pte., k. in a., F., 12/7/16.

ROBERTS, T. J., b. Bersham, 26077, Pte., d. of w., F., 19/5/16.

ROBERTS, T. R., b. Llanarmon, 204123, Pte., k. in a., F., 1/5/18.

ROBERTS, W., b. Leigh, 25828, Pte., k. in a., F., 14/3/16.

ROBERTS, W., b. Llanfwrog, 37194, Pte., k. in a., F., 9/7/16.

ROBERTS, W., b. Llantrisant, 61140, Pte., k. in a., F., 3/9/18.

ROBERTS, W., e. Colwyn Bay, 240824, Pte., k. in a., F., 29/8/17.

ROBERTS, W. J., b. Ystrad Rhondda, 37328, Pte., d. of w., F., 19/7/16.

ROBERTS, W. J., b. Llandwrog, 59749, L/Cpl., k. in a., F., 31/7/17.

ROBINSON, S., b. Dukinfield, 251117, Pte., k. in a., F., 12/7/16.

ROBINSON, T., b. Salford, 267060, Pte., k. in a., F., 31/7/17.

ROBINSON, W., b. Barwell, 60398, Pte., k. in a., F., 29/8/17.

ROBISHAW, W., e. Royton, 60081, Pte., d. of w., F., 18/3/18.

ROGERS, C., b. London, 76297, Pte., k. in a., F., 12/9/18.

ROGERS, P. S., b. Ponkey, 200400, L/Cpl., k. in a., F., 4/11/18.

ROGERSON, L., b. Manchester, 266891, Pte., k. in a., F., 25/8/18.

ROSE, J., b. Hadfield, 235431, Pte., d. of w., F., 21/4/18.

ROSS, A., b. Swansea, 54877, Pte., k. in a., F., 4/9/18.

ROUTLEDGE, E., b. Cambridge, 27903, Pte., k. in a., F., 10/7/16.

ROWLAND, I., b. Llanishen, 94159, Pte., k. in a., F., 29/10/18.

ROWLANDS, M., b. Penmynwdd, 25670, Pte., d. of w., F., 20/1/16.

ROWSON, O., b. Church Pulverbatch, 25617, Sgt., k. in a., F., 22/1/16.

ROYLE, W., b. Bolton, 45128, Pte., k. in a., F., 31/7/17.

ROYSTON, F. F., b. Colne, 56173, Cpl., k. in a., F., 30/8/18.

RYLES, G., b. Rhyl, 12794, Pte., k. in a., F., 28/3/18.

SANGER, J., b. Ruabon, 55512, Pte., k. in a., F., 2/2/17.

SAUNDERS, W. H., b. Bewdley, 36131, Cpl., d. of w., F., 7/11/18.

SEARS, S. C., b. London, 27764, Cpl., k. in a., F., 21/4/18.

SHARP, L. W., b. London, 25793, Pte., k. in a., F., 14/1/16.

SHEPHERD, J. W., b. Norden, 266951, Pte., k. in a., F., 28/7/17.

SHEPPARD, A., b. Bristol, 93661, Pte., k. in a., F., 3/9/18.

SHERIDAN, J., b. Kildare, 25149, Pte., d. of w., F., 26/8/18.

SHINTON, A., b. Bilston, 56129, Pte., k. in a., F., 13/8/18.

SHUTTLEWORTH, T., b. Burnley, 72888, Pte., k. in a., F., 4/9/18.

SIMMS, C., b. Cowbridge, 94093, Pte., k. in a., F., 4/11/18.

SLATER, T. H., b. Liverpool, 37227, Pte., k. in a., F., 9/7/16.

SMITH, N. S., e. Hitchen, 235252, Pte., k. in a., F., 31/7/17.

SMITH, W., b. Harthill, 25006, Pte., d., F., 15/3/16.

SMITH, W. J., b. Seven Sisters, 26206, Pte., k. in a., F., 12/7/16.

SNOOKS, W., b. Birmingham, 76331, Pte., k. in a., F., 1/9/18.

SPEAKMAN, R., b. Wavertree, 60535, Pte., k. in a., F., 31/7/17.

SPENCER, A., b. Wanbury, 43899, Pte., k. in a., F., 30/8/18.

SPENCER, S. J., b. Caldicott, 267920, Pte., d. of w., F., 2/9/18, M.M.

SPINKS, F., b. Brownhills, 25635, L/Cpl., k. in a., F., 29/10/17.

STACEY, J. W., e. Ramsey, 202404, Pte., k. in a., F., 6/6/18.

STALLARD, W., b. London, 27950, L/Cpl., d., Home, 22/7/16.

STEELE, T., b. Crewe, 242263, Pte., k. in a., F., 26/6/18.

STEVENSON, T., b. Burslem, 25702, Cpl., k. in a., F., 4/9/18, M.M.

STEWART, J. H., b. London, 54039, Pte., k. in a., F., 30/8/18.

STOTT, F., b. London, 22807, Pte., k. in a., F., 8/10/18.

STRAND, A., e. Ramsgate, 56166, L/Cpl., k. in a., F., 31/7/17.

STRATTON, A. J., b. Bristol, 25707, Pte., k. in a., F., 9/5/18.

SURRIDGE, E. W., b. Harpole, 60591, Pte., k. in a., F., 29/8/17.

SUTTON, H., b. Blackburn, 20304, Pte., d. of w., Home, 27/3/17.
SWALLOW, W. H., b. Beaconsfield, 75331, Pte., k. in a., F., 16/5/18.
TABBOTT, J., e. Cwm, 268192, Pte., d., Home, 3/10/17.
TERRY, E. V., b. London, 25716, Pte., d. of w., F., 27/4/16.
THOMAS, D., b. Mold, 25583, Pte., k. in a., F., 9/7/16.
THOMAS, D., e. Cardiff, 57117, Pte., d., F., 6/11/16.
THOMAS, E., b. Llanrwst, 203587, Pte., k. in a., F., 27/10/18.
THOMAS, F., b. Pentraeth, 25105, Pte., d. of w., F., 7/2/17.
THOMAS, H. D., b. Ruthin, 31324, Pte., k. in a., F., 14/7/16.
THOMAS, J., b. Briton Ferry, 26190, Pte., k. in a., F., 6/7/16.
THOMAS, J., b. Festiniog, 26369, Pte., k. in a., F., 8/10/18.
THOMAS, J. E., b. Abernant, 40215, Cpl., k. in a., F., 30/8/18.
THOMAS, J. G., b. Nevin, 203778, Pte., d. of w., F., 29/10/18.
THOMAS, L. J., b. Pembroke, 94123, Pte., k. in a., F., 21/10/18.
THOMAS, O., e. Carnarvon, 56941, Pte., k. in a., F., 26/9/17.
THOMAS, P., b. Mold, 54582, Pte., d. of w., F., 1/9/18.
THOMAS, W., b. Llanwnnog, 55519, Pte., k. in a., F., 14/2/17.
THOMAS, W. C., b. Tredegar, 94132, Pte., k. in a., F., 29/10/18.
THOMAS, W. J., b. Clydach, 94122, Pte., k. in a., F., 29/10/18.
TIPPING, J., b. Walker, 60541, A/Cpl., d. of w., F., 24/5/18.
TOWERS, D., b. Barry, 25452, Cpl., k. in a., F., 2/2/17, M.M.
TREHERNE, O. T., b. Hereford, 13146, Pte., k. in a., F., 11/10/17.
TURNER, C. C., b. Pontypool, 94311, Pte., d. of w., F., 29/10/18.
TURNER, H., b. Wallasey, 70470, Pte., k. in a., F., 1/5/18.
WAINE, S., b. Homesfield, 26153, Pte., d. of w., F., 2/7/18.
WALES, J. T., b. Earith, 235258, Pte., d. of w., F., 29/8/17.
WALSH, J., b. Blackburn, 33142, Pte., k. in a., F., 15/2/16.
WALTERS, F., b. Salford, 59279, Pte., d. of w., F., 5/5/18.
WARBURTON, J., b. Hawarden, 25415, Pte., d. of w., Home, 22/7/16.
WARD, A. E., b. Kidwelly, 235597, Pte., k. in a., F., 4/11/18.
WATERS, W. G., b. London, 41740, Pte., k. in a., F., 26/9/17.
WATKIN, M. T., b. Llanbrynmair,

55529, Pte., k. in a., F., 31/7/17.
WATSON, T., b. Llanrwst, 94083, Pte., d. of w., F., 29/10/18.
WAUGH, J., b. Harrington, 25952, Sgt., k. in a., F., 1/5/18.
WEARE, G., e. Pontypridd, 45253, Pte., d. of w., F., 30/9/17.
WEBSTER, J., b. Kerry, 55538, Pte., k. in a., F., 1/9/18.
WELLS, T., b. Hyde, 45055, Pte., d. of w., F., 12/10/17.
WHITE, R. C., b. Ystrad, 94128, Pte., k. in a., F., 29/10/18.
WHITE, W., b. Dukinfield, 46365, Pte., k. in a., F., 31/7/17.
WHITTAKER, F., b. Market Drayton, 267701, Pte., d. of w., F., 8/3/18.
WHITTLE, J., b. Preston, 26209, Pte., d. of w., F., 8/8/17.
WILDE, C., b. Denbigh, 25007, C.Q.M.S., d., F., 20/2/16.
WILKINSON, W. J., b. Llanbeblig, 26039, Pte., k. in a., F., 19/6/17.
WILLIAMS, A., b. Clydach, 59761, Pte., k. in a., F., 12/4/18.
WILLIAMS, A., b. Swansea, 243271, Pte., k. in a., F., 4/9/18.
WILLIAMS, A. R., b. Bettws-y-Coed, 26070, Pte., k. in a., F., 21/5/16.
WILLIAMS, C., b. Bodfari, 345806, Pte., d., F., 1/11/18.
WILLIAMS, D. G., b. Trawsfynydd, 40433, Pte., k. in a., F., 3/9/16.
WILLIAMS, E., b. Oswestry, 43508, Pte., d. of w., F., 4/8/17.
WILLIAMS, E. D., e. Carnarvon, 265441, Pte., k. in a., F., 1/9/18.
WILLIAMS, E. O., b. Bethesda, 25543, Pte., k. in a., F., 14/7/16.
WILLIAMS, H., e. Llangefni, 26062, Pte., k. in a., F., 31/7/17.
WILLIAMS, H. G., b. Llanidloes, 25232, Pte., k. in a., F., 8/4/17.
WILLIAMS, H. P., b. Brymbo, 25169, Pte., k. in a., F., 23/12/16.
WILLIAMS, J., b. Llanerchymedd, 25576, Pte., d. of w., F., 26/8/17.
WILLIAMS, J., b. Hanley, 26145, Pte., k. in a., F., 9/7/16.
WILLIAMS, J., b. Pentraeth, 26333, Pte., k. in a., F., 9/7/16.
WILLIAMS, J., b. Bodedern, 59743, Pte., d. of w., F., 8/7/17.
WILLIAMS, J. O., b. Bersham, 26028, Pte., k. in a., F., 6/7/16.
WILLIAMS, L. O., b. Ystradgynlais, 53984, L/Cpl., k. in a., F., 8/10/18.

WILLIAMS, O., b. Bodedern, 20949, Pte., k. in a., F., 31/7/17.
WILLIAMS, P., e. Llangefni, 24882, Pte., k. in a., F., 31/7/17.
WILLIAMS, R., b. Rhydwern, 59744, Pte., k. in a., F., 16/6/17.
WILLIAMS, R., b. Llanllechid, 26137, Pte., k. in a., F., 12/7/16.
WILLIAMS, T., b. Beaumaris, 26338, Pte., k. in a., F., 9/7/16.
WILLIAMS, T. H., b. Ruabon, 26373, Pte., k. in a., F., 11/5/16.
WILLIAMS, W., b. Byngwran, 25838, Pte., k. in a., F., 31/7/17.
WILLIAMS, W., b. Wrexham, 55536, A/Cpl., d. of w., F., 9/3/18.
WILLIAMS, W., b. Ynyscynhaiarn, 203646, Pte., d. of w., F., 8/10/18.
WILLIAMS, W. A., b. Llanferres, 25504, Pte., k. in a., F., 31/7/17.
WILLIAMS, W. C., b. London, 59714, Pte., d. of w., F., 10/9/18.
WILLIAMS, W. J., b. Briton Ferry, 25578, L/Cpl., k. in a., F., 6/8/18.
WILLIAMS, W. J., b. Bodorgan, 26396, Pte., d. of w., F., 17/10/16.
WILLIAMS, W. J., b. Holyhead, 265729, Pte., k. in a., F., 31/7/17.
WILLIAMS, W. M., b. Prestatyn, 241093, Pte., d. of w., F., 28/4/18.
WILLIAMS, W. T., b. Gwersyllt, 43856, Pte., d. of w., F., 5/1/17.
WILLIAMS, W. T., b. Llandudno, 43901, Pte., k. in a., F., 8/10/18.
WILLOUGHBY, S., b. Hunstanton, 44307, Pte., k. in a., F., 23/11/17.
WILSON, A., b. Birmingham, 37144, Pte., k. in a., F., 28/3/18.
WILSON, W. T., e. Gladestry, 55533, Pte., k. in a., F., 5/8/17.
WINTERBOTTOM, R., b. Roby Mill, 93393, Pte., k. in a., F., 29/10/18.
WOLFENDEN, R., b. Bury, 52056, Pte., k. in a., F., 28/8/17.
WOOD, W., b. Wybunbury, 291683, Pte., k. in a., F., 4/9/18.
WORTHINGTON, S., b. St. Helens, 25830, Pte., d. of w., F., 15/7/16.
WREN, R. C., e. Hertford, 235260, Pte., d. of w., Home, 8/4/18.

WRIGHT, W., b. Liverpool, 29979, Pte., d. of w., F., 29/8/18.

WYNNE, E. L., b. Mold, 25430, Pte., k. in a., F., 12/7/16.

YARWOOD, H., b. Reddish, 26234, Pte., d. of w., F., 24/4/18.

YATES, S., b. West Bromwich, 26429, Pte., k. in a., F., 7/2/16.

18th BATTALION

ANDREWS, J., b. London, 35144, Pte., d., Home, 25/12/15.

BELL, J. H., b. Carlisle, 26924, Pte., d., Home, 24/2/17.

BUTTERWORTH, A., b. Macclesfield, 26039, Pte., d., Home, 21/3/17.

EVANS, H., b. Kentish Town, 26567, Pte., d., Home, 11/5/15.

HEXT, W. C., b. Stocklanch, 26768, Pte., d., Home, 15/3/17.

HUGHES, D. A., b. Haverfordwest, 44743, Pte., d., Home, 7/5/16.

JONES, E., b. Leeswood, 20162, Pte., d., Home, 22/6/17.

KENT, J. H., b. Northwich, 26641, Pte., d., Home, 11/5/17.

NOBLE, W., b. Ashton-under-Lyne, 52371, Pte., d., Home, 5/7/18.

NORBURY, A. B., b. Chester, 35457, Pte., d., Home, 1/5/16.

19th BATTALION

ACKLAND, H., b. Bethnal Green, 45711, Pte., k. in a., F., 19/6/16.

ALCOCK, A., b. Fenton, 29188, Pte., k. in a., F., 6/5/17.

AMOS, H., b. Belfast, 28279, Cpl., d., F., 25/12/17.

ASTLEY, A., b. Blackburn, 201704, Cpl., d. of w., F., 4/12/17.

BAILEY, G. W., b. Lytham, 29184, Pte., k. in a., F., 20/6/16.

BAILEY, U., b. Smallthorne, 28588, Pte., d. of w., F., 28/4/17.

BAILEY, W., b. Altrincham, 28278, Pte., k. in a., F., 23/11/17.

BARKER, C. J., b. Stoke-on-Trent, 24473, L/Sgt., k. in a., F., 14/8/17.

BARNETT, C. T., b. Cobridge, 29224, Pte., d. of w., F., 15/7/16.

BARTON, G., b. Liverpool, 45744, Pte., k. in a., F., 14/8/17.

BATES, A., b. Newcastle, 28962, Pte., k. in a., F., 14/6/16.

BENFIELD, A., b. Longton, 28311, Pte., d., Home, 23/3/18.

BENNETT, F. A., b. Little Drayton, 268003, Pte., k. in a., F., 23/11/17.

BETTS, E. W., e. Gateley, 53990, Pte., k. in a., F., 23/11/17.

BINGHAM, R. E., b. London, 21828, Pte., k. in a., F., 24/11/17.

BIRCHALL, P., b. Bolton, 28503, Pte., d., Home, 10/1/18.

BOLTON, A., b. Blackburn, 33144, Pte., d. of w., F., 22/4/17.

BONNETT, J. T., b. Salford, 28896, Pte., k. in a., F., 12/6/16.

BORST, E., b. London, 66541, Pte., d. of w., F., 25/11/17.

BOWEN, F. B., b. Llandilo, 29628, Pte., k. in a., F., 24/11/17.

BOYLAN, W. H., b. Longton, 28963, Pte., k. in a., F., 31/8/16.

BURKE, P., b. Manchester, 28916, Pte., k. in a., F., 24/11/17.

BURROWS, T. A. W., b. London, 45783, Pte., k. in a., F., 6/5/17.

BUTLER, J., b. Clayton le-Moors, 20101, Pte., k. in a., F., 23/11/17.

CALLINAN, T., b. Cardiff, 73708, Pte., k. in a., F., 15/12/17.

CASSELL, A., b. London, 45620, Pte., k. in a., F., 24/11/17.

CHADWICK, H., b. Walkden, 28469, L/Cpl., k. in a., F., 23/11/17.

CHADWICK, H., b. Hyde, 46310, L/Cpl., k. in a., F., 24/11/17.

CHAMBERLAIN, C., b. Newport, 45561, L/Cpl., k. in a., F., 23/11/17.

CHIDLEY, H., b. Smethcote, 54910, Pte., d. of w., F., 24/11/17.

CLARK, E., b. London, 29000, Pte., d., Home, 25/12/16.

CLOWES, W., b. Manchester, 29300, Pte., k. in a., F., 21/4/17.

COCK, J., b. Buckland, 30286, Cpl., k. in a., F., 23/11/17.

COLCLOUGH, W. J., b. Hanley, 28967, Sgt., d., F., 19/6/16.

CONNOR, J., b. Warrington, 28606, Pte., k. in a., F., 4/5/17.

COOPER, L., b. Manchester, 45590, Pte., d. of w., Home, 9/3/18.

COX, A., b. Hanley, 28777, Sgt., k. in a., F., 6/5/17.

COX, G. H., b. Warrington, 45738, Pte., d. of w., F., 12/9/16.

COX, R., b. Trealaw, 61335, Pte., k. in a., F., 15/1/18.

CULLEN, J., b. Stockport, 45502, Pte., k. in a., F., 23/11/17.

CULLEN, S., b. Swansea, 61187, Pte., k. in a., F., 24/11/17.

DAVIES, A. H., b. St. Bride's, 66915, Pte., k. in a., F., 24/11/17.

DAVIES, E., b. Caerphilly, 61574, Pte., k. in a., F., 24/11/17.

DAVIES, G., b. Henllan, 44781, Pte., k. in a., F., 25/11/17.

DAVIES, J., b. Llanfagdalen, 28917, Pte., d. of w., F., 20/5/18.

DAVIES, J., b. Caersws, 55393, Pte., d. of w., F., 26/11/17.

DAVIES, R. E., b. Llanuwchllyn, 61020, Pte., k. in a., F., 3/2/18.

DONOVAN, J. T., b. Salford, 29276, Sgt., d. of w., F., 8/5/17.

DRAPER, E., b. Liverpool, 29445, Pte., k. in a., F., 25/8/18.

DURHAM, W. H., b. Swynnerton, 28920, Pte., k. in a., F., 24/11/17.

EDWARDS, A., b. Somerstown, 35053, Pte., d., F., 12/5/18.

EDWARDS, J. A., b. Birkenhead, 45704, Pte., d. of w., F., 24/11/17.

EDWARDS, J. J., b. Brymbo, 61254, Pte., k. in a., F., 12/5/18.

EDWARDS, S., b. Wrexham, 45584, Pte., d. of w., F., 21/10/16.

ELLIS, J., b. Liverpool, 45565, Pte., d. of w., F., 31/12/17.

EVANS, D. J., b. Festiniog, 20237, Pte., k. in a., F., 2/10/16.

FAIRCLOUGH, J. E., b. Burtonwood, 45622, Sgt., d. of w., F., 18/10/16.

FARREN, T. E., b. Manchester, 29443, Pte., k. in a., F., 12/5/18.

FELTON, G., b. Burslem, 28603, Pte., d., F., 3/2/17.

FITTON, H., b. Heaton Norris, 61227, Pte., k. in a., F., 23/11/17.

FITZPATRICK, F., e. Wrexham, 57009, Pte., k. in a., F., 23/11/17.

FOOTE, J., b. Manchester, 52660, Pte., k. in a., F., 6/5/17.

FRATER, G., b. Thornaby-on Tees, 73556, Pte., k. in a., F., 15/12/17.

FREEMAN, A. B., b. Brimington, 45770, Pte., d. of w., F., 10/4/18.

FREEMAN, E. A., b. Fenton, 24383, L/Cpl., k. in a., F., 23/11/17.

FRYERS, H. A., b. Chorlton-on-Medlock, 29162, Pte., k. in a., F., 23/11/17.

FURNER, J. L., b. Rye, 45632, Pte., k. in a., F., 12/9/16.

GARNER, W. C. E., b. St. Helens, 75418, Pte., k. in a., F., 18/1/18.

GERRARD, W., b. St. Helens, 45623, Pte., d. of w., F., 3/1/17.

GIBBS, A. E., b. Bristol, 19699, Pte., k. in a., F., 24/11/17.

GREY, J. W., b. Scarborough, 45550, Pte., k. in a., F., 21/4/17.

GOODWIN, D., b. Chester, 44971, Pte., k. in a., F., 28/9/17.

GRIFFITH, E. H., b. Liverpool, 28595, Pte., k. in a., F., 4/7/16.

GRIFFITHS, A., e. Wrexham, 200670, Pte., k. in a., F., 24/11/17.

GRIFFITHS, W. D., b. Festiniog, 20272, Pte., k. in a., F., 24/11/17.

HALSALL, P., b. Southport, 55049, Pte., d. of w., F., 24/11/17.

HAMPSON, T., b. Oldham, 267010, Cpl., k. in a., F., 24/11/17.

HAYNES, J., b. Liverpool, 29279, Pte., d. of w., Home, 13/5/17.

HEARN, G., b. London, 45551, Pte., k. in a., F., 15/12/17.

HENNIGAN, P., b. Hanley, 28377, Pte., d. of w., F., 17/9/16.

HICKTON, D., b. Burslem, 28872, Pte., d. of w., F., 1/12/17.

HINKSMAN, A., b. Bromyard, 21934, L/Cpl., d. of w., F., 5/9/18.

HOLMES, A., b. Manchester, 266942, Pte., d. of w., F., 2/12/17.

HOPKINS, A., e. Swansea, 202671, Pte., k. in a., F., 23/11/17.

HOPWOOD, H., b. Manchester, 267228, Pte., k. in a., F., 23/11/17.

HORRIGAN, T., e. Newport, 45571, Pte., d., F., 16/9/17.

HUGHES, G. T., b. Llanllyfni, 29447, Pte., d. of w., F., 6/6/17.

HUGHES, W. J., b. Llanbeblig, 29122, L/Cpl., k. in a., F., 4/1/17.

JOHN, D. H., b. Llandow, 55563, Pte., d., F., 12/5/18.

JOHNSON, S., e. Liverpool, 241681, Pte., k. in a., F., 15/12/17.

JONES, A. E., b. St. Asaph, 265828, Pte., k. in a., F., 24/11/17.

JONES, D., b. Middlesbrough, 28381, Pte., k. in a., F., 6/5/17.

JONES, E., e. Wrexham, 69314, Pte., d., F., 31/10/18.

JONES, E. W., b. Tryddyn, 29384, Pte., k. in a., F., 6/5/17.

JONES, H., b. Newtown, 201221, Pte., k. in a., F., 15/12/17.

JONES, H., b. Rhuddlan, 53938, Pte., k. in a., F., 24/11/17.

JONES, H., b. Conway, 54623, Pte., d. of w., F., 18/2/17.

JONES, J., b. Ruabon, 28419, Pte., k. in a., F., 10/9/16.

JONES, J., b. Llantrisant, 28428, Pte., k. in a., F., 21/4/17.

JONES, J. J., b. Manchester, 28416, Pte., k. in a., F., 2/1/17.

JONES, J. R., b. Llanfaelog, 28975, Pte., k. in a., F., 23/11/17.

JONES, J. R., b. Bangor, 28854, L/Cpl., k. in a., F., 28/9/18.

JONES, L., b. Penrhyndeudraeth, 28359, Pte., d. of w., Home, 6/6/17.

JONES, R., b. Llandysilio, 28906, Pte., k. in a., F., 28/9/17.

JONES, W., b. Loch Wynnoch, 28320, Pte., d. of w., F., 26/9/16.

JONES, W., b. Glyn, 54369, Pte., k. in a., F., 23/11/17.

JONES, W. H., b. Welshpool, 203066, Pte., k. in a., F., 23/11/17.

KELLY, J., b. Hadfield, 29345, Pte., d. of w., F., 24/4/17.

KELLY, P., b. Gibraltar, 23979, R.S.M., d., Home, 18/3/16.

KINLEY, C., b. Salford, 28890, Pte., k. in a., F., 12/6/16.

KNOWLES, J., b. Sheffield, 28365, Pte., k. in a., F., 10/9/16.

KNOWLES, J., b. Brynn, 28489, Pte., d., Home, 18/1/16.

KNOWLES, W. T., b. Llanrug, 28251, Pte., k. in a., F., 23/11/17.

LANE, J., b. Manchester, 28751, Pte., k. in a., F., 23/11/17.

LAWES, H. E., b. London, 268124, Pte., d. of w., F., 19/12/17.

LAWRENCE, E., b. Essex, 28942, Pte., d. of w., F., 19/6/16.

LAWTON, T., b. Manchester, 28441, Sgt., k. in a., F., 25/9/17.

LEACH, T., b. Bury, 54363, Pte., k. in a., F., 21/4/17.

LEE, J., b. Ashton-under-Lyne, 29248, Pte., k. in a., F., 22/4/17.

LEES, E. H., b. Stalybridge, 45529, Pte., d., F., 17/11/17.

LEES, J. J., b. Rochdale, 28628, Pte., d. of w., F., 25/11/17.

LEWIS, A. J., b. Blaenavon, 73766, Pte., d. of w., F., 8/9/18.

LEWIS, W., b. Trefeglwys, 73765, Pte., d. of w., F., 15/12/17.

LILLEY, W., b. Kettering, 45662, Sgt., k. in a., F., 6/5/17.

LLOYD, J., b. Rhos, 54392, Pte., d. of w., F., 23/11/17.

LLOYD, M. G., b. Llanfair, 61085, Pte., k. in a., F., 23/11/17.

LOMAS, S., b. Congleton, 28764, Pte., d. of w., F., 27/10/17.

MALE, J. T., b. London, 45723, Pte., k. in a., F., 27/5/18.

MALONE, M., b. London, 27430, Pte., k. in a., F., 24/11/17.

MARSDEN, J., b. Manchester, 39747, Pte., k. in a., F., 21/10/16.

MARSHALL, W., b. Talysarn, 59142, Pte., k. in a., F., 23/11/17.

MARTIN, M., b. Pontypridd, 54391, Pte., d. of w., F., 26/11/17.

MATTHEWS, E., b. Wrexham, 29363, Pte., k. in a., F., 16/10/16.

MAUND, J. M., b. Knowbury, 267681, Pte., k. in a., F., 20/9/17.

MAWBY, J., b. London, 45696, Pte., d. of w., F., 25/4/17.

McDERMOTT, W., b. Dublin, 45664, Pte., k. in a., F., 6/5/17.

McMANUS, J., b. Manchester, 29167, Pte., k. in a., F., 25/1/17.

MELLOR, A., b. Oldham, 28711, Pte., d. of w., F., 30/4/17.

MELVIN, W. C., b. Barry, 73772, Pte., d. of w., F., 24/8/18.

MEREDITH, J. A., b. Ruabon, 200257, Pte., d. of w., F., 19/12/17.

MEREDITH, T., b. Liverpool, 29454, Pte., k. in a., F., 10/9/16.

MILLS, R., b. Heywood, 29298, Pte., d., F., 15/6/17.

MOORE, A. J., b. London, 21926, L/Cpl., k. in a., F., 31/1/18, M.M.

MOORE, E., b. Cardiff, 54335, Pte., k. in a., F., 25/8/18.

MORRIS, G., b. Cardiff, 29308, Pte., k. in a., F., 21/4/17.

MORRIS, G. E., e. Colwyn Bay, 54573, Pte., d., Home, 31/12/17.

MORRIS, R., b. Cowbridge, 73783, Pte., k. in a., F., 12/5/18.

MUNRO, G., b. Manchester, 28727, Pte., d. of w., F., 21/10/16.

MURRAY, L. P., b. Dublin, 28515, Cpl., d. of w., F., 20/8/16.

OATLEY, A., b. Crosscombe, 28879, Pte., k. in a., F., 24/11/17.

O'BRIEN, G. H., b. Manchester, 28943, Pte., k. in a., F., 31/8/16.

OLD, W. A., b. Maid Newton, 45521, Pte., k. in a., F., 28/12/16.

OLIVER, D., b. Bethesda, 54631, Pte., k. in a., F., 3/9/18.

OWEN, G., b. Llanllyfni, 37461, Pte., k. in a., F., 24/11/17.

OWEN, J., b. Penrhynside, 75428, Pte., k. in a., F., 8/1/18.

OWEN, J. E., b. Llandrinio, 202966, Pte., k. in a., F., 24/12/17.

OWEN, T., b. Stonehouse, 29057, L/Sgt., k. in a., F., 2/10/16.

OWEN, T. A., b. Conwill, 73785, Pte., d. of w., F., 2/1/18.

OWEN, W., b. Llanfaethlin, 73789, Pte., k. in a., F., 23/12/17.

PARRY, J., e. Holywell, 54636, Pte., d. of w., F., 28/9/17.

PARRY, R. A., b. Hope, 19884, Pte., k. in a., F., 23/11/17.

PENFOLD, C. E., b. London, 45727, Pte., d. of w., F., 24/11/17.

PERCIVAL, H., b. Wrexham, 29302, Pte., k. in a., F., 21/10/16.

PERRY, J., b. Longton, 28348, Pte., d. of w., F., 26/11/17.

PERRY, W., b. Longton, 29400, Pte., d. of w., F., 21/6/16.

PETERS, L., b. Brymbo, 28266, Sgt., d. of w., F., 10/8/16.

PLANT, H., b. Burnley, 73687, Pte., k. in a., F., 15/12/17.

PLATT, H., b. Longton, 29062, Pte., k. in a., F., 24/11/17.

POWELL, J., b. Wednesbury, 201658, Cpl., k. in a., F., 24/11/17.

PRICE, L., b. Burry Port, 201543, Pte., d. of w., F., 11/8/17.

PUDDY, E., b. Mark, 72842, Pte., k. in a., F., 24/11/17.

READER, H. W., b. London, 45752, Pte., d. of w., F., 23/6/17.

REDGE, G., b. Abingdon, 45691, Pte., k. in a., F., 14/9/17.

RICE, A., b. Newton, 29180, Pte., k. in a., F., 23/11/17.

RIDGE, G. E., b. Meifod, 203111, Pte., k. in a., F., 25/5/18.

ROBERTS, A., b. Ruthin, 28331, Pte., d., Home, 4/10/16.

ROBERTS, D., b. Llangar, 29449, Pte., k. in a., F., 24/11/17.

ROBERTS, D. J., b. Ystrad, 20447, Sgt., d. of w., F., 24/11/17.

ROBERTS, H., b. Penmaenmawr, 267408, Pte., k. in a., F., 23/11/17.

ROBERTS, H. J., b. Llanystumdwy, 61017, Pte., k. in a., F., 23/11/17.

ROBERTS, H. T., e. Carnarvon, 268228, Pte., k. in a., F., 23/11/17.

ROBERTS, J. E., b. Whittington, 10910, Cpl., k. in a., F., 15/2/17.

ROBERTS, O. J., b. Llanbedrgoch, 29399, Cpl., k. in a., F., 21/4/17.

ROBERTS, W., b. Wrexham, 200063, Pte., d. of w., F., 29/11/17.

ROGERS, D., e. Tonypandy, 267872, Pte., d. of w., F., 24/11/17.

ROWLANDS, J. F., e. Bala, 291737, Pte., d. of w., F., 27/11/17.

RUDDOCK, C. H., b. Liverpool, 45507, Pte., k. in a., F., 6/5/17.

RYLANCE, J. F., b. Birkenhead, 204997, Cpl., k. in a., F., 23/11/17.

SALT, H., b. Ebenezer, 73812, Pte., k. in a., F., 8/1/18.

SEALE, J., b. Kensington, 28702, Cpl., d., F., 5/8/16.

SELF, E. C., b. London, 45742, Pte., k. in a., F., 24/11/17.

SHAWCROSS, E., b. Manchester, 29255, Pte., d. of w., F., 24/4/17.

SIMMONDS, J., b. London, 45621, Pte., k. in a., F., 23/11/17.

SIMON, W. T., b. Ruabon, 28771, Pte., d. of w., F., 27/11/17.

SLACK, W., b. Manchester, 29355, Pte., k. in a., F., 23/11/17.

SMITH, E. S., b. Rhondda, 29395, Pte., k. in a., F., 24/11/17.

SMITH, J., b. Hesketh Bank, 201769, Pte., k. in a., F., 9/9/17.

SPENCER, H., b. Blackburn, 201695, Pte., d. of w., F., 23/11/17.

TANNER, H., b. Mangotsfield, 9179, Pte., k. in a., F., 26/7/17.

TAPLIN, G. E., b. Cadishead, 28858, Pte., k. in a., F., 16/6/17.

THOMAS, D. A., b. Middlesbrough, 23819, L/Cpl., k. in a., F., 30/9/16.

THOMAS, G., b. Llangerniew, 36810, Pte., k. in a., F., 23/11/17.

THOMAS, R., b. Bangor, 28728, Pte., k. in a., F., 24/11/17.

THOMAS, R., b. Llansamlet, 201518, Pte., k. in a., F., 18/9/17.

TOOTH, T., b. Longton, 28969, Pte., k. in a., F., 14/6/16.

TRAVIS, G. T., b. Gorton, 29181, Pte., k. in a., F., 23/4/17.

TUNSTALL, E., b. Burslem, 28305, Pte., d. of w., F., 24/4/17.

TURNBULL, W., b. Manchester, 73666, Pte., k. in a., F., 15/1/18.

WAGG, A., b. Stoke, 45771, Pte., k. in a., F., 8/1/18.

WALSH, F., b. Dublin, 45537, Pte., d. of w., F., 21/4/17.

WALSH, W., b. Dublin, 45505, L/Cpl., k. in a., F., 21/4/17.

WARBURTON, G., b. Warrington, 45690, Pte., k. in a., F., 31/8/16.

WARDLE, P., e. Manchester, 28544, L/Cpl., k. in a., F., 24/11/17.

WEBSTER, H., b. Sheffield, 45549, Pte., k. in a., F., 1/10/16.

WHEATCROFT, H., b. Chorley, 73676, Pte., k. in a., F., 25/8/18.

WHITE, C., b. Rhondda, 12166, L/Cpl., k. in a., F., 29/8/17.

WHITE, J., e. London, 52752, Pte., k. in a., F., 8/1/18.

WHITE, P., b. Blackwell, 28905, Pte., k. in a., F., 24/11/17.

WHITTAKER, J. E., b. Rawtenstall, 56479, Pte., k. in a., F., 15/1/18.

WHITWORTH, H. W., b. Bury, 45552, Pte., k. in a., F., 21/4/17.

WILLDING, A., b. Pontypridd, 202797, Pte., k. in a., F., 24/11/17.

WILLIAMS, D. W., e. Denbigh, 205025, Pte., k. in a., F., 24/11/17.

WILLIAMS, E., b. Gelligaer, 54375, Pte., d. of w., F., 30/12/17.

WILLIAMS, E. J., b. Bethesda, 45679, Pte., d. of w., F., 17/12/17.

WILLIAMS, G., b. Llanllechid, 20609, Pte., k. in a., F., 14/8/16.

WILLIAMS, I., b. Treorchy, 20471, Sgt., k. in a., F., 20/10/16.

WILLIAMS, R., b. Carnarvon, 28566, Pte., k. in a., F., 18/10/16.

WILLIAMS, R., b. Llangean, 61137, Pte., k. in a., F., 24/11/17.

WILLIAMS, R. J., b. Wrexham, 28430, Pte., k. in a., F., 25/9/17.

WILLIAMS, R. T., b. Llandysilio, 29488, Pte., d. of w., Home, 17/5/17.

WILLIAMS, W. G., b. Llanelly, 202672, Pte., d. of w., F., 13/9/17.

WOOD, W., b. Yspytty, 29440, Pte., k. in a., F., 24/11/17.

WOOLLEY, A. F., b. Castleford, 45674, Pte., d., F., 5/2/18.

WRENCH, R., e. Conway, 29466, Pte., d., F., 9/5/17.

YALES, T., b. Wellington, 31708, Pte., k. in a., F., 24/11/17.

YARWOOD, G., b. Widnes, 45677, Pte., d. of w., F., 22/8/18.

YOUNG, F., b. Liverpool, 67205, Pte., d. of w., F., 24/11/17.

YULE, C. S. J., b. Penarth, 45769, Cpl., d., Home, 19/12/16.

20th BATTALION

COUGHLIN, A., b. Ashton-under-Lyne, 20966, Pte., d., Home, 1/12/15.

DAVIES, D., e. Bangor, 37327, Pte., d., Home, 26/3/16.

JOHN, R. T., b. Nantymoel, 19429, Pte., d., Home, 8/1/16.

JOHNSON, R. E., b. Manchester, 31704, Pte., d., Home, 29/10/15.

OWEN, R., b. Dinas-Mawddwy, 37022, Pte., d., Home, 1/4/16.

PARTINGTON, J., b. Liverpool, 30416, L/Cpl., d., Home, 4/6/17.

PEAKE, T. J., b. Corwen, 31946, Pte., d., Home, 1/3/16.

SHORTMAN, J., b. Bristol, 21447, Pte., d., Home, 1/3/16.

TAYLOR, E. J., b. London, 22070, Pte., d., Home, 4/3/16.

TYRER, W. T., e. Bethesda, 18797, Pte., d., Home, 1/3/16.

WILKINSON, E., b. Manchester, 39384, Pte., d., Home, 13/4/16.

21st BATTALION

HUMPHREYS, J. R., b. Dolgelly, 39079, Pte., d., Home, 19/4/16.

22nd BATTALION

MATTHEWS, A., b. Merthyr, 40614, Pte., d., Home, 12/4/16.

ROBERTS, E., b. Peniel, 40781, Pte., d., Home, 16/4/16.

23rd BATTALION

AUCHINCLOSS, J. M., b. Bridgeton, 64482, Pte., d., Home, 9/2/18.

DAINTY, J., b. Birmingham, 97303, Pte., d., Home, 9/11/18.

EVANS, C., b. Llandudno, 267970, Cpl., d., Home, 30/6/18.

JONES, W. H., b. Carnarvon, 315542, Pte., d., Home, 11/2/17.

NESBITT, M., b. Leeds, 316778, Pte., d., Home, 9/4/17.

SIBLEY, E. R., e. Brighton, 91687, Pte., d., Home, 11/8/18.

WILLIAMS, G., b. Liverpool, 91674, Pte., d., Home, 1/8/18.

WILLIAMS, R., b. Talsarnam, 315636, Pte., d., Home, 5/9/17.

24th BATTALION

ARMSTRONG, G., b. Bassenthwaite, 51506, Pte., d., F., 9/9/18.

BACKHOUSE, J., b. Darwen, 345465, L/Cpl., k. in a., E., 31/10/17.

BALL, E., b. New Brighton, 345158, L/Cpl., k. in a., E., 27/12/17.

BANHAM, J., b. Llanbeblig, 265520, Sgt., k. in a., F., 28/6/18.

BARLOW, W. H., b. Llanbeblig, 266357, Pte., k. in a., E., 27/12/17.

BEBB, D., e. Trefynant, 345270, Pte., k. in a., F., 19/9/18.

BELLIS, R. H., b. Hawarden, 203529, Pte., k. in a., F., 31/10/18.

BENNETT, A., b. Thornton, 63791, Pte., d., At Sea, 15/4/17.

BENTLEY, E., e. London, 345472, Pte., k. in a., E., 27/12/17.

BIBBY, R., b. Liverpool, 345663, Pte., d. of w., F., 9/9/18.

BINNER, J. L., e. Wrexham, 345250, Pte., d. of w., E., 6/11/17.

BORE, A. E., b. St. Andrew's, 36514, Pte., k. in a., E., 27/12/17.

BOWDEN, J., b. Bollington, 63651, Pte., d., At Sea, 15/4/17.

BOWERS, E., e. Manchester, 63270, Pte., d., At Sea, 15/4/17.

BRADBURY, W., b. Macclesfield, 73050, Pte., k. in a., F., 31/10/18.

BRADLEY, W. F., b. Egremont, 57785, Pte., d. of w., Home, 21/10/18.

BRIDGE, W. C., b. Risca, 57781, Pte., d. of w., F., 6/10/18.

BUNN, H. T., b. Ipswich, 63792, Pte., d., At Sea, 15/4/17.

BUNN, R. F., b. London, 345478, Pte., k. in a., E., 31/10/17.

BURTON, L., b. Peterborough, 61789, Pte., k. in a., F., 18/7/18.

CAPPER, A., b. Hyde, 73060, Pte., k. in a., E., 31/10/17.

CASEY, W. J., b. Newport, 57789, Pte., k. in a., F., 25/8/18.

CLARKE, T., b. Farnworth, 73329, Pte., k. in a., F., 20/9/18.

COLES, F. T., b. Bristol, 63833, Pte., d., At Sea, 15/4/17.

COPE, S., b. Hyde, 345668, Pte., d. of w., E., 1/2/18.

CORFE, S., e. Wrexham, 345282, Pte., d. of w., F., 11/9/18, M.M.

CRAIG, G. H., b. Manchester, 63857, Pte., d., At Sea, 15/4/17.

DAVIES, B., e. Pembroke, 235731, Pte., d. of w., F., 28/6/18.

DAVIES, E., b. Llangollen, 345092, Sgt., d. of w., E., 28/12/17.

DAVIES, G., e. Pontypridd, 21418, Pte., k. in a., F., 5/8/18.

DAVIES, H., b. Meifod, 203617, Pte., k. in a., F., 23/7/18.

DAVIES, H. O., b. Festiniog, 345489, Pte., d. of w., E., 1/11/17.

DAVIES, W., b. Worsley, 73019, Pte., d. of w., F., 6/11/18.

DAVIES, W. H., b. Llanfair-is-Gaer, 315505, Pte., k. in a., F., 7/9/18.

DAVIES, W. L., b. Mynyddislwyn, 93310, Pte., d. of w., F., 29/8/18.

DAWSON, J., b. Blackburn, 242676, Pte., k. in a., E., 31/10/17.

DAWSON, W., b. Blackpool, 57805, Pte., k. in a., F., 22/9/18.

DOCKER, W., b. Lindal-in-Furness, 345679, Pte., k. in a., E., 27/12/17.

DODD, E., e. Ashton-under-Lyne, 93332, Pte., d. of w., F., 12/9/18.

DUCKETT, R. A., e. Wrexham, 345500, Pte., k. in a., E., 31/10/17.

DUMBLE, E., b. Leigh, 73053, Pte., k. in a., E., 31/10/17.

DYSON, T., b. Middleton, 63856, Pte., d., At Sea, 15/4/17.

EDWARDS, J., e. Wrexham, 200664, Pte., k. in a., F., 31/10/18.

ELLERY, T., b. Bodmin, 345507, Pte., k. in a., E., 31/10/17.

EVANS, C. G., b. Llanvair, 57815, Pte., k. in a., F., 29/9/18.

EVANS, G. P., b. Eccleshall, 315984, Pte., k. in a., F., 25/7/18.

EVANS, H., b. Glyn Ceriog, 267549, Pte., d. of w., F., 7/9/18.

EVANS, T., b. Carno, 203527, Pte., d. of w., F., 24/7/18.

EVANS, T., b. Ystrad, 345689, Pte., k. in a., F., 7/8/18.

EVANS, W. L., b. Gresford, 345172, L/Cpl., k. in a., E., 27/12/17.

FALLOWS, B. W., b. Hawarden, 345089, L/Cpl., k. in a., F., 7/9/18.

FENDER, H., b. Bridgwater, 59852, Pte., k. in a., E., 31/10/17.

FISHER, T. H., b. Tipton, 345691, Pte., k. in a., E., 27/12/17.

FLEW, A. C., b. Portsmouth, 242684, Pte., k. in a., E., 27/12/17.

FODEN, F., b. Biddulph, 31910, Sgt., k. in a., F., 31/10/18.

FOWLES, W., b. Northwich, 93463, Pte., k. in a., F., 7/9/18.

FRANCE, T. G., b. Montgomery, 43997, Pte., k. in a., F., 5/7/18.

GREAVES, G. C., e. Birmingham, 59887, Pte., k. in a., F., 8/8/18.

GRIFFITHS, J. P., b. Broughton, 345085, Pte., d., F., 5/11/18.

GRIFFITHS, R., e. Porth, 69416, Pte., k. in a., F., 31/10/18.

GRIFFITHS, W., e. Wrexham, 345356, Pte., k. in a., E., 27/12/17.

GRIFFITHS, W. E., b. Holyhead, 73007, Pte., k. in a., E., 27/12/17.

GROOM, T., b. Wrexham, 54555, Pte., k. in a., F., 28/6/18.

HARRISON, F., e. Wrexham, 54524, Pte., k. in a., F., 31/10/18.

HEWLETT, E., b. London, 242641, Pte., k. in a., E., 27/12/17.

HICKERTON, W. R. S., e. Birmingham, 59862, Pte., d. of w., F., 24/7/18.

HILL, H. J., b. Barmouth, 345702, Pte., d., E., 19/5/17.

HOCKLEY, S. J., b. Epping, 242640, Pte., k. in a., E., 27/12/17.

HOLMES, F., b. Birkenhead, 345529, Pte., k. in a., E., 27/12/17.

HONE, W., b. Liverpool, 63682, Pte., d., At Sea, 15/4/17.

HUGHES, J. H., e. Wrexham, 345291, Pte., d. of w., E., 4/11/17.

HUGHES, O., b. Penycae, 345537, Pte., k. in a., F., 7/9/18.

HUGHES, R. O., e. Blaenau Festiniog, 345709, Cpl., k. in a., E., 27/12/17.

HUGHES, T. L., b. Corwen, 45117, Pte., k. in a., F., 28/6/18.

HUGHES, W., b. Northop, 73010, L/Cpl., k. in a., F., 30/10/18.

HUMPHREYS, J., b. Ludlow, 63831, Pte., d., At Sea, 15/4/17.

IRVINE, R. H., b. Llanrwst, 345176, Pte., d. of w., F., 8/11/18.

JACKS, T., b. Tregeiriog, 345543, Pte., k. in a., E., 31/10/17.

JAMES, E. A., b. Ruabon, 63848, Pte., d., At Sea, 15/4/17.

JAMESON, R., b. Hebburn, 345713, I/Sgt., d. of w., E., 22/12/17.

JAMIESON, G. R., b. Aberdeen, 63668, Pte., d., At Sea, 15/4/17.

JENKINS, E. J., b. Efailisaf, 63794, Pte., d., At Sea, 15/4/17.

JENKINSON, W. G., b. West Ham, 59875, Pte., k. in a., E., 31/10/17.

JEWELL, W., b. Morwenstow, 69405, Pte., d. of w., F., 7/9/18.

JOHN, T. R., b. Dulais Higher, 54996, Pte., d., E., 15/4/17.

JOHNSON, J. W., e. Lancaster, 73149, Pte., d., E., 23/11/17.

JOHNSON, L., b. Swinton, 31360, Pte., k. in a., E., 27/12/17.

JOHNSON, L. H. G., b. Plymouth, 242716, Pte., d. of w., E., 23/4/17.

JONES, A., b. Buckley, 345796, Pte., d. of w., E., 29/12/17.

JONES, C., b. Greenfield, 203256, Pte., k. in a., E., 31/10/17.

JONES, C., b. Corwen, 345002, Sgt., k. in a., F., 27/8/18.

JONES, C. S., b. Llanegwad, 292718, Pte., k. in a., E., 27/12/17.

JONES, E., b. Bangor, 57851, Pte., d. of w., F., 16/11/18.

JONES, J., b. Birkenhead, 73056, Pte., d. of w., E., 2/11/17.

JONES, J. W., b. Llangollen, 73233, Pte., k. in a., F., 7/9/18.

JONES, O., b. Llannor, 316032, Pte., k. in a., E., 27/12/17.

JONES, S., b. Chester, 63238, Pte., d. of w., F., 8/11/18.

JONES, T. C., b. Penycae, 345724, Pte., k. in a., E., 27/12/17.

JONES, T. M., b. Merthyr, 315771, Pte., k. in a., E., 27/12/17.

JONES, W., e. Rhyl, 53932, Pte., d., At Sea, 15/4/17.

JONES, W., b. Colwyn Bay, 345406, Pte., d. of w., F., 8/9/18.

KAY, W. F., b. London, 345553, Sgt., k. in a., E., 27/12/17.

KELLEY, J. A., e. Wrexham, 345229, Pte., d., E., 6/9/17.

KIDWELL, W. S., b. Swansea, 345556, Pte., k. in a., E., 27/12/17.

KIRK, R., b. Failsworth, 57857, Pte., k. in a., F., 22/8/18.

LAKIN, W. B., b. Atherstone, 345557, Pte., k. in a., E., 27/12/17.

LLOYD, J. E., e. Wrexham, 345344, Pte., k. in a., E., 27/12/17.

LLOYD, R., b. Denbigh, 345565, Pte., d. of w., E., 8/11/17.

LLOYD, S. T., b. London, 345732, L/Cpl., k. in a., E., 9/12/17.

LOFTUS, J., b. Flint, 241950, Pte., k. in a., E., 31/10/17.

LOWE, C. C. M., b. Scarborough, 63686, Pte., d., At Sea, 15/4/17.

LUND, W., b. Foulridge, 242689, Pte., k. in a., E., 31/10/18.

MALKIN, C. F., b. Stafford, 345735, L/Sgt., d. of w., E., 31/10/17.

MARTIN, J. b. Rawtenstall, 63490, Pte., d., At Sea, 15/4/17.

MAUNDERS, S., b. Swansea, 58531, Pte., k. in a., F., 18/9/18.

MAYES, W. G., b. London, 24044, L/Cpl., d., At Sea, 15/4/17.

MORGAN, W. D., b. Briton Ferry, 345741, Pte., k. in a., F., 31/10/18.

MORRIS, A. S., b. Liverpool, 63507, Pte., d., At Sea, 15/4/17.

MORRIS, D. R., e. Wrexham, 345299, A/Cpl., k. in a., F., 4/9/18.

MORRIS, E., b. Mold, 345574, Pte., k. in a., F., 31/10/18.

NAYLOR, H., e. Wrexham, 345303, Pte., k. in a., E., 31/10/17.

NEALE, C. F., b. Cromlin, 63501, Pte., d., At Sea, 15/4/17.

NEWTON, P., b. Oldham, 345579, Pte., k. in a., F., 21/9/18.

OLIVER, J. E., b. Tregynon, 203639, Pte., k. in a., E., 31/10/17.

OWEN, R., b. Clynnod, 203715, Pte., d. of w., F., 28/6/18.

OWENS, D., b. Llanwynddyn, 345583, Pte., k. in a., E., 27/12/17.

PARKINSON, J., b. Bolton-le-Sands, 345749, Pte., k. in a., E., 27/12/17.

PEARSON, J. S., e. Wrexham, 345279, Pte., d. of w., F., 12/9/18.

PERCIVAL, H., e. Chadderton, 58490, Pte., d., F., 24/6/18.

PETERS, G. V., b. London, 345593, Pte., k. in a., E., 31/10/17.

PETRIE, T., b. Rochdale, 345595, Pte., k. in a., F., 8/8/18.

PHILLIPS, W. J., e. Neath, 89185, Pte., d. of w., F., 6/11/18.

PHŒNIX, J., b. Wrexham, 345103, L/Cpl., k. in a., F., 21/8/18.

PIERCE, J. H., b. Meliden, 345062, Sgt., k. in a., F., 7/11/17.

PIERCE, R., b. Wrexham, 345596, Sgt., d. of w., F., 10/11/18.

PLANT, W., b. Brierley Hill, 345754, Pte., k. in a., F., 22/9/18.

POWELL, E., b. Wrexham, 345599, Pte., d., Home, 7/10/18.

POWELL, F., b. Birmingham, 59869, Pte., k. in a., E., 31/10/17.

POWELL, S., e. Wrexham, 345233, Pte., k. in a., E., 31/10/17.

PRICE, I., b. Rhosddu, 345037, Cpl., d. of w., F., 11/9/18.

PRITCHARD, J. D., b. Cefn Mawr, 204964, Pte., k. in a., F., 8/9/18.

RAWCLIFFE, J., b. Oswaldthwistle, 63526, Pte., d., At Sea, 15/4/17.

ROBERTS, D., b. Wrexham, 69319, Pte., k. in a., F., 31/10/18.

ROBERTS, E., b. Llanfihangel, 203969, Pte., d., E., 20/11/17.

ROBERTS, G., b. Llaneilian, 69694, Pte., d. of w., F., 7/9/18.

ROBERTS, J. E., b. Llangollen, 201130, Pte., d. of w., E., 14/11/17.

ROBERTS, J. O., b. Trefnant, 37120, Pte., d., At Sea, 4/5/17.

ROHUN, E., b. Bulwell, 19466, A/Sgt., k. in a., E., 15/4/17.

ROWLANDS, H., e. Eccleston Camp, 345218, Pte., d. of w., F., 19/7/18.

RUSH, J., b. London, 63512, Pte., d., At Sea, 15/4/17.

SALMON, A., b. London, 242650, Pte., d. of w., E., 3/1/18.

SCOTT, F. A., b. London, 59878, Pte., k. in a., E., 31/10/17.

SEAMAN, R., e. Wrexham, 345327, Pte., k. in a., F., 22/9/18.

SHARP, J., b. Richmond, 345617, L/Cpl., k. in a., F., 23/9/18.

SMITH, A., b. Great Crosby, 267001, Pte., k. in a., F., 31/10/18.

SMITH, A. H., b. Brixham, 242697, L/Cpl., k. in a., E., 6/3/18.

SMITH, W., b. Hyde, 54112, Pte., d., At Sea, 15/4/17.

SOURBUTTS, H., b. Accrington, 63043, Pte., d., At Sea, 15/4/17.

STARLING, G., e. Wrexham, 345302, Pte., k. in a., E., 27/12/17.

STEPHENS, G. H. C., b. London, 26969, A/Sgt., d., At Sea, 15/4/17.

STORRAR, K. C., e. Eccleston Camp, 345220, A/C.S.M., k. in a., F., 29/9/18.

TAYLOR, D. M., b. Rochdale, 63852, Pte., d., At Sea, 15/4/17.

THOMAS, H., b. Morriston, 345628, Pte., d., E., 26/5/17.

THOMPSON, R. N., e. Carnarvon, 265654, L/Cpl., k. in a., E., 31/10/17.

TINKER, A., e. Birkenhead, 345274, Pte., d., E., 3/9/18.

UNSWORTH, T., b. Widnes, 73018, Pte., k. in a., E., 3/3/18.

UNSWORTH, W., b. Leigh, 73030, L/Cpl., k. in a., E., 31/10/17.

WALMSLEY, J., b. Blackburn, 63353, Pte., d., At Sea, 15/4/17.

WATSON, J., b. Beaumont, 345777, A/Cpl., d. of w., F., 31/10/18.

WATTS, H., b. Newtown, 290792, Pte., k. in a., F., 31/10/18.

WATTS, T., b. Ulverston, 242910, Pte., k. in a., F., 28/6/18.

WAYNE, E. A., e. Swansea, 345638, Pte., d. of w., F., 1/11/18.

WEBB, M., b. Preston Brook, 93345, Pte., k. in a., F., 17/7/18.

WEBBER, T. M., b. Cardiff, 60291, Pte., k. in a., F., 8/9/18.

WHEATLEY, R. S. P., e. Wrexham, 345318, Pte., d., E., 10/3/17.

WHITE, T., b. Leicester, 345645, Pte., k. in a., E., 27/12/17.

WHITTINGHAM, R. C., b. Bickerton, 345192, Pte., k. in a., E., 27/12/17.

WILKINSON, K., b. Blythe Bridge, 345646, Pte., d. of w., E., 2/11/17.

WILKS, S. T., b. Wrexham, 345100, Pte., k. in a., E., 31/10/17.

WILLIAMS, D., b. Llangollen, 345784, Pte., d., F., 8/11/18.

WILLIAMS, D. H., e. Colwyn Bay, 345314, Pte., d. of w., E., 1/11/17.

WILLIAMS, H., b. Bootle, 63157, Pte., d. of w., E., 11/2/18.

WILLIAMS, R., b. Capel Curig, 345654, Pte., d. of w., E., 16/7/17.

WILLIAMS, T. C., e. Liverpool, 49807, Pte., d., At Sea, 15/4/17.

WILLIAMS, W., e. Rhyl, 203155, Pte., d. of w., F., 14/9/18.

WILLIAMS, W. M., b. Colwyn Bay, 345389, Pte., d. of w., E., 2/11/17.

WINDSOR, H., b. Malpas, 60004, Pte., k. in a., F., 1/7/18.

WOOD, J., b. Wheelock Heath, 345657, Pte., d. of w., F., 21/9/18.

YOUNG, G. E., b. Liverpool, 345194, Pte., k. in a., E., 27/12/17.

25th BATTALION

ANDREW, W., e. Welshpool, 355314, Pte., k. in a., F., 21/9/18.

ANDREWS, R., b. Warrington, 356047, Pte., k. in a., E., 30/11/17.

ASHCROFT, C. H., b. Liverpool, 62381, Pte., d. of w., E., 31/10/17.

ASTLEY, W. T., e. Welshpool, 355230, Pte., k. in a., F., 16/9/18.

BARRITT, F., b. Oldham, 60029, Pte., k. in a., F., 16/9/18.

BEADLES, T. E., e. Newtown, 355759, Pte., k. in a., F., 8/9/18.

BEDDOES, C., e. Welshpool, 355359, Pte., k. in a., F., 21/9/18.

BERRILL, H., b. Emberton, 60087, Pte., k. in a., F., 18/9/18.

BOOTH, G., b. Holcombe, 24435, Pte., k. in a., F., 18/9/18.

BOYES, A., b. Bagillt, 200579, Cpl., k. in a., E., 30/11/17.

BREESE, G., e. Welshpool, 355441, Pte., d., E., 22/11/17.

BRODERICK, S., b. Newport, 355947, Pte., k. in a., E., 30/11/17.

BURGE, W., b. Manchester, 75732, Pte., k. in a., F., 18/9/18.

BURKE, J., b. Canning Town, 355826, Pte., k. in a., F., 5/9/18.

BURNETT, T., b. Old Cleave, 355580, Pte., d. of w., F., 17/11/18.

BUTLER, T. J., b. London, 21776, L/Cpl. k. in a., P., 23/4/17.

CAIN, G. H., b. I.O.M., 57753, Pte., d. of w., F., 20/7/18.

CARSWELL, T., b. West Bromwich, 60015, Pte., k. in a., F., 21/9/18.

CHANDLER, P., b. Wilby, 355944, Pte., k. in a., E., 31/10/17.

COLEMAN, R. T., e. Welshpool, 355360, Pte., d. of w., E., 5/12/17.

CONDON, M., b. Swansea, 355651, Pte., k. in a., F., 21/9/18, D.C.M. and M.M.

CORFIELD, J., b. Church Stoke, 355097, Pte., k. in a., E., 31/10/17.

CULL, J. L., b. Trehafod, 88628, Pte., d. of w., F., 18/10/18.

CURTIS, A., b. Faringdon, 355054, Pte., d. of w., E., 12/3/18.

DARRICOT, F., b. Blackburn, 315318, Pte., k. in a., F., 21/9/18.

DAVENPORT, W. J., b. Knighton, 355055, Pte., k. in a., E., 8/12/17.

DAVIES, C. M., b. Glamorgan, 355147, Pte., k. in a., F., 18/9/18.

DAVIES, D. E., b. Morriston, 355773, Pte., k. in a., E., 30/11/17.

DAVIES, D. J., b. Blaenporth, 355816, Pte., k. in a., F., 8/9/18.

DAVIES, D. W., b. Pennant, 355317, Pte., d. of w., F., 25/9/18.

DAVIES, E. H., b. Merthyr Tydvil, 356018, Pte., k. in a., E., 30/11/17.

DAVIES, G. H., e. Hay, 355297, Pte., d. of w., E., 27/12/17.

DAVIES, I., b. Carnarvon, 75483, Pte., k. in a., F., 19/8/18.

DAVIES, I., e. Welshpool, 355426, Pte., d. of w., E., 4/12/17.

DAVIES, L. J., e. Newtown, 355817, L/Cpl., d. of w., Home, 26/10/18.

DIGGERY, C. A., b. South Africa, 51310, Pte., d. of w., E., 1/11/17.

DILLON, T., b. Dublin, 355850, L/Cpl., d. of w., F., 6/9/18.

DINGLE, E. A., b. Cardiff, 72955, Pte., d. of w., F., 10/9/18.

DOPSON, W., b. Hungerford, 355769, Pte., k. in a., E., 30/11/17.

DOWN, A. E., b. Burgess Hill, 72978, Pte., k. in a., E., 9/3/18.

DOYLE, J., b. Cloone, 15449, Pte., k. in a., E., 31/10/17.

DUNN, A. T., b. Burslem, 355476, Pte., d. of w., E., 18/11/17.

DUXBURY, F., b. Burnley, 201717, Pte., k. in a., F., 19/9/18.

EDWARDS, D. H. P., e. Welshpool, 355399, Pte., k. in a., E., 30/11/17.

EDWARDS, J. H., b. Llangedwyn, 355036, Sgt., k. in a., E., 9/3/18.

EVANS, A. B., b. Manchester, 58408, Pte., k. in a., F., 18/9/18.

EVANS, E., b. Montgomery, 355865, Pte., k. in a., E., 17/4/17.

EVANS, E., b. Newcastle-Emlyn, 72988, Pte., d. of w., F., 19/9/18.

EVANS, R., b. Llanrhaiadr, 355109, Pte., k. in a., E., 31/10/17.

EVANS, T., e. Newtown, 355753, A/Cpl., k. in a., E., 31/10/17.

FANNING, B., b. Manchester, 64296, Pte., k. in a., F., 19/9/18.

FEARN, B., b. Macclesfield, 60024, Pte., k. in a., P., 9/3/18.

Fox, J., b. Southport, 315324, Pte., k. in a., E., 30/11/17.

FRANCIS, A., b. Trefonen, 355146, Pte., d., F., 5/11/18.

GARBETT, C., b. Mansfield, 21096, Sgt., d. of w., F., 11/3/18.

GELL, H., b. Blackburn, 201494, Pte., k. in a., F., 18/9/18.

GILBURT, A. E., b. London, 56029, Cpl., d. of w., F., 6/9/18.

GILL, E., b. Sheffield, 30216, Pte., k. in a., E., 30/11/17.

GLEAVE, R., b. Bollington, 315863, Pte., d. of w., Home, 4/11/18.

GOODISON, H., b. Stockport, 315685, A/L/Cpl., k. in a., E., 30/11/17.

GORDON, H., b. Aberdeen, 72987, Pte., k. in a., F., 20/7/18.

GRAYSTON, H., b. Bilsborough, 315235, Pte., k. in a., E., 31/10/17.

GREEN, G. B., b. Oxford, 60104, Pte., k. in a., E., 30/11/17.

GRIFFIN, W., b. Llanhilleth, 57761, Pte., k. in a., F., 26/9/18.

GRIFFITHS, W., e. Welshpool, 355223, Pte., d., E., 13/7/17.

GRUNDY, T. H., b. Manchester, 315230, Pte., k. in a., F., 18/9/18.

GUNSTONE, W., b. Swansea, 355631, L/Sgt., k. in a., E., 31/10/17.

HANNAM, A., b. Valley, 355468, Pte., d. of w., E., 10/12/17.

HARRIS, W. H., b. Llanwonno, 355543, L/Sgt., d. of w., F., 23/8/18.

HAYNES, F., b. Ellesmere, 355808, Pte., d. of w., E., 2/11/17.

HEIL, B., b. London, 355837, Pte., k. in a., E., 30/11/17.

HIBBOTT, C., b. Welshpool, 356019, Pte., d. of w., E., 18/11/17.

HIGGINBOTHAM, J., b. Bagillt, 12929, Pte., k. in a., P., 11/3/18.

HILL, G. H., b. Hyde, 72986, Pte., k. in a., E., 31/10/17.

HOLMES, J., b. Preston, 315256, Pte., k. in a., E., 30/11/17.

HUGHES, C., b. Gwersyllt, 355892, L/Cpl., k. in a., F., 26/9/18.

HUGHES, J., e. Wrexham, 54504, Pte., k. in a., F., 21/9/18.

HUMPHREYS, S., b. Llanerfyl, 355048, C.S.M., k. in a., E., 10/3/18.

HUTT, E. D., e. Llandrindod Wells, 355286, Cpl., k. in a., E., 31/10/17.

INGHAM, E., b. Burnley, 201681, A/L/Cpl., k. in a., F., 21/9/18.

INGRAM, J., b. Guilsfield, 355478, Pte., k. in a., E., 31/10/17.

INNS, H., e. Colwyn Bay, 201097, Pte., k. in a., F., 15/9/18.

JAMES, E., e. Welshpool, 355412, Pte., k. in a., E., 30/11/17.

JAMES, E., b. Cardiff, 355623, C.S.M., d. of w., F., 19/9/18, D.C.M.

JAMES, L. T., e. Llandrindod, 355220, Pte., k. in a., F., 18/9/18.

JOHN, N., b. Cardiff, 355863, Pte., d. of w., E., 10/12/17.

JOHNS, W. R., b. Cardiff, 355617, L/Cpl., d. of w., F., 19/9/18.

JONES, A. M., b. Llantrisant, 355919, Sgt., d., F., 20/9/18.

JONES, D., b. Cefncoch, 355148, Pte., k. in a., E., 31/10/17.

JONES, D., b. Carnarvon, 356011, Pte., k. in a., E., 11/3/18.

JONES, E., b. Llanrhaiadr, 355093, Pte., k. in a., F., 18/9/18.

JONES, E., e. Welshpool, 355373, Pte., k. in a., E., 31/10/17.

JONES, E. T., b. Mold, 356028, Pte., k. in a., E., 31/10/17.

JONES, H., b. Birkenhead, 315079, Pte., k. in a., F., 18/9/18.

JONES, J., b. Carmarthen, 355164, Pte., k. in a., F., 21/9/18.

JONES, L., b. Bagillt, 60616, Pte., k. in a., F., 21/9/18.

JONES, O., b. Prescot, 355815, Pte., k. in a., E., 30/11/17.

JONES, O., b. Llanerchymedd, 29614, Pte., d. of w., F., 18/9/18.

KENDRICK, J., b. Oswestry, 355145, A/L/Cpl., d. of w., E., 31/10/17.

LANGLEY, W. J., b. Abertillery, 78328, Pte., k. in a., F., 21/9/18.

LARWOOD, E., b. Yarmouth, 45781, Sgt., k. in a., F., 8/9/18, M.M.

LEECH, W., b. Lees, 93315, Pte., k. in a., F., 18/9/18.

LEWIS, H., b. Glasbury, 355154, Cpl., d. of w., E., 11/3/18.

LEWIS, W., e. Welshpool, 355347, Pte., k. in a., E., 31/10/17.

LEWIS, W., e. Welshpool, 355347, Pte., k. in a., F., 18/9/18.

LLOYD, S. R., b. Llanidloes, 355075, Cpl., k. in a., F., 18/9/18.

LOFTUS, W. L., e. Wrexham, 43784, L/Cpl., k. in a., F., 19/9/18.

LUCAS, R., b. Ashford, 55063, Pte., k. in a., F., 21/9/18.

MARSDEN, E. J., b. London, 54034, Pte., k. in a., F., 28/8/18.

MATTHEWS, E. A., b. Llanidloes, 91415, Pte., k. in a., F., 21/9/18.

MEDCROFT, F., b. Gloucester, 355878, L/Cpl., k. in a., F., 21/9/18.

MERCHANT, L., b. Burslem, 28322, Cpl., d., E., 28/9/18.

MINTON, J., b. Lydbury, 355239, Pte., k. in a., F., 20/7/18.

MORGAN, E. P., b. Llangurig, 355031, C.Q.M.S., d., E., 14/2/18.

MORGANS, D. E., b. Llanelly, 72957, Pte., d. of w., E., 10/3/18.

MORRIS, A., b. Llansillan, 355067, Pte., k. in a., F., 18/9/18.

MORRIS, C., b. Tredegar, 56827, Pte., d. of w., F., 24/4/17.

MORRIS, D., e. Welshpool, 345575, Pte., k. in a., F., 12/7/18.

MOUNTJOY, W. D., b. Bideford, 355598, Pte., k. in a., E., 30/11/17.

NEWBURY, H. A., b. Alveston, 355560, L/Cpl., k. in a., E., 30/11/17.

OLDFIELD, C., b. Darwen, 93321, Pte., d. of w., F., 23/9/18.

O'MALLEY, T. J., b. London, 355575, Pte., k. in a., F., 19/8/18.

OWEN, O., b. Carnarvon, 40905, L/Cpl., k. in a., E., 31/10/17.

OWEN, J. R., e. Welshpool, 355456, Pte., k. in a., F., 21/9/18.

OWENS, O. T., b. Blaenau Festiniog, 356034, Pte., k. in a., E., 31/10/17.

OWENS, R., b. Wrexham, 14310, Pte., k. in a., F., 21/9/18.

PARKINSON, T., b. Burnley, 73637, Pte., d. of w., F., 24/8/18.

PARR, A., b. Burslem, 355494, Pte., k. in a., E., 30/11/17.

PARRY, A., b. Llangollen, 68453, Pte., k. in a., F., 20/9/18.

PARRY, W. J., e. Welshpool, 355190, C.S.M., k. in a., F., 20/10/18.

PEBERDY, F., b. Bourne, 355714, Sgt., d. of w., E., 6/11/17.

PHILLIPS, B., b. Tregynon, 355461, Pte., d. of w., F., 19/8/18.

PIGHILLS, F. H., b. Soulby, 355258, Pte., k. in a., E., 31/10/17.

POTTS, J. T., b. Kimbolton. 355768, A/L/Sgt., k. in a., F., 21/9/18.

POWELL, E., b. Great Malvern. 290893, Pte., d. of w., F., 18/9/18.

POWIS, W., b. Clungunford. 355376, Pte., d. of w., E., 31/10/17.

PRICE, A., b. Llangollen, 16602, Pte., k. in a., F., 16/7/18.

PRICE, C., e. Newtown, 355866, Pte., k. in a., F., 18/9/18.

PRICE, I. T., b. Llanigon, 355153, Pte., k. in a., E., 30/11/17.

PRICE, J., e. Llandrindod Wells, 355397, Pte., d. of w., E., 1/11/17.

PRICE, R. S., b. Glazebury, 355162, A/L/Sgt., k. in a., E., 31/10/17.

PRICE, T., e. Knighton, 355312, Pte., k. in a., E., 30/11/17.

PRITCHARD, J., e. Tregynon, 355302, A/L/Sgt., k. in a., E., 31/10/17.

PRYCE, G. H., b. Llandyssil, 355463, Pte., d., At Sea, 1/1/17.

READ, R., b. Ystalyfera, 335546, A/Sgt., k. in a., E., 31/10/17.

REGAN, P., b. Cwmbran, 61486, Pte., k. in a., F., 8/9/18.

REID, P., b. Birmingham, 17293, Pte., k. in a., F., 10/9/18.

RICHARDS, J. A., e. Welshpool, 355357, Pte., k. in a., E., 10/3/18.

ROACH, W., b. Fernshop, 356001, Pte., d. of w., E., 13/3/18.

ROBERTS, E., b. Buttington. 355013, C.Q.M.S., d., E., 31/1/18.

ROBERTS, H. H., e. Welshpool, 355407, Pte., k. in a., E., 31/10/17.

ROBERTS, T., b. Rhos-y-Bol, 355889, Pte., k. in a., E., 30/11/17.

ROGERS, T., b. Londonderry, 46894, Pte., k. in a., F., 20/9/18.

ROURKE, H., b. Liverpool, 72948, Pte., k. in a., F., 17/7/18.

ROWLANDS, T. E., b. Llanfechain, 355465, Pte., k. in a., F., 20/7/18.

RUSHTON, J. B., b. Farnworth, 73460, Pte., k. in a., F., 16/9/18.

SHAW, C., b. Bistre, 355813, A/L/Cpl., k. in a., F., 6/9/18.

SINCLAIR, J. L., b. Liverpool, 57757, Pte., k. in a., F., 21/9/18.

SINGLETON, W. H., b. Newmarket, 267127, Pte., d. of w., F., 4/10/18.

SMITH, G., e. Welshpool, 355221, Pte., k. in a., F., 18/9/18.

STRAUGHTON, W., b. Cardiff, 72968, Pte., k. in a., F., 18/9/18.

SYMONDS, H., b. Much Marcle, 355180, Pte., k. in a., E., 28/6/17.
TAPPIN, W., b. London, 355825, Pte., k. in a., E., 9/3/18.
THEODORE, J. F., b. Alberbury, 355276, Pte., k. in a., F., 18/9/18.
THOMAS, J. H., b. Meifod, 355138, L/Cpl., d. of w., F., 23/7/18.
THOMAS, J. R., b. Penboyr, 355874, Pte., k. in a., E., 30/11/17.
THOMAS, M., b. Harlech, 78403, Pte., k. in a., F., 8/9/18.
THOMAS, R. J., b. Tregynon, 355510, Pte., k. in a., F., 20/10/18.
TOMLINSON, W., b. Buckley, 356037, Pte., k. in a., E., 30/11/17.
TURNER, E., e. Stockport, 238106, Pte., d. of w., F., 6/9/18.
VEZEY, E. E., b. London, 22019, Pte., k. in a., E., 30/11/17.
WARD, F. J. E., b. Henley, 355682, Pte., k. in a., F., 18/9/18.
WARING, W., b. Welshpool, 355014, L/Sgt., d. of w., F., 8/10/18, V.C. and M.M.
WATKIN, A., b. Llanfyhangel, 355030, Pte., k. in a., F., 30/11/17.
WATKIN, D., b. Rhostie, 355973, Pte., k. in a., E., 31/10/17.
WHITE, D., e. Llandrindod Wells, 355217, Pte., k. in a., F., 18/9/18.
WHITE, F. W., b. Liverpool, 355257, Pte., k. in a., E., 21/4/17.
WHITING, M. J. A., e. Cardiff, 355767, Pte., d. of w., F., 3/11/18.
WHITTALL, G., e. Welshpool, 355324, Pte., k. in a., F., 20/9/18.
WILLIAMS, J., b. Newborough, 21411, Pte., d. of w., F., 27/8/18.
WILLIAMS, J. H., b. Ellesmere Port, 56245, Pte., d. of w., F., 10/9/18.
WILLIAMS, J. S., b. Welshpool, 355337, Pte., d. of w., E., 1/11/17.
WILLIAMS, R., b. Llanfechan, 355213, Pte., d. of w., F., 2/11/17.
WILLIAMS, W. G., b. Llanberis, 51713, Pte., k. in a., E., 9/3/18.
WILLIAMS, W. O., b. Llanllyfni, 355893, Sgt., d. of w., Home, 21/12/18.
WOODHOUSE, W. F., b. Warrington, 57768, Pte., d. of w., F., 18/9/18.
WRIGHT, G. E., b. Leeds, 355512, Pte., k. in a., F., 18/9/18.

26th BATTALION

BARTROP, B., b. Sheffield, 42477, Pte., d., F., 5/10/18.
DAVENPORT, H., b. Ashton-under-Lyne, 71895, Pte., d. of w., F., 5/10/18.
FRANKLING, W., b. Westbury, 48857, L/Cpl., k. in a., F., 4/10/18.
GILES, G. W., b. Dulwich, 93477, Pte., k. in a., F., 9/8/18.
GILLING, R., b. Saffron Walden, 206354, Sgt., d., F., 15/9/18.
GRAHAM, E., b. Oldham, 46786, Pte., k. in a., F., 29/7/18.
HAYES, G., b. Dutton, 52290, Pte., d., F., 5/11/18.
HESKETH, A., b. Manchester, 42523, Pte., k. in a., F., 4/10/18.
JOHNSON, W., e. Brecon, 91173, Pte., d., F., 31/10/18.
LIGHTFOOT, G., b. Middlewich, 77780, Pte., k. in a., F., 29/9/18.
McCAFFERTY, H., b. Kilbirnie, 57190, Pte., k. in a., F., 3/8/18.
MORRIS, R., b. Westbourne Park, 72239, Pte., d. of w., F., 9/8/18.
NOBLE, L., b. Oldham, 87522, Pte., k. in a., F., 5/10/18.
ROTHWELL, S., e. Ashton-under-Lyne, 82213, Pte., k. in a., F., 3/10/18.
SALMON, F., b. Tunstall, 57538, Pte., k. in a., F., 3/10/18.
SEDDON, H., b. Manchester, 62931, Cpl., d., F., 11/11/18.
SMITH, T., b. Merthyr, 82304, Pte., k. in a., F., 12/9/18.
SMITH, W., b. Manchester, 87749, Pte., k. in a., F., 18/10/18.
WHARTON, F., b. Thornton, 46935, Pte., k. in a., F., 8/8/18.
WILLIAMSON, J. W., b. Manchester, 87777, Pte., d., F., 27/10/18.

DEPOT

ASTALL, H. W., e. Altrincham, 345464, Pte., d., Home, 30/10/18.
BATTEN, C., b. London, 53993, Pte., d., Home, 7/11/18.
BORLEY, A. J., e. Cardiff, 53075, Pte., d., Home, 8/3/18.
BRIDGEMAN, C. E., b. Burwell, 202274, Pte., d., Home, 21/4/18.
CLARKE, J. H., e. Liverpool, 75368, Pte., d., Home, 27/9/18.
CUEL, A., b. Oswestry, 31320, A/Sgt., d., Home, 13/12/15.
CURRAGH, J. H., b. Birmingham, 7911, Pte., d., Home, 6/11/17.
DAVIES, B., b. Cardiff, 31264, Pte., d., Home, 24/4/18.
DEAN, A., b. Burslem, 28584, Pte., d., Home, 19/9/18.

GALLAGHER, P., b. Liverpool, 36189, L/Cpl., d., Home, 16/9/17.
GRIFFITHS, G., e. Llanberis, 37326, Pte., d., Home, 2/4/17.
GRIFFITHS, R., b. Kilvey, 5600, Pte., d., Home, 21/2/15.
HARKER, J., b. Darlington, 17946, Pte., d., Home, 4/1/15.
HESLOP, A., b. London, 35271, Pte., d., Home, 15/5/17.
HODGKINS, J., e. Wrexham, 8112, Pte., d., Home, 15/12/16.
HUGHES, J. E., e. Rhosymedre, 54087, Pte., d., Home, 16/7/18.
JENKINS, F., b. Swansea, 38271, Pte., d., Home, 30/1/18.
LEACH, H. F., b. London, 26878, Pte., d., Home, 3/9/18.
MINTON, A. P., b. Shrewsbury, 7156, Pte., d., Home, 28/11/14.
MOSS, T. N. K., b. Manchester, 8470, A/Cpl., d., Home, 13/10/18.
PAGE, J., b. Cardiff, 33258, Pte., d., Home, 22/8/15.
PARRY, W., b. Chwrlog, 203183, Pte., d., Home, 3/9/18.
PUGH, C., b. Bishop's Castle, 33806, Pte., d., Home, 8/11/18.
SMITH, J., b. Wrexham, 201189, Pte., d., Home, 24/10/18.
SMITH, J., b. Great Saughall, 55973, Cadet, d., Home, 29/12/17.

1st GARRISON BATTALION

DONOVAN, J., b. Blaenavon, 33524, Pte., d., Gib., 27/4/16.
GRIFFITHS, J., b. Monington, 15877, Pte., d., Home, 10/2/17.
HARTY, J., e. Liverpool, 67871, Pte., d., At Sea, 27/6/17.
JENKINS, T., b. Merthyr, 33869, Pte., d., Gib., 5/10/17.
JENKINS, T., b. Briton Ferry, 34167, Pte., d., Home, 30/8/15.
MANNING, P., b. Llandovery, 33779, Pte., d. Gib., 15/5/18.
McAULIFFE, T., b. Cork, 33879, Pte., d., Gib., 9/12/16.
MOORE, C., b. Cardiff, 34311, L/Cpl., d., Gib., 18/11/15.
MORTIMORE, T., b. Newport, 33566, Pte., d., Home, 4/12/15.
PALMER, A., b. Ystradfywg, 34032, Cpl., d., Gib., 1/10/17.
PAYNE, G. A., b. Hereford, 34139, Pte., d., Gib., 1/11/18.
ROBERTS, R., b. Ruabon, 28291, Pte., d., Gib., 12/1/17.
THOMAS, T. D., b. Aberdare, 33588, Pte., d., Gib., 26/10/18.
WILLIAMS, C., b. Abertillery, 6523, Pte., d., Gib., 23/8/17.

2nd GARRISON BATTALION

AITKENHEAD, W., b. Cathcart, 243303, Pte., d., E., 8/3/18.
CARROLL, G., b. Upper Brighton, 68832, Pte., d., E., 22/10/18.

DIXON, J., b. Seaton, 72222, Pte., d., E., 6/11/18.

DOBBS, E., b. Wigan, 49707, Pte., d., E., 19/10/18.

DYAS, D., b. Welshpool, 11508, Pte., d., E., 6/8/17.

EDWARDS, E., b. Bangor, 33327, Pte., d., Home, 4/12/15.

EDWARDS, J., b. Southport, 39594, Pte., d., E., 9/11/18.

EVANS, E. J., b. Penygraig, 38733, Pte., d., E., 6/11/18.

EVANS, T., b. Pendergast, 38532, Pte., d., E., 13/6/16.

FOOT, J., b. Ebbw Vale, 38137, Sgt., d., Home, 13/11/15.

FUGE, T. J., b. Ebbw Vale, 68140, Pte., d., E., 29/10/18.

GRIFFITHS, A., b. Barry, 38547, Pte., d., E., 4/11/18.

HARDING, J., e. Ormskirk, 51731, Pte., d., E., 5/11/18.

HEYWOOD, W., e. Garswood Park, 38444, L/Cpl., d., E., 12/10/18.

HICKEY, J., b. Bootle, 42383, Pte., d., E., 12/8/18.

HOLLANDS, D., b. Bramley, 38040, A/Cpl., d., E., 12/9/17.

HOLLINS, E. G., b. Birmingham, 6663, Pte., d., E., 1/2/17.

JENKINS, D., b. Port Talbot, 38754, Pte., d., E., 3/11/18.

JENKINS, E. T., e. Pentre, 243422, Pte., d., E., 6/11/18.

JONES, E., b. Neath, 38574, Pte., d., Home, 18/5/16.

JONES, J., b. Capel Garmon, 20249, Pte., d., E., 16/4/17.

JONES, J. W., b. Wrexham, 12158, Sgt., d., At Sea, 1/1/17.

JONES, L. C., b. Ross, 243286, Cpl., d., E., 7/11/18.

LLEWELLYN, G. D., b. Narberth, 38605, Pte., d., E., 4/3/17.

MITCHELL, E. J., b. Arundel, 38146, A/Sgt., d., E., 7/11/18.

MURPHY, J., b. Rhondda, 42122, Pte., d., E., 2/11/18.

OWEN, F., b. Kerry, 6635, Pte., d., E., 5/3/18.

PERRY, T. W., b. London, 38230, L/Cpl., d., E., 4/11/18.

PLEITCH, H., b. Edinburgh, 243298, Pte., d., E., 3/11/18.

POOLER, W., b. Glossop, 51879, Pte., d., E., 11/11/18.

ROBINSON, J., b. Winewall, 38407, Pte., d., E., 17/12/16.

SHERRATT, J., b. Rugeley, 20798, Pte., d., E., 21/4/16.

SIMPSON, F. J., b. Chester, 68142, Pte., d., E., 6/11/18.

TOWNLEY, P. G., b. Manchester, 72379, Pte., d., E., 27/3/18.

WILLIAMS, D., b. Carnarvon, 33371, Pte., d., E., 6/11/18.

WILLIAMS, D., b. Cardiff, 49772, Pte., d., E., 26/12/17.

WILLIAMS, E., b. Hereford, 38108, Pte., d., E., 3/11/18.

WILSON, A., b. Manchester, 38686, A/Cpl., d., E., 1/7/17.

3rd GARRISON BATTALION

ADAMS, C. J., b. London, 27987, L/Cpl., d., Home, 25/4/16.

ALLEN, G. W., b. Liverpool, 51977, Pte., d., Home, 24/1/17.

ARMSTRONG, G. H., b. Manchester, 62631, Pte., d., Home, 31/12/16.

BEVERIDGE, C., b. York, 67350, Pte., d., Home, 27/4/17.

BRADBURY, H., e. Macclesfield, 64098, Pte., d., Home, 24/2/17.

BRIDGE, C., e. Caerphilly, 42103, L/Cpl., d., Home, 30/12/16.

CLARK, W. G., b. Marple, 72555, Pte., d., Home, 24/9/18.

CLARKE, H. J. B., b. Dunster, 66656, Pte., d., Home, 19/2/17.

DAVIES, F. V., e. Goodwick, 47247, Pte., d., Home, 19/9/16.

DUNN, J., b. Rochdale, 71671, Pte., d., Home, 5/4/18.

FINNIGAN, M., b. Salford, 58940, Pte., d., Home, 28/7/17.

GAY, W. H., b. London, 63464, Pte., d., Home, 9/2/17.

GOLDSWORTHY, H., b. Carlisle, 64073, Pte., d., Home, 14/2/17.

GRADY, A., b. Liverpool, 67650, Pte., d., Home, 12/2/18.

HAND, T. H., b. Manchester, 66599, L/Cpl., d., At Sea, 15/4/17.

HENDRY, R. A., b. Liverpool, 71882, Pte., d., At Sea, 10/10/18.

HYDE, W., b. Stalybridge, 63650, Pte., d., Home, 6/2/17.

JONES, J., b. Denbigh, 63445, Pte., d., Home, 1/1/17.

JONES, O. S., b. Criccieth, 66674, Pte., d., Home, 3/2/17.

KAYS, T., b. Salford, 63635, Pte., d., Home, 18/1/17.

LANGFIELD, S., b. Oldham, 90490, Pte., d., At Sea, 10/10/18.

LATCHFORD, F., e. Macclesfield, 66243, Pte., d., Home, 5/2/17.

LUNDY, J. W., b. Sunderland, 87831, A/L/Cpl., d., At Sea, 10/10/18.

MAKIN, S., b. Bury, 86749, Pte., d., Home, 30/10/18.

NEWMAN, J., b. London, 35329, d., Home, 9/3/17.

NORCROSS, W. E., b. Sabden, 67125, Pte., d., Home, 19/5/17.

PICKLES, H., b. Burnley, 86900, Pte., d., At Sea, 10/10/18.

PRICE, H. S., e. Wrexham, 90280, Pte., d., Home, 20/9/18.

SMITH, A., b. Ystalyfera, 76582, Pte., d., Home, 19/5/18.

SUTTON, J. H., b. Manchester, 63870, Pte., d., Home, 13/1/17.

WALKER, W., b. Dudley, 87949, Pte., d., At Sea, 10/10/18.

WILKINSON, H., b. Peel Green, 71605, A/Cpl., d., At Sea, 10/10/18.

4th GARRISON BATTALION

ALLEN, J., b. Birmingham, 47217, Pte., d. of w., F., 3/8/18.

BINGHAM, S., b. Dover, 57401, Pte., d., F., 19/12/17.

HILL, T. J., b. Liverpool, 47071, Pte., d., F., 5/2/17.

MOORE, J., b. Liverpool, 47121, Pte., d., Home, 3/6/18.

MURPHY, J., b. Cork, 58812, Pte., d., F., 5/4/17.

PETERS, B., b. Briton Ferry, 47331, Pte., d., F., 10/3/17.

WATKIN, J., b. Liverpool, 46956, Pte., d., Home, 5/6/16.

5th GARRISON BATTALION

LYNCH, H., b. Merthyr, 58764, C.S.M., d., Home, 13/1/17.

SUTCLIFFE, J. A., b. Halifax, 64337, Pte., d., Home, 18/5/17.

6th GARRISON BATTALION

DEARDEN, W., b. Lancaster, 61621, Pte., d., E., 21/10/18.

FISHER, C. S., e. London, 61892, Pte., d., Home, 18/10/16.

GARDNER, W., b. Hadley, 62524, Pte., d., E., 3/9/17.

GARSIDE, H., b. Harpurhey, 243016, Pte., d., S., 6/11/18.

GREY, J. E., e. Carlisle, 62371, Pte., d., Home, 17/10/16.

HARRISON, J., b. Birmingham, 62157, L/Cpl., d., E., 9/10/17.

KAVANAGH, H., b. Manchester, 61819, Pte., d., E., 20/9/17.

KIRK, A., b. Bugsworth, 243591, Pte., d., E., 18/8/18.

LOWE, G., b. Runcorn, 242247, Pte., d., E., 17/10/18.

McLEAN, J. J., b. Liverpool, 61736, Pte., d., E., 16/9/17.

MOSCROP, W., b. Stockport, 61855, Pte., d., S., 5/11/18.

PARLBY, D., b. Henley, 68046, Pte., d., S., 5/11/18.

ROBBINS, A., b. Ross, 204933, Pte., d., E., 31/10/17.

SCULLEY, M., b. Widnes, 62248, Pte., d., S., 11/11/18.

WARREN, J., e. Stockport, 62017, Pte., d., Home, 27/12/16.

WATKIN, R. A., e. Welshpool, 355340, Pte., d., E., 23/11/17.

WEAVER, E., b. Dorrington, 62267, Pte., d., E., 28/10/18.

4th BATTALION (T.F.)

ABBOTT, B., b. Shepton Mallet, 242966, Pte., d., F., 24/11/18.

ARMITAGE, H., b. Mirfield, 10430, Pte., k. in a., F., 5/10/16.

ARMSTRONG, C. T., b. Stevenage, 202261, Pte., d. of w., F., 15/4/18.

ASKEY, J., b. Llanwrog, 8780, Pte., d., F., 24/11/16.

ASTLEY, W. P., e. Welshpool, 203413, Pte., d., F., 30/3/17.

AVIS, F., b. London, 46278, Cpl., k. in a., F., 9/6/18.

BAILEY, H., b. Oswestry, 200446, L/Sgt., k. in a., F., 6/4/18.

BALL, J., b. Rhosddu, 7341, Pte., d. of w., F., 22/7/15.

BANKS, T., b. Leeds, 202241, Cpl., k. in a., F., 18/8/18.

BATHER, W., b. Llansaintffraid, 8540, Pte., k. in a., F., 3/9/16.

BAYLEY, J., b. Oswestry, 9336, L/Cpl., d., Home, 19/11/16.

BEARD, J., b. Flint, 77934, Pte., Pte., d., Home, 2/7/18.

BECKETT, R., b. Oswestry, 315983, Pte., k. in a., F., 22/3/18.

BEE, T., b. Llanbeblig, 265541, Pte., d. of w., F., 26/3/18.

BELTON, J., b. Minera, 200403, Cpl., d. of w., F., 22/3/18.

BENN, A., b. Barnsley, 202047, Pte., k. in a., F., 5/11/18.

BENNION, T., e. Wrexham, 200954, Pte., d., F., 20/8/18.

BINGHAM, G. H., b. Ossett, 202055, Pte., d. of w., F., 7/7/17.

BLACKSHAW, T., b. Blackburn, 96461, Pte., d., Home, 29/10/18.

BOWEN, E., b. Meifod, 203663, Pte., d., Home, 27/2/17.

BOWLES, J. J. S., b. Birmingham, 8843, Pte., d. of w., F., 18/8/16.

BOWSHER, W., b. London, 202268, Pte., k. in a., F., 15/9/16.

BRADWICK, J. T., b. Loughborough, 202287, Pte., k. in a., F., 6/10/18.

BRAMPTON, J., e. Birmingham, 36394, Pte., k. in a., F., 2/9/18.

BREEZE, J. S., b. Rhosllanerchgrugog, 6897, Pte., k. in a., F., 3/4/15.

BROWN, H., b. Kirkby, 267006, Pte., d. of w., F., 14/4/17.

BROWN, H. J., b. Fowlmere, 202288, Pte., k. in a., F., 10/6/17.

BUNN, W., e. Wrexham, 200811, Pte., d. of w., F., 6/10/18.

BURGOYNE, G., b. Hanwood, 6862, L/Cpl., k. in a., F., 24/12/16.

CARRINGTON, C., b. Bagillt, 6137, A/L/Sgt., k. in a., F., 9/5/15.

CHAMBERS, A. E. J., b. Stoke, 202306, Sgt., k. in a., F., 6/4/18, M.M.

CLARKE, A. C., b. Little Harrowden, 202292, Pte., d. of w., F., 24/3/18.

COLE, F., b. Great Gransden, 10723, Pte., d. of w., F., 18/9/16.

COLE, F. G., b. Biggleswade, 202302, Pte., d. of w., F., 6/4/18.

COLLINS, G., b. Esclusham, 7473, L/Sgt., k. in a., F., 18/9/16.

CONWAY, A., b. Old Colwyn, 201108, Pte., k. in a., F., 23/3/18.

COOPE, A. R., b. Kersley, 70536, Pte., d., F., 7/5/18.

COOPER, H., b. Peterborough, 202310, Pte., k. in a., F., 28/2/17.

CORBETT, F. J., b. Llandaff, 291962, Pte., k. in a., F., 6/4/18.

CORKE, S. P., b. Chirk, 3240, Pte., k. in a., F., 9/5/15.

CRESSWELL, W., b. Altofts, 202075, Pte., d. of w., F., 28/5/17.

CUMMINGS, J., b. Pontypridd, 8854, Pte., k. in a., F., 18/8/16.

CUMMINS, J. J., b. Christchurch, 201227, Pte., k. in a., F., 23/3/18.

DAVIES, A., e. Ystradgynlais, 203315, Pte., k. in a., F., 13/9/17.

DAVIES, A., e. Wrexham, 200987, Pte., d. of w., F., 6/4/18.

DAVIES, A., b. Chirk, 6165, Sgt., d. of w., F., 11/5/15.

DAVIES, D., b. Ruabon, 4936, Pte., k. in a., F., 6/6/15.

DAVIES, J., e. Neath, 242468, Pte., k. in a., F., 5/4/18.

DAVIES, J., b. Stalybridge, 315222, Pte., d., F., 20/8/18.

DAVIES, J. H., b. Hanley, 202927, Pte., k. in a., F., 20/2/17.

DAVIES, R. E., b. Welshpool, 6509, A/Cpl., d., F., 16/3/15.

DAVIES, S., b. Liverpool, 204614, Pte., d. of w., F., 11/6/18.

DAVIES, T. P., e. Denbigh, 8179, Pte., k. in a., F., 6/10/16.

DAVIES, T. T., b. Glais, 96444, Pte., d., Home, 31/10/18.

DAVIES, W. G., b. Manordeifi, 204710, Pte., d. of w., F., 6/12/17.

DAWSON, J., b. Liverpool, 75735, Pte., d. of w., F., 8/8/18.

DENSON, W., b. Breton, 3367, L/Cpl., k. in a., F., 9/5/15.

DILWORTH, W. W., b. Liverpool, 70544, Pte., k. in a., F., 6/4/18.

DOBBINS, T. A., b. Holt, 201070, Pte., k. in a., F., 23/3/18.

DUTTON, F., b. Wrexham, 201293, Pte., k. in a., F., 6/4/18.

EAST, W., b. Preston, 315680, Pte., k. in a., F., 2/4/18.

EDWARDS, D., b. Cefn Mawr, 7178, Pte., k. in a., F., 26/9/15.

EDWARDS, D., b. Llanrhaiadr, 44203, Pte., k. in a., F., 13/5/18.

EDWARDS, E., b. Chester, 5549, Sgt., k. in a., F., 9/5/15.

EDWARDS, E. W., b. Oswestry, 235660, Pte., k. in a., F., 2/9/18.

EDWARDS, G., b. Cefn, 201023, Pte., k. in a., F., 22/3/18.

EDWARDS, J. S., b. Mold, 6798, Pte., k. in a., F., 21/8/15.

ELLIOTT, S. E., b. Liverpool, 70550, Pte., k. in a., F., 6/4/18.

ELLIS, A., b. Buckley, Flint, 240446, Pte., d., F., 15/8/18.

ELLIS, C., b. Dewsbury, 202092, Pte., k. in a., F., 6/4/18.

ELLIS, J., b. Ellesmere, 7419, Pte., k. in a., F., 9/5/15.

ELLIS, S. P., e. Wrexham, 8269, Pte., k. in a., F., 6/10/16.

ELMS, J. J., b. Liverpool, 267235, Pte., k. in a., F., 20/7/17.

EVANS, C. E., e. Wrexham, 8153, Pte., d. of w., F., 12/1/16.

EVANS, D., b. Dowlais, 8860, Pte., d. of w., F., 20/8/16.

EVANS, D. T., b. Pontypridd, 8833, Cpl., d. of w., F., 18/9/16.

EVANS, E., b. Rhosllanerchgrugog, 7299, Pte., k. in a., F., 25/1/15.

EVANS, G., b. Weston Rhyn, 6168, Pte., d. of w., F., 21/9/15.

EVANS, H. W., b. Llanuwchllyn, 8968, Pte., k. in a., F., 15/8/16.

EVANS, T., b. Bala, 203782, Pte., d., Home, 25/2/17.

EVANS, W., e. Brecon, 235394, Pte., k. in a., F., 2/9/17.

EVANS, W., b. Denbigh, 6077, L/Cpl., k. in a., F., 9/5/15.

EYTON, F., e. Wrexham, 7630, Pte., k. in a., F., 4/5/16.

FAIL, W., b. Rhosllanerchgrugog, 5621, Pte., k. in a., F., 25/1/15.

FELL, T., b. Burnley, 201486, L/Cpl., k. in a., F., 1/9/17.

FIRTH, A., b. Buller Thorpe, 202105, Pte., k. in a., F., 23/3/18.

FODEN, A. E., b. New Zealand, 203044, Cpl., d., F., 15/8/18.

FORREST, A., b. Bradford, 202106, Pte., k. in a., F., 6/4/18.

FOSTER, C., b. Wrexham, 8657, Pte., k. in a., F., 15/8/16.

FRANCIS, J. W., e. Wrexham, 200694, Pte., d. of w., F., 28/3/18.

GEORGE, D., b. Ystalyfera, 235395, Pte., k. in a., F., 4/8/17.

GOLDSTONE, S., b. Leeds, 267134, Pte., k. in a., F., 5/4/18.

GRIFFITHS, A. D., b. Borfl-Wen, 202941, Pte., d. of w., F., 26/3/18.

GRIFFITHS, E., b. Rhosllanerchgrugog, 200504, Pte., d. of w., F., 5/5/18.

GRIFFITHS, G., b. Newbridge, 200435, Pte., k. in a., F., 6/4/18.

GRIFFITHS, J., b. Rhosllanerchgrugog, 6843, Pte., k. in a., F., 25/1/15.

LIEUTENANT-COLONEL FRANCE HAYHURST.

GRIFFITHS, J., b. Rhosymedre, 6994, Cpl., k. in a., F., 31/3/15.

GRIFFITHS, P. H., e. Welshpool, 202883, Pte., k. in a., F., 21/3/18.

HALL, C. E., b. Barnsley, 202128, Pte., k. in a., F., 3/12/17.

HALL, H. V., e. Wrexham, 202600, Pte., k. in a., F., 26/8/17.

HALL, L., b. Haydock, 202119, Pte., k. in a., F., 6/4/18.

HALL, N., b. Chorley, 241871, Pte., k. in a., F., 3/9/18.

HAMER, A. J., e. Kington, 203056, Pte., d. of w., F., 7/4/18.

HANNABY, A., e. Wrexham, 7713, Pte., k. in a., F., 19/7/15.

HARPER, G., b. Bettisfield, 8616, Pte., k. in a., F., 18/8/16.

HASELTINE, H., b. Darrington, 10677, Pte., k. in a., F., 5/10/16.

HAZELWOOD, W., b. Earl's Heaton, 202116, Pte., d. of w., F., 3/1/18.

HERBERT, J. P., b. Cribyn, 40970, L/Cpl., k. in a., F., 16/8/18.

HESTER, J., b. Stockport, 292257, Pte., k. in a., F., 23/8/18.

HICKSON, H., b. Chester, 75901, Pte., k. in a., F., 9/6/18.

HIGGINS, J., e. Normanton, 202126, Pte., k. in a., F., 6/4/18.

HIGGINS, W. H., b. Gwersyllt, 7441, Pte., k. in a., F., 25/1/15.

HILL, A. H., b. Liverpool, 57352, Pte., d. of w., F., 5/4/18.

HOLT, C., b. Rhosymedre, 6688, Pte., d. of w., F., 29/12/14.

HOLT, J., b. Burnley, 315255, Pte., Pte., d. of w., F., 5/4/18.

HOUGHLAND, G., e. Wrexham, 7610, Pte., d. of w., F., 5/10/15.

HOWARD, G. E., e. St. Albans, 202346, Pte., k. in a., F., 6/4/18.

HOWSON, W., b. Emberton, 202343, Pte., k. in a., F., 10/5/17.

HOYLAND, J., b. Silkstone, 202121, Pte., d. of w., F., 7/4/18.

HUDSON, J., b. Doncaster, 10521, Pte., k. in a., F., 18/9/16.

HUGHES, E., b. Llangollen, 7508, Pte., k. in a., F., 24/12/14.

HUGHES, F., b. Mold, 7066, L/Cpl., k. in a., F., 5/1/15.

HUGHES, F., b. Chirk, 200363, Pte., k. in a., F., 9/9/17.

HUGHES, H., b. Wellingborough, 10780, Pte., d. of w., F., 18/9/16.

HUGHES, R. I., e. Colwyn Bay, 202528, Pte., k. in a., F., 6/4/18.

HUGHES, R. O., e. Wrexham, 7533, Pte., k. in a., F., 29/3/15.

HUGHES, R. T., b. Denbigh, 7284, Pte., k. in a., F., 25/9/15.

HUGHES, W., e. Wrexham, 7530, Pte., k. in a., F., 9/5/15.

HUGHES, W., e. Wrexham, 7755, Pte., k. in a., F., 17/9/16.

HUGHES, W. E., b. Wrexham, 202029, Pte., d., F., 7/12/18.

HUMPHREYS, I., b. Broughton, 200247, Pte., d., Home, 26/10/18.

JEFFREYS, J. R., b. Esclusham, 200569, Pte., k. in a., F., 7/12/17.

JEFFREYS, R., b. Wrexham, 6794, L/Cpl., k. in a., F., 28/5/15.

JERMAN, J. E., b. Llanidloes, 203015, Pte., d. of w., F., 25/3/18.

JONAS, H., b. Manchester, 316938, Pte., d. of w., F., 3/4/18.

JONES, A., e. Wrexham, 200693, Pte., k. in a., F., 22/3/18.

JONES, D., e. Wrexham, 200818, Pte., d. of w., F., 27/3/18.

JONES, D., e. Wrexham, 200602, Pte., d. of w., F., 19/4/18.

JONES, D. E., b. Brymbo, 7128, Pte., d., Home, 11/9/14.

JONES, D. J., b. Bersham, 6474, Pte., k. in a., F., 13/3/15.

JONES, D. T., b. Glyn, 201290, Pte., k. in a., F., 10/7/17.

JONES, E., b. Gwespyr, 200536, Pte., d. of w., F., 10/6/17.

JONES, E., b. Denbigh, 200591, Cpl., d., F., 19/4/18.

JONES, E., e. Wrexham, 200906, Pte., d. of w., F., 7/4/18.

JONES, E., b. Wrexham, 7471, Pte., k. in a., F., 25/1/15.

JONES, E., b. Tanyfonwent, 203419, Pte., d., F., 13/12/18.

JONES, E. A., b. Denbigh, 200165, Cpl., k. in a., F., 9/4/17.

JONES, E. D., b. Carnarvon, 201329, Pte., k. in a., F., 6/4/18.

JONES, E. S., b. Denbigh, 200585, Pte., k. in a., F., 3/12/17.

JONES, E. S., e. Southsea, 200914, Pte., k. in a., F., 6/4/18.

JONES, E. S., b. Llanidloes, 266789, Pte., d., F., 1/12/18.

JONES, F., e. Wrexham, 7657, L/Cpl., k. in a., F., 3/10/16.

JONES, F., b. Newtown, 203286, Pte., k. in a., F., 3/12/17.

JONES, G. H., b. Cefn Mawr, 200422, Pte., d., At Sea, 4/5/17.

JONES, G. R., b. Meifod, 203068, Pte., d. of w., F., 8/4/18.

JONES, H., e. Wrexham, 8243, Pte., k. in a., F., 4/5/16.

JONES, H. H., b. Llangynog, 6397, Pte., k. in a., F., 27/3/15.

JONES, J., b. Castleford, 202134, Pte., d. of w., F., 17/4/18.

JONES, J. A., b. Gresford, 7219, Pte., d. of w., F., 2/2/15.

JONES, J. C., b. Wrockwardine, 91478, Pte., d., Home, 27/8/18.

JONES, J. E., b. Ruthin, 318u2, Pte., d. of w., F., 4/9/18.

JONES, J. E., b. Stockport, 6779, Pte., k. in a., F., 25/3/15.

JONES, J. J., e. Wrexham, 7705, Pte., k. in a., F., 19/7/15.

JONES, J. M., b. Rhosllanerchgrugog, 7329, Pte., k. in a., F., 10/3/15.

JONES, J. T., b. Wrexham, 200155, Pte., k. in a., F., 18/9/16.

JONES, L., e. Wrexham, 7602, Pte., k. in a., F., 7/6/15.

JONES, O., b. Minera, 200404, Pte., d., F., 8/9/18.

JONES, O. M., b. Ebenezer, 203399, Pte., k. in a., F., 6/4/18, M.M.

JONES, R., b. Holyhead, 61188, Pte., k. in a., F., 13/5/18.

JONES, R., b. Wrexham, 200302, Sgt., k. in a., F., 7/6/17, M.M.

JONES, R. J., b. Llanwrog, 7421, Pte., d., Home, 14/6/15.

JONES, T., b. Broughton, 6893, L/Cpl., k. in a., F., 11/3/15.

JONES, T. E., e. Liverpool, 40934, Pte., k. in a., F., 2/9/18.

JONES, W., b. Broughton, 200374, Pte., k. in a., F., 2/2/18, M.M.

JONES, W., e. Wrexham, 200687, L/Cpl., k. in a., F., 6/4/18.

JONES, W. A., b. Llanarmon, 201164, Pte., d. of w., F., 14/4/18.

KELLY, P., b. Dewsbury, 202138, Cpl., d., Home, 28/5/17.

KING, H., b. Bersham, 200564, Cpl., d. of w., F., 10/6/18, M.M.

KNOTT, G., e. Uppingham, 202359, Pte., d., Home, 8/11/18.

KNOWLES, E., b. Wombwell, 202142, Pte., k. in a., F., 23/3/18.

KNOWLES, H., b. Hyde, 316840, Pte., d. of w., F., 24/3/18.

LAMBERT, J., e. Rhosymedre, 200904, Pte., d. of w., F., 14/9/17.

LEAROYD, C. E., b. Barnsley, 202149, Pte., k. in a., F., 6/4/18.

LEWIS, A., b. Rhosllanerchgrugog, 7135, Pte., k. in a., F., 9/5/15.

LEWIS, W., b. Cwmglo, 201349, Pte., k. in a., F., 3/12/17.

LITTLE, W., b. Carlisle, 315359, Pte., d. of w., F., 25/3/18.

LLOYD, A., b. Rhostyllen, 200573, Pte., d., F., 4/11/18.

LLOYD, E., e. Wrexham, 7573, Pte., k. in a., F., 9/8/15.

LLOYD, E., b. Guilsfield, 12226, Pte., k. in a., F., 13/1/17.

LLOYD, E., e. Wrexham, 7752, Pte., k. in a., F., 19/1/16.

LLOYD, J., b. Ruabon, 6069, L/Cpl., d. of w., F., 11/3/15.

LLOYD, P., b. Cefn, 6514, Pte., k. in a., F., 3/6/15.

LLOYD, T., b. Bersham, 200495, Pte., d. of w., F., 13/4/18.

LOVELOCK, T. J., b. Northop, 5829, Pte., d. of w., F., 9/6/18.

MATTHEWS, G., b. Bersham, 200496, Cpl., d. of w., F., 24/3/18.

MATTOCK, C. J., b. Tenbury, 241616, A/Sgt., d., Home, 11/8/18.

MCLAREN, J. D., b. Wrexham, 5641, Sgt., d. of w., F., 6/10/16.

MEREDITH, W., b. Gresford, 8566, Pte., k. in a., F., 23/8/16.

MILLINGTON, J., e. Wrexham, 7552, Pte., k. in a., F., 9/5/15.

MILLS, F., b. Welshpool, 203086, Pte., d. of w., E., 14/4/18.

MINNEY, F., b. Harold, 202366, Pte., d. of w., F., 21/3/18.

MORGAN, E., b. Stansty, 6050, Pte., k. in a., F., 25/1/15.

MORGAN, J. C., e. Welshpool, 203090, Pte., k. in a., F., 26/8/17.

MORGAN, J. T., e. Ruabon, 8592, Pte., d., F., 21/1/17.

MORRIS, E., e. Wrexham, 200614, Pte., k. in a., F., 6/4/18, M.M.

MORRIS, E., e. Welshpool, 203093, Pte., d. of w., F., 15/6/17.

MORRIS, J., b. Llangedwyn, 201081, Pte., k. in a., F., 23/3/18.

MORRIS, W., b. Llanrhaiadr, 203092, Pte., k. in a., F., 23/8/18.

MORRIS, W. T., e. Wrexham, 200844, Pte., d. of w., F., 10/6/17.

MULVEY, P., b. Wrexham, 201078, Pte., d., F., 20/8/18.

MYDDLETON, A. E., b. Denbigh, 7263, Pte., d. of w., F., 11/5/15.

NADIN, B., b. Wrexham, 7480, L/Cpl., k. in a., F., 7/6/15.

NICHOLSON, A., b. Catworth, 202376, Pte., k. in a., F., 3/6/17.

OAKLEY, R., b. Willian, 202378, L/Cpl., k. in a., F., 23/3/18.

OSTLER, T., b. Cadoxton, 8888, Pte., d., F., 19/8/16.

OVEREND, A., b. Pendleton, 242526, Pte., k. in a., F., 16/8/18.

OWEN, E. F., b. Llandudno, 201174, L/Cpl., d., F., 16/2/18, M.M.

OWEN, E. J., b. Llanfairfechan, 9234, Pte., d. of w., F., 1/2/17.

PADDOCK, C., b. Ellesmere, 6111, Pte., k. in a., F., 22/6/17.

PALMER, W., b. Barnsley, 202168, Pte., d. of w., F., 10/6/18.

PARKER, W., b. Wrexham, 200421, Pte., k. in a., F., 5/4/18.

PARRISH, H., b. Chirk, 201094, Pte., k. in a., F., 6/4/18.

PARRY, A., b. Holywell, 8670, Pte., k. in a., F., 15/8/16.

PARRY, D., b. Rhosllanerchgrugog, 200090, Pte., d. of w., F., 12/6/17.

PARRY, D. J., e. Carnarvon, 203396, Pte., k. in a., F., 6/9/17.

PARRY, J., b. Rhosymedre, 6775, Pte., k. in a., F., 9/3/15.

PARRY, J. P., e. Cardiff, 77172, Pte., d., Home, 21/4/18.

PARRY, R., b. Crook, 6138, Cpl., k. in a., F., 25/1/15.

PARRY, R. J., e. Wrexham, 7615, Pte., k. in a., F., 6/9/15.

PARSONS, J. W., b. Liverpool, 200588, Sgt., d. of w., F., 22/12/17, D.C.M.

PATTLE, J., b. Bury St. Edmunds, 201403, Pte., k. in a., F., 23/3/18.

PEMBERTON, J., b. Esclusham, 6846, Pte., k. in a., F., 9/1/16.

PENLINGTON, T., e. Wrexham, 200698, Pte., d., F., 3/12/18.

PERKS, J. W., b. Wrexham, 8687, Pte., k. in a., F., 5/10/16.

PETERS, S. I., b. Trumpington, 10815, Pte., k. in a., F., 9/11/16.

PHYTHIAN, J. A., e. Wrexham, 202603, Pte., k. in a., F., 23/3/18.

PICKERING, J., b. Barnsley, 202244, Cpl., d. of w., F., 11/6/17.

PINK, T. W., b. Brough Green, 202380, Pte., k. in a., F., 6/4/18.

POTTER, E., e. Luton, 10812, Pte., k. in a., F., 15/9/16.

POWELL, E., e. Neath, 73792, Pte., k. in a., F., 23/3/18.

POWELL, E., b. Brymbo, 200567, L/Cpl., k. in a., F., 20/4/17.

PRESCOTT, A., e. Rhos, 6448, Dmr., k. in a., F., 25/1/15.

PRICE, A., e. Wrexham, 8123, Pte., k. in a., F., 1/9/18.

PRICE, B., b. Rhosllanerchgrugog, 7255, Pte., d., Home, 5/8/14.

PRICE, H., b. Wrexham, 200348, Cpl., k. in a., F., 6/4/18.

PRICE, J., b. Wrexham, 200217, L/Cpl., k. in a., F., 3/9/18.

PRICE, M., b. Rhosymedre, 7151, Pte., d. of w., F., 7/6/15.

PRIDDLE, C., b. Chard, 68765, Pte., d. of w., F., 9/6/18.

PRITCHARD, C., b. Hanley, 6850, Pte., d., Home, 5/8/14.

PRYCE, S., b. Pentre Voelas, 8526, Pte., d. of w., F., 6/10/16.

RATHBONE, W. A., b. Gwersyllt, 6084, L/Cpl., k. in a., F., 19/7/15.

REID, J., b. Steeple Gidding, 202391, Pte., k. in a., F., **6/4/18.**

RICHARD, E. T., e. Wrexham, 200671, Pte., d. of w., F., 13/6/17.

RICHARDS, H., b. Cefn Mawr, 200508, Pte., k. in a., F., 18/8/18.

RIDGE, R., b. Chirk, 200455, Pte., d. of w., F., 22/3/18.

RILEY, B., b. Burnley, 66634, Pte., k. in a., F., 22/8/18.

ROBERTS, E. D., e. Carnarvon, 235002, Pte., d. of w., F., 4/9/18.

ROBERTS, I., b. Bersham, 200119, Pte., d. of w., F., 24/3/18.

ROBERTS, J., b. Stockport, 267654, Pte., d., F., 20/8/18.

ROBERTS, J. H., b. Bersham, 3894, C.S.M., k. in a., F., 18/7/15.

ROBERTS, L., b. St. Asaph, 201267, Pte., d. of w., Home, 31/7/17.

ROBERTS, R., b. Bersham, 200465, Pte., k. in a., F., 6/4/18.

ROBERTS, T., b. Llanfwrog, 4217, Pte., k. in a., F., 25/1/15.

ROBERTS, W., e. Wrexham, 200608, Pte., d., F., 17/3/17.

ROBERTS, W., b. Sontley, 201005, Pte., d. of w., F., 6/4/18.

ROBERTS, W., b. Ponkey, 203408, Pte., k. in a., F., 26/8/17.

ROBINSON, J., b. Haydock, 7000, Pte., d. of w., F., 12/1/15.

ROGERS, E., e. Wrexham, 200912, Pte., k. in a., F., 6/4/18.

ROGERS, H., e. Wrexham, 8167, Pte., d. of w., F., 9/10/16.

ROGERS, J. E., b. Meifod, 202930, Pte., k. in a., F., 22/3/18.

ROGERS, J. E., b. Rhosllanerchgrugog, 7333, Pte., k. in a., F., 9/5/15.

ROGERS, J. I., b. Aberdare, 8901, Pte., k. in a., F., 15/8/16.

ROWLANDS, D., b. Bersham, 6887, L/Cpl., d. of w., F., 2/1/17.

ROWLANDS, G., b. Ferryhill, 7439, Pte., k. in a., F., 9/5/15.

SHARPE, T., e. Wrexham, 8065, Pte., k. in a., F., 18/5/16.

SHARWOOD, H. H., b. Doddington, 202415, Pte., d. of w., F., 12/12/17.

SMALL, B., b. Houghton Regis, 10831, Pte., d. of w., Home, 11/1/17.

SMITH, A., b. Leeds, 202198, Pte., k. in a., F., 28/3/17.

SOMERS, W. R., b. Scarborough, 202189, Pte., d., F., 20/8/18.

SQUIRES, E., b. Gawthorpe, 202184, Pte., k. in a., F., 6/4/18.

STOKES, C. E., b. Whittington, 7073, Pte., k. in a., F., 25/1/15.

STOKES, R. T., b. Rhosllanerchgrugog, 6898, Pte., k. in a., F., 22/10/15.

SWAILES, J., b. Whitehaven, 204344, Pte., d. of w., F., 13/5/18.

TAYLOR, A. R. J., b. Kettering, 202418, Pte., k. in a., F., 22/7/17.

TAYLOR, E., b. Great Staughton, 202420, L/Sgt., k. in a., F., 6/4/18.

THELWELL, J., e. Wrexham, 200721, Sgt., k. in a., F., 19/1/18, D.C.M.

THOMAS, D. R., e. Wrexham, 202912, L/Cpl., k. in a., F., 6/4/18.

THOMAS, H. C., e. Brecon, 243063, Sgt., k. in a., F., 13/5/18.

THOMAS, H. W., b. Liverpool, 235100, Pte., k. in a., F., 7/6/17.

THOMAS, J., e. Wrexham, 7613, Pte., d. of w., F., 19/9/15.

THOMAS, J., e. Cefn, 200724, Pte., k. in a., F., 6/9/17.

THOMAS, J., b. Festiniog, 203457, Pte., k. in a., F., 6/4/18.

THOMAS, J. B., b. Mumbles, 69770, Pte., d. of w., F., 9/6/18.

THOMAS, J. P., b. Henllan, 7370, Pte., k. in a., F., 25/1/15.

THOMAS, N., b. Worthen, 203434, L/Cpl., k. in a., F., 22/3/18.

THOMAS, R., e. Wrexham, 203456, Pte., k. in a., F., 3/12/17.

THOMAS, W. C., b. Penmachno, 203435, Pte., k. in a., F., 22/3/18.

THOMPSON, G. F., b. Swinton, 202216, Pte., k. in a., F., 23/3/18.

THOMPSON, H., b. Castleford, 10622, Pte., d. of w., F., 16/9/16.

TOMPKINS, W. H., e. Wrexham, 7621, Pte., k. in a., F., 25/1/15.

TRAVERS, H., e. Crewe, 203453, Pte., k. in a., F., 6/4/18.

TULLY, R. W., e. Pembroke, 317018, Pte., d. of w., F., 17/8/18.

TURTLE, A., b. Birkenhead, 8600, Pte., d. of w., F., 4/10/16.

VERITY, W. B., b. Halifax, 202251, Pte., k. in a., F., 6/4/18.

WALTERS, H., b. Newcastle, 10867, Pte., d. of w., F., 18/9/16.

WARBURTON, L. R., b. Walton, 24439, Sgt., d. of w., F., 22/8/18.

WEBB, W., b. Sudbury, 202437, Pte., d. of w., F., 6/4/18.

WEEDON, E., b. Eaton Bray, 10866, Pte., d. of w., F., 5/10/16.

WHITEMAN, F., b. Stanley, 202234, Pte., d., F., 20/8/18.

WILDE, W. S., b. Wrexham, 6315, Pte., d. of w., F., 7/4/15.

WILKES, J., b. Ruabon, 201139, Pte., k. in a., F., 6/4/18.

WILLIAMS, A., b. Brithdir, 8831, Pte., k. in a., F., 5/10/16.

WILLIAMS, A. H., b. Cerrig-y-Druidon, 201051, Pte., k. in a., F., 6/4/18.

WILLIAMS, C., b. Cerrig-y-Druidon, 201074, Pte., k. in a., F., 9/6/18.

WILLIAMS, E., b. Welshpool, 290869, Pte., d. of w., F., 3/12/17.

WILLIAMS, E., e. Wrexham, 200931, Pte., k. in a., F., 22/3/18.

WILLIAMS, E. T., b. Penley, 202027, Pte., k. in a., F., 20/8/18.

WILLIAMS, G., b. Wrexham, 201150, Pte., k. in a., F., 6/4/18.

WILLIAMS, H., b. Rhosymedre, 200255, Pte., d. of w., F., 18/4/18.

WILLIAMS, J., e. Wrexham, 6848, Pte., d., F., 30/10/16.

WILLIAMS, J., e. Wrexham, 200641, L/Cpl., k. in a., F., 6/9/17.

WILLIAMS, J. H., e. Bangor, 76037, Pte., k. in a., F., 9/6/18.

WILLIAMS, P., b. Merthyr Tydvil, 201258, Pte., k. in a., F., 19/3/18.

WILLIAMS, R., b. Edeyon, 203819, Pte., d. of w., Home, 27/3/18.

WILLIAMS, R. E., b. Corwen, 201133, Pte., k. in a., F., 22/3/18.

WILLIAMS, S., e. Wrexham, 7797, Pte., d. of w., F., 30/3/15.

WILLIAMS, S. J., e. Brecon, 203313, Pte., k. in a., F., 23/3/18.

WILLIAMS, S. J., e. Carmarthen, 202990, Pte., k. in a., F., 26/8/17.

WILLIAMS, W., b. Ruabon, 6147, Pte., k. in a., F., 7/10/16.

WILLIAMS, W., b. Ruthin, 200419, Pte., k. in a., F., 6/4/18.

WILLIAMS, W., b. Caerwys, 201198, Pte., k. in a., F., 9/6/18.

WOOD, J., e. Wrexham, 203220, Pte., k. in a., F., 3/9/18.

WOOLHAM, J., e. Ellesmere, 201288, Pte., k. in a., F., 23/3/18.

WOOLMER, W. J., b. Weekley, 202422, Pte., d. of w., F., 22/3/18.

WRIGHT, A., b. Sheffield, 202222, Pte., k. in a., F., 6/4/18.

WRIGHT, A., b. Fairburn, 10645, Pte., k. in a., F., 15/9/16.

WYNNE, C., e. Wrexham, 7646, Pte., d. of w., F., 23/10/16.

2/4th BATTALION

BAKER, A., e. Queensferry, 9667, L/Cpl., d., Home, 26/7/16.

BILSBOROUGH, J., e. Blackburn, 10050, Pte., d., Hofe, 23/8/16.

CURWEN, E., b. Liverpool, 204417, Pte., d. of w., Home, 16/1/18.

DUXBURY, T., b. Darwen, 10051, Pte., d., Home, 24/6/16.

GOVAN, T., b. Birmingham, 203842, Cpl., d., Africa, 3/7/18.

JONES, J., e. Wrexham, 8070, Pte., d., Home, 7/11/15.

MORLEY, H., b. Derby, 8104, Pte., d., Home, 16/6/15.

POWELL, A. W., e. Pembroke, 204617, Pte., d., Home, 5/7/17.

SMITH, W., b. Blackburn, 9890, Pte., d., Home, 23/11/16.

STACK, J., b. Bootle, 68801, Pte., d., Home, 14/1/18.

3/4th BATTALION

DAVIES, T. P., b. Wrexham, 8172, Pte., d., Home, 8/7/15.

DAVIES, W. T., b. Trefriw, 8655, Pte., d., Home, 6/4/16.

MORRIS, A., b. Newtown, 9046, Pte., d., Home, 19/4/16.

ROBERTS, H., b. Port Dinorwic, 8992, Pte., d., Home, 16/6/16.

4th RESERVE BATTALION

ABEL, J. P., b. Llangurig, 203677, Pte., d., Home, 21/2/17.

DAVIES, R. L., b. Llanidloes, 203603, Pte., d., Home, 14/2/17.

EVANS, D., b. Trefeglwys, 291280, Pte., d., F., 5/3/17.

GRIFFITHS, G., b. Beddgelert, 203628, Pte., d., Home, 26/2/17.

HUGHES, M., b. Nevin, 203968, Pte., d., Home, 31/3/17.

HUGHES, W. R., b. Holyhead, 40893, Pte., d., Home, 1/7/18.

HUMPHREYS, A., b. Newtown, 290070, Pte., d., Home, 17/10/18.

JONES, D. T., b. Llanefyl, 203546, Pte., d., Home, 13/2/17.

JONES, E. D., b. Machynlleth, 203755, Pte., d., Home, 15/8/17.

JONES, H. O., b. Llangadfan, 203734, Pte., d., Home, 5/3/17.

JONES, J. H., b. Bootle, 1021, Pte., d., Home, 28/10/16.

JONES, L. R., b. Trefriw, 203626, Pte., d., Home, 18/2/17.

JONES, R., b. Penrhosligwy, 203590, Pte., d., Home, 17/2/17.

JONES, S., b. Llanidloes, 203602, Pte., d., Home, 14/2/17.

LUCAS, W. C., e. Wrexham, 11372, Pte., d., Home, 5/2/17.

McLAREN, T., b. Wrexham, 200298, Pte., d., Home, 24/12/17.

OWEN, G., b. Llanfaelog, 78005, Pte., d., Home, 13/4/18.

PARRY, R. J., b. Garn Dolbenmaen, 203695, Pte., d., Home, 28/2/17.

PROSSER, G., b. Swansea, 87205, Pte., d., Home, 25/6/18.
ROBERTS, R. T., b. Denbigh, 200556, A/Sgt., k. in a., E.A., 12/4/18.
ROBERTS, W. E., b. Beddgelert, 203754, Pte., d., Home, 19/2/17.
THOMAS, J. O., b. Rhos, 7443, Pte., d., Home, 4/12/15.
WILLIAMS, E., b. Llandwrog, 203630, Pte., d., Home, 8/2/17.

5th BATTALION (T.F.)

ALLSOPP, B., b. West Bromwich, 241594, A/Cpl., d. of w., E., 19/9/18.
AMIS, D. E., b. Greenfield, 1206, Pte., d., Malta, 30/11/15.
BAKER, J., b. Withington, 41511, Pte., d., E., 22/4/18.
BALDWIN, G., b. Blackburn, 66258, Pte., d., At Sea, 4/5/17.
BARNETT, W. J., e. Rhyl, 241110, Pte., k. in a., E., 20/4/17.
BAXTER, F., b. Pontnewynydd, 1608, Pte., k. in a., G., 10/8/15.
BELLIS, J., b. Salop, 2120, Pte., k. in a., G., 10/8/15.
BENTHAM, J. J., b. Flint, 240660, Pte., k. in a., E., 26/3/17.
BEVAN, T., b. Pontypool, 241949, L/Cpl., k. in a., E., 26/3/17.
BEWLEY, J. H., e. Queensferry, 3660, Pte., d. of w., E., 5/8/16.
BIRTALL, W. C., b. Chester, 40573, A/L/Cpl., d. of w., E., 30/4/18.
BOTT, S., b. Widnes, 63576, Pte., k. in a., E., 1/2/18.
BRAY, H., b. Manchester, 1456, Pte., d. of w., At Sea, 16/8/15.
BROWN, F., b. Patricroft, 240643, Pte., d. of w., E., 7/11/17.
BRYAN, G., b. Mold, 2365, Pte., d. of w., At Sea, 23/8/15.
BUTLER, J. W., b. Greenfield, 240802, Pte., k. in a., E., 26/3/17.
CALVER, F., b. London, 242951, Pte., k. in a., E., 26/3/17.
CAMPINI, B., b. Shrewsbury, 2554, Pte., k. in a., G., 10/8/15.
CAPEL, F. J., b. Llangeinor, 13201, Pte., d., At Sea, 4/5/17.
CATHERALL, E. G., e. Buckley, 241382, Pte., k. in a., E., 26/3/17.
CATHERALL, E., b. Hawarden, 240261, A/C.S.M., k. in a., E., 26/3/17, D.C.M.
CLEGG, L., b. Chester, 2354, Pte., d., E., 6/9/15.
CLEWS, J., b. Flint, 882, Pte., k. in a., G., 10/8/15.
CLIFF, T. W., b. Mostyn, 240201, Pte., k. in a., E., 26/3/17.
CONNOLLY, W., b. Old Colwyn, 2622, Pte., d. of w., E., 30/8/15.

CONSTANTINE, J., b. Liverpool, 61174, Pte., k. in a., E., 7/11/17.
CONWAY, H., b. Flint, 240692, L/Cpl., k. in a., E., 26/3/17.
CONWAY, J., b. Flint, 713, Pte., k. in a., G., 22/8/15.
COX, W., b. Buckley, 241332, Pte., k. in a., E., 26/3/17.
DAVID, W., b. Barry, 241565, Pte., k. in a., E., 26/3/17.
DAVIES, A., e. Colwyn Bay, 240894, Pte., k. in a., E., 26/9/17.
DAVIES, A., b. Flint, 240634, Pte., d., E., 26/3/17.
DAVIES, D. J., b. Mold, 2407, Pte., k. in a., G., 10/8/15.
DAVIES, E., b. Rossett, 890, Pte., d., Home, 17/6/15.
DAVIES, G., b. Birkenhead, 240409, L/Sgt., k. in a., E., 26/3/17.
DAVIES, H., b. Mold, 2271, Pte., d. of w., G., 14/8/15.
DAVIES, J., b. Abergele, 2648, Pte., k. in a., G., 10/8/15.
DAVIES, J., b. Oldham, 241564, Pte., k. in a., E., 9/3/18.
DAVIES, J. D., b. Ruabon, 1514, Pte., k. in a., G., 10/8/15.
DAVIES, T., b. Mold, 2265, Pte., d., Malta, 5/11/15.
DAVIES, W., b. Flint, 349, Sgt., d., Malta, 14/9/15.
DENNIS, D., b. Stagget, 975, Pte., k. in a., G., 10/8/15.
EGAN, T., b. Co. Tipperary, 59946, Pte., k. in a., E., 1/2/18.
ELLIS, H. R., b. Rhyl, 241181, Pte., k. in a., E., 26/3/17.
ELLIS, J., b. Bagillt, 2459, Pte., d., Home, 16/1/16.
ELLIS, J. D., b. St. Asaph, 241341, Pte., k. in a., E., 26/3/17.
EDWARDS, D. R., b. Ruabon, 241933, Pte., k. in a., E., 26/3/17.
EDWARDS, E., b. Llanrhaiadr, 36774, Pte., k. in a., E., 9/3/18.
EDWARDS, E., b. Mold, 241465, Pte., k. in a., E., 26/3/17.
EDWARDS, J., b. Mold, 2341, Pte., k. in a., G., 15/8/15.
EDWARDS, P., b. Rhyl, 876, Pte., k. in a., G., 10/8/15.
EDWARDS, R., e. Flint, 241143, Pte., k. in a., E., 26/3/17.
EDWARDS, R., b. Chester, 241520, Pte., k. in a., E., 7/11/17.
EDWARDS, R. T., b. Flint, 241604, Pte., k. in a., E., 26/3/17.
EVANS, E., b. Queensferry, 240263, Pte., d. of w., E., 9/3/18.
EVANS, J., e. Colwyn Bay, 2981, Pte., d., Mudros, 26/9/15.
EVANS, J., b. Flint, 573, Pte., k. in a., G., 13/9/15.
EVANS, T., b. Oakenholt, 241471, Pte., d., E., 28/9/18.
EVANS, W., e. Cefn, 200722, Pte., d., E., 18/7/18.

EVANS, W. E., e. Shotton, 240978, Pte., d. of w., E., 28/3/17.
FAULKNER, J., b. Farnworth, 241566, Pte., k. in a., E., 26/3/17.
FAZAKERLEY, B. G., b. Wavertree, 565, C.Q.M.S., d., Home, 27/12/16.
FISHER, W. J., b. Llysfaen, 240585, Pte., d., E., 20/6/18.
FLETCHER, J., b. Castleton, 59273, Pte., d., F., 2/3/17.
FOULKES, J., b. Llandyrnog, 201125, Pte., k. in a., E., 26/3/17.
FOULKES, T., b. Ysceifiog, 241448, Pte., k. in a., E., 26/3/17.
FURNISH, T. W., b. Llanddulas, 2701, Pte., k. in a., G., 10/8/15.
GEORGE, J., b. Flint, 240709, Pte., k. in a., E., 9/3/18.
GITTENS, T. E., e. Flint, 2286, Pte., k. in a., G., 10/8/15.
GREENWOOD, J., b. Holyhead, 63088, Pte., d., At Sea, 4/5/17.
GRIFFITHS, T. J., b. Pennffordd, 241397, Pte., k. in a., E., 26/3/17.
GRIFFITHS, T. J., b. Carnarvon, 265492, Pte., k. in a., E., 26/3/17.
GRIFFITHS, W., b. Tregarth, 201354, Pte., k. in a., E., 26/3/17.
GRIFFITHS, W., b. Holywell, 240307, L/Cpl., k. in a., E., 9/3/18.
GRIFFITHS, W., b. Mold, 240848, Pte., d., E., 7/10/18.
GUNTHER, A., b. Flint, 714, Pte., d. of w., G., 14/9/15.
GWILLIAM, H. W., e. Oswestry, 201314, L/Cpl., k. in a., E., 26/3/17.
HAINES, J., b. Rhyl, 1596, Pte., d. of w., At Sea, 16/8/15.
HALL, G., b. Blaenavon, 58887, Pte., d., Home, 24/2/17.
HALL, J., b. Stalybridge, 241827, Pte., k. in a., E., 26/3/17.
HALL, R., b. Ashton-under-Lyne, 240465, Pte., k. in a., E., 7/11/17, M.M.
HANDS, J., b. Whiston Potteries, 241702, Pte., k. in a., E., 26/3/17.
HARGREAVES, J., b. Newcastle-on-Tyne, 240158, Sgt., d. of w., E., 26/3/17.
HARRINGTON, J., b. Onibury, 241381, Pte., d., E., 2/4/17.
HARVEY, W., b. Headington, 62163, Pte., d., E., 3/10/18.
HAYES, J., e. Holywell, 2917, Pte., d., G., 8/10/15.
HAYES, W. H., b. Buckley, 240341, Pte., k. in a., E., 26/3/17.
HEMMINGS, A., b. Mold, 241473, Pte., k. in a., E., 26/3/17.
HERRINGAN, P., e. Ashton-under-Lyne, 63217, Pte., d., At Sea, 4/5/17.

HENSHAW, H., b. London, 242755, Pte., d., At Sea, 15/4/17.

HEWITT, T., b. Flint, 1377, Pte., k. in a., G., 10/8/15.

HOGAN, E., b. Bangor, 265816, Pte., k. in a., E., 9/3/18.

HOPWOOD, J., e. Mold, 241010, Pte., d. of w., E., 21/4/17.

HOWE, J., b. Coventry, 37101, Pte., d., At Sea, 4/5/17.

HUGHES, A., b. Connah's Quay, 528, Pte., d. of w., G., 12/8/15.

HUGHES, J., b. Mold, 1541, Pte., k. in a., G., 10/8/15.

HUGHES, J., e. Colwyn Bay, 240994, Pte., k. in a., E., 26/3/17.

HUGHES, J., b. Conway, 241213, Pte., k. in a., E., 26/3/17.

HUGHES, J. T., b. Mold, 2281, Pte., k. in a., G., 15/9/15.

HUGHES, M., b. Capel Curig, 241127, Pte., k. in a., E., 26/3/17.

HUGHES, M. H., b. Ruthin, 240666, Pte., d., E., 3/9/18.

HUGHES, N., b. Rhyl, 240562, Pte., k. in a., E., 26/3/17.

HUGHES, R., b. Glan Conway, 241092, L/Cpl., k. in a., E., 26/3/17.

HUGHES, T. G., e. Flint, 2268, Pte., d., Home, 11/7/16.

HUGHES, W., b. Flint, 1151, Pte., k. in a., G., 18/8/15.

JACKSON, P., b. Plumbley, 66206, Pte., d., At Sea, 4/5/17.

JACKSON, S., e. Manchester, 63105, Pte., d., At Sea, 4/5/17.

JAMES, R., b. Flint, 2177, Pte., k. in a., E., 7/1/16.

JENKINS, G., b. Llansamlet, 909, Dmr., d. of w., At Sea, 21/8/15.

JOHNSON, R. E., b. Flint, 1208, Pte., k. in a., G., 22/9/15.

JONES, A., b. Wrexham, 240104, A/L/Sgt., d. of w., E., 22/4/17.

JONES, C. H., b. Leeswood, 200300, Sgt., d. of w., E., 14/2/18.

JONES, D., b. Llanbeblig, 265005, Pte., k. in a., E., 26/3/17.

JONES, D., b. Rhuddlan, 1287, Pte., k. in a., G., 10/8/15.

JONES, E., b. Flint, 1144, Pte., d. of w., At Sea, 20/8/15.

JONES, E., b. Rhyl, 241128, Pte., d. of w., E., 1/4/17.

JONES, E. L., b. Carnarvon, 242753, Pte., d., At Sea, 15/4/17.

JONES, E. P., e. Colwyn Bay, 240969, L/Cpl., k. in a., E., 26/3/17.

JONES, F., b. Holywell, 1220, Pte., k. in a., G., 19/8/15.

JONES, I., b. Mostyn, 999, Pte., k. in a., E., 1/9/15.

JONES, J., b. Pontblyddyn, 2376, Pte., k. in a., G., 11/8/15.

JONES, J., b. Holywell, 2194, Pte., k. in a., G., 10/8/15.

JONES, J. E., b. Rhos-y-cae, 20862, Pte., d., At Sea, 4/5/17.

JONES, J. O., b. Festiniog, 49804, Pte., d., At Sea, 4/5/17.

JONES, L., b. Halkyn, 241260, Pte., d. of w., E., 27/4/18.

JONES, L. E., b. Llanfair, 17935, Sgt., d. of w., 7/11/17.

JONES, R., b. Colwyn Bay, 2011, Pte., d., Malta, 18/9/15.

JONES, R. A., b. Newtown, 291426, Pte., k. in a., E., 9/3/18.

JONES, S., b. Mold, 240572, Pte., k. in a., E., 10/8/15.

JONES, T., e. Rhyl, 3273, Pte., d. of w., E., 4/8/16.

JONES, T. J., b. Llanllyfni, 23283, Pte., k. in a., E., 15/4/17.

JONES, W., b. Rhyl, 857, Pte., k. in a., G., 10/8/15.

JONES, W. D., b. Llanbrynmair, 2426, Pte., d., At Sea, 31/8/15.

JONES, W. R., b. Llanberis, 265175, Pte., d., E., 25/12/17.

KENYON, S., b. Preston, 64065, Pte., d., E., 29/8/18.

KIRKHAM, S., b. Liverpool, 241407, Pte., k. in a., E., 26/3/17.

LAMBERT, J., b. Rhyl, 240735, Pte., k. in a., E., 9/3/18.

LANCELOT, J. R., e. Holywell, 240939, L/Cpl., k. in a., E., 26/3/17.

LATHAM, H. S., b. Queensferry, 1326, Pte., k. in a., G., 21/8/15.

LEATHERBARROW, J., b. Wigan, 788, Cpl., k. in a., G., 10/8/15.

LEWIS, E., b. Penmachno, 201357, Pte., k. in a., E., 9/3/18.

LLOYD, F., b. Llanarmon, 201425, Pte., k. in a., E., 9/3/18.

LLOYD, O., e. Llanrwst, 3089, Pte., k. in a., G., 22/9/15.

LLOYD, T., e. Carnarvon, 265677, Pte., k. in a., E., 26/3/17.

LOADER, F., b. Hinckley, 2690, Dmr., k. in a., G., 10/8/15.

MACHIN, H., b. Kingsway, 241377, Pte., k. in a., E., 9/3/18.

MANLEY, A., b. Birkenhead, 242760, Pte., k. in a., E., 26/3/17.

MARTIN, T., b. Birmingham, 243011, Pte., k. in a., E., 26/3/17.

MATHER, F., b. Mold, 240541, Cpl., k. in a., E., 26/3/17.

McCUNNIFF, T., b. Flint, 240711, Pte., k. in a., E., 9/3/18.

McWICKER, B., b. Bacup, 28895, Pte., d. of w., E., 12/11/17.

MILLINGTON, A., b. Buckley, 241498, Pte., k. in a., E., 26/3/17.

MORGAN, E. T., e. Birmingham, 37096, Pte., d., At Sea, 4/5/17.

MORRIS, D. I., e. Llanrwst, 240826, Pte., k. in a., E., 26/3/17.

MORRIS, E., b. Colwyn Bay, 240860, Pte., k. in a., E., 26/3/17.

NADIN, P., b. Shotton, 201414, Pte., d. of w., E., 6/11/17.

OLIVER, C., b. Chester, 553, L/Cpl., k. in a., G., 15/8/15.

OWEN, G. J., b. Llanddeiniolen, 44030, Pte., d., At Sea, 4/5/17.

OWEN, H., b. Nantgwynant, 241432, Pte., k. in a., E., 26/3/17.

OWEN, H., b. Ynseynhaiarn, 266378, Pte., d. of w., E., 27/5/17.

OWEN, W. H., b. Taldrwst, 1140, Pte., k. in a., G., 10/8/15.

OWEN, W. L., b. Rock Ferry, 203645, Pte., k. in a., E., 9/3/18.

PARRY, J. W., b. Mold, 2694, Pte., k. in a., G., 22/9/15.

PIERCE, F. E., b. St. Asaph, 726, Pte., d., E., 29/8/15.

PIERCE, P., b. Dyserth, 241204, Pte., k. in a., E., 7/11/17.

PIERCE, W., e. Mold, 2933, Pte., d. of w., At Sea, 5/9/15.

POLLARD, J., b. Partington, 35455, Pte., d., At Sea, 4/5/17.

POWELL, F., b. Northop, 241348, Pte., k. in a., E., 7/11/17.

PRICE, D., b. Brynford, 2206, Pte., d. of w., G., 29/8/15.

PUGH, S., b. Wrexham, 1050, Pte., k. in a., G., 11/8/15.

RECKLESS, E. W., b. Urmston, 2032, C.Q.M.S., d. of w., At Sea, 23/8/15.

ROBERTS, D., e. Flint, 2282, Pte., d., Home, 30/1/15.

ROBERTS, D. O., b. Capel Curig, 241112, Pte., k. in a., E., 26/3/17.

ROBERTS, E., b. Bistre, 2423, Pte., k. in a., G., 18/8/15.

ROBERTS, F., b. Mold, 1337, Pte., d., E., 5/12/15.

ROBERTS, G., b. Broseley, 242736, Pte., d., At Sea, 15/4/17.

ROBERTS, J., b. Barryford, 2117, Pte., d., At Sea, 2/10/15.

ROBERTS, J., e. Flint, 2309, Pte., k. in a., G., 18/8/15.

ROBERTS, J., b. Liverpool, 49867, Pte., d., At Sea, 4/5/17.

ROBERTS, J., b. Northop Hall, 3646, Pte., d. of w., E., 5/8/16.

ROBERTS, R., b. Flint, 526, Pte., d. of w., At Sea, 28/8/15.

ROBERTS, R., b. Ffynnongroew, 240959, Pte., k. in a., E., 29/4/18.

ROBERTS, T., b. Flint, 1387, Pte., d. of w., Home, 29/12/16.

ROWLANDS, J., b. Holt, 240960, Pte., k. in a., E., 9/3/18.

SALT, A. J., e. Colwyn Bay, 240970, Pte., k. in a., E., 9/3/18.

SCHOFIELD, H., b. Salford, 59465, Pte., d., At Sea, 4/5/17.

SHORT, S., b. Newton Abbot, 56925, Pte., k. in a., E., 3/11/17.

SIMSON, A. J., e. Rhyl, 3295, Pte., d. of w., At Sea, 11/9/15.

SLATER, J., b. Accrington, 242953, Pte., k. in a., E., 26/3/17.

SLEIGH, J., b. Manchester, 241373, Pte., k. in a., E., 26/3/17.

SMITH, T., b. Northop, 240419, Sgt., k. in a., E., 26/3/17.

THOMAS, A., e. Carnarvon, 268247, Pte., d. of w., E., 10/3/18.

THOMAS, C., b. Gresford, 1547, Pte., k. in a., G., 17/8/15.

THOMAS, H. P., b. Llandilo, 53067, Pte., d., At Sea, 4/5/17.

THOMAS, J. E., e. Flint, 2315, Pte., d., Home, 15/1/15.

THOMAS, W., b. Hope, 1550, Pte., k. in a., G., 17/8/15.

THOMAS, W. T., b. Whitford, 241515, Pte., d. of w., E., 9/3/18.

TOWNLEY, W., b. Manchester, 240547, Cpl., d., E., 10/7/18.

TUCK, F. D., b. Hawarden, 1097, Pte., d., E., 5/10/15.

TUCK, T. J., b. Hawarden, 1496, Pte., d., At Sea, 22/8/15.

VAUGHAN, J., b. Llanrwst, 2764, Pte., k. in a., G., 10/8/15.

VERNON, G. A., b. Stockport, 242740, Pte., d., At Sea, 15/4/17.

VERNON, J. T., b. Winsford, 2433, Pte., d., E., 18/11/15.

WALLSGROVE, J., b. London, 38953, L/Cpl., k. in a., E., 9/3/18.

WALLWORTH, L. A., b. Liverpool, 968, Sgt., k. in a., G., 10/8/15.

WARREN, E. C., b. Plymouth, 59959, Pte., k. in a., E., 9/3/18.

WELSH, E., b. Flint, 2334, Pte., d., E., 17/12/15.

WHEELER, W. E., b. Portsmouth, 241229, Pte., k. in a., E., 26/3/17.

WHITE, A. E., b. St. Margaret's, 266133, Pte., k. in a., E., 26/3/17.

WHITEHEAD, N., e. Wrexham, 202609, Pte., d., E., 17/1/18.

WHITLEY, E., b. Mold, 1100, Pte., d. of w., At Sea, 16/8/15.

WHITLEY, J., b. Mold, 946, Pte., k. in a., G., 20/8/15.

WHITLEY, J., b. Flint, 2418, Pte., d., G., 29/11/15.

WIGGINS, R., b. Wolverhampton, 240192, Pte., d., E., 21/10/18.

WILLIAMS, E., b. Preston, 1053, Pte., k. in a., G., 22/9/15.

WILLIAMS, E., b. Flint, 883, Pte., k. in a., G., 16/8/15.

WILLIAMS, E., b. Holywell, 60955, Pte., k. in a., E., 4/5/17.

WILLIAMS, E. R., b. Conway, 2162, Pte., k. in a., G., 29/11/15.

WILLIAMS, F., b. Wrexham, 2697, Pte., k. in a., G., 10/8/15.

WILLIAMS, H., b. Hawarden, 1484, Pte., k. in a., G., 19/8/15.

WILLIAMS, J., b. Llysfaen, 2111, L/Cpl., k. in a., G., 10/8/15.

WILLIAMS, J. A., b. Bagillt, 2231, Pte., k. in a., G., 10/8/15.

WILLIAMS, O., b. Holywell, 2381, Pte., d., Home, 22/9/15.

WILLIAMS, R. T., b. Denis, 241884, Pte., k. in a., E., 26/3/17.

WILLIAMS, T., b. Prion, 201372, Pte., d. of w., E., 12/11/17.

WILLIAMS, T. R., b. Holyhead, 2156, Pte., d. of w., F., 30/9/15.

WILLIAMS, W., e. Flint, 240798, Pte., d. of w., E., 20/6/18.

WILLIAMS, W., b. Broughton, 241333, Pte., k. in a., E., 26/3/17.

WILLMORE, A., b. Bilston, 1574, Pte., d. of w., G., 22/9/15.

WILSON, C., b. Cardiff, 240163, L/Cpl., k. in a., E., 7/11/17.

WILTON, W., b. Erith, 1585, Sgt., k. in a., G., 10/8/15.

WOODS, H., b. Rock Ferry, 242769, Pte., k. in a., E., 26/3/17.

WOODWARD, D., b. Mold, 201375, Pte., d. of w., E., 27/3/17.

2/5th BATTALION

BRAYSHAW, R. H., b. Lancaster, 242565, Pte., d., Home, 19/12/17.

ELLIS, A., b. Flint, 2233, Pte., d., E., 2/7/16.

GOODWIN, A., b. Hyde, 4925, Pte., d., Home, 27/10/16.

PARR, A., e. Rhyl, 2997, Pte., d., Home, 14/8/16.

3/5th BATTALION

HOWELLS, J., b. Wellington, 1578, Pte., d., Home, 16/9/16.

HUGHES, E., b. Mold, 2360, Pte., d., Home, 15/8/16.

LEA, J., b. Capenhurst, 3822, Pte., d., Home, 9/2/17.

6th BATTALION (T.F.)

ASTALL, T. J., b. Liverpool, 265786, Pte., k. in a., E., 28/12/17.

BANKS, W., b. Barnton, 267328, Pte., k. in a., E., 6/11/17.

BARBER, N., b. Darlington, 22, Cpl., d., G., 28/11/15.

BARTON, A., b. Llanbeblig, 904, Pte., d., Malta, 8/9/15.

BEAVER, A., b. Mottram, 267329, Pte., k. in a., E., 31/10/17.

BOLAND, W., b. Liverpool, 266495, Pte., k. in a., E., 26/3/17.

BORASTON, L., b. Liverpool,

267334, Pte., d. of w., E., 27/3/17.

BURTON, G. F., e. Carnarvon, 2644, Pte., k. in a., G., 10/8/15.

CLAYS, A., e. Wrexham, 200956, Pte., d., E., 17/10/18.

CLIFTON, B. F., b. Leamington, 6922, Cpl., k. in a., E., 10/3/18.

COUNTER, R. A., e. Plymouth, 242667, Pte., k. in a., E., 14/6/18.

COX, W., b. London, 1066, L/Cpl., d. of w., At Sea, 21/8/15.

CUSH, J., b. Holyhead, 266465, A/Cpl., d. of w., E., 4/8/18.

DAVIES, D. B., Port Dinorwic, 265501, Pte., d. of w., E., 1/5/17.

DAVIES, E., e. Rhyl, 3248, Pte., d. of w., G., 22/8/15.

DAVIES, E. A., e. Denbigh, 202597, Pte., k. in a., E., 6/11/17.

DAVIES, H., b. Bethesda, 266558, Pte., d., E., 9/3/17.

DAVIES, J., b. Llanfairfechan, 4061, Pte., d., E., 4/8/16.

DAVIES, R., b. Maenan, 266366, Pte., k. in a., E., 10/3/18.

DAVIES, R. L., e. Carnarvon, 2830, Pte., k. in a., G., 26/10/15.

DAVIES, T., b. Mold, 906, Pte., d., G., 30/11/15.

DAVIES, T., e. Carnarvon, 2512, Pte., d., E., 15/11/15.

DAVIES, W. R., b. Pentre, 265436, Pte., d. of w., E., 8/11/17.

DAWSON, T., b. Todmorden, 7992, Pte., d., E., 21/10/18.

DONE, A., b. Weston Point, 267346, Pte., d. of w., E., 20/11/17.

DOWELL, E. O., b. Penmaenmawr, 968, Pte., k. in a., G., 10/8/15.

DOWNS, S., e. Stockport, 51830, Pte., k. in a., E., 6/11/17.

EARDLEY, H., e. Carnarvon, 2893, Pte., d. of w., E., 19/8/15.

EDWARDS, R., e. Carnarvon, 265978, Pte., k. in a., E., 26/3/17.

EVANS, E., b. Carnarvon, 265702, Pte., k. in a., E., 6/11/17.

EVANS, G., b. Llanbeblig, 265448, Pte., d. of w., E., 27/4/18.

EVANS, H. R., b. Llandwrog, 1098, Cpl., k. in a., G., 21/8/15.

EVANS, J., b. Abersoch, 203589, Pte., k. in a., E., 6/11/17.

EVANS, J. S., e. Carnarvon, 265413, Pte., d. of w., E., 5/5/17.

EVANS, R., e. Carnarvon, 265671, Pte., k. in a., E., 6/11/17.

EVANS, R. H., b. Llanfair, 266411, Pte., d. of w., E., 7/1/18.

FARRELL, J. H., b. Birkenhead, 267352, Pte., k. in a., E., 6/11/17.

FELLOWS, H. H., b. Holyhead, 266348, Pte., k. in a., E., 28/12/17.

FOULKES, J., b. Bangor, 266381, Pte., d. of w., E., 9/4/17.

FOULKES, W., b. Bangor, 1594, Pte., d. of w., G., 28/8/15.

GREEN, W., b. Denio, 265259, A/L/Sgt., k. in a., E., 28/12/17.

GRIFFITHS, H. O., b. Llanberis, 265870, Pte., k. in a., E., 6/11/17.

GRIFFITHS, W., b. Nevin, 1606, Pte., d., Home, 24/2/15.

HOWARD, J., b. Dublin, 923, Pte., d. of w., G., 23/8/15.

HOWELLS, H., e. Plymouth, 242670, Pte., k. in a., E., 10/3/18.

HOWELLS, H., b. Abernant, 266645, Pte., k. in a., E., 6/11/17.

HUGHES, E., e. Carnarvon, 3249, Pte., k. in a., G., 14/8/15.

HUGHES, E. J., e. Carnarvon, 3211, Pte., d. of w., G., 27/11/15.

HUGHES, H., b. Llanengan, 1604, Pte., d., E., 8/7/16.

HUGHES, J., e. Carnarvon, 1445, Pte., d., Home, 9/6/16.

HUGHES, J., b. Pwllheli, 265171, Pte., d. of w., E., 17/11/17.

HUGHES, J., b. Llanllyfni, 265304, Pte., k. in a., E., 26/3/17.

HUGHES, J., b. Llangybi, 265478, Pte., k. in a., G., 10/8/15.

HUGHES, J., b. Aberffraw, 266406, Pte., k. in a., E., 27/3/17.

HUGHES, J. H., b. Cwm-y-Glo, 1878, Pte., k. in a., G., 11/8/15.

HUGHES, O., e. Carnarvon, 1844, Pte., d., E., 5/5/16.

HUGHES, R., b. Pwllheli, 266395, Pte., d., At Sea, 15/4/17.

HUGHES, R., b. Llanerchymedd, 267318, Pte., k. in a., E., 6/11/17.

HUGHES, T. H., b. Glyn Ceiriog, 1522, A/L/Cpl., k. in a., G., 26/10/15.

HUGHES, W., e. Carnarvon, 3161, Pte., d. of w., G., 11/8/15.

HUGHES, W., b. Conway, 265315, Pte., k. in a., E., 26/8/17.

HUGHES, W. J., e. Carnarvon, 1473, Pte., k. in a., G., 11/8/15.

HUGHES, W. J., e. Carnarvon, 3156, Pte., k. in a., G., 11/8/15.

HUGHES, W. S., b. Bangor, 1597, Pte., d., Home, 17/7/16.

HUMPHREYS, J. T., b. Llanwnda, 266486, Pte., k. in a., E., 6/11/17.

HUMPHREYS, T., b. Penybont, 203688, Pte., k. in a., E., 6/11/17.

JACKSON, J. H., b. Conway, 265032, A/Cpl., k. in a., E., 6/11/17.

JOHN, J. D., b. Cil-y-Bebyll, 20878, Pte., d. of w., E., 7/11/17.

JOHNSON, N., b. Southport, 88078, Pte., d., E., 26/10/18.

JOHNSON, W., b. Leeds, 59921, Pte., d., E., 20/1/18.

JONES, A. W., e. St. Albans, 31841, Cpl., k. in a., E., 6/11/17.

JONES, B. V. H., b. London, 267944, Pte., k. in a., E., 28/12/17.

JONES, D., b. Coedana, 1770, Pte., d. of w., At Sea, 3/9/15.

JONES, E., b. Cemmaes Bay, 268541, Pte., d., E., 9/11/17.

JONES, E., b. Llanberis, 1136, Pte., k. in a., G., 17/8/15.

JONES, E., b. Chwilog, 266216, Pte., d., Home, 28/3/18.

JONES, E., b. Criccieth, 266448, Pte., d., E., 18/10/18.

JONES, E. H., e. Carnarvon, 3177, Pte., d., G., 28/11/15.

JONES, G., b. Ynyscyhaiarn, 980, Pte., k. in a., G., 11/8/15.

JONES, G., b. Pwllheli, 202773, Pte., k. in a., E., 6/11/17.

JONES, H., e. Carnarvon, 3074, Pte., d. of w., At Sea, 12/8/15.

JONES, H., b. Llanrug, 1034, Pte., d., At Sea, 30/9/15.

JONES, H., b. Llangrin Abersoch, 1559, Pte., d., G., 15/10/15.

JONES, H., b. Llanddyfnan, 266463, Pte., k. in a., E., 6/11/17.

JONES, H., b. Bodorgan, 266715, Pte., k. in a., E., 26/3/17.

JONES, H. E., b. Dwygyfylchi, 265111, L/Cpl., k. in a., E., 30/11/17.

JONES, H. P., b. Llanrwst, 1570, Pte., k. in a., G., 17/8/15.

JONES, J., b. Clynog, 1332, Pte., d., G., 23/8/15.

JONES, J., b. Holyhead, 266139, Pte., k. in a., E., 6/11/17.

JONES, J. G., e. Carnarvon, 2443, Pte., d., E., 3/9/15.

JONES, J. H., e. Carnarvon, 1890, Pte., k. in a., G., 11/8/15.

JONES, J. O., b. Llanddansant, 265473, Pte., k. in a., E., 6/11/17.

JONES, J. R., b. Conway, 265320, A/L/Cpl., k. in a., G., 10/8/15.

JONES, J. R., b. Bangor, 266589, Pte., d. of w., E., 24/11/17.

JONES, J. S., b. Blaenau Festiniog, 291399, Pte., k. in a., E., 26/3/17.

JONES, J. T., e. Carnarvon, 265932, A/L/Cpl., k. in a., E., 6/11/17.

JONES, L., b. Holyhead, 2279, Pte., d., Malta, 17/9/15.

JONES, O., b. Holyhead, 265723, Pte., d. of w., E., 10/11/17.

JONES, O., b. Bethesda, 266710, Pte., d. of w., E., 28/3/17.

JONES, O. O., b. Llandwrog, 266524, Pte., k. in a., E., 6/11/17.

JONES, R., b. Penmaenmawr, 265469, L/Sgt., d., E., 17/6/18.

JONES, R., b. Llanllyfni, 631, Sgt., k. in a., G., 11/8/15.

JONES, R., e. Carnarvon, 2792, Pte., d., G., 29/11/15.

JONES, R., b. Bangor, 265427, L/Cpl., k. in a., E., 26/3/17.

JONES, R., e. Bethesda, 266047. Pte., d., E., 3/4/18.

JONES, T. I., b. Llandudno, 266380, Pte., d. of w., E., 7/11/17.

JONES, T. J., e. Carnarvon, 266095, Pte., d., E., 18/9/17.

JONES, W., b. Llandewyn, 334, Cpl., d. of w., E., 20/12/15.

JONES, W., b. Corwen, 787, L/Cpl., k. in a., G., 11/8/15.

JONES, W., b. Llanbeblig, 1530, Pte., d. of w., At Sea, 25/8/15.

JONES, W., b. Carnarvon, 1920, Pte., d., G., 13/9/15.

JONES, W., e. Carnarvon, 265670, Sgt., k. in a., E., 9/3/18.

JONES, W., b. Llanberis, 265875, L/Cpl., k. in a., E., 6/11/17.

JONES, W., b. Aberffraw, 266249, Pte., d., E., 12/12/17.

JONES, W., b. Bodedern, 266342, Pte., k. in a., E., 6/11/17.

JONES, W., b. Llanfairfechan, 266438, Pte., k. in a., E., 28/12/17.

JONES, W., b. Bodwrog, 266513, Pte., d., E., 16/4/17.

JONES, W. H., b. Bangor, 265821, Sgt., k. in a., E., 6/11/17.

JONES, W. L., b. Llanbeblig, 266317, Pte., k. in a., E., 26/3/17.

JONES, W. M., b. Llandegai, 266194, Pte., k. in a., E., 9/3/18, M.M.

LATHAM, G. H., b. Cakemore, 38939, Pte., k. in a., E., 28/12/17.

LEACH, G., b. Blackburn, 268535, Pte., k. in a., E., 6/11/17.

LEAVETT, J. W., e. Carnarvon, 2504, Pte., k. in a., G., 22/8/15.

LEWIS, O., b. Penmon, 3413, Pte., d., E., 31/10/15.

LLOYD, J., b. Horbury, 315279, Pte., k. in a., E., 9/3/18.

LLOYD, J., b. Llanllyfni, 1171, Pte., k. in a., G., 11/8/15.

LLOYD, M., b. Llanllyfni, 961, Pte., k. in a., G., 11/8/15.

LLOYD, S., b. Holyhead, 265755, Sgt., d. of w., E., 9/11/17.

MAIDEN, E., b. Dawley, 267374. Pte., k. in a., E., 6/11/17.

MANLEY, L. T., b. Alberbury, 203660, Pte., d., E., 16/10/18.

MARTIN, J. H., b. Long Eaton, 59923, Pte., k. in a., E., 6/11/17.

McGLONE, J., b. Carlisle, 315369, Pte., k. in a., E., 10/3/18.

MICHAEL, D., b. Pensarn, 267315, Pte., d. of w., E., 7/11/17.
MORELAND, H., b. Stonehouse, 1110, Sgt., d., E., 20/9/16.
MORRIS, L., b. Aber, 3270, Pte., d., Home, 7/9/15.
MULLARKEY, P., b. Lichfield, 266655, Pte., k. in a., E., 6/11/17.
NAGLE, J., b. Manchester, 34228, Pte., k. in a., E., 6/11/17.
NANNEY, W. R., e. Carnarvon, 1488, Pte., d. of w., G., 20/8/15.
NEWSHAM, C. R., e. Birkenhead, 267375, Pte., k. in a., E., 27/3/17.
OWEN, E. R., e. Carnarvon, 2290, Pte., d., Home, 24/1/15.
OWEN, G., b. Carnarvon, 2227, Pte., d. of w., At Sea, 14/8/15.
OWEN, G., e. Carnarvon, 3264, Pte., d., G., 3/9/15.
OWEN, H., b. Bethesda, 265302, Pte., d., E., 5/11/18.
OWEN, H. J., b. Nantgwynant, 266510, Pte., k. in a., E., 26/3/17.
OWEN, H. H., b. Llanllyfni, 265059, Pte., k. in a., E., 6/11/17.
OWEN, J., b. Beaumaris, 266542, Pte., d. of w., E., 3/5/17.
OWEN, M. J., e. Carnarvon, 1957, L/Sgt., k. in a., G., 11/8/15.
OWEN, T., e. Carnarvon, 266270, Pte., d. of w., E., 2/11/17.
OWEN, W., b. Llanllyfni, 265218, L/Cpl., k. in a., E., 6/11/17.
OWEN, W., b. Talsarnau, 267281, Pte., k. in a., E., 4/11/17.
OWEN, W. R., b. Menai Bridge, 266723, Pte., d., E., 2/3/17.
OWENS, J., b. Llangefni, 201411, Pte., k. in a., E., 9/3/18.
PARRY, E. R., b. Llanberis, 1278, Pte., d. of w., G., 17/9/15.
PARRY, J. E., b. Pentraeth, 265692, Pte., d., E., 21/11/17.
PARRY, J. H., e. Carnarvon, 3034, Pte., d., G., 29/11/15.
PARRY, O. W., b. Bangor, 265231, Pte., d. of w., E., 27/3/17.
PARRY, R. R., b. Llanberis, 265342, Sgt., d. of w., E., 29/12/17, M.M. and Clasp.
PARRY, W., b. Ebenezer, 1349, Pte., d., E., 17/7/16.
PARRY, W. H., b. Llanbeblig, 838, L/Cpl., k. in a., G., 23/8/15.
PECKETT, J. H., b. High Burton, 59925, Pte., k. in a., E., 6/11/17.
PICKARD, L., b. Sandon, 267378, Cpl., k. in a., E., 30/4/18.
PIERCE, O. R., b. Abererch, 265281, Pte., d. of w., E., 28/12/17.
PIERCE, S., b. Kidderminster, 268539, Pte., d., E., 30/1/18.
POWELL, W., b. Church Aston, 266679, A/Sgt., k. in a., E., 6/11/17.

PRITCHARD, I., b. Holyhead, 2217, Pte., d., Home, 31/3/15.
PRITCHARD, O., b. Criccieth, 266274, Pte., d., E., 7/10/17.
PUGH, D. S., e. Carnarvon, 265781, Pte., k. in a., E., 10/3/18.
READ, H., b. Conway, 265358, A/Sgt., k. in a., E., 9/3/18.
REED, T. H., b. Copperas, 17156, Pte., k. in a., E., 6/11/17.
REES, B. J., e. Carnarvon, 2075, Pte., k. in a., G., 17/8/15.
RICE, T., e. Carnarvon, 266033, Cpl., d. of w., E., 29/12/17.
RICHARDSON, R. E., b. Pudsey, 74051, Pte., d., E., 1/9/18.
RIDLEY, A., b. Ynyscynhaiain, 265596, Pte., d., At Sea, 30/12/17.
ROBERTS, C. H., b. Dolwyddelan, 204032, Pte., k. in a., E., 6/11/17.
ROBERTS, D. G., e. Carnarvon, 1414, Pte., d., At Sea, 12/9/15.
ROBERTS, D. J., b. Dwygyfylchi, 292, A/Cpl., d., Malta, 24/8/15.
ROBERTS, H., e. Carnarvon, 2560, Pte., k. in a., G., 11/8/15.
ROBERTS, J., e. Carnarvon, 3190, Pte., d. of w., G., 5/11/15.
ROBERTS, J. E., e. Carnarvon, 2412, Pte., k. in a., G., 23/11/15.
ROBERTS, M., b. Cwm-y-Glo, 266737, Pte., k. in a., E., 6/11/17.
ROBERTS, N. A., e. Carnarvon, 265672, Pte., k. in a., E., 6/11/17.
ROBERTS, O., b. Talysarn, 1774, Pte., k. in a., G., 22/8/15.
ROBERTS, R., b. Pont Llynffyn, 265481, Pte., k. in a., E., 6/11/17.
ROBERTS, R., b. Bangor, 1081, L/Cpl., k. in a., G., 11/8/15.
ROBERTS, R. E., b. Conway, 265086, L/Cpl., k. in a., E., 26/3/17.
ROBERTS, R. J., e. Menai Bridge, 268534, Pte., k. in a., E., 6/11/17.
ROBERTS, S., b. Wrexham, 266660, Pte., k. in a., E., 6/11/17.
ROBERTS, T., b. Carnarvon, 265621, L/Cpl., k. in a., E., 6/11/17.
ROBERTS, W., b. Conway, 223, A/Sgt., k. in a., G., 10/8/15.
ROBERTS, W. J., e. Carnarvon, 268259, A/C.S.M., d., Home, 5/11/18.
ROGERS, L., b. Talysarn, 267301, Pte., d., At Sea, 15/4/17.
ROWLANDS, G. A., b. Llanrug, 266478, Pte., d., E., 12/10/17.
ROWLATT, G., b. London, 64019, Pte., k. in a., E., 6/11/17.
SALTHOUSE, W. B., b. Openshaw, 268556, Pte., k. in a., E., 6/11/17.
SAUNDERS, W. H., b. St. Helen's,

266664, Pte., k. in a., E., 6/11/17.
SEAMARKS, H., b. Gt. Linford, 266671, Pte., d., E., 10/6/18.
SEFTON, H., b. Liverpool, 315937, Pte., d. of w., E., 18/4/18.
SHERRATT, G., b. Warrington, 315478, Pte., k. in a., E., 10/3/18.
SIMMS, D. J., b. Llansamlet, 20942, Pte., k. in a., E., 6/11/17.
STEWART, A., b. Dublin, 601, L/Cpl., k. in a., G., 19/8/15.
THOMAS, A., b. Manchester, 315390, Pte., k. in a., E., 28/6/18.
THOMAS, J., b. Dwygyfyleli, 230, L/Sgt., k. in a., G., 10/8/15.
THOMAS, R., e. Carnarvon, 1369, Pte., d., Home, 8/1/16.
THOMAS, R. J., b. Llanberis, 151, Pte., d., E., 21/9/15.
TURNER, W., b. Harlon, 31396, Pte., d. of w., E., 9/4/18.
WALKER, W. H., b. Manchester, 265115, Pte., d. of w., E., 29/12/17.
WARD, M., b. Bangor, 1075, L/Cpl., d., Home, 20/2/15.
WEBB, E. J., e. Carnarvon, 1442, Cpl., d. of w., At Sea, 15/8/15.
WEYMAN, J., b. Conway, 1261, Pte., k. in a., G., 10/8/15.
WHELAN, C. T., b. Dublin, 605, Sgt., k. in a., G., 11/8/15.
WILKINSON, H., b. Carnarvon, 1527, Pte., k. in a., E., 26/10/15.
WILLIAMS, D. O., b. Llanwndr, 1178, Pte., d., Malta, 14/2/16.
WILLIAMS, D. R., b. Bangor, 2682, Pte., d. of w., At Sea, 15/8/15.
WILLIAMS, D. R., e. Conway, 1342, Pte., d., G., 3/9/15.
WILLIAMS, E., b. Beaumaris, 266597, Pte., k. in a., E., 26/3/17.
WILLIAMS, E., e. Carnarvon, 53875, Pte., k. in a., E., 28/12/17.
WILLIAMS, G., e. Carnarvon, 3273, Pte., k. in a., G., 6/11/15.
WILLIAMS, H., e. Carnarvon, 1921, Pte., d., E., 2/12/15.
WILLIAMS, H., b. Llandwrog, 3578, Pte., d., E., 18/5/16.
WILLIAMS, J., e. Holywell, 240989, Pte., k. in a., E., 6/11/17.
WILLIAMS, J., b. Criccieth, 265230, Pte., d., E., 15/8/18.
WILLIAMS, J., b. Rhoscolyn, 266181, Pte., k. in a., E., 6/11/17.
WILLIAMS, J., b. Denio, 266202, Pte., d. of w., E., 28/3/17.
WILLIAMS, J., b. Llanrug, 265519, L/Cpl., k. in a., E., 6/11/17.
WILLIAMS, J. J., b. Carnarvon, 1978, Pte., d., G., 30/11/15.

WILLIAMS, M. P., e. Carnarvon, 1374, Pte., k. in a., G., 20/8/15.
WILLIAMS, O., e. Carnarvon, 2743, Pte., d. of w., G., 18/8/15.
WILLIAMS, R., b. Conway, 361, L/Cpl., k. in a., G., 12/11/15.
WILLIAMS, R., e. Carnarvon, 265580, Sgt., d. of w., E., 13/11/17.
WILLIAMS, R., b. Llanfair P.G., 266405, Pte., k. in a., E., 26/3/17.
WILLIAMS, R., b. Holyhead, 266426, Pte., k. in a., E., 26/3/17.
WILLIAMS, R. C., b. Menai Bridge, 831, Pte., d. of w., At Sea, 18/9/15.
WILLIAMS, R. E., b. Llanfairfechan, 1062, Pte., d. of w., G., 11/8/15.
WILLIAMS, R. T., e. Carnarvon, 1459, Pte., d., Malta, 6/3/16.
WILLIAMS, T. D., b. Llanbeblig, 1509, A/L/Cpl., d., Home, 14/3/16.
WILLIAMS, T. J. A., b. Llandudno, 1095, Pte., d. of w., Home, 9/10/15.
WILLIAMS, T. W., b. Carmel, 267403, Pte., k. in a., E., 26/3/17.
WILLIAMS, W., b. Llanbeblig, 1305, Pte., d. of w., G., 20/8/15.
WILLIAMS, W., b. Deganwy, 265359, Pte., k. in a., E., 26/3/17.
WILLIAMS, W. B., b. Liverpool, 252, Cpl., d., Home, 19/12/15.
WILLIAMS, W. H., b. Penmaenmawr, 1210, Pte., k. in a., G., 13/8/15.
WILLIAMS, W. J., b. Bangor, 1637, Pte., k. in a., G., 21/8/15.
WILLIAMS, W. R., e. Carnarvon, 1977, Pte., k. in a., G., 11/8/15.
WOOD, A., e. Carnarvon, 2876, Pte., d., G., 30/11/15.
WOOD, T. J., b. Bangor, 1731, Pte., k. in a., G., 10/8/15.
WRIGHT, H., b. Bangor, 265312, Sgt., k. in a., E., 26/3/17.

2/6th BATTALION

BRANWOOD, L., e. Carnarvon, 2785, Pte., d., Home, 14/11/15.
COLLINS, F., b. Bury, 4762, Pte., d., Home, 18/5/16.
ECKERSALL, A., e. Stockport, 267648, Pte., d., Home, 19/4/17.
HUGHES, G. J., e. Carnarvon, 1809, Pte., d., Home, 8/11/16.
JONES, H., b. Groeslon, 2845, Pte., d., Home, 20/5/15.
JONES, O., b. Llandwrog, 3354, Pte., k. in a., G., 10/8/15.
McDONALD, J., b. Bromborough,

267472, Pte., d., Home, 30/9/17.
O'NEILL, J., e. Liverpool, 4490, Pte., d., Home, 9/6/16.
PYE, W., b. Southport, 266766, Pte., d., Home, 3/2/17.
ROBERTS, D. G., b. Llanfairfechan, 2828, Pte., k. in a., F., 25/8/16.
ROBERTS, H. J., e. Carnarvon, 2028, Pte., d., At Sea, 28/10/15.
SMITH, P., e. Seaforth, 266774, Pte., d., Home, 2/3/17.
THOMAS, W., e. Carnarvon, 2408, Pte., d., Home, 19/7/16.
WILLIAMS, H., e. Carnarvon, 1659, A/L/Cpl., d., Home, 12/1/16.

3/6th BATTALION

WILLIAMS, O., b. Llandwrog, 3967, Pte., d., Home, 20/3/16.
WILLIAMS, R. H., b. Llandwrog, 4029, Pte., d., Home, 4/4/16.

5/6th BATTALION

CRONIN, J., b. Kings Co., 74010, Pte., d., E., 21/10/18.
DARBEY, J. E., e. Shotton, 241043, Pte., d., E., 31/10/18.
JONES, G., b. Pwllheli, 201212, Pte., d., E., 9/11/18.
LANGMAN, S., e. Pontypridd, 268518, Pte., d., E., 25/10/18.
MOODY, W. M., b. Penmaenmawr, 266427, Pte., d., E., 8/8/18.
MOULTON, R. A., b. Saltney, 241517, Pte., k. in a., E., 1/2/18.
PARRY, W., b. Flint, 240671, Pte., d., E., 22/10/18.
ROE, W., e. Blackburn, 70760, Pte., d., E., 18/10/18.
SEMMENS, A., b. London, 268533, Pte., d., E., 11/11/18.

7th BATTALION (T.F.)

ALLSOBROOK, J. A., b. Manchester, 315193, Pte., k. in a., E., 10/3/18.
APPLEBY, J., b. Beswick, 70734, Pte., k. in a., E., 6/11/17.
ARTHUR, F., b. Guilsfield, 290819, Pte., k. in a., E., 4/11/17.
ASTLE, C. E., b. Oak Thorpe, 291865, Pte., k. in a., E., 19/4/17.
BAILEY, J., b. Macclesfield, 291810, Pte., k. in a., E., 26/3/17.
BALL, G., e. Macclesfield, 291814, Pte., k. in a., E., 26/3/17.
BALSHAW, J., b. Ormskirk, 70642, Pte., k. in a., E., 6/11/17.
BARDSLEY, W. B., b. Hyde, 291816, Pte., k. in a., E., 26/3/17.

BARNSHAW, T., b. Bollington, 291866, Pte., k. in a., E., 26/3/17.
BEBB, F., b. Kerry, 3030, Pte., d., Home, 30/10/14.
BENNETT, D. W., b. Llandinam, 290812, Pte., k. in a., E., 26/3/17.
BENNION, G., b. Llanfyllin, 290839, Pte., k. in a., E., 26/3/17.
BEVAN, T., b. Kidderminster, 290897, Pte., k. in a., E., 26/3/17.
BIRKS, J., b. Pendleton, 291616, Pte., k. in a., E., 10/3/18.
BLACK, J. W., b. London, 290432, L/Cpl., k. in a., E., 6/11/17.
BLANCHE, H., b. Oldham, 52229, Pte., k. in a., E., 6/11/17.
BOSTON, H., b. Congleton, 291818, Pte., k. in a., E., 26/3/17.
BRAMPTON, C. W., b. Adbaston, 70668, Pte., k. in a., E., 6/11/17.
BRATT, G., b. Manchester, 292807, Pte., k. in a., E., 6/11/17.
BREESE, J., b. Newtown, 290005, Sgt., k. in a., E., 6/11/17.
BREEZE, W. E., b. Welshpool, 290821, Pte., d., E., 28/10/18.
BROCK, A. C., b. Newtown, 199, L/Cpl., k. in a., G. 10/8/15.
BROMILOW, C. W., b. Liverpool, 73089, Pte., k. in a., E., 6/11/17.
BROUGH, J., b. Liverpool, 70601, Pte., d. of w., At Sea, 6/12/17.
BROWN, A., b. Wolverhampton, 3626, Pte., k. in a., G., 10/8/15.
BROWN, W. E., b. Llanfyllin, 290126, L/Cpl., k. in a., E., 26/3/17.
BUCKLEY, P., b. Manchester, 292809, Pte., k. in a., E., 30/12/17.
BUTTERS, S., b. Crewe, 291817, Pte., k. in a., E., 6/11/17.
CARTER, G., b. Manchester, 292813, Pte., k. in a., E., 6/11/17.
CAWLEY, R., b. Chester, 291873, Pte., k. in a., E., 26/3/17.
CHAPMAN, C. G., b. London, 292955, Pte., d., E., 28/10/18.
CHILD, A. W., b. Purley, 34812, Pte., d., E., 18/9/17.
CLEATON, R. F., b. West Derby, 292815, Pte., k. in a., E., 6/11/17.
COLLIER, N. M., b. Macclesfield, 291822, Pte., k. in a., E., 27/12/17.
COLLINS, A., b. Llandinam, 1094, Pte., k. in a., G., 10/8/15.
COPE, S., b. Crewe, 291682, L/Cpl., d., At Sea, 30/12/17.
CROOK, F. G., b. Newport, 2732, Cpl., d. of w., Home, 28/1/16.
CURETON, C., b. Didsbury, 88121, Pte., d., E., 5/11/18.
DALEY, J., e. Harlech, 291149, Pte., k. in a., E., 6/11/17.

DAVIES, C., b. Newtown, 290097, Pte., k. in a., E., 26/3/17.

DAVIES, C., b. Welshpool, 290120, Sgt., k. in a., E., 6/11/17.

DAVIES, D., b. Llanyblodwell, 152, A/Cpl., k. in a., G., 10/8/15.

DAVIES, D., b. Manllwyd, 290920, Pte., k. in a., E., 26/3/17.

DAVIES, D., b. Llanidloes, 291167, Pte., d. of w., E., 6/11/17.

DAVIES, D., b. Welshpool, 290297, Pte., k. in a., E., 6/11/17.

DAVIES, D. J., e. Dolgelly, 291274, Pte., d., E., 3/10/17.

DAVIES, D. M., b. Bala, 2160, Sgt., d., E., 23/7/16.

DAVIES, E. T., b. Llanfyllin, 291175, Pte., d., E., 24/10/17.

DAVIES, G., b. Dolgelly, 290537, Pte., k. in a., E., 29/3/18.

DAVIES, G. O., b. Welshpool, 290261, L/Cpl., k. in a., E., 26/3/17.

DAVIES, J. D., b. Bontddu, 290479, Pte., k. in a., E., 25/4/17.

DAVIES, L., b. Newtown, 3118, Pte., d. of w., E., 17/8/15.

DAVIES, R., b. Llanaber, 291410, Pte., k. in a., E., 27/10/17.

DAVIES, R., b. Dolgelly, 290368, Pte., k. in a., E., 26/3/17.

DAVIES, R., b. Darowen, 705, L/Cpl., d. of w., Malta, 20/12/15.

DAVIES, R., e. Blaenau Festiniog, 290592, L/Cpl., k. in a., E., 20/4/17.

DAVIES, S., b. Kerry, 290774, Pte., k. in a., E., 6/11/17.

DAVIES, T. O., b. Llangollen, 2288, Sgt., k. in a., G., 10/8/15.

DAVIES, W., b. Tidsley, 73146, Pte., k. in a., E., 6/11/17.

DAVIES, W., b. Newtown, 291119, Pte., d. of w., E., 6/11/17.

DYKES, M., b. Liverpool, 290180, Pte., k. in a., E., 26/3/17.

EASTHAM, J., b. Blackburn, 70678, Pte., k. in a., E., 6/11/17.

EDGE, R., b. Farndon, 268102, Pte., d. of w., E., 11/3/18.

EDWARDS, A., b. Birkenhead, 70604, Pte., d. of w., E., 9/11/17.

EDWARDS, E. W., b. Rhyl, 203320, Pte., k. in a., E., 6/11/17.

EDWARDS, J., b. Dolgelly, 2694, Pte., k. in a., G., 10/8/15.

EDWARDS, R., b. Dolgelly, 2739, Pte., k. in a., G., 10/8/15.

EDWARDS, W. T., b. Blaenau Festiniog, 291439, Pte., d. of w., E., 29/12/17.

ELLIS, D. R., b. Festiniog, 291534, Pte., k. in a., E., 26/3/17.

ELLIS, H. P., b. Towyn, 291501, Pte., d., E., 19/10/17.

ELLIS, W., e. Blaenau Festiniog, 291305, Pte., k. in a., E., 10/7/18.

EVANS, D. W., b. Welshpool, 291417, Pte., d. of w., E., 20/9/18.

EVANS, G., b. Llandyssil, 291083, Pte., d., E., 29/11/17.

EVANS, G., b. Llanigryn, 290588, Pte., k. in a., E., 22/2/18.

EVANS, G. H., b. Welshpool, 290252, Pte., k. in a., E., 26/3/17.

EVANS, J., b. Llanfairfechan, 3211, Pte., k. in a., G., 10/8/15.

EVANS, J. H., b. Dolgelly, 290581, Pte., k. in a., E., 26/3/17.

EVANS, J. W., b. Welshpool, 290999, Cpl., k. in a., E., 28/12/17.

EVANS, L., b. Harlech, 1002, Pte., k. in a., G., 10/8/15.

EVANS, T., b. Trawsfynydd, 291530, Pte., k. in a., E., 26/3/17.

EVANS, T. J., b. Penybont Fawr, 3188, Pte., k. in a., G., 10/8/15.

EVANS, W., b. Talley, 290285, Cpl., k. in a., E., 26/3/17.

EVANS, W. L., b. Dolgelly, 2824, Pte., k. in a., G., 10/8/15.

FIELD, T. G., b. Chertsey, 2926, Pte., d. of w., At Sea, 16/8/15.

FLOY, J., b. Macclesfield, 291825, Pte., d., E., 13/4/18.

FOULKES, D., b. Carnarvon, 290453, L/Cpl., k. in a., E., 6/11/17.

GOSEN, G., b. Treharris, 14710, Pte., k. in a., E., 27/12/17.

GOULD, F., b. Liverpool, 290347, Pte., k. in a., E., 27/12/17.

GREEN, C. H., b. Stoke-on-Trent, 655, Pte., k. in a., G., 10/8/15.

GREENHALGH, J., b. Kearsley, 70607, Pte., k. in a., E., 6/11/17.

GRIFFITHS, J. E., b. Newmarket, 73136, Pte., k. in a., E., 6/11/17.

GRIFFITHS, R. O., e. Blaenau Festiniog, 4315, Pte., d., E., 4/9/16.

GRIFFITHS, T., b. Broseley, 290662, Pte., k. in a., E., 26/3/17.

GRIFFITHS, W., e. Blaenau Festiniog, 290635, Pte., k. in a., E., 6/11/17.

GWYNNE, H. H., b. Newtown, 291116, Pte., k. in a., E., 26/3/17.

HACKING, J., b. Darwen, 70610, L/Cpl., k. in a., E., 6/11/17.

HATTON, J., b. Kerridge, 291832, Pte., k. in a., E., 6/11/17.

HIGGINS, G., b. Leighton, 1033, L/Cpl., d., Malta, 15/11/15.

HIRONS, L. E., b. Shrewsbury, 3643, Pte., k. in a., G., 10/8/15.

HIRST, S., b. Mossley, 70609, Pte., k. in a., E., 6/11/17.

HODGE, T. E., b. Brecon, 290955, Pte., k. in a., E., 26/3/17.

HOLLOWAY, J., b. Welshpool, 3516, Pte., d. of w., Malta, 24/8/15.

HOPKINS, H., b. Framfield, 290293, Sgt., k. in a., E., 26/3/17.

HUGHES, E., b. Liverpool, 73092, Pte., k. in a., E., 6/11/17.

HUGHES, E., b. Pwllheli, 291405, Pte., k. in a., E., 26/3/17.

HUGHES, E. E., b. Llwyngwril, 3410, Pte., k. in a., G., 10/8/15.

HUGHES, J. E., b. Llangollen, 70608, Pte., k. in a., E., 27/12/17.

HUGHES, J. P., b. Blaenau Festiniog, 2517, L/Cpl., k. in a., G., 10/8/15.

HUGHES, T., b. Festiniog, 290401, Pte., d. of w., E., 28/10/17.

HUGHES, T. O., b. Blaenau Festiniog, 291545, L/Cpl., k. in a., E., 28/12/17.

HUGHES, W., b. Llanbrynmair, 291246, Pte., k. in a., E., 26/3/17.

HUMPHREYS, F. C., b. Cardiff, 291696, Pte., k. in a., E., 6/11/17.

JAMES, A. L., b. Llanfaircaerinion, 1194, Pte., k. in a., G., 10/8/15.

JARVIS, S. R., b. Welshpool, 290291, Pte., k. in a., E., 26/3/17.

JENKINS, L. H., b. Aberystwyth, 290235, Pte., k. in a., E., 26/3/17.

JENKINS, T. L., b. Newtown, 995, Pte., k. in a., G., 10/8/15.

JOHNSON, J., b. Whitegate, 70657, Pte., k. in a., E., 6/11/17.

JONES, A., b. Newtown, 290728, Pte., k. in a., E., 26/3/17.

JONES, D., b. Llandinam, 290289, Sgt., k. in a., E., 6/11/17.

JONES, E., b. Blaenau Festiniog, 4325, Pte., d., E., 5/8/16.

JONES, E., b. Glynawern, 993, Pte., d., Home, 16/2/15.

JONES, E. G., e. Blaenau Festiniog, 201313, Pte., k. in a., E., 6/11/17.

JONES, E. L., b. Towyn, 2034, C.Q.M.S., d. of w., At Sea, 11/8/15.

JONES, E. T., b. Cefnfair, 291390, Pte., k. in a., E., 26/3/17.

JONES, E. W., b. Berriew, 1041, Pte., d., E., 26/4/16.

JONES, F. J., b. Liverpool, 292833, Pte., d. of w., E., 5/1/18.

JONES, G., b. Dolgelly, 2620, L/Sgt., k. in a., G., 10/8/15.

JONES, G., b. Towyn, 2525, Pte., k. in a., G., 10/8/15.

JONES, G. E., b. Penrhyndeudraeth, 2913, Pte., k. in a., G., 10/8/15.

JONES, H., b. Dolgelly, 2742, Pte., k. in a., G., 10/8/15.

JONES, H., b. Festiniog, 290514, Pte., d., E., 19/9/17.

JONES, H., b. Holyhead, 290532, Sgt., k. in a., E., 26/3/17.

JONES, I., b. Bala, 2630, L/Cpl., d., Malta, 3/1/16.

JONES, J. b., Guilsfield, 290855, A/Cpl., d. of w., E., 11/11/17.

JONES, J., b. Llangclynin, 2566, Cpl., d. of w., At Sea, 12/8/15.

JONES, J., b. Llanfair Waterdine, 201289, Pte., k. in a., E., 6/11/17.

JONES, J. C., e. Welshpool, 291291, Pte., k. in a., E., 26/3/17.

JONES, J. F., b. Llanidloes, 290081, Pte., k. in a., E., 26/3/17.

JONES, J. O., b. Llanfrothen, 291467, Pte., k. in a., E., 26/3/17.

JONES, J. P., b. Pwllheli, 290651, L/Sgt., d. of w., E., 30/10/17.

JONES, J. P., b. Llangollen, 2200, L/Cpl., k. in a., G., 10/8/15.

JONES, J. R., b. Llanidloes, 290177, L/Cpl., k. in a., E., 6/11/17.

JONES, J. R., b. Machynlleth, 290255, Pte., k. in a., E., 26/3/17.

JONES, J. T., b. Llwyngwril, 290907, Pte., d., Home, 28/10/18.

JONES, J. T., b. Llandyssil, 290349, Pte., d. of w., E., 8/11/17.

JONES, L. H., b. Bemnia, 291432, Pte., k. in a., E., 26/3/17.

JONES, R. B., b. Festiniog, 290371, C.S.M., k. in a., E., 6/11/17.

JONES, R. H., b. Blaenau Festiniog, 2509, Sgt., k. in a., G., 8/12/15.

JONES, R. L., b. Llanerfyl, 291797, Pte., k. in a., E., 28/12/17.

JONES, T., b. Llanidloes, 291193, Pte., k. in a., E., 26/3/17.

JONES, T., b. Llanidloes, 292714, Pte., d. of w., E., 10/11/17.

JONES, T. H., b. Llanidloes, 290939, Pte., k. in a., E., 26/3/17.

JONES, T. P., b. Arddleen, 1186, Pte., d., Home, 12/11/14.

JONES, W., b. Llanfihangel, 2606, Pte., k. in a., G., 10/8/15.

JONES, W., b. Llaniestyn, 242614, Pte., d., E., 28/9/18.

JONES, W., e. Blaenau Festiniog, 291199, Pte., k. in a., E., 26/3/17.

JONES, W. R., b. Caersws, 290193, L/Cpl., k. in a., E., 26/3/17.

JORDAN, A. E., b. Newtown, 1088, L/Cpl., k. in a., G., 10/8/15.

LANGRICK, W. T., b. Ingoldsby, 290302, Pte., k. in a., E., 11/10/17.

LEWIS, I. M., b. Llanenwyn, 291109, Cpl., k. in a., E., 26/3/17.

LEWIS, R., b. Newtown, 290096, Pte., k. in a., E., 26/3/17.

LEWIS, R., b. Gwyddelwern, 2564, Pte., k. in a., G., 8/11/15.

LEWIS, W. J., b. Dolgelly, 291018, Pte., k. in a., E., 6/11/17.

LLOYD, A., e. Blaenau Festiniog, 291479, Pte., k. in a., E., 26/3/17.

LLOYD, E., b. Harlech, 291538, Pte., k. in a., E., 26/3/17.

LLOYD, G. E., b. Penrhyndeudraeth, 290626, Pte., k. in a., E., 26/3/17.

LLOYD, J., b. Montgomery, 290314, L/Cpl., k. in a., E., 6/11/17.

LLOYD, J. E., b. Festiniog, 290471, L/Cpl., k. in a., E., 26/3/17.

LLOYD, T., b. Llandinam, 290817, Pte., d. of w., E., 28/10/17.

LLOYD, W., e. Welshpool, 291605, Pte., k. in a., E., 26/3/17.

LLOYD, W. T., b. Llangedwyn, 290866, Pte., k. in a., E., 26/3/17.

LONGMAN, E. E., b. Kerry, 290274, Pte., k. in a., E., 26/3/17.

MANGNALL, S., b. West Houghton, 70717, Pte., k. in a., E., 6/11/17.

MASSEY, G. H., b. Wilmslow, 291886, Pte., k. in a., E., 26/3/17.

MILLER, J., b. Stalybridge, 291712, Pte., k. in a., E., 26/3/17.

MILLS, G. M., b. Llanmerewig, 290991, Pte., k. in a., E., 26/3/17.

MILLS, J. B., b. Llanidloes, 2907, Pte., d. of w., At Sea, 11/8/15.

MILLS, W., b. Newtown, 816, Pte., d. of w., G., 16/8/15.

MOORHOUSE, R. J., b. Llanymynech, 1043, Pte., k. in a., G., 10/8/15.

MORGAN, R., b. Llanymawddwy, 290276, Pte., k. in a., E., 26/3/17.

MORRIS, C., b. Kerry, 3249, Pte., k. in a., G., 10/8/15.

MORRIS, F., b. Llanaber, 2917, Pte., k. in a., G., 10/8/15.

MORRIS, F., b. Towyn, 2513, Pte., d. of w., At Sea, 11/12/15.

MORRIS, J., b. Welshpool, 290998, Pte., k. in a., E., 26/3/17.

MORRIS, J., b. Dolgelly, 291272, Pte., k. in a., E., 26/3/17.

MORRIS, R., b. Festiniog, 2485, Pte., k. in a., G., 13/8/15.

MOSS, S., b. Stockport, 291863, Pte., k. in a., E., 26/3/17.

MUMFORD, G. H., b. Newtown, 290312, Sgt., k. in a., E., 26/3/17.

MURRAY, J., b. Liverpool, 70684, Pte., d., E., 26/10/18.

MYERS, J. T., b. Birkenhead, 70620, Pte., k. in a., E., 6/11/17.

OLDFIELD, G., b. Rainow, 291846, Pte., k. in a., E., 10/3/18.

OLIVER, C. K., b. Llanllwchalarn, 291230, Pte., d., E., 14/7/17.

OWEN, A., b. Llanfihangel, 290464, Pte., k. in a., E., 6/11/17.

OWEN, E., b. Machynlleth, 39, Sgt., k. in a., G., 10/8/15.

OWEN, E., b. Harlech, 2791, L/Sgt., k. in a., G., 10/8/15.

OWEN, E., e. Blaenau Festiniog, 290637, Pte., k. in a., E., 26/3/17.

OWEN, E. L., b. Llanidloes, 291168, Pte., k. in a., E., 6/11/17.

OWEN, R., b. Llanymynech. 290108, Cpl., k. in a., E., 26/3/17.

OWEN, S., b. Newtown, 3248, Pte., d., E., 28/11/15.

OWEN, T., b. Festiniog, 290428, Sgt., k. in a., E., 26/3/17.

OWEN, T. E., b. Machynlleth, 290052, L/Sgt., d., E., 28/11/16.

OWEN, T. E., b. Forden, 290292, Cpl., d., E., 3/4/17.

OWEN, T. W., b. Newtown, 811, Pte., k. in a., G., 10/8/15.

OWEN, W. R., b. Dyffryn, 291073, Pte., k. in a., E., 6/11/17.

PARRY, H. O., e. Blaenau Festiniog, 290638, Pte., k. in a., E., 26/3/17.

PARRY, S., b. Wrexham, 290112, Pte., d., E., 25/8/17.

PATTISON, J., b. Tallyllyn, 1025, Pte., d. of w., G., 10/8/15.

PEARCE, A. E., b. Machynlleth, 2471, Sgt., k. in a., G., 10/8/15.

PEARCE, R., b. Montgomery, 290941, Pte., k. in a., E., 26/3/17.

PEARSON, S., b. Marston, 291686, Pte., k. in a., E., 26/3/17.

PETTIT, C., b. Calton, 291252, Pte., k. in a., E., 6/11/17.

PEYTON, T., b. St. Helen's, 13879, Pte., k. in a., E., 6/11/17.

PHILLIPS, P., b. Corwen, 290435, Pte., k. in a., E., 26/3/17.

PHILPOTT, S., b. Montgomery, 290280, Pte., k. in a., E., 6/11/17.

PIERCE, J., b. Oswestry, 290908, Pte., k. in a., E., 6/11/17.

POPPLE, W., b. Welshpool, 290210, Pte., k. in a., E., 26/3/17.

POWELL, J., b. Wrexham, 290254, Sgt., k. in a., E., 26/3/17.

POWELL, R., e. Blaenau Festiniog, 291354, Pte., d. of w., E., 28/3/17.

POWELL, T. W., b. Wem, 291717, Pte., k. in a., E., 26/3/17.

POWNALL, C., b. Macclesfield, 70626, Pte., k. in a., E., 6/11/17.

PRICE, E., b. Clun, 290899, L/Cpl., k. in a., E., 26/3/17.

PRICE, W. J., b. Cwmpark, 740, L/Cpl., d., G., 7/9/15.
PRICE, W. R., b. Kerry, 290831, Pte., k. in a., E., 26/3/17.
PRIESTLEY, J., e. Blackpool, 292844, Pte., k. in a., E., 6/11/17.
PRITCHARD, J., b. Llanfaelog, 291376, Pte., k. in a., E., 6/11/17.
PRITCHARD, T. E., b. Llanmerewig, 3507, Pte., d. of w., G., 29/11/15.
PRITCHARD, W., b. Newtown, 290827, L/Cpl., k. in a., E., 6/11/17.
PROCTOR, A. W., b. Llanidloes, 1131, Pte., k. in a., G., 10/8/15.
PRYCE, T. O., b. Newtown, 1048, L/Cpl., d., At Sea, 17/8/15.
PRYSE, J., b. Trefeglwys, 291321, Pte., k. in a., E., 26/3/17.
PUGH, H., b. Bithdir, 291412, Pte., k. in a., E., 26/3/17.
PUGH, J., b. Trefeglwys, 291285, Pte., k. in a., E., 26/3/17.
PUGH, J. A., b. Llanymynech, 3024, Pte., d., G., 6/10/15.
PUGH, P., b. Llanyblodwell, 290877, Pte., k. in a., E., 26/3/17.
REES, D., b. Corwen, 290395, Sgt., k. in a., E., 26/3/17.
RICHARDS, D., b. Llawrgilyn, 291281, Pte., k. in a., E., 6/11/17.
RICHARDS, E. L., b. Llanegryn, 2042, L/Cpl., k. in a., G., 13/8/15.
RICHARDS, J., b. Dyffryn, 2785, Pte. k. in a., G., 10/8/15.
ROBERTS, D., b. Rhosddu, 2600, Pte., k. in a., G., 10/8/15.
ROBERTS, D., b. Dinas Mawddwy, 291701, Pte., d. of w., E., 22/6/17.
ROBERTS, E., b. Amlwch, 203705, Pte., k. in a., F., 20/9/17.
ROBERTS, J. T., b. Blaenau Festiniog, 2500, L/Cpl., k. in a., G., 10/8/15.
ROBERTS, L. W., b. Machynlleth, 290266, Sgt., k. in a., E., 26/3/17.
ROBERTS, R., b. Carnarvon, 204476, Pte., k. in a., E., 10/3/18.
ROBERTS, R., e. Blaenau Festiniog, 291171, Pte., d. of w., E., 1/4/17.
ROBERTS, R. F., b. Festiniog, 290473, Pte., d., E., 25/11/17.
ROBERTS, R. H., b. Penrhos, 3005, Pte., k. in a., G., 10/8/15.
ROBERTS, T., e. Dolgelly, 2850, Pte., k. in a., G., 10/8/15.
ROBERTS, T., e. Welshpool, 291289, Pte., k. in a., E., 6/11/17.
ROBERTS, T., b. Amlwch, 291382, Pte., k. in a., E., 26/3/17.
ROBERTS, T. E., b. Rhosddu,

2602, L/Cpl., k. in a., G., 8/12/15.
ROBERTS, W., b. Llanuwchllyn, 290888, Pte., k. in a., E., 6/11/17.
ROBERTS, W. J., b. Llanfaelog, 291380, Pte., k. in a., E., 26/3/17.
ROGERS, F., b. Llanidloes, 105, C.S.M., k. in a., G., 10/8/15.
ROWLANDS, D., b. Penrhyndeudraeth, 290558, Pte., d. of w., E., 9/11/17.
ROWLANDS, J., e. Cleckheaton, 3462, L/Cpl., d., G., 6/9/15.
ROWLEY, A., b. London, 5886, C.S.M., d. of w., G., 8/8/15.
SAPPLE, D. C., b. Newtown, 1140, Pte., k. in a., G., 10/8/15.
SMITH, A. C., b. Jarvis Brook, 293174, Pte., d., E., 3/11/18.
SMITH, S. S. C., b. Southampton, 291894, Pte., k. in a., E., 26/3/17.
SMITH, W. C., b. Berriew, 291254, Pte., k. in a., E., 26/3/17.
STONES, F., b. Darwen, 292854, Pte., k. in a., E., 27/12/17.
STRONGMAN, A. J., b. Market Harborough, 290629, A/Sgt., d. of w., E.A., 2/8/17.
SYKES, F., b. Almondbury, 3457, Pte., k. in a., G., 1/12/15.
TAYLOR, W., b. Stockport, 291897, Pte., k. in a., E., 28/12/17.
THICKENS, J., b. Llandinam, 290795, L/Sgt., k. in a., E., 26/3/17.
THIRLWALL, S., b. Wilmslow, 70647, Pte., k. in a., E., 6/11/17.
THOMAS, J. R., b. Llanerfyl, 291241, Pte., k. in a., E., 6/11/17.
THOMAS, J. W., b. Festiniog, 290390, Pte., k. in a., E., 26/3/17.
TINCKLER, F., b. Liverpool, 70637, Pte., k. in a., E., 6/11/17.
TISDALE, T., b. Warrington, 291898, Pte., d. of w., E., 31/12/17.
TISDALE, W. E., b. Penrhos, 3275, Pte., d., G., 12/11/15.
TUDOR, W., b. Penegoes, 291251, Pte., k. in a., E., 26/3/17.
TURNER, E. J., b. Pwllheli, 203323, Pte., d. of w., E., 12/11/17.
VAUGHAN, E. L., b. Church Stoke, 290327, Pte., k. in a., E., 6/11/17.
WALMSLEY, T. A., b. Walton-le-Dale, 70701, Pte., k. in a., E., 22/2/18.
WATKIN, G. L., b. Llanfaircaerinion, 290282, A/Sgt., k. in a., E., 6/11/17.
WATKINS, C., b. Llanwron, 290864, Pte., k. in a., E., 6/11/17.
WATKINS, J., b. Coston, 290755, Pte., k. in a., E., 26/3/17.

WILCOX, R. N., b. Church Bank, 291518, Pte., k. in a., E., 26/3/17.
WILDING, D., e. Welshpool, 291288, Pte., k. in a., E., 26/3/17.
WILKINSON, W., b. Welshpool, 290863, Pte., d. of w., E., 17/5/17.
WILLIAMS, B., b. Welshpool, 782, Pte., k. in a., G., 10/8/15.
WILLIAMS, D., b. Festiniog, 2612, Pte., k. in a., G., 10/8/15.
WILLIAMS, D., b. Llangollen, 290478, Cpl., d. of w., E., 29/12/17.
WILLIAMS, E., e. Blaenau Festiniog, 291240, Pte., k. in a., E., 26/3/17.
WILLIAMS, E., b. Newtown, 1161, Pte., k. in a., G., 10/8/15.
WILLIAMS, E., e. Blaenau Festiniog, 291133, Pte., k. in a., E., 6/11/17.
WILLIAMS, E. R., b. Tallyllyn, 291464, Pte., d. of w., E., 11/11/17.
WILLIAMS, G., b. Llandinam, 291057, Pte., k. in a., E., 26/3/17.
WILLIAMS, H., b. Montgomery, 291010, Pte., k. in a., E., 26/3/17.
WILLIAMS, J., b. St. Asaph, 290300, Pte., k. in a., E., 26/3/17.
WILLIAMS, J., b. Port Dinorwic, 291375, Pte., k. in a., E., 29/12/17.
WILLIAMS, J., b. Moelfre, 291857, Pte., d., E., 26/8/17.
WILLIAMS, J., b. Trecastle, 292712, Pte., k. in a., E., 6/11/17.
WILLIAMS, J. E., b. Newtown, 820, Pte., k. in a., G., 10/8/15.
WILLIAMS, J. P., b. Welshpool, 895, Pte., k. in a., G., 10/8/15.
WILLIAMS, L. E., e. Penrhyndeudraeth, 291338, Pte., d. of w., E., 22/11/17.
WILLIAMS, L. J., b. Bangor, 14974, Pte., d., E., 25/10/18.
WILLIAMS, M. R., b. Knockin, 1158, Pte., k. in a., G., 10/8/15.
WILLIAMS, M. R., b. Dolgelly, 291911, Pte., d., At Sea, 15/4/17.
WILLIAMS, O., b. Llansantffraid, 760, Pte., k. in a., G., 10/8/15.
WILLIAMS, R., b. Corwen, 2727, Pte., d., G., 14/10/15.
WILLIAMS, R., b. Towyn, 290539, Sgt., k. in a., E., 26/3/17.
WILLIAMS, R., e. Towyn, 291270, Pte., d. of w., E., 29/12/17.
WILLIAMS, R. E., e. Blaenau Festiniog, 291192, Pte., k. in a., E., 26/3/17.
WILLIAMS, T. J., b. Penrhyn, 290431, L/Cpl., k. in a., E., 6/11/17.

WILLIAMS, W., b. Blaenau Fes-
  tiniog, 2591, Pte., d., G.,
  29/11/15.
WILLIAMS, W. F., b. Berriew,
  3710, Pte., k. in a., G.,
  10/8/15.
WILLIAMS, W. J., b. Llanbedr,
  290560, A/L/Sgt., k. in a., E.,
  6/11/17.
WILSON, R. H., b. Warton,
  315177, Pte., d., E., 10/11/18.
WOOD, H., b. Tottington, 59309,
  Pte., d., E., 27/10/18.
WOOD, H. E., b. Wibsey, 291082,
  Pte., k. in a., E., 26/3/17.
WOODS, J., b. Llandyssil, 291207,
  Pte., k. in a., E., 26/3/17.
WRIGHT, J. J., b. Blackpool,
  70639, Pte., k. in a., E.,
  6/11/17.
WRIGHT, W., b. Congleton,
  291860, Pte., k. in a., E.,
  4/11/17.

2/7th BATTALION

EDWARDS, E. W., b. Blaenau Fes-
  tiniog, 290521, d., Home,
  23/1/17.
EVERALL, J. E., b. Lydbury, 3470,
  Pte., d., Home, 20/2/15.
HEROD, H., e. Bury, 4600, Pte.,
  d., Home, 11/5/16.
JONES, W. H., e. Carnarvon, 1815,
  L/Cpl., d., Home, 20/3/16.
REYNOLDS, H., b. Newtown, 822,
  Pte., d., Home, 22/4/15.

3/7th BATTALION

DAVIES, G., b. Llandinam, 63,
  Pte., d., Home, 5/7/16.

EDWARDS, E., b. Llangar, 4237,
  Pte., d., Home, 3/3/16.
EVANS, J. R., e. Machynlleth,
  291699, Pte., d., Home,
  14/1/17.
EYNON, L. T., b. Towyn, 2214,
  Pte., d., Home, 14/3/16.
GRIFFITHS, J., e. Blaenau Fes-
  tiniog, 3900, Pte., d., Home,
  27/2/16.
JOHN, T. I., b. Morriston, 4713,
  Pte., d., Home, 9/8/16.
JONES, G. H., b. Blaenau Fes-
  tiniog, 2637, Pte., d., Home,
  25/4/16.
LEWIS, P., b. Machynlleth, 4352,
  Pte., d., Home, 3/5/16.
LLOYD, W., b. Llanfair, 4343,
  Pte., d., Home, 28/3/16.
THOMAS, A., e. Machynlleth,
  4382, Pte., d., Home, 15/9/16.
WILLIAM, F., b. Abergwynolwyn,
  2814, Pte., d., Home, 7/6/16.

1/1st WELSH HORSE, YEOMANRY

BRIDGMAN, A. J., b. Stroud, 42,
  Pte., d., Home, 12/6/16.
CANNING, W. F., b. Portsmouth,
  205, Pte., d., Home, 19/12/16.
CLAY, H., b. Liverpool, 48, Cpl.,
  d. of w., At Sea, 21/12/15.
DAVIES, P., b. Llanelly, 182, Pte.,
  k. in a., G., 20/11/15.
EVANS, L., b. Newcastle Emlyn,
  136, L/Cpl., k. in a., G.,
  20/11/15.
EVERINGHAM, R., b. Tynemouth,

1098, Pte., k. in a., G.,
  10/12/15.
HENRY, J., b. Swansea, 306, Pte.,
  k. in a., G., 1/12/15.
HUMPHREYS, E. J., b. Griffiths-
  town, 18, Pte., k. in a., G.,
  20/11/15.
JONES, A. G., b. Leominster, 246,
  Pte., k. in a., G., 20/11/15.
JONES, L., b. Llangeler, 540, Pte.,
  k. in a., G., 20/11/15.
JONES, W., b. Llandyssul, 565,
  Pte., d., E., 14/11/15.
KENNAUGH, F., b. I.O.M., 346,
  F.Q.M.S., d., G., 30/10/15.
LEWIS, W. C., b. St. Peter's, 137,
  Pte., k. in a., G., 20/11/15.
LOVEGROVE, A., b. Crookham, 79,
  Pte., k. in a., G., 20/11/15.
McCRAE, R. D., e. Cardiff, 679,
  Pte., d. of w., At Sea,
  21/10/15.
MORRIS, T., b. Hirnant, 1200,
  Pte., d., E., 14/4/16.
MORRIS, T. H., b. Aberdare, 233,
  Pte., k. in a., G., 13/12/15.
MUCKART, D., b. St. Vigean's,
  190, Pte., d., E., 14/11/15.
REES, R., b. New Quay, 322, Pte.,
  k. in a., G., 20/11/15.

2/1st WELSH HORSE, YEOMANRY

OWEN, E. J., e. Newtown, 655,
  R.S.M., d., Home, 12/4/15.
REES, W., b. Porth, 640, Pte.,
  d., Home, 16/1/16.
WYCHERLEY, J. E., e. Newtown,
  1533, Pte., d., Home, 19/4/16.

APPENDIX IX

REGIMENTAL GOATS

MOST battalions seem to have been presented with or acquired a goat during the War. The 1st Battalion took its goat to Flanders, but it was sent home immediately and arrived at Wrexham on the 22nd October 1914. The 3rd Battalion presented a white goat to the 2nd Battalion which arrived in France on the 22nd February 1917; this was the animal they had such difficulty in bringing back with them.

With the exception of this white goat there is no record of a battalion having one permanently in France or Flanders, or any other theatre of war. Fitful mention is made of goats which apparently disappeared quickly.

APPENDIX X

THE FLASH

PERMISSION to wear the flash in Service dress, all ranks, was given on the 13th May 1915. Size, 5 inches. (See Vol. II, Appendix IX.)

APPENDIX XI
BADGES

DISTINGUISHING badges were worn by certain battalions.

10th Battalion. Battalion Headquarters wore purple shoulder-straps ; A Company, blue ; B Company, yellow ; C and D Companies, green.

The 13th, 14th, 15th, and 16th Battalions wore the collar badge in place of the cap badge.

Other distinguishing badges in the 38th Division Battalions were : 13th Battalion a red flannel triangle half-way between shoulder and elbow, 14th Battalion a blue, 15th Battalion a yellow, 16th Battalion a green, 17th Battalion a salmon-pink square.

The officers of the 19th Battalion wore two strips of ribbon on the sleeve, the upper red, the lower blue.

APPENDIX XII
THE WAR MEMORIAL

THE unveiling and the dedication of the War Memorial of the Royal Welch Fusiliers took place on Saturday, 15th November 1924, at Wrexham, the depot of the regiment.

The Memorial perpetuates the sacrifices made by nearly 10,000 officers and men of the 42 battalions of the R.W.F. who fell in the Great War. It was unveiled by Lieutenant-General Sir Francis Lloyd, G.C.V.O., K.C.B., D.S.O., the Colonel of the Regiment, and the dedication ceremony was conducted by the Archbishop of Wales.

Before the ceremony the troops paraded at the Barracks, and with the ex-Service men marched to the Guildhall, where they were joined by the Mayor of Wrexham (Mr. C. E. Hickman), the Corporation, and officials. The procession then moved off in the following order :

Band and Drums 2nd Battalion, R.W.F., under Mr. Clancy.
Major H. V. Venables Kyrke, D.S.O., Officer commanding the Depot.
Detachment 7th Battalion, R.W.F.
Detachment 6th Battalion, R.W.F.
Guard of Honour, Depot R.W.F., in command of Lieutenant W. P. Kenyon, M.C.
The Colours of the 2nd Battalion, R.W.F., Lieutenant R. W. C. Martin in charge of
    the Regimental Colour.
Firing Party, Composite Battalions R.W.F., T.A.
Detachment 5th Battalion, R.W.F.
Detachment 4th Battalion, R.W.F.
Old Comrades, R.W.F.
Mayors of Boroughs of North Wales.
Mayor and Corporation of Wrexham.

On arrival at the site they took up their allotted positions and were joined by the Lord Kenyon, Lord-Lieutenant of Denbighshire, Sir W. W. Wynn, Bart., C.B., Lord-Lieutenant of Montgomeryshire, the Hon. H. N. Gladstone, Lord-Lieutenant of Flintshire, Viscount Southwell, the Rev. Mgr. Canon G. Nightingale, V.G., Sir E. Pryce Jones, Bart, etc., then followed the clergy, viz. the Vicar of Wrexham (Canon Lewis Pryce), the Rev. T. Owen Jones (representing the Evangelical Church Council), and the Archbishop of Wales (Dr. Edwards).

Immediately afterwards Lieutenant-General Sir Francis Lloyd, G.C.V.O., K.C.B., D.S.O., Colonel of the Royal Welch Fusiliers, arrived attended by his staff officer, Captain J. G. Bruxner-Randall, and 3 A.D.C.s, Lieutenant H. C. Stockwell, 2nd Battalion, Lieutenant S. Farthing, 6th Battalion, and Captain Fitzsimmons, 25th Service Battalion.

The following C.O.s were also present : Colonel C. I. Stockwell, C.B., C.M.G., D.S.O., 2nd Battalion, Lieutenant-Colonel G. C. W. Westbrooke, 4th (Denbighshire) Battalion T.A., Major H. M. Davies, 5th (Flintshire) Battalion T.A., Major G. R. D. Harrison, 7th (Montgomeryshire) Battalion T.A.

The Territorial detachments were under the charge of Captain A. Wynne, 4th Battalion, Captain J. Mostyn, M.C., 5th Battalion, and Captain A. M. Trustram Eve, M.C., 6th Battalion.

Amongst the officers present were Lieutenant-General Sir C. Dobell, Brigadier-General R. A. Berners, Brigadier-General O. de L. Williams, Brigadier-General Minshull-Ford, Colonel the Lord Mostyn, Lieutenant-Colonel Judge Ivor Bowen, K.C., Lieutenant-Colonel J. B. Cockburn, Colonel T. A. Wynne Edwards, Lieutenant-Colonel Alan Gough, Colonel Gwyther, Lieutenant-Colonel the Viscount Hill, Colonel T. E. F. Lloyd, Lieutenant-Colonel C. C. Norman, Colonel R. Williamson, Lieutenant-Colonel Jones-Williams, Lieutenant-Colonel Walwyn, Lieutenant-Colonel Peters, Lieutenant-Colonel J. E. H. Davies, Colonel Luther, Major G. J. P. Geiger, Major E. R. Kearsley, Major Sir Horace McMahon, Bart., Major H. M. Richards, Major E. O. Skaife, Major Venables, D.S.O., Major Harvey Lloyd, Major W. Norman Withers, Major Marston, Major Paris, Major Hugh Peel, and many others.

On arrival Sir Francis Lloyd was received with a General Salute, after which he inspected the Guard of Honour.

The proceedings opened by the singing of the hymn, " O God, our help in ages past." Prayers were then read by the Vicar of Wrexham, the lesson was read by the Rev. T. Owen Jones, and the hymn, " O Fryniau Caersalem," sung. At the close of the singing the troops presented arms, and Sir Francis Lloyd then unveiled the Memorial with the following words : " In the name of the Ever-blessed, Glorious, and Undivided Trinity, and in memory of the gallant men of the Royal Welch who gave their lives for King and Country, I unveil this Memorial."

The Union Jack which covered the Memorial then fell and everyone saluted. The Archbishop read the short dedicatory prayer, and the firing party fired three volleys. This was followed by the buglers sounding the Last Post and then the Réveillé.

Sir Francis Lloyd, addressing the troops, said that that day their great historic regiment celebrated perhaps the greatest epoch in the history of the world, certainly the greatest page in its own history, the page covering the years 1914 to 1918. Forty-two battalions, 77 battle honours, and between 9,000 and 10,000 dead on the various battle-areas of the World War were what they commemorated that day. That was what had been beautifully depicted in their Memorial by the greatest sculptor of Wales and its foremost artist.

This sculpture carried the mind back to the great epoch of the regiment in the eighteenth century, through the figure of an early Fusilier holding the flag, the emblem of loyalty, over the men who gave everything so willingly and so lovingly in the Great War.

It had always been the same. When the regiment assaulted the Fort of Namur, it was given the place of honour to keep the gate. When the Fusiliers stormed the trenches at Dettingen, it was with like gallantry ; and it was in the same good heart that the Fusilier Brigade, of which it formed an integral part, marched through the rose-garden at Minden, under the blood-draining volleys of the French troops. They followed Rowe when he marched up to the palisades at Blenheim, and forced his sword into them before he was shot dead. At Ramillies it was the same, and on the bloodstained field of Albuera the French Marshal said of them, " What are these men ? They cannot be soldiers. I have turned their right ; I have turned their left ; I have forced their centre ; but they do not budge."

At Waterloo they stood firm and fast under a merciless pounding of French cannon-balls, playing their part in the great victory. It was the same at Alma and Inkerman. It was the same in the Great War, with all its untold horror and miseries. No one did better than gallant Wales, who sent the flower of her race from the ancient cradle of the Cymry. The Welch Fusiliers upheld in every possible manner the traditions of the British race and British armies.

The first note struck by the monument, Sir Francis went on to say, was one of sadness, for with all the horrors of battle and all the joy of victory they could not forget those who gave their all, nor the women of Britain who inspired those men to the work they did. Their sympathy and sorrow went out to such a noble race of women as the nation possessed. And joy, too, with the men, who, like a great river in flood, had gone forth to battle, straight of limb, true of eye, steady and aglow. They were staunch to the end against uncounted odds. They fell with their faces towards the foe. Those men had gone " over the top " into the tornado of shot and shell and horror, as though they were going to a feast, and in the torrent of battle and death could there be a prouder moment in life than to know, as the sands of life died out, that the sacrifice was being made for King and Country, for Humanity and for Christianity !

It was the pride of Wrexham, and the pride of Wales, that they had one of the finest memorials there to remind them that that was not all. They had got to live for what those men had died for. He knew that many would say, " Oh, but I am only a poor unit, what can I do ? What effect will it have if I do handle my arms well ? " Every soldier knew the great effect that the individual men who tried to do their best had on the whole. What had made the regiment was the great endeavour of each individual in it. It was what made the regiment great in the past, what made it great to-day, and what would make it great in the future. That was the message of their Memorial.

Sir Francis Lloyd closed his speech by formally handing over the Memorial to the Mayor and Corporation of Wrexham.

During the singing of the hymn, " O valiant hearts, who to your glory came," wreaths were laid at the foot of the statue.   The first was laid by Sir Francis Lloyd, then followed tributes from all sections of the regiment, and private individuals.

The band of the 2nd Battalion had come from Pembroke Dock to take part, and their rendering of Chopin's " Marche Funèbre," given while wreath after wreath was laid on the base of the Memorial, provided one of the most touching incidents of the ceremony.

The pronouncement of the Benediction by the Archbishop, the sounding of the Réveillé, and the singing of " Hen wlad Fy Nhadau " and the National Anthem brought to a close this most memorable ceremony.

In the evening the " Old Comrades " held their reunion dinner in the Barracks, Lieutenant-General Sir Francis Lloyd presiding.   A telegram was dispatched to H.M. the King and a cable of greeting was sent to the 1st Battalion in India.

The Memorial consists of a fine group in bronze by the distinguished Welsh sculptor, Sir William Goscombe John, R.A.   It represents two Fusiliers, one in the uniform of the regiment of the Marlborough period holding the Colours over the other, a Fusilier of the " Great War " period, who carries his rifle, bayonet, " tin hat," and gas mask.

The group stands on a stone pedestal which bears the inscription : " To the immortal memory of the Royal Welch Fusiliers, 1914–1918. Duw Cadw'r Brenin."   The total height of the monument is about 20 feet, the bronze group being about 10 feet. The site, which was given by the Borough of Wrexham, is at the corner of Grosvenor Road and Regent Street.

APPENDIX XIII

COMMANDING OFFICERS

1st Battalion

H. O. S. Cadogan .	to 30 Oct.	1914
R. E. P. Gabbett .	. Feb.	1915
J. R. Minshull-Ford	. 24 March	1915
G. E. F. Dickson .	. 15 April	1915
R. E. P. Gabbett .	. 17 May	1915
R. A. Berners	. 30 Sept.	1915
J. R. Minshull-Ford	. 3 Feb.	1916
C. I. Stockwell	. 16 Sept.	1916
W. G. Holmes	. . Oct.	1918
L. A. Alston.	. .	

2nd Battalion

H. Delmé-Radcliffe	.	
O. de L. Williams	. to 7 June	1916
C. H. R. Crawshay	. 25 Jan.	1917
W. B. Garnett	. . 6 May	1918

IV—26

G. E. de Miremont	. July	1918
J. B. Cockburn	. .	

3rd Battalion

H. R. Jones Williams	to 16 March	1918
A. R. P. Macartney-Filgate		

4th Battalion

F. C. France-Hayhurst	to 9 May	1915
G. E. Pereira	. . 2 Oct.	1916
G. G. Otley .	. . 10 Nov.	1916
G. E. Pereira	. . 20 Jan.	1916
W. C. W. Hawkes	. 3 Feb.	1917
J. H. Langton	. . July	1917
W. H. Mathews	. . Jan.	1918
H. Marshall .	. . Aug.	1918
J. H. Langton	. .	

5th Battalion

B. E. Philips.	.	10 Aug.	1915
F. H. Borthwick	.	9 Oct.	1915
C. S. Rome	.	28 Jan.	1916

(Amalgamated with 6th Bn.)

F. H. Borthwick	.	23 Sept.	1916
W. Beswick	.	7 Nov.	1916
F. H. Borthwick	.	

6th Battalion

T. W. James	.	9 Oct.	1915
C. S. Rome	.	17 July	1916
F. Mills	.	10 Sept.	1916
C. S. Rome	.	5 April	1917
F. Mills	.	19 March	1918
E. H. Evans	.	

7th Battalion

A. E. J. Reveley	.	28 Dec.	1915
J. O. W. Williams	.	8 March	1916
T. H. Harker	.	26 Aug.	1916
Owen Owen	.	2 Oct.	1916
T. H. Harker	.	24 June	1917
Owen Owen	.	7 Aug.	1917
T. H. Harker	.	

8th Battalion

A. R. Hay	.	5 Feb.	1917
M. D. Gambier Parry	.	to Armistice	
E. A. Stretch	.	

9th Battalion

Sir H. W. McMahon	.	to July	1915
H. J. Madocks	.	25 Sept.	1915
C. Burrard	.	23 Dec.	1915
R. A. Berners	.	20 Nov.	1916
L. F. Smeathman	.	Sept.	1917
Lord Howard de Walden	Dec.	1917	
L. F. Smeathman	.	25 April	1918
Lloyd Williams	.	Oct.	1918
L. F. Smeathman	.	

10th Battalion

W. R. H. Beresford-Ash	to 5 Feb.	1916	
S. S. Binny	.	9 March	1916
G. R. Crosfield	.	31 March	1916

F. A. Samuel	.	6 April	1916
A. M. L. Long	.	3 April	1917
Compton Smith	.	26 Sept.	1917
A. J. S. James	.	

11th Battalion

Hon. U. de R. B. Roche	to 23 Feb.	1915	
G. W. D. B. Lloyd	.	23 March	1916
A. H. Yatman	.	

12th Battalion

G. W. Lilly	.	to 8 April	1915
H. Delmé-Radcliffe		

13th Battalion

T. A. Wynne-Edwards	to 19 Nov.	1914	
C. E. Willis	.	20 Sept.	1915
O. S. Flower	.	13 July	1915
R. O. Campbell	.	4 Nov.	1917
J. F. Leman	.	

14th Battalion

D. Davies	.	to 17 June	1916
G. H. Gwyther	.	12 July	1916
H. V. R. Hodson	.	16 June	1917
E. W. P. Uniacke	.	12 March	1918
W. P. Weldon	.	31 March	1918
B. W. Collier	.	12 July	1918
D. Brock Williams	.	2 Aug.	1918
B. W. Collier	.	11 Nov.	1918
C. C. Norman	.	

15th Battalion

W. A. L. Fox Pitt	.	to 13 Nov.	1915
J. C. Bell	.	19 Sept.	1916
C. C. Norman	.	July	1917
R. H. Montgomery	.	

16th Battalion

T. A. Wynne Edwards	to Dec.	1915	
R. C. Carden	.	10 July	1916
A. N. G. Jones	.	20 June	1917
H. F. N. Jourdain	.	6 Dec.	1917
E. J. de P. O'Kelly	.	July	1918
C. E. Davies	.	

17th Battalion

H. R. H. Lloyd Mostyn	to 15 Nov.	1915
J. A. Ballard . .	July	1916
J. B. Cockburn . .	Aug.	1917
H. J. Taylor . .	22 Feb.	1918
J. B. Cockburn . .	5 July	1918
C. C. Norman . .	Sept.	1918
R. L. Beasley . .		

18th Battalion

I. Bowen . .

19th Battalion

O. L. J. Evans .	to 12 Nov.	1915
B. J. Jones . . .	14 Sept.	1917
J. F. Plunkett . .		

20th Battalion

C. E. Wynne-Eyton	to 20 April	1916
R. M. C. Glynn . .		

21st Battalion

T. A. Wynne-Edwards .

22nd Battalion

O. L. J. Evans . .

23rd Battalion

G. R. Tod . . .

24th Battalion

H. N. H. Clegg . .

25th Battalion

Lord Kensington .	to Aug.	1918
J. G. Rees . .		

26th Battalion (also 4th Garrison Bn.)

G. W. Priestley .	to 6 June	1916
E. H. Thurston .	23 July	1918
H. H. Lee . . .		

1st Garrison Battalion

A. J. Arnold . .

2nd Garrison Battalion

W. H. Hussey-Walsh	to 7 Nov.	1918
W. R. Howell . .		

3rd Garrison Battalion

E. H. Thurston .	to 6 June	1916
G. W. Priestley . .	1 June	1917
C. E. Willis . .		

5th Garrison Battalion

J. F. Wolseley . .

6th Garrison Battalion

E. C. M. Lushington .

7th Garrison Battalion

W. McG. Armstrong .

APPENDIX XIV

1st GARRISON BATTALION

THE 1st Garrison Battalion served abroad, but not in a " war area." The Battalion arrived at Gibraltar on 23rd August, 1915, and left Gibraltar for Crowborough on the 4th November, 1919. The Battalion was disbanded on the 14th February, 1920.

APPENDIX XV

BATTALION ESTABLISHMENT (WAR)

(Expeditionary Force, 1914)

	Personnel.						Horses.				
	Officers.	Warrant Officers.	Staff Sergeants and Sergeants.	Drummers and Buglers.	Rank and File.	Total.	Riding.	Draught.	Heavy Draught.	Pack Cob.	Total.
Headquarters . .	4	1	8	—	61	74	7	22	—	1	30
Attached H.Q. . .	1	—	1	—	5	7	1	—	—	—	—
Machine Gun Section .	1	—	1	—	16	18	1	—	—	—	—
4 Companies . .	24	—	40	16	828	908	4	—	8	8	20

DETAILS LEFT AT BASE

	Officers.	Warrant Officers.	Staff Sergeants and Sergeants.	Drummers and Buglers.	Rank and File.	Total.	Riding.	Draught.	Heavy Draught.	Pack Cob.	Total.
Storemen, first reinforcements, etc. .	1	—	4	—	95	100	—	—	—	—	—

DETAILS OF BATTALION

	Officers.	Warrant Officers.	Staff Sergeants and Sergeants.	Drummers and Buglers.	Rank and File.	Total.	Riding.	Draught.	Heavy Draught.	Pack Cob.	Total.
Headquarters.											
Lieutenant-Colonel .	1	—	—	—	—	—	2	—	—	—	—
Major . . .	1	—	—	—	—	—	1	—	—	—	—
Adjutant . . .	1	—	—	—	—	—	1	—	—	—	—
Quartermaster . .	1	—	—	—	—	—	1	—	—	—	—
Transport Officer (Sub. from Battalion) .	—	—	—	—	—	—	1	—	—	—	—
Sergeant-Major . .	—	1	—	—	—	—	—	—	—	—	—
Quartermaster Sergeant	—	—	1	—	—	—	—	—	—	—	—
Orderly Room Clerk .	—	—	1	—	—	—	—	—	—	—	—
Sergeant Drummer .	—	—	1	—	—	—	—	—	—	—	—
Sergeant Cook . .	—	—	1	—	—	—	—	—	—	—	—
Transport Sergeant .	—	—	1	—	—	—	1	—	—	—	—
Sergeant Shoemaker .	—	—	1	—	—	—	—	—	—	—	—
Drivers, 1st line vehicles	—	—	—	—	9	—	—	18	—	—	18
Drivers, spare animals	—	—	—	—	2	—	—	3	—	1	4
Batmen . . .	—	—	—	—	6	—	—	—	—	—	—
Pioneer Sergeant .	—	—	1	—	—	—	—	—	—	—	—
Pioneers . . .	—	—	—	—	10	—	—	—	—	—	—
Signaller Sergeant .	—	—	1	—	—	—	—	—	—	—	—
Signaller Corporal .	—	—	—	—	1	—	—	—	—	—	—
Signaller Privates .	—	—	—	—	15	—	—	—	—	—	—
Stretcher Bearers .	—	—	—	—	16	—	—	—	—	—	—
Orderlies for M.O. .	—	—	—	—	2	—	—	—	1	—	1
R.A.M.C. attached .	1	—	—	—	5	—	1	—	—	—	1
Armourer . . .	—	—	1	—	—	—	—	—	—	—	—
A.S.C. Drivers . .	—	—	—	—	4	—	—	—	8	—	8
Machine Gun Section											
Subaltern . . .	1	—	—	—	—	—	1	—	—	—	—
Sergeant . . .	—	—	1	—	—	—	—	—	—	—	—
Corporal . . .	—	—	—	—	1	—	—	—	—	—	—
Privates . . .	—	—	—	—	12	—	—	—	—	—	—
Drivers, 1st line trans. .	—	—	—	—	2	—	—	4	—	—	—
Batman . . .	—	—	—	—	1	—	—	—	—	—	—

BATTALION ESTABLISHMENT—*continued*

	Personnel.						Horses.				
	Officers.	Warrant Officers.	Staff Sergeants and Sergeants.	Drummers and Buglers.	Rank and File.	Total.	Riding.	Draught.	Heavy Draught.	Pack Cobs.	Total.
Company.											
Major or Captain .	1	—	—	—	—	—	1	—	—	—	—
Captain (2nd in command) . . .	1	—	—	—	—	—	—	—	—	—	—
Subalterns. . .	4	—	—	—	—	—	—	—	—	—	—
Company Sergeant-Major . .	—	—	1	—	—	—	—	—	—	—	—
Company Q.M. Sergeant	—	—	1	—	—	—	—	—	—	—	—
Sergeants . . .	—	—	8	—	—	—	—	—	—	—	—
Drummers. . .	—	—	—	4	—	—	—	—	—	—	—
Corporals . . .	—	—	—	—	10	—	—	—	—	—	—
Privates . . .	—	—	—	—	188	—	—	—	—	—	—
Drivers, 1st line trans..	—	—	—	—	3	—	—	—	2	2	4
Batmen . . .	—	—	—	—	6	—	—	—	—	—	—

DETAILS LEFT AT BASE

Orderly Room Sergeant	—	—	1	—	—	—	—	—	—	—	—
Sergeant of Band .	—	—	1	—	—	—	—	—	—	—	—
Sergeant Master Tailor	—	—	1	—	—	—	—	—	—	—	—
Storemen . . .	—	—	—	4	—	—	—	—	—	—	—
First reinforcement .	1	—	2	—	91	94	—	—	—	—	—

FIRST LINE TRANSPORT

	Vehicles.	Drivers.	Draught.	Heavy Draught.	Pack.
Headquarters.					
Bicycles for Signallers . .	9	—	—	—	—
Carts :					
S.A.A.	5	5	10	—	—
Maltese. . . .	1	1	1	—	—
Water	2	2	4	—	—
Wagons limbered G.S. . .	2	2	4	—	—
Drivers for spare animals . .	—	2	3	—	—
Machine Gun Section.					
Wagons, limbered G.S. . .	1	1	2	—	—
Cart, S.A.A. . . .	1	1	2	—	—
Pack Cobs for Ammunition (2 per Company)	—	8	—	—	8
Travelling Kitchen (1 per Company)	4	4	—	8	—
Train.					
H.Q. Wagons for baggage, stores and supplies	4	4	—	8	—

APPENDIX XVI
BATTLE HONOURS
THE GREAT WAR
(42 Battalions)

Mons, Le Cateau, Retreat from Mons, **MARNE, 1914,** Aisne, 1914–18, La Bassée, 1914, Messines, 1914, '17, '18, Armentières, 1914, **YPRES, 1914, '17, '18,** Langemarck, 1914, '17, Gheluvelt, Givenchy, 1914, Neuve Chapelle, Aubers, Festubert, 1915, Loos, **SOMME, 1916, '18,** Albert, 1916, '18, Bazentin, Delville Wood, Pozières, Guillemont, Flers-Courcelette, Morval, Le Transloy, Ancre Heights, Ancre, 1916, '18, Arras, 1917, Scarpe, 1917, Arleux, Bullecourt, Pilckem, Menin Road, Polygon Wood, Broodseinde, Poelcappelle, Passchendaele, Cambrai, 1917, '18, St. Quentin, Bapaume, 1918, Lys, Bailleul, Kemmel, Scherpenberg, **HINDENBURG LINE,** Havrincourt, Epehy, St. Quentin Canal, Beaurevoir, Selle, Valenciennes, Sambre, France and Flanders, 1914, '18. Piave, **VITTORIO VENETO,** Italy, 1917, '18, **DOIRAN, 1917, '18,** Macedonia, 1915, '18, Suvla, Sari Bair, Landing at Suvla, Scimitar Hill, **GALLIPOLI, 1915, '16,** Rumani, **EGYPT, 1915, '17, GAZA,** El Mugheir, Jerusalem, Jericho, Tell'Asur, Megiddo, Nablus, Palestine, 1917, '18, Tigris, 1916, Kut al Amara, 1917, **BAGHDAD,** Mesopotamia, 1916, '18.

Names in BLOCK LETTERS are on Colours.

INDEX

For Roll of Honour, see pages 287-397.

INDEX

INDEX

INDEX

INDEX

INDEX

INDEX

INDEX

INDEX

INDEX

INDEX

INDEX

INDEX

Printed in the United Kingdom by
Lightning Source UK Ltd., Milton Keynes
140855UK00001B/39/A